PENGUIN BOOKS

THE COMPLETE PROSE OF MARIANNE MOORE

Marianne Moore was born in Kirkwood, Missouri, on November 15, 1887, and spent much of her youth in Carlisle, Pennsylvania. After graduation from Bryn Mawr College in 1909 she taught for four years at the Carlisle Indian School. Her poetry first appeared professionally in *The Egoist* and *Poetry* magazines in 1915, and she moved to New York City in 1918. Her first book, *Poems*, was issued in England by the Egoist Press in 1921. *Observations*, published three years later in America, received the Dial Award. From 1925 to 1929 she served as acting editor of *The Dial*, the preeminent American literary periodical. She moved to Brooklyn in 1929, where she lived for the next thirty-six years. In 1935 *Selected Poems*, with an Introduction by T. S. Eliot, brought her work to the attention of a wider public.

Three additional books of poetry were followed, in 1951, by her *Collected Poems*, which won the Bollingen Prize, the National Book Award, and the Pulitzer Prize. She went on to publish a verse translation of the complete *Fables of La Fontaine*, a collection of critical essays, and three more volumes of poems.

Among the many awards Marianne Moore received are the National Institute of Arts and Letters Gold Medal for Poetry, the Poetry Society of America's Gold Medal for Distinguished Achievement, and the National Medal for Literature, America's highest literary honor. A member of the National Institute of Arts and Letters since 1947, she was elected to the American Academy of Arts and Letters in 1955. In 1967 she was made Chevalier de l'Ordre des Arts et des Lettres by the French Republic, and in 1969 she received an honorary doctorate in literature from Harvard University, her sixteenth honorary degree. Marianne Moore died in New York City, in her eighty-fifth year, on February 5, 1972.

Patricia C. Willis is the Curator of Literature (including the Marianne Moore collection) at The Rosenbach Museum & Library in Philadelphia.

BY MARIANNE MOORE

The Complete
Prose of
Marianne
Moore

EDITED AND WITH AN INTRODUCTION BY
PATRICIA C. WILLIS

Elisabeth Sifton Books
PENGUIN BOOKS

ELISABETH SIFTON BOOKS · PENGUIN BOOKS
Viking Penguin Inc., 40 West 23rd Street,
New York, New York 10010, U.S.A.
Penguin Books Ltd, 27 Wrights Lane, London W8 5TZ
(Publishing & Editorial) and Harmondsworth,
Middlesex, England (Distribution & Warehouse)
Penguin Books Australia Ltd, Ringwood,
Victoria, Australia
Penguin Books Canada Limited, 2801 John Street,
Markham, Ontario, Canada L3R 1B4
Penguin Books (N.Z.) Ltd, 182–190 Wairau Road,
Auckland 10, New Zealand

First published in the United States of America by
Viking Penguin Inc. 1986
Published in Penguin Books 1987

LIBRARY OF CONGRESS CATALOGING IN PUBLICATION DATA
Moore, Marianne, 1887–1972.
The complete prose of Marianne Moore.
"Elisabeth Sifton books."
Includes index.
I. Willis, Patricia C.   II. Title.
[PS3525.05616A14   1987]   818'.5208   87-2319
ISBN 0 14 00.9436 9

Printed in the United States of America by
R. R. Donnelley & Sons Company, Harrisonburg, Virginia
Set in Bodoni Book

INTRODUCTION

I bring up, in the course of time, the subject of writing, touch in a light, apparently unconsciously affectionate manner, upon the possibilities of the art. Also say there are times when I should give anything on earth to have writing a matter of indifference to me. Then add with a glance modestly askance, that it is undeniably convenient, in time of expressionary need, to be able to say things to the point. And, irrelevantly, that I like the thing for the element of personal adventure in it.

Marianne Moore, as a college junior in 1907, portrayed the struggle of a young writer in her story, "Pym." With half a century of her craft behind her, she echoed her Pym's dilemma in "Profit Is a Dead Weight":

I doubt that anyone who is uncurably interested in writing as I am, and always doing it, has had as much difficulty as I have in expressing what I fanatically find myself determined to say: How get it all in—compact, unmistakable—set down as if spontaneously.

Writing never became "a matter of indifference" to her; "personal adventure" and "expressionary need" were to urge her to publish, in addition to her marvelous and enduring poetry, more than four hundred prose pieces.

Marianne Moore recognized the desire to write at age nineteen while attending Bryn Mawr College. She was elected to the board of the college literary magazine, *Tipyn o'Bob*, and published there eight short stories and one review, as well as eight brief poems. Her professional debut in prose occurred in the pages of *The Egoist*, *Poetry*, William Rose Benét's *Chimaera*, and *The New York Times*, beginning in 1916—six short pieces of which two, reviews of William Butler Yeats' *The Wild Swans at Coole* and T. S. Eliot's *Prufrock and Other Observations*, were to suggest her ability to take on both a senior and an upstart major poet. By 1918 when she moved from her hometown, Carlisle, Pennsylvania, to New York, her work had come to the attention of her contemporaries among the modernist poets whose unofficial leader, Ezra Pound, was soon to propel her career as a critic to a leading position in American letters.

The Dial, which claimed the parentage of the Margaret Fuller–Ralph Waldo Emerson *Dial* of the 1840s, became in the 1920s the most prominent American magazine of arts and letters under the ownership of Scofield Thayer and Dr. J. Sibley Watson, Jr. When Ezra Pound suggested to Thayer that he invite Marianne Moore to write prose for *The Dial*, he initiated for her an extraordinary decade as a critic. Prior to 1920, her serious efforts to find work as a book reviewer had met with minimal acceptance. Suddenly, her prose was in demand, and she was to publish 187 prose pieces in *The Dial* along with the poems which brought her book, *Observations*, the Dial Award in 1925. That same year she succeeded Thayer as editor, a position she held until *The Dial* was discontinued in July 1929.

As a writer for *The Dial*, Marianne Moore forged her style as reviewer and essayist. She resolved, as she later noted that Leo Stein said of himself, "never to review a book unless essentially in sympathy with it and never to proffer . . . critical verdict without at the last again consulting the book to be sure that what [was] written was apt and dependable." Her library and manuscripts, now part of the Marianne Moore Archive at the Rosenbach Museum & Library in Philadelphia, bear witness to her diligence: review copies contain her long indices of choice quotations, notes point to the many other works consulted for a review, and manuscripts show extensive reconsideration. Her method as a critic was to display an author's achievements by the quotation of passages which reflected elements she thought essential to good writing. Principal among these elements are accuracy of perception of detail and verisimilitude in portrayal, precision and compactness of language which "admits of no interpretation of accent but the one intended," gusto and idiosyncrasy in expression, and finally, intensity, "the test for what purported to be art" at *The Dial*. She sought a writer's "consanguinities," his or her relation to writers of the past, and she called upon the work of writers ranging from seventeenth-century prose masters to her contemporaries to illustrate her assessment of the book at hand. Her correspondence is testimony to the fact that the writers whose work she reviewed found illumination, prescience, and occasional alarm in the rightness of her judgments.

Marianne Moore wrote twenty-five article-length reviews for *The Dial;* she also published six prose pieces elsewhere during the decade. Her subjects were chiefly the leading poets of the day, Wallace Stevens, T. S. Eliot, E. E. Cummings, William Carlos Williams, and H. D., although such writers of prose as George Moore and Gertrude Stein also received her attention.

As editor of *The Dial*, she wrote the monthly "Comment," a two- or three-page unsigned essay on topics of her choosing: books, maps, painting, fashion, auctions, serpents, the circus, the Holland Tunnel—the record of a poet's curiosity and investigation. Here one finds the wit, the wide-ranging awareness of life and literature, the delight in quotation, and the unlikely juxtapositions that mark her poems. Indeed, during her five years as editor, she wrote no poetry: the "Comment" pieces are, in their way, its substitute.

The Dial carried each month about eight anonymous one-paragraph reviews in a section called "Briefer Mention." Marianne Moore wrote 121 of these pieces, many of them notices of books on subjects quite different from those of her long reviews—travel, history, philosophy, biography, and other nonfiction. The compression dictated by the single-paragraph format resulted in the tours de force of precise diction and the inventive splicing of quotations that make these reviews extraordinary reading.

The demise of *The Dial* with the July 1929 issue, due largely to the withdrawal of Thayer's financial support when serious illness left him unable to participate in the magazine, had a devastating effect on Marianne Moore. At forty-two, she found her career as a successful editor brought to a crashing end. There was no other magazine like *The Dial* to which she might have applied her talents nor, in that year of financial crisis, other means of making a living as an editor. Marianne Moore had to turn to free-lance work, but only after a fallow period during which she was unable to write. In the fall of 1929 she moved to Brooklyn and eventually began again to publish in *Poetry* and other American and British little magazines. Her position as the last editor of *The Dial* and her intensity as a reviewer brought requests for comments, but she did not hesitate to face rejection slips when trying to promote the work of new writers whose merit she discerned. New books of poetry continued to be her primary interest, but throughout these middle years she also considered such topics as film, Trollope, Charlotte Brontë, and Anna Pavlova, and she published one short story, "A Farm Show." Her longest review, of Pound's *A Draft of XXX Cantos*, has the authority of her extensive reading of Pound from 1911 through 1930, evidenced by 105 footnotes intended not for publication but for the eyes of *Poetry*'s editor, Harriet Monroe. Another long essay, "Henry James as a Characteristic American," like the Pound review, suggests the importance to her of the novelist's or the poet's nonfiction. The war years elicited two polemical and uncharacteristic pieces, "We Will Walk Like the Tapir" and "Who Has Rescued Whom," which decry the waste of natural and human resources and the horror of fascism.

During this middle period, Marianne Moore published three books of poetry, and began to lecture on poetry at colleges and writers' workshops. She continued, as her notebooks and appointment books indicate, her extensive reading and regular attendance at lectures, concerts, and museum exhibitions. She maintained a vigorous correspondence with her modernist compeers, agreed to suggest material for anthologies, and encouraged the editors of new little magazines.

Marianne Moore's sixtieth year, 1947, was marked by the death of Mary Warner Moore, her mother, closest friend, and most diligent critic. In her grief, Marianne plunged into her current project, a translation of all of the fables of La Fontaine, with an intensity that helped her through a long period of recovery. Following Ezra Pound's advice about her translations, she strove to follow English sentence structure, "subject, predicate, object," a practice which led her to reflect on the functions of grammar, sentence structure, and sound effects from a new perspective. Her first essays on poetics and literary technique followed, marked by an intensified simplicity of style which carried over into her poetry.

Major honors for poetry attended Marianne Moore in her last two decades, beginning with the recognition of her *Collected Poems*, 1951, by the awarding of the Pulitzer Prize, the Bollingen Award, and the National Book Award. Her translations of La Fontaine's *Fables* and *Predilections*, her first book of essays, brought her the attention of a new readership, as did essays on a variety of nonliterary subjects—jewels, miniature knives, the delights of the zoo, the Brooklyn Bridge. Editors requested autobiographical pieces about her life in Brooklyn and her development as a poet; publishers sought dust jacket blurbs; awards proliferated. The audience for her prose expanded further when she wrote for such wide-circulation magazines as *Harper's Bazaar, Vogue,* and *The Atlantic.* A "Profile" in *The New Yorker* and a *Life* picture story showed the poet of the tricorne hat and the poet laureate of baseball, if not the serious editor of *The Dial* who could reject a poem by Yeats, revise Hart Crane's work, and help to discover Louis Zukofsky. But from her first collegiate efforts, through those of the prestigious editor of *The Dial* and, later, woman of letters, Marianne Moore's prose commands attention as the work of a major intelligence of gifted subtlety and complexity. The idiosyncratic mosaic of these many worlds, seen through the eyes of a superb observer, characterizes Marianne Moore's prose. Her criticism, as Eliot said of Pound, is significant because it is "the writing of a poet about poetry"; it must be read "in the light" of the poetry. And her other prose, while demonstrating the breadth of her ideas, concerns, and enthusiasms, succeeds in performing the major function she ascribed to the prose of both Pound and Eliot: it "italicizes" her poetry. It is, as she noted in her best-known poem, "Poetry," "the raw material of poetry in / all its rawness . . . a place for the genuine."

A NOTE ON THE TEXT

IN 1967, Marianne Moore gathered her *Complete Poems* for publication, culling just 120 poems and a few translations with the warning, "omissions are not accidents." It was her practice to revise by subtraction, giving laborious attention to work she would stand behind. This collection of her prose has not been subjected to her refining choices; had she been its compiler, it would have been a much slimmer volume. Without her instructions to the contrary, completeness seems indicated. Nevertheless, while many items in the present book have previously escaped bibliographical detection, it is certain that others will surface in the future, only to expand a remarkable record of the writer at work.

This collection includes Marianne Moore's published prose with the following exceptions: printed items in whose publication Marianne Moore did not participate, letters, interviews, and quotations. The copy texts are the last published versions supervised by the author. In cases where there are obvious errors in transmission, manuscripts, proofs, and annotated versions have been consulted and the author's intentions, when explicit, have been honored. Her endnotes are included after the texts with which they appeared. Translations of foreign language passages and uniform identification of books reviewed have been supplied. The Appendix contains prose in forms other than essays, reviews, and short fiction.

When editor of *The Dial*, Marianne Moore employed the house spelling style which was chiefly but not consistently British, and British editors converted her American spelling to theirs. Following Marianne Moore's customary practice, spelling in this collection conforms to American usage. Foreign names transliterated from other alphabets are given in the version of the original publication. During Marianne Moore's sixty-one years of prose publication, house styles of punctuation varied widely, and frequently the author did not correct proof. Punctuation which is either incorrect or misleading has been made to conform to modern usage—practices involving ellipses, periods after abbreviated titles, the position of quotation marks, the use of italics, and the lack of any punctuation after set-off quotations from poems which end sentences. Marianne Moore's own style of punctuation which affects grammatical expression has been retained.

PATRICIA C. WILLIS
Ewing, New Jersey

ACKNOWLEDGMENTS

In preparing this edition, I have incurred debts to both friends and strangers who offered information or access to needed material. My thanks to Frances E. Anderson, Russell Baker, J. Robert Barth, S. J., Stan V. Baum, Robert Bertholf, Robert L. Blackmore, James D. Bloom, Mary Boccaccio, Helen M. Cannon, Alice R. Cotton, Rosemary L. Cullen, Leo Dolenski, Ellen S. Dunlap, Monroe Engel, Kathleen Farley, Evelyn W. Feldman, Aaron M. Fine, Ralph Franklin, Donald Gallup, Philip G. Gates, Celeste Goodridge, Blanche E. Grant, Joseph Grucci, Anna Marie Hager, Jack Hagstrom, Bonnie Hoenigsblum, Mary Kennedy, Vernon Jordan, Helen Klaviter, Clay Lancaster, Jean S. Lindsay, Kenneth A. Lohf, Robert M. Makla, Taffy Martin, Alice Z. Meyer, James E. Miller, Jr., Herbert Mitgang, Timothy D. Murray, Carol Jones Neuman, Gerald Neuman, Dorothy S. Norman, Dorothy Nyren, Peter Quartermain, Robert Rosenthal, Perdita Schaffner, David Schoonover, Grace Schulman, Lewis Sckolnick, Charles Skelley, Virginia Smyers, Dorothy L. Swerdlove, David Szewczyk, Lola Szladits, Emily Mitchell Wallace, the late James S. Watson, Jr., Lloyd Wengrow, Robert L. Wilbur, Robert A. Wilson, Norman Wiltsie, and my colleagues at the Rosenbach Museum & Library.

Particular gratitude is owed to Elisabeth Sifton whose enthusiasm and understanding graced this project; to the late Charles B. Cannon whose knowledge of copyright law guided and corrected me; to Robert J. Willis, my husband, untiring supporter and proofreader; and to Clive E. Driver, Marianne Moore's friend and Literary Executor, and my generous collaborator.

CONTENTS

I. THE EARLY YEARS
1907-1919

YORROCKS

London, June 5, 19—.

My dear Pen,—This chap is a loan. He is a bit of my studio property, so don't knock him over if his loquacity jars on you. I propose that he look after your garden, trim your hedge and pose for you, while you feed him and see that he doesn't commit suicide. He goes by the name of Yorrocks, and I think you'll be keen about him. Yours.

Thomas II.

Now, Pennel was an artist. But more than all he was a vagabond. A hatred of "drawing rooms," journalists and surging thoroughfares had driven him from town. He loved color, he loved weeds, he loved solitude. After a London winter, he gloried in the country roads, the sunny hillsides, the warm, lifting winds of Hampstead. And they were glorious sacrifices to the idol of self-gratification, those armfuls of scarlet-weeds and millet that he was always placing upon the hearth of his yellow-walled living room. It was living, indeed, to stand by a small-paned window in his own quiet house and gaze at the sweeps of pale evening color while his straight curtains drew back and forth across the sash.

It was with reluctance that Pennel felt about his clothes for a match, one evening. He was hating to break the spell of deepening shadows and trilling toads when he saw his etching late returned. He bent over it with eagerness. He looked hard at the words, "First Prize," and smiled approvingly at his signature, "Novgorod." With a careless glance at the whole, he was thinking to himself, "That meadow is rather a jolly bit," when, clack! the brass goose fell against the oak with a short, hard knock, and there stood Yorrocks of the note. Pennel had glared at the boy with American ferocity. He had read the proffered note, read it twice and then said, "John, come in"—he refused to say Yorrocks. "we shall not work tonight. We shall have some food and then go upstairs."

A week had passed. The boy now followed Pennel like a dog. The more forbidding the man, the more devoted the boy. The boy often went hatless because Pennel did so. For the same reason he often cut a switch to carry with him on a ramble. Pennel could not in self-respect object to the latter misdemeanor on the part of his devotee and curse, but he forced Yorrocks to wear a hat. "Would you hobject hif I was to wear no 'at?" the boy would ask. "Yes, it's not done," Pennel would answer. The devil of uncharitableness was strong in the man. He was cutting and unrestrained.

"Mr. Pen-nile," Yorrocks would say, as the man worked, "will you be in want of me this afternoon?" "No," Pennel would answer. "I work in the morning, and call me 'James' if you can't say 'Pennel.' " "Well, Mr. James, Mr. James?" "Yes." "You know Mr. Hayden's pictures. You do know Mr. Hayden's pictures, don't you? Well, when you've been looking at 'is pictures the people you see look wrong."

"Pretty neat"; and Pennel smiled as he reached for a drawing-block and a heavy pencil. "How do you like that man in the corner?" he said, unbending.

"I like that, I do like hit, but I guess I'd like the man better."

"You would, John, yes you would," responded Pennel with decent pleasantry. "You may go now," he added, "but you've got to be more quiet tomorrow and you've got to sit still. You made me spoil a draught that was pretty tolerable for a 'penny-Whistler.' " The boy slid from his chair with evident reluctance. He was not pleased to substitute the fascinations of the garden for the fascinations of the studio. "Mr. James," he said, " 'ow much is that picture worth, habout?"

"This 'pencil' of yourself? It's not finished, John." "Oh, just as it is?" "Why, about three pounds," the man responded, as he fitted a fine point to a very long handle.

"May I be toppered!" gasped the boy.

"Too much?" inquired the man.

"You do 'ave cheek," said the boy.

"Well, a man's done a good deal when he's caught the magic of your face," Pennel remarked dryly.

"Well, take hanything to do, han it's tough," the boy responded in all seriousness.

Pennel smiled again. "You may go," and he said it conclusively.

Against a wall of the toolhouse, peaches were ripening and the boy gazed at them, his body motionless, his head directed upward. The tanbark of the path was soft, the sun was warm, the time was one for thought. Pennel seemed to think so. He stepped into the garden, passed through the gate and began to move slowly down the road. But Yorrocks had seen him and rushed after. "O, Mr. Pen-nile, Mr. James, I'll go with you," and his voice had a delightful ring of assurance. Pennel turned about sharply.

"No," he said, "you can't. You like pictures," he added. "Go into the house, go upstairs, look at anything you see."

He tramped on past meadows, hedges and estates.

"I cannot stand that lout," he muttered. "Intimated that he didn't approve my work. I like him, for that. It shows discrimination. But the fellow jars on me to a degree that's frightful. He has a well-shaped head and takes fascinating attitudes, but what's a pose? It was infernally presumptuous of Hayden. I shall tell him so."

Now Pennel possessed in high degree the "gentle art of making enemies." He should have been grateful to Hayden for his even constant friendship, but a particularly cutting smile flickered about his mouth when he thought of the man. In haste he turned, but it was late when he regained the cottage. He entered the studio with an air of determination. He looked over the sketches just made. "They are rotten!" he exclaimed as he twisted the roll up and tossed it in the direction of a squat jar which stood on the fireplace. He passed to the other room, sat down and wrote:

Heath End, Hampstead.

My Dear Hayden:—

At that juncture he paused. "Guess I'll tell the little beggar *now*," he said, with a return of the high spirits upon which the offensive little Yorrocks had cast a gloom.

"Oh John," he called. "John." There was no response and Pennel rose. He looked into the cool, quiet garden and made a tour of the house, delaying in the studio to enjoy the shadows which fell on the pale gray walls and the lights which gleamed on the fire-dogs. In his bedroom he found a note.

"Dear Mr. James," it ran. "I have gone. Mr. Hayden said he thought you were solitary. 'Deuced solitary' was what he said. I don't see it that you are.

"Yorrocks.
"P. S.—I should find my way, so don't worry."

Pennel breathed again. He breathed as he had not done for weeks.

At tea he spoke hardly once to the woman who prepared his meals and kept house for him. The joy of uninterrupted thought was too delicious.

Toward bedtime, however, his thoughts wandered. He jerked a volume of Balzac from the shelf. Balzac was generally inspiration, entertainment, anything he wished, but tonight he slammed the book shut when half through

"The Conscript." "London's a fine rat-hole for the youngster, suppose he does get there safe." And he rushed from the house. He strode along the moonlit highway as only a vagabond can. The night was soothing, but still the man suffered. "That lonely house. It's nauseous," he muttered.

Tipyn o'Bob, 4 (January 1907), 3–4.

A BIT OF TAPESTRY

"I F it is true that you must renounce this divine land, for one more rugged, then, smooth roads and a blue sky, Bertram—Eleanor D., of Volquesse. But stop—a single leaf must not be at the same time good-morrow, good-night and farewell. Come to that smallest hall which opens from Count Athol's if you would see me, and by twelve I shall appear. The place is Paradise, with dogs and men all gone."

Bertram cut a pen and wrote. A very gash of a frown disfigured his face; the toes of his pointed shoes drooped submissively over the edge of the footstool, the quill shook blots on the page and again scratched merrily.

"At last," he growled. "Here, boy, to the Duchess." A little green-clad sprout received the roll, eyed its red silk tying with an awestruck, falling glance and departed.

Bertram made a start as if to recall the boy, then turned back with resignation, dropped the quill and said quietly, "It's unforgivable that one so powerful should be so proud, and gracious and yet so unapproachable. As for me, I do not believe I can stand it. I will not go tonight, and yet Heaven knows I—will."

With an effort to forget justifiable resentment, he left the manor and followed his legs till they brought him to a copse, upon the hazy tufts of which his eye had often rested.

Beneath a sapling he lay down and closed his eyes. It was not long, however, till the beat of hoofs smote upon his ears, and he turned upon one elbow. "Do monks, lords or damozels pass by?" he said. Leaves obstructed his view. He descried the heads of the mounts, however, and dismissed his curiosity with a shrug. Then, glancing up, "Pray do not cease your twittering, birds," he said. "You funny little speckled Puckchasers, I like it vastly." And he sighed. He watched the birds a long time, he trod upon the twisting tunnels of the mole, and dabbled his hands in the brook, in the kind of water that makes one's hands feel clean and cold. In short, he moved now here, now there, and the afternoon was gone.

At twelve he found himself in the great manor. He paced the floor and a rose drooped from his clenched teeth. His arms were folded. Now and again he glanced toward one of the several doors about him. The Duchess of Volquesse did not appear, however. She was in the hall of state.

"Heigh-ho," cried the restive Prince, "where can she be? and why this infidel delay when she cares not a jack about me."

"I'll go." He caught up his great cloak and was gone without half a glance back.

A taper had been marking the hours. The wick of it curled over, and, falling in a pool of its own making, marked the hour of twelve and a half.

"Well, I must go," said the Duchess of Volquesse to Harry the seneschal.

"Well, as to the young Prince; from your vehement defense of the knave, you might easily be in love with him."

"I am—I'm very much in love with him," said Eleanor, returning. "I now must tell him so."

Harry gazed upon her with intense admiration.

"I gave him to know in writing that I prized his companionship, but I'll have to interpret my words, no doubt. You won't forget about the bridge, nor yet about the weather-vane."

Thrusting head and shoulders into the atrium, she paused, then walked to the great door which stood open. How strangely discolored the sky, she thought. How very restless the dogs, as she caught the fading wail of a hound.

She turned about and moved now here, now there. She picked up a rose and, having stripped some skin from the stem, threw it down, for it was wilting. She pressed her hands to her eyes.

"Oh my! why doesn't he come?" she yawned.

Reflecting on his Duchess' words, the seneschal stepped out that night with a mind to arrive at the Jolly Brown Frog in the course of his wanderings.

"A dainty pair," he mused, wiping a stray smile from his lips, when,— "Ho, what haste, sweet boy?" he called as he spied a figure moving steadily before him. And then, "By the breath of my body, it's Bertram," he said in a wondering voice. "And who may you be?" said Bertram. "Who am I?" said the man with an air of abstraction. "Why, Harry, the seneschal, handsome Harry." Then quickly, "Whence coming and whither going, my dainty-throated starling?"

"From your castle, bold friend, to the farthest place ten demons can take me," said the youth.

"I saved you from drowning and I'll save your life presently with a bottle of sack, but you mustn't rush off with despair, my lad."

"And is it *you?*" said Bertram. "The ten devils are laughing ones. I'll not bear you grudge, though, and if my throat can swallow, why not die drinking," he blurted out with a jerk of the shoulder. "If I stay two hours at a tavern, though, I might have waited there all night."

"By holy John, my charter-book," gasped the seneschal, stopping short. "Friend, as you love me, fetch it," he said with appealing eyes. And then, becoming unmistakably serious, "Go back, I'll wait for you. Look in the first small room on your right as you enter the great door." Bertram glanced at the man half indignant. He gazed with abstraction ahead, and then, with a resigned heave of the chest, turned about.

"I'll rest me here till you're back," called Harry, with artistic disregard for the truth.

Tipyn o'Bob, 4 (February 1907), 13–15.

THE DISCOURAGED POET

IT was midsummer. The dust hung thick about the poet and his little horse, and the flowers, which knocked together behind the retreating heels of the horse, looked gray to the poet.

"The famous bard is quite right, I do not know enough ever to become famous. I shall not try to write," he said. He was lurching comfortably in the saddle, but he spoke wearily, for he was thinking hard of his visit to the sage.

> " 'You'd like to dream for hours and hours
> Of nodding gardens, tall with flowers?
> Of reddening vines and small round towers?' "

"My, but it's bad! Isn't it bad, Jack?" he said, crushing the paper in his hands regardless of the shadowy neatly blocked oblongs of writing which covered it. The little horse tossed his forelock and switched his tail. The roll dropped by the road and the poet lifted the sagging rein and dug gently into the animal's ribs.

They jogged on easily for a mile or so. Then, when the gray line of the town, and the rounding masses of green, and the bits of red chimney, and the swallows had come into view once more, the poet dropped the bridle again and slipped from the horse's back, with care not to alight on more dandelions than he could help. He patted the creature's neck, then turned it loose, for it did not belong to him, and, with a last glance over his shoulder, trudged on by himself till he had come before the great door of his, and his guardian's, abode.

He gazed at the forbidding door, looked into the gray-green distance, and then, glancing at the ground, sat down to examine a flower which had been blooming during his absence. He remained for some time, with his hands clasping his knees; then, having made up his mind to enter the house, he got to his feet and was soon in his guardian's presence.

"My lord," he said, "I have come to say that I am no longer a poet." Then he paused. "You are glad, perhaps?"

The old man looked hard at the youth and said:

"I am glad indeed—more glad than I can say, my son."

There was another long silence, during which the youth worked his toe through imaginary fringe.

"My lad," said the guardian, with a frown, "you are young. You do not know enough to write."

The poet turned away, and there was an angry look about him. He wandered through various rooms and entries, till he found a large dark windowsill, upon which he sat down. And he made no motion save to rub an eyelash from one of his eyes and to pass his hand slowly along his calm, tilted chin.

"I don't know?" he queried, hesitatingly. "The bard—may know, but you—my careful guardian, you don't know about verse—or me. To the winds with distemper. I'll roam the woods and then, if I wish, I'll write." He jumped up and strode back through room after room. He passed his guardian, but paid no attention to him, and paused only long enough on the sill of the great, forbidding doorway, to adjust a shapeless cap upon his determined head.

The guardian plucked a companion by the sleeve and remarked, "This new decision becomes him, friend. Should you not say so?"

Tipyn o'Bob, 4 (April 1907), 24–25.

A PILGRIM

H E came out of the wood, a lad tall and willowy. From between the closed fingers of one hand a delicate end of creeper hung down, and over the brim of his hat hung a plume which now shook, now stood still, like a vibrating curl of fine wire.

He proceeded for some time along the bank of a stream which led from the wood, until he perceived a hut, a clump of willows, and a very old pensive man.

"Good man, I have lost my way," he remarked. "Could you direct me?"

"Toward what land do you journey?" inquired the old man.

"Toward the land of heart's desire." The boy's eyes twinkled and grew dark, as he drew himself up, and half-turned to face the breeze. "It is a place," he said, "where people do as they please. The flowers gleam, and there are always poets about, and actors and artists and architects. Time is to be had for the asking, and the finding of an occupation is not short of a pleasure. And when a man grows tired of what he has been doing, and begins something new, a new and needful kind of luck is with him. Some say it is a sloping meadow, this land, which rises to a great height and looks over the sea, with a forest of pines behind it and a great pile of white cliffs in front of it. I have been there, and as I remember it, it was no meadow. I shall be able to tell more fully of that land, however, when I have got back there." The boy gave his cloak a hitch and folded his arms carelessly.

"I cannot direct you," said the old man. "There is a road beyond that cluster of trees, very wild and little frequented. It dips into the mist here and there, and is very much talked of by the venturesome."

The boy's mouth acquired a set look, and his arms fell slack, whereupon the old man said warmly:

"Give up this way-side existence, my boy. If you are willing to help me with my work you may come and live with me. The work before me is the pruning of yonder willows and the digging of a well."

"Ah, my good sir!" The youth shot an arch, haughty glance at the old man, and then, with careless patience, gazed aloft.

"The work is not hard," said the old man. "Compared with making verses and roaming the high-roads it is play."

"It is not that I cannot do it, but that I hate it." The lad moved back a step to gain the support of a tree. He glanced down and then up, and his face wore an arch expression, this time confidential, and his eye had a glint in it of latent capability.

"You would do nothing at all?"

The youth smiled and said: "Theoretically. I can't say just that," he added, "I merely object to working steadily." Then, fastening his eyes on the old man, "I—I shall help you for a week or two."

On the following day the sun shone brightly and the work began. It was not long, however, till the boy shook his head and sat down on the grass to rest. The old man reminded him that time was slipping by.

"If we had a time-piece we could watch time go, and it would then not go so fast," the youth replied, adding as he jumped up, "We shall have a sun-dial before night." Again, when at work upon the well, he stopped impulsively to build a stone foundation in the stream, in the form of an oval. But of this he soon tired. When he had brought the stones up even with the surface of the water, he said to the old man:

"When the elder-bushes bloom and are reflected in that, you will have a mirror with a lady's flowers across it."

He was always dropping down on the grass to rest. He was always consulting the half-finished sun-dial or interpreting the clouds.

"Now it's a sail-boat, and now the map of England, and now a lion rampant," he would say.

One day, when the trees had been trimmed and large stones had been laid in a circular mosaic about the mouth of the well, he looked into the black round of water and said, with his eye upon his reflection:

"You are rather young. You did not know it. Oh, yes, my dear." He then smiled contentedly. The childish turn of his mind and the precise sound of his words pleased him. Upon glancing up, he was annoyed to find the old man beside him, and he was suddenly prompted to say, without the effort which he had expected the words to cost him:

"Master, I must leave tomorrow." One's own words are reassuring, and despite the lad's fondness for the old man, upon the following day he was all eagerness to be off. The old man watched him go, and then turned to his fishing.

It was toward evening when he came upon a bedraggled feather. He began to miss the owner of it. He had learned to love the boy's warmth of feeling, which smoldered and flashed by turns; and he was wondering how the youth might be faring, when a voice called from outside:

"I could not find my way. May I rest?" A figure leaned in the doorway, in its own shadow, and a dark thing like a hat flopped down on the floor. "The prince is obliged to content himself with the rôle of poor penny."

The old man looked dazed. The speaker paused, considering for a moment, and then went out. The old man had stared coldly.

"Heaven knows," the ruffled boy said, "it is the fault of luck that I am back here. It is not my custom to intrude." He took a seat on the grass and, resting his chin on his hand, gazed up at the crescent moon which was beginning to glimmer above the willows. "I stumble on the ideal life and curse myself," he meditated. "I recognize my mistake, and find it unself-respecting, not to say impossible, to make amends for it. Patron Saints! He who dances—"

"Lad," called the man. The youth curled a hand about his knee and looked behind him. "Lad, will you draw me some water?"

"Yes," returned the youth wearily. "I should love to." The full meaning of his words then dawned upon him, and he laughed a ringing laugh. "Father?" he called. There was no sound, and he shouted out, "I really meant that, father. I should love to—."

Tipyn o'Bob, 5 (November 1907), 15–17.

PYM

January 28.

WELL again and out. But can I ever forget it, the faintly medicinal smell of things, the glare, the dazzling bed-spread, the wilted, sickly droop of my clothes on the half-open door of the closet!

And a *fire* once again. In the light of it, the past begins to look fairly serene, and the future (from a safe distance to be sure), fairly tranquil.

But Daniel, big aggressive brute! I wonder whatever possessed Alden to give him to me. I think if there ever was an inexcusable perpetration of kindness, he is guilty of it. I see now why he is such a cynic. The cynics in life are the people who are always trying to do things for people who don't *want* things done for them.

And Charles! That man! No domestic could be more utterly a failure. The joy of a house untenanted by servants! I am thinking fairly hard. Things are beginning to materialize. I rest my eye fixedly upon my portrait of the unknown lady in the green dress. I watch an occasional diagonal of fire-light splash a path across her dark slippery hair, across the zig-zag light parts in her dress, and over her hands. My words, I realize, are coming unusually well—when—knock, thump. Charles! to suggest if he may be allowed, that it is late—also, that I might be glad of something to eat, might I not? I feel the lateness of the hour to be discouraging but in no way "disconcerting." Food, I do not mention.

January 30.

What can be ailing me. My looks are a reflection of the civilization of my country and my feelings have no right to seek counterparts, even in *Paganism*. It's a pity anyone can play the spiritless old fowl under so little justifiable pressure. My work is bad also. I can no more write according to Cob's requirements and at the same time approve what I write, myself, than I can make it rain. I've got to buck up. Now that I've begun I have to stick it out. Revolting beast that Cob. I can hardly stand him. Says I am supersensitive, effeminate and perverse, charged too heavily with "scruples," always full of excuses and explanations. I may have bad judgment and fall short of the mark a little too often, but conscience—! If I can scrape a pretext, in the shape of one provocation more, I shall throw up the sponge. A derelict life has in some ways attractions, it can't be denied. It is in all the copy-books that a man may lay down his life for his individualism. I begin to be convinced.

I have certainly been getting on no better, with no more satisfaction to myself than before I was ill. The whole confounded situation is worse than before.

If Uncle Stanford comes out strongly and says he is sorry he drove me to this and made me take him seriously when he was joking, if he wants to meet me squarely and says he wants me to come back and live with him again, and be social and a gentleman and start out again and try law (for I *was* promising in my profession), I am doubtful as to whether I can resist him. He took an unfair advantage of my youth and irascibility though, and my foolish early conception of what it is to be "game" (*really* game). I shall approach him contritely (of my own accord) under *no* circumstances whatever. If I am playing the part of unregenerate prodigal, I surely have character enough to sustain it. I shall pray that too much pressure be not brought to bear at once, on *either* side, the side of conscience or the side of self-respecting, righteous wrath. Uncle Stanford is "playing" me consciencelessly in his amused paternal patronage of me, and Cob is "trying" me to the last degree with his harshness and materialism. I daresay, my break with Uncle Stanford was unjustifiable. It was more or less his fault, though. If he had said, *"Don't* 'play' so much," I should very probably have said, "In future I shan't." But when he said, "You impose on my good nature, child, with all this literary trifling. As you love what is good for you, read law," it was natural in the extreme, for me to attempt to prove to him that he was wrong and old-fashioned (in the old-fashioned sense of the word). Indeed, if Uncle Stanford comes, I shall become as hard-frozen as my premises, for despite the fact that I know I acted rashly, I cannot retract, unless I act the repentant prodigal, and I could not do that, with any great comfort, if Uncle Stanford were an angel in Heaven.

February 10.

He has been and has gone. (For a reticent man he certainly has a compelling manner.) I bluff and chatter and hang fire the whole time without giving him or myself a grain of satisfaction. On the surface of it, it was all pretty funny. Uncle Stanford rather guilefully, "Are you feeling perfectly up to the mark, Alexander?" I, assuming a judicial air, "I'm *thoroughly* myself—anything hectic about my appearance?" I suggest that I may appear subdued, from the great extent to which I have recently been giving my attention to depressing subjects. I say that the involved, unhappy side of existence interests me a good deal—a good deal more than the happy-go-lucky surface aspect. I then refuse to elaborate. I come to the conclusion that I have been talking about myself unduly. I don't as a general thing approve of putting checks on spontaneity. One's conversational and more practical abilities suffer somehow, through a straining to appear judicial and mature. One gets to the point where coercion is indispensable to accomplishment. It is advisable, however, for the young at all costs to avoid in the presence of the old and critical the appearance of being effervescent.

I bring up, in the course of time, the subject of writing, touch in a light, apparently unconsciously affectionate manner, upon the possibilities of the art. Also say there are times when I should give anything on earth to have writing a matter of indifference to me. Then add with a glance modestly askance, that it is undeniably convenient, in time of expressionary need, to be able to say things to the point. And, irrelevantly, that I like the thing for the element of personal adventure in it.

Well, so much for Uncle Stanford. He sees through me and very evidently disapproves of me. Fond of me or not, he may go hang—(if he cannot take the trouble to come down to realities with me, and bring about an understanding). I like him, though—as much as he likes me, I rather think.

February 20.

The die is cast! "Manuscript and hesitations seek the flames together." I have been a fool and should have "turned" long before. I *would* have but for that dastardly instinctive dread of equinoxial effects which is present with the most of us at all such inconvenient times as this. That I could be worse off than I have been is, of course, as a matter of fact, impossible. In friendly surroundings mental discomfort is quite endurable. I am relieved, however, that I have at last come to the conclusion that false pride is too serious an obstruction to happiness to be put up with. My encounter with Cob, amusing—strong element of the unexpected in it. I give him my article, and turn to go. He stops me, asks me some insolent, trivial question and I start again for the office door.

"This done?" he pursues.

I nod and say, "I *think* so."

"Are you coming on better?" he inquires. I meditate a clever rejoinder and, in so far as I am a judge, a creeping disgust spreads over my features.

"I like what I have just given you better than *you* will, but—"

"You think it's worth something?"

"Since you force me to it, *that* is what I think of it," and without having the least intention of it, slip open the little iron door of the office stove and shoot the whole mass onto a bed of little, feathering flames. I remark coolly, "I am developing a passion for frankness, Cob."

The question is now, how I can explain my crazy zig-zag course to Uncle Stanford with all due regard for my own proper feelings on the question. I cannot say that I am tired of being alone. I cannot say that I am unable to stand the strain of analytical, attentive work. I am reduced to the truth. And having never yet told anyone I was sorry (when I was anything but jesting—Allah!).

I feel that I may have been a little stubborn. One must be pertinaciously ingenious as well as genuinely a little blind, to follow long a course which insists upon maintaining its original, experimental character.

If I am not traveling toward my ideas with rapidity now though, I should like to know what is happening. I've spoiled my chances for greatness, I surmise, by having made a bull in my career at the very start. I can to a certain extent, however, redeem myself, if I put my mind on the task. Ineffective as I have been hitherto, I have a good deal behind me. I could afford to be, however, much more keenly alive to things than I generally manage to be. I shall go in for some actual experience and prepare to grow mentally acquisitive. I am all too conscious of my having a "point of view." I here and now put off the semblance of dignity and for a short time ostentatiously consecrate myself to *toil*.

February 22.

I must telegraph Uncle Stanford and *leave*. My love of the material tends to interfere with all this sudden display of method and efficiency. I tend to place a restraining hand upon the silly fools that affect a claim upon me, while I stand like the idiot Celt, head back, mouth open, eyes gleaming, my mind gone from me with a conviction of the existence aloft of a new "possibility." (I may be said I think to have a very delicious appreciation of the humorous.)

My surroundings certainly have been decently congenial. Their calm, fond aspect, their inability to shrivel fills me with an unbounded admiration and affection for them, and they prove to me, poor things (more satisfactorily than their animate associates) that I have a sympathetic side to me, and a faint suggestion of something more potential. And they are not an everlasting test of one's bigness.

The portrait and my dark blue rug, with its all-over snail-shell pattern, I shall take with me. All else I shall abjure, with employer, servant, and dog. Living is a fairly simple matter, for me to have made such a mess of it. In the effort to compass things in an original manner, however, anything can be made to come failure-end up. The effort of individual isolation, above all others. Nothing done for effect, is worth the cost.

"God knows you can enter the game if you'll only pay for the same, and the price of the game is a candle, one single flickering candle—"

But enough of this reflection and melancholy, or a moment more, and I shall have forgotten mayhap what I am going to do. Here goes for a beginning—"Dear Uncle—"

Tipyn o'Bob, 5 (January 1908), 13–17.

THE BOY AND THE CHURL

THE situation was, upon its face, simple enough. My nephew was twelve and I twenty. He was lively, sensitive to appreciation, and much at ease wherever he went. I was self-centered and uncommunicative, benevolently inclined occasionally, appreciative to a high degree of the humorous. When given the chance of my nephew's society for a month, I readily undertook the responsibility of him. I liked his name—"Gregory"—I had liked his "manner"—whenever I had come in contact with him, at family parties. It was the second or third day, however, after his arrival, and I found myself beginning to cherish an undefinable resentment toward him. We were pulling on opposite ends of a rope. I said to myself it must have been a chance generous impulse on his part that had ever made me think I could exercise authority over him. I concluded lazily that with fluctuating youthful ardor, the boy was preparing to hate me. I stood by a window, ruminating, when he appeared.

"Gregory," I said, "I must find out what the matter is. Your behavior is unconscionable."

He dug his foot into the ground viciously.

"Do you dislike me? Why is it that you disobey me?" I fixed the lad with my eye.

"No I don't—dislike you."

"Where have you been?" I saw the advisability of proceeding rapidly.

"Camping—on the left bank of the creek."

"In this freezing weather?"

"Yes. Mr. Carson has a cabin there, and it's great."

"Your father said you might do nothing without asking my permission and *really*"—I interrupted myself to bring the knot of the boy's tie into line with his collar, while he stood with face averted—"*really*, you must change your ways."

My nephew turned away, glanced back half annoyed, hesitated, then walked away in silence. In a moment he gave a leap and began to run, shaking his heels out after him in a way that made me smile—in spite of myself.

"It's insufferable," I reflected, "all that modified resentment, suppressed indignation, and restiveness under correction. I can't see the justification for it even in a baby." I had been reading a book and an envelope marked the place. I brought the latter to coincide with the corner of a page and steadied it with two fingers, while I reflected.

"He is not so young as to be thoroughly irresponsible," I argued, "and I am not old enough to know just how far I have a right to expect him to *be* responsible. I detest the child, and sometimes he fascinates me. I like the way he clasps his hands behind his head and roams about while he discourses. Few people know enough to make themselves properly at home." I then thought of the boy's dislike for me, and bit my lip. I had the irritable fondness for him that we have for all people that seem at one time spontaneously to like us and at another to be made actively unhappy by us.

"I just came back with my gloves. I don't want them. The snow's too wet." My nephew was out of breath and scarcely looked at me.

"Yes."

"Do you mind?"

"No. Only don't forget to come home early. In time for dinner."

"Well."

"I *mean* that, Gregory. I don't intend to have you disobedient, all the time."

"I don't understand."

"You don't?"

"No. I'm afraid I don't." The boy's nostrils dilated. "You mean I shouldn't have gone off the way I did? For I don't see. Nothing could possibly have happened to me."

"You should not have gone. But what I mean is, that I don't want you to be doing that kind of thing any more, and if you do, I simply will not take care of you."

The boy stared.

"You think I don't take care of you?"

"I think I take care of myself. I think I do." My nephew shot me a glance. His eyes under ordinary circumstances were dark; they now were cold and unfeeling as a parrot's, and glittered.

"You drive me wild," I said, "when you look at me that way."

"I just don't see, Catherine. That's all." An amenable temper always impressed me, and I said:

"What's the matter? Are you tired of staying here shut up alone in the house with me?"

"No." The boy twisted a tired, puzzled glance at me and sighed. "No, only you never play with me, and I like to get out sometimes."

"You hate me, I'm afraid." I was tactless and forcing things, but if enmity were the result, it would not be enmity at close quarters forever.

"I *don't* hate you. I like you an awful *lot*. But you keep making me do things, and make me behave all the time and—and I can't. I'm sorry I dropped the cat on your dress yesterday. I didn't think it would stick its claws out. My cat wouldn't have. (It's a tiger cat, with great big green eyes and stiff whiskers. It's a nice cat. Only I don't keep it in the house—not much. It's not an angora cat.)" The boy put out his hand to a frill that ran from my neck, part way down the front of my waist, and began turning it this way and that, stopping suddenly to grasp me about the neck with both hands and bring an upward pressure to bear upon my chin. I blinked menacingly and he withdrew.

My sensations became instantly like paper twisting in the flame, but I pursued:

"My dress was altogether too long. It was not your fault that it got torn."

"*All* your clothes—well, maybe not."

"Clothes, what?"

"Act as if they were made just to be looked at."

"You don't mean that! *Gregory!*" I put my hands on the boy's shoulders, and almost instantly removed them. Something in him seemed to shrivel.

"May I go?" His eye rested on me by accident, but neither of us took account of the fact, so perfect was the misunderstanding between us.

"Yes. Please do."

"And if I don't come back right away you'll know where I am, and not be worried?"

I made no answer.

The strain of warm reflection was too much for me, and I began to walk about from room to room through the house.

"It's queer! When the boy is away I feel that I know just about how to take him. Then, as soon as we come together it is sniff and snarl and off with a bang." I was standing with my foot on the rung of a chair, watching the fire, intent on easing my spirit, "I am a screw, I know. How people are to make themselves over, unassisted however, is hard to see." The fire shot up and sank, sending up a shower of sparks that flew out and vanished with a snap. I leaned forward and listened. A branch must have been scraping the window. I sank back again into vacuous discontentment. The hour grew later and later, and, unwilling to get up and go to bed, unable to see anything, with the firelight in my eyes, I sat fixed, as if a spell had been cast upon me.

Toward morning I came to my senses. The wind had died down. The sky was growing light near the horizon and the firs, still somewhat black and indistinct, were becoming a dead, mud-green. I rose and stepped outside, feeling, as I gazed about, like a man with a reach of two or three miles of barren seacoast to traverse. Hardly stopping to think why I was so bent on "setting forth," I started briskly from the house and pushed an entrance between the tangled snowy firs. The cold set my teeth on edge, and having walked for some time, I turned mechanically, and slowly began to retrace my steps. Almost back at my own door, I stopped, thinking I heard the fragment of a song.

" 'Heave way, heave way.' "

I ground my heel into the snow with a crunch, and put my hand on the door knob.

" 'For far away Australia.' "

I entered the house and slammed the door—then paused.

"An Australian crew is a very fine crew
If your boat's leak proof,

As a wooden shoe.
'Heave way, heave way,
For far Australia.' ' "

With my head still turned to one side, I caught a glimpse of my distraught face in the window, and fell to wondering how I could have done such a thing as sit up all night.

"I came back for my other gloves." Glancing up, I beheld my nephew.

"Oh, C—Catherine!"

"What?"

"You needn't have gotten up to *get* them for me."

I simulated a smile, and after a pause remarked:

"You'd better get warm, hadn't you?"

"Guess I had." The boy glanced at me curiously, and not being one of those individuals so unused to modern social and architectural conventions as to find difficulty in maintaining their equilibrium on polished floors, he acted upon my suggestion with a rapidity which made me smile.

At first wary, he could hardly trust me in my smiling consideration of him, and made a remark only occasionally, maintaining for a great time a suspicious silence. Yet there was something in my manner which seemed to flatter him, and in the midst of an explanation as to how rabbit tracks might be imitated, his chest fell and he said:

"If you'd only been along. I was coming back for you, but I hated to after all I'd said about your being snappish with me. Come on, I'll take you right away and show you where I made a little line of tracks this morning—coming back."

I replied with a trifle less sparkle perhaps than was fitting under the circumstances:

"We'll go back to yesterday, afterwhile. Don't let's be monkeys, yet. There'll be time enough to pick up the nuts we threw at the moon, when we've had some breakfast."

Tipyn o'Bob, 5 (March 1908), 12–16.

PHILIP THE SOBER

"HEAVENS what a spectacle!" Philip sat up in bed with a start, and half closing his eyes, gazed stupidly at a scarlet cloak which lay voluminous and unfolded across a chair, then glanced downward at an undried pool of rainwater glittering red beside it.

"Very disagreeable—must say. Such things are not often seen in a man's bed-room." His close squint relaxed and he sank back, leaving stars on the coverlet, where he had clutched it. He seemed to take for a moment a whimsical satisfaction in the uncertainty of some hidden thought. Then closing his eyes, he extended his feet rigid, the length of the bed, and gave himself up to enjoyment of a grateful sound, that of rain-drops pattering down heavily on large leaves outside the window.

A prince, Philip had the misfortune to be in love with a countess. Not that a countess is a mean personage, but that Philip was a prince and in many ways a foolish prince,—with strange ideas about the value of crowns and titles and other accidental trifles of a perishable character. He was almost in horror of those in whose lives tradition played no part. He had a superstitious feeling that under no circumstances could the ways of the unanointed be the ways of kings.

Instinctive in his desire to make the countess—Isabella—like him, he was, in all his efforts to make her do so, successful. He could never be quite sure, however, that he *wished* to have her like him—the flesh was strong, the spirit weak. An ordinary man with aristocratic tendencies would, in Philip's position as prince, bound by tradition to marry a princess, have swept away all considerations of marrying another, but Philip, of a nature intense and persevering, speculated a great part of the time as to whether he cared to marry "the fair Isabella" or whether he did not.

He was correct in supposing that he had a chance of doing so, could he make up his mind to. He had quite a talent for conversation and a rather high-bred particular fashion, set off by a rather agreeable voice, of drawling his vowels and crisping his consonants. He was extremely handsome, moreover, his face being at the same time spirited and thoughtful. He had a broad, low forehead with a suggestion of a diagonal furrow down it; eyebrows sweeping apart like a bird's wings; a mouth which closed with sensitive determination more firmly on one side than on the other, and that permanent deep coloring held to be indicative of a high level of fine feeling.

With the effect produced, of the imaginary carnage, still in his mind, he dressed with lazy care. Without emotion or visible pride he looked at himself in the mirror, then stepping back, touched his foot idly to the surface of the pool of rain-water which lay upon the floor still undried, and moved to the window. Planting his hands on the sill he was greeted by the deceptive hot-house aroma of a spring morning, and seized with a desire to be in the air— the rain having stopped—he descended the private stair from his apartment and was soon riding forth unprotected by a cloak or wrap of any description.

He walked his horse for a time through shallow puddles and drying mud, his head bowed, in his eyes a look of vacant concentration. Then, as one subconsciously conscious of a person's presence, glances up, he thought he must be in the neighborhood of what he had fancifully termed the Forbidden Mount, and looking up, found that it was so. He went chop-chopping along for a moment, oblivious to anything which might be happening, then glanced back. Catching sight of what he thought was a glimpse of something at a window, he took off his hat with a graceful sweep. His hand slackened on the rein and turning in a slow curve he urged his horse back at a rapid walk to the castle just passed. He abandoned his horse at the gate, as was the custom of the times, without fastening it, then, without waiting long enough for his patience to be tried, was admitted.

"I thought, Philip—"

"I was *passing*," answered Philip, mock-prim and jocose. The chivalrous ring of the words was of a character so pronounced as not to appeal to one so fond of the direct and the uncomplimentary as was Isabella.

"Of course," she smiled. She knew his ways. "I am glad the ceremony is so easily impelled." An evanescent spark of admiration lit her eye which pleased Philip, as he had come to regard the object of his affection as almost imperturbable. He reached out rather mock-ceremoniously a sprig shoot which he had stuck in his doublet and upon which he had been gazing down from time to time admiringly.

"Not that an addition to your attire is in any way necessary, if I may be so crude."

Isabella took it, twirled it absentmindedly for a moment, stroked her knee first with one tuft and then with another, and after a moment, let it fall to the ground unnoticed. Philip folded his arms and said with precision:

"Isabella—" Then with a flash of ardor so hot and unexpected as to startle even his Promethean-trained sensibilities—"I want you to marry me. Will you?"

A flickering smile played over the countess' down-cast features. Then with a look of determination she smiled again and shook her head.

Philip dropped his head back and said with calm persistence:

"You won't?" He planted his hands on the table. "Why not? In the course of time, you know, you would wear a crown, Isabella (to be inartistically worldly)."

"I know I should; and that is just it. It is not in the nature of things that I should. Not that you do not *want* me to." She gazed at Philip searchingly.

"You cannot care to marry me," remarked Philip with subtle carelessness.

"I care a great deal. It is from the *fact* that I care that I will *not* marry you," Isabella responded. "I do not believe in acquiescing in the things people that I care for ask me to do, as if their requests were matters of indifference to me."

"You cannot think me so frivolous, Isabella, as not to think I intend that you shall marry me, if you wish to, when I ask you to." Philip fixed his eyes on the ceiling, and Isabella, having walked the length of the room away from him, watched him for a long time, unobserved, her head slightly drawn back, her impassive, delicate features expressing a severity and sensitiveness contradicted by the look in her eyes. She felt that Philip possessed an underlying defect; that somehow he needed to be brought to his senses. She felt vaguely that his offer to marry her was, in a way which she could not detect, insincere. She felt subconsciously that he had had to persuade himself against his will to make the offer, that to make it he must have been carried on a tide of feeling which obliterated all feelings but those of the moment. A smile of evanescent conceit played for a moment upon her downcast features. She sighed, and advanced across the room, a deliciously pungent fragrance floating out from the folds of her skirt as it came hitching along carelessly after her.

"You do *not*, Philip, in your heart of hearts, Philip, want me to marry you. I am not going to—marry you."

The young prince glanced up at his accuser with doglike humility, and forbore to contradict her.

"My principles of life are crude and lawless from your point of view. An end is justified to my way of thinking, by any means, and you scorn that way of doing."

Nothing was being said. Isabella reached for a scrap of paper which lay on the table, lined with words in Philip's handwriting.

"May I read?" Her hand, lying across her knee, rose in protest as the author of the words stirred forward unconsciously solicitous.

"Philip!" The outburst had nothing to do with the words. "I am disappointed in you. You have no—" The girl gazed up at the ceiling. "You *lack* something."

"What?"

Taking a step forward, her fingers twisting together lightly behind her, the countess bent her gaze on the table, paused, and bit her lip, cutting off all possible speculation as to the probability of her intention. Rising and drifting near her mechanically, Philip paused, and with his head bent remained motionless. He jumped as if stabbed.

"You have what?" He began to arrange with care an already orderly part of his clothing.

"I have always liked you, Philip—*always;* but, unlike the most of people, you make it hard for one to like you." Philip smiled, vaguely flattered. "You remind me—of Pharaoh, you cannot decide."

She drew up her shoulders slowly, then smiled and gazed intently downward.

"Thoughtlessly heartless, ambitiously proud."

"Isabella?"

"Yes?" Philip took Isabella by the hand and led her to a window. Her hand dropped, inert and heavy, against the soft slippery silk of her dress. With a slow gaze of reproach she turned away and at some distance from her companion sat down. He stood gazing through the window.

"Isabella? Isabella, I can't think what I was saying. Are you ill? What is the matter?"

Shaking her head vigorously, she replied with slight disdain something it was impossible to hear.

"You want me to go?" The girl rose and, standing primly, inclined her head. "I—shall return—Isabella, if you will allow me." Philip advanced, then, with a helpless glance about him, withdrew from the apartment.

He traveled homeward, slowly, and producing the paper Isabella had been reading, he read over to himself a part of it.

"They come, I see them come this way,
    Advancing in a ring
    Upon their bending ranks,
    A thing which glitters as they swing."

"And then they crown him—And I—They do?" He twisted his scrawl into a spiral and swallowed calculatingly. Then, dragging down the bit and turning short, he galloped back on his tracks. The madness of a sudden hope caused him to spur his horse unmercifully.

"What fools are they who pray to crowns." He crisped the syllables contemptuously.

"Isabella, I am back. If I were a peasant instead of a king, you would marry me. If I were to cast every crown, farthing, stone, in my possession, into your lap, to be sold for alms, would you marry me?"

He smiled at his gravity, feeling that he argued weakly.

"You never would."

Isabella looked up gravely questioning.

"Don't you see, Isabella? I now understand. See how well," and he fairly shouted, " 'What fools are they who pray to crowns.' You do see now, don't you? and you will?"

Despite the surprise that shone upon it, Isabella's face betokened that she would.

Tipyn o'Bob, 5 (April 1908), 6–11.

IN A BALCONY

In a Balcony was given, March sixth, 1909, for the benefit of the Endowment Fund.* The play, with a plot which consisted only in the variation upon the dramatic moment, presented difficulties in the production, which were overcome, to the amazement of those who saw it. The sustained sentimental and dramatic conception was remarkable. Miss Elliott, '08, as Constance, not only satisfied the demand of beauty, particularly in the first scene as she stood against the balcony, but when it came to the climax of the play in the second scene, her artistic power gave the intellectual lines a tense dramatic vigor. Norbert, played by Miss Fox, '08, was handsome and impassioned. He betrayed his sex, however, in the breathlessness of his gesticulation. Miss Schenck's rendering of the queen's infatuation showed a remarkable mastery of a difficult rôle. When she came in she was haggard and old. As realization dawned upon her she became youthful, almost fervid. Miss Schenck achieved a counterpart to her effect in her assumption subsequently of the sinister.

The effect in the scenery, of darkness and height, was perfect, the Italian precision of it, assisted by the eavesdropping and ghostly statue. The whole effect was enhanced by the fitful music.

Four hundred and fifty dollars was made.

Tipyn o'Bob, 6 (April 1909), 18–19.

*In a Balcony, by Robert Browning (1855), was staged by Bryn Mawr College alumnae to raise money for the Endowment Fund.

WISDOM AND VIRTUE

THE rug had been swept, the floor waxed, the candle-sticks polished and set with fresh candles.

"Annie! Bring the flowers in." Miss Duckworth walked to the mantle, ran her fingers down the smooth irregularities of the candles, finally turned and walked from the room. She came back carrying a pot of brilliant yellow tulips in a small round dish, the shape and color of an acorn-cup. This she set on the table, moved off to get the effect, then sat down and taking a book from the table, began to read. The bell rang. She glanced toward the adjoining room, read a line or two and getting up deliberately, walked to the door. She slipped on the rug, pulled it straight with her foot and opened the door.

"Come in, Uncle Jack. I'm so glad to see you." Mr. Duckworth entered in a slouch hat and heavy overcoat, an expression of pleasure on his face in response to that occasioned by his arrival, threw down his hat and coat; his niece revolved uneasily behind him. He bestowed a brief glance on her dress, and on the ornament, a greenish pearl set in jasper which she wore around her neck, then he followed her into the drawing-room.

The house was a flat, centering about a small hallway; against the wall was a carved bench contrasting oddly with the reddish paneling behind it. In the drawing-room, a room with a low ceiling and heavy window frames, divided by small mullions, a Turkish rug covered the center of the floor. Straight curtains of a silky texture and vague pattern hung at the windows. Miss Duckworth held one of the curtains aside and gazed out at the river. The apartment was high, overlooking on the one hand a great stretch of smoky city, on the other a long line of river bank. Trees lined either bank; a stretch of clouds was settling down over the trees, which already wore a furry aspect in the evening light. Ice was floating along in the stream, a paddle-boat shoving about in the middle of it.

Mr. Duckworth was the owner of a publishing concern, had a taste for books and a fair amount of polish. The fact of his niece's existence had occurred to him and he had written to her that if she could set aside the Bohemian custom, as he understood it existed, of looking upon visitors as "enemies or a bore," he would come to see her.

"How are things going? It's cold in here." He followed the remark with a suggestive glance about the room and pulled out his handkerchief. It fell from his hand in a small cascade.

"Yes, a trifle; you asked me a question, did you not?" Miss Duckworth rose and turned on the heat. Her uncle was not an intellectual enough man to be forgiven physical inertia on the ground of mental activity, but she decided to get what pleasure she could from his conversation.

"What did you ask me, Uncle Jack?"

"I asked you how your work was going."

"Wretchedly." Miss Duckworth studied the carpet. "I feel a little bewildered."

"Yes, I've heard the tumultuous indolence of Bohemia has rather a peculiar effect on the inhabitants. Hardly a deadening one, though." Mr. Duckworth smiled.

"Bohemia is a very different sort of place, I imagine, from the sort of place you think it is. We can scare up a scandal or two to satisfy your craving for sensation, but it's purely from a willingness to be obliging. I could entertain you all night."

"I shan't force you to."

Miss Duckworth looked bored.

"See my cat." She pointed awkwardly to a pearl-colored Angora cat which was making its way about the room.

"Since when have you had that?" Mr. Duckworth took off his glasses and smoothed his eyebrows apart with his fingers, thoughtfully. "A cat is so suggestive."

"Of protracted domesticity? It *is*, rather. Baudelaire put the notion in my head." She laughed and opened the book she had been reading. "I think you would like it." She thrust the book into her uncle's hands. He glanced at it scornfully.

"Though it is the exceptional point of view, very much like your own, you might find it stale." The man puzzled.

"I think I generally agree with people."

"But in such a way that the implication is plain. Disagreement is a little too energetic a mode of self-defense to find favor with you."

Presumptuousness was not exactly the sort of thing to stimulate Mr. Duckworth to gallantry, nor was emphasis placed upon feminine professionalism. Pious women, clever men, and obedient children, were the order of things in his world; his curiosity, however, with regard to the profession in question, overmastered reserve.

"What made you go into this?"

"Painting, do you mean?"

"Yes, I shouldn't think you would be so consumingly bored." Mr. Duckworth glanced at the burnished lead candle-shades and the silver fire irons.

"Is that meant for sarcasm? Your significances mystify me. Funny thing about Bohemia," Miss Duckworth ran on without giving her uncle time for reply. "The experiences derived, exasperating as they are, you feel to be superior to the experiences to be derived at any other place. You probably don't see that they are. I expect you to agree with me, though, on a number of points—"

"I'm a little supercilious about what's expected of me."

"Well,—" a pause ensued, "if you come with me, I'll show you some pictures."

Mr. Duckworth rose, a smile played about his lips; instantly he suppressed it.

"I hate to show you these things. You won't like them and you'll feel obliged to."

"I shan't, I assure you."

A keenness for self-characterization always roused Miss Duckworth's interest. "Say anything that occurs to you," she urged.

"An invitation to the gallows." Mr. Duckworth smiled. A few cryptic remarks came floating into his head and a remembrance of forgotten technicalities, but he dismissed them.

"Horrible place, is it not?"

Miss Duckworth held back a curtain and exposed to view a large room. A square patch of light fell on the floor from a skylight in the ceiling. The floor was dingy and cluttered with scraps and thumbtacks, pushed into the wood to the head. Easels stood about encroaching upon each other, groups of unframed pictures leaned against the wall. A set of drawings by Jerome filled the middle space of the main wall, there was a general air of invitation to zeal if anything were to be accomplished.

Miss Duckworth stood idly, jerked a portrait out from where it stood against an easel in the shadow, and set it in the light.

"Ah!" Mr. Duckworth moved up close, then stood off. The picture showed a girl in a white dress, an orange rock behind her, a brilliant patch of sea toward the left.

"Landscape portraiture is going out, but I rather like it. It looks windy that side"; Miss Duckworth glanced critically.

"Is that yours?" Her uncle looked with indulgent scorn at a cigarette which lay on the edge of a table.

"No." His niece brushed it into a waste-basket with a fastidiousness which argued sincerity.

"Almost too ascetic to be in character, aren't you?" Mr. Duckworth put his hands up to his face and lit a pipe.

" 'Angels are not happier than men because they are better than men,' but because they don't investigate each other's spheres." The stroke fell boldly.

"You don't separate pedantry from art, I see." Mr. Duckworth was above resenting the impertinence.

"No, my patron saints are job affairs."

Mr. Duckworth flashed her a frightened glance. He set up for a connoisseur, but she failed to make the application personal.

"This needs to be simplified." She held her hands up parallel and brought them down emphatically.

"Rather a puddle, I should say. It takes art to get art *out* of things like that."

"That's one of the best things I've done," Miss Duckworth said stiffly, annoyed at the ambiguity of the words and the shadow of egotism which they cast upon her. The picture showed a poplar tree, which looked like a banyan-tree, beside a roadway, which looked like a small stream; "and that's not bad," she pointed to a violinist in an entirely different style, a street musician, the hands and chin strikingly blocked, a clear, diagonal running from a flower in his coat to a glare of light on his nose. "The jaw's good, shaped like a sugar scoop, if you notice."

"How about this?" With the air of a dog which sees another dog of his own kind, Mr. Duckworth walked up to a picture of a man, named, according to Miss Duckworth's explanation, Thomas Dagley. The light struck sharply across the forehead, cutting into a number of small planes above the eye.

"Pretty, isn't it, the way the color works into it there and that green eye. He's very clever, a curious combination of ambition and indifference." Miss Duckworth followed her train of thought with interest.

"You speak complacently for a person who is going into a decline. He looks shy."

"He is not, that's his art."

"What is that?"

"That?" Miss Duckworth bent down. "That is my signature." A small reddish device lay scrawled against a purple oblong. "It's an earthworm, rather like one, don't you think? Suppose we go." Her eyes reverted to the worm and a settled gloom appeared to descend upon her.

"Well, yes," Mr. Duckworth held the curtain aside, but glanced back at the portrait, "his hands sag down on his pockets too much and his elbows stick out. It's like a woman to construct the thing that way. Are you coming?" He glanced imperiously.

Too charmed with the comment to be annoyed at the insult, Miss Duckworth followed.

"Very good judges such as yourself consider enthusiasm a wild delusion, I know, and perhaps it is. But there's a fascination about it."

"I've no doubt there is," Mr. Duckworth mused. "I'm glad to see you encouraged with regard to your prowess. You are foolish to allow your ambition to be measured by attainment."

"Yes, do you suppose people who have anything to them ever do?"

Mr. Duckworth was silent. The clock struck three,—four, five, six, precipitately.

"I must go."

"Can't you stay? It was careless of me not to think of it before, but I've been so absorbed in what you were saying. Dinner in Bohemia is a different thing from a Bohemian dinner, but I think if you stay, I may sufficiently recover from my lugubrious mood to be able to make you wish to come back."

"I *shall* come back." Mr. Duckworth hesitated, his niece avoided his glance. He finally left. Carrying the Baudelaire to the bookcase, Miss Duckworth stood the volume in its place, then glanced at the door through which her uncle had departed.

"Gloomy, Janus-headed man. Wisdom palls upon him." A smile flashed across her countenance.

Tipyn o'Bob, 6 (June 1909), 11–15.

SAMUEL BUTLER

BUTLER is a black thorn stick in the hand of the optimist. "Surely we may do whatever we like, and the better we like it, the better we shall do it," illustrates his ideas of the value of literary boundaries and prohibitions. To set the matter forth uncurtailed: "It has been said, 'Thou shalt not masquerade in costumes not of thine own period,' but the history of art is the history of revivals. Surely we may do whatever we like, and the better we like it, the better we shall do it. The great thing is to make sure that we like the style we choose better than we like any other; that we engraft on it whatever we hear that we think will be a good addition, and depart from it wherever we dislike it. If a man does this, he may write in the style of the year one, and not be an anachronism."

The fact of Butler's unwillingness to assume the official character of "scrutineer" has not impaired his serviceability. One does not love a man the less for his unwillingness to say, "I have examined the credentials of other people; I have plucked masks from hypocrites' faces; I have stood nearby to see that no undeserving person got a crumb." What does impair his serviceability is a disability, shared by him in common with most staves—the inability to enjoy the progress which he was able to promote.

Chimaera, 1 (July 1916), 55–56.

THE ACCENTED SYLLABLE

F O R the most part, in what we read, it is the meaning rather than the tone of voice which gives us pleasure. In the case of the following groups of words, however, I am inclined to think that the meaning has very little to do with the pleasure the words give us.

Then Louisa went into the kitchen and cried for it is exasperating to be unjustly accused. (Strindberg: *Easter and Other Plays*)

And verses? Why I even composed a whole drama in imitation of Manfred. Among the characters was a ghost with blood on his breast, and not his own blood observe, but the blood of all humanity. (Turgenef: *Rudin*)

Tom when very young, had presented Sophia with a little bird which he had taken from the nest, had nursed up and taught to sing. (*Tom Jones*)

One would hate to have to live in the world which Mr. X describes but one is delightfully conscious of the fact that one will never have to. (J. B. Kerfoot: *Life*)

As I have said over and over again if I think something that I know and greatly like (in music) no matter whose it is, is appropriate, I appropriate it. (Butler: Note 122)

A cognate essay is on *Description in Poetry* by Mr. A. Clutton-Brock, who contends, firstly, that beauty in poetic description is *irrelevant* unless it adds to the cumulative powers of the whole, and secondly, that it must be judged not by absolute standards but by its *relation* to the theme. Sound notions, these. The first might be taken to heart by certain modern bards; the second, by their critics. (Books of the Month: *English Review*, January, 1912)

It is true enough to say that everybody is selfish provided we add, and unselfish. (Cabot: *What Men Live By*)

Does Mr. Shaw admit that he has blundered? Not a bit of it. He assures the spectators that while in one sense the theme is not the "opening theme" because it does not open the work, in a higher, subtler sense it is the opening theme inasmuch as the music passes into it by "an irresistible gravitation." Mr. Shaw's week I suppose, begins with Tuesday afternoon. ("The Arts and Crafts of Bernard Shaw." Reprinted in the *Transcript*, Boston, September 16, 1914)

Of course I knew all that down in the cellars of my being, but upstairs all the same I had the sense of guilt and expiation, this anxious doubt that perhaps all that great, gloomy, medieval business of saints and nuns and bones and relics and miracles and icons and calvaries and cells and celibacy and horsehair shirts and blood and dirt and tears, was true after all! (Zangwill: *Dreamers of the Ghetto*)

Androcles is probably Mr. Shaw himself and right glad we are to see him. (*English Review*, October, 1913)

Impartial? Never. (*Life*)

and the English of the footnote to one of Augier's plays:

Three chops well peppered.

By the tone of voice I mean that intonation in which the accents which are responsible for it are so unequivocal as to persist, no matter under what circumstances the syllables are read or by whom they are read. Often the recital of a passage is termed monotonous when the dominant accents only are monotonous and it is made up of an infinite number of varied accents; if an author's written tone of voice is distinctive, a reader's speaking tone of voice will not obliterate it.

An author's tone of voice repels or compels us. It rarely happens that this tone of voice varies from time to time as the author writes under one classification of prose, say history, or under another, say fiction; but we have an instance of this in the case of Poe. Poe's narrative tone of voice is flavored with artifice, and with the artifice of the drawing-room, not with the artifice of the detective-story expert, the italicized words serving only to make the effect more rigid. The ideas stand muster and the sentences are carefully interrelated so the slightly repellant flavor of the writing is to be attributed to the tone of voice rather than to the trend of the ideas. In the case of Poe's papers on the *Literati* of New York, the critical opinions expressed are in many cases not sound, and in some cases argue a complete lack of imagination as in the flouting of Cornelius Matthews' "feathers darker than a thousand fears," on the ground that feathers are not of the same substance as fears and are not to be compared with them. Moreover, in these papers—

and in the "Rationale of Verse"—there is a tincture of the artificiality which characterizes the narratives, there is a slight grandiloquence, a straining for rarity, and an unmistakable tone of condescension, but the intensity of the writing is very fine and an intonation of gusto lends to the whole an imperativeness which the tales can never have. Compare the tone of voice of the tales with the critical tone of voice in this passage:

> I think I could manage the point myself (the writing of Greek hexameters): For example:
>
>> Do tell when may we hope to make men of sense out of
>>   the pundits.
>> Born and brought up with their snouts deep down in the
>>   mud of the frogpond?
>> . . . or downright, upright nutmegs out of a pineknot?

> The proper spondee predominance is here preserved; some of the dactyls are not so good as I could wish, but upon the whole the rhythm is very decent, to say nothing of the excellent sense.

And in this:

> The truth is that cant has never attained a more owl-like dignity than in the discussion of dramatic principle. A modern stage critic is nothing if not a lofty condemner of all things simple and direct.

In these extracts we have a distinctive, written, personal tone of voice.

It is true that written tones of voice may resemble each other and that a distinctive tone of voice employed by one author may resemble that same tone of voice as employed by another author. The following observations of Poe's are like some of Samuel Butler's notes as any of Butler's notes are like each other:

> An argument (prefixed to a poem) is but another form of "this is an ox," subjoined to the portrait of an animal with horns.

> The deepest emotion aroused within us by the happiest allegory is a very imperfectly satisfied sense of the writer's ingenuity in overcoming a difficulty which we should have preferred his not having attempted to overcome. . . . Under the best circumstances it must interfere with that unity of effect which to the artist is worth all the allegories in the

world. . . . Pleasure will be derived from the reader's ability to keep the allegory out of sight or his inability to comprehend it.

But the fact that a tone of voice is not invariably a distinctly personal one does not alter the fact that the tone of voice does contribute to or detract from the aesthetic effect of a piece of writing.

In the case of rhymed verse, a distinctive tone of voice is dependent on naturalistic effects, and naturalistic effects are so rare in rhyme as almost not to exist. By a naturalistic effect I mean the sort of thing we have in Hamilton Sorley's "Barrabas," D. F. Dalston's "Blown," and Wallace Stevens' "As Before."

> Little live, great pass.
> Jesus Christ and Barrabas
>   Were found the same day.
>   *Spectator*, May 27, 1916.

> It was all my own,
> I have tended it carefully
> For its sake full many a crop have I sown.
> I have guarded it well from the winds that have blown
>   So bitterly.
>   *English Review*, June 1914.

> He will be thinking in strange countries
> Of the white stones near her door;
> But it is me he will see
> At the window, as before.
>   *Poetry*, July 1916.

So far as free verse is concerned, it is the easiest thing in the world to create one intonation in the image of another until finally one has assembled a bouquet of vocal exclamation points. I can read the following advertisement with a great deal of pleasure but I am not sure that it would give me pleasure to read this identical advertisement every day in the week. An intonation must have meaning behind it to support it, or it is not worth much:

> Venus pencils are made in seventeen black and two copying degrees, each degree guaranteed never to vary: softest and blackest, very very soft and very black, very soft and very black, very soft and black, soft and black, soft, soft medium, firm, medium hard, hard, very hard, extra hard,

very very hard and firm, extra extra hard and firm, extra extra hard and extra firm, hardest and firmest.

The Egoist, 3 (October 1916), 151–52.

A NOTE ON T. S. ELIOT'S BOOK

I T might be advisable for Mr. Eliot to publish a fangless edition of *Prufrock and Other Observations* for the gentle reader who likes his literature, like breakfast coffee or grapefruit, sweetened. A mere change in the arrangement of the poems would help a little. It might begin with "La Figlia che Piange," followed perhaps by the "Portrait of a Lady"; for the gentle reader, in his eagerness for the customary bit of sweets, can be trusted to overlook the ungallantry, the youthful cruelty, of the substance of the "Portrait." It may as well be admitted that this hardened reviewer cursed the poet in his mind for this cruelty while reading the poem; and just when he was ready to find extenuating circumstances—the usual excuses about realism—out came this "drunken helot" (one can hardly blame the good English reviewer whom Ezra Pound quotes!) with that ending. It is hard to get over this ending with a few moments of thought; it wrenches a piece of life at the roots.

As for the gentle reader, this poem could be followed by the lighter ironies of "Aunt Nancy," the "Boston Evening Transcript," etc. One would hardly know what to do with the two London pieces. Whistler in his post-impressionistic English studies—and these poems are not entirely unlike Whistler's studies—had the advantage of his more static medium, of a somewhat more romantic temperament, and of the fact that the objects he painted half-hid their ugliness under shadows and the haze of distance. But Eliot deals with life, with beings and things who live and move almost nakedly before his individual mind's eye—in the darkness, in the early sunlight, and in the fog. Whatever one may feel about sweetness in literature, there is also the word honesty, and this man is a faithful friend of the objects he portrays; altogether unlike the sentimentalist who really stabs them treacherously in the back while pretending affection.

Poetry, 12 (April 1918), 36–39.

Review of *Prufrock and Other Observations*, by T. S. Eliot (Egoist).

JEAN DE BOSSCHÈRE'S POEMS

THIS Frenchman, like certain modern poets of our own language, sees the characteristics, as of individual life, which lurk in inanimate objects and even in situations, as well as in living beings. He feels what might be called the soul of these. This form of vision is perhaps mysticism, but it is entirely apart from, though not contradictory to, theological mysticism. To one with a developed sensitiveness this form of individuality is a thing as real—in this world of illusions—as material appearances are. Much of Harold Monro's poetry is on this theme, and one may trace it in some poems of H. D., of Pound, Eliot, and others. One can find a slight similarity between Amy Lowell and Jean de Bosschère in the exaggerated form of the expression of their vision, though there is a heat and an artistic self-abnegation in the French poet which Miss Lowell does not attain, perhaps does not wish to attain.

"Homère Mare,"* for example, is a story-poem about the attachment of the human soul to the souls of his surroundings, and its estrangement from them. It has the serene, subdued beauty of a sunny pebbled road through a fair country.

"L'Offre de Plebs"† is probably the most beautiful poem in the volume— one can hardly over-praise its peculiar beauty. The subject is sympathetic with the poet's temperament, and its gloom and playfulness express a depth of sensitiveness rarely reached. It is the perfect image of a mood—desire for solitude; and in spite of wistfulness it has no trace of sentimentality:

> Je veux qu'il ait un Dieu!
> Et qu'il brûle en sacrifices toutes ses amours
> Et ses maisons;
> Et que, pour moi, son esprit prenne
> La robe des moines
> Close comme la peau des grenouilles.
> Je veux qu'il ait un Dieu!
> Il faut que cela soit moi. . . .[i]

*"Homeric Marsh" (Flint's translations, not supplied by M. M.)
†"The Offering of Plebs"

Review of *The Closed Door*, by Jean de Bosschère. Illustrated by the author, with a translation by F. S. Flint and an introduction by May Sinclair (John Lane).

And:

> Je ne veux pas d'un coeur qui ait aimé;
> Je ne veux d'un ami qui sera hérétique.
> Il y a la chair et le diable de l'esprit.
> Il y a les arbres et aussi les parfums;
> Il y a des ombres, des souvenirs;
> Il y a des images, des rêves,
> Et il y a l'espoir
> Et la douleur. [ii]

"Ulysse Bâtit son Lit"* is the expression of an individual soul in a small or large village—it might be in France, Argentina, or America, for it is everywhere the same. The poem is a perfect embodiment of the pettiness of the village spirit, which in this case resented a man's way of "building" his bed! God help these bed-builders of France, Argentina, or America.

The latter parts of the volume express more personal emotions and are less unlike the work of other poets. The themes of "Doutes," "Gridale," "Verger," "La Promesse du Merle,"† have been treated in poetry in various forms. "Doutes" and "Gridale" are in places rhetorical, but always lit with a weird and sometimes quaint fire which is the poet's own. Parts of them form complete poems, like these about his father and mother from "Doutes":

> Il fumait sa pipe avec intégrité.
> On se collait près de lui
> Pour tirer par le nez son odeur d'homme.
> . . . .
> Et la mère etait le pain et le beurre,
> La rosée froide de six heures, et la cerise,
> Les draps blancs au réséda,
> Et le rond chaud des levres sur la joue. [iii]

In "La Promesse du Merle" the somberness is relieved by the lightness of touch:

> Ce n'est pas fier de finer
> Toujours à moitié! . . .
> De jeter trois notes de feu
> Qui ouvrent le coeur fané
> Avec des ézardes de faim et de soif. [iv]

---

*"Ulysses Builds His Bed"
†"Doubts," "Gridale," "Orchard," "The Blackbird's Promise"

In this poem, as well as in some of the others, the poetic height and depth of the emotion sometimes appear strained, but that depends on the temperament and even on the mood of the reader.

In the illustrations one can find the influence of Kandinsky's black-and-white—haunting patterns often like spilled and partly dried water. Also there may be a suggestion of Alfred Kubin—compare for instance Kubin's illustrations to his romance with De Bosschère's at the end of "Doutes." He is trying to escape Beardsley, and usually succeeds—indeed, he is on the whole self-expressive. One wishes that our American illustrators would give us, as intimately as these men, their own happy or somber individualities.

The translation is too servile, and lacks charm, especially toward the end of the book. But printing the French and English versions on opposite pages is too severe a test for any translator.

> i I wish Him to have a God!
> It must be I . . .
> I wish him to have a God,
> And to burn as a sacrifice all his loves
> And his houses;
> I wish him to clothe his mind for me
> In a monk's frock,
> Close-shut like the skin of a frog.
> I wish him to have a God!
> It must be I. . . .

> ii I want no heart that has loved;
> I want no friend who will be a heretic.
> There is the flesh and the daemon of the mind;
> There are the trees and also the perfumes;
> There are shadows and memories;
> There are images and dreams,
> And there is hope
> And sorrow. . . .

> iii He smoked his pipe with integrity.
> You pressed yourself close to him
> To snuff the man's smell of him.
> . . . .
> And my mother was the bread and butter,
> The cold dew of evening and the sweetness of the cherry,
> The white sheets smelling of mignonette,
> And the warm circle of lips on my cheek.

> iv It is not such a great thing
> Always to stop half-finished!

> . . . .
> To strike three fiery notes
> That open the faded heart
> With cracks of hunger and thirst.

Poetry, 12 (April 1918), 48–51.

WILD SWANS

FOR a poet with such a personality as Yeats, it seems almost indecorous to bare it before us, in the midst of our social, political and literary lives. Yeats makes poetry out of the fact that he is a proud, sensitive, cultivated Irishman. He hardly has to make poetry—except the rhymes, which don't matter; he just lets his heart talk, as in the poems about the dying lady.

In a despondent mood, the poet, like some of the admirers of his earlier manner, longs for the leopards of the moon, and complains of the harsh and timid sun. Whatever the lights are of "Ego Dominus Tuus," "Presences," "Men Improve with the Years," "The Collarbone of a Hare," "The Fisherman," "The Hawk," they shine. The invading hawk too, if not indecorous, is unfair, as unfair as some similarly naive passages in the Bible are:

> What tumbling cloud did you cleave,
> Yellow-eyed hawk of the mind,
> Last evening? that I who had sat
> Dumbfounded before a knave,
> Should give to my friend
> A pretense of wit.

The weighing and measuring, the critical care evidently spent on this thin volume, save the reviewer most of his labor. If the longer poems seem to him, in spite of their shrewdness and spells of passion, somewhat old-fashioned, he is willing to bend to the opinion of the author of the others. One can not but pay reverence to a poet who, after having written poetry for many years, can still be read with the same critical alertness that one

---

Review of *The Wild Swans at Coole, Other Verses and a Play in Verse*, by W. B. Yeats (The Cuala Press).

would give to the best of the younger poets. And if there is a drooping line here and there, the author is too proud, too able, and too conscientious to arouse misgivings that he will ever bank on his reputation.

Here is Yeats in a very gentle mood:

Presences

The Night has been so strange that it seemed
As if the hair stood up on my head:
From going-down of the sun I have dreamed
That women laughing, or timid or wild,
In rustle of lace or silken stuff,
Climbed up my creaking stair. They had read
All I had rhymed of that monstrous thing
Returned and yet unrequited love.
They stood in the door and stood between
My great wood lectern and the fire,
Till I could hear their hearts beating.
One is a harlot, and one a child
That never looked upon man with desire,
And one it may be a queen.

In "Ego Dominus Tuus," the beautiful poetic dialogue which appeared first in *Poetry* and is reprinted here and in his latest prose volume, the poet would have us believe that great poems are the result of the poet's "opposite" image—an expression of what the poet is not. I think this opposite, and not his little everyday thoughts and actions, *is* the poet; Dowson's drunkenness, and Dante's lecherous life, are somewhat beside the mark, as their effects on the poet's soul are mainly those of health and sickness. They are ethical and civil sins, but hardly poetic *sins*. Their scars on the poet are not of the same character as Turner's miserliness, or as malice, envy, etc. But even these, when present, are hardly more than masks of the poet's soul—perhaps hardly more than masks of any soul; it is in his poems that the real soul can be seen. Nor is indulgence due, as Yeats thinks, to the poet's desire to escape from himself; but rather, in so far as it is more than mere exhaustion, due to his desire to find himself. It is the disappointment with pleasure, and life's egging on.

At the Hawk's Well, beautiful as it is as poetry and as a poetic play, does not to me seem to be a Noh play in the full sense of the term. The Noh play is based on something nearer to the lives of the Japanese people than a legend. A modern Noh play, to have a similar appeal, would have to be based on something nearer the lives of the Irish people. A play based on Davitt or Parnell might come nearer the Japanese; or perhaps best, a play based on something in modern life treated mystically. But it has the great merit of being the first attempt at a Noh play in English.

Poetry, 13 (October 1918), 42–44.

OLD AND NEW MASTERS IN LITERATURE

THIS new volume, by Robert Lynd, contains a group of twenty-seven biographical and critical studies in which are set forth in their essential character the genius and personality of each of the authors forming the subject of these essays.

Dostoevsky's world is to Mr. Lynd, "an inferno—a multiplicity of action . . . in which even the talk is of actions more than of ideas." "As strongly repelled by Dostoevsky's shrieking Pan Slavism as by his sensationalism among horrors," Turgenev is "a welcome presence . . . one of those authors whose books we love because they reveal a personality sensitive, affectionate, pitiful." His chief distinction as a novelist is to Mr. Lynd, the creating of noble women; his chief fault, a "lack of exuberance." Jane Austen is one to whom "conversation is three-fourths of life . . . the first English novelist before Meredith to portray women with free personalities," and, like Meredith, a "satirist of the male egoist." Mr. Lynd regards Shaw as "genial beyond the majority of inveterate controversialists and propagandists . . . not hesitating to wound and not hesitating to misunderstand, but free from malice"; he is a champion of truth and a "master of laughter," gifted with a "genuine comic sense of character." James is characterized as a "realist of civilized society, in which both speech and action have to be sifted with scientific care before they will yield their grain of motive," and as has been noted by James' amanuensis, Miss Bosanquet, Mr. Lynd notes the striking analogy between James' literary method and that of his hero in "The Death of the Lion"—"loose, liberal, confident." Of *The Middle Years*, he says, "It is precious in every page for its wit . . . and those who can

Review of *Old and New Masters in Literature*, by Robert Lynd (Scribner's).

read it at all will read it with shining eyes"; while of James as a critic, he says, "he is never more human than when he is writing about books. It is not inconceivable that he will live as a critic long after he is forgotten as a novelist."

To admirers of Hardy it would seem that the moving quality of this novelist's work has escaped the critic. One finds fault with the statement that Hardy is not a great poet, not because the critic has failed to enjoy Hardy's poetry, but because the statement implies an insufficient grasp of Hardy's prose. To apply Hudson's definition of a poet, Hardy is an "interpreter of life through the medium of the emotions"; the verse is, if you like, a variation on the prose; superfluous if one does not care for the prose, indispensable if one does. So far as Hardy's meter is concerned, it will not strike the most ardent admirer of Hardy as being uniformly felicitous, but is it fair to say that Hardy is "neither sufficiently articulate nor sufficiently fastidious to be a great poet?"

Mr. Lynd says of Conrad: "There is no other living writer who is sensitive in anything like the same degree, to the sheer mysteriousness of the earth," and he has felt to be conspicuous, throughout Conrad's interpretation of life, a "passionate morality." "In some ways," he says in the chapter on Browning, "Mr. Conrad's is the most heroic imagination in contemporary literature." Though Conrad himself has said that it is *The Nigger of the Narcissus* by which he wishes his success as an artist to be judged, Mr. Lynd thinks his fame will rest chiefly upon three of his volumes of short stories, *Typhoon*, *Youth*, and *'Twixt Land and Sea*.

In Yeats, Mr. Lynd regrets the "self-consciousness of the priest"; he feels that "Mr. Yeats is not a genius with natural readiness of speech." Those who think of Mr. Yeats as a conversationalist, a master of clean-cut, luminous prose, will find it difficult to credit this last statement, but will none the less be satisfied that Yeats' magic has been felt when Mr. Lynd speaks of "the deep passion which has given shape to his verse," when he denominates him "a genius outside the landmarks, . . . too original, too secret . . . to capture an imagination that has fixed the outlines of its kingdom."

The "left-handedness" of Masefield "moves" Mr. Lynd "to impatience." Keats, Mr. Lynd declares, is "great among the second, not among the first, poets." Rossetti is to Mr. Lynd "one who always sought to bring peace to his soul by means of ritual." Browning is "the poet of love," whose "imagination was a soaring eagle," who has achieved in "Childe Roland," if it has been "anywhere in literature, the summit of tragic and triumphant music."

In addition to the authors mentioned, Mr. Lynd writes of Mr. G. K. Chesterton and Mr. Hilaire Belloc, Wordsworth, J. M. Synge, Villon, Pope,

James Elroy Flecker, Strindberg, Ronsard, Tchekov, Lady Gregory, Mr. Cunninghame Graham, Swinburne, Mr. J. C. Squire, Mr. Rudyard Kipling, and Thomas M. Kettle. Mr. Lynd's criticism of Kettle remains in the mind; it is this essay perhaps more than any other which makes one wish to own the book, and to urge it upon one's friends.

The New York Times Book Review, 12 October 1919, p. 536.

II. *THE DIAL* YEARS
1921-1929

REVIEWS AND
ESSAYS

JACOPONE DA TODI

THE life of Jacopone da Todi is a highly romantic, dramatic narrative; it is a background for religious poetry as beautiful as any that we have; more than anything else, however, it is as the name indicates, a spiritual biography. Of the conspicuously romantic episode of Jacopone's conversion, too much, perhaps, has been made. It is not more romantic nor dramatic than each of the successive phases of his life as a friar and scarcely more than alluded to by Miss Underhill, the tragedy is one of which he, himself, has seen fit not to speak at all. At the age of thirty-seven or eight—in one of the years between 1265 and 1267—he was married to Vanna, daughter of Bernardino di Guidone of the lesser Umbrian aristocracy, of a house Ghibelline in politics as was his own. The ideal wife he has told us, should be "beautiful and healthy, well-bred and sweet-natured. She must have a large dowry and must not have a nagging tongue." We infer that Vanna was the personification of his requirements with perhaps the exception of the dowry and the fact that she was desirous of living a life of religious seclusion. Accommodating herself outwardly to Ser Jacomo's requirements, she had accompanied him to the home of an acquaintance on the occasion of a marriage festival and during the progress of the ball, was dancing on a balcony when the balcony fell and she was mortally hurt. When her injuries were being cared for, it was discovered that beneath her magnificent garments, she wore a shirt of hair. "Life he must have": says his biographer; "he needed its color, its perpetual calls to action, its romance. Now his temporal life lay in ruins around him: but through the rents in its wall, eternal life was suddenly disclosed." "Mystics," she says, "do not spring full-grown from the wreck

Review of *Jacopone da Todi, Poet and Mystic—1228–1306: A Spiritual Biography*, by Evelyn Underhill. With a selection from the spiritual songs— the Italian text translated into English verse by Mrs. Theodore Beck (E. P. Dutton).

of their worldly careers. They pass for the most part through a period of spiritual childhood and hard education, marked by the child's intensity of feeling and distorted scale of values, its abounding vitality, dramatic instinct and lack of control. . . . In this, Jacopone was true to type." He had led the life of the intellect for nearly forty years. "When others went to Mass or to hear a sermon, he preferred to stay at home and have a good dinner and a little music." From having thus deferred to the dictates of intellect and sense, he now became wildly ascetic—subject on the one hand to wild states of rapturous adoration, recalling in exuberance the "French-like rejoicings" into which St. Francis is said to have broken out, and on the other hand to "profound reactions of self-hatred and despairing grief," going so far beyond the requirements of convent piety that he was refused admittance into the Convent of San Fortunato at Todi.

We do not know where the years were spent until 1278; we do know that the "superficial character of mere physical austerities" had at this time become clear to him; he found that he had "but exchanged one kind of wealth for another." He had achieved a conquest over the senses; he now felt it to be essential that he should make a complete sacrifice of his personal will and with the end in view of subjecting himself to the uncongenial restraints of convent life, he again sought admittance to the Convent of San Fortunato and was received.

His entrance into the convent was no more a matter of satisfaction to the friars than it was to him for "although the Spiritual party and those who followed the 'relaxed' rule, had alike accepted Holy Poverty theoretically, as theoretically, ordinary Christians have accepted the Sermon on the Mount," they felt "the continuance and success of the primitive Franciscan methods" to be a reproach to them; nor was Jacopone, we read, "easily transformed into the pattern friar." Contemplation was not in accord with his disposition. "Fasting and prayer were welcome—indeed, he loved them to excess—but it was long before he learned to accept with meekness the small mortifications of daily life." The poem on impatience cited by Miss Underhill in this connection shows how difficult for him was the conquest of hot temper and self-esteem (Lauda XXVIII).

Of Impatience, Which Brings All Our Gains to Nothing

I labored long, I strove with might and main:
And yet I cannot keep the good I gain.

Yea, I have been a monk full many a year,
Have suffered much, and wandered far and near,
Have sought and found—yet held not,—till I fear
    That nothing can I show for all my pain.

In calm retreats my truest joy I found;
I strove in prayer with no uncertain sound;
I fed the poor for many miles around;
    In sickness, very patient have I lain.

In uttermost obedience did I dwell,
In suffering and poverty as well;
Yes, I was chaste and happy in my cell,
    So far as my poor powers could attain.

Famished and weak, I fasted many a day;
Dried up by heat and pierced by cold I lay;
I was a pilgrim on a weary way,
    Or so it seemed, in sunshine and in rain.

To pray, I daily rose before the sun;
Mass did I hear before the dark was done;
To tierce and nones and vespers would I run,
    And, after compline, still to watch was fain.

And then was said to me a scornful word:
—Deep in my heart the poisoned arrow stirred,—
At once my tongue was ready when I heard,
    With fierce and burning fury to complain.

Now see how great and wealthy I must be!
I heap my gains for all the world to see;
Yet one poor word so fiercely angers me,
    That I must strive to pardon it in vain!

Affectation of learning was to him an acute source of discipline, and one notes that it is pride of intellect, not learning which he condemns—that for instance, in Laude XVII and XXXI, he "expresses merely the contempt felt by the inheritor of a solid culture and an unassailable social tradition for the thinly-veneered imitation—the intellectual 'beggar on horse-back.' " The works characteristic of his middle period are "remarkable for their insistence on order and measure." "There is something deeply impressive," Miss

Underhill says, "in the spectacle of this vehement nature thus capitulating to the austere Augustinian concept of love as to the very principle of order itself at the moment in which it is still swept by the tempest of feeling—ready to justify its own impassioned state."

Having triumphed over the senses and the will, the supreme achievement yet remained to him—the conquest of the spirit. He finds that "still the busy intellect has not been put in its place. It continues to possess its own ideas, and therefore to be possessed by its own limitations. Entangled in these, it ranges around, seeking to understand; only to find that the brick-built conceptual universe intervenes between it and reality." This transcendence of separateness, says Jacopone, "is the testing-house where the academic and the real mystic part company. The first is still held in the realm of speculation; lofty indeed yet tethered to the earth like a captive balloon. The second has the free flight of a bird . . . not needing to see because it is at home." Jacopone was imprisoned by Pope Boniface VIII in 1298, and we infer that it was at this time that he entered upon his third stage of mystical development. Only life can speak of life, and his words are testimony to the fact of an unprecedented vital force within. He speaks of personal oppositions having at last been transcended and says that he is "no longer troubled by the temptation to take an interest in his food," that "when it is nice, he refers its flavors to God" but that he permits himself such gratitude only as is permitted to those who can refer everything to God. In the attainment of power through acceptance of the untoward circumstances of life, he reminds one of the live oak which cannot be killed by cutting, with its tent-like foliage and contradictory intricateness of growth. The genius for attaining to sphere after sphere of spiritual development is a secret even when explained, but what Boethius has defined as the "total and perfect possession of unlimited life at a single moment" seems less far removed from the world of experience when its transcendence is seen to stand out in as bold relief as in the present instance.

It is, as Miss Underhill says, Jacopone's poems upon which we base our knowledge of his inner life. The Italian text of certain of these laude is printed at the end of the book with the translation beside it. The selections vary in interest but each is a work of marked individuality. The author's ability to sustain a key, his passion for symmetry, and the dramatic instinct are apparent throughout. Repetition, the bane of some writing, is in the laude a powerful adjunct and the writer's accomplished use of accent is a rare delight. Although one involuntarily prefers the language in which the poems are written, to a translation, it is due the translator to note that the English version has here and there more charm than the original, as in the lines (Lauda XXV):

My vanity is lying in the tomb;
My flesh decayed, my bones take little room;

and (Lauda C)

O human nature, dark and poor and low,
Like withered grass a-droop for death to mow.

In the Italian, more is presented to the eye at a glance than in the English; the correspondence between the rhythm and the frame of mind of the writer is also more apparent in the Italian than in the English; one tone-deaf and form-blind must admit the felicity of the opening lines of Lauda XXV:

Quando t'alegri, omo de altura
va', pone mente a la sepultura.

Our religious consciousness today, is so far removed from the medieval consciousness in its expression of love for God in terms of human love, that we can but theoretically enter into Jacopone's imagery; nevertheless, it is clearly depersonalized passion of which we read.

In Lauda XC—the Amor de Cantare—the velocity, concentration, and irrepressible expansiveness of the writer's nature converge to a most august expression. Quoting, with omissions:

Glowing and flaming, refuge finding none,
    My heart is fettered fast, it cannot flee;
It is consumed, like wax set in the sun;
    Living, yet dying, swooning passionately,
It prays for strength a little way to run,
    Yet in the furnace must it bide and be:
Where am I led, ah me!
        To depths so high?
        Living I die,
    So fierce the fire of love.

For I have lost my heart, my will, my wit,
    My hopes, desires, my pleasures and my taste;
Beauty seems vile, corruption crawls on it,
    Riches, delights and honors all are waste.

My friends, who loved me, called me oft away,
    Far from this bitter path, this arid track;

> But how can kingship sink to serfdom? nay—
> Who gives himself hath given and takes not back.
>
> Now we are one, we are not separate;
> Fire cannot part us nor a sword divide;
> Not pain nor death can reach these heights so great
> Where Love hath snatched and set me by His side:
> Far, far below, I see the world gyrate,
> Far, far above, my heart is satisfied.

In preparing the life, Miss Underhill has been at pains to put one in possession of all her sources, and that the subject's spirit should make the impression on one that it does, so different in the resonant note that it strikes, from that made on one by other Christian mystics and medieval writers, is the result of no mere abstract literary intention. The biographer's comprehension of the worldly accomplishments of her subject and her equal insight into his spiritual attainments, is strikingly the counterpart of that two-sidedness which she emphasizes in the man himself—his instinct for the superlative among those interests which are transient, and his ability to unfold the most intensive of mystical doctrines.

The bibliography apart from its immediate value as indicating the sources of the present work, will be of service to those interested in the whole subject of Christian mysticism.

The Dial, 70 (January 1921), 82–88.

THE SACRED WOOD

THE Sacred Wood is a thoughtful book; its well-knit architecture recalls Trollope's comment upon Castle Richmond. It has "no appearance of having been thrown out of its own windows." As a revival of enjoyment it has value, but in what it reveals as a definition of criticism it is especially rich. The connection between criticism and creation is close; criticism naturally deals with creation but it is equally true that criticism inspires creation. A genuine achievement in criticism is an achievement in creation; as Mr. Eliot says, "It is to be expected that the critic and the creative artist should frequently

---

Review of *The Sacred Wood*, by T. S. Eliot (Alfred A. Knopf).

be the same person." Much light is thrown on the problems of art in Mr. Eliot's citing of Aristotle as an example of the perfect critic—perfect by reason of his having the scientific mind. Too much cannot be said for the necessity in the artist, of exact science.

What Mr. Eliot says of Swinburne as a critic, one feels to be true. "The content," of Swinburne's critical essays "is not, in any exact sense, criticism." Nor, we agree, is it offered by Swinburne as such; he wrote "as a poet, his notes upon poets whom he admired." Mr. Eliot allows Swinburne, perhaps, a sufficiently high place as a poet; to imply that he does not, is to disregard the positively expressed acceptance of his genius; nevertheless, in the course of the essay on Swinburne as Poet, he says, "agreed that we do not (and I think that the present generation does not) greatly enjoy Swinburne," et cetera. Do we not? There is about Swinburne the atmosphere of magnificence, a kind of permanent association of him with King Solomon "perfumed with all the powders of the merchants, approaching in his litter"— an atmosphere which is not destroyed, one feels, even by indiscriminate browsing—and now in his verse as much as ever, as Swinburne says of the Sussex seaboard, "You feel the sea in the air at every step." There is seeming severity in stripping a poet of his accepted paraphernalia and bringing him forth as he is, but in the stanza from "Atalanta":

> Before the beginning of years
>   There came to the making of man
> Time with a gift of tears;
>   Grief with a glass that ran . . . .

is it not undeniable, as Mr. Eliot says, that "it appears to be a tremendous statement, like statements made in our dreams; when we wake up we find that the 'glass that ran' would do better for time than for grief, and that the gift of tears would be as appropriately bestowed by grief as by time?" True, Swinburne "is concerned with the meaning of the word in a peculiar way: he employs or rather 'works,' the word's meaning." The "flap of wings and fins" in him—to quote from "A Cameo," is very apparent. As for "the word" however, invariably used by him as a substitute for "the object," is it always so used? "When you take to pieces any verse of Swinburne," says Mr. Eliot, "you find always that the object was not there—only the word." What of

> The sea slow rising
>   . . . .
> the rocks that shrink,
> the fair brave trees with all their flowers at play?

One of the chief charms, however, of Mr. Eliot's criticism is that in his withholding of praise, an author would feel no pain. But when his praise is unmixed, the effect is completely brilliant as in the opening paragraphs of the essay on Ben Jonson. In his profound appreciation of the genius of Jonson, Mr. Eliot is perhaps more revealing than in any other of the studies in this volume and is entirely convincing in his statement that Ben Jonson is not merely the "man of letters" but is the "literary artist," who if played now, would attract thousands. The eminent robustness of Jonson appears in the lines from *The Silent Woman*, which Mr. Eliot quotes:

> They shall all give and pay well, that come here,
> If they will have it; and that, jewels, pearl,
> Plate, or round sums to buy these. I'm not taken
> With a cob-swan or a high-mounting bull,
> As foolish Leda and Europa were; .
> But the bright gold, with Danaë. For such price
> I would endure a rough, harsh Jupiter,
> Or ten such thundering gamesters, and refrain
> To laugh at 'em, till they are gone, with my much suffering.

One recognizes the truth of the statement that Jonson's "skill is not so much skill in plot as skill in doing without a plot" and that "what holds the play together is a unity of inspiration that radiates into plot and personages alike." The distinction made in Ben Jonson's case between brilliance of surface and mere superficiality, is well made. As Mr. Eliot notes, the liveliness of Fletcher and Massinger covers a vacuum, whereas the superficies of Jonson is solid; "The superficies *is* the world." Could the victim of an all-conspiring luxury inspire a thorn more commensurate with himself than:

> I will have all my beds blown up, not stuft;
> Down is too hard; and then, mine oval room
> Fill'd with such pictures as Tiberius took
> From Elephantis, and dull Aretine
> But coldly imitates. Then, my glasses
> Cut in more subtle angles, to disperse
> And multiply the figures, as I walk. . . .

"He did not get the third dimension, but he was not trying to get it."

In these studies it is interesting to note that truth is to the author a fundamental attraction. He defines the strangeness of Blake as "merely a peculiar honesty, which in a world too frightened to be honest, is peculiarly terrifying." He says:

And this honesty never exists without great technical accomplishment. Being a humble engraver, he had no journalistic-social career open to him, nothing to distract him from his interests, and he knew what interested him and presents only the essential—only what can be presented and need not be explained. He was naked, and saw man naked, and from the center of his own crystal. He approached everything with a mind unclouded by current opinions. There was nothing of the superior person about him. This makes him terrifying.

Blake's humanly personal approach to any subject that he treated, preserves him to us; he is a greener figure to the eye than Dante. It is not personal transcendence; it is as Mr. Eliot observes, the combination of philosophy, theology, and poetry, which makes Dante strong and symmetrical. A conclusion with regard to Dante which has been largely held no doubt by many, is accurately expressed by Mr. Eliot when he says that "Dante, more than any other poet, has succeeded in dealing with his philosophy in terms of something *perceived*." We enjoy, furthermore, the critic's ability to separate the specious from the sound when he says apropos of Landor's failure to understand Francesca: "Francesca is neither stupefied nor reformed; she is merely damned; and it is a part of damnation to experience desires that we can no longer gratify. For in Dante's Hell souls are not deadened, as they mostly are in life; they are actually in the greatest torment of which each is capable."

Although Swinburne was not as Mr. Eliot says he was not, "tormented by the restless desire to penetrate to the heart and marrow of a poet," it is apparent that Mr. Eliot is. In his poetry, he seems to move troutlike through a multiplicity of foreign objects and in his instinctiveness and care as a critic, he appears as a complement to the sheen upon his poetry. In his opening a door upon the past and indicating what is there, he recalls the comment made by Swinburne upon Hugo:

Art knows nothing of death; . . . all that ever had life in it, has life in it forever; those themes only are dead which never were other than dead. No form is obsolete, no subject out of date, if the right man be there to rehandle it.

The Dial, 70 (March 1921), 336–39.

KORA IN HELL BY
WILLIAM CARLOS WILLIAMS

''THE unready would deny tough cords to the wind because they cannot split a storm endwise and wrap it upon spools.''

This statement exemplifies a part of what gives to the work of William Carlos Williams, "a character by itself." It is a concise, energetic disgust, a kind of intellectual hauteur which one usually associates with the French.

The acknowledgment of our debt to the imagination, constitutes perhaps, his positive value. Compression, color, speed, accuracy and that restraint of instinctive craftsmanship which precludes anything dowdy or labored—it is essentially these qualities that we have in his work. Burke speaks of the imagination as the most intensive province of pleasure and pain and defines it as a creative power of the mind, representing at pleasure the images of things in the order and manner in which they were received by the senses or in combining them in a new manner and according to a different order. Dr. Williams in his power over the actual, corroborates this statement. Observe how, by means of this rehabilitating power of the mind, he is able to fix the atmosphere of a moment:

> It is still warm enough to slip from the weeds into the lake's edge . . . and snake's eggs lie curling in the sun on the lonely summit.

> Calvary Church with its snail's horns up sniffing the dawn—o' the wrong side!

> Always one leaf at the peak swirling, swirling and apples rotting in the ditch.

"By the brokenness of his composition," he writes, "the poet makes himself master of a certain weapon which he could possess himself of in no other way." We do not so much feel the force of this statement as we feel that there is life, as there is in Sir Francis Bacon—in the ability to see resemblances in things which are dissimilar; in the ability to see such differences, a special kind of imagination is required, which Dr. Williams has. Despite his passion for being himself and his determination not to be at the mercy of "schoolmasters," it is only one who is academically sophisticated who could write:

Review of *Kora in Hell: Improvisations*, by William Carlos Williams (The Four Seas Company).

Fatigued as you are, watch how the mirror sieves out the extraneous,

and:

> Of what other thing is greatness composed than a power to annihilate half truths for a thousandth part of accurate understanding.

"Often," he says, "a poem will have merit because of some one line or even one meritorious word. So it hangs heavily on its stem but still secure, the tree unwilling to release it."

Such an observation certainly is not the result of purer intuition or of any informally, semi-selfconsciously exercised mental energy. It is not after all, the naïve but the authentic upon which he places value. To the bona fide artist, affectation is degradation and in his effort to "annihilate half truths," Dr. Williams is hard, discerning, implacable and deft. If he rates audacity too high as an aesthetic asset, there can be no doubt that he has courage of the kind which is a necessity and not merely an admired accessory. Discerning the world's hardness, his reply is the reply of Carl Sandburg's boll weevil to threats of sand, hot ashes and the river: "That'll be ma HOME! That'll be ma HOME!"

"Where does this down hill turn up again?" he says.

"Driven to the wall you'll put claws to your toes and make a ladder of smooth bricks."

Though restive under advice, he is resigned under the impersonal, inevitable attrition of life.

"One need not be cast down," he says, "because he cannot cut onyx into a ring to fit a lady's finger. . . . There is neither onyx nor porphory on these roads—only brown dirt. For all that, one may see his face in a flower along it—even in this light. . . . Walk in the curled mud crusts to one side, hands hanging. Ah well."

To discuss one's friends in print may or may not be necessitated by fealty to art but whether there is beauty or not in Dr. Williams' discussions of persons as there is in his discussion of life—in citing the idiosyncracies of friends, note his calmness:

> B. pretends to hate most people, . . . but that he really goes to this trouble I cannot imagine.

Additional marks of health are to be found in his use of idiom. He says:

If a woman laughs a little loudly one always thinks that way of her.

Throw two shoes on the floor and see how they'll lie if you think it's all one way.

The sharpened faculties which require exactness, instant satisfaction and an underpinning of truth are too abrupt in their activities sometimes to follow; but the niceness and effect of vigor for which they are responsible, are never absent from Dr. Williams' work and its crisp exterior is one of its great distinctions. He again reminds one of the French. John Burroughs says of French drivers of drays and carts, "They are not content with a plain matter-of-fact whip as an English or American laborer would be, but it must be a finely modeled stalk, with a long tapering lash, tipped with the best silk snapper."

"It is silly to go into a puckersnatch," Dr. Williams says, "because some brass-button-minded nincompoop in Kensington flies off the handle and speaks openly about our United States prize poems."

In the following passage, the words "black and peculiar" would seem to be the snapper:

> A mother will love her children most grotesquely. . . . She will be most willing toward that daughter who thwarts her most and not toward the little kitchen helper. So where one is mother to any great number of people she will love best perhaps some child whose black and peculiar hair is an exact replica of that of the figure in Velasquez' Infanta Maria Theresa or some Italian matron whose largeness of manner takes in the whole street.

Despite Dr. Williams' championing of the school of ignorance, or rather of no school but experience, there is in his work the authoritativeness, the wise silence which knows schools and fashions well enough to know that completeness is further down than professional intellectuality and modishness can go.

"Lamps carry far, believe me," he says, "in lieu of sunshine."

> What can it mean to you that a child wears pretty clothes and speaks three languages or that its mother goes to the best shops? . . . Men . . . buy their finery and indulge in extravagant moods in order to piece out their lack with other matter.

> Kindly stupid hands, kindly coarse voices . . . infinitely detached, infinitely beside the question . . . and night is done and the green edge of yesterday has said all it could.

In middle life the mind passes to a variegated October. This is the time youth in its faulty aspirations has set for the achievement of great summits. But having attained the mountain top one is not snatched into a cloud but the descent proffers its blandishments quite as a matter of course. At this the fellow is cast into a great confusion and rather plaintively looks about to see if any has fared better than he.

Dr. Williams' wisdom, however, is not absolute and he is sometimes petulant.

"Nowadays poets spit upon rhyme and rhetoric," he says. His work provides examples of every rhetorical principle insisted on by rhetoricians and one wonders upon what ground he has been able to persuade himself that poets spit upon rhyme? Possibly by rhetoric, he means balderdash; in this case then, we are merely poorer by one, of proofs for his accuracy.

"It is folly," he says, "to accept remorse as a criticism of conduct."

One's manners, good or bad, are conventionalized instincts and conduct as a combination of manners and volition, predicates whatever is the result of it, so remorse is automatically a criticism of conduct; but Dr. Williams is essentially a poet. It is true, as he says, that "by direct onslaught or by some back road of the intention the gifted will win the recognition of the world." His book is alive with meaning; in it, "thoughts are trees" and "leaves load the branches." But one who sets out to criticize him, has temerity since he speaks derisively of the wish of certain of his best friends to improve his work and after all, the conflict between the tendency to aesthetic anarchy and the necessity for self-imposed discipline must take care of itself.

As for leaving nothing unsaid—or to be accurate, something unsaid—there is no topic which a thoughtful person would refuse to discuss if gain were to result; but so far as one can see, the peculiar force of Dr. Williams' work does not gain by an allusion to topics of which the average person never thinks unless inescapably for humanitarian reasons. Dr. Williams is too sincere to wish to be fashionable and that one so rich in imagination should have to be thrifty in the use of poetic material is preposterous. One's perspicacity here meets a stone wall.

So disdainful, so complex a poet as Dr. Williams, receives at best, half treatment from the average critic or from the ambitious critic, such untruthful, half specific approbation as, "Ah, quite deep! I see to the bottom." This is to be expected. There is in Dr. Williams, an appetite for the essential and in how many people may one find it? How many poets, old or new, have written anything like "January Morning" in *Al Que Quiere!*, like the second paragraph of "Improvisation XVII" in the present volume, and pre-eminently, the "Portrait of the Author" in a recent number of *Contact?* Withholding comment upon the title, this poem is a super-achievement. It preserves the atmosphere of a moment, into which the impertinences of life cannot intrude. In the sense conveyed, of remoteness from what is detestable, in the effect of balanced strength, in the flavor of newness in presentation, it is unique.

Contact 4 (January–March 1921), 5–8.

DEVELOPMENT

DEVELOPMENT is the study of a mind in the formative process—perhaps one should say of a scholarly mind. The interacting of intellectual interests as the heroine combats imposed restraints and herself, takes the place of what might be required as plot and the recital will please those who, with a recent contributor to *The Spectator*, like the "novel neat" and "regret that delightful descriptions of Swiss mountains and Italian plains should be subordinated to an amatory plot." Juxtaposed, we have impetuosity and philosophic endurance of what cannot be helped. Miss Bryher says of her heroine that "she could never remember a time when she had not wanted to go to sea. True, when she was fourteen she would run away and be a sailor, but that was ten years distant; it was so long to wait that sailing ships might be then, as she heard them say, 'extinct.' " Of Nancy at school she says, "The glare of many faces, weary and uniform in expression, was about her. Surely this was the feeling out of which was born the many-headed dragon of myth. . . . As the class ended, she rose like the Athenian follower of Nikias, his body compelled to obedience, his soul freer than ever."

Nancy's aloofness was not the apathy of a captive enslaved but of a busy man kept from work. She was impelled to write a history

> which would become almost the history of the Mediterranean, from the beginnings of Egypt, through Phoenicia, Greece and Carthage, to the end of Saracen and Norman, the gradual dying of the Middle Age. It was not alone to be a history. All the life of the time, the customs, the armor, especially the trade, would be depicted, the tiny details she missed in the longest histories, all she wanted to know and was told she was "too young to understand." She would labor to make it perfect . . . till it became the very epic of the South, till all could read in one volume the knowledge

Review of *Development*, by W. Bryher. Preface by Amy Lowell (Macmillan).

she was seeking in books, in fragments, in pictures, in stones, in the whole of the land itself.

The roots of things interested her. Middleton, Lyly and Marston gave her the inside of an age. . . . It was indeed a mad world, curious mingling of a very ferocity of strength with the "light-color summer stuff" out of which Euphues, Campaspe and Rosalynde were fashioned.

Naturally enough the modern opus was to her but a

lump of unwrought material, a long preparation for something which never happened, heavy, blunted, barren of definite aim. The "romantic" volumes set out to be wicked, and drowned themselves in a mire of untrue psychology and false emotion. The realists photographed the time, but somehow managed to omit the spirit. There was no mingling of irony with loveliness; the unpleasant truths of existence were blurred with a false perspective or were never faced at all. Discouragement marched in the train of this futility, and from these pages of degenerate weakness, Nancy turned with relief to Tom Jones.

One might easily expect to find conclusions arrived at by the small heroine, immature; and possibly in her protest against woman's *rôle* as a wearer of skirts—in her envying a boy his freedom and his clothes—her view is somewhat curtailed. One's dress is more a matter of one's choice than appears; if there be any advantage, it is on the side of woman; woman is more nearly at liberty to assume man's dress than man is able to avail himself of the opportunities for self-expression afforded by the variations in color and fabric which a woman may use. Moreover, women are no longer debarred from professions that are open to men, and if one cares to be femininely lazy, traditions of the past still afford shelter. There is nothing unripe, however, in Nancy's comment upon her schoolmates, who on the last day of school "besought mistresses to write to them, whom, a week before, they had hoped never to see again," or in her simple answer, "They are the South," when a flock of goats occasioned shivering on the part of a fellow traveler, who "loved" little green shutters and said, "Nancy, you don't realize how wonderfully romantic it all is. I don't believe you appreciate traveling at all." There is something dramatic in winning by force of intention; and in every case in which a lack of comprehension is recorded such as the foregoing, one feels that Nancy's silence under fire is a victory. Her oppressive companion might feel—should she read the following description, that sightseeing included more than green shutters:

The sea was a wide mass of luminous metal, faint silver here and there where a flickering light caught it, or a grey hollow revealing the tumult underneath. A parting of the waves, a vivid shout, and the lifeboat slid into the water, vanishing in the hollows, or flung, a struggling fish, upright against a roll of wave.

This book is a flower cluster mounted on a tall spike—a raceme of lilies; and for the lily the flower level of development is sufficient, but in human development the flowering stage is many times this side of maturity. One awaits eagerly the higher stages of maturing, which, in *Development*, Miss Bryher leads one to anticipate.

The Dial, 70 (May 1921), 588–90.

A METROPOLITAN HERMIT

IN all artists, there is a tendency towards hermitry and a desire for justification from those who know what beauty is. The man has a disgust for humanity; the artist expresses himself in symbols which only humanity can read. In Mr. Mitchell's work, a self-evolved independence as a result of this conflict we feel very much. We are conscious of hauteur, yet a contempt for the occasions to hauteur—for the tyranny, panic, and fetishism of urban life: the passion in these poems is real and the coldness is real: there is sensuous beauty and a desire to replace susceptibility to it with something more fundamental. It is not always possible to tell whether a man or a woman is designated in certain of the poems and this is as it should be; in so far as a poem is a work of art, one does not wish to know, and must not know too definitely, the facts which underlie the expression. Mr. Mitchell feels the aesthetic value of courage, but he also has courage.

He makes no concessions; he forces nothing on one and although the very quality which makes the craftsman cautious and technically competent, hampers expression, in Mr. Mitchell's poems thought and feeling triumph over formality and while a radical might object to the method, one is always sure that the underlying thought has justified the writing. There is honesty and depth in these poems; there seems to be extant in this author a power of self-expression which is not self-conscious—which is devoid of that blatantly self-analytical aggressiveness which is characteristic of certain modern contortionists.

Review of *Poems*, by Stewart Mitchell (Duffield).

In the decorative detail, note the actuality in "Autumn": "Webs of grey mist, a glitter of black wings, life circled with fire," and in "From a Garden": "the purple well of night walled with the elms like shadows of vast fountains." The sea is treated with great distinction, both allusively and directly. We have in "Ego," "Out of the contending light and darkness, springs the tempest on the sea" and in "Sea Side," reversing the stereotyped order of comparison, Mr. Mitchell says:

> The waters tremble where the grey wind sets
> His blue lips to the body of the sea,
> Cloud over as your face, now it forgets
> Some vague pledge common between such as we—
> Startled to hear my tedious regrets
> That you it was who were the death of me.

One's taste in verse forms varies as one's taste in gems varies. It may vary with the occasion but it is essentially a matter of temperament. For a poet not to know this is to throw away his power of attack. For Mr. Mitchell to be erratic or showy would be to forfeit distinction. There is something very pleasing about the arrangement of the words in the following line: "Till life shall be as love may please" and in Mr. Mitchell's work throughout, the faceted correctness of the verse structure gives pleasure. There are in it, various best things—"Ego," "Sea Side," "Lucretius," "A Theorist," "Astarte," "Helen," and, especially in "Ipswich Dunes," the sea is brought before us in all its calm, savage finality:

> If ever we could love them who art sped,
> Out of the world with swift and trackless feet,
> I should have known your England from my bed,
> In fields of poppies sown through deep, green wheat
> ·
> Stretched on these dunes—white sand, sweet-smelling bay,
> I think I taste the draught of your disdain—
> Only what you have told of Beauty, we,
> Who love you best, remember—turn away
> From idle fancy, and your age-old vain
> Unprofitable comradeship with pain,
> On wings of light, wings that desire the sea.

The Dial, 70 (June 1921), 692–93.

GEORGE MOORE, AESTHETE

GEORGE Moore's experience of life has been exceptional, and there are phases of life with which he is not familiar but it is his idiosyncrasy not to qualify. He is an aesthete, a man of supreme accomplishment in presenting sensation. To any but one who has made a specialty of sensation, he seems superficial, but a nerve is a nerve and his expertness as an observer makes one feel as if sensation might at any time wander all the way to the heart as indeed it does in *Esther Waters.* His introducing in his work so many imagined instances of suffering illustrates this aesthetic sensitiveness and is a marvel of contrast to the unconcern of such a writer as Defoe, who tells in *Robinson Crusoe* of the hungry wildcat:

> I tossed her a bit of biscuit, though by the way I was not very free of it, for my store was not great: however, I spared her a bit, I say, and she went to it, smelled of it, and ate it, and looked (as pleased) for more, but I thanked her, and could spare no more; so she marched off;

and of the sleeping lion:

> I took the best aim I could with the first piece to have shot him in the head, but he lay so with his leg raised a little above his nose, that the slugs hit his leg about the knee, and broke the bone. . . . I took a second piece immediately, and though he began to move off fired again, and shot him into the head, and had the pleasure to see him drop, and make but little noise, but lay struggling for life. . . . This was indeed game to us, but this was no food, and I was very sorry to lose three charges of powder and shot upon a creature that was good for nothing to us. . . . I bethought myself, however; . . . at last we got off the hide of him, and spreading it on top of our cabin, the sun effectually dried it in two days' time and it afterward served me to lie upon.

Defoe is austere; George Moore, the obverse; the sense of sense is so poignant that there is no room for pity. In *Hail and Farewell,* he speaks of his and Yeats' altering of Edward Martyn's play *The Tale of a Town,* with Edward Martyn in an adjoining room and says, "We were like two boys threading a bluebottle." Héloïse said, "I cannot sit reading with the skin of the animal about my knees that howled to me for help" and Héloïse and Abélard "continued talking through a cloudy morning of May, puzzled to discover in their imagination how a wolf and her cub had come by their deaths." There is a tinge of misery in this pathological humanitarianism.

Aesthetic feeling sometimes plays Mr. Moore false, for narrator though he is, apparently impeccable in conversation and in his conception of dramatic interval, there are in *Héloïse and Abélard,* passages in which crudeness, mawkishness, indecision and lame unnatural cadence spring out at one: "A good baby, the best of babies Héloïse said; I believe that there was never so good a child. . . . Dear wife, dear wife! he said overcoming the suffocation of the moment." *The Spectator* remarks that Mr. Moore has chosen to write "in a kind of diluted Wardour Street," that "his characters do not say Tush! or Zooks!" and that "he has avoided the worst blunders of the 'hath done' style, but . . . there is too much talk of 'ousels' and 'willow beds;' " a not unfair criticism. One is merely aware of these flaws upon perfection as a minor blemish of cover and print. One expects the taste of an aesthete to be impeccable; then why the pale print and clamorous bourgeois binding of the American edition?

In common with other aesthetes, Mr. Moore sacrifices the austere beauty of the athlete; this would perhaps be his defense for so repeatedly making a study of themes which involve the disintegrating factor of sensuality. Perhaps he would have one charitably transfer to him Héloïse's defense of Abélard when she says, "If we are to have genius we must put up with the consequences of genius, a thing the world will never do; it wants geniuses but it would like them to be just like other people." The average person has seen genius walking erect too many times to accept the implication that genius progresses best when it crawls; innate sensuality is a mildew and in defense of an author who is aesthete pure and simple, one recalls Abélard's observation respecting Madelon: "We owe her a good deal . . . and we are paying with our patience all that we owe her."

As in *The Brook Kerith* Mr. Moore is not a theologian, so in *Héloïse and Abélard,* he is not a philosopher. His knowledge is a knowledge of living, not a concept of life; his philosophical discussions no more attain the illusion of realness than he seems in them, like Socrates. To those deeply interested in philosophy, it is irritating that philosophy should be made a backdrop to "a rampage of the passions," but Mr. Moore's imperviousness to disapproval is part of his virtue and in *Héloïse and Abélard,* it is not twelfth century scholastic philosophy but George Moore that we read. In Abélard, Madelon, Héloïse and Fulbert, we have four aspects of him.

In Abélard, we have the Arabian nights concept of masculine favor in which the grand vizier indicates with his sceptre, which maiden shall advance—a contrast indeed, to the "charity in armour" of medievalism—to Rudel of whom Abélard says that he walked "with a stoop, deep in his dream, seeing his princess far more clearly than the women about him" and to the romantic self-abasement of the seventeenth century:

Mon Dieu, aide-moi!*
That I with the primroses of my fresh wit;
May tumble her tyranny under my feet.
Donc je serai un jeune roi.†

Instead of being "animated by a durable ecstasy . . . which rendered him capable of haughty thoughts and valiant deeds," Abélard was demoralized, finding in Héloïse, man's natural enemy; this fact Mr. Moore elaborates, quoting Proverbs, "I have found woman bitterer than death; . . . her hands are chains"; citing Adam and how "the first woman brought about the banishment of man from paradise"; Samson, "brought to such despair that he buried himself . . . under the ruins of the temple"; Solomon who "lost his reason through a woman"; Socrates, whose sufferings should "cause the most thoughtless to ponder"; and Job, "for it was against his wife that Job, that holy man, fought the last and hardest fight of all." Mr. Moore shares the oriental conception that to be inescapably associated with woman, is degradation. Although, as he says, "in every life there is an adventure that sums up lesser adventures," and in Abélard's case, "Héloïse was this summary," he causes Abélard to reflect that "if he had not met her his life would have continued to be an ever-swirling adventure." "He hated to think of himself as an animal at tether, moving circlewise, always equidistant from the center, never able to project himself even a few feet farther into the unknown." In reading George Moore, one cannot but feel the retentiveness of his mind and in his attributing to Abélard a remarkable memory, one is aware of his own highly specialized faculty. When Abélard says to Héloïse: "If the Georgics were lost, we could recover them all from our memories, for where mine failed thou wouldst come to my aid, and together we could give back to the world the book it had lost," we are reminded of *Avowals* in which Mr. Moore says, "Your memory is better than mine . . . in this instance, certainly" and Mr. Gosse replies, "Thank you for this tribute, which it is an honor to receive from one of prodigious memory, though of slight reading."

In Madelon, we have the foil to reflection—corresponding to that which we have in the Gosse of *Avowals*.

In Héloïse, we have Mr. Moore's concept of woman as man's satellite and handmaid, Héloïse is like the Lady Malberge of the Hermit's ballad: "She has no real being except in me; she is here, and nowhere else, and the Hermit pointed to his heart." Life at Argenteuil was to her after leaving

*My God, help me!
†Thus shall I be a young King.

Abélard, "shadowy as the world she saw about her when she left the library and walked into the open air" and "there was nothing true in her except her love for Abélard, whom she would follow into the gulfs of hell rather than live in paradise without." "And in one intense moment of vision," says Mr. Moore, "she saw into life as it is offered to women, the obliteration of themselves in marriage or the obliteration of themselves in convent rules; . . . convent or marriage, it's always that for a woman." Another phase of Mr. Moore's notion of woman's subordinate rôle, we have in the young Astrolabe's ennui at being obliged to stay in the convent with the nuns and with his mother; he said, "I don't want to live here shut up with a lot of women" and upon being asked, "And what will you do, little sir, when you are older? I do not know so much what I shall do, Astrolabe answered. I shall escape away from women of whom I have seen enough." Although Mr. Moore apparently supports the illusion of Héloïse's erudition, her Ovid and Virgil do not as presented make her seem learned. She is like Tappé's Miss Pellicoe, "circumspect and tidy, polite and tractable, working away behind closed doors at deportment, penmanship, Latin, Greek and botany." "Moreover," says Tappé, "Miss Pellicoe is not six forever; she eventually achieves the academic age of sixteen and with it the dignity of profound hours in a college library." It is dignity of this sort that Héloïse seems to us to have attained. In insisting upon her indifference to religion, Mr. Moore departs possibly a little from the original. Roman Catholicism is a formal religion and she was negatively its disciple although she had also, it is true, definite interests of the intellect and of the emotions.

But if, according to Mr. Moore, she was indifferent to religion, she was not more so than Fulbert in whom we have a fourth phase of Mr. Moore's aesthetics of materialism. "He had gone for a handful of nuts and a tankard of wine," says Mr. Moore. "He sat cracking and skinning the nuts and drinking large draughts in silence." Despite the fact that Mr. Harris lauds Mr. Moore's moderation, anything more unequivocally sottish, it would be impossible to imagine. Fulbert remarks that "when the belly suffers, the heart is hard," and other like allusions are made, as that of the robber. The Canon speculates upon "the shortsightedness of servants governed always by the seeming need of the moment" and upon the advisability of "throwing himself upon the charity of a new servant who, though she might not have the faults that Madelon had, would have other faults . . . and the thought of Madelon's dismissal was dropped almost as quickly as it had come." His appreciation of creature comfort has no less conspicuous a counterpart in Abélard and Héloïse than in Madelon, who is made to say of the pigeon that he "is better if he be laid out between slices of good beef, for the neighborhood of the beef favors him" and "when the king of fishes, the shad, was laid before them: of more delicate flavor than the bass, better than the turbot, a fish that makes the sole seem common, said Abélard." Abélard is made to speak "of a vexing puffing wind, that carries us a little way and then leaves us" and many times in this book as in others of his books, one notes Mr. Moore's appraisement of the pain of being thwarted. When Héloïse inquired about Abélard, "As the student gave ear to him, thinking he was about to speak of Abélard. But it was of the fine weather they spoke."

In the matter of architectural setting which is essentially a matter of feeling, in the crafty, leisurely advance, one is conscious of no flaws. The fact that Mr. Moore tells a story different from the one on which his narrative is based, does not matter. The proportioned, unhurried spaciousness of design—so much the reverse of what is usual—excites admiration. Buildings of great size are often complained of as not being set in sufficient greensward; similarly, one must give architectural advantage to an experience of colossal size and this Mr. Moore does. There is an orchestral quality, a premonitory note in his deliberate advance upon his theme, whereby he carries one "like a fish in net drawn along." In the beginning, one notes this atmosphere of veiled suspense, in the uncertainty which surrounds Héloïse's future. The possibility of her becoming an abbess is mentioned and of her being forced into a marriage abhorrent to her. Madelon is made to say, "I have my doubts thou'lt ever get back to Argenteuil." She is made to "ask herself for the first time . . . if she had a destiny, glad or sad . . . and waited for an answer that did not come."

Mr. Moore's conception of narrative is supported, moreover, by his predilection for reverie—by the romantic warpedness of his imagination. He speaks of "the sense of sadness inseparable from a river," of how "the dead have a hold upon us that the living haven't." He says of Héloïse, that "her thoughts seemed to fall into nothing" and speaks of "innumerable peacocks, ghostly birds in the mild moonlight, whose long white tails set Madelon crying: 'ghosts or angels; let us away.' " "Is it not strange," Abélard said to himself, "that what I love best in the world should bring me back to the country most antagonistic to me and my ideas, and reining in his horse he pondered in front of the city on hatred and love, asking himself which was the deeper feeling." Observe, moreover, how in Héloïse's meditation on the soul and the body, he gives a facsimile of the mental process in which the mind picks up and drops an idea and picks it up again:

> She returned to the window overlooking the Seine; unable to take up the book again, she fell to thinking instead of the Poet whom Christianity unites with paganism in honoring: and her eyes returning to the page, she

reread that Iris . . . descended to liberate the soul from the body. But why liberate the soul from the body? she asked, since the two are inseparable as we know them.

Mr. Moore has said in *Avowals*, "Whosoever keeps humor under lock and key is read in the next generation, if he writes well, for to write well without humor is the supreme test"; nevertheless, sleights of mind should not count for nothing. "In difficult and thorny questions an adjournment of the debate is always welcome"; "the false always being accepted, rather than the true, . . . small satisfaction it is to us that the truth shall prevail in the end, Abélard said"; "Why, indeed, said Romuald," should one come between friends who have chosen to quarrel, "since swordsmanship proceeds out of friendship, like the egg from the hen; we can't have one without the other." These things amuse us but we agree that they are subsidiary to the structure. Mr. Moore's flawless transcript of the surface of things makes him powerful; in his reverence for himself as an artist—his willingness to "pick a thing to threads and reweave," he is essentially the writer, interested in elegance and lucidity. The tendency to experiment with punctuation—to take away unnecessary detail that one may exhibit the meaning—is characteristic only of those who are interested in the mechanics of language and his abandoning of quotation marks perhaps necessary to an understanding of the meaning as one feels by their absence, is not the less a phase of the spirit which enables him to say, "The exception to the rule must return to the rule for fortification against eccentricity" and "she awoke suddenly though she had not been asleep." His artificial simplicity—"corrupt simplicity" so called— is the artificial simplicity of every fashion expert and it is not to our discredit that we like it. When in *Hail and Farewell*, he says, "We never grieve for anybody, parent or friend as we should like to grieve and are always shocked by our absentmindedness," when he says, "The trouvère getting the better of the philosopher he forgot faith and reason and said: the beauty of the larches is enough," the demure, assured quality, the ripeness as of meat well hung yet not decayed—so recognizable as to be signed without a name— is none the less expert for the consciousness of its effort to be sensational. It is the writer rather than the experiencer who says, "Life is more elaborate in its processes than we think for"; who says of Abélard that "he never said anything twice in the same way," who causes Abélard to say that "all similes are defective if pressed too far," who quotes from the two gleemen: "At first our differences were slight, and it amused us to wrangle over an art that was dear to both of us; but in the second year we wearied of our differences." "Buried shade is a strange expression," said Héloïse and reminding one of

Avowals, she speculates further on the refinements of language when she says, "But why, uncle, do we not write as the pagans wrote?" Mr. Moore exhibits in his sentence structure with its echo of "The House that Jack Built," a seventeenth century fastidiousness:

> It may seem to thee that I am talking only as the mad talk. . . . But I am not talking, Abélard, I am thinking; I am not thinking, Abélard, I am dreaming; I am not dreaming, Abélard, I am feeling; and in this moment I am consonant with the tree above me and the stars above the tree; I am amid the roots of the hills.

It is only one who has analyzed the secret of emphasis who could say, "protracted farewells may be borne only by those whose hearts are cold"; "it is always coming and going from the convent to the world, and from the world to the convent"; and "the longer the immortality, the more perfect it becomes, time putting a patina on the bronze and the marble and . . . I think upon the texts."

Note the outcome of sober observation, the accurate, crafty transcript of human behavior and of nature—of the veracious, intentionally conspicuous lack of sentimentality in the following characterization:

> Of a sudden the voices ceased, and, turning her head, Héloïse saw a short man, of square build, who, although well advanced in the thirties, still conveyed an impression of youthfulness; for though squarely built his figure was well knit, his eyes bright, and his skin fresh and not of an unpleasing hue, brown and ruddy. The day being warm, he walked carrying his hat in his hand, looking round him pleased at the attendance, and it was this look of self-satisfaction that stirred a feeling of dislike in Héloïse. He seemed to her complacent and vain; and she did not like his round head, his black hair, his slightly prominent eyes: . . . the only feature that forced an acknowledgment from her was his forehead, which was large and finely turned. . . . She could not imagine Aristotle or Plato . . . or Seneca, or Virgil, or Ovid, or Tibullus . . . converging to the type that Abélard represented so prominently. . . . Half an hour must have been spent in the donning of the laces at his cuffs and another in choosing the buckles of his shoes. But her criticism of his apparel was quickly swept away again by the sound of the rich, smooth, baritone voice, and this time she perceived that the voice was accompanied by an exquisite courtesy, and that the manner in which he walked addressing those who gathered about him to admire and to listen was kindly, although it was plain that though familiarity from him would be an honor he would resent it quickly in another.

The account of Héloïse's behavior upon her second visit to the Canon, moreover—the intense, introspective captiousness of youth—is psychologically accurate and is one of the most close-textured, distinctive episodes in the book:

The Canon stopped speaking so that Héloïse might ask him some questions that would lead to a further unwinding of a story which had begun to seem to him more inveigling than he knew it to be before he began it. But Héloïse said nothing, and after waiting for a question from her, he said: where are thy thoughts? My thoughts, uncle, were—I do not know where they were. I suppose I must have been thinking. Can anyone think without words? Ah, now I remember; I was asking myself if Abélard's story would have revealed to me the man whom I saw and heard in the cloister. . . . If thou hadst heard his story from me before seeing him? Yes, uncle; and her face still deep in a cloud of meditation, she confessed that it was not until she heard him in the cloister that she began to see that what she saw and heard were not two different things but one thing for he would not be himself without—Without what, niece? the Canon asked, for he was amused by Héloïse's embarrassment, and to continue it he added: his beauty? The sneer threw Héloïse off her guard, and she answered that nobody could call Abélard an ugly man. A stocky little fellow, the Canon persisted. And he would have said more of the same kind if Héloïse's face had not warned him not to proceed further with his teasing. He spoke instead of Abélard's forehead, which he admitted to be of the Socratic type in its amplitude; but he averred that the likeness between the two men ceased at the forehead, for whereas Socrates was of the ascetic temperament, Abélard was by his face notably a free liver, a disparagement that seemed to Héloïse like a challenge. She asked the Canon to mention a feature that would testify to the truth of this, and the spirit of battle being upon him he could not keep back the words: his singing of French songs. You never spoke to me before of Abélard as one divided between free living and philosophy. Nor is it many minutes since you were speaking of him as the intellectual descendant of Aristotle and Plato; your present sneers of him cannot be else than an attempt to anger me, and we would do better, mayhap, to talk of matters on which we are agreed.

Later in the narrative, the characterization of Astrolabe—spoiled and egotistical but a child of parts—is true to the child mind and entertains us throughout. While the snare for the ducks was being woven, "he practised quacking, becoming quickly so skillful that his quacking deceived the nuns." He wished to have a lute or a ribeck and was affronted for a day or two by being offered a pair of regals when he recovered his humor enough to ask for a gittern. "One has to learn these instruments early when one is young just as I am, else it is difficult to learn them later. But I heard thee say thou wert going to be a Crusader. Can't I be both, mother, gleeman and Crusader?" His mind was like a genie in a box demanding freedom. "And Héloïse was jealous of Abélard and asked why he should have possessed himself so completely of his offspring."

Of equal distinction with these characterizations are Mr. Moore's description of nature. The Comte de Rodeboeuf says of a parrot, "I bought a grey bird, whose wrinkled eyelid fell over an eye that seemed to know all things"; the sense of Argenteuil's remoteness from Paris is felt and its lack of austerity, in "the nuns . . . walking in their convent garden finding young spiders weaving glittering threads from spray to spray." We have an epitome of bird life in the "tall boles rising fifty or sixty feet from the roadway, the nests in the high branches, and a great clamor about them. The wayfarers stopped to admire the parent rook crawling gingerly into the nest with some snail or grub for the squeakers within it," in the swallows at dusk "flying more madly than ever, as if to lose a minute were a loss." In the description of the snowstorm, we have a unified, perfectly fused fragment of atmosphere—in "the sky copper and sulphur . . . along the horizon, betokening more snow," in "the thin wintry day, a small passage of daylight between the long nights" and "people walking in the middle of the street to avoid the drip." Abélard's reference to his life in the monastery of Saint-Gildas remains in the mind as vividly as the longer description does of the forest—"Saint-Gildas among the rocks where the tides are moaning always if they are not crashing." To Madelon, discoursing of the practical properties of the oak, "Thou'rt forgetting, Madelon, the power of the oak over the mind, said Abélard; the oak grove was the cathedral of our ancestors. Not a whit does that surprise me, said Madelon, for who can walk in these shades without awe?" Abélard remarks that "the silence of the forest is different from any other" for "the forest is never silent" and we are told how they "rode beneath the boughs not yet in full leaf, following the path as it wound through hollows, losing it and finding it amid rocks, pushing their way through thickets that seemed impenetrable at a distance but did not prove so hard to force through as they had appeared"—of how "stooping low in their saddles, they broke through somehow," of how Abélard "pointed to a dark ragged line of pines flowing down the northern sky" and of "the fringe of birch-trees that encircled with their pallor the great district of pines that showed in black masses over against Etampes . . . the pines rising up naked and bare some fifty or sixty feet, some straight, some leaning in endless aisles." "Like the spears, Héloïse said, of Crusaders going into battle." What one does not like in Mr. Moore is not what one thinks of as one reverts to these verisimilitudes; one honors genius which is able to spin out of itself, the fabric of its illusions. As Fulbert says: "We must not ask more of paganism than it can give; its gift is beauty."

Broom, 2 (May 1922), 124–32.

IS THE REAL ACTUAL?

THE preoccupation today is with the actual. The work therefore of Alfeo Faggi[1] exhibited last year and with important additions this year at the Bourgeois Gallery, is especially for the thinker, presenting as it does solidly and in a variety, a complete contrast to the fifty-fathom deep materialism of the hour. Spiritual imagination as is apparent, is especially potent in interpreting subjects which are spiritual, seeming to derive feeling from the subject rather than to have to bring feeling to it as in the theme which is palpable and easily comprehensible; therefore as could be expected, in the recent exhibition, the more purely philosophic and intellectual concepts— the Ka and the Dante—make the most powerful impression; and although one would not naturally classify the Robert Jones with the Dante, it is entirely congruous that the same mind that could reach the heights and depths of spirituality which would produce the Dante, could marginally produce that which is so highly aesthetic as the Jones; a thing so illusory in its effect of poetic distillation as the mask of Noguchi; a portrait so distinguished as that of Robert Frost; so pliant as the Eve with its early-in-the-morning atmosphere, recalling Spenser's swans:

> even the gentle streame, the which them bare,
> Seem'd foule to them, and bade his billows spare
> To wet their silken feathers.

The astutely chosen medium in which each study is executed, bears out what one feels, in the sensitive development of the subject in hand—the smooth dark surface of the Tagore like a ripe olive, the bone-white, weathered aspect of the Frost, the misty waxlike bloom on the Eve as on bayberries or iris stalks, the tarnish and glint of fire of the Dante. However great the range of subject, there is a creative unity; complementary curves and repeated

[1] Reproductions of Mr. Faggi's sculptures have appeared in *The Dial* for March, 1921 (Madonna, Yoné Noguchi, and Pietà) and in April, 1922 (Dante).

motive of lines or angles in hands or drapery—which instantly mark the subjects as being one man's work; there is moreover as in the work of any disciplined mind, an absence of stentorian insistence on the work's right to attention—the scorn of self-extenuation as in the case of Dante, Socrates, and Christ. Remembering C. H. Herford's comment upon Sir Thomas Browne's contemporary, Alexander Ross, one hesitates to appraise work—even to praise it—the inspiration of which is spiritual. Herford says: "The formidable Alexander Ross in his *Medicus Medicatus*, drove his heavy bludgeon this way and that through the tenuous fabric of the *Religio* without damaging a whit its spiritual substance 'for it was as the air invulnerable.' " Corrupted by the conventions of the banal and the bizarre, under contract to compass every novelty, there are many critics or so-called artists qualified to judge of such work only in so far as they are able to discriminate between Hepplewhite and Sheraton. The most hasty, however, the most errant, will feel in Mr. Faggi's Ka as in all his work, the controlled emotion, the mental poise which suggests the Absolute—a superiority to fetishism and triviality, a transcendence, an inscrutable dignity—a swordlike mastery in the lips, which suggests the martyr secure in having found the key to mystery, a reserve which recalls Dante as pictured by Croce, "absorbed and consumed by his secret, unwilling that vulgar and gossiping folk should cast their eyes upon it: 'and he smiling looked at them and said nothing.' " Face to face with such sincere expressions, one suspects that in the vulgarity and peremptoriness of one's passions, either in praise or blame, one may be as St. Augustine says he was prior to his conversion, "like a dog snapping at flies." A reverence for mystery is not a vague, invertebrate thing. The realm of the spirit is the only realm in which experience is able to corroborate the fact that the real can be also the actual. Such work as Mr. Faggi's is a refutation of the petulant patronage which for instance assigns Plato to adolescents— which remarks: "How Plato hated a fact!"

To grasp the nature of the phenomenon which Dante represents, is perhaps impossible to many of us since one cannot discern forces by which one is not oneself unconsciously animated. As Symons has remarked, "We find the greatest difficulty in believing that Socrates was sincere, that Dante was sincere." One feels that even with a profound critical interest in Dante, Boccaccio could not, as Symons says, comprehend a nature more metaphysical than his own. However, those who have studied biographical conjecture and the historical certainties of Dante's life, will be grateful to Mr. Faggi for his synthesis of what is the feeling or at least the apprehension of so many. In this robustly compact bronze like some colossal gold ingot stood erect, obviously intended to represent a man but not brutishly male, with the look of the athlete made lean, with the action in repose of the spiritual potentate, one sees the man as one has imagined him, the student of "philosophy, theology, astrology, arithmetic, and geometry, turning over many curious books, watching and sweating in his studies," with a view of the world founded as Croce says, on faith, judgment, and bound by a strong will, commanding like a wall of solid water, the incredulity of minds egotistical and as shallow as a fish-wafer—too idle to think. In the intellectuality, the distilled impersonal spiritual force of Mr. Faggi's Dante, one recalls Giotto's superiority to interest in masculinity or femininity *per se;* the inadvertent muscularity and angelic grace of his male figures—the faces of his madonnas and female saints, like the faces of stalwart boys. In the shoulders compact like a bulldog's, in the nostrils built for expansion under physical stress sunk under long imposed restraint, the horizontal eyebrows, raised cheekbones of the ascetic, the iron skull, the substantial character of the face as of an iron crow, the mobile expression of the mouth—not incompatible with the gaiety of which Croce and other authorities are convinced—the cap like war, set from the face as if to indicate hope; the collar, round like an ecclesiastic's, the wakeful reserve of the lowered eyes—we have "the ardor, admiration and fury" of the politician, the distilled supersensory sentience of the seer—the man who was "the product of a nation of scholars and doctors who were artists." In the animating force of this bronze in its setting of physical power, is embodied the spiritual axiom that Dante has come to be.

The Dial, 73 (December 1922), 620–22.

A PORTRAIT OF GEORGE MOORE

TAKING for granted that the biographer is affectionately predisposed, a portrait constructed from a man's work is the most justifiable and the justest sort of biography. In the effort to understand and exhibit Mr. Moore's achievements and idiosyncrasies, Mr. Freeman his been self-effacing, profound, and unhurried. One does not share every detail of his admiration, but his appreciation is never blind eulogy and now and again he is startlingly fearless in his aloofness, as when he says of *Lewis Seymour and Some Women* revised, that it is to him like a certain respectable brick building upon which was

---

Review of *A Portrait of George Moore in a Study of His Work,* by John Freeman (D. Appleton and Company).

imposed "a new stucco front with an elaborate cornice above which the old roof still rose steep. The stucco was finished to look like stone, but the stone refused to look like stucco, and the building remains now a sad and haunting image of uncostly sham."

The more acute an artist is in recognizing perfection, the more alert he is in recognizing blemishes, but it is not to give a photographically accurate bad likeness that Mr. Freeman is working. Few artists have chosen and developed a subject with a deeper affection or more insight. In the ingenious selection, moreover, of passages from Montaigne to stand at the beginnings of chapters as indices, we are much enriched—in the lines for instance, prefixed to Chapter II as applying to George Moore in Paris and to *The Confessions of a Young Man*, but we are warned by Mr. Freeman to use discernment in distinguishing the fact from the fiction of these seemingly frank revealings, not however, that the fiction is false. "I often hazard upon certaine outslips of minde for which I distrust myself," says Montaigne, "and certaine verbal wilie-beguiles, whereat I shake mine eares"; and although Mr. Freeman admits that "the display of shabby dissoluteness, of crude and pushy splendor" of the *Confessions* "illuminates a certain aspect of Moore's early work," he points out that it "is obviously remote from the diligence and aristocracy of his mind."

In *Esther Waters*, that wolf-lean, unforgettable romance, "the only English novel that treated a servant-girl seriously," we have George Moore, one would like to think, as his most unself-conscious self—if not, in a *rôle* which is his most magnificent assumption. He has produced an epic, a life cycle in bleakness, and despite his Paris skin so recently sloughed, not one tawdry sparkle attaches to it. "The most English of all novels," Mr. Freeman says, "if *Tom Jones* and *David Copperfield* be added." As a line in George Moore's portrait, it is especially commemorative and is fittingly dedicated to Colonel Maurice Moore who called "the surrender of his brother to the stables, 'truly Irish carelessness'—a 'little kid of nine,' riding as he pleased about the country, until through the success of a horse named *Master George*, Master George was snatched from the horses and sent to school."

Of *Hail and Farewell*, the first volume of which appeared in 1911, Mr. Freeman says one of George Moore's distinctions is to have "modified an old form so as virtually to turn it into a new one in his autobiographic writings; making grave things light, using mockery and malice for those intellectual revenges which the very kindest of us condone." He regrets "a dozen wanton pages" in *Vale*. "If it be urged," he says, "that you must take an author as he is, the answer is simple: Moore as he essentially is does not raise this offense. It comes from a spirit which he oddly fancies to be a spirit of moral and intellectual liberty. Such episodes signify a brief maddening failure of the artistic." Referring to Mr. Moore's "subtle constructive surgery," he says, "It has been Moore's fortune and ours, that sitting opposite his friends, he has not simply torn them to pieces, but also put them together again—making them different perhaps, but making them whole." One especially admires the condensed: "romantic biography as well as romantic autobiography, and when all is said, it remains equally admirable and inexcusable."

Although verse rhythms and cadences are analyzed today with great particularity, prose rhythms are not less important. One is influenced and somewhat overawed by Mr. Freeman's analytic knowledge of the values and harmonies of Mr. Moore's prose. The adjective "staccato" is used in objection, whereas one not a classicist would say the staccato sentence is permissible as expressing spontaneously positive sentiment; and although one perceives Mr. Moore's evolution and feels that his later work is "characterized by a new cunning," of the so-called "unfortunate" early work, one would say merely that the early lacks the subtlety and elegance of the later. As Mr. Freeman says, Mr. Moore's art is "a thing of clarification and effusion" like "a Corot landscape": "The movement of the prose, the undulations never wandering past control, the unheightened and unlapsing phrasing, the color and the quietness, the simplicity, the depth, the brightness—all these, the mere names of qualities, as trees are mere names of mysteries, are the artist's rendering in his proper medium of that which his youth has breathed, and which was in his veins before consciousness awoke." Any writer of strong personality is a stylist, the style varying from the stereotyped in rhetoric and sentiment as the personality varies. Moreover, as Mr. Moore himself says, "the impersonality of the artist is the vainest of delusions" and in this portrait it would seem that George Moore the man of letters and George Moore the man, are identical. In the artist as in the man, we have the same "intricate simplicity," the same incapacity for indifference, the adhering to prejudice, the same *hauteur* and subservience; for as Mr. Freeman says, "His temptation has not been to court the world but to shock it, a subservience as illseeming as any compliance"; he has indeed "redeemed portraiture from gentleness and made butchery a pleasure"—the same individual who "would not care to leave Max on 'Servants' lying about in his house, for fear that if a servant read in it she might think it superior and inconsiderate." "Too much absorbed in observing and remembering life, to be interested in moral ideas," he is yet according to Mr. Freeman, interested in religion—"in the personal aspect of it"; exercising sobriety and moderation, yet with unreserve of judgment, revealing "thoughts which most of us rebuke into snake-like stillness," he "is equally isolated by his virtues and his faults."

One feels with Mr. Freeman very heartily that *Avowals* is Mr. Moore's

Odyssey. Defining these "serenely nimble conversations" as "a kind of innocent thinking aloud," he perceives "an ease, a vivacity, a brilliance and a simplicity" in them; stressing this charm above the weight of the critical opinions expressed. Certain it is that the imaginative inventive realism of the conversations, the drawing-room quality, native grace, and candid speculation take precedence in one's mind, of other merits, the paraphrase of Defoe having the qualities of Defoe himself—preciseness without apparent effort to be precise, the effect of discursiveness unrehearsed—the holding power of prose reduced to its lowest terms. "*Robinson Crusoe,* the most English of all books," says Mr. Moore: "We are islanders, Crusoe was one. Our business is the sea. Crusoe was constantly occupied going to and fro from a wreck. We are a prosaic people, what the French would call *terre à terre.* Nobody was more *terre à terre* than Crusoe." One finds an enigma in Mr. Moore's indifference—professed indifference perhaps one should say— to Henry James. The word envy as applied to James' attitude to *A Modern Lover* seems fantastic; as for his "unresponsiveness to the imagination of others," suggested by Mr. Freeman in this connection, one is bewildered when one remembers James in his letters struggling to catch the reflection of his correspondents' thoughts in every query. On the other hand, there is the justness of Mr. Moore's admiration for Hawthorne, the apt characterization of Zola's mind as "a coarse net through which living things escape," and the aesthetic soundness of his prejudice against Tolstoi in his assertion that "Tolstoi writes with a mind as clear as an electric lamp, a sizzling white light, crude and disagreeable." Mr. Moore succeeds in seeming "unaware of conventional appreciations"; undependable as a critic—inspired as an appreciator of those writers with whom he is in sympathy.

With regard to *Héloïse and Abélard,* named as one of Mr. Moore's supreme achievements, we are less tempted to speak in the superlative than in the instance of *Avowals*—dependable and absorbing as all of Mr. Freeman's comments are. We feel perspicacity in the contrast between Pater's interpretation of Abélard and Mr. Moore's: " 'true child of light'—Pater's phrase"; "those sins, that thwarted passion, that pride, that madness of mind and body—the features of Moore's portrait," and we relish Mr. Freeman's ingenious assertion that while "it would be untrue to say that George Moore has given you the Abélard of the letters, it is true that he has given you something at least of the Abélard whose passions were abjured and lamented by the Abélard of the letters"; most adroit, his answer to the criticism that the book is monotonous, "if that term be meant as equivalent to monotoned, it can be admitted." He laments that an early proclivity has smirched the book as it smirched *Hail and Farewell,* but pronounces it none the less, "the work of a mature unaging mind, the prose masterpiece perhaps of our time." Of Astrolabe, Mr. Freeman says it is strange "that the writer who has so often been dismissed as affected should almost alone have created the natural and beloved child." "Natural" and obviously beloved, is he lovely? He justifies the description of him by Mr. Moore in the question, "Why should nature have given him such witty eyes?" His resentful grief, however, at the death of the musician is scarcely that of a child; and captivating and diverting though he is, when one recalls his relentless investigating activity, his conflicting ambitions, the snare for the ducks, the wish to be a gleeman, his determination to go on a crusade, and his superiority at the age of eleven or less, to his mother's society and that of her companions—the only society he had known—one feels that to have such a child in tow would deprive one of reason.

Not so much a composite as a gallery of aspects from childhood to maturity, Mr. Freeman's portrait is surprisingly augmented by the addendum of Mr. Henry Danielson's bibliography of Mr. Moore's works. The connoisseur here sees in the notes appended, the price approximated at which volumes may be obtained and exults or is abased accordingly.

Exemplifying his own ideal of portraiture, Mr. Freeman has set forth "the character, the spirit, the inward history" that Mr. Moore's work "has expressed or suggested," giving a portrait so faithful that a detractor could not say that he has suppressed blemishes or idealized his subject; moreover in refusing to minimize an unbeautiful feature, he has not immortalized it. He is at every point his own man and Mr. Moore's deepest admirer could not wish a more glowing likeness or a finer light.

The Dial, 73 (December 1922), 664–68.

HYMEN

DR. MAHAFFY says in his essay "The Principles of the Art of Conversation," that artificiality is an evidence of some kind of dishonesty. Undoubtedly respect for the essence of a thing makes expression simple and in reading the present collection of poems by H. D., the hasty mind is abashed by the measure of intention and the exacting sincerity which prevail from the beginning to the end of the volume. Mr. Glenway Wescott praises the sternness of H. D.'s translations. "No race of men ever subsisted on

---

Review of *Hymen*, by H. D. (Henry Holt & Company).

sweet rhetorical distinction," he says and in her work, it is life denuded of subterfuge—it is the clean violence of truth that we have. Only as one isolates portions of the work, does one perceive the magic and compressed energy of the author's imagination, actuality in such lines as the following, being lost in the sense of spectacle:

> dark islands in a sea
> of gray olive or wild white olive
> cut with the sudden cypress shafts;

fingers

> wrought of iron
> to wrest from earth
> secrets; strong to protect,
> strong to keep back the winter.

One recognizes here, the artist—the mind which creates what it needs for its own subsistence and propitiates nothing, willing—indeed wishing to seem to find its only counterpart in the elements; yet in this case as in the case of any true artist, reserve is a concomitant of intense feeling, not the cause of it. In H. D.'s work, there is not so much reserve as insistence upon certain qualities; nature in its acute aspects is to her, a symbol of freedom. A liking for surf for instance, makes the contemplation of still water seem like loathing as in Swinburne when one recalls his comparison of Childe Harold and Don Juan:

> They are like lake water and sea water; the one is yielding, fluent, in-
> variable: the other has in it a life and pulse, a sting and swell, which
> touch and excite the nerves like fire or like music; the ripple flags and
> falls in loose lazy lines, the foam flies wide of any mark, and the breakers
> collapse here and there in sudden ruin and violent failure. But the violence
> and weakness of the sea are preferable to the smooth sound and equable
> security of a lake.

In the following lines as in H. D.'s work throughout, wiry diction, accurate observation and a homogeneous color sense are joint phases of unequivocal faithfulness to fact:

> Though Sparta enter Athens,
> Thebes wreck Sparta,
> each changes as water,

> salt, rising to wreak terror
> and fall back;
>
> a broken rock
> clatters across the steep shelf
> of the mountain slope,
> sudden and swift
> and breaks as it clatters down
> into the hollow breach
> of the dried water course.

Color and careful detail may arrest without commanding, but here—physical beauty emends other beauties and H. D.'s concept of color makes it hard to disassociate ideas from the pageant that we have of objects and hues—Egyptian gold and silver work, a harmonious, tempera-like procession of dyes and craftsmanship—of these "flocks of amber on the dolphin's back," "white cedar and black cedar," "the shore burned with a lizard blue," "the light shadow print cast through the petals of the yellow iris flower," in "the paved parapet" on which "you will step carefully from amber stones to onyx." In this instinctive ritual of beauty, at once old and modern, one is reminded of the supernatural yellows of China—of an aesthetic consciousness which values simultaneously, ivory and the chiseled ivory of speech, finding "in the hardness of jade, the firmness of the intelligence; in its sound with the peculiarity of ceasing abruptly, the emblem of music, in the sharpness of its angles, justice; in its splendor, the sky and in its substance, the earth." "Beauty is set apart," H. D. says:

> Beauty is cast by the sea
> a barren rock,
> beauty is set about
> with wrecks of ships,
> upon our coast, death keeps
> the shadows—death waits
> clutching toward us
> from the deeps.

In the bleakness as in the opulence of "The Islands" from which the above lines are taken, one remembers Ezekiel's Tyre, "a barren rock, a place for the spreading of nets in the midst of the sea—" the Tyre which commanded with her wares, "emeralds, purple and broidered work, fine linen, coral and rubies, horses, war-horses, wine and white wool, bright iron, casia and calamus, precious cloths for riding, horns of ivory and ebony, wares in wrappings of blue and broidered work and in chests of rich apparel bound with cords and made of cedar—replenished and made very glorious in the heart of the seas."

Talk of weapons and the tendency to match one's intellectual and emotional vigor with the violence of nature, give a martial, an apparently masculine tone to such writing as H. D.'s, the more so that women are regarded as belonging necessarily to either of two classes—that of the intellectual free-lance or that of the eternally sleeping beauty, effortless yet effective in the indestructible limestone keep of domesticity. Woman tends unconsciously to be the aesthetic norm of intellectual home life and preeminently in the case of H. D., we have the intellectual, social woman, non-public and "feminine." There is, however, a connection between weapons and beauty. Cowardice and beauty are at swords' points and in H. D.'s work, suggested by the absence of subterfuge, cowardice and the ambition to dominate by brute force, we have heroics which do not confuse transcendence with domination and which in their indestructibleness, are the core of tranquillity and of intellectual equilibrium.

Broom, 4 (January 1923), 133–35.

GENTLE SORCERY

IN these tales selected from four volumes published previously, the outstanding impression is that of moral sensibility; a heightened sense of the appropriateness of outward beauty to inward—as in the case of Mr. Housman's novel, *The Sheepfold*. But whereas the austerity and calm but torrential force in *The Sheepfold* make it unique, there is variableness in the symmetry and in the power of the telling of these later stories. The fairy-tale, like the question, bespeaks faith in the outcome of what is not yet evolved; and in their prime quality of illusory credibility, Mr. Housman's tales command belief. One reads eagerly until the end has been reached, infinitesimally disaffected by an occasional flaw. Although usually in the fairy-tale, good triumphs over evil and virtue is synonymous with beauty, an appearance of moral insouciance is essential; and in a number of these stories, one sees perhaps too plainly, the wish to bless. Also, evolving from an affection for

---

Review of *Moonshine and Clover* and *A Doorway in Fairyland*, by Laurence Housman (Harcourt Brace and Company).

the child mind and perhaps from a wish not to labor the matter, we have from time to time a kind of diminutive conversation as of an adult in the nursery, which is death to the illusion of make-believe. There is poetic security, however, in the statement, "he closed his eyes, and, with long silences between, spoke as one who prayed," and in the observation that Toonie's wife when her husband did not return, "became a kind of widow"; the pace is especially businesslike in this story of Toonie. Minute rapier-like shafts of crossing searchlights seem to play upon the "tight panting little bodies" whose sentinel Toonie outwitted, "picking him up by the slack of his breeches, so that his arms and legs trailed together along the ground." In "The Traveler's Shoes," one is infected with the poison of

> Sister, sister; bring me your hair,
> Of our mother's beauty give me your share.
> You must grow pale, while I must grow fair!

and sophisticated imagination in the metamorphosis by the blue moon of a pale country, is no enemy to realness: "All the world seemed carved out of blue stone. . . . The white blossoms of a cherry-tree had become changed into turquoise, and the tossing spray of a fountain as it drifted and swung was like a column of blue fire."

In the tradition of the house that Jack built, and of the stick that beat the dog, the fire that burned the stick, the water that put out the fire, there is newness in the evolving of the Prince's birth-day present.

"His fairygodmother had sent him a bird, but when he pulled its tail it became a lizard, and when he pulled the lizard's tail it became a mouse, and when he pulled the mouse's tail, it became a cat. . . . He pulled the cat's tail and it became a dog, and when he pulled the dog's it became a goat; and so it went on till he got to a cow. And he pulled the cow's tail and it became a camel, and he pulled the camel's tail and it became an elephant, and still not being contented, he pulled the elephant's tail and it became a guinea-pig. Now a guinea-pig has no tail to pull, so it remained a guinea-pig." Intricately perfect as a pierced ivory mosque, "The Prince with the Nine Sorrows" is a tale of nine sisters enchanted into peahens. Eight having refused to regain their identity at the sacrifice of their brother's life, the ninth after pecking out his heart, pecked out her own in remorse, substituting it for his and he, "taking up his own still beating heart, laid it into the place of hers so that which was which they themselves did not know."

In these two books there is a disparity in favor of *Moonshine and Clover*, there being perhaps but one story in *A Doorway in Fairyland*, "The Rat-catcher's Daughter," which may surely be depended upon to remain in the mind. In this most civilized obverse of fox-hunting ethics, a gnome having got himself caught in a trap with a view to entrapping his captor, is found apparently "wriggling and beating to be free." As the price of freedom, he consents to give the ratcatcher all the gold in the world and to make his daughter pure gold so that the king's son will marry her. Then when the ratcatcher finds that the prince will marry her only in the event that she can be made natural, in order to effect a retransformation, he is obliged to relinquish to the gnome his last penny. "The White Doe" maintaining throughout the image of a creature springing this way and that across a narrow forest stream, "A Capful of Moonshine" with its theme of the man who wished to know "how one gets to see a fairy," "The Gentle Cockatrice" monumentally patient despite a recurring desire to identify its tail, and "The Man Who Killed the Cuckoo," are tales one does not forget. This Mr. Badman's progress, told with a laconic wonder and embodying newly as it does, the moral contained in the story of Midas, is an account of a man who "lived in a small house with a large garden" and "took no man's advice about anything." Finding that the poisonous voice that he had disliked at a distance proceeded from himself, he "felt his eyes turning inwards so that he could see into the middle of his body. And there sat the cuckoo." We find him eventually "sailing along under the stars," tied into a bed of cuckoo feathers, "complete and compact; and inside him was the feeling of a great windmill going round and round and round."

One must not monopolize; one need not avenge oneself; in improving the morals of the world, one should begin by improving one's own; these are the mordant preoccupations about which Mr. Housman's fancy plays.

The Dial, 75 (September 1923), 293–95.

AN EAGLE IN THE RING

THE outstanding impression made by Mr. Lindsay's collected poems is that the author pities the fallen, deplores misunderstandings, and is saddened that the spirit should so often be at the mercy of the body. One cannot but revere his instinctive charity and determination to make a benevolent ordering of the universe possible. One knows that it is not an assumed attitude which leads Mr. Lindsay to say:

Review of *Collected Poems*, by Vachel Lindsay (The Macmillan Company).

> I want live things in their pride to remain.
> I will not kill one grasshopper vain,
> Though he eats a hole in my shirt like a door.
> I let him out, give him one chance more.
>
> Love's a gamble, say you. I deny.
> Love's a gift. I love you till I die.
> Gamblers fight like rats. I will not play.
> All I ever had I gave away.

It is a fine courage that enables a writer to let himself loose in the religious revival sense of the term at the risk of being thought an unintentional clown. It is impossible not to respect Mr. Lindsay's preoccupation with humanitarianism, but at the same time to deplore his lack of aesthetic rigor. In a lover of the chant, one expects a metronomelike exactness of ear; it is the exception, however, when the concluding lines of Mr. Lindsay's stanzas are not like a top which totters, or a hoop which rolls crazily before it finally stops. We have:

> Murdered in filth in a day,
> Somehow by the merchant gay!

and as the final lines of a poem:

> The urchins of the sky,
> Drying their wings from storms and things
> So they again can fly.

It is difficult to enunciate the words in such lines as:

> With my two bosomed blossoms gay

> Like rivers sweet and steep,
> Deep rock-clefts before my feet

> You were a girl-child slight.

One is disaffected even in the mood of informal discursiveness by adjacent terminal words such as calculation, Appalachian; whole, jowl; ore, floor; trial, vile; fire, the higher; and

> Join hands,
> Poets,
> Companions

is a metrical barbarism. Why, in "A Dirge for a Righteous Kitten," "His shirt was always laundried well"? What of the prose lines, "A special tang for those who are tasty"? And in the phrase, "when the statue of Andrew Jackson . . . is removed," we have that popular weak misuse of the present tense which we have in such an expression as "I hope he gets there." There is a lack of neat thinking in such phrases as "Lining his shelves with books from everywhere" and "All in the name of this or that grim flag." There is inexactness of meaning in

> The long handclasp you gave
> Still shakes upon my hands.

Usefulness is contradicted by the copybook concept of Dante:

> Would we were lean and grim, and shaken with hate
> Like Dante, fugitive, o'erwrought with cares,

and to speak of "Christ, the beggar," is inexact since it has never been said of Christ that he begged; he did without. One questions the cogency of Mr. Lindsay's thought when he says in alluding to the San Francisco earthquake, "Here where her God has scourged her." Not that San Francisco was or is a godly city, but many another city has gone unscourged.

As a visionary, as an interpreter of America, and as a modern primitive— in what are regarded as the three provinces of his power, Mr. Lindsay is hampered to the point of self-destruction by his imperviousness to the need for aesthetic self-discipline. Many poets have thoughts that are similar, in which case, only heedlessness prevents the author of the less perfect product from giving place to the author of the stronger, and much of Mr. Lindsay's collected work is unfortunate in thus provoking comparison with attested greatness. Unfortunate also, is the conscious altering of great familiar expressions:

> The times are out of joint! O cursed spite!
> The noble jester Yorick comes no more

> What Nations sow, they must expect to reap

> Within the many mansions,
> [the hosts] . . .
> Slept long by crooning springs.

> Did you waste much money
> To deck a leper's feast

and the context, provoke comparison with "The Vision of Sir Launfal." In "The Mysterious Cat," the line repeated three times, "Did you ever hear of a thing like that," recalls "The Three Blind Mice"; "Eden in Winter" recalls Ralph Hodgson's "Eve." "Star of My Heart," "At Mass," and "Foreign Missions in Battle Array," recall such classics as "We Three Kings of Orient Are" and "Onward, Christian Soldiers," and "The Last Song of Lucifer" seems like a mild transcript of *Paradise Lost*.

> In that strange curling of her lips,
> That happy curling of her lips,

comparison is simultaneously provoked, with E. E. Cummings and with Poe. "The Fairy Bridal Hymn" embodies without the aureole of distinguished effect of separateness, the feeling in Blake's account of a fairy's funeral and in "The Wedding of the Lotus and the Rose," the lines:

> Above the drownèd ages,
> A wind of wooing blows,

unconsciously to Mr. Lindsay no doubt, but suicidally, recall Swinburne.

Although it was not intended that the poems should be read to oneself, they will, on occasion, be so read, and so surely as they are it is inevitable that the author will in certain respects be presented amiss. Certain repetitions suggest the pleonasm of the illiterate preacher who repeats a phrase in order to get time to formulate another:

> Love is not velvet, not all of it velvet

> When a million million years were done
> And a million million years beside . . . .

We have not that reinforcing of sentiment which we have in reiteration by Yeats:

> She pulled the thread and bit the thread,
> And made a golden gown.

In his essay on Poetic Diction, Robert Bridges says, "The higher the poet's command of diction, the wider may be the field of his Properties; . . . and this is a very practical point, if a writer with no command of imaginative diction, should use such Properties as are difficult of harmonization, he will discredit both the Properties and the Diction." Despite the fact that Mr. Lindsay's properties are abundant and often harmonious as in the fantasy of the gypsies:

> Dressed, as of old, like turkey-cocks and zebras,
> Like tiger-lilies and chameleons,

the grouping is often conspicuously self-destructive. One feels that

> Percival and Belvidere
> And Nogi side by side

distract one from the poet's meaning as do the statesmen, artists, and sages, in "The Litany of the Heroes": Amenophis Fourth—Hamlet and Keats "in one"—Moses, Confucius, Alexander, Caesar, St. Paul, "Augustine," Mohammed, St. Francis, Dante, Columbus, Titian, Michael Angelo, Shakespeare, Milton, Napoleon, Darwin, Lincoln, Emerson, Roosevelt, Woodrow Wilson, Socrates. Like paintings in public buildings of the world's cultural and scientific progress, such groups sacrifice impact to inclusiveness. "Johnny Appleseed" is marred, one feels, by such phrases as "the bouncing moon," and

> He laid him down sweetly, . . .
> Like a bump on a log, like a stone washed white.

We rejoice in the resilience of imagination in the idea of a grasshopper as "the Brownies' racehorse," "the fairies' Kangaroo"; and in "The Golden Whales of California," there is controlled extravagance in the enumeration of "the swine with velvet ears," "the sacred raisins," "the trees which climb so high the crows are dizzy," "the snake fried in the desert," but "the biggest ocean in the world," and the whales "whooping that their souls are free," suggest the tired European's idea of America and the fantasy which visualizes St. Francis in the mere literal appropriateness of an etymological pun, offends by its conception of:

> The venturesome lovers . . .
> In a year and a month and a day of sailing
> Leaving the whales and their whoop unfailing
> On through the lightning, ice and confusion
> North of the North Pole,
> South of the South Pole
> And west of the west of the west of the west.

Objecting further, it is impossible not to say that Mr. Lindsay's phrases of Negro dialect are a deep disappointment. A familiarity with Negroes and the fact that the adaptations are intentional cannot absolve such Aryan doggerel as:

> And we fell by the altar
> And we fell by the aisle,
> And found our Savior
> In just a little while.

Such lines are startlingly at variance with real Negro parallelism as we have it in:

> Oh, Hell am deep 'n Hell am wide
> an' you can't touch bottom on either side"

and are incompatible with that perfect fragment of Negro cadence which Mr. Lindsay has combined with it, "Every time I hear the spirit moving in my heart I'll pray." A stentorianly emphatic combining of the elements of the black genius and the white, but emphasizes their incompatibility. In "The Congo," the "Baboon butler in the agate door," "And hats that were covered with diamond-dust" are pale substitutes for

> Baboon butler at the door,
> Diamond carpet on the floor.

In the "Booker Washington Trilogy,"

> . . . the oak secure,
> Weaving its leafy lure,
> Dreaming by fountains pure
> Ten thousand years

recalls "The Charge of the Light Brigade." "The Daniel," and "Simon Legree" have intermittently fantasy and beat, but the refrain, fabricated or authentic, "Let Samson be coming into your mind" is inexplicable from any point of view. In stage directions, the most expert craftsmen such as Shaw and Yeats barely escape pedantry and one feels that however necessary to Mr. Lindsay's conception of the spoken word particular information may be, when he asks us "to keep as lightfooted as possible," to read "orotund fashion," "with heavy buzzing bass," et cetera, one can but feel, unfairly or not, that he is subordinating a poorly endowed audience to wit which he proposes to furnish.

Some of Mr. Lindsay's work would lead one to infer that "a man is out on three wide balls but walks on four good strikes." The literary reader tends not to be compensated by moral fervor for technical misapprehensions, but there is life in any kind of beauty and in these poems avoidance of grossness and the entirely vengeful, is fortifying. "Why I Voted the Socialist Ticket" is full of contagious vigor:

> I am unjust, but I can strive for justice.
> My life's unkind, but I can vote for kindness.
> I, the unloving, say life should be lovely.
> I, that am blind, cry out against my blindness,

but in his "Curse for Kings," Mr. Lindsay gives the effect of an emotional pacifism which is incompatible with earnestness.

"This whole book is a weapon in a strenuous battlefield," Mr. Lindsay says; "practically every copy will be first opened on the lap of some person . . . trying to follow me as I recite as one follows the translation of the opera libretto." He is not to be refuted. There is a perhaps not very exact analogy between him in his *rôle* of undismayed, national interpreter, and a certain young eagle conveyed by American naval officers to the Philippines, styled "an American rooster," and pitted invariably with mortal consequence against Philippine gamecocks.

If a reader felt no responsibility for a writer, and were merely culling felicities, certain of Mr. Lindsay's poems would undoubtedly give complete pleasure; disregarding as a whole the poem, "How a Little Girl Danced," there is a fine accuracy in the line:

> With foot like the snow, and with steps like the rain.

There is suggested fragility in the poem game of yellow butterflies:

> They shiver by the shallow pools. . . .
> They drink and drink. A frail pretense!

There is beauty in "The Dandelion"; especially also, in "The Flower of Mending":

> When moths have marred the overcoat
> Of tender Mr. Mouse.

And the lines:

> Factory windows are always broken.
> Somebody's always throwing bricks,

are expertly captivating. Lincoln is not added to, but he is not travestied in "Abraham Lincoln Walks at Midnight"; there is glory in the conception of Alexander Campbell stepping "from out the Brush Run Meeting House"; and reality in Bryan:

> With my necktie by my ear, I was stepping on my dear. . . .
> The earth rocked like the ocean, the sidewalk was a deck.
> The houses for the moment were lost in the wide wreck.

We have in this poem, some of Gertrude Stein's power of "telling what you are being while you are doing what you are doing," and there is "blood within the rhyme" in

> The banjos rattled and the tambourines
> Jing-jing-jingled in the hands of Queens.

The Dial, 75 (November 1923), 498–505.

WELL MOUSED, LION

I T is not too much to say that some writers are entirely without imagination— without that associative kind of imagination certainly, of which the final tests are said to be simplicity, harmony, and truth. In Mr. Stevens' work, however, imagination precludes banality and order prevails. In his book, he calls imagination "the will of things," "the magnificent cause of being," and demonstrates how imagination may evade "the world without imagination"; effecting an escape which, in certain manifestations of *bravura*, is uneasy rather than bold. One feels, however, an achieved remoteness as in Tu Muh's lyric criticism: "Powerful is the painting . . . and high is it hung on the spotless wall in the lofty hall of your mansion." There is the love of mag-

---

Review of *Harmonium*, by Wallace Stevens (Alfred A. Knopf).

nificence and the effect of it in these sharp, solemn, rhapsodic elegant pieces of eloquence; one assents to the view taken by the author, of Crispin whose

> . . . mind was free
> And more than free, elate, intent, profound.

The riot of gorgeousness in which Mr. Stevens' imagination takes refuge, recalls Balzac's reputed attitude to money, to which he was indifferent unless he could have it "in heaps or by the ton." It is "a flourishing tropic he requires"; so wakeful is he in his appetite for color and in perceiving what is needed to meet the requirements of a new tone key, that Oscar Wilde, Frank Alvah Parsons, Tappé, and John Murray Anderson seem children asleep in comparison with him. One is met in these poems by some such clash of pigment as where in a showman's display of orchids or gladiolas, one receives the effect of vials of picrocarmine, magenta, gamboge, and violet mingled each at the highest point of intensity:

> In Yucatan, the Maya sonneteers
> Of the Caribbean amphitheatre
> In spite of hawk and falcon, green toucan
> And jay, still to the nightbird made their plea,
> As if raspberry tanagers in palms,
> High up in orange air, were barbarous.

One is excited by the sense of proximity to Java peacocks, golden pheasants, South American macaw feather capes, Chilcat blankets, hair seal needle-work, Singalese masks, and Rousseau's paintings of banana leaves and alligators. We have the hydrangeas and dogwood, the "blue, gold, pink, and green" of the temperate zone, the hibiscus, "red as red" of the tropics.

> . . . moonlight on the thick cadaverous bloom
> That yuccas breed . . .

> . . . with serpent-kin encoiled
> Among the purple tufts, the scarlet crowns.

and as in a shot spun fabric, the infinitude of variation of the colors of the ocean:

> . . . the blue
> And the colored purple of the lazy sea,

the emerald, indigos, and mauves of disturbed water, the azure and basalt of lakes; we have Venus "the center of sea-green pomp" and America "polar purple." Mr. Stevens' exact demand, moreover, projects itself from nature to human nature. It is the eye of no "maidenly greenhorn" which has differentiated Crispin's daughters; which characterizes "the ordinary women" as "gaunt guitarists" and issues the junior-to-senior mandate in "Floral Decorations for Bananas":

> Pile the bananas on planks.
> The women will be all shanks
> And bangles and slatted eyes.

He is a student of "the flambeaued manner,"

> . . . not indifferent to smart detail . . .
> . . . hang of coat, degree
> Of buttons . . . .

One resents the temper of certain of these poems. Mr. Stevens is never inadvertently crude; one is conscious, however, of a deliberate bearishness—a shadow of acrimonious, unprovoked contumely. Despite the sweet-Clementine-will-you-be-mine nonchalance of the "Apostrophe to Vincentine," one feels oneself to be in danger of unearthing the ogre and in "Last Looks at the Lilacs," a pride in unserviceableness is suggested which makes it a microcosm of cannibalism.

Occasionally the possession of one good is remedy for not possessing another as when Mr. Stevens speaks of "the young emerald, evening star," "tranquillizing . . . the torments of confusion." "Sunday Morning" on the other hand—a poem so suggestive of a masterly equipoise—gives ultimately the effect of the mind disturbed by the intangible; of a mind oppressed by the properties of the world which it is expert in manipulating. And proportionately, aware as one is of the author's susceptibility to the fever of actuality, one notes the accurate gusto with which he discovers the Negro, that veritable "medicine of cherries" to the badgered analyst. In their resilience and certitude, the "Hymn from a Watermelon Pavilion" and the commemorating of a Negress who

> Took seven white dogs
> To ride in a cab,

are proud harmonies.

One's humor is based upon the most serious part of one's nature. "Le

Monocle de Mon Oncle"; "A Nice Shady Home"; and "Daughters with Curls":
the capacity for self-mockery in these titles illustrates the author's disgust
with mere vocativeness.

Instinct for words is well determined by the nature of the liberties taken
with them, some writers giving the effect merely of presumptuous egotism—
an unavoided outlandishness; others, not: Shakespeare arresting one continually with nutritious permutations as when he apostrophizes the lion in
A Midsummer Night's Dream—"Well moused, lion." Mr. Stevens' "junipers
shagged with ice," is properly courageous as are certain of his adjectives
which have the force of verbs: "the spick torrent," "tidal skies," "loquacious
columns"; there is the immunity to fear, of the good artist, in "the blather
that the water made." His precise diction and verve are grateful as contrasts
to the current vulgarizations of "gesture," "dimensions" and "intrigue." He
is able not only to express an idea with mere perspicuity; he is able to do
it by implication as in "Thirteen Ways of Looking at a Blackbird" in which
the glass coach evolved from icicles; the shadow, from birds; it becomes a
kind of aristocratic cipher. "The Emperor of Icecream," moreover, despite
its not especially original theme of poverty enriched by death, is a triumph
of explicit ambiguity. He gets a special effect with those adjectives which
often weaken as in the lines:

> . . . That all beasts should . . .
>   . . . be beautiful
> As large, ferocious tigers are

and in the phrase, "the eye of the young alligator," the adjective as it is
perhaps superfluous to point out, makes for activity. There is a certain
bellicose sensitiveness in

> I do not know which to prefer . . .
> The blackbird whistling
> Or just after,

and in the characterization of the snow man who

> . . . nothing himself, beholds
> The nothing that is not there and the nothing that is.

In its nimbleness *con brio* with seriousness, moreover, "Nomad Exquisite"
is a piece of that ferocity for which one values Mr. Stevens most:

> As the immense dew of Florida
> Brings forth

> The big-finned palm
> And green vine angering for life.

Poetic virtuosities are allied—especially those of diction, imagery, and cadence. In no writer's work are metaphors less "winter starved." In "Architecture" Mr. Stevens asks:

> How shall we hew the sun, . . .
> How carve the violet moon
> To set in nicks?
>
> Pierce, too, with buttresses of coral air
> And purple timbers,
> Various argentines

and "The Comedian as the Letter C," as the account of the craftsman's un"simple jaunt," is an expanded metaphor which becomes as one contemplates it, hypnotically incandescent like the rose tinged fringe of the night blooming cercus. One applauds those analogies derived from an enthusiasm for the sea:

> She scuds the glitters,
> Noiselessly, like one more wave.
>
> The salt hung on his spirit like a frost,
> The dead brine melted in him like a dew.

In his positiveness, aplomb, and verbal security, he has the mind and the method of China; in such controversial effects as:

> Of what was it I was thinking?
> So the meaning escapes,

and certainly in dogged craftsmanship. Infinitely conscious in his processes, he says

> Speak even as if I did not hear you speaking
> But spoke for you perfectly in my thoughts.

One is not subject in reading him, to the disillusionment experienced in reading novices and charlatans who achieve flashes of beauty and immediately contradict the pleasure afforded by offending in precisely those respects in which they have pleased—showing that they are deficient in conscious artistry.

Imagination implies energy and imagination of the finest type involves an energy which results in order "as the motion of a snake's body goes through all parts at once, and its violation acts at the same instant in coils that go contrary ways." There is the sense of the architectural diagram in the disjoined titles of poems with related themes. Refraining for fear of impairing its litheness of contour, from overelaborating felicities inherent in a subject, Mr. Stevens uses only such elements as the theme demands; for example, his delineation of the peacock in "Domination of Black," is austerely restricted, splendor being achieved cumulatively in "Bantam in Pine-Woods," "The Load of Sugar-Cane," "The Palace of the Babies," and "The Bird with the Coppery Keen Claws."

That "there have been many most excellent poets that never versified, and now swarm many versifiers that never need answer to the name of poets," needs no demonstration. The following lines as poetry independent of rhyme, beg the question as to whether rhyme is indispensably contributory to poetic enjoyment:

> There is not nothing, no, no, never nothing,
> Like the clashed edges of two words that kill

and

> The clambering wings of black revolved,
> Making harsh torment of the solitude.

It is of course evident that subsidiary to beauty of thought, rhyme is powerful in so far as it never appears to be invented for its own sake. In this matter of apparent naturalness, Mr. Stevens is faultless—as in correctness of assonance:

> Chieftain Iffucan of Azcan in caftan
> Of tan with henna hackles, halt!

The better the artist, moreover, the more determined he will be to set down words in such a way as to admit of no interpretation of the accent but the one intended, his ultimate power appearing in a selfsufficing, willowy, firmly contrived cadence such as we have in "Peter Quince at the Clavier" and in "Cortège for Rosenbloom":

> . . . That tread
> The wooden ascents
> Of the ascending of the dead.

One has the effect of poised uninterrupted harmony, a simple appearing, complicated phase of symmetry of movements as in figure skating, tight-rope dancing, in the kaleidoscopically centrifugal circular motion of certain medieval dances. It recalls the snake in *Far Away and Long Ago*, "moving like quicksilver in a rope-like stream" or the conflict at sea when after a storm, the wind shifts and waves are formed counter to those still running. These expertnesses of concept with their nicely luted edges and effect of flowing continuity of motion, are indeed

> . . . pomps
> Of speech which are like music so profound
> They seem an exaltation without sound.

One further notes accomplishment in the use of reiteration—that pitfall of half-poets:

> Death is absolute and without memorial,
> As in a season of autumn,
> When the wind stops. . . .
> When the wind stops.

In brilliance gained by accelerated tempo in accordance with a fixed melodic design, the precise patterns of many of these poems are interesting.

> It was snowing
> And it was going to snow

and the parallelism in "Domination of Black" suggest the Hebrew idea of something added although there is, one admits, more the suggestion of mannerism than in Hebrew poetry. Tea takes precedence of other experiments with which one is familiar, in emotional shorthand of this unwestern type, and in "Earthy Anecdote" and in the "Invective against Swans," symmetry of design is brought to a high degree of perfection.

It is rude perhaps, after attributing conscious artistry and a severely intentional method of procedure to an artist, to cite work that he has been careful to omit from his collected work. One regrets, however, the omission by Mr. Stevens of "The Indigo Glass in the Grass," "The Man Whose Pharynx

Was Bad," "La Mort du Soldat Est Près des Choses Naturelles (5 Mars)" and "Comme Dieu Dispense de Graces":

> Here I keep thinking of the primitives—
> The sensitive and conscientious themes
> Of mountain pallors ebbing into air.

However, in this collection one has eloquence. "The author's violence is for aggrandizement and not for stupor"; one consents therefore, to the suggestion that when the book of moonlight is written, we leave room for Crispin. In the event of moonlight and a veil to be made gory, he would, one feels, be appropriate in this legitimately sensational act of a ferocious jungle animal.

The Dial, 76 (January 1924), 84–91.

SIR FRANCIS BACON

In his *Studies of Extraordinary Prose*, Lafcadio Hearn says, "You cannot appeal to the largest possible audience with a scholarly style." This would seem to be true; but expressions of deep conviction, in all ages, weather coldness, and Sir Francis Bacon's "exact diligence" and pleasing defiances anticipated not only the mind of close successors, but of our own age. "There is no excellent beauty that hath not strangeness in the proportion" recalls Burke's statement, in his essay "On the Sublime and the Beautiful," that beauty is striking as deformity is striking—in its novelty; also Ruskin's summary of beauty as beauty of behavior affirms the statement, "No youth can be comely but by pardon and considering the youth." When Bacon says of masques that the eye must be relieved "before it be full of the same object," since "it is a great pleasure to desire to see that it cannot perfectly discern," one is reminded of Santayana's observation that "nothing absorbs the consciousness so much as what is not quite given."

There is a renovating quality in the work of early writers, as also in so-called "broken" speech in which we have the idiom of one language in the words of another. Sir Francis Bacon surely has this raciness, as when he says, "I have marveled sometimes at Spain how they clasp and contain so large dominions with so few natural Spaniards," and defines moss as "a rudiment between putrefaction and an herb"; the vigor of the writer's nature being, of course, the key to his "efficacy," as when he says of anger, "To seek to extinguish anger utterly is but a bravery of the Stoics. We have better oracles"; and what of, "A civil war is like the heat of fever but a foreign war is like the heat of exercise"? In Sir Francis Bacon, conclusiveness and contempt for tact are always at variance with caution, his desire for efficiency pertaining even to death: "I would out of a care to do the best business well, ever keep a guard, and stand upon keeping faith with a good conscience. And I would die together, and not my mind often, my body once."

His insight into human idiosyncrasy has a flavor of Machiavelli, as when he says, "I knew one that when he wrote a letter, he would put that which was most material in the postscript as it had been a bye matter"; of boldness, "It doth fascinate and bind hand and foot, those that are shallow in judgment and weak in courage, and prevaileth with wise men at weak times." Of blindness to one's own defects, he remarks that there is a confidence "like as we shall see it commonly in poets, that if they show their verses and you except to any, they will say that that line cost them more labor than all the rest." Of pulling down the ambitious, he says, "The only way is the interchange continually of favors and disgraces, whereby they may not know what to expect and be as it were in a wood." "As for jest, there be certain things which ought to be privileged from it," he says. "Men ought to find the difference between saltness and bitterness. Certainly, he that hath a satirical vein, as he maketh others afraid of his wit, so need he be afraid of others' memory."

Bacon admires Machiavelli's suiting of form to matter; he feels letters to be an "even more particular representation of business" than "chronicles or lives"; and says those who have returned to Caesar's *Commentaries* after a first compulsory reading will perhaps agree that in "Caesar's history, entitled only a commentary," there are solid weight of matter, real passages, and lively images of actions and persons, expressed in the greatest propriety of words and perspicuity of narration that ever was." Moreover, his differentiation of poetry from prose is entertaining. Poetry, he says, has "more unexpected and alternative variation," and in "being not tied to the laws of nature, may at pleasure join that which nature has severed and sever that which nature hath joined."

A student of human nature and of words ought to be able to tell a story, and Bacon winds quickly into the heart of an episode—in *The New Atlantis;* in the essays, as when he says, "It is sport to see when a bold fellow is out of countenance, at a stay like a stale at chess"; and in *The Advancement of Learning,* in the account of Xenophon's prowess and Falinus' skepticism " 'If I be not deceived, young gentleman, you are an Athenian and I believe you study philosophy and it is pretty that you say, but you are much abused if you think your virtue can stand the king's power.' Here was the scorn," says Bacon. "The wonder followed." Not only as he exposits mythology in *The Wisdom of the Ancients* but as narrator of facts in *The History of Henry VII*, he is a siren of ingenuity. The circumstantial manner of a novel continually refreshes the content, as when the queen's coronation is likened to a christening that has been put off until the child is old enough to walk to the altar; and exact without being labored, Bacon says the king "was a comely personage, a little above just stature, well and straight limbed but slender. His countenance was reverend, and a little like a churchman. But it was to the disadvantage of the painter for it was best when he spake." Could anything be more chiseled than the closing sentences of this history? "He was born at Pembroke Castle, and lieth buried at Westminster, in one of the stateliest and daintiest monuments of Europe, both for the chapel and the sepulchre. So that he dwelleth more richly dead, in the monument of his tomb, than he did alive in Richmond or any of his palaces."

The essays have perhaps absorbed interest which belongs to the other writings and have stood as a barrier to the daring of the other. The aphorisms and allusions to antiquity have an effect of formula; quoted wisdom from the Greek, Roman, Hebrew and Italian sages tending to excuse attention as much as to concentrate it. One thinks of the early essays in relation to the *History of Henry VII* somewhat as one thinks of an anthology in relation to a novel. "Even in divinity," Bacon says, "some writings have more of the eagle than the others"; and in *The Advancement of Learning* there is conspicuously much of the eagle. It is understandable that Bacon should say, "If the first reading will make an objection, the second will make an answer."

The Dial, 76 (April 1924), 343–46; *Predilections*.

THE MAN WHO DIED TWICE

THROUGHOUT Mr. Robinson's work, one feels his admiration for "courage that is not all flesh recklessness." This emphasis upon the predominance of the soul's conflicts over those of the intellect, is conspicuous in *The Man Who Died Twice*. A musician, gigantically endowed—who has "mistaken hell for paradise," since he is not

---

Review of *The Man Who Died Twice*, by Edwin Arlington Robinson (The Macmillan Company).

> . . . the sanguine ordinary
> That sees no devils and so controls itself,
> Having nothing in especial to control—

has died, but not completely. Brought back to life, he finds in moral triumph, "more than he had lost," and gives what is left of his reviving genius to those who have reclaimed him. An early friend descried him among

> The caps and bonnets of a singing group
> That loudly fought for souls,

> . . . beating a bass drum
> And shouting Hallelujah with a fervor
> At which . . . no man smiled.

Reserved though he is, and non-committal in respects in which the psychoanalysis-infected poet is not, Mr. Robinson is entirely explicit in trusting the reader with his beliefs, tastes, and judgments; and his intuitively dramatic expanding of a theme carries conviction even in respect to "the success of failure," a subject which he repeatedly presents, and without collapse of interest develops at length as in *The Man Who Died Twice*. In it as in his other work, the triumph of truth is galvanically thrilling. In its pursuit, he declares, you may not untroubled enjoy "the perennial weed Selfishness": "No doubt you call it Love"; on the other hand, "hell shall have . . . No laughter to vex down your loyalty." His inability to think selfishly with blind aboriginal zeal, differentiates him from the sybarite or mere connoisseur; and in this basic spiritual sensitiveness, he recalls Hardy, although one feels no consanguinity of dogma between these poets, Hardy's tenacious incredulity and Mr. Robinson's persistently tentative credulity being obversely helpful. It is in an extra-normal sense of responsibility that one feels a resemblance—in the capacity for suffering and the incapacity intentionally of inflicting it; in a sense of "the eternal tragedies" that render as Mr. Robinson says, "hope and hopelessness akin": this fidelity to experience leading him to visualize "sunlit labyrinths of pain" as it has actuated Hardy to uphold in his "pleasing agonies and painful delights" with titanic inevitableness, a concept of romance which in its superiority to actuality, is surely deathless.

Mr. Robinson deplores "the brain-waste of impatience," and as a concomitant of deliberate, searching scholarship, we perceive in his work, the dominance without protest, of humility. With an acuteness of perception and of speech which are the attributes of a truly sentient view of life, he shows us Fernando Nash, now "disintegrated, lapsed and shrunken,"

> The king who lost his crown before he had it,
> And saw it melt in hell,
>
> Pounding a drum and shouting for the lost.

Yet Mr. Robinson seems not to be immune from the aggressive superficiality of critics who share least, the basic quality of his reserve; and at a time when

> The ways of unimaginative men
> Are singularly fierce . . .

wise craftsmanship must suffer not the ridicule but the ridiculousness of final dictum as unsubstantiated as a Hollywood substitute for medieval masonry when it affirms his writing to be "aurad with the dim halo of futility"; as it must suffer also, the appraisal which resembles praise. As Mr. Robinson has said,

> The dower of ignorance is to distrust
> All that it cannot feel,

and one recalls with gratitude Professor Saintsbury's good sense in refusing to place posterity's verdict upon the work of living writers.

Mr. Robinson's work is completely self-vindicating, however, in its sensitive, self-corroborating, rhetorically measured, elegant articulateness. It is true that in a capacious treatment of large themes which embody more than one climax, parts of the design must be subordinate and the necessary line which is not emotionally inevitable, is sometimes a difficulty. In the poems "Merlin" and "Lancelot," the reader's imagined familiarity with the subject-matter puts the author at the disadvantage of being more than adequately splendid, but Mr. Robinson is at all times a poet—at all times circumstantially exact, the actuality of his treatment of characters in the Bible and in history making it difficult to think of him as restricted to one place or to an epoch. His intuitively aesthetic use of experience is notably embodied in the fluently sustained, aristocratic manipulating of what passes for casual talk in the play, *Van Zorn;* and in *The Man Who Died Twice*, there is the actual sound of

> . . . those drums of death, which, played by Death
> Himself, were beating sullenly alone.

This tale of Fernando Nash with its "flaming rain," and the "competent plain face of Bach" as its presiding influence, exhibits that personal attitude of

Mr. Robinson's—of care for humanity and for art which makes his work stand out with a self-sustaining stiffness which is not mere exterior North American correctness, and gives it an aspect of solitary, mystical security of possession. Captain Craig's biographer says: "I felt the feathery touch of something wrong," and in a day of much shallowness, muddy technique, and self-defended mystery, one is grateful for this highly developed obedience to a sensibility which is a matter not only of the nerves, but of the whole man.

The Dial, 77 (August 1924), 168–70.

THISTLES DIPPED IN FROST

MAXWELL BODENHEIM'S work has been honored in almost every notable type of current publication; in that published for the politically conservative seriously cultured person, in the contumaciously aesthetic uncompromisingly intellectual magazine, in the "poet's garland," in newspapers, and in the fashionable woman's Lady-Book-and-Shopping-Guide. As is to be expected of a writer for many persons, Mr. Bodenheim is many things: social philosopher, literary critic, novelist, and poet; but it is to be regretted that as a critic of modern life, he goes but part of the way, sparing himself accurate exposition of the things he advocates, impetuously dogmatizing so that one is forced in certain instances to conclude that he is self-deceived or willingly a charlatan. Our anger is stirred by his epitome of Christ's "mistakes" in emancipating humanity. He says Christ approved the repressing of instinct and that he "told people to believe with their feelings and let their minds go on a vacation." As it were in passing, Mr. Bodenheim offers definitions which detain without enriching. In comparison with Chesterton's compact, expansive consideration of mysticism, his definition of it is not thorough, nor are his definitions indeed definitions, but assertions. When he says to a grass blade,

> You reach the sky because your face
> Is not turned toward it,

Review of *Against This Age,* by Maxwell Bodenheim (Boni and Liveright), and *Crazy Man,* by Maxwell Bodenheim (Harcourt, Brace and Company).

one feels a shrewdness of which the logic is not sound; eventually one doubts the authoritativeness of opinions which have the effect of being aphorisms; aphorisms in which there is often the mischievousness of half-statement or a slovenly abandoning of what at first had seemed to the author to be interesting. "Modern poets . . . frequently sneer at philistines, hypocrisies, and conservative postures," says Mr. Bodenheim, "and this reiterated attitude reveals a baffled longing for vengeance." Can a poet sneer? Is not Mr. Bodenheim's interest in retaliation at variance with creative power? Moreover, side by side with much candor, sensitiveness, and emancipated judgment, this author's concept of woman puzzles one. Surely there is false perspicacity in an analysis which results always in the exhibiting of woman's "enticing inferiority"; which finds her an embarrassing adjunct, "cooing and crawling for your money," a creature of perfumed effeteness, of "interminable evasions," "waving surrender in the foreground," never other than a receiver of "men's ornaments and poverties." The writer's attitude of pronouncement reaches its apex in the statement made by one of his *dramatis personae*, that there is zest in bagging a woman who is one's equal in wits; the possibility of bagging a superior in wits not being allowed to confuse the issue. Suspecting that Mr. Bodenheim has but half sifted the facts in his observations as cited above, one feels a false approach to life in certain of his ironies. "Highly imaginative men are accused of being demented, and consequently belittled," he says. If they are, it is perhaps because they are not laborious— not so severe in judging themselves as in judging others. In his interpretation of Christ, his attitude to woman, his impatience with his readers, one feels a grudging view, a lack of breadth, of noble reverie, of the detachment of faith.

There is more for us, however, in Mr. Bodenheim's writing than cause for objection. In one of his poems he makes the crystal statement that "simplicity demands one gesture and men give it endless thousands," and he is in his own fiction somewhat stark and emphatic, showing dispatch and quick firm action, with that condensed finality of implication which is an attribute of the genuine narrator. There is too, an acid penetration which recalls James Joyce's *Dubliners* in the statement, "[his] eyes greeted the darkness as if it were an advancing mob." One values the compactness of, "the sea had lent her its skin," the power of accurate observation in the poem, "Old Man,"

> You turn your hammock and surrender limbs
> To sunlight, and increase the hammock's swing,

and the pliant irony of some of Mr. Bodenheim's underworld vernacular:

He asks me to please keep quiet! I said, "Gee, you've got a big opinion of yourself, haven't you?" . . . and he answers, "No, it's not that, but I know in advance everything that you're going to say so there's no need of me hearing it."

But again we disagree with him when he says, "The novel should be far more interested in style than in message." It is Mr. Bodenheim's misfortune that he has attained this ideal, since in his work, there is much to arrest one yet not enough to detain; his work lacks substance—his unscientifically careless pronouncement for the bettering of fiction, explaining the lack on his own part of a genuine triumph; for is not style invariably a concomitant of content—the prototype of personality? Mr. Bodenheim says, "Man has a far more plaintive interior than the sexologist dares to admit." We agree, and apropos of his further statement that "intellectual curiosity, emotional whimsicality, the decorative poetic touch, ironical strength, and even a plausible realism are . . . absent from American novels of the present," are hopeful of what he may give us, only to be astounded in his proffer of *Crazy Man*—a staggering dream of fleshly discontent.

It is to his poetry that we owe most; although in it, as in his prose, there is the elected right to be superficial. Aboriginal enticing femininity has been completely written of by the Greeks; again with freshness, by Restoration poets. Such subject-matter requires magical treatment if it is to receive a second glance. Emotion, truth, intellect, revenge, money, are topics about which universal sciences have been built. How then, can we accept a stinginess of content in certain of Mr. Bodenheim's poems which deal with these themes, the poet deifying "the workshop of his mind," the matter in hand eluding him?

The mechanism of Mr. Bodenheim's mind is delicate and his predilection for "tombstones, skulls, and lilies" is by no means ridiculous, nor is it surprising that he should be alive to the beauty of death; but among poems of distinction, there are some self-consciously macabre conceits, for example, "Emotional Monologue"—a weightless, miasmal brittle, "studio" extravaganza in which we have the hobby for death at its worst.

Waiving the matter of content, Mr. Bodenheim's technique varies in soundness. He says, "No longer do poets linger over their output, seeming to emulate the men who turn out collars and automobiles." Then why when expectation has been awakened by the piquancy and proper reserve of opening lines such as "Gingerly the poets sit," is it not fulfilled? And how is it that in what one ventures to call a very bad poem such strokes of excellence occur, as:

> Men sit and feign industrious respect,
> With eye-brows often slightly ill at ease—
> Cats in an argument are more erect?

Mr. Bodenheim's aloofness from the faults of the day would not lead one to expect the weak last lines which mar many of his poems—in some lines, a not sustained effortful crispness of implication which seems an evasion, a faith in words rather than in logic, and that pitfall of aesthetic natures, the convention of the bizarre in which poetry instantaneously and disaffectingly becomes prose. Mr. Bodenheim invents with firmness:

> Black angels and muscular contortions
> On panels of taffeta,

and inquires with what is to the reviewer, engaging *esprit*,

> Maiden, where are you going,
> With impudence that makes your arms and legs
> Unnecessary feathers?

Admitting such a thing as exotic diction, one can sometimes applaud Mr. Bodenheim's "madness" although feeling his most daring prose to be not entirely cohesive or transparently accurate. As has been said of his "tall adjectives" and verbal sleights, in one of those gentle and distinguished analyses that have been accorded him by literary experts: "Such tricks, although they often steal distinction from surprise, wear out the power of the brain to respond, and eventually develop a resentment toward the kind of verse that leaves us jaded." A certain form of soliloquy resorted to by Mr. Bodenheim has not one's entire sanction. The soliloquy is, at its best, creatively a make-shift, and when not used with consummate address, has the effect of being a not quite natural, ripe vehicle for conveying meaning; for example, "Turmoil in a Morgue," "Impulsive Dialogue," "Dialogue Between a Past and Present Poet," "When Spirits Speak of Life," "A Chorus Girl Speaks in a Dream to a Former Lover." Perfect diction we have, in "Advice to a Blue-Bird":

> Who can make a delicate adventure
> Of walking on the ground,

in that allusion to the "woman in penitent lavender," and in this interpretation of despair:

> She killed herself, believing
> That he might become to her in death
> A figure less remote and careful.

Yet why, in prose that is the work of a precisian, should one encounter unintentional rhymes: "Their heads cleared and the past night reappeared," "the sickly brawls and vapid scandals of streets and halls"? Why in either verse or prose, the words "boresome," "peeked," "glimpsed," "tawdrily," the phrase "apt to induce," and the effete one, "moments of rare insight"?

There is that in Mr. Bodenheim's work which is delicately moving, as when he calls the butterfly, "aimless petal of the wind" and in

> . . . you will have a wife
> Like a thistle dipped in frost.

> . . . your life will
> Stand in a desperate majesty.

And far beyond mere sensibility, in certain work, a laconic violence with exactness persuades one of more than sensory impressionableness, as in the lines:

> An effervescence of noises
> Depends upon cement for its madness.

Dissatisfied with the irony and unrest of Mr. Bodenheim's spirit, we await an exposition of that which to him would make life satisfactory. He writes in one of his poems of a man who in 1962:

> . . . died with a grin at the fact
> That literature and art in America
> Were still presenting a mildewed, decorous mien.

Is the implication accurate? And if it is, is not the best corrective, an exemplifying at white heat of the accuser's indigenous, individual genius?

HISTRIONIC SECLUSION

In Mr. Moore's *Conversations in Ebury Street*, are to be found a criticism of Balzac, the already published lecture in French on Balzac and Shakespeare, a discussion with an American, and a number of "portraits"—notably that of Dujardin: in these discussions of novels, of the theater, of painting, and of poetry, the honor of "prodigious memory" and much wit being shared with John Freeman, Walter de la Mare, Cunninghame-Graham, Edmund Gosse, and Granville-Barker. Reminding us by its tempo and method, of *Avowals*, this volume presents certain of Mr. Moore's sensitively cruel, aesthetically flawless foibles: that intentional distorting of judgment, that pleased contemplation of the resolving of a promised climax into contradiction, that ever enlivening ingenuity and formal virtue. Certain characteristic crochets present themselves with new vigor: the mischievousness of journalism: the unhelpfulness of "all the many Sirs" who have written about Shakespeare; as Mr. Moore says, *"Il y a un proverbe français qui dit que les arbres nous empêchent de voir la forêt"*: he reiterates, "Of French literature I know but a corner, and of the French language not much more": he reminds us that "education is of no help to anybody except teachers": alludes to "a quiet corner and a grave": and by emphasis upon "the simple reality" of certain chicken, and "the boycott of bass" which may "oblige" him "to organize a Bass Club," we are reminded of "that animality which is" to him, "our better part."

There are depths of color in these imaginings and there are flaws. As the verbal virtuoso, Mr. Moore is sometimes disappointing, presenting the paradox of a naturalness as oral as Bunyan's; and a naturalness so studied as to annihilate itself. There are inharmonious echoes of the Bible and of the English prayer-book, and an intentional impertinence that on occasion becomes insult; one feels the lack of aesthetic tone in Mr. Moore's displeasure with Hardy.

If, however, Mr. Moore seems to succeed in his intention not to be sound, certain of his imaginary sentiments are most amusing, as when he says of true love: "It is nothing to inspire it, the difficulty is to feel it," and our admiration is engaged by his cat's play with painting—his exposition of a method untrammeled by the necessity for drawing or values—"the tap, tap, tap method" by which the pupil is enabled "to escape from a quality not easily distinguishable from linoleum."

Review of *Conversations in Ebury Street*, by George Moore (Boni and Liveright).

The actuality of the eliciting principle as employed in these conversations, recalls Plato's dialogues, *The Life and Death of Mr. Badman,* some of Jacob Abbott's most dramatically lifelike colloquies, and Landor; Mr. Moore far surpassing the *Imaginary Conversations* one feels, in the circumstantial quality of parry and thrust. The disciplined celerity of the story-teller as we have it in the instantaneous evoking of a scene, moreover, arrests and takes possession of one as development succeeds development; studious economy of exposition being in no respect more conspicuous than his precision of epithet, as when he denominates Ann Brontë, "a sort of literary Cinderella" and is apprehensive of Wyndham Lewis as "the new Beelzebub." This positive precision, exemplified in his attitude to the work of others, appears in his reflecting that Balzac

> did not *write;* he registered his ideas, and his ideas are always so interesting that you read without noticing the ruts of verbal expression he slips into . . . until we come to translate or to read very, *very* attentively, the page appears to us to be not only well but splendidly written;

as in a flank attack upon journalism, his saying:

> At certain seasons locusts fall upon a country and devour it leaf by leaf, and in the same way French words have within the last few years fallen upon the English language and are eating up English words.

In that verbal dovetailing which is his passion, and that trouble-taking propensity in matters in which it pleases him to take trouble, we note the clearness obtained by repetition, item being added to item with an almost violent exactness; and in the following sentences, his sincere if somewhat ostentatious insistence that mechanism and literary effect are indivisible:

> During the first fifty pages of *The Brook Kerith* I tried to stint myself to the miserable *you,* which is not a word but a letter of the alphabet, at least in sound; but to weed out the *yous* means something more than grammatical changes; every sentence has to be recast; the rearrangement of the verbs is difficult sometimes, but of very nearly the same disciplinary advantage as the use of meter.

This attentiveness of the writer to the business of writing has resulted in Mr. Moore's case, in some of the most accurate correct speaking known to one as when he says: "In reading the Elizabethans we are in salt water always; the verse is buoyant," and thus deprecates a metropolitan theater:

"Mean streets and a tangle of tramways from which we have to run for our lives like cats before pavement skaters, shatter our dreams."

"A book must go to a tune," he says, and plainly in his own writing, "the composition is balanced within and without." Just as one is alive to the more easy euphony of such phrases as "the epistle of an apostle," a "taxi, who took us in tow," "Augustus being among the gone," one is alive to more difficult harmonies—to the neat machinery, the grace, the impetuosity, the finality, of this writing which is, one ventures to feel, perfectly a counterpart to "a good play"—a definition of which is attributed by Mr. Moore to Mr. Granville-Barker:

> By a good play I do not mean a play that will run as long as a public house, but one that will encourage and enrapture those who seek pleasure in thought.

The Dial, 78 (March 1925), 225–27.

BESITZ UND GEMEINGUT*

DR. BRANDES has in this biography remembered what Goethe counsels the biographer not to forget—that succeeding generations have a flimsy idea of preceding periods; that nothing is to be assumed, everything is to be related. We should, however, welcome a consideration of *Dichtung und Warheit*† fuller than the slender chapter which Dr. Brandes vouchsafes us, and are defrauded in the absence of any but cursory allusions to Goethe's letters, essays, and reviews. Furthermore, one feels Dr. Brandes to be a more "trusting" student of Goethe than one is oneself when he says that "by the mere touch of his spiritual personality Goethe had initiated Carlyle into life and literature"; that in "publishing under his own name the most beautiful poems Marianne von Willemer ever produced," he "conferred honor when he took." Dr. Brandes' gift of epithet is manifest in his alluding to Bettina's

*Personal Property and Communal Property.
†*Poetry and Truth.*

Review of *Wolfgang Goethe*, by Georg Brandes. Translated by Allen W. Porterfield (Nicholas L. Brown).

"burrlike hanging on" and "youthful boldness," to Schiller's "noble and striving nature"; in his characterizing Frau von Klettenberg as "a Protestant nun" and Goethe as "a fortress, not an open town"; his military pre-empting of judgment, however, would scarcely convert one to his admiration for Goethe if one did not already share it. A certain infelicity of speech is heightened, one suspects, by the translation, in which, notwithstanding the translator's confessed loyalty to the text, his idea of idiom seems a false one, resulting as it does in such phrases as "quite a few," "quite a while," "measured up," "forever and a day" "apt to be full of," and "time out of mind."

That of which one is above all, and always delightfully, conscious throughout the work is Goethe's lyric power, especially valuing what is said of his "musical skill" and "tonal depth"—as a result of which greater effects have "never been produced by fewer words and simpler means." Although certain poems quoted by Dr. Brandes do not seem to us "immortal masterpieces," we feel "the fire," "the manly seriousness," "the tenderness," "the real humor," "the great glamour," the "inner richness of Goethe's being, which makes it impossible for even a short stanza to be empty."

We are especially indebted to Dr. Brandes for his paragraphs upon Goethe as counsel for the defense in certain legal cases and for his comment upon Goethe's discoveries in anatomy, geology, and botany, for which, he says, "we feel a respect nearly deeper than that evoked by his purely poetic creations."

"Casting off works in the process of self-creation," describing his life as "the incessant turning and lifting of a stone that had to be turned and lifted once more," Goethe is himself, as Dr. Brandes implies, his greatest work of art. This man who "never rode on a railway train, never sailed on a steamship, who read by a tallow lamp and wrote with a goosequill," who "never saw Paris, never saw London, never saw St. Petersburg, never saw Vienna," and caught but a fleeting glimpse of Berlin, "was within himself a whole and complete civilization." "He was among minds," as Dr. Brandes says, "what the Pacific Ocean is among the waters of the earth. In reality only a small part of it is pacific." We see an evolving enthusiasm in which a preference for Gothic is "wheeled about" to a preference for the art of ancient Greece, "somewhat as one would turn a fiery charger." Aloof from politics, yet as a passionate economist he appears "in the person of the singular uncle in *Wilhelm Meister's Wanderejahre*, whose watchword, '*Besitz und Gemeingut*,' was inscribed round about on his various buildings somewhat as the Oriental peoples adorn the walls of their houses with excerpts from the Koran." We see his spiritual independence, his love of liberty as "the opposite of coercion, but not the opposite of a voluntary subjection to such coercion as that of moral discipline, or that of metrics, or social forms, or reasonable law"—a concept embodied in his saying, *"Und das Gesetz nur kann uns Freiheit geben."** We recall with Croce his "opposing that in French literature which was intellectualistic and ironical, aged and correct like an old lady," as against his reviling "those Germans who were wont to justify every unseemliness they wrote by saying that they had 'lived it.' " We see his unconquerably social nature, as evinced by his many friends; a distrust of his age, on the other hand, such that "when finally as a result of extraordinary exertion he had finished the second part of *Faust,* he sealed the manuscript with seven seals and laid it aside for posterity, convinced that his contemporaries would simply misunderstand it." By this "development of the soul in accord with its inborn ability," we are reminded of "that manifoldness in simplicity of mountains" which Goethe himself admired.

*And it is the law alone that gives us freedom.

The Dial, 78 (June 1925), 508–10; *Predilections.*

"THE BRIGHT IMMORTAL OLIVE"

WE have in these poems, an external world of commanding beauty—the erect, the fluent, the unaccountably brilliant. Also, we have that inner world of interacting reason and unreason in which are comprehended, the rigor, the succinctness of hazardous emotion. And in the entire volume, one is conscious of a secure, advancing exactness of thought and of speech. There is here, an immortalizing of minutiae that is both personal and cosmic, whereby we may observe, "the wind-indented snow," the sea "painting the lintel of wet sand with froth," "the staggering ships," the boat that "climbs—hesitates—drops—climbs—hesitates—crawls back," the cliff temple, "white against white," "the serpent-spotted shell" of the swan's egg,

> the broken hulk of a ship
> hung with shreds of rope,
> pallid under the cracked pitch.

We have the "stiff ivory and white fire" of cyclamen flowers,

---

Review of *Collected Poems of H. D.* (Boni and Liveright).

a petal
with light equal
on leaf and under-leaf,

the illusory behavior of the marine creature,

this sea-gliding creature,
this strange creature like a weed,

the unanticipated, unforgettable mutations of aquatic color,

where rollers shot with blue
cut under deeper blue,

and

as the tide crept, the land
burned with a lizard-blue
where the dark sea met the sand.

As the verisimilitude of this outer world remains with one, no more is the author's emotional intensity to be evaded—in which "flesh shudders," and the mind waits "as a wave-line may wait to fall"—that intensity in which pleasure is painful and pain is painful, in which emotion can, like beauty, "crowd madness upon madness."

Since form and content corroborate each other, it is not surprising to find that the technique of these poems should, like the substance, present a fastidious prodigality—an apparent starkness which is opulence. One resists, mistakenly perhaps, what seems a too consistently insisted-upon avoidance of the small glib particle, the climax in certain instances submerged in a lesser climax, a sometimes distracting long digression. Yet, in the never monotonous, ever recurring device of the alternate repeated word—"torture me not with this or that or this"—in a careful mosaic of rhymes such as we have in "Lais":

Lais is now no lover of the glass,
seeing no more the face as once it was,
wishing to see that face and finding this;

we have the verbal continuity, the controlled ardor, the balanced speech of poetry. The sensitive advancing rhetoric of "Sitalkas," of "Pygmalion," of

"Sea Gods," suggests by its momentum, water inundating cove after cove of an irregular coast:

> you will curl between sand-hills—
> you will thunder along the cliff—
> break—retreat—get fresh strength—
> gather and pour weight upon the beach.

There is present the sense of honey and salt, an ever implied query:

> . . . which is more sweet,
> the sweetness
> or the bitterness?

the suggestion of paean, plaint, and madrigal that we associate with Swinburne, as in "We Two":

> have we two met within
> this maze of daedal paths
> in-wound mid grievous stone,
> where once I stood alone?

Yet on each page of original verse or of translation, a personal spirit manifests itself. In the making of classic personages or situations, symbols of present ones; in the concept of color and form, as in the rhetoric, we find, intensive, unmixed, and unimpeded, the white fire of the poet—of one who, repudiating miscellany, is immemorially garlanded, not with orange flowers nor cyclamen, but as H. D. has said of Sappho, with "the frail silver leaf of the bright scentless and immortal olive."

The Dial, 79 (August 1925), 170–72.

"LITERATURE THE NOBLEST OF THE ARTS"

O F these essays and papers by George Saintsbury, two have not before been printed. In all, there is "the old gay pugnacity" of one not thus far "disabled";

Review of *The Collected Essays and Papers of George Saintsbury, 1875–1920* (Dent and Company).

and an impenitent Toryism so opposed in every nerve to "the washy semi-Socialism, half sentimental, half servile, which is the governing spirit of all but a few politicians today," that it would seem in its own right to exemplify "that single-hearted and single-minded insanity of genius which carries a movement completely to its goal."

We feel it is the novelist speaking, as well as the critic, in the biographical summaries and paraphrases of plot; in the statement that Xenophon's *Cyropaedia* "is a philosophical romance for which its author has chosen to borrow a historic name or two"; and that one critic at least has an acute understanding of "the very important division of human sentiment, which is called for shortness, love." What relish for life there is in this elaborating of the Ettrick Shepherd's statement that "A' contributors are in a manner fierce." "The contributor who is not allowed to contribute," says Mr. Saintsbury, "is fierce, as a matter of course; but not less fierce is the contributor who thinks himself too much edited, and the contributor who imperatively insists that his article on Chinese metaphysics shall go in at once, and the contributor who, being an excellent hand at the currency, wants to be allowed to write on dancing; and, in short, as the Shepherd says, all contributors."

It is Mr. Saintsbury's conviction that "the greatest part, if not the whole of the pleasure-giving appeal of poetry, lies in its sound rather than in its sense"—that "no 'chain of extremely valuable thoughts' is poetry in itself." Objections suggest themselves, and one can understand the comment on Matthew Arnold: "I cannot quite make out why the critic did not say to the poet, 'It will never do to publish verse like this and this and this and this,' or why the poet did not say to the critic, 'Then we will make it worth publishing' and proceed to do so."

Despite trifling divergence from impartiality in the appeal to "any fit reader," to "any competent judge," to "any tolerably intelligent critic," one cannot fail to be exhilarated in these pages by its ever-present equity, as in the statement, "It will be only in a way for [a man's] greater glory if you find out where and wherefore he is sometimes wrong." Essentially "a thoughtful person" in the desire to give facts "without violating the sanctity of private life," Mr. Saintsbury admits that he "may have 'most politely, most politely' made some authors uncomfortable," but reminds one that, to reviewers, "Stiletto and pole-axe, sandbag and scavenger-shovel, are barred"—that one "can administer sequins as well as lashes, and send a man to ride round the town in royal apparel as well as dispatch him to the gallows."

The work vibrates with contempt for "twentieth-hand learning"—is alive with a voracity that has "grappled with whole libraries." "I have seen disdainful remarks," says Mr. Saintsbury, "on those critics who, however warily, admire a considerable number of authors, as though they were coarse and omnivorous persons. . . . A man need not be a Don Juan of letters to have a list of almost *mille e tre* loves in that department." The impassioned temper of these essays is in itself a pleasure, as when we have Macaulay "not only 'cocksure' but cock-a-hoop," and "the average mid-century Liberal" regarding Carlyle as "a man whose dearest delight it was to gore and toss and trample the sweetest and most sacred principles of the Manchester School." Mr. Saintsbury recalls to us "the massive common sense and nervous diction" of Dryden, whom he denominates "a poetical schoolman"; "the extraordinary command of meter which led Swinburne to plan sea-serpents in verse in order to show how easily and gracefully he can make them coil and uncoil their enormous length"; and says of Mr. Scarborough's family, in connection with Trollope's "economy and yet opulence of material," "If you have any sense of the particular art you can't help feeling the skill with which the artist wheels you along till he feels inclined to turn you out of his barrow and then deposits you at his if not your destination."

One does not correct the speech of those who make our speech correct, but Mr. Saintsbury's "Heaven knows" seems a needless superlative on completeness. "With the imperiousness natural to all art," however, "style absolutely refuses to avail itself of, or to be found in, company with anything that is ready made," and as might be expected in the work of one who has written a *History of English Prosody*, we have here a style in which there is often "a perfection of expression which transmutes the subject"; security which can say, "There is no wing in Crabbe, there is no transport." These essays have wing, a grace that recalls the Bible, Cicero, the seventeenth century, and "the engaging idiom of the Gaul."

Referring to Carlyle's life of Sterling, Mr. Saintsbury says, "I have seldom been able to begin it again or even to consult it for a casual reference, without following it right through." So with any piece of writing by George Saintsbury, one must follow it through, grateful forever to the essays on Lockhart, "Some Great Biographies," to those on the grand style, on Macaulay, "Bolshevism in Its Cradle," and "The Life and Opinions of William Godwin."

The Dial, 79 (October 1925), 345–47; *Predilections*.

"AN ILLUSTRIOUS DOCTOR ADMIRABLE FOR EVERYTHING"

THOSE who find modern autobiographic fiction disenchanting and unreal, may acclaim perfection in Henry Adams Bellows' recent translation of Abélard's autobiographic letter, *The Story of My Misfortunes*. Not everyone, however, has agreed with John of Salisbury that Abélard was "an illustrious doctor admirable for everything." In his *Historical Sketches*, Cardinal Newman observes: "Supposing Abélard to be the first master of scholastic philosophy, as many seem to hold, we shall have still no difficulty in condemning the author, while we honor the work." "Abélard was not a great character," says Henry Osborn Taylor, "apart from his intellect. He was vain and inconsiderate, a man who delighted in confounding and supplanting his teachers, and in being a thorn in the flesh of all opponents." Ralph Adams Cram, furthermore, in introducing *The Story of My Misfortunes*, says with temerarious fluency, "We know that during his early years in Paris Abélard was a bold and daring champion in the lists of dialectics; brilliant, persuasive, masculine to a degree; yet this self-portrait is of a man timid, suspicious, frightened of realities," and Dr. Maurice De Wulf speaks of him as "challenging all and sundry to philosophical controversies in which he always boasted of victory in advance." In the statement, "I pitched the camp of my school outside the city," it is obvious that the wisdom suggested is "gladiatorial wisdom," nor does one doubt the appropriateness of the assertion that Abélard was, when confronted by the tribunal who accused him of heretical belief in three separate gods, as "a bound wild rhinoceros." But why not? Under such circumstances, surely it is inevitable that one's "natural promptness" should assert itself, rather than the gentleman's talent of "not offending." In an age of "savants' cockfights," when men "preferred new and hazardous doctrines to those that were truer, but appeared superannuated," and "scorned what seemed too clear"; when it was said by a disgusted contemporary that the subtleties of dialectics were "like a fine and minute dust blinding the eyes of those who stir it up," Abélard's clear vigor separates itself from the manner of the times, and nicely florescent writers might well refresh their faculties in an examination of his pliant, severely careful methods.

We have in the *Historia Calamitatum*, throughout, the naturalness of the

Review of *Historia Calamitatum: An Autobiography*, by Peter Abélard. Translated by Henry Adams Bellows. With introduction by Ralph Adams Cram (Thomas A. Boyd).

literary genius with a native orderliness and an enticing gift of subordination and emphasis, which in combination would seem to constitute the essence of good story-telling; the instinct for method which is the animating principle of suspense, being especially conspicuous in such statements as the following:

> First I was punished for my sensuality, and then for my pride. . . . now it is my desire that you should know the stories of these two happenings . . . the very facts . . . and the order in which they came about.

Although Abélard is said to have been "greatly in love with his own discernment," and innate humility is not to be observed in the statement, "It was my wont to win success, not by routine but by ability," the manner of the *Historia* is striking in its utter simplicity with a kind of laconic despair—whether combined with arrogance or pruned of it. Of the sentimental preoccupation which insulated him from philosophical research, he wearily remarks:

> It became loathsome to me to go to the school or to linger there. . . . I had become nothing more than a reciter of my former discoveries,

and although he had said of William of Champeaux,

> the more his envy pursued me, the greater was the authority it conferred upon me. Even so held the poet, "Jealousy aims at the peaks,"

he repudiates his own hauteur, observing:

> But prosperity puffs up the foolish. . . . Thus, I, who by this time had come to regard myself as the only philosopher remaining in the whole world, . . . I departed alike from the practice of the philosophers and the spirit of the divines,

and says of his failure to inculcate sobriety in the monks of St. Gildas:

> I considered how of old I had been of some service to the clerics whom I had now abandoned for the sake of these monks, so that I was no longer able to be of use to either; how incapable I had proved myself in everything I had undertaken or attempted, so that above all others I deserved the reproach, "This man began to build, and was not able to finish."

Abélard was not perhaps, "the first philosopher of his time," in the body of thought which he bequeathed to us, but his methods "emancipated reason by giving it confidence in its own forces," and although a boast of priority is self-adulatory no doubt, one values the intelligence of the critic who remarks in quoting what Abélard so unselfprotectively said of himself, "If he was wrong to say it, perhaps he was right in thinking it."

The arresting combination of explicitness with aloofness emphasizes in the *Historia Calamitatum,* the contrast in literary skill between the mawkish accounts by untalented writers, of the author's relationship with Héloïse, and his own magisterial candor. *The Story of My Misfortunes,* far from being as one might infer from allusions to it, *The Story of My Misfortune*—the mere record of a sentimental tragedy—is rather, a many-angled record of a life of multiform hardship.

For the "peevishness" to which Mr. Cram refers in the introduction to this letter, one looks in vain. We do perceive a desperate melancholy in the statement:

> The only way of escape seemed for me to seek refuge with Christ among the enemies of Christ.

Abélard speaks of being "horrified," "stunned by fear," but does it not at all fearfully; it is suffering rather than fear that is emphasized when he says:

> I am driven hither and yon, a fugitive and a vagabond even as the accursed Cain. . . . "Without were fightings, within were fears,"

and

> amid the dreadful roar of the waves of the sea, where the land's end left me no further refuge in flight, I was like one who in terror of the sword that threatens him dashes headlong over a precipice, and to shun one death for a moment rushes to another.

In writing this letter as a specific for another's despair—of whose we cannot be sure—Abélard has bequeathed to us a masterstroke of sensibility and understanding. He has narrated simply, with many graces of exactness, the particulars of his experience and he has done it with incomparable éclat.

The Dial, 79 (November 1925), 425–28.

"NEW" POETRY SINCE 1912

IN America what is often referred to as modern poetry received marked impetus in 1912. Converted from the manner of *A Dome of Many-Coloured Glass* (1912) to the apparent newness of Imagisme (1913), Amy Lowell became "the recognized spokesman of the Imagist group." Inaugurally arresting, however—that is to say really inaugural—Ezra Pound invented the term Imagisme; and "A Few Dont's by an Imagist" presented by him in 1913 in the March issue of *Poetry, A Magazine of Verse,* advocated composing "in sequence of the musical phrase, not in sequence of a metronome; direct treatment of the thing, whether subjective or objective; the use of absolutely no word that does not contribute to the presentation"; and in 1914 with work of his own, appeared poems by Richard Aldington, F. S. Flint, H. D., Amy Lowell, Skipwith Cannell, William Carlos Williams, James Joyce, John Cournos, F. M. "Hueffer," and Alan Upward.

Mr. Braithwaite felt in Imagisme, "an intensifying quality of mood," Richard Aldington felt it "an accurate mystery," and in answer to the objection that Imagist poetry was "petty poetry, minutely small and intended to be so," Miss May Sinclair observed that the critic "is not justified in counting lines." Of image-making power as "common to all poets," she remarked, "When Dante saw the souls of the damned falling like leaves down the banks of Acheron, it is an image, it is also imagery. It makes no difference whether he says *are* leaves or only *like* leaves. The flying leaves are the perfect image of the damned souls. But when Sir John Suckling says his lady's feet peep in and out like mice he is only using imagery." H. D.'s "Pines," *i. e.,* "Oread," which appeared first in Wyndham Lewis' *Blast* (1914), Richard Aldington's "The Poplar," and Ezra Pound's "The Garret" seem to one incontrovertibly illustrative of the Imagist doctrine.

In 1915 and 1916, under the direction of Richard Aldington, "The Poets' Translation Series" was published by The Egoist Press, which was under the direction of Miss Harriet Shaw Weaver, and the starkness and purity of these translations is allied in one's mind with Imagism and Vorticism—Ezra Pound and certain of his Imagists being identical with certain of Wyndham Lewis' Vorticists.

The "new" poetry seemed to justify itself as a more robust form of Japanese poetry—that is perhaps to say, of Chinese poetry—although a specific and more lasting interest in Chinese poetry came later. In 1913, coincident with the translating into English of "Gitanjali," Rabindranath Tagore visited the United States, was termed by our press, "The creator of a new age in literature," and W. B. Yeats wrote in "The Athenaeum," "A whole people, a whole civilization, immeasurably strange to us, seems to have been taken up into this imagination; and yet we are not moved because of its strangeness, but because we have met our own image; as though we had walked in Rossetti's willow wood, or heard, perhaps for the first time in literature, our voice as in a dream." Felt by public and poets alike to be important, *North of Boston* by Robert Frost, appeared in 1914, *A Boy's Will* having been published the previous year.

The Egoist, Poetry of Chicago, and *The Little Review* of Chicago, were hospitable to "new" poetry, as was Alfred Kreymborg's *Others*. With a subsequently diverse and justifiable use of no rhyme, part rhyme, all rhyme, Alfred Kreymborg had to some, in his early practice of vers libre and his encouragement of the "vers libertine" as Louis Untermeyer denominates the writer of free verse—the aspect of a Cambodian devil-dancer. One recalls the emphatic work of William Carlos Williams whose book, *The Tempers* had appeared in 1913; a sliced and cylindrical, complicated yet simple use of words by Mina Loy; an enigmatically axiomatic "Progression of the Verb 'To Be' " by Walter Arensberg, and a poem by him entitled "Ing" which corroborated the precisely perplexing verbal exactness of Gertrude Stein's "Tender Buttons"—a book which had already appeared.

Ing

Ing? Is it possible to mean ing?
Suppose
 for the termination in *g*
  a disoriented
  series
 of the simple fractures
  in sleep.
  Soporific
has accordingly a value for soap
  so present to
  sew pieces.
  And *p* says: Peace is.
And suppose the *i*
  to be big in ing
  as Beginning.
   Then Ing is to ing
as aloud
 accompanied by times
and the meaning is a possibility
  of ralsis.

In Ezra Pound one recognized that precise explicit "positiveness"—felt in him by Wallace Stevens—and he was the "new" poetry's perhaps best apologist as he reiterated in articles contributed to Miss Monroe's magazine, his feeling that "there should be in America the *gloire de cénacle.*' " "He is knowledge's lover," as Glenway Wescott has said, "speaking of it and to it an intimate idiom which is sometimes gibberish," and if his equivalents for that which is "dead" or foreign seems to some not always perspicuous, his contagiously enjoyable enjoyment of and his unpedantic rendering of "dead" language have done as much as have his own poems, one feels—to create an atmosphere in which poetry is likely to be written. Adelaide Crapsey's apartness and delicately differentiated footfalls, her pallor and color, were impressive. Wallace Stevens' sensory and technical virtuosity was perhaps the "new" poetry's greatest ornament and the almost imperceptibly modern, silver-chiming resonance of "Peter Quince at the Clavier" did much to ameliorate popular displeasure. One recalls in "Primordia" an insisted upon starkness:

> The blunt ice flows down the Mississippi,
> At night

and a complexity of apprehension:

> Compilation of the effects
> Of magenta blooming in the Judas-tree
> And of purple blooming in the eucalyptus.

As Kenneth Jewett remarked (in *The Transatlantic Review*, April, 1924) "his perfected, two-dimensional still lifes stand like rests or held chords in the progression of his complete harmony." T. S. Eliot's scrutiny of words and of behavior was apparent in his "Portrait of a Lady." Mr. Eliot "has not confined himself to genre nor to society portraiture," says Ezra Pound. "His

> lonely men in shirt sleeves leaning out of windows

are as real as his ladies who

> come and go
> Talking of Michelangelo.

Writers of free verse were, for the most part, regarded as having been influenced by Laforgue, Rimbaud, and other French poets. Alfred Kreymborg, Maxwell Bodenheim, Carl Sandburg, Marsden Hartley, Muna Lee, Wallace Gould, Man Ray, Adolf Wolff, Helen Hoyt, Orrick Johns, Conrad Aiken, Amy Lowell, Evelyn Scott, Lola Ridge, Marjorie Allen Seiffert, Donald Evans, Emanuel Carnevali, Arthur Davison Ficke, and Witter Bynner, contributed to making respectable as poetry, verse which was not rhymed. In 1916, certain of these, under the names of Emanuel Morgan, Anne Knish, Elijah Hay, purporting to be a new school termed themselves Spectrists. Vachel Lindsay's declamatory and in some respects unaesthetic pictorialism (1915–16), pleased, displeased, and pleased the public—his originality in "trading rhymes for bread" having earlier made a good impression. Resisted and advertised, Edgar Lee Masters' *Spoon River Anthology* (1915) seemed a technical pronunciamento.

One associates with 1921 rather than with 1913, 1915, 1916, or 1917, the morosely imaginative and graphic work of D. H. Lawrence and recalls his introversive but in mood none the less emancipated poem, "Snake":

> He drank enough
> And lifted his head, dreamily as one who has drunken,
> And flickered his tongue like a forked night on the air,
>   so black,
> Seeming to lick his lips,
> And looked around like a god, unseeing into the air.

In 1920 and 1921, readers of new poetry noted the work of E. E. Cummings—its sleights of motion and emotion. A great deal has been made of the small "i" as used by Mr. Cummings and of certain subsidiary characteristically intentional typographic revivals and innovations on his part. While "extreme," he is, however, "only superficially modern," as has been pointed out by Dr. W. C. Blum, and truly major aspects of his work are "feeling for American speech," "rapid unfailing lyrical invention," ability to convey the sense of speed, "of change of position," "the sensations of effective effort."

Various child poets received, in 1920, the respectful attention of the public. American Indian poetry has also, at intervals, been introduced to us, as has the Negro spiritual. Leon Srabian Herald, though as yet without full command of technique, Glenway Wescott, and Yvor Winters—the one somewhat delicately Persian, the other somewhat constricted—R. Ellsworth Larsson, Harold Monro, Peter Quennell, Edith Sitwell, Osbert and Sacheverell Sitwell, have produced work which is, if not purely modern, properly within the new movement. Catholic in using either rhyme or no rhyme, certain others, not modern, yet by no means old-fashioned, manifest vigor which predominates it would seem, over newness. In Joseph Auslander, for example, we find a centaur-like and entrenched individuality of this non-conforming variety.

One recognizes in Ralph Cheever Dunning's depth and sobriety of treatment, a phase of contemporary watchfulness against ineptness. Although not especially recent, Mr. Dunning evinces, as Ezra Pound has observed, "clarity of impact," "surety," "exact termination of expression," "originality" in being superior to current fashions in verse.

Categorically "formal," as are George Dillon and Archibald MacLeish, Scofield Thayer is a new Victorian—reflective, bi-visioned, and rather willfully unconventional. We have a mixture, apparently, of reading and of asserted detachment from reading, emotion being expressed through literal use of detail:

> I agitate the gracile crescent
> Which calls itself a fern:

and through what seems a specific reviving of incident. Tension affords strength, as is felt in certain verbally opposed natural junctures of the unexpected—"a gentle keenness," "gradual flames," "concision of a flame gone stone"—the mechanics being that of resistance.

It is perhaps beside the point to examine novel aspects of successive phases of poetic expression, inherited poetry having been at one time new, and new poetry even in its eccentricities seeming to have its counterpart in the poetry of the past—in Hebrew poetry, Greek poetry, Chinese poetry. That which is weak is soon gone; that which has value does, by some strange perpetuity, live as part of the serious continuation of literature.

In William Stanley Braithwaite, ed. *Anthology of Magazine Verse for 1926*. Boston: B. J. Brimmer, 1926, pp. 172–79.

PEOPLE STARE CAREFULLY

ONE has in Mr. Cummings' work, a sense of the best dancing and of the best horticulture. From his *Forty-One Poems* and lest one seem to stutter,

---

Review of *XLI Poems*, by E. E. Cummings (The Dial Press), and *&* by E. E. Cummings (privately printed).

seventy-nine, emerge the seasons, childhood, humanity selectly and unse-
lectly congregated, war, death, *l'amour* with a touch of love, music, painting,
books, and a fine note of scorn. In finding Picasso a sculptor among "un-
interesting landscapes made interesting by earTHQuake," Mr. Cummings is
fanciful, yet faithful to that verisimilitude of eye and of rhetoric which is so
important in poetry.

Settling like a man-of-war bird or the retarded, sonambulistic athlete of
the speedograph, he shapes the progress of poems as if it were substance;
he has "a trick of syncopation Europe has," determining the pauses slowly,
with glides and tight-rope acrobatics, ensuring the ictus by a space instead
of a period, or a semi-colon in the middle of a word, seeming to have placed
adjectives systematically one word in advance of the words they modify, or
one word behind, with most pleasing exactness.

In being printed phonetically, although decorously spelled, these poems
constitute a kind of verbal topiary-work; not, however, in the manner of the
somewhat too literal typographic wine-glasses, columns, keys, and roses
approved by Elizabethan poets and their predecessors. We have, not a replica
of the title, but a more potent thing, a replica of the rhythm—a kind of
second tempo, uninterfering like a shadow, in the manner of the author's
beautiful if somewhat self-centered, gigantic filiform ampersand of symbolical
"and by itself plus itself with itself." The physique of the poems recalls the
corkscrew twists, the infinitude of dots, the sumptuous perpendicular appearance of Kufic script; and the principle of the embedded rhyme has
produced in "Post Impression XI" and "Portrait III" of *And*, in the big A,
the big N, and the big D, which mark respectively each third of the book,
some sublimely Mohammedan effects. "TUMTITUMTIDDLE THE BLACK
CAT WITH THE YELLOW EYES AND THE VIOLIN," advances metro-
nomically through the rest of the poem and

ta
ppin
g
toe

hip
popot
amus Back

gen
teel-ly
lugu-
bri ous

descends the page "as fathandsbangrag."

There is in these poems, a touch of love perceived in allusions to unconscious things—horses' ears and mice's meals. Also, there is a more egotistic and less kind emotion which has the look of being in its author's eyes, his most certain self. One wishes that it weren't. Love is terrible—even in the East where the Prince who wished to find a perfectly beautiful woman commissioned the Arabs rather than the nobility to find the girl, convinced that "the quickest and best judges of a man or a woman are the very same persons who are the best judges of a horse or a cow." But when love is presented under the banner of Watteau, as a philtre, not to say the menu, it is not terrible; it is merely circumstantial, or at most phenomenal. An admirer of the dead languages—"an Oxford scholar in a scarlet gown" let us say, who reads no Latin but Petronius—lacks certitude. That the academy-tinctured, modern books of a western poet, should preserve no more than the devouring, in the sense that it is the destroying passion of master for slave, robs testimony, even poet's testimony, of its terror.

If there is not much love in these pages, however, there is glamour—verbal as figurative:

> . . . horses of gold
> delicately crouching beneath silver
> youths   the leaneyed
>
> Caesars borne neatly through enormous
> twilight. . .
>
> . . . while the infinite processions
> move like moths and like boys and
> like incense and like sunlight

There is Spring like a

> Hand in a window
> (carefully to
> and fro moving New and
> Old things,while
> people stare carefully
> moving a perhaps
> fraction of flower here placing
> an inch of air there)and
>
> without breaking anything.

The Woolworth building becomes "the firm tumult of exquisitely insecure sharp algebraic music." "SNO" falls:

>tiny,angels sharpen:themselves
>
>(on
>   air)
>don't speak

There is verbal excitement in the renaissance of certain important words— of marvelous, of perfect, of beautiful, of wonderful:

>And if, somebody hears
>what i say—let him be pitiful:
>because i've traveled all alone
>through the forest of wonderful,
>and that my feet have surely known
>the furious ways and the peaceful,
>
>and because she is beautiful

If we have not Karnak and the pyramids, we have in these pages, a kind of engineering which includes within it, the jewelry of Egypt and the panting sense of those who wore it. We have the spryness of Vienna—the spun glass miniature object, porcupine or angel-fish—and we have an object from Crete.

There is in the art museum at Eighty-Second Street and Fifth Avenue, a late Minoan ivory leaper. Suspended by a thread, the man swims down with the classic aspect of the frog. As a frog startled, palpitating, and inconsequential, would seem in the ivory man to have become classic, so Mr. Cummings has in these poems, created from inconvenient emotion, what one is sure is poetry. There is here, the Artificiall Changling of John Bulwer's *Anthropometamorphosis*—"the mad and cruell Gallantry, foolish Bravery, ridiculous Beauty, filthy Finnesse. . . of most Nations."

The Dial, 80 (January 1926), 49–52.

THE SPARE AMERICAN EMOTION

EXTRAORDINARY interpretations of American life recur to one—*The Finer Grain, In the American Grain, The Making of an American, The Domestic Manners of the Americans.* We have, and in most cases it amounts to not having them, novels about discontented youth, unadvantaged middle age, American materialism; in *The Making of Americans,* however, we have "not just an ordinary kind of novel with a plot and conversations to amuse you, but a record of a decent family progress respectably lived by us and our fathers and our mothers, and our grand-fathers, and grand-mothers." One is not able to refrain from saying, moreover, that its chiseled typography and an enticing simplicity of construction are not those of ordinary book-making.

By this epic of ourselves, we are reminded of certain early German engravings in which Adam, Eve, Cain, and Abel stand with every known animal wild and domestic, under a large tree, by a river. *The Making of Americans* is a kind of living genealogy which is in its branching, unified and vivid.

We have here a truly psychological exposition of American living—an account of that happiness and of that unhappiness which is to those experiencing it, as fortuitous as it is to those who have an understanding of heredity and of environment natural and inevitable. Romantic, curious, and engrossing is this story of "the old people in a new world, the new people made out of the old." There are two kinds of men and women Miss Stein tells us, the attacking kind and the resisting kind, each of which is often modified by many complex influences. Mr. Dehning who was of the resisting kind, "never concerned himself very much with the management of the family's way of living and the social life of his wife and children. These things were all always arranged by Mrs. Dehning." Yet "they could each one make the other one do what they wanted the other one to be doing"—this "really very nice very rich good kind quite completely successful a little troubled american man and woman." The insufficiency of Alfred Hersland who married Julia Dehning, is shown to be largely a result of his mother's anonymity, of incompetent pedagogy, of spoiling, and of his father's impatient unconsidering wilfulness. The Dehnings were happy; the Herslands were under the impression that they too, were happy. As Miss Stein says:

Review of *The Making of Americans Being the History of a Family's Progress,* by Gertrude Stein (Three Mountains Press).

And all around the whole fence that shut these joys in was a hedge of roses, not wild, they had been planted, but now they were very sweet and small and abundant and all the people from that part of Gossols came to pick the leaves to make sweet scented jars and pillows, and always all the Herslands were indignant and they would let loose the dogs to bark and scare them but still roses grew and always all the people came and took them. And altogether the Herslands always loved it there in their old home in Gossols.

In persons either of the resisting or of the attacking kind, contradictions between "the bottom nature and the other natures" result in hybrids; as in Napoleon—in Herbert Spencer—in various other kinds of nature. Disillusionment, sensitiveness, cowardice, courage, jealousy, stubbornness, curiosity, suspicion, hopefulness, anger, subtlety, pride, egotism, vanity, ambition—each phase of emotion as of behavior, is to Miss Stein full of meaning. "Someone gives to another one a stubborn feeling," she says, "when that one could be convincing that other one if that other one would then continue listening," and "it is very difficult in quarreling to be certain in either one what the other one is remembering." Of the assorting of phenomena in "an ordered system" she says, "Always I am learning, always it is interesting, often it is exciting."

There is great firmness in the method of this book. Phillip Redfern we are told, "was a man always on guard, with every one always able to pierce him." The living rooms of Julia Dehning's house "were a prevailing red, that certain shade of red like that certain shade of green, dull, without hope, the shade that so completely bodies forth the ethically aesthetic aspiration of the spare american emotion." Her mother's house was, on the other hand, of a different period. "A nervous restlessness of luxury was through it all. . . . a parlor full of ornate marbles placed on yellow onyx stands, chairs gold and white of various size and shape, a delicate blue silk brocaded covering on the walls and a ceiling painted pink with angels and cupids all about, a dining-room all dark and gold, a living room all rich and gold and red with built-in couches. . . . Marbles and bronzes and crystal chandeliers and gas logs finished out each room."

We "hasten slowly forward" by a curious backward kind of progress. "Sometimes I like it," Miss Stein says, "that different ways of emphasizing can make very different meanings in a phrase or sentence I have made and am rereading." To recall her summary of washing is to agree with her:

It's a great question this question of washing. One never can find any one who can be satisfied with anybody else's washing. I knew a man once who never as far as any one could see ever did any washing, and yet he described another with contempt, why he is a dirty hog sir, he never does any washing. The French tell me it's the Italians who never do any washing, the French and the Italians both find the Spanish a little short in their washing, the English find all the world lax in this business of washing, and the East finds all the West a pig, which never is clean with just the little cold water washing. And so it goes.

Repeating has value then as "a way to wisdom." "Some children have it in them." "Always more and more it has completed history in it" and "irritation passes over into patient completed understanding."

Certain aspects of life are here emphasized—the gulf between youth and age, and the bond between these two; the fact of sentimental as of hereditary family indivisibility—such that when Julia Dehning was married, every one of the Dehnings had "feeling of married living in them."

The power of sex which is palpable throughout this novel, is handsomely implied in what is said of certain uncles and cousins in the Dehning family,

generous decent considerate fellows, frank and honest in their friendships, and simple in the fashion of the elder Dehning. With this kindred Julia had always lived as with the members of one family. These men did not supply for her the training and experience that helps to clear the way for an impetuous woman through a world of passions, they only made a sane and moral back-ground on which she in her later life could learn to lean.

The ineradicable morality of America is varyingly exposited, as in the statement that to Julia Dehning, "all men that could be counted as men by her and could be thought of as belonging ever to her, they must be, all, good strong gentle creatures, honest and honorable and honoring." Contrary to "the french habit in thinking," "the american mind accustomed to waste happiness and be reckless of joy finds morality more important than ecstacy and the lonely extra of more value than the happy two."

There is ever present in this history, a sense of the dignity of the middle class, "the one thing always human, vital, and worthy." Of a co-educational college of the west, Miss Stein says:

Mostly no one there was conscious of a grand-father unless as remembering one as an old man living in the house with them or as living in another place and being written to sometimes by them and then having died and that was the end of grand-fathers to them. No one among them was held responsible for the father they had unless by some particular notoriety that had come to the father of some one. It was then a democratic western institution, this college where Redfern went to have his college education.

As Bunyan's Christian is English yet universal, this sober, tender-hearted, very searching history of a family's progress, comprehends in its picture of life which is distinctively American, a psychology which is universal.

The Dial, 80 (February 1926), 153–56.

MEMORY'S IMMORTAL GEAR

CERTAIN of his contemporaries found it upon their consciences to wonder whether Sir Thomas Browne were or were not an atheist; and it is perhaps to be expected that a man's admirers today, in superfluously extenuating non-existent demerits, should sometimes say things which must astonish him. If one must go to an extreme it should be, one feels, in avowing the obverse of the statement that Mr. Hardy is "a pessimist" and that "his verse throughout has no touch of lyric smoothness." "Discouragement," "Premonitions," "Questionings," are very essential parts of answers and there is uncommonly an effect of spiritual security in the statement that "When Dead,"

> This fleeting life-brief blight
>   Will have gone past
> When I resume my old and right
>   Place in the Vast.
>
> And when you come to me
>   To show you true,
> Doubt not I shall infallibly
>   Be waiting you.

Themes calculated to "persuade" one, are usually aesthetically disaffecting. In this collection of reveries, ballads, "songs," and love-songs, however, certain poems which have the force of argument are indubitably poems. "The

---

Review of *Human Shows, Far Phantasies, Songs, and Trifles*, by Thomas Hardy (The Macmillan Company).

Sheep Fair," "Bags of Meat," "Horses Aboard," the poem about the itinerant vendors with "No Buyers," and "The Flower's Tragedy." One stands condemned by the "reproachful stare" of

> . . . the timid, quivering steer,
> Starting a couple of feet
> At the prod of the drover's stick,
> And trotting light and quick,

and yet more mutely histrionic is the cat, in "Snow in the Suburbs":

> Every branch big with it,
>   Bent every twig with it;
> Every fork like a white web-foot;
> Every street and pavement mute;
> Some flakes have lost their way, and grope back upward, when
> Meeting those meandering down they turn and descend again.
>   . . . .
> The steps are a blanched slope,
>   Up which, with feeble hope,
> A black cat comes, wide-eyed and thin;
>   And we take him in.

In addition to this ever operative solicitude of Mr. Hardy's, there are in his work certain unmistakably distinctive traits of eye, an awareness of architecture, a sense of the hour, an intense particularity and originality in the characterizing of nature. His elms are "by aged" rather than by playful "squirrels' footsteps worn." Eels "even cross, 'tis said, the turnpike-road"; when "among the evergreens around," rooks are awed by "sundry thrills about their quills," it is autumn, not spring. And the moon, much as it belongs to everyone, probably pertains especially to the poet, and to the kind of poet who can say:

> The moon's glassed glory heaved as we lay swinging
> Upon the undulations. Shoreward, slow,

who remembers how "At Rushy-Pond" the wind

> . . . stretched it to oval form;
> Then corkscrewed it like a wriggling worm.

The sense of masonry with shadows on it, of Gothic ogives and mullions, enriches what would without it, perhaps, still be poetry, but how insistent are these imagined interiors and exteriors. How desperate are these glimpses of recumbent figures, "chiseled in frigid stone; In doublets are some; some mailed, as whilom ahorse they leapt"; and most indelible perhaps is "A Cathedral Facade at Midnight":

> The lunar look skimmed scantly toe, breast, arm
> Then edged on slowly, slightly,
> To shoulder, hand, face; till each austere form
> Was blanched its whole length brightly.

The artist gravitates instinctively toward that subject-matter over which he has command, as we see in this volume, by the many allusions to songs, local superstitions, and old documents. Always in Mr. Hardy, one perceives a justly dramatic interest in the significance of what seems insignificant, in those ironies which comprehend simultaneously the shine of the satin dress and the shine of a corpse; the once living man interred in the once living wood; the unease of the man who cures an emotion which when cured he misses; the sexton's reply to "The Fading Rose," in speech which flowers can understand:

> "She must get to you underground
> If anyway at all be found,
> For, clad in her beauty, marble's kin,
> 'Tis there I have laid her and trod her in."

One must here accept as poetic, certain apparently unpermissible plots. There is the dying man, who, not suspecting disloyalty, wishes before dying to kiss a wife who is in prison upon the charge of having poisoned him. A neighbor consents to impersonate the absent wife, and the doubly deceived man dies happy. There are the lovers alone at the inn, who, married each to another, must for the sake of propriety, pretend in parting to be man and wife. How strangely Mr. Hardy's is the poem about the funeral of the young woman with unmarried men as pallbearers—and the footnote: "In many villages it was customary after the funeral of an unmarried young woman to ring a peal as for her wedding while the grave was being filled in, as if Death were not allowed to balk her of her bridal honors."

With death ever in attendance and love momentarily outwitting it, these poems are ballads—*trouvère*-like dirges of the lover fainting and undone, records of a moment with attached to it, "A Shiver." Romance is said to be inseparable from that which is sinister, and perhaps it is. In Mr. Hardy's work it is usually attended by forebodings and is associated with "love's fresh found sensation." How very aesthetic, furthermore, in comparison with those of certain other writers, Mr. Hardy's lovers are. His inferences are, while not at variance with them, entirely different from those experienced modern findings which allege that if a man would not be "Dick who takes me to the theatre or Jack who sends me flowers, he must vary his suggestions since habits enable one to get more into one's life but seldom allow one to get so much out." Mr. Hardy can feel as well as look at cosmic malady. "That mortal moan begot of sentience" is not to him a matter of topical interest; he does it the honor to write of it not as yours but as his.

The lover, who vexed "by tones now smart, now suave," "would flee in ire, to return a slave," has the somewhat inconsequent lightness of Goldsmith's "Secluded from domestic strife, Jack Bookworm led a college life," and contrary to one's wish, one can be reminded of Poe by the lines:

> As I enter chilly Paul's
> With its chasmal classic walls.
> —Drifts of gray illumination
> From the lofty fenestration

but certainly "The Echo-Elf Answers," is an antidote to reckless rhyme, and an austere counterpart to the method of "The Raven":

> How much shall I love her?
> For life, or not long?
> "Not Long."

> Alas! When forget her?
> In years, or by June?
> "By June."

> And whom woo I after?
> No one or a throng?
> "A throng."

> Of these shall I wed one
> Long hence or quite soon?
> "Quite soon."

> And which will my bride be?
> The right one or the wrong?
> "The wrong."

> And my remedy—what kind?
> Wealth-wove, or earth-hewn?
> "Earth-hewn."

With an aesthetic vision as exacting and unvaryingly posited as his real one, Mr. Hardy's technical idiom is as distinctive as his mental one. The graveyard "where bristled fennish fungi, fruiting naught," the creature "pinched and pent," or "looking all so down and done," commend an essential alliteration which is not easy. The unaccented terminal rhyme is not used by many so well as by Mr. Hardy and such words as "subtant," "circuiteer," and "tele-graph," are set by him in the context so deftly as to be scarcely evident. One cannot gainsay "bees leg-laden," or "the rain clams her apron till it clings." If words are to be innovated, let it be in this way. Concepts of "smoothness" differ, but the ear of this reader is not alive to any rhythmic heresy, in "specters rose like wakened winds that autumn summons up" or in "that winter did not leave last year for ever after all."

A seer more even than a craftsman, Mr. Hardy is concerned with the nature and responsibility of existence and with love as life's complicator. His work is "chasmal," never gruesome. He deprecates life's "dinning gear," but how immortal that gear is, to those who know his carriers' vans, unhappy honeymoons, missed trains, and twilit heaths; to say nothing of the woman who emerges in muslin vesture from a mansion's front—to whom he says:

> You stand so stock-still that your ear-ring shakes
> At each pulsation which the vein there makes.

The Dial, 80 (May 1926), 417–21.

LAND AND SEA AND SKY AND SUN

I N each of three contemporary poets, Miss Mabel Simpson, Leon Srabian Herald, and Melville Cane, the unimplicated mere reader seems to distin-guish a unanimity which is not conspicuously prevalent among contemporary

---

Review of *January Gardens*, by Melville Cane (Harcourt, Brace and Com-pany); *Poems*, by Mabel Simpson (Harold Vinal); *This Waking Hour*, by Leon Srabian Herald, with an introduction by Zona Gale (Thomas Seltzer).

poets—that is to say, reverence for mystery and for deity. There is also most diversely manifested by these three poets, a love of "land and sea and sky and sun."

Mr. Cane has, in his view of the external world, a distinctly formulated, approvedly decorative concept of color. Mauve, gray, blue, white, silver, black, he finds in what he sees, making best use perhaps, of black. In time of snow and fog, he buries "deep the black world underneath the white," says of fireflies, "Sparks fly, . . . Through the thick black foliage of my soul," and there are occasions upon which to him

> Indistinguishable lie
> Black sea, black sky.

The artist in that he will and can preserve the sense and aspect of what has meant much to him, Mr. Cane is able, alas, to dismay as to delight. One syllable too much, one impropriety of diction, and illusion is lost. The reader regrets "exquisitely," "flavorous," "to get the leaves used to it," "kitchenetted souls," "infant rainbows," and can scarcely accept as poetically appropriate, "cowed waves slinking at their feet." There is on the other hand, in the following epitome of "Northwinds in May," a moving truthfulness: "panic clutches the bushes"; as in the concept of the sandpiper: "It rides an instant on the shifting swell." And how fine:

> The rich moon with its broadly streaming flood
> Washes with light
> The earth whereon I stand.
> The icy ether fires my smoldering blood.

Miss Simpson is one of the least demanding and one of the most receptive of writers. Those who cannot read but as they run, who dispatch simplicity as insipidity and equipoise as inertness, will not perceive the dynamic intensity of her work. An apparent philosophy of resignation is distasteful to some, religious feeling partakes to some, of fatuousness, and studious technical symmetry seems to some to lack ingenuity. In her world of patient apartness, however, there is force of emotion such that it is possible for her to say that in one hour, "then swept the surge, then rose the sea." There is conviction without protest. Her reflections upon mortality, the body, the spirit, "the bright dead," are perhaps in a world of cleverness, arcane. But they are not insignificant; they mean a great deal. One finds in this book, most integrally and instinctively self-corroborating, a sense of the sky, of the shapes of trees, of the sound of the wind, of dark storms that darken

the landscape; of snows "that fill the fields with light again." Miss Simpson's
fastidious compelling of form appropriate to thought is apparent in the shapes
of her poems and in her frequent use of a first line as a title. One cannot
always feel that a climax is perfectly a climax, that each line is as hard and
spare as every other line; but what careful, technically self-sustained work
this is; how shapely and nocturnal are the lines upon "Sleep":

> Pale on the pallid
> Deep does float
> The shaped shadow
> Of her boat,
> Her white oars murmur note on note.

Although by no means a compendium of perfect integers, Mr. Herald's
This Waking Hour is an impressive book. There is in the thought, an innocence, a mere not knowing, which is not that callow *naïvete* of the ambitious
aspirant to early laurels. There is here something rapt; an atmosphere of
culture, the more certainly that no such thing is bespoken. The writer is
cognizant of attendant circumstances and sentiments, aesthetically insatiate,
yet importunate. Horror at ignorant living and ignorant thinking is here
acute, yet decorous and gentle. Although Mr. Herald reveres the university,
apostrophizing it as

> Fire, into whose flame I would hurl myself.
> Suns are molded in your flame,

he resents learned questioners, replying to them, "I am a question myself,
that comes not after the word or sentence, but before." One suspects that
the learned could be of use to him, but perhaps he too suspects it.

"People have been telling me the wrong thing always," he says, "With
their mouths they only talk and eat things coming out of the ground. I am
an animal like a star. I am a bird. . . ."

Although the rhythm of certain of these poems is satisfactory, that of others
is not, and Mr. Herald's diction is at once a source of weakness and of
strength. "I dart my needles on the wind, / At the earth my cones unwind"
seems to one poetry and the "green-green sandals" of "My Nephew Spring"
are appropriate. "A Babylon of tongues" is perhaps an inadvertence, but "I
will make trees of widest leaves" is not.

An eastern to us unselfprotective as it seems abandon, in opening one's
heart and in finding similitudes for one's open heart, seems sometimes to
impair characteristic poetry of the east. Unconscious and unthinking fear-

lessness of saying too much, can however inspire envy and in Mr. Herald's work, a tincture of this rhapsodic confidentially intimate self-exposition is present, merely serving, however, to emphasize his free, untrammeled condition. Observant and full of feeling, he writes of nature, of others, of himself, in a manner detached yet implicated, faithful to the usualness and the excellence of life. He has observed the bay where wilting rain-storms meet and a "Tree First in Bloom" of which he says,

> I lie beneath
> And watch your many, many milky ways,
> Crossing each other, circling
> And circling all around you.

In characterizing "The Four Winds," he says of one of them, "I seek a cool place to avoid her," and of another, "She persuades me to my very door / Which I slam in her face / And draw my window panes / And double them with heavy curtains." "At Love's Manger" is a group of poems, thoughtful and strange like its name. In *This Waking Hour*, indeed, "flocks of thoughts scatter into the pasture."

Mr. Cane's flowers, Miss Simpson's quiet, Mr. Herald's sententious simplicity are, if they are not products of peace, conducive to it. One is pleased when poets who live in America are sufficiently pleased with America to seem so; and the exciting charm of American vegetation, gardens, weather, and people, is indubitably felt in the work of these three poets.

The Dial, 81 (July 1926), 69–71.

NATIVES OF ROCK

IN this collection of twenty poems, we have such "polished facets and relics devotedly adorned," "symmetrical relations," and "evidence of intelligence" as Mr. Wescott likes to find in a poet's book. In "those days" as he calls 1922 and the years prior to it in which he wrote these poems, he "had taken here and there a devious circumlocution to avoid awkwardness of grammar," "had removed a connective, or forced a noun to modify a noun as if it were

---

Review of *Natives of Rock*, by Glenway Wescott, with decorations by Pamela Bianco (Francesco Bianco).

an adjective or as if English were German." He has "once or twice" come
upon a word or a phrase which he cannot understand and has omitted it or
has put in its place "an exact word for what it probably meant." In anxiety
about one's past poetic self, there is something perhaps dangerously leisured,
but such anxiety is natural and it is literary, and we should like to assure
the author that we find here, much besides "souvenirs" and "facets."

Although there are typographical errors as ingeniously undetectable as
the book is decorative, such errors recede. Strangely, yet perhaps not strangely,
in proportion as authors are disturbed by unaccountable defects in their
work, they are miraculously absolved of them.

The New Mexico country—a heightened, poetic equivalent of the literal—
is here. Verbal harmony and cadence are here, and a veritable Scheherazade's rainbow-garmented, many-ply tissue of color. "Peaches in Bloom"
are

> . . . Froth of
> cherries,
> red bees, and fingers
> spread in a star. . . .

With the "Penitent in the Snow," are three figures—two walking,

> . . . and Christ
> carried overhead—
> his red cotton robe
> flaring
> over wooden loins,
> his face as if whittled
> in green wax.
>
> Kin of the calla,
> of fish-brown orchids,
> of the rubber plant
> and fuchsia. . . .

Embedded in ornament and "gaiety of enamel," the concept sometimes
simulates its background—as similarly, one cannot at first see what one is
seeing, in Miss Bianco's dense, clear, geometric pomegranates, petunias,
trumpet-flowers, gloxinias, salpiglossus, orange-flowers, and orchids. The
turkey "moves his embossed body of gun-metal and gold in the stubblefield";

> . . . the twig-horned deer
> whets his haunches
> on the air;

horses stand in the river, "their feet on the reflected sun"; the human body
is

> Simple as a snake
> to the eye, but curious
> in motions. . . .

In having a sumptuously feathered, tropic, tribally adorned aesthetic progress
of that which is elaborately unusual, one is without something else and feels
in this instance a need for more of the "snake," or "rivers walked by snipe,"
of "the spotted flock . . . like a stream of water flowing in a crevice."

But cadence is "something" and color is something—violet, pink, primrose, maroon,

> in the plaza, where autumn
> is thin, tinged
> like a fish-scale.

Exactly tinted and unexaggeratedly denominated *Natives of Rock*, intangible
"Magnolias" and the "Intangible Horse of New Mexico" become in this book,
a possession even of those who have not seen them.

The Dial, 81 (July 1926), 69–72.

THE WAY WE LIVE NOW

IN speaking of the art of literary portraiture, "If the drawing be undertaken,"
says Mr. Saintsbury, "let it be faithful." Memoirs, subjective and objective,
seem to have usurped the place of the "mere" novel. Indeed, one perhaps

---

Review of *All Summer in a Day, An Autobiographical Fantasia*, by Sacheverell Sitwell (Duckworth).

unconsciously extends a reprieve to the form of certain stories and novels because one has encountered in them the author's inviolate living—a personal essence superior to chapter-headings and machinery.

Of autobiography, we are familiar with several varieties. There is the devoir so to speak, conceived by a writer out of respect for his past and in solicitude for the rights of posterity. There is also, what might be called the personal cyclorama—a thing of expletives, italics, and untriumphant puns. *I Have This to Say* by Violet Hunt is a book of this kind—a book which, despite many an unsayable saying, moves one. Its mentality has regard for the mentality of others and is not impatient of those "who have not novels to write, but gain their living in a less nervous way." Much that purports to be much, has dwindled it seems in the printing; and as a mere matter of literary style one cannot but be aware that an enquiry is sometimes more conclusive than dogmatic pronouncement, but even in the suspect realm of the-hero-by-an-eye-witness there are particulars in this book, which in all asceticism and gossipless renunciation, we should have. Certain photographs, "My Niece," and "Henry James" by Miss Boughton, are talismanic and one recognizes as essential the verbal portrait of Henry James holding between his open palms, "my last new Persian kitten . . . which was too polite and too squeezed between the upper and the nether millstones of the great man's hands, to remind him of its existence."

There is a kind of reminiscence, may we add, which is religious, rapt, a thing inner and final—such writing as has been given us by The Venerable Bede, by W. B. Yeats, by Henry James, and by less conspicuous exemplars of what is burnished and priestly.

In the personal record which is somewhat remote, so also in that which is informal, one may have a devout "interiority." One is aware of it in Mr. Sacheverell Sitwell's Autobiographic Fantasia, *All Summer in a Day.* A wealth of unhackneyed metaphor, to be sure, has the effect occasionally, of being not quite serviceable to imagination; and as the rapid enlargement of face or other object in a motion picture may seem to one too large, "Part Two" seems "large." Habits of indocility furthermore, may permit some readers to reverse the author's characterization and find in the half of the book which tells of childhood—"a low and sad half"—"some ground for optimism," and in the half of the book which tells of "the winter walk"—"equivalent to spending one's afternoon in a cistern"—and of an Italian theater's "groves and pavilions of comedy"—a slight sadness in sophistication. But the likeness in both to the way we live now, is faithful. (When Anthony Trollope told us of *The Way We Live Now*, that way of course was different.) In "the world of things one's eyes could see," there was as Mr. Sitwell saw it before he "had grown tall enough to fit his coffin," much that we ourselves, now coffin size, corroborate: the grass, "like the schoolboy's pocket-knife which will never shut properly from ill-usage . . . bent back and trampled upon"; "a long brick wall, white-washed in a nautical manner"; the music of Chopin which "has such an immediate and overwhelming effect when one is young and first hears it"; and Dürer's water-colors—"the bunch of violets, the rose-tree, the rabbit, the jay's feather, the cornfield." Mr. Sitwell's human things, Colonel Fantock and Miss Morgan, are truer even perhaps than his inanimate ones. And a certain sail-boat is, as made to behave in these pages, "sempiternally" marine.

When, as in the Italy of this Fantasia, Mr. Sitwell "distorts the present, so as to make it full of anecdote and mythology like the past," it pleases us less than when he had tea with the Polish musicians, "at a round table, which was hidden like a baby in long white clothes," in a house "with seven great windows coming right down to the floor and two more of them at the end of the room." Less curiously and baroquely apical than Italy, these times enchant us when he was "too young to realize that we are in a condition of absolute liberty, except in so far as we may punish ourselves by too much greed or curiosity." But the "ghosts," early and later, of this his "private mythology" recalled in accordance with "oral and visual memory," are properly poetic and fantastic and one cannot but identify them. What could be more undeniable than the appearance when traveling, of the "interior scene . . . outside the window as though it was traveling along beside the train," "my five fellow-passengers counterfeited on the left-hand side instead of the right, so that while it was true that they now surrounded me, I was none the less able to keep a watch on them which they could not inflict on me, for they were too far away to catch any distinct reflection of the carriage." Mr. Sitwell's oral memory is not a ragged one, as we know from what he has to say of music in the theater where "everything glided continuously into the next thing," and of music in the hotel: "No one stared and there was a noisy peace." And it is a pardonable phonetic mimicry that preserves to us the French châteaux which Miss Morgan "always attributed to the reign of 'Angry Cat,' giving by these words to the debonair and vulgar Henri Quatre a kind of fantastic alertness and sharpness of whisker that was not out of keeping with the dandyism and self-assertion of those buildings."

If one seems to be assenting to this "caparison of ghosts . . . which all came from their tombs at the band's harsh breath" as to something in which everyone has participated, is the compliment less than it would be were one speaking of life? In having said that Mr. Sitwell faithfully describes our analytic habit of subjecting experience to a poetically scrutinizing modern consciousness, we have not said how much we like his portrait or how friendly we are to certain of his sentiments as he "sat in safety behind that bed of

sunflowers," particularizing "those sentiments because of their florid openness and their gilt and rayed ornament to so large and simple a center."

The Dial, 82 (January 1927), 66–68, published under the pseudonym "Peter
Morris."

i compose curves

MR. E. E. CUMMINGS is under the impression as are others of us,
that two and two is five, and by a similarly superstitious triumph over logic,
one tries to feel in reading *Is Five* that poems which detract from other poems,
detract nothing and that it is possible to be pleasing when one is entirely
displeasing.

The untrammeled terminology of hampered sensibility, psychoanalytic
sententiousness, and the elaborated allusion to what sounds interesting when
thought of as an impropriety—exact of the arbiter, unegotistic, unparalleled
toughness of spirit; and although such fortitude is sometimes found in parents,
the hedonist prefers usually to do something other than to endure poetry.
Wary lest fearless fooling become stereotyped novelty and originality be mere
cleverness, inceptors of poetry do not trust themselves unreservedly to poets,
even to best ones and may in the instance of *Is Five* be casual with disrespectful amplitude; but they have also reason to be grateful.

Mr. Cummings reenforces offended justice in its disapproval of approved
enormities—of war, of sartorial heroics, of unimagination, of upper-class
triviality, of any overbearing rightness. He likes the cathedral, the procession, the hilltop; a mouse, lizard ladies;

> Cats which move smoothly from neck to neck of bottles, cats
> smoothly willowing out and in between bottles. . . .

Modulations, musics, subsidiary to larger ones, and fugue-like progres-
sions of corresponding enumerations "compose curves" of reptilian, imperceptibly segmented continuity. There are too, the monumental minutiae of
emotion, transfigured moments in which an insulating externality encloses
"faithful and mad" unstared-at drama.

The Forum, 177 (February 1927), 316.

Review of *Is Five*, by E. E. Cummings (Boni & Liveright).

A POET OF THE QUATTROCENTO

IT was Ezra Pound's conviction some years ago, that there could be "an age of awakening in America" which would "overshadow the quattrocento." Hopeful for us at that time, "our opportunity is greater than Leonardo's," said Mr. Pound; "we have more aliment," and never really neglectful of us, he has commended in us, "Mr. Williams' praiseworthy opacity." "There is distinctness and color," he observed, "as was shown in his 'Postlude,' in 'Des Imagistes'; but there is beyond these qualities the absolute conviction of a man with his feet on the soil, on a soil personally and peculiarly his own. He is rooted. He is at times almost inarticulate, but he is never dry, never without sap in abundance."

This metaphor of the tree seems highly appropriate to William Carlos Williams—who writes of seedling sycamores, of walnuts and willows—who several years ago, himself seemed to W. C. Blum "by all odds the hardiest specimen in these parts."[1] In his modestly emphatic respect for America he corroborates Henry James' conviction that young people should "stick fast and sink up to their necks in everything their own countries and climates can give," and his feeling for the *place* lends poetic authority to an illusion of ours, that sustenance may be found here, which is adapted to artists. Imagination can profit by a journey, acquainting itself with everything pertaining to its wish that it can gather from European sources, Doctor Williams says. But it is apparent to him that "American plumbing, American bridges, indexing systems, locomotives, printing presses, city buildings, farm implements and a thousand other things" are liked and used, and it is not folly to hope that the very purest works of the imagination may also be found among us. Doctor Williams is in favor of escape from "strained associations," from "shallowness," from such substitutes as "congoleum—building paper with a coating of enamel." The staying at home principle could not, he is sure, be a false one where there is vigorous living force with buoyancy of imagination—as there was apparently in Shakespeare—the artist's excursion being into "perfection" and "technical excellence." "Such names as Homer, the blind; Scheherazade, who lived under threat—their compositions have as their excellence, an identity with life since they are as actual, as sappy as the leaf of the tree which never moves from one spot." He has visited places and studied various writings and a traveler can as Bacon says, "prick in some flowers of that he hath learned abroad." In the man, however, Doctor Williams' topics are American—crowds at the movies

[1]Cf. "American Letter," by W. C. Blum, *The Dial*, May 1921.

with the closeness and
universality of sand,

turkey nests, mushrooms among the fir trees, mist rising from the duck pond, the ball game:

It is summer, it is the solstice
the crowd is

cheering, the crowd is laughing

or

It is spring. Sunshine . . . dumped among factories . . . down a red dirt path to four goats. . . . I approach the smallest goat timidly. . . . It draws away beginning to wind its tie rope around the tree. . . . I back the creature around the tree till it can go no further, the cord all wound up. Gingerly I take it by the ear. It tries to crowd between me and the tree. I drive it around the tree again until the rope is entirely unwound. The beast immediately finds new violent green tufts of grass in some black mud half under some old dried water-soaked weedstalks. . . . To the right of the path the other goat comes forward boldly but stops short and sniffs. . . . It ventures closer. Gna-ha-ha-ha-ha! (as in hat). Very softly. The small goat answers.

O spring days, swift
and mutable, wind blowing
four ways, hot and cold.

Essentially not a "repeater of things second hand," Doctor Williams is in his manner of contemplating with new eyes, old things, shabby things, and other things, a poet. Meter he thinks of as an "essential of the work, one of its words." That which is to some imperceptible, is to him the "milligram of radium" that he values. He is rightly imaginative in not attempting to decide; or rather, in deciding not to attempt to say how wrong these readers are, who find his poems unbeautiful or "positively repellant." As he had previously asked, "Where does this downhill turn up again? Driven to the wall you'd put claws to your toes and make a ladder of smooth bricks."

Facts presented to us by him in his prose account of "The Destruction of Tenochtitlan," could not be said to be "new," but the experience ever, in encountering that which has been imaginatively assembled is exceedingly new. One recalls in reading these pages, the sense augmented, of "everything which the world affords," of "the drive upward, toward the sun and the stars"; and foremost as poetry, we have in a bewilderingly great, neatly ordered pageant of magnificence, Montezuma, "this American cacique," "so delicate," "so full of tinkling sounds and rhythms, so tireless of invention."

One sees nothing terrifying in what Doctor Williams calls a "modern traditionalism," but to say so is to quibble. Incuriousness, emptiness, a sleep of the faculties, are an end of beauty; and Doctor Williams is vivid. Perhaps he is modern. He addresses himself to the imagination. He is "keen" and "compact." "At the ship's prow" as he says the poet should be, he is glad to have his "imaginary" fellow-creatures with him. Unless we are very literal, this should be enough.

The Dial, 82 (March 1927), 213–15.

A HOUSE-PARTY

"THE sea lay three parts round the house, invisible because of the wood. . . . The people who had the house were interested in the wood and its silence." "Poverty and pride, cant and candor, raw flesh and velvet" seem collectively to ask, "Are we never to have any peace, only adventure and pain?" to say "there is no good will left anywhere in the world."

They were Drusilla Taverner—"Scylla"; Carston, an American; Picus "unnaturally supple"; Carston "had seen him pick up something behind him with his hands as if it had been in front"; Clarence "with a feeling for decoration best served in cities." "One rougher and shorter, fairer, better bred, called Ross. Then a boy, Scylla's brother, Felix Taverner."

"Ross arranged their chairs in the veranda while the storm banged about." "For an hour it rained, through sheet lightning, and thunder like a departing train, the hills calling one to another."

The Sanc-Grail is supposed to have been fished from the well, but "Picus had taken his father's cup . . . had run to small mystifications . . . had whistled up mystery with what was now undoubtedly a victorian finger-bowl."

" 'We don't seem to have cleared up anything,' said Clarence. 'Cleared up,' said Picus chattering at them. . . . In this there was something that was not comic, in the dis-ease he imparted."

When consulted about disposing of the cup the vicar suggests replacing

---

Review of *Armed with Madness*, by Mary Butts (Albert and Charles Boni).

it where they got it. " 'It seems to like wells,' " he said. " 'And truth, if she prefers not to talk, can return to one.' "

" 'Good,' said Picus, 'learn it to be a toad.' "

One sees the artist in Miss Butts, in her liking to watch "how violently, strangely, and in character people will behave," though an attitude of being surprising in matters of personal freedom seems needless. The iron hand of unconvention can be heavier than the iron hand of convention; and heresy in respect to this or that orthodoxy is perhaps a greater compliment to it than one sets out to pay, amounting really in the vehemence of protest, to subjection; to marriage and various other kinds of conformity Miss Butts pays compliments of this grudged, paining variety.

There are gruesome things here, as there were continually in the minds of the maddened conversers—"while high over them the gulls squalled like sorrow driven up." But there are many graces. And it is a triumph for the author that it is a mistake to recount anything she writes without recounting it in her own words. Sensitiveness sponsors defiance; it also sponsors homage to beauty. Strictness of touch and accurate drawing give "the endless turf-miles which ran up a great down into the sky"; "above the thunder a gull repeating itself . . . a little noise laid delicately upon the universal roar of air"; Carston "beautifying himself scrupulously and elaborately as a cat"; Picus' father, a collector with "a theory of the rights of owners to their property"—"prupperty: prupperty: prupperty"; Lydia (in London) "in a too short frock and a too tight hair-wave and a too pink make-up, reading the *Romaunt de la Rose*"; and Lydia's husband. "His method was to cut conversation, to interrupt whatever was said, and when he spoke, interrupt himself, so there should never be any continuity. Perfectly sound. . . . Could show them that not being a gentleman was worth something."

Little thicknesses are chipped away. Emphasis of writing and of attitude are equal, and as a change from the periodic sentence a syncopated rhetoric is pleasant; though emphasis without interruption amounts to no emphasis and one has the feeling that a mixture of code and declarative sentence may be best. There is much to notice, as one proceeds—rejecting, accepting, renovated and attentive. Would a Bostonian say, "I reckon" in the way in which Carston says it? Is flavor contributed or sacrificed by the elegiac curfew chime of current literacy—that is to say, by the interpolated aphorism: "When we were very young"; "meaning of meaning"; "portraits of the artist"; things from the Bible? But to doubt is merely a part of liking, and of feeling. One need not read Mary Butts if one has not a feeling for feeling. Her presentation of what one feels is here as accurate as of what one sees. Scylla "wished the earth would not suddenly look fragile, as if it was going to start shifting about. . . . There was something wrong with all of them, or with their world. A moment missed, a moment to come. Or not coming. Or either or both. Shove it off on the War; but that did not help." The "trick on Carston was ill-mannered, a little cruel. Also irrelevant." "What he could not have done [to others], others could do [to him]." It is a compassionate view Miss Butts takes of this informed, formless party; of its "insolent insincerity" and seeming insufficiency—of Clarence smiling back at Picus "as if he had to smile under pain, his own, any one's," listening "till the time came when he could listen no longer, and hid his face, the awful pain rising in him drowning Picus' presence." "There was something in their lives spoiled and inconclusive like the Grail," she says. Some would say nothing in them was like the Grail. But Miss Butts is not palming anything off on us. We may make what we may of it. It is sympathy she offers us in Carston's reply when the vicar wonders "whether a true picture of the real is shown by our senses alone." "All I can say is that I've never never been so bothered, never behaved so like a skunk, never so nearly fell dead in my tracks till I got down here and began to think about such things. It's unfashionable now, you know—"

The Dial, 85 (September 1928), 258–60.

COMMENT

WHEN writers of plays or of novels create plots which are similar, the possibility of imitation occurs to one—of what was in Poe's time called plagiarism. Reflection might easily persuade one that neither author has been aware of the work of the other and that neither piece of work is invaluably original. Similarly, in the work of poets, resemblances in performance sometimes lead one to attribute to an author, dependence upon sources of which he knows nothing. It is apparent, however, that among poets, aesthetic consanguinity is frequent. The fire, the restraint, the devout paganism of H. D. are unequivocally Greek. Wallace Stevens' morosely ecstatic, trembling yet defiant, multifarious plumage of thought and word is to be found, also, in France. By no means a chameleon, Ezra Pound wears sometimes with splendor, the cloak of medieval romance. Employing diction which is not infrequently as decorous as it is instructed, E. E. Cummings shares with certain writers of the fourteenth and sixteenth centuries, a manner as courtly and decisive as it is sometimes shabby. T. S. Eliot often recalls to us, the verbal parquetry of Donne, exemplifying that wit which he defines as "a tough reasonableness under . . . lyric grace."

Amy Lowell most conspicuously provides an illustration of this genetic sharing of tradition. Unequivocally paying tribute to Keats in her first book, *A Dome of Many-coloured Glass*, she has to some readers appeared to be now an imagist, now a vorticist, now a writer of polyphonic prose. Granting a various method, one discerns in all that she has written, pre-eminently a love for the author whom she commemorates in her last work. One cannot but find in her imagination, an analogy to the "violets," the "nightingale," the "tiger-moth," the "rich attire" of Keats. When she says:

> I have no broad and blowing plain to link
> And loop with aqueducts, no golden mine
> To crest my pillars, no bright twisted vine
> Which I can train about a fountain's brink . . . ;

when as a pointillist she says of trees after a storm:

> They are blue,
> And mauve,
> And emerald.
> They are amber,

> And jade,
> And sardonyx.
> They are silver fretted to flame
> And startled to stillness . . .

one is in the world of "chimes," of "perfume," and of "falling leaves"—
Endymion's world of "poppies," of

> . . . visions all about my sight
> Of colors, wings, and bursts of spangly light.

Nor is the atmosphere of sentiment, of hospitality, and leisure, at variance
with the character of this self-dependently American, sometimes modern
American writer. The death of Amy Lowell but emphasizes the force of her
personality. Cosmopolitan yet isolated, essentially distinct from "the imagist
group," of which she has been called "the recognized spokesman," she has
by a misleadingly armored self-reliance, sometimes obscured a generosity,
a love of romance, the luster of a chivalry which was essentially hers.

The Dial, 79 (July 1925), 87–88.

• • •

"ACTION, business, adventure, discovery," are not prerogatives exclu-
sively American; and obversely, creative power is not the prerogative of
every country other than America. That it is not, moreover, we have had
abundant evidence during March, in Room 303 of The Anderson Galleries—
a brief, memorable "depository" for the work of John Marin, Arthur G. Dove,
Marsden Hartley, Paul Strand, Alfred Stieglitz, Charles Demuth, and Georgia
O'Keeffe.

We are pleased that Marin has conceived the possibility of "a wind blowing
pigment," the more rather than less that Botticelli and Turner observed the
metamorphosis of clothes and water by the wind. We are consciously indulgent, perhaps, towards certain of Arthur Dove's idiosyncrasies—towards
"10-Cent-Store Still-Life" and "Mary Goes to Italy"; examining his "Storm-
Clouds in Silver" and his "Garden, Rose, Gold, Green," however, we agree
that we'd "rather have the impossible than the possible," that we'd "rather

have truth than beauty," and that we'd "rather have a soul than a shape"; the soul and the truth sometimes conveniently as in this case, having "beauty" and a "shape." Wary, yet eager snappers-up of the uninsistent masterpiece, like certain fish, we sometimes pre-empt something that we may afterward reject; and nearly always prefer precisely those works for which the author himself, cares least. Although certain of Marsden Hartley's stark austerities not here, are preferred by us to some that are, his tessellated representations of landscape and still-life correct the jocund American tendency to guess rather than to know. Canaletto and the charts of seventeenth-century botanists have but prepared our vision for the reredos of buildings, for the architecture of weeds, for the machinery of Paul Strand, than which nothing is more veracious. We welcome the power-house in the drawing-room when we examine his orientally perfect combining of discs, parabolas, and verticals—when we perceive the silver flexibility of skin or the depth of tone upon the anaconda-like curves of central bearings. We agree with Gaston Lachaise that "personality is expressed by Alfred Stieglitz in a profound and penetrating comprehension of character, as by daguerreotypes in their enchanting manner": here, by his clouds—his "Equivalents," characteristically interrogatory. Charles Demuth's jewelry of apples reinforced by pieces of green glass or black, pleases us as well as their Chinese counterparts—mandarins and insects painted upon silk. Certain of Miss O'Keeffe's petunias and "Portraits of a Day" check the impact of precursory consent. The unvariegated burning brass of her autumn leaves, however, assures us as an interpreter of her work has said, that she "wears no poisoned emeralds." Her calla lilies, gladiolas, and alligator pears, have upon them, the luster of mosques, of lotus flowers, of cypress-bordered pools. They have the involute security of Central African, of Singhalese and Javanese experienced adornment.

Doubtless there are admirers of American aesthetic performance who would revert to Whistler's Mother; to the grasshopper weather-vane of gilded copper with glass eye, made by an American for Faneuil Hall in 1742; to the silk embroidered lady in an empire dress, half kneeling under a willow tree by George Washington's tomb; to the early American kitten held by an early American child—or to the work of John Singer Sargent, admiration for whose portraits has now honoringly, in the year of his death assumed "patriotic proportions." Yet obviously, past and present, creative effort is here—conscious of which, we participate in that for which Yeats pleads: the old culture "that came to man at his work, which was not at the expense of life, but an exaltation of life itself."

The Dial, 79 (August 1925), 177–78.

• • •

This is perhaps our nearest approach to a definition of Beauty: that it is a supreme instance of Order, intuitively felt, instinctively appreciated.

DENMAN WALDO ROSS

IN 1854, in a report made by the librarian of The Astor Library, New York City—we read: "The young fry of today employ all the hours they are not in school, reading trashy current fiction such as Scott, Cooper, Dickens, Punch, and The Illustrated News." From this statement it would appear that young people may be spontaneously attracted to that which is educative, and one is reminded that education has been defined as, "any activity which we value not for its direct results but for its indirect effects upon the capacity of the man who is engaged therein"—a wise version, it is obvious, of the banal dogma that compulsory study of helpful subjects is invariably baneful. One observes the desultoriness of children whose adult associates are superficial and artificial. Energy and imagination are, however, never greater than in childhood; and it is possible to find even today, on the part of some children, purposefulness and originality which are extraordinary.

The recent exhibition at The Metropolitan Museum, of work done in the Education Department of the Worcester Art Museum, is diverting—indeed most enriching—to those who have observed the power implicit in the child's imagination. The work exhibited, comprising formal and pictorial designs, is the product of children from eight to thirteen years of age, who have come voluntarily to The Worcester Museum—have studied there, the pottery, textiles, and paintings, and have been instructed in accordance with the theories of Dr. Denman Waldo Ross.

A project which is aesthetic must be undertaken, Dr. Ross affirms, "just for the satisfaction, the pleasure, the delight of it," yet he reminds us that in the practice of pure design, the sense of order which we all have, must be educated. "The process," he says—to quote further from his manual, *A Theory of Pure Design*—"is one of experimenting, observing, comparing, judging, arranging and rearranging, taking no end of time and pains to achieve Order, the utmost possible Order, if possible the Beautiful."

To those who forget, as well as to those who remember, that at the age of thirteen, one feels older than one can every really be, the stability of the work of which we have been speaking could not be other than impressive. None of the themes upon which the designs are based, is far fetched; indeed, the formal unit of the printed designs is in each case, startlingly familiar, yet the result has been personal and distinguished. The circle, the violet, the trefoil, the Parthenon horse, have been used with the utmost exactitude— the identity of the unit being revealed only upon analytic study. Tone harmony has been heightened by the accuracy of the printing; the feeling for scale and texture, is sure and consonant with the best examples that one knows, of formal decoration.

The monotonous, would-be usualness of the work of children is a byword; one cannot but abandon caution, however, in this composite, yet strangely homogeneous exhibition. One is conscious of the unstrained-for *esprit*, the energy, and the fertility of these designs, the manner of which is controlled and by no means unintentional or grotesquely entertaining. Again to quote Dr. Ross, "important work comes only from important people," yet "it constantly happens that in pleasing ourselves, we please others." "The House in the High Wood," "Summer," "Adventure," "Excitement," "Anger," "Hurry," "Happiness," "The Sea"—these themes so evidently productive of emotion in the designer, are in their varied interpretations, most imaginative. It is poetically right that ducks should, in their progress toward the water, hurry; that happiness should be symbolized by flowers, red and blue; that excitement should be symbolized by a purple shark with orange eyes, in pursuit of purple fish with orange eyes, between blue rocks, through crimson water.

The tendency to multiply detail is instinctive. There is in this work, however, a sense of simplifying rather than of complication, of restraint rather than of "decoration." It is evident that "additions are, as a rule, to be avoided." The force of omission is especially felt in the design entitled "The Sea"—a composition, the few lines and flat tones of which, consummately suggest, wind, weight, and violence. The adjusting of form, tone, and sentiment, is perhaps even more experienced in the composition called "Anger"; jagged bayonets of yellow, green, black, red, and blue, having been so used that the effect of descending force prevents all sense of counter-movement. In these diverse designs by children of varied association as of nationality, unanimity of accomplishment is proof that imagination gains rather than loses by guidance and one is assured that the creating of beauty is, like the appreciating of beauty, in part the result of instruction.

The Dial, 79 (September 1925), 264–66.

. . .

A voluntary descent from the dignity of science is perhaps the hardest lesson which humility can teach.

DOCTOR JOHNSON

DR. ELIOT, the President Emeritus of Harvard, regards as our foremost educators during the last 2300 years, Aristotle, Galen, Leonardo da Vinci, Sir Francis Bacon, Milton, Shakespeare, John Locke, Immanuel Kant, Sir Isaac Newton, and Ralph Waldo Emerson. Advantaged by his fearlessness to choose, one acknowledges that one might choose similarly, and is reluctant to remember that one's predilection for these justly celebrated persons has in some measure been instructed.

Shakespeare perhaps must be excepted. One may not have known him before having seen his plays acted and may yet be sure that from the time one is able to read, to have evaded his intoxicating sovereignty would be impossible. For the most part, however, has not the domination of these ten sages been implicit in that of lesser sages? Has the compactness of Aristotle who, as a schoolmaster, "goeth for the best author," been more alluringly succinct than Roger Ascham's motto, "He who teaches, learns"—*Qui docet, discit?* Emerson's attitude of friendship has seemed to one surely, not less a platitude than the devout firmness of Maria Edgeworth in *The Parent's Assistant.* In Kate Greenaway—a writer and a painter too, like Leonardo da Vinci—one has found an indelible simplicity:

> The king said he liked apples,
> The Queen said she liked pears,
> And what shall we do to the blackbird
> Who listens unawares?

Has one consciously been more in debt to Galen's subtlety than to Doctor Goldsmith's therapy of man and dog, or less in debt to Luther Burbank whose witchcraft we are told is merely the suncraft of an observer, than to Sir Isaac Newton? Since, having been made to understand how five hundred kinds of fruit may be produced on one tree, how white blackberries, stoneless plums, spineless cactus, and sweet lemons may be successfully "designed," one cannot but understand somewhat of the water, of the air, and of the sun which contributed to produce these curiosities. Admiring in *The Adventures of Mr. Verdant Green,* Cuthbert Bede's infectious plea for learning, one has become aware of the classic cosmos of Sir Francis Bacon—of "those influences which possess the mind almost imperceptibly and are yet of primary importance in the formation of character," surrounded by which Mr. Verdant Green "had to bear contradictions and reproof, progressing in that knowledge of himself which has been found to be about the most useful of all knowledge." Ever within the range of our vision, yet distant—a kind of poetic Mt. Everest—Milton's greatness has in certain instances, been less to us than the great simplicity of Isaac Watts; one agrees with Doctor Johnson that, "Every man acquainted with the common principles of human action will look with veneration on the writer who is at one time combating Locke and at another time making a catechism for children in their fourth year." Jacob Abbott's ethical deductions "About Right and Wrong" are perhaps the most potent preparation for Kant's crabbed insistence that "if there is in an act, the least admixture of any motive other than the moral, it loses its moral worth," and general acceptance of the educational ideal, "a sound mind in a sound body," may be attributed as much to the influence of *The Compleat Angler* as to the influence of Locke.

Unmenaced as is the greatness of Dr. Eliot's decemvirs, the unbookish are intimidated by greatness so inclusive. Indeed it is perhaps an imaginary America which pores over either a preeminent or a miniature greatness. Rabbi Israel Goldstein deplores the "characterless Apollos and cynical Minervas of our metropolis, whose attitude toward parents is arrogant, toward moral standards flippant, toward duty as such, recalcitrant," and one wishes that our disgracing juniors might exemplify, if not the simplicity of art, the simplicity of artlessness.

The Dial, 79 (November 1925), 443–44.

• • •

THE Editors of *The Dial* have had pleasure in proffering to William Carlos Williams, *The Dial*'s award for 1926.

May we repeat ourselves: "Our insistence that *The Dial*'s award is not a prize is frequently taken to be a characteristic pedantry on our part, almost as reprehensible as the use of the preferred spelling in our pages. We can only reply that the dictionary and good usage are the pedants, not ourselves; we are using words in their accurate and accepted sense when we say that

a prize is something contested for and that an award is something given. . . .
The Dial's award 'crowns' no book, nor does it imply any moral or even
aesthetic judgment of superiority. It indicates only that the recipient has
done a service to letters and that, since money is required even by those
who serve letters, since the payment in money is generally inadequate when
good work is concerned, *The Dial* is in a way adding to the earnings of a
writer, diminishing, by a little, the discrepancy between his minimum requirements as a citizen in a commercial society and his earnings as an artist.
We have never believed that the recipient has, or will have, done exactly
two thousand dollars' worth of service to letters. We haven't the standard of
measurement for such delicacy of judgment."

William Carlos Williams is a physician, a resident of New Jersey, the
author of prose and verse. He has written of "fences and outhouses built of
barrel-staves and parts of boxes," of the "sparkling lady" who "passes quickly
to the seclusion of her carriage," of Weehawken, of "The Passaic, that filthy
river," of "hawsers that drop and groan," of "a young horse with a green
bed-quilt on his withers." His "venomous accuracy," if we may use the
words used by him in speaking of the author of "The Raven," is opposed to
"makeshifts, self-deceptions and grotesque excuses." Among his meditations
are "Chickory and Daisies," "Queen-Ann's-Lace," trees—hairy, bent, erect—
orchids, and magnolias. We need not, as Wallace Stevens has said, "try
to . . . evolve a mainland from his leaves, scents and floating bottles and
boxes." "What Columbus discovered is nothing to what Williams is looking
for." He writes of lions with Ashur-ban-i-pal's "shafts bristling in their
necks," of "the bare backyard of the old Negro with white hair," of "branches
that have lain in a fog which now a wind is blowing away." "This modest
quality of realness which he attributes to 'contact' with the good Jersey dirt
sometimes reminds one of Chekhov," says a connoisseur of our poetry. "Like
Chekhov he knows animals and babies as well as trees. And to people who
are looking for the story his poems must often seem as disconnected and
centrifugal as Chekhov's later plays." We concur that "his phrases have a
simplicity, solid justice." He "is forthright, a hard, straight, bitter javelin,"
said William Marion Reedy. "As you read him you catch in your nostrils
the pungent beauty in the wake of his 'hard stuff,' and you begin to realize
how little poetry—or prose—depends on definitions, or precedents, or forms."
You do.

A child is a "portent"; a poet is a portent. As has been said of certain
theological architecture, it is the peculiarity—we have noticed—of certain
poetic architecture that "the foundations are ingeniously supported by the
superstructure." The child

> Sleeps fast till his might
> Shall be piled
> Sinew on sinew.

In the arboreally imaginative world of thought as in the material world,

> creeping energy, concentrated
> counterforce—welds sky, buds, trees.

We have said that Carlos Williams is a doctor. Physicians are not so often poets as poets are physicians, but may we not assert confidently that oppositions of sciences are not oppositions to poetry but oppositions to falseness. The author of the *Religio Medici* could not be called anything more than he could be called a poet. "He has many verba ardentia," as Samuel Johnson has observed—"forcible expressions, which he would never have found, but by venturing to the utmost verge of propriety; and flights which would never have been reached, but by one who had very little fear of the shame of falling."

The service which it is our pleasure to acknowledge is "practical service. Service not to that Juggernaut, the Reading Public,—that Juggernaut which is well served in being served badly. Service rather to the Imaginative Individual, to him who is in our world always the Marooned Individual."

In one of Doctor Williams' books we find a poem entitled, "To Wish Courage to Myself." It is to wish courage to him and in the inviting of his hardy spirit, to wish it to ourselves, that we have—inadequately—spoken.

The Dial, 82 (January 1926), 88–90.

· · ·

IN modern collections of short stories, in the would-be microcosm of aesthetic or political opinion, in anthologies of verse or of prose, there is apparently none of that skillful anonymity which was characteristic of definite periods in the past. Contemporary audacity of dissimilarity recalls the assertion that opposition is wise, since to be in agreement with everyone is as bad as being alone. Certainly in *The Hogarth Essays*,[1] we have an impressive example of disparateness. The reader unforewarned must start, at this fraternal confluence of sentiments and techniques as he encounters variously, studiousness, experience, inexperience, effrontery, decorum, dullness, inconsequence, discernment, wisdom—indeed genius.

Those whose meditative enjoyment of art is always being violated by the hasty, cannot but find consolation—as has been intimated by *The Dial*[2]—in Mr. Roger Fry's *The Artist and Psycho-Analysis*; and a similar sensitiveness is felt in Miss Bosanquet's essay, *Henry James at Work*, in which, unprofaning yet observant, we have not merely a portrait of Henry James at work, but what seems a "life" of him. Biographies of writers often read as if they had unsuperstitiously been compiled by persons innocent of the writings to which the author's life had been devoted. And now when many a novel tells us what "has happened in life but what cannot happen in a novel," one is glad to be reminded that Henry James used his friends "not as the material of his art, but as the sources of his material," and remembers appropriately that his present biographer had not only read his books but had actually written them. So impervious to "the American accent and the English manner that he seemed only doubtfully Anglo-Saxon," Henry James is exhibited here as nowhere else outside of his own books—"paternally responsible for two distinct families," "treating the printed pages like so many proof sheets of extremely corrupt text"—aware that "the tenderness of growing life is at the mercy of personal tyranny"—with "a horror of interfering, or seeming to interfere with the freedom of others."

The novel is the form of art which the public is least willing to ignore; and loath as one is to brand this inherence of permanence with the term Victorian, Edwardian, Georgian, modern, one is involuntarily attentive to each new pronouncement upon progress. With an occasional strange phase of syntax, or strong generalization not entirely conclusive, the evolution of the novel is again honored under the assured and flippant label, "Mr. Bennet and Mrs. Brown." Mrs. Brown—that is to say, character-making power in the art of the novel—will, Mrs. Woolf tells us, some day be caught.

In his *Journal of the Retreat of the Fifth Army from St. Quentin*, Mr. Herbert Read may surely be immune from the literary asperities of those who find his workmanship tired, his diction not quite spare, and his sentences unmusical. Regarding with a perhaps justifiable "bitterness," "certain states of forgetfulness in the minds of non-combatants," he shows us much that is sorrowful—men and horses "debonaire and well fed," "harness jingling, the sun shining on well-polished accoutrements,"—"old men, many old women, a few young women," trudging along beside carts "hand-pulled or yoked to bony horses." Having thought to encounter ingenuities evolved in a bookman's retreat, we have more valuably perhaps, a reiterating of the truism that really great things cannot be accomplished with guns; we find soldiers to be, not conquerors, but creatures with "hearts like taut drum skins, beaten reverberantly by every little incident."

Pained by the starkness of Mr. Read's truthfulness, one needs if one is fully to enjoy it, already to have read *Histriophone*. In this dialogue on dramatic diction, Mr. Bonamy Dobrée's willowy, almost too educated fastidiousness, brings us now and then into the atmosphere of what we like— although one's remoteness from the acropolis and too great intimacy with the market, could lead one possibly to prefer impersonal treatment of what has here been presented in the form of a dialogue.

By no means wearily yet warily, we examine generalizations with regard to poetry, and unimpaired by their studious constraint, T. S. Eliot's epitomes and hypotheses are in their inherent equilibrium, detaining. It is our whim to enjoy in the essay on Marvel, one of those "undesirable" images which in Mr. Eliot's opinion, "support nothing but their own misshapen bodies":

> And now the salmon-fishers moist
> Their leathern boats begin to hoist;
> And, like Antipodes in shoes,
> Have shod their heads in their canoes.

By "notions of the critic's" here "preserved in cryptogram," however, pleasure is revived in that omnipotence of Dryden's which we prefer to a certain kind of lyric loveliness—although we know it is not *better*. Mr. Eliot reinfects one with a liking for satire which has the fineness of stroke to "separate the head from the body and leave it standing in its place." And "that precise taste of Marvel's which finds for him the proper degree of seriousness for every subject which he treats," has never been presented more firmly. In these three essays, "Homage to John Dryden," "The Metaphysical Poets," and "Andrew Marvel," the distinctiveness of an age is revived—that "wisdom, cynical perhaps but untired," of the Elizabethan and Jacobean mind— that "wit" which is felt by Mr. Eliot to be so nearly synonymous with wits.

To this collection of essays, others are being added. It is a luxury to have large truths in modest form and gratitude should perhaps hinder the beneficiary from being entirely sure that he knows the difference between large truths and little ones.

[1] *The Hogarth Essays*. Vol. I: *Mr. Bennet and Mrs. Brown* by Virginia Woolf. Vol. II: *The Artist and Psycho-Analysis* by Roger Fry. Vol. III: *Henry James at Work* by Theodora Bosanquet. Vol. IV: *Homage to John Dryden* by T. S. Eliot. Vol. V: *Histriophone* by Bonamy Dobrée. Vol. VI: *In Retreat* by Herbert Read. Vol. VII: *Fear and*

Politics: A Debate in the Zoo by Leonard Woolf. Vol. VIII: *Contemporary Techniques of Poetry* by Robert Graves. Vol. IX: *The Character of John Dryden* by Alan Lubbock. Published by Leonard and Virginia Woolf at the Hogarth Press, London.
² Cf. Review by W. C. Blum, "Improbably Purity." *The Dial*, April, 1925.

The Dial, 80 (February 1926), 176–78.

• • •

> *I am sure there is a common Spirit that plays within us,*
> *yet makes no part of us.*
>
> SIR THOMAS BROWNE

THE brittle, brilliant character of life today is varyingly exposited. Speed and sport are, it would seem, indigenous to this country. We have the canoe, but ignore the punt and one could inspect the craft belonging to any American yacht-club without finding as a name, the continentally approved *Pas Pressé*. We are accustomed in America to admitting that "the prosperous, good-looking, domineering woman is a very attractive being." Our most presentable young people seem to share in the attitude of haste, and are accused of irreverence, ingratitude, and flippancy. We are, however, encouraged to suspect beneath the mannerism of quick self-sufficiency, a root of serious-ness. In a recent book, *The Religion of Undergraduates*,¹ opinions are re-vealed which have been expressed in private conclave and in answers to questionnaires. In apparent contrast with the insobriety of the present day, these opinions involving moral issues, could not, one suspects, have been heard on the campus or in undergraduate meetings during the early days of American colleges, despite the recorded circumspect bearing of those times. In few novels is the "mystical," the "medievally intense" atmosphere of the university, so prepossessingly and so exactly suggested as incidentally in these impressions of "the silent quadrangle suddenly filled with color and purposeful movement resembling some sedate folk-dance of processional figures on the green." No subjects of enquiry seem more living than those skeletons and scientific queries brought forth by students in unembarrassed freedom of discussion: Is there a truly desirable profession? In how far has one responsibility for others? What place has sex in one's life? What is immortality?

"We, it seems, are critical," says Emerson in "The American Scholar."

"We cannot enjoy anything for hankering to know whereof the pleasure consists; we are lined with eyes; we see with our feet; the time is infected with Hamlet's unhappiness." Prompted by those perennial "two selves, one actual; the other ideal," various questions are asked: "Is one's conduct ethical because good ethics have been found to be good for the race and because one has the habit?" "How good must one be to be good?" "What am I?" "I seem to be at war with myself. Two forces fight for possession of me. Sometimes I take sides with one, sometimes with the other. More often I merely look on." "I feel a sort of cheerless pity for myself. I am an animal, not a brain or a soul." These not complacent statements and inquiries point to the fact that there is in an age of lightness, a desire for the essential—that "the unstable estimates of men crowd to him whose mind is filled with a truth, as the heaped waves of the Atlantic follow the moon." It would seem that "in an age of wonders" there is "room for wonder." One is pleased to maintain an illusion of the university as "a grove of everbearing trees," and recalls, not in irony, a much read non-academic student's concept of the undergraduate as a Myron's Discobolus descending marble steps between ivory pillars.

¹ *The Religion of Undergraduates*, by Cyril Harris. Charles Scribner's Sons.

The Dial, 80 (March 1926), 265–66.

• • •

Quicquid loquemur, ubicunque, sit pro sua scilicet portione perfectum.*
QUINTILIAN

To exclude the speciously attractive, is difficult. The ideal director of a "zoo," we are told by Mr. William Hornaday, must at this time when tempted to "take on" mammals, birds, and reptiles, be a master in the art of refusing. The avowed artist must also, unless we are to have fads rather than individuality, be an artist in refusing. In each phase of art, interrelated influences of technique are apparent. The writer, however, seems in certain respects, either more pridelessly or more recklessly than others, susceptible to current

*Whatever we may say, and wherever, may it be perfect, at least according to its own kind.

cleverness. Much as the victim of the fashionable *couturier* participates in successive epidemics of cut and color—of shutter green, serpent blue, or Venetian fuchsia—of the wet seal *coiffure* or the powdered wig, the sciolist subscribes to the tyranny of timelessness, of delightful dubiety, of what is acute or effective. Imagism, the *hokku*, the coon song, the story true-because-I-have-lived-it, a morality of immorality, significantly concocted equine unselfconsciousness, these several modes have found prompt adherents.

There cannot be too much excellence. *Wilhelm Meister, Phineas Phinn, The Golden Bowl, The Lost Girl, Dubliners, Esther Waters,* we may admire, and the shock of admiration may serve us as an incentive to writing, quite as may that which has been experienced by us; but like the impelling emotion of actual experience, literary excitement must be assimilated before it can be reproduced. Experiences recorded verbatim are not fiction and verbiage is not eloquence. Much may be learned by consciously noting the merits of other writers. Apperception is, however, quite different from a speedy exchange of one's individuality for that of another. There is a certain briskness of execution which reminds one of the medieval undisciplined disputant who "like the fighting-cock, was armed with a redoubtable 'therefore:' " (*ergot*, spur).

Among rules recommended by Robert of Sorbon to the scholar who desired to make progress in his studies, were a summarizing of what had been read, a fixing of the attention upon it, and a conferring with fellow pupils. This counsel to precision and this permission to discussion, were signally if unconsciously exemplified by Doctor Johnson, whose life by Boswell presents itself to us just now, simultaneously in two editions—in two volumes, with notes by Roger Ingpen;[1] and again, in three volumes with notes by Arnold Glover and introduction by Austin Dobson, in the Dent, Dutton edition.[2] Based upon the sixth edition somewhat dutiful in appearance and heavy in the hand, the three Dutton volumes give us six prefaces and the dedication, a facsimile of the original title page, the Boswell foot-notes and notes by the editor, the "chronological catalogue of the prose works of Samuel Johnson," and an index. With decorous animation, Mr. Dobson tells of the houses in which Doctor Johnson lived and of places where he dined. One delights to be reminded of The Crown and Anchor, Apollo Chamber, The Pine Apple in New Street, likes to be told of Doctor Johnson's patronizing The Turk's Head because it "had not much business," and to reread the testimony of Ozias Humphrey, the miniature painter, that Doctor Johnson was "so sententious and so knowing" that it was "impossible to argue with him," that "when he began to talk, everything was 'as *correct* as a *second edition*.' "

A FONDNESS for compactness and severity of format, tempts one to wish to keep one's Oxford Boswell; but in honesty one admits that it is possible for this most self-sufficient narrative to be enhanced by portraits and drawings. To commend a work of art by saying that one is unaware of it, is doubtful praise, but the typographic—perhaps calligraphic—minute severity of the sketches by Herbert Railton, renders them a species of printers' flowers, affixed but not intruded.

Boswell's folly is in its egregious indocility, classic; nevertheless it is as Sir Edmund Gosse observes, through Boswell, that "a great leader of intellectual society was able after his death to carry on unabated, and even heightened, the tyrannous ascendency of his living mind." Boswell allows "his hero to paint his own portrait." He is indeed the artist, demonstrating as he does, "that in no writings whatever can be found more *bark and steel for the mind*" than in those of Doctor Johnson, and aware of his vanity, one is deeply affected by his irrelevantly modest request to posterity: "If this work should at any future period be reprinted, I hope that care will be taken of my orthography." The relation between Boswell and Doctor Johnson "must sometimes be admitted even by friends," says Professor Saintsbury, "as that of bear and monkey, a contrast diverting and effective, but almost too violent for the best art." Nevertheless, he says also, of Boswell: "He is often actually on the scene: he is constantly speaking in his own person; and yet we never think of him as the man with the pointing-stick at the panorama, as the beadle at the function, as the ring-master of the show. He seems to stand rather in the relation of the epic poet to his characters, narrating, omnipresent, but never in the way. No other biographer, I repeat, seems to me to have reached quite this pitch of art."

In this age of curiosity, of excursiveness and discursiveness, one is impelled by the thoroughness even more than by the virtuosity of Doctor Johnson. One may say of him as he said of Sir Thomas Browne, that he "used exotick words which if rejected, must be supplied by circumlocution; . . . in defense of his uncommon words and expressions, we must consider that he had uncommon sentiments." "I'll mind my own business," said Doctor Johnson, and accuracy was apparently part of that business. He felt, says Boswell, that if accuracy is to be habitual, one must never suffer any careless expression to escape one or attempt to deliver thoughts without arranging them in the clearest manner. In alluding to "a certain female friend's 'laxity of narration, and inattention to truth,' 'I am as much vexed (said he) at the ease with which she hears it mentioned to her, as at the thing itself.' " Gracefully to enlarge upon slight and untested premises is a temptation, for scarcely any one loves toil for its own sake. Diligent though not inclined to diligence, Doctor Johnson is the author of what one may justifiably term "works." In his writings we have so competent a grasp of what was to be said, that we have the effect of italics without the use of them. There is also an abundant naturalness, and a simplicity which like that of Abraham Lincoln, was not ashamed to be vulnerable to distress. "Beauclerk had such a propensity to satire," says Boswell, "that at one time Johnson said to him, 'You never open your mouth but with the intention to give pain; and you have often given me pain, not from the power of what you said, but from seeing your intention.'" Doctor Johnson's prodigiousness, vociferousness, and fighting form are made much of. His dialectic has sometimes the aspect of a bout at quarter-staff, but is also, vibrant with sensibility, and one cannot dismiss from one's mind the boldness and the humility of those unselfdefensive words to Thomas Warton: "You will be pleased to make my compliments to all my friends; and be so kind, at every idle hour, as to remember, dear Sir, Yours," and "I have a great mind to come to Oxford at Easter; but you will not invite me. Shall I come uninvited, or stay here where nobody perhaps would miss me if I went? A hard choice! But such is the world to, dear Sir, Yours." Consciousness of lack or of disappointment is an odd part of self-sufficiency and an unselfconscious attributing of value to the minute is seen in the statement: "Nothing is little to him that feels it with great simplicity; a mind able to see common incidents in their real state is disposed by very common incidents to very serious contemplations." Confident and businesslike, his "gorgeous declamation" is sometimes "splendid," never showy. "I think," he says, "there is some reason for questioning whether the body and mind are not so proportioned, that the one can bear all which can be inflicted on the other; whether virtue cannot stand its ground as long as life, and whether a soul well principled will not be sooner separated than subdued." In its remoteness from fashion, the style of this passage recalls Sir Thomas Browne. And in "the uniform vivid texture" of other of his prose, surely it is not a mistake to perceive that "subtlety of disquisition and strength of language" which he found in the author of *The Religio*.

One cannot perhaps be an "unofficial head of English literature," but one may be an apprentice, inferring much from the analytical thinking and "spoken essays" of one who *was*, of one who remarked in speaking of Dryden: "He who excels has a right to teach, and he whose judgment is incontestable, may without usurpation, examine and decide." Waiving as one may, certain of Doctor Johnson's "judgments," one can ill afford to disregard his example. That is to say, one may if one will, avoid faults of negligence; one need not—if one has read and thought—be on the watch for novelty; one may be "lofty without exaggeration"; "the force of one's disapproval may go into personal affirmation."

[1] *Boswell's Life of Johnson* edited, with notes, by Roger Ingpen. Bath. G. Baytun.
[2] *Boswell's Life of Johnson* edited, with notes, by Austin Dobson. Illustrated. E. P. Dutton and Company.

The Dial, 80 (April 1926), 353–56.

.   .   .

I T is true that "peculiar style must precede peculiar expression" and that literary fastidiousness is for the most part, implicit in precise, brilliant thinking. Nevertheless, there is a kind of virtuosity or prodigiousness of diction which is distinctly associated in one's mind with some rather than all, good writers. We attribute to let us say Machiavelli, Sir Francis Bacon, John Donne, Sir Thomas Browne, Doctor Samuel Johnson, a particular kind of verbal effectiveness—a nicety and point, a pride and pith of utterance, which is in a special way different from the admirableness of Wordsworth or of Hawthorne. Suggesting conversation and strengthened by etymology there is a kind of effortless compactness which precludes ornateness, a "fearful felicity," in which like the pig in the churn, imagination seems to provide its own propulsiveness. We have it in Gabriell Harvey's "right Iuggler, as ful of his sleights, wyles, fetches, casts of Legerdmaine, toyes to mocke Apes withal, odde shiftes and knauish practizes, as his skin can holde," and in Sir Thomas Browne's "Bees, Ants, and Spiders": "In these narrow Engines there is more curious Mathematicks"—than in whales, elephants, dromedaries, and camels—"and the civility of these little Citizens more neatly sets forth the Wisdom of their Maker."

Perfect diction is not particularly an attribute of America. We have it, however, in the geometrically precise, snow-flake forms of Henry James. In Poe's criticism, there are crystals if not absolute symmetry, and Whistler is our perhaps outstanding example of verbal *esprit*. There is in Wallace Stevens a certain irony, dignity, and richness: in Ezra Pound, a vigilant exactness: and E. E. Cummings is admirably synthetic. It is true that in America, we sometimes lack altitude and as masters of slang, we do, as we are often told, excel.

To a recent tract of The Society for Pure English,[1] Doctor Robert Bridges contributes an article upon Anglo-American Vocabulary, in which most rewardingly he quotes Professor F. N. Scott: "Where," it is asked, "will the

Englishman learn the esoteric meaning of 'key-noter,' 'he's the berries,' "
and "how will he translate our 'poor' series,—'poor fish, poor shrimp, poor
dub?' " Of the three suggested classes of vernacular, "the idiom of slang or
'violent colloquialism,' " of "the idiom of commonplace reality," and of "the
idiom of intellectual interests," he quotes Professor Scott as saying that "in
all the words and patterns of speech used to express the profoundest and
most useful ideas . . . the two languages differ slightly, if at all."

"The literary as distinguished from the learned," will find these tracts of
The Society for Pure English, persuasively fastidious. We have in the present
issue a consideration by Mr. H. W. Fowler of "the use of italic," and of
"fused participle"; also notes on various words—replace and substitute,
standpoint, onto, due, and Mahomet. Apropos of standpoint, point of view,
or viewpoint, "the perplexed stylist," says Mr. Fowler, "is at present inclined
to cut loose and experiment with *angle*." New spellings are recommended,
among which we find malease for *malaise*, memorandums for memoranda,
medieval for mediaeval, and peony for paeony.

A "rough but reliable statement of the Society's finances" is offered so
pleasantly that it cannot share the fate of most tables of statistics, and one
is impelled also by the method of the following paragraph with regard to the
price of the tracts, to quote it:

> Times have been unfavorable to cheap production; and the decent style
> which we consider indispensable has had an enhanced value since 1914.
> But one gentleman wrote that in his experience "Tracts" were usually given
> away. That is true in some departments of Tractation, especially of Tracts
> as no mortal would dream of buying: but, though one cannot tell what
> prosperity or calamity may be in store for us, it seems unlikely that we
> shall ever embrace this desperate expedient of philanthropy.

In Sir Richard Paget's article, "The Nature of Human Speech," despite
a special application to Great Britain, there are for any reader, potent
provocations to discussion and to reflection. "A pure language," says Sir
Richard, "may be compared with a pure style in architecture," in which
"similar structural problems are dealt with by similar methods." The "I be,
thou be, we be, you be, they be," of the West Country, he finds "a far more
advanced form of Pure English than the "I am, thou art, he is, we, ye, or
they are" of Standard Southern English. "Again," he says, "there is another
criterion by which language may reasonably be judged, viz. the audibility
of its elemental sounds. In this respect we find our Standard Southern English
very inferior to the 'Wessex' dialect, and it is actually worsening."

In the comment following Sir Richard's article, the question is asked, would it be possible to discard unvoiced sounds and if so, "would it be well to do so?" To do so is impossible, it is answered, "unless the recent mechanical reproductions of speech . . . should supplant them by their voiced forms." As for the second question—whether the discarding of these sounds would be aesthetically an improvement or impoverishment of the language: this is an aesthetic question, on which our prejudices are so strong that we can scarcely trust our opinion; but it does seem to us unmistakable that if *z, v,* and *dh,* were substituted for *s, f,* and *th,* whenever these occur in our speech, the result would be a great loss of lightness and variety with a definite effect of trammeled monotony. It is, however, impossible to imagine everyone saying *vah ov* for *far off.* . . . And we utterly repudiate the principle that speech should be made only of sounds which can be easily heard fifty yards off." "The displacement of *larboard* by *port,* was secured by an Admiralty instruction of 1844 'because the distinction between *starboard* and *port* is so much more marked.' But . . . conversation and what is called table-talk cannot be ruled by the wide acoustics of a ship's bridge in a gale, or of public halls and monster meetings."

When in Maine the harbor-master is the *habba-masta,* when in New York seabirds are *seaboids,* when as in the Negro vernacular, the tenth becomes the *tent,* certainly is *certainy,* and Paris is *Parus,* the curiosity of the unprofound, with regard to the acoustics of speech, may seem like that of Esquimaux listening for the first time to a phonograph. Our completely fascinated interest in these matters is, however, not to be disguised and our desire to know what topics may occupy the attention of the fastidious, is genuine.

[1] S. P. E. Tract No. XXII. "The Nature of Human Speech." By Sir Richard Paget, Bart. "On the Use of Italic, Fused Participle, etc." By H. W. Fowler. "Reviews & Miscellaneous Notes." By Robert Bridges. The Oxford University Press, American Branch, New York.

The Dial, 80 (May 1926), 444–48.

• • •

W E are often reminded that the civilized world is uncivilized. The malevolence of a protective tariff seems to be as great as that of the "trust." We are begged to realize that among human beings, "there should be no power to exploit and no fear of being exploited." We sometimes scrutinize our national charitableness and wish that we could cancel the indebtedness to us of our various foreign debtors—not that we might buy goodwill, but that we might enjoy the sense of friendliness.

The world of art also is assailed by a spirit of domination, gainfulness, or expediency. "No one," says Roger Fry,[1] "however much he admires a bronze on purely aesthetic grounds, fails, if he is going to purchase it, to find out how many exactly similar pieces the artist purposes to make. Its rarity is part of its value to almost any owner." And depressingly but justifiably he defines as an "opifact," "any object made by man not for direct use but for . . . various forms of ostentation."

An even less veiled accentuating of one's "personal worth either in his own or . . . in others' eyes," we have in our present economically irresponsible detailed ornateness and cleverly demure exalting of what is anatomically decorative. Clement of Alexandria with the averted eye of the jailer, deplored as it were prophetically, an admiration for green stones and for pearls and wished that "our life might be anything rather than a pageant." Anton Theodor Hartmann's "The Hebrew Woman at her Toilette and in her Bridal Character,"[2] "weeded" by De Quincey "of that wordiness which has made the original unreadable," is as readable as it is modern in its complement of reticulated foot-wear, of trellis-work sandals, of veils, and *bijouterie*. What but contemporary is the mania of which we read, for "*Suns* and *Moons*" and "half-moons," for "golden snakes" and pigments—a "black rim" being "traced about the eyelid . . . to throw a dark and majestic shadow over the eye"; to give it "a lustrous expression; to increase its apparent size; and to apply the force of contrast to the white of the eye."

When persons contribute to the support of a hospital or to a fund for eastern relief or to the support of orphans, some point out that charity is advertising and that benefactors to causes in which there may be Jewish orphans or invalids, are probably Jewish, and are in a sense giving to themselves. Civic projects for entertaining industrial workers, or feeding children in tenement districts, are deprecated as being a subterfuge on the part of ostentatious people, to amuse themselves or to make themselves prominent.

In his voluntary poverty as in his conviction that "industry must be spiritualized" Mahatma Gandhi can, however, scarcely be thought to have resorted to a clever means of enriching himself. The late William Rockhill Nelson, unhamperingly so far as one can see, provides that the presidents of three universities shall appoint trustees to establish and maintain in Kansas City under one of the largest art foundations in this country, an art museum. The wish of Mr. Rockefeller that there should be a new museum of antiquities in Egypt seems generous; and what species of self-exultation is evinced by the recent anonymous gift to one of our universities of a million dollars for the establishing of an art school? Sir Henry Lunn has created a foundation to promote unity among the churches of the world and peace among the nations of the world. Adding to it himself, Samuel Yellin has made the Philadelphia Award received by him this past year, a fund for assisting ironworkers to go abroad to study beautiful metal-work in the museums and buildings in Europe. The John Simon Guggenheim Memorial Foundation Fellowships for Advanced Study Abroad have been established: "To improve the quality of education and the practice of the arts and professions in the United States, to foster research, and to provide for the cause of better international understanding." It does seem to us that there is active today, an altruism which is disinterested. Can it be possible that we are stupendously naïve in the face of what is merely sublime knavery?

If Phoenecian trivialities seem to find more favor with us than The Barnard Cloisters, early American furniture, or the records of The Smithsonian Institute, a lugubrious conclusion need not be drawn. The Huxley Memorial Medal has been for the second time awarded by The Royal Anthropological Society of Great Britain, to an American. Certain German chemical discoveries; the steam engine made in England, the telephone, the airplane, and certain noted electrical inventions of America, are not local property. To part with a valuable thing without losing it, bespeaks for this thing, a very special kind of value.

The basic selfishness of human nature, the elaborate crookedness, and the irrelevant lightness of civilization are, of course, not a myth. "No deed of ours, I suppose, on this side of the grave," says Lewis Carroll, "is really unselfish." In view of events of the past year, however, it is not so Alice-in-Wonderland-like as it may sound, to say that no deed of ours does look to us in its every aspect, selfish.

[1] *The Hogarth Essays: Art and Commerce* by Roger Fry. The Hogarth Press.
[2] *Toilette of the Hebrew Lady Exhibited in Six Scenes* by Thomas De Quincey. Edwin Valentine Mitchell.

The Dial, 80 (June 1926), 532–34.

• • •

POETRY, that is to say the poetic, is a primal necessity. Condoned as a labored flight, the concept in Rasselas of the happy valley in Abyssinia, is typically expressive of the universal need for something which transcends the literal. "On one part were flocks and herds feeding in the pastures, on another all the beasts of the chase, frisking in the lawns; the sprightly kid was bounding on the rocks, the subtle monkey frolicking in the trees, and the solemn elephant reposing in the shade." It would seem that the more seriously careful responsibility is, the greater the need for imagination and the surer, an apperception of it.

Unfortunately, the romantic book which is insistently advertised as a compendium of fire and flavor, may darken more than it diverts and often it is in the child's book that one finds the really potent principle of which we hear so much. No doubt successive editions of Hawthorne's *Wonder Book*, of *The Wind in the Willows*, *The Little White Bird*, of Padraic Colum's "children's books," and of *Alice in Wonderland*,[1] are required by grown people whose patience with the mode is at an end. Seeming to some in childhood incomprehensibly epic in character, Lewis Carroll is to mature taste, appropriate *espièglerie*. Overcoming all sense of the somnambulistic predetermined formlessness of a conscious trance, certain qualities are beyond cavil. There are the personable, self-contained, human completeness of the rabbit, and the attentive uncontradictoriness of Alice. A precision of unlogic in Lewis Carroll, is logic's best apologist—a hypothetically accurate illogical law of cause and effect. And the connection between the kitten as precipitating the dream and the fact that all the poems are about fish, is most precise.

In commending technical merits, one pays tribute to a deeper power, and is in this instance in debt to something which is in many senses, poetic. We may read in an English weekly of a raven which built a nest in a cypress-tree with the assistance of a boy, the boy handing the sticks and the raven building the nest; and find in the idea of Alice's "going messages for a rabbit" or watching a mousehole for the cat, an equally satisfactory unliteralness. The colloquy in the railway carriage, of the gentleman dressed in white paper, of the Goat, the Beetle, the Gnat, and the Lass, is plausibly fantastic because so unplausible, as is the metamorphosis of the grunting baby—which "held out its arms and legs in all directions, 'just like a starfish,' thought Alice." "So she set the little creature down, and felt quite relieved to see it trot away quietly into the wood. 'If it had grown up,' she said to herself, 'it would have made a dreadfully ugly child: but it makes rather a handsome pig, I think.' "

Books proffered as children's books are sometimes for older readers. Babies' books, indeed, Jules Lemaître's *Alphabet* for instance, and Anatole France's children's books, *The Mad Dog*, *John Gilpin's Ride*, and *The House*

That Jack Built, are philosophically for the man; and a literary monument—let us say *Robinson Crusoe*—seems sometimes to those who are not grown up, a kind of apocalyptic aesthetic revelation. *Tom Brown's Schooldays* sounds more limber than it is; *The Water Babies,* and Hans Andersen seem old for children, and to the unsuspecting, very young reader, *Alice in Wonderland* is complex. Lewis Carroll's books are now, however, as Mr. Woollcott says in the introduction to this present edition—folk-lore. Alice has become our mentor and is at no one's mercy. The rather grown-up, fashionable, white and red board covers are for the patient adult, but the illustrations are by John Tenniel, and for one's own part, the polite, indoor, lighthaired, straighthaired aspect of an as he sees her extraordinary ordinary child, could not be supplanted.

Mr. Woollcott speaks of the many languages into which *Alice in Wonderland* has been translated, of satires upon her, plays about her, music and illustrations which have been made for her. He tells us something of Lewis Carroll, the "shy, retreating man" whose life was scholastic and whose spirit was immaculate. If not all of these introductory words are shy and retreating or sparely scholastic, they ungrudgingly invite us to share the pleasure and the power that only a certain kind of uncommon nonsense can impart.

[1] *Alice in Wonderland. Through the Looking Glass. The Hunting of the Snark* by Lewis Carroll. Illustrations by John Tenniel. Introduction by Alexander Woollcott. Boni and Liveright.

The Dial, 81 (August 1926), 177–78.

• • •

In a tabernacle of a toure,
As I strode musying on the mone,
A crouned quene, most of honoure,
Apeared in gostly syght ful done.
'I may nat leue mankynde allone.'
MIDDLE ENGLISH LYRIC

A C C U S E D not long since, of a disaffecting tendency to find ourselves of more concern than the cosmos, we are charged also it seems, with failing to find these cosmic selves amusing—of maintaining in robe and cowl, an atmosphere of cloistered gloom. One cannot be annoyed to be associated with cowls and cloisters, admirable as they are on the stage and in history; but one may have at the same time, a taste for chess tournaments and whippet races, and if we are open to the charge of publishing that which is less hopeful than we are ourselves, we can but recall as conducive to equipoise, the experience of many a positive spirit who has been misunderstood. William Blake, who died in August one hundred years ago and was in most respects exceedingly human, seems to be regarded even today as a victim of the cabbala; Shelley has been regarded as wicked; Edwin Valentine Mitchell reminds us in *Book Notes* for June—July, that Havelock Ellis was at first felt by some, to be "a serpent of immorality" and notes Lord Morley's dissatisfaction in 1866, with Swinburne's *New Poems*. "Mr. Swinburne is much too stoutly bent," said Lord Morley in *The Saturday Review*, "on taking his own course to pay any attention to critical monitions as to the duty of the poet, or any warnings of the worse than barrenness of the field in which he has chosen to labor."[1]

Fortified in examining its "humble beginnings," we do aspire to common sense, foregoing confetti. There is much in life and there is much in art that is not productive of complaisance. One enjoys a sense of magnanimity in George Washington's dismounting to assist a stranger to right an overturned carriage, and denies implication in the slave auction—in the "sickly" creature's going for little and the "good" one's selling for more; but both incidents are really ourselves and are in the eye of honesty, to be verified. Benefits become obsolete and abuses become obsolete as is easily apparent in glancing at the years 1776, 1876, and the present time. In every age the egotist strives to devour leaner spirits, but has not so far as one can see, outwitted the aesthetic judiciary. Although we have come to be easily embarrassed by prosperous luckiness according to formula, the prevailing happy ending of the novel of 1876 is not yet outmoded. Life is often painful, however, and it is inevitable that art should not ignore the fact. An uneducated reader of one public library novel a week, deprecates as a misleading title, *Tess of the D'Urbervilles*, but finds the book "gripping." Something beneath the surface, a sense of life and of roots, is attested by work which is aesthetically serious—a scientifically potent energy which seems to involve us in a centripetal force of its own. As Mr. Roger Fry remarks in his article upon "Art and Commerce," "a really creative design has a certain violence and insistence, a spiritual energy, which is disquieting to people at first sight, however much they may come afterwards to like it." It is evident that art can wait to be discerned and our own unfashionably awful intensity is frequently beguiled by an occasional "peece of the World discovered" or "pretie discourse of honest Loue, very pleasant for all Gentlemen to reade, and most necessary to remember."

[1] *Notorious Literary Attacks* edited with an introduction by Albert Mordell. Boni and Liveright.

The Dial, 81 (September 1926), 267–68.

• • •

I T seems sometimes as if "printing has virtually ceased to exist and mere publication has taken its place." One does not feel that in order to be pleasant reading, a thing must be expensive or limited, and often the well printed book is too fine. But certain lovers and producers of good typography there are in America, modest and intentional, as is evinced by a recent exhibition at The Grolier Club. One welcomes any willingness "to Rescue from the Iron Teeth of TIME, the Original of that Noble MYSTERY, which gives Immortality even to Learning it Self, and is the great Conservator of all other Arts and Sciences,"[1] finding significance even, in subtleties analogous to those of printing: in the Indian pictograph[2] and in the arranged grace of such tall lower-case characters as appear on a rock in the giants', unicorns', and Dragon's lair near Mixnitz, Austria.[3]

Among importations there is often the very thing we like: we cannot hope to initiate the Dutch, German, English, French, or Spanish printers into any very much higher beauty than that which they have known. The Deutsche Buchgewerbeverein in Leipsic has sent us its recent issue, in which are to be found some regal title pages and other specimen pages. Conspicuously experienced and agreeable to the *Bucherskorpion*, are the impressions from wood, exhibiting the grain and silky texture of the block.

T H E woodcuts on view at The Public Library are as "early" and orderly as one could wish, showing customary respect to Dürer, to a Lucas Cranach "Repose in Egypt" and a Holbein "Erasmus." Some fifteenth-century anony-mous Italian book illustrations of a-monk-in-a-garden sentiment are there, and some severely fluent early French designs. Excitement resides chiefly, however, in the books—in a first issue of the first edition of a block book copy of the German *Biblia Pauperium* printed in black ink on one side only of the paper and illuminated. The intensively stiff Lorenzo de Medici-like augustness of the Breydenbach fifteenth-century *Perigrinatio* detains one as does the perpendicular *esprit* and fencing-foil erectness of the lines on the page at which the 1491 *Schatzbehalta* is open, and there is a 1499 Aldus edition—open at pairs of elephants, flutes, harps, banners, and other constituents of a triumph. To have shown certain pre-Anthony Cole early first American work seems unjustly thorough. As for the present moment, Eric Gill, Gordon Craig, J. J. Lankes, and Hunt Diederich, are there, and others, not; some master hands are missing.

WE are told by Mr. Karl Čapek that Europe wasted her time for many thousands of years and that this is the source of her inexhaustibility and fertility—that America's predilection for huge dimensions, for speed and success, is corrupting the world. Ambition provokes action, however. Having left Europe under the auspices of "the most Invincible King of Spain," the eight pomegranates of Granada, the castles of Castile, and the lions of Aragon, Columbus—"admiral of the ocean fleet" of three caravels on its two hundred twenty-four day voyage to Cipano[4]—says in his narrative of discovery,[5] "I remained in no place longer than the winds have forced me," and adds that the rewards of arrival "would have been much greater if I had been aided by as many ships as the occasion required." He found the natives "timid and full of fear" and says that "the women appear to work more than the men," prompting perhaps no inevitable comparison with the present. Assisted by the typewriter, the sewing-machine, and the telephone, the American white woman—and with her, every other—seems as time goes on, more serviceable and less servile and the "natives" are, one likes to think, becoming more at home. Columbus might approve; and Burgomasters, Schout, and Schepen might not. Of these last-named model councillors, more later.

[1] *An Essay on the ORIGINAL, USE and EXCELLENCY, of the Noble ART and MYSTERY of PRINTING* by GEORGE LARKIN, Senior, *Typographer*. DUBLIN: Printed by A. Rhames in the Year MDCCXXII. In the possession of Douglas C. McMurtrie.

[2] *Universal Indian Sign Language of the Plains Indians of North America*, by William Tompkins.

[3] Illustration—*Journal of The American Museum of Natural History*, May–June, 1926.

[4] Reaching Fernandino and Isabella, Columbus supposed that he was in the neighborhood of Japan, sailed south, and on the 28th of October, reached Cuba.

[5] *The Letter of Columbus on the Discovery of America*. From the originals in the Lenox Library. A Facsimile of the Pictorial Edition, with a New and Literal Translation and a Complete Reprint of the Oldest Four Editions in Latin. The New York Public Library, 1892.

The Dial, 81 (October 1926), 356–58.

• • •

THE menace and the mecca which we regret to be and are glad to be, is mirrored to us from time to time in impressions of us published by distinguished visitors to America, and impersonal or self-conscious as one may be when reminded of the adequacy or inadequacy of our cities and our citizens, there was much to interest one the past summer in the exhibition descriptive of the history of New Netherland, at the New York Public Library. Among the engravings the well-known but to genealogists of Dutch New York, never hackneyed 1717 William Burgis map of the south prospect of New York commends itself—depicting cattle and cattle-pen, the French Church, the English Church, the Dutch Church, the Fort, the Chappel in the fort, "Collonel Morris' Fancy turning to windward with a sloop of common mould," under the not entirely it would seem characteristically American legend, *Arte non Impeto.*

Without an interior decorator's fondness for cartography or a placing of insistence upon first things, one may yet enjoy Girolomo da Verrazzano's fearlessly definite and unusual map of the world—the first map of Italian origin with the name America on it, and as an associate *tyrannus rex* of geographical daring, the 1529 Diego Ribera. Curiosity, and tenacity with boldness are implicit in these books, maps, and pamphlets relating to and written by first visitors to America, and may well counteract in the contemporary American, one feels, our prevailing tendency to remove as one man to Europe.

CHILDREN'S Book Week bespeaks as annually, the irrelevantly necessary enthusiasm of grown people. In writing for children one may not, as Anatole France has said, assume a style—one must think; and too, in making pictures for children no indifferent species of thinking is operative. Pictorially descriptive officious assistance is its own ostracist and on the other hand as in the instance of the Brownie Books by Palmer Cox, illustrations and text may be disassociable. If it is possible to be both hidebound and hospitable, children's books presented collectively can perhaps more than others, make one so.

THE death of Doctor Charles W. Eliot is notable in its reminding us primarily of life and only incidentally of death. An educator as it seems to us, even when a student, Doctor Eliot recalls to us Ruskin's remark that education is not the equalizer but the discerner of men. We associate with him an instinct for the development of character, a "passion for justice and for progress"—for education in the sense in which Matthew Arnold, Cardinal Newman, and Aristotle conceived it, not as attainment but discipline. Alert aesthetically to his not ungentle classic restraint and a "deceptive mildness" which has never deceived us, we have been aware of much else. The power residing in his so seldom anticipated, not to be evaded judgments upon life can never be to us other than an enduring vitality.

The Dial, 81 (November 1926), 447–48.

*   *   *

> *Besides the Howres, many things also belonging to Geography, Astrology, and Astronomy, are by the Sunnes shadow made visible to the eye.*
>   FATHER HALL

"IT is seldom that the professed grounds correspond with the real motives of a war," we are told, and in the drawing room one is familiar with that form of preamble to hostilities which is said to have been Renan's: "You are right, a thousand times over." The attainment of international, even of national harmony, is always it would seem deliberate, and one perceives that it is only in the world of aesthetics that a tendency toward universal harmony is unconscious. The unquiet nature of the artist is proverbial, genius being in some sense always in revolt. But hostile though specific theories may be and riotous as the artist may sometimes seem in his attitude toward the existing body of art, in so far as a thing is really a work of art it confirms other works of art. The incompatibility of Whistler and Ruskin is a by-word: imagination, however, transcends that which is personal and expressed divergencies of belief but point to the fact that of those interested in certain subject-matter not all are of the same hatching. Annoyed by Ruskin's "teachings," Whistler was obviously unable to remove his works of art from that world of art in which were Ruskin's corroborating masterpieces; and a sinuously alert aesthetic sensibility conspicuously unites certain living philosophers, be they philosophically ever so distinct from one another. The aesthetic malcontent is out of court, for wherever there is art there is equilibrium— a basic adjustment toward which the most distinguished and the most extinguished works of art alike converge. As we are aware, it is determination with resistance, not determination with resentment, which results in poise. In blindly disparaging another, one shows merely that one envies him his realness and wishes that he were what one says he is. Agitated in the disposing of his own turbulent business as were "the Egyptian sculptors who set themselves problems a little beyond their comfort," the artist is in a state of profound activity, emerging from darkness into light like the grain which he eats, unable often to recognize in himself that "summer in December" of which enduring art consists. The ruffled genius might in his acuteness realize that sometimes he fights with that with which he is agreeing, and is like the hour, marked by a shadow which seeming to cut the sun, defines it. Although "the judgment of experts on one another is at variance," their genius is not; perception is always as Traherne would say, "innocent": insurrection being contrary to that sensitiveness and receptiveness which

> . . . like the fairest glass,
> Or spotless polished brass,
> Themselves soon in their object's image clothe.

In making works of art, the only legitimate warfare is the inevitable warfare between imagination and medium and one finds it impossible to convince oneself that the part of the artist's nature which is "rash and combustible" has not been tamed by the imagination, in those instances in which the result achieved is especially harmonious.

The Dial, 81 (December 1926), 535–36.

• • •

As is observed by a writer upon St. Francis in a recent article in *The Spectator*, humility is a quality which attracts us—though not to imitation. One is impressed today by the assured manner of the writing world, by the disfavor into which "we" has fallen—by a bold omitting and by an equally bold, supercilious much using of the designation, "Mr"; by the piquant or predatory as one likes to look at it, transparent utilizing by novelists, of story and style as found ready made in the lives of their friends. Far from being a disgrace, awkwardness is often an excellence and the Downright Scholar is not resented, whose "mind is too much taken up with his mind . . . who has not humbled his meditations to the industry of compliment." But literary "neatness" implies a certain decorum of manner as of matter. A theme had, like a house, better not have "the appearance of having been thrown out of its own windows." Egotism is usually subversive of sagacity. Critical remarks at all events, which are uncongenial to the object of them, are often uncongenial to others, and having had a great deal of such careless grandeur, we seem now to require a corrective—as sick dragons, wild lettuce; that is to say, care and uninflation.

Pressure of business modifies self-consciousness and genuine matter for exposition seems to aid effectiveness; in for instance, Darwin's scientific descriptions. A similar faithfulness to the scene—to the action and aspect of what makes the scene important, alive or stationed there—rewards one in the writings of Audubon, the ornithologist.[1] A certain method of "gentility" may annoy one—an allusion to "the wild luxuriance of untamed nature," or to "the husbandman cheerily plying his healthful labors"; but "The American Woodsman's" delineation of America a hundred years ago, is an able one. Quite as opportune as the American Turkey Cock, the Great American Hen and Young, as the Trumpeter Swan turning upon the surface of the glassy ripples it has made, to snap at an unwary insect—is his portraiture of places, animals, and persons. "Its gait, while traveling," says Audubon of the opossum, "and at a time when it supposes itself unobserved, is altogether ambling: in other words, it, like a young foal, moves the two legs of one side forward at once." He sees or rather experiences a hurricane in such a way that we also seem to feel its impact. Ice in the Mississippi when beginning to break, "split," he says, "with reports like those of heavy artillery," the congealed mass breaking into large fragments, "some of which rose nearly erect here and there, and again fell with thundering crash." Reminiscences of turtles, "turtlers," birds and "eggers," are no more precise than those of persons—of "Colonel Boone," of Thomas Bewick, and of the mild, gruesome, Poe-Beardsley-like, exotically ignorant Monsieur de T., who is ceremonially present as an "eccentric naturalist."

Francis Hobart Herrick has assembled, with an introductory biography, and the omission only of "Remarks on the Form of the Toes of Birds," what now that we have it, seems in Audubon's *Delineations of American Scenery and Character*, indispensable. These "episodes" written to relieve the tedium of descriptive ornithology and to accompany the 435 double elephant folio plates published in London during the years 1826 and 1838—do relieve tedium. The cut-throats, the barbecues, the "coon" and 'possum hunts, the Cane-Brakes, the loneliness and discomfort of pioneer life in Audubon's America, seem strange to us; and in a way, since we are not quite free or improved, so does his saying:

Large roads are now laid out, cultivation has converted the woods into fertile fields, taverns have been erected, and much of what we Americans call comfort is to be met with. So fast does improvement proceed in our abundant and free country.

But there is apparently a consensus of opinion that we are "rapid," an adjective much used by Audubon in alluding to his own actions. Paul Morand[2] accuses our trans-continental railway system of having shot him through America like a surgical needle, aware as he is at the same time of our fifty-story modern Chaldean architecture; of the little anonymous way-station with its old Ford—the new world's one ruin; of our wheat-fields undulating like music, of snow overhead on the sides of *Les Rockies;* of what seems, one infers, our attention to business in hand at the expense of perspective—our ostrich-like concentration and would-be emancipation from consequences. And a study of our domestic manners provokes not unprofitably, enquiry into this analogy of the ostrich.

Bertrand Russell has reminded us that the Puritan was concerned with happiness; the contemporary man, with pleasure. The progress, if one may so speak of it, of manners, fashions, sport, and art, recurs to one. An aesthetic agrarianism, humanitarianism, society's permission to play an instrument, to paint pictures, to act, and dance, prevail: and various infamies—the competitive spirit in undertakings which should be spontaneous, a supplant-ing in baseball, football, tennis, walking, and swimming, of the amateur spirit by the professional spirit. Even in the province of good looks, we are brow-beaten. It is insisted upon by cities, states, and countries, that we have them—our embarrassment in competition being mitigated only by the superlatively similar humiliation of sister nations. All these "developments" are irrelevant so far as one can see, to happiness, very much as provincially exaggerated collegiate interest in athletics has always seemed to the under-graduate with literary tastes, irrelevant to reading.

In *Our Times*, Mark Sullivan[3] has presented to us, songs, clothes, vehicles, and town talk which we had almost forgotten; and in *The Elegant Eighties*[4] by Henry Collins Brown, we have further moments of amused incredulity with as it were, the brought-to-light collection of photographs and stereop-ticon, or the album with hasps. New York "still had" in the eighties, "a strong frontier atmosphere about it—half mining camp and half Mayfair," says Mr. Brown. How curiously preserved to us both appearances are today, with the Columbus Circle monument jacked protectively out of the way of the new subway, and peculiar to ships' rats and migratory birds, a residen-tially changing polarity among our florists, dress-makers, and art dealers. "The charming old home-town feeling" which prevailed in the city as it then was—that city between Maiden's Lane and "the goats"—may still be felt by the superstitious among us, in the region about Trinity Church and in the streets near Washington Square. The elbow in Broadway caused by the importance of the apple orchard in "an old farm owned by Henry Brevoort," is preserved to us by Mr. Brown, as are various notable contests—the fight to remove women's hats in the theater, the crusade against wearing feathers; the battle to compel shopkeepers to provide seats for their clerks.

Henry Bergh's founding of The Society for the Prevention of Cruelty to Animals, the courts, the theaters, the hotels, homes, streets, torchlight processions, tally-ho excursions, "the crack Lawn Tennis Players, Sears, Dwight, Beeckman, and Taylor," the prides, misfortunes, and whims of one-time New York, are richly present in this book. One values Mr. Brown's "observatory nerves" as Audubon would say. Indeed, as Greek architecture rendered domestic by Thomas Jefferson, seems colonial, New York seems as one reads of it in Valentine's *Manuals*, national; and although an occasional rococo facetiousness scarcely augments vividness, one's rhetorical ear pardons to enthusiasm, incidental offenses.

[1] *Delineations of American Scenery and Character* by John James Audubon. With an Introduction by Francis Hobart Herrick. G. A. Baker and Company.

[2] *Rien que la Terre* par Paul Morand. Bernard Grasset, Paris. Reviewed in *The Dial*, January 1927, page 59.

[3] *Our Times: The United States 1900–1925*. Volume I: "The Turn of the Century" by Mark Sullivan. Charles Scribner's Sons. Reviewed in *The Dial*, November 1926, page 446.

[4] *New York in the Elegant Eighties, Valentine's Manual No. 11* by Henry Collins Brown. Illustrated. Henry Collins Brown.

The Dial, 82 (March 1927), 267–70.

• • •

ORIGINALS are better than replicas and a modern book got up to look precisely like an old one inspires no veneration, though like a photograph of an old binding or book page it may be informing. Real fondness for the unique copy will not however pretend indifference to one of Arber's reprints, to the publications of the Early English Text Society, or other redeeming of what only the nation can afford to own.

In a recent book on William Caxton,[1] the author has appended Caxton's prologues, epilogues, and what she names—significant interpolations. The antique strengths and refinements of speech and thought in these originals, kindle by their substance and manner, enthusiasm for exactness of production and depth of learning—far removed as we may feel ourselves to be from the composite cunning of this original and originating—editor, translator, illustrator, printer, and author.

SOME while ago *The New York Times* recorded the fact that a writer in *The Manchester Guardian* had discovered a suggestion by " 'somebody in America' that Dear Sir should be omitted at the beginning of business letters." The English writer inferred that the innovation had been proposed because the salutation sounds insincere says the writer in *The Times*, but defending the salutation as too obviously insincere even to be thought so, he remarks that "in letters the ceremonious is as a rule more welcome than attempted originality." However cold or inadvertently ironic an epistolary "dear" or "yours" may be, formal approach to and departure from the business seems inevitable. Complete absence of salutation of course as in certain impassioned letters of Keats, Shelley, and Diderot, arrests the attention as the formal salutation is unable to arrest it. Yet in these letters the conclusion is not lacking and one particularly admires that shapely mechanics in which the complimentary close is indivisibly a part of what came before it.

Short-cuts to culture are commended by present-day advertisers to those who would converse fluently, dance correctly, address audiences impressively, speak any foreign language like a cultured native. One can with difficulty place perfect faith in formulae which profess to remedy every mental deficiency; nor thus far has the secret of writing letters been imparted to the undeserving. Professor Saintsbury is sure that "the more the spoken word is heard in a letter the better." Some letters seem more reasoned than speaking. One likes those which are particular without being malapert and charm seems absent where there is not naturalness. Delightful things were to be found in *The American and English Autograph Collection of Mr. A. C. Goodyear*,[2] sold at The Anderson Galleries during February. In the handwriting of some of these letters the author's individuality as we have conceived it seemed curiously evident; and Shenstone does indeed seem to speak rather than write, to the Doctor Percy of the *Reliques:* "I have also read ye Essay on ye present state of learning, written by Dr. Goldsmith, whom you know; and whom such as read it will desire to know." There were letters by Abraham Lincoln and a remarkable letter from Zachary Taylor to his son-in-law, Jefferson Davis. In many of the American letters one feels the tension of crisis; the English letters are companionably philosophical. Southey writes to John May: "There are three classes of people in whose society I find pleasure. Those in whom I meet with similarity of opinion—those who from a similarity of feeling tolerate difference of opinion, & those to whom long acquaintance has attached me, who neither think nor feel with me, but who have the same recollections & can talk of other times, other scenes. . . ."

Of things purporting to be transitory, letters can be seriously a pleasure and as permanently a monument as anything which has been devised. With John Donne one "makes account that this writing of letters when it is with any seriousness, is a kind of extasie, and a departure and secession and suspension of the soul, which doth then communicate itself to two bodies." One can safely affirm at any rate that a writer of letters is not one of those who know much and understand little.

¹ *Caxton—Mirrour of Fifteenth-Century Letters* by Nellie Slayton Aurner. Houghton Mifflin Company.
² Catalogue of The American & English Autograph Collection of Mr. A. C. Goodyear, Buffalo, N.Y. Brochure. The Anderson Galleries.

The Dial, 80 (April 1927), 359–60.

• • •

ACADEMIC feeling, or prejudice possibly, in favor of continuity and completeness is opposed to miscellany—to music programs, composite picture exhibitions, newspapers, magazines, and anthologies. Any zoo, aquarium, library, garden, or volume of letters, however, is an anthology and certain of these selected findings are highly satisfactory. The science of assorting and the art of investing an assortment with dignity are obviously not being neglected, as is manifest in "exhibitions and sales of artistic property," and in that sometimes disparaged, most powerful phase of the anthology, the museum. Persons susceptible to objects of "extreme significance" may remember with gratitude in the late Lieutenant Commander William Barrett's Naval and Marine Collection at the Anderson Galleries, an albino tortoise shell decorated in scrimshaw with an American clipper ship in full sail; and in the Spanish collection of Señor D. Raimundo Ruiz, at the American Art Galleries in December, a remarkable Gothic forged iron gate and "some small objects." A two-edged Dresden rapier from the armory of the Fortress Hohenwerfen (The Anderson Galleries) seemed to one, super-eminent—the serpent-like nudity of the interlacing spirals about the grip suggesting Swinburne's comment upon Rossetti's *The Song of Lilith:* "It has the supreme luxury of liberty in its measured grace and lithe melodious motion of rapid and revolving harmony, the subtle action and majestic recoil, the mysterious charm as of soundless music which hangs about the serpent when it stirs or springs." One cannot be dead to the sagacity inherent in some specimens of sharkskin, camellia-leaf, orange-peel, semi-eggshell, or sang-de-boeuf glaze; nor be blind to the glamour of certain "giant," "massive," "magnificent" objects in pork-fat or spinach-green jade as shown last winter in the collection of Mr. Lee Van Ching at the Anderson Galleries.

THE selective nomenclature—the chameleon's eye if we may call it so—of the connoisseur, expresses a genius for differences; analogous dissimilarities in Man Ray's *Of What Are The Young Films Dreaming*, exemplifying variously this art of comparison and synthesis. In what degree diverse subject-matters lend themselves to association, is a question. Comprehensive paper, cloth, and leather "libraries" attest the public's docility towards editors and its respect for transcriptions. We owe much to "the excellent Mr. Bohn" and are conscious of multiple value received, in Cassell's ten-cent paper series. No books in miniature could be more pleasing or in a sense more rare than Gowan's *Nature Books*, or more accomplished in providing that which could not be omitted, than the Frederick A. Stokes "Painters" Series. In issuing *The Pamphlet Poets*,[1] Simon and Schuster credit us with a fondness for poetry irrespective of the year in which it was written. Lincoln MacVeagh in his *The Little Books of New Poetry*[2] assumes that we can enjoy what has not had a fuss made about it; though *The Weed in the Wall*, and *Sussex Poems*, we find conspicuously unobscure. In James A. Woodburn's and the late Alexander Johnson's collection of *American Orations*,[3] we have phenomenally an effect of history recalled as experience. Mr. George H. Putnam, Chairman of the American Committee instituted to give co-operation in the establishment in London University of a chair for instruction in American History, emphasizes in his introduction to the fifth edition of these documents, their value as documented *feeling*. Unfamiliar yet actual, like an animal reconstructed from certain bones, they curiously evoke the past, constituting in their chronological sequence, an anthology which results as a skeleton should, in being a "body."

However expressive the content of an anthology, one notes that a yet more distinct unity is afforded in the unintentional portrait given, of the mind which brought the assembled integers together.

[1] *The Pamphlet Poets: Carl Sandburg* edited by Hughes Mearns; *Elinor Wylie* edited by Laurence Jordan; *Walt Whitman* edited by Louis Untermeyer; *Ralph Waldo Emerson* edited by John Erskine; *Nathalia Crane* edited by Hughes Mearns; *H. D.* edited by Hughes Mearns. Simon and Schuster.

[2] *The Little Books of New Poetry: The Portrait of the Abbot* by Richard Church; *Sussex Poems* by Bennett Weaver; *The Weed in the Wall, and Other Poems* by James McLane;

Beethoven Deaf, and Other Poems by Alec Brown; *A Sorbonne of the Hinterland* by Jacques LeClercq; *A Poet Passes* by D. L. Kelleher. Lincoln MacVeagh. The Dial Press.

³ *American Orations: Studies in American Political History* edited by Alexander Johnson and James Albert Woodburn. With an introduction to the Fifth Edition by George Haven Putnam. Two Volumes. G. P. Putnam's Sons.

The Dial, 82 (May 1927), 449–50.

•   •   •

The Sun's Light when he unfolds it
Depends on the Organ that beholds it.
WILLIAM BLAKE

"THOUSANDS of people can talk," Ruskin says, "for one who can think; but thousands can think for one who can see. To see clearly is poetry, prophecy, and religion all in one." A special kind of seeing, "mental strife," "rapture and labor," are characteristic of few persons indeed, and of no one perhaps to the degree in which they are characteristic of Blake. The incontrovertible actuality of seen impossibilities as he portrayed or told of them, we need scarcely be reminded of—as when in conversation he thus revisualized a fairy's funeral: "I heard a low and pleasant sound and knew not whence it came. At last I saw the broad leaf of a flower move and underneath I saw a procession of creatures of the size and color of green and grey grasshoppers, bearing a body laid out on a roseleaf, which they buried with songs, and then disappeared. It was a fairy's funeral." Contrariwise, "the spiritual apparition of a Flea" is fearsomely circumstantial—though in connection with John Varley's "test of the truth of these visions" as recorded in *A Treatise on Zodiacal Physiognomy* it is interesting to read that "the neatness, elasticity, and tenseness of the Flea are significant of the elegant dancing and fencing sign, Gemini."

As for labor, "the hard wiry line of rectitude and certainty in the actions and intentions" of Blake teaches one to dispel hope—and fear—that great art is "the fruit of facility." In a letter, the property of Mr. W. A. White, written to James Linnell on August 25th, 1827, he says, "I am too much attached to Dante to think much of anything else. I have proved the six plates and reduced the Fighting devils ready for the copper. I count myself sufficiently paid if I live as I now do and only fear that I may be unlucky to my friends and especially that I may be so to you." He could "see," and could work—his home being not the age nor the house in which he lived, but his mind. The placing of a stone near the site of his grave in Bunhill

Fields, and of a tablet to his memory in St. Paul's, is rightly commemorative, as are reproductions and exhibitions of his works. In being urged to prepare for the Blake centenary, however, we are a little at a loss. If we are not already prepared, it is difficult to know how we are to become so.

The Dial, 82 (June 1927), 540.

• • •

A recent bulletin[1] of The University of South Carolina draws our attention to the peculiarities of Gullah dialect, the term Gullah coming possibly "from the name of the Liberian group of (African) tribes known as Golas, living on the West Coast between Sierra Leone and the Ivory Coast." The one-time environment of these Negroes as rice and cotton laborers on South Carolina and Georgia plantations is brought before us in this study, as also the aspect today of the estates stretching "in an irregular chain along the coast, inlets, and tidal rivers, each with the gray-weathered dwelling-house in its moss-draped grove of live-oaks; the big barns and slave-quarters off to one side, consisting of a double row of one-story cabins, now in ruins, lining the 'street.' "

Over-emphasis as occasionally felt in these pages—minimizes the imperativeness of what is set forth. And one is reluctant to infer monkey-nut, a Negro term for cocoa-nut, to have arisen "probably from the resemblance of the hairy nut to a brown monkey's head." But the pamphlet is not a lazy thing and is as benefiting as it is ungreedy of thanks.

Gullah dialect is distinguished by short-cuts Mr. Smith observes—short-cuts of tense, without distinctions of gender. An equivalent of *nicht wahr* or *n'est-ce pas, enty* may mean "isn't, aren't, didn't, doesn't, don't, you, she, it, they, we." And the instance is given of a Georgetown Negro who said in offering a conductor a ticket for his wife—"Dis one fuh him"; and a ticket for himself—"and dis one fuh we."

What is said of the historical background, of the literary background, and of the dialect of the Gullah Negroes, is followed by a discussion of their Spirituals, allusion being made to that tendency on the part of white singers to "render a Spiritual as though it were a Brahms song or to assume a Negro 'unctuousness' that is obviously false and painfully so." The Charleston Society whose admitted object is the Preservation of Negro Spirituals, is however, exonerated of would-be-helpful unusefulness; and also, not by contrast but synonymously, strong effort is being made we are told, to encourage the Negroes to sing their own rather than other men's songs.

Blinded by no subjective penny of infallibility, this pamphlet affords comprehensive bibliographies of writings—good and bad—about subject-matter discussed, and quotes Mr. N. G. J. Ballanta as feeling that the characteristics of certain American Negro music could be traced to an African stem. [2] Believing as we do in the Negro's primeval richness, we should like to suppose that they could.

O U R passion for the new becomes cold on occasion through finding it though new, not living; but some months ago at a presentation arranged by Paul Rosenfeld, of work by Aaron Copland, Roger Sessions, Theodore Chanler, William Grant Still, Avery Claflin, and Harold Morris, severally, at the New School for Social Research, we were enriched by novelty plus vigor. Paintings are usually not painted for the painter by somebody else, and the fortunate credulous as well as those who insist upon authenticity of interpretation were happy in the playing by composers of their own compositions, as in the assisting by them of each other; and may one say—not parenthetically—that Violinist and 'Cellist, Mr. Edwin Idler and Mr. Paul Gruppe were devout in their earnestness and not more earnest than accomplished.

The two movements from Mr. Chanler's "Violin Sonata in F Minor" were marked by a strange rich elegiac thoughtfulness with helpfully recurrent emphases—the ripple widening beneath sensitively formal gusts of marine willfulness. We were ineptly tardy, so were defrauded of hearing Mr. Copland's "Passacaglia," but are told that structurally it would not have seemed faint to us, exaggeratedly adherent though we are to Bach and Frescobaldi. (Not so much though as because, should one say.) It is probably not ultimate musical felicity that an instrument's characteristic sound can be made to simulate a bird, a cricket, a human being, a bell, or a banjo; but a plucking, a rattling of skeleton leaves, a kind of orchestrated Aeolian equinox, may be music not chaos and Mr. Copland's "Serenade" was magnificently impersonated. His polyphonic security is frightening but his seriousness saves us.

To Mr. Still's "Dialect Songs" one could be attentive—particularly had "Winter's Approach" been the starting-point of a progress. Spheroid and positive, Mr. Morris' "Fantasy" was eloquent rather than mysterious; and Mr. Claflin also perhaps was inclined to meet us more than half way. In his "Four Pieces from an Unfinished Ballet" he was to us, especially in the Allegro molto ben marcato, a very handsome "turn." Certain depths on the other hand can be all but too deep for one. Mr. Sessions' "Three Coral Preludes for Organ" exacted a far from stupid faithfulness to musical intention and the punitively many who have not the ear to hear all there is in a thing are unruly beneficiaries. These preludes, however, had been written for the organ and their masonry—vital and careful—was to one through its fine logic, veritably a song of the congregation, marvelously assisting Mr. Rosenfeld's little family of geniuses to seem large.

[1] *Gullah*. By Reed Smith. Bulletin of the University of South Carolina. November 1, 1926.

[2] *St. Helena Island Spirituals*. Recorded and transcribed at Penn Normal, Industrial, and Agricultural School, St. Helena Island, Beaufort County, S.C., by Nicholas George Julius Ballanta of Freetown, Sierra Leone, West Africa. Introduction by George Foster Peabody. Press of G. Schirmer, Inc.

The Dial, 83 (July 1927), 88–90.

• • •

T H E usefulness, companionableness, and gentleness of snakes is sometimes alluded to in print by scientists and by amateurs. Needless to say, we dissent from the serpent as deity; and enlightenment is preferable to superstition when plagues are to be combated—army-worms, locusts, a mouse army, tree or vegetable blights, diseases of cattle, earthquakes, fires, tornadoes, and floods. Destruction such as was experienced by us in western states and in Florida the past winter, from tornadoes and from the Mississippi in the spring, could not have been more portentously afflicting or more usefully admonitory had we believed ourselves to have been preyed upon by an aquatic serpent or by a wind god. A certain ritual of awe—animistic and animalistic—need not, however, be effaced from our literary consciousness. The serpent as a motive in art, as an idea, as beauty, is surely not beneath us, as we see it in the stone and the gold hamadryads of Egypt; in the turtle zoomorphs, feathered serpent columns, and coiled rattlesnakes of Yucatan; in the silver-white snakes, "chameleon lizards," and stone dragons of Northern Siam. Guarding the temple of Cha-Heng in Nan, the hundred yard long pair of blue-green-yellow painted monsters [1]—with reared head and flowing, skin-like rise of body—are, one infers from Reginald le May's description and partial photograph, majestic worms. Nor does the mythologic war between serpent and elephant seem disproportionate when one examines a stone dragon [2] which guards rice fields in Northern Siam from raiding herds of elephants. As Edward Topsall has said in his *Historie of Serpents*, "Among all the kinds of serpents there is none comparable to the Dragon," and the fact of variants seemed to Aldrovanus, no detraction. "Dragons there are in

Ethiopia ten fathoms long" and there are little ones. In an old letter to the public we read: "Thirtie miles from London, this present month of August, 1614"—and the news is attested by two men and by a Widow Woman dwelling near Faygate—there lives a serpent "or dragon as some call it," "reputed to be nine feet, or rather more, in length. It is likewise discovered to have large feet, but the eye may be there deceived" and "two great bunches" "as some think will in time grow to wings; but God, I hope, will defend the poor people in the neighborhood, that he shall be destroyed before he grow so fledged. Farewell. By A. R. He that would send better news, if he had it."

The death of our own two carnivorous dragons—brought last year from the Island of Komodo—was an evil of the opposite sort: punitive possibly; in any case a victory, making emphatic to us our irrelevance to such creatures as these, and compulsorily our mere right to snakes in stone and story.

ANTHONY Trollope remarked in his *Autobiography*, "I do not think it probable that my name will remain among those who in the next century will be known as the writers of English prose fiction." The Oxford Press, however, sees fit to include various of his novels[3]—also the *Autobiography*— in its series of World's Classics; and by other publishers, as was brought to one's attention during the war, the complete novels were issued with view to augmenting the number of valuable books available to those at the front. One had not looked upon Trollope's work in the light of an overture to battle; his novels bring within the reader's experience, nevertheless, a titanically courageous sense of justice and, as Mr. Michael Sadleir has said, a period of English life in which it was as though society said to the individual, "you will help and not hinder; and you will help by denying to yourself the indulgences that no one withholds from you. Because such denial will be made of your own volition, you will yourself become the more free and as a servant of the community the more profitable."

"I think," says Trollope, "the highest merit which a novel can have consists in perfect delineation of character." He invariably secures to the tale which he tells—and conspicuously we see this in his outlines of prospective novels— that "central tie-beam" or "omnipresence of subject" to which Mr. Saintsbury refers in his essay, "Some Great Biographies." And also, looked at as characterization, the work though never about himself, is himself. A craftsman whose "spare-times were more than odd-times," a man not grasping, but thrifty and generously helpful for thrift makes opportunity for generosity, Trollope is still able to give us something. Tolerant of frailty as Mr. Sadleir points out, but aggressive toward the strong, "he learnt, when the limits of his tolerance were overstepped, to choose the moment for a blow and the best way of giving it." Determined "neither to accept nor to solicit literary favor," he has had to accept help now and again—and recently from Mr. Sadleir, a most perfected kind of help. In *Anthony Trollope: A Commentary*[4] "experienced selecting," "careful mixing" of evidence, and unegotistic emphasizing of others' work compel thanks. Detail is impressive because properly subordinated as in the comment upon the brilliance of Trollope's "black eyes, which, behind the strong lenses of his spectacles, shone . . . 'with a certain genial fury of inspection' "; and his "family group"—especially the characterization of Mrs. Trollope, the novelist's mother—is really portraiture. Admiring the strength of the biography, one is troubled now and again by what seems an ungentleness of literary demeanor—a lesser thing to be sure—as not in character with Trollope, but it is perhaps not legitimate to suggest that biographers be literary chameleons; and Mr. Sadleir is far from requiring that a subject be chameleon to his biographer. Ambitious that mid-Victorianism emerge as it was—as something quite other than "portentousness," "rococo ornament," and "dowdy morality"—he makes Trollope seem and permits him to let himself seem "the articulate perfection of its normal quality."

[1] *An Asian Arcady* by Reginald le May. W. Heffer & Sons, Ltd., Cambridge.

[2] Photographed by Mr. Ernest Shoedsack of the Paramount Famous Lasky Corporation Expedition to Northern Siam under the leadership of Mr. Shoedsack and Major Merian C. Cooper. Reproduction in the photogravure section of *The New York Times*, April 21st, 1927.

[3] *Framley Parsonage. Barchester Towers. Et alii.* The World's Classics, The Oxford University Press, American Branch.

[4] *Anthony Trollope: A Commentary* by Michael Sadleir. Introduction by A. Edward Newton. Houghton Mifflin Company.

The Dial, 83 (August 1927), 178–80.

• • •

> *The religion of literature is a sort of Pantheism. You never know where the presence of the Divine may show itself, though you should know where it has shown. And you must never forbid it to show itself, anyhow or anywhere.*
> GEORGE SAINTSBURY

IF our choice in youth were the choice of age and our choice in age were that of youth our usefulness to ourselves would be doubled. We value the modern spirit of *The Manchester Guardian* as depending on the un-aging discernment of Mr. C. P. Scott whose eighty-first birthday occurs this October. No work of art certainly is old which was ever new, as no one is dead who ever was alive.

It is reasonable to expect to find in the young more sap than in the old and inexperience is not always crassness. In undergraduate magazines for example, there is often more to detain one than there is in the popular product with which the news-dealer papers his cubicle. Not that youthful impetus is always admired or is always able to admire itself. An early editor of the *Oxford Undergraduate* seems to have felt aloofly distinct from what he regarded as "the Careless or greater division of non-reading men," from "the Philosophers" who "will not enter into any plan of study because they do not see the *good* of it," from "Quacks" and "Procrastinators"—indeed from most of his fellow gownsmen in each of whom he had expected to find a savant, a genius, or a wit. "My ideas of their conversation," he says, "were taken from the humor of Addison and of their customs from the rules in the Statute Book." It must be admitted that Oxford undergraduates of our own day sometimes lend their attention to specimens from America of what might be called our rag and bone fiction—not that we may easily scorn Oxford for reading what Yale or Harvard has written. We need not be seriously horrified by scholastic digressions, cultural playfulness, or intellectual wastefulness of aesthetic abundance. The unprecedented sybaritism at Harvard for instance, of the brother of the late President Eliot in having dared when an undergraduate to add a carpet to his room-furnishings seems not to have presaged perdition. The past has not at any time been entirely without liveliness and no period was ever without resemblance to other periods— our own age included. Gabriell Harvey's report of intellectual assumptiveness at Cambridge applies equally to our halls of residence:

all inquisitiue after Newes, newe Bookes, newe Fashions, newe Lawes, newe Officers, and some after newe Elementes, and some after newe Heauens, and Helles to. . . . Castels builded in the Ayre: much adoe, and little helpe: Iacke would faine be a Gentlemanne: in no age so little so muche made of, euery one highly in his owne fauour, thinking no mans penny so good siluer as his own: . . . but Agent, and Patient muche alike, neither Barrell greatly better Herring. . . . Olde men and Counsailours amongst children: Children amongst Counsailours, and olde men: Not a fewe dubble faced Iani, and chaungable Camelions: ouer-manye Clawbackes, and Pickethanks: Reeds shaken of euerie Wind: Iackes of bothe sides: Aspen leaues: painted Sheathes, and Sepulchres: Asses in Lions skins: Dunglecockes: slipperye Eles: Dormise: I blush to thinke of some, that weene themselues as fledge as the rest, being God wot, as Kallowe as the rest:

"The younger American writers" are accused of "a pseudo-hardness and clarity of mind which makes sharp distinctions and is really singularly inexpressive." Certain of the most presentable specimens of modern art are called "sophisticated, modern, trivial" and the even graver charge is brought against us of being nothing and of being too much—of not being serious and of being indecent. We seem so conspicuously to have outstripped our best champion of a "natural morality"—George Moore—that he says or is quoted as saying, "Now I can't keep up with them and don't want to. They have made it all so carnal."

Should we be tweaked by these compliments, it is still truer perhaps that we have not been quenched. The striving for "a reasoned form," the main- taining of a toehold upon progress, our manifold ferocities and ungainly graces, are after all a corollary to momentum. It is common sense, rather than blindness to Dean Inge's spiritual significance, that sustains us under the somewhat aggressively withering remark that "It is not necessary to 'make' a cubist or a free-verse writer; he has unfortunately been 'born.' " And one recalls in good part the fearless effacing of futurism and cubism by Theodore Roosevelt: "There is no reason why people should not call themselves Cub- ists, or Octagonists, or Parallelopedonists, or Knights of the Isosceles Tri- angle, or Brothers of the Cosine, if they so desire; as expressing anything serious and permanent, one term is as fatuous as another. . . . The paleo- lithic artist was able to portray the bison, the mammoth, the reindeer, and the horse with spirit and success, while he still stumbled painfully in the effort to portray man. This stumbling effort in his case represented progress, and he was entitled to great credit for it. Forty thousand years later, when entered into artificially and deliberately, it represents only a smirking pose of retrogression and is not praiseworthy."

Our attachment is to the art of Egypt and the Primitives rather than to the later Renaissance and to Impressionism and many of us are "not praise- worthy." Our apparently conglomerate methods and our wilfulness are, how- ever, not so hurtful we hope as to some elegant and seemly minds they are distasteful. One has, like the inaugurator of The Oxford Student in 1750, a feeling for being one's self and if as is possible in the subsequent progress of art, we should never be heard of, we cannot in advance regret our eclipse nor anticipating it, spare diligence. And with this student, should it be our good fortune, at the moment or later, to have "disgusted the frivolous, abashed the vicious, and awed the virtuous," we cannot be sorry.

The Dial, 83 (October 1927), 358–60.

• • •

ONE sometimes encounters in one's reading an implication that book-reviewing is not criticism, and admitting that sometimes it is not, asks perhaps inhumanely, why print it? The reviewer, or should one say critic, ought to be collaterally informed and a kind of writing would be welcome in which "everything is easy and natural, yet everything is masterly and strong." Common sense is not innately favorable to Dick Minim, "the great investigator of hidden beauties," and has no particular need of the writer who is so obsessed with his own identity that he cannot refrain from deploring what is merely deplorable. *The Dial* may be abecedarian on occasion, despite its liking for naturalness, substance, and simplicity; but it would rather exposit the treasurable than advertise mediocrity. It agrees with the editor of Copleston's warning to reviewers[1] that "the unbearable repartee" is silence, and though it licenses as antiquarianism an occasional cock-fight, the hurtful inhumanity of Gifford, Wilson, and Judge Jeffrey, never make it envious. A business-like rancor may exist in the heart of one who has learned from Erasmus "the smoothest form for each suggestion of politeness," but ill-nature on the part of those who have not learned politeness from Erasmus results usually in a collapse of unequestrianism. If criticism is "the effect of the subjection of the product of one mind to the processes of another," is not the reviewer's own mind disparaged by him in resorting to an inconsequent and disrespectful *ruade*?

Those who are displeased by an unduly academic literary mechanics may consider the advantages of verbal unfearfulness, in the recently inaugurated little cinema review, *Close Up*.[2] To burst into feeling so to speak, and praise an art through a medium other than its own, without having mastered the terms of the auxiliary art is surely an experiment; but zeal, liberty, and beauty are allied phenomena and apart from oddity there are in *Close Up* to reward us, besides certain other items, a poem about light by H. D.; a report of "Kopf Hoch Charley" that holds the attention; a contribution entitled "Mrs. Emerson" by Miss Stein; and a letter to the editor: *"About cinemas. I do not care for them, but I do not know why I don't. . . . I think my prejudice is hardly justified. But I couldn't write about it. I've nothing to say. I'm so sorry."* We like the letter and we like the movies. We have said something about the theater's undeserved, sanctified background as compared with the reluctantly accepted celluloid permanence of the movies[3] and we feel, with

Close Up, that intelligence is " 'sadly lacking' " in the films' critics as in
the film world. In producing films, "brains and education" ought not to be
"dead weights against you" and often "one wants to see films one has missed."

We are not sure that *Close Up* is in the strict sense informing though
it tells us that "all Americans in France, Switzerland, England, are printing their books at the shop of the master printer, Maurice Darantière,
Dijon." We read advertisements as we read the body of a magazine and
like the impression of energy and ability conveyed by the announcement
that the firm of John and Edward Bumpus is to the reader what the camera
is to the film.

Perquisites are of secondary importance; motive is the lively factor, and
we find here a zeal for enjoyment and for not keeping that enjoyment to one's
self. Despite stock phrases, ambiguities, italics, capital type, superlatives,
and certainties so sanguine as somehow to seem like uncertainties, there is
friendliness here. "By mixing more in the world," "a healthy enjoyment of
the business of life is imparted" as Mr. Larkyns, the rector, was able to
convince Mr. Verdant Green's father. It is incumbent upon us occasionally
to consent to be lured into the society of others who have, like ourselves, a
special fondness for art.

¹ *Advice to a Young Reviewer With a Specimen of the Art* by Edward Copleston.
Houghton Mifflin Company.
² *Close Up.* Published monthly by Pool, Riant Château, Territet, Switzerland.
³ *The Dial*, February 1927, page 178.

The Dial, 83 (November 1927), 449–50.

• • •

The trees have wisdom, for they sleep
. . .
But man claps on his coat of brown,
His badger coat,
When winter whistles through the town
And sledge is boat.
DOUGLAS AINSLIE

HERMAN Patrick Tappé would be sorry to have us outgrow the Christmas
of Bracebridge Hall and a garland, tinsel diadem, or "so personal" wreath

of mistletoe refuting skepticism, he is justly reminded of Lord Chesterfield's conviction that " 'the manner of giving shows the genius of the giver more than the gift itself.' " The Christmas battered, that is to say the Christmas-gift-battered heart, however, inclines to the scene outside "where white winds blow" and to James Joyce's dislike of gifts that are appropriate—"a spellingbee book for Rosy Brooke"; "scruboak beads for beatified Biddy": "for Camilla, Dromilla, Ludmilla, Mamilla, a bucket, a packet, a book and a pillow."

"I am compelled to celebrate Christmas in some way, but I had much rather not," Bernard Shaw is quoted as saying and the complaint is far from outrageous. We have observed the bareness of giving which is not inclusive of the giver, yet the preposterous aspect of a thing ought not to do away with the thing itself; it is apparent that counterfeits are not able to make people dislike money. What we probably need, as Mr. Shaw shows, is not judiciousness but continuity. "I have no quarrel with the Christmas feeling" he goes on to say, "but I think it should be spread over the whole year," and Washington Irving, Lowell, Dickens, Mr. Tappé, and certain of us by nature more sardonic than these, would agree with him.

The Dial, 83 (December 1927), 540.

• • •

> *Piety: Why, did you hear him tell his dream?*
> *Christian: Yes, and a dreadful one it was, I thought; it made my heart ache*
> *as he was telling of it, but yet I am glad I heard it.*
>   JOHN BUNYAN

IN the work of Thomas Hardy as in the writings of Bunyan, there is the sense of mortality,—not divided from immortality. We are spoken to by a wisdom in which there is "something of ecstasy" and by a spirit kindly concerned with the "phantasmal variousness" of existence. Deprecating Vanity Fair and the town where "this lusty fair is kept," Bunyan says, "he that will go to the [Celestial] city, and yet not go through this town, must needs go out of the world." Mr. Hardy's guidance of us through "the pleasing agonies and painful delights" of an imagined world has, like Bunyan's, caused ordinariness to be clothed with extraordinariness. Irrefutably, seductively, severely, unselfconsciously urgent in their verisimilitude, the rude incidents and the elate, the work of his hands and the travel of his feet, constitute the life and flower of a pilgrim's universe. Humanity has perhaps forgotten how, "sepulchre-clad" with insincerity, it visited abuse upon Tess of the D'Urbervilles and other of Mr. Hardy's apologues for purity and goodness. In adjudging as he did, he has made it ever after, less possible that convention should "perish the understanding." His martyr-like sincerity drew the world as an undertow toward true vision and into respect for his un-overbearing certitude. Such propriety of enchantment and the ancient wisdom emerging from reverie, we can be proud to show to succeeding ages.

In life as in death a great man cannot be saved from pursuit by the curious, but Mr. Hardy's suppliant silence, his sequestration so native as to seem kind, should protect him even now from intrusion. We remember, in *A Laodicean*, his remark, "incurious unobservance is the true attitude of cordiality." The quickset privacy of Max Gate, with its concealed entrance, which seems unapproachable rather than forbidding, is not at variance with the fact that it stands "on the road" and calls itself by the name of the adjacent once used toll-gate.

Home-loving and apart as he was, nothing was more remote from his intention than that a region which he felt to be his retreat should be conspicuous with monuments pre-eminently his. But no named memorial can be so poignantly commemorative as certain unpremeditated reminders. The figure of The White Hart with gilded eyes, antlers, and chain; the ancient bridge over The Frome; the cattle market; The King's Arms; "the grizzled church" of Saint Peter; "the peremptory clang" of its curfew chime at eight in the evening as a signal for the shops to close; and that of the alms-house, "with a preparative creak of machinery more audible than the note of the bell"; fixed in one's consciousness as when received in the bright rain of summer, these stay in the mind like the *timbre* of heard speech. With yet more immanence perhaps, the black yews in Stinsford churchyard, the headstones with sculptured angels above graves of members of his family, the peal of bells and the Norman font, are component with what Mr. Hardy has told us. And their important seclusion is his.

The Dial, 84 (February 1928), 179–80.

.   .   .

A N art not dissociated from writing is handwriting and what might at first be an idle or curious interest in the significance of one's capitals and small letters can lead to the mending of serious defects of character. There are various published expositions of the principle of graphology, a new one having just been added;[1] and even more engrossing, are the "artistic and paleographical criticisms" of Roger Fry and E. A. Lowe, in a Tract on English Handwriting[2] compiled under the auspices of The Society for Pure English. Doctor Lowe finds "an increase in freedom, boldness, and originality . . . in the performances of the last half-century." Mr. Fry feels that free writing "appears to surpass in sheer linear beauty any kind of writing in which the letters are formed consciously" and says, "Perhaps the most interesting result for me of the whole inquiry has been the discovery that the aesthetic excellence of a handwriting depends so little on the unit forms chosen." The specimens reproduced provoke study and tempt comparison with specimens not reproduced—with a spacious, compact, versatile page by Molière in The British Museum, a romantic Erasmus and a polite Newton in the Fitzwilliam Museum, and with specimens one has seen of handwriting by Gordon Craig, Doctor von Bode, Havelock Ellis, John Eglinton, and other contemporaries. The hesitantly experienced antennaelike candor of Mr. Fry's judgments in this matter—and a certain elegant obduracy in plate 28— prepossessingly emphasize the axiom that aesthetic dogma sometimes gains importance inversely as it pre-empts it.

T O accept congratulation is almost like self-gratulation; nevertheless praise from contemporaries is grateful. A brother journal, published weekday afternoons in Denver, finds our verses, articles, and short stories, capital and a contributor—one might say a cousin, for we are less ashamed of nepotism than of seeming to quote without acknowledgement—said not long ago in the office that he was pleased we had offered The Dial Award to Ezra Pound; that Mr. Pound has the intuitive mind in a degree to which few people have it, "a mind that moves back and forth like sea-weed."

We confessed to admiring instinctiveness, concentration, and tentativeness; to realizing that gusto is not incompatible with learning, and to favoring opulence in asceticism. It is apparent also in lines by Sung Lien[3] that such liking is not recent:

> In the dormitory I had two meals a day, but nothing fresh, fat, or of any good taste. All other schoolmates were dressed up in fine silk and

with embroidery; their hats were decorated with jewels; their girdles made of white jade. Every one bore a sword on his left, and perfume at his right. They looked as shining and dignified as angels. While living among them I wore my cotton robe and tattered clothes, but had not the slightest desire to be like them, for I had my enjoyment focused upon something different, knowing not that my bodily wants were not as well supplied as those of others.

It is possible to conceive of victory achieved at a leap. If over-confident, however, or over-curious with regard to the manner of a career, one could not fail to derive benefit from the kind, if uncomfortably practical advice to young actors, which George Arliss gives in his memoirs. In accepting it one seems not to picture oneself incommoded by a storm of applause. His honorable and unusual convictions with regard to punctuality are particularly impressive—and the sin that it is for one man to waste the time of another, however great that man's position, may be by comparison.

A E is here, and having held out a welcome to him for many years, it is not likely that, as the newspapers suggest, we shall confuse his identity with that of George W. Erskine Russell, of Bertrand Russell, or of another. At first not quite hearing him since our fellow-townsmen are, under excitement, spectators rather than audience, but entirely believing him, we can accept his implication that poetry is invariably at the core of reanimation in Ireland.

Susceptible to Irish magic in its various strengths, we cannot say we are not enchanted with disenchantment in *The Plough and the Stars;* that we are indifferent to certain of James Joyce's lyrics "carved from the air and colored with the air" as Mr. Russell denotes them; or to George Moore's "novel," *Hail and Farewell.*

The Venerable Bede finds that "when some persons have been bitten by serpents, the scrapings of leaves of books that were brought out of Ireland, being put into water, and given them to drink, have immediately expelled the spreading poison, and assuaged the swelling." And we are grateful that there should have been administered to our restiveness, the poems and thoughts which Mr. Russell has brought us.

[1] *Mind Your P's and Q's* by Jerome S. Meyer. Simon and Schuster. See also: *Character From Handwriting* by Louise Rice. Frederick A. Stokes Company.

[2] *S. P. E. Tract No. XXIII. English Handwriting* by Roger Fry & E. A. Lowe. With Thirty-four Facsimile Plates and Artistic & Paleographical Criticism. Oxford University Press, American Branch.

[3] Translated from the Chinese by Kwei Chen. *Literary Magazine of the University of Wisconsin*, December, 1927.

The Dial, 84 (March 1928), 268–70.

.   .   .

PROFUSENESS, magnificent special editions, and a campaign of conquest through activity, seem at times characteristic of present-day book-making. When Mr. Henry McBride remarked not long ago in *The Sun* that "Americans at heart still love costumes but have less and less courage for them," it is obvious that he was referring to society rather than to publishing. New illustrations to old favorites seem uningenuous and illustrations to a book other than those made by the author, add usually rather than reiterate. But the manner of using illustration is more legitimately one's concern perhaps than a favoring or excluding of pictures.

The subtleties and atmospheric depth of naturalistic painting and drawing are disturbing in a book, says a writer on Text and Illustration in the Printing Number issued with a *London Times Literary Supplement*, since "in reading you look 'at' the page; in looking at a realistic illustration you look 'through' it." That is to say formality of style is needed which will keep the work in relation with type; as in "the wonderful series of books designed and produced by William Blake, in which a method of engraving invented by himself produced a unity comparable to that of early illuminated manuscripts." In the Nonesuch India paper volume of Blake's poetry and prose,[1] the printing of illustrations on the same page with text is a pleasure and compactness compensates for a tenuousness which perhaps verges on transparency. Thin pages opaque enough to permit of printing on both sides are to the bibliophile without bookshelves by no means a bibliographic mistake.

A progress in pictures commends itself and especially a progress in pictures so rare as certain engravings reproduced in Mr. Randolph C. Adams' *The Gateway to American History*.[2] In assembling unique specimens, however, there is danger of incoherence; of incongruity of fount so to speak—since harmony is not merely a matter of printing on one kind of paper—on coated paper throughout, or on text paper throughout. The "right relation of illustration to text" has its counterpart, moreover, in the pictures. But a book which is good for children is far from childish and one values as much as children could, the symmetrical representation of stags in flight, of sea-monsters bewildered by barrels, of coats of arms accorded "piracy that has reached patriotic proportions," of astrolabes, indigo-plantations, and the ceremonious savagery of savages and courtiers.

EARLY maps with emphasized shore-lines and rivers have much in common with the modern air-view. Though the photograph may seem as art somewhat "easier," both styles of likeness confer unrealistic distinction, so that New York as foreshortened in a view taken recently by The Airmap Corporation of America, wears the delicately engraved aspect of a sand-dollar or cluster of barnacles. Our master-production, The Clifford Milburn Holland Vehicular Tunnel, is not visible. In close approach to entrance or exit it is scarcely more perceptible than a wormhole, but pourings of traffic toward Broome Street or from Canal Street indicate sand-adder selfhelpfulness within and encourage one to feel that occupancy will presently have become indigenous i.e. that the tunnel will presently have paid for itself and be free to the public. We are glad to have civic prowess subjacent. Expenditure does not seem expenditure when the result is a benefit.

¹ *The Centenary Edition of Blake's Poetry and Prose* edited by Geoffrey Keynes. Complete in one volume. The Nonesuch Press; Random House.
² *The Gateway to American History* by Randolph C. Adams. Illustrated. Little, Brown and Company.

The Dial, 84 (April 1928), 359–60.

* * *

> *My intentions are all directed to worthy ends, to do good to all and evil to none. And now let your graces judge whether a man who means this, does this, and makes it his only study to practise all this, deserves to be called a fool.*
>
> DON QUIXOTE

CERVANTES is not in need of being rescued from oblivion. Though he calls *Don Quixote* a legend as dry as a rush, destitute of invention, in a wretched style, poor in conception and void of learning, no one has agreed with him. Monuments such as the colossal Dulcinea to be erected at Toboso are evidence merely that a world going the opposite way declares his, admirable. With much patience Signor Unamuno remarks in his eloquent commentary:[1]

> The best listeners are the goatherds, accustomed to the voices of woods and fields. The others do not receive your words with inner silence and virgin attention; however you sharpen your explanations, they will not sharpen their understandings; not they.

In an age of philanthropy and self-entrenchment as squire to philanthropy, however, the cooperation of the knight and squire usefully suggest "for the comfort of our discomfort," "goodness and humanness." The knight's prowess was mystical—without thought of defeat or reward. While Sancho was crouching under Dapple for protection, or "awaiting death in its cruelest form, hunger," Don Quixote was at attention or composing a poem; "born in an age of iron, to revive in it that of gold," he was not sometime to rest in a silver coffin on seventy-eight crowns of khans and princes; or to outshine in death Jelalu-'d-din, or the King of Ur. His courteously fraternal dying—with Sancho, the priest, the notary, the niece, the housekeeper, and the bachelor beside him, is conspicuously incomparable with the punctilio of the "hecatomb" and its arranged rows of wives, appropriately in attendance but without belongings of their own since "it was not their grave but the king's."

Don Quixote seems proverbial of extremes—the measure of impracticality; typical also, of right as more sovereign than rights. When the "short-winged and sharp-beaked" "domestic impediment of his heroism" asks her uncle why he should try to make himself out vigorous when old, strong when sickly, and be able to put straight what is crooked when he himself was bent by age, he admits the body to be withered and the armor rusty. Put to the test, however, he exclaims, in defiance of "Panza" 's prejudice against an attack upon the twenty Yanguesans by a pair who were "not more than one and a half," "I count for a hundred." Sublime inferences are inevitable.

By the properties of the novel—courtly, confiding, Asiatically detailed yet "not swerving a jot from the truth"—the attention is enticed and involved in the mystery of a continuously imaginary verisimilitude, the smaller included in greater and the greater as Heine has said, like a tree of India. We are familiar with the intimidating sheep—the mighty Duke of Nerbia whose device was an asparagus-bed, and Brandabarnaran of Boliche armed with a serpent's skin and a gate of the temple which Samson pulled down; and with the funeral cortège amid "about a dozen of tall beeches," "not one of them without the name of Marcela written and engraved on its smooth bark"—the "twenty shepherds clad in jerkins of black wool, crowned with garlands, some of which were of yew and some of cypress," and the Lycidas-like hero; the flowers, the books and "great number of papers, some open and some folded," that "lay round him on the bier." And most important perhaps, is the exploit in which Don Quixote falls with drawn sword on the puppet Moors, decapitating, maiming, and demolishing. In every age there are regalia and insignia that are nothingness.

The humble grandeur which Don Quixote achieved through "good sense and good conduct," "modesty, liberality, courtesy," "chaste ears and compassionate deeds," has somehow acquired an angelic quality—akin to what Mr. Henry McBride finds in the painting by El Greco—a "curiously lambent inner glow" that gives it "an unearthly impressiveness." The world has been unwilling to pay the tribute of imitation but has offered its admiration. In Unamuno's commentary, knight and squire signify love for humanity, its spirit and body; "not the two halves of a whole, but a single being viewed from either side." And this your graces cannot question, having read "the History of the Famous Don Quixote de La Mancha, who in the opinion of all the inhabitants of Campo de Montiel, was the chastest lover and most valiant knight that had appeared in those parts for many years."

[1] *The Life of Don Quixote and Sancho, according to Miguel de Cervantes Saavedra.* Expounded with Comment by Miguel de Unamuno. Translated from the Spanish by Homer P. Earle. Alfred A. Knopf.

The Dial, 84 (May 1928), 448–50.

• • •

I T is his resolve, Leo Stein tells us, never to review a book unless essentially in sympathy with it and never to proffer his critical verdict without at the last again consulting the book to be sure that what he has written is apt and dependable. Though we are sufficiently like "Prussolini" to feel that we should, possibly, have the same impression of a book after writing about it that we had had of it before, we agree with Mr. Stein in choosing, when we can, to analyze what we instinctively like. Volcanics seem pardonable when they are one's own, but in others it is some species of poetics usually which attracts one, and in search of pure art we tend to feel betrayed when experts tell us merely where it is not. There is, to be sure, a kind of destruction which is not destruction, nor is enlarged experience in any sense an impertinence—those little folded and cut, scissors-lace conceits of Hans Andersen: a balloonist, a chimney-sweep, a lover-and-gallows, or inscribed as by the writing-master, a *MARIE* continuous with the geometric garland which surrounds it.

We have been so fortunate—dog being interested in dog—as now and then to happen, in print, upon phases of cordiality. Arthur Davison Ficke as imaginary counselor to an imaginary poet has offered what it seems to us is sound advice—suggesting as evidence of sincerity, the willingness to work for a time without recognition; the study of great masters of the past, a learning the lesson of their method not merely of their manner, disbelief in the fable of the poet's attic, and ability to earn a living entirely apart from the writing of poetry. A kind of every-author-his-own-Whittington fantasia of the studios seems at times not entirely repellent; but a superiority achieved by ant-like industry need not be even to uncommercial eyes, illiterate or mildewed. Messrs W. and G. Foyle, the London booksellers for instance, are satisfactorily romantic in their conviction that "any book which has eluded your search hitherto may be speedily obtained." (Their first catalogues were, they say, transcribed by hand and distributed with the request, "Please return when used," and both members of the firm were so young at the time of this first venture that it seemed to them judicious when possible to reply by post to inquirers since a customer had mistaken one of them for the office-boy.)

Among other persuasions of literature there have been lectures by and articles about AE. "The remarkable thing about AE," Padraic Colum says, "is not the vitality which permits him to get so much done in his day, but the eagerness, the freshness of interest, which seems to be always his . . . as if he had a charm to prevent the world wearying him. Or perhaps it is a technique—a technique which saves his vitality from flagging and goes with his deliberate practice of concentration and meditation."

The cynic's tooth is again evaded with delicacy in a recent discussion of Marc Chagall by Christian Zervos. Susceptible to the subordinated minutiae of such things as the boat, bridge, and metropolitan architecture in the "Self-Portrait, 1918," we know Chagall to be technical and exact and yet, as Mr. Zervos says, "one who lives in a state of enchantment and gracious absorption"; we respond to his "capacity for receiving impressions, his tenderness, something subtle, sensitive, feverish, impatient, emotional, timid and arrogant." "And so one cannot too much encourage artists who strive to bring back unity, who perceive new sources of ecstasy, who all their lives love something not to be found in this world. . . ."

The Dial, 84 (June 1928), 539–40.

• • •

*In der Zeit verliche mir Gott Fleiss, dass ich wol lernete.**
ALBRECHT DÜRER

DÜRER'S "Rhinoceros," Pollajuolo's "Battle of the Nudes," and various concepts by Mantegna and by Leonardo da Vinci, have for us that attraction which originality with precision can exert, and liking is increased perhaps when the concept is primarily an imagined one—in the instance of the rhinoceros, based apparently on a traveler's sketch or description. The conjunction of fantasy and calculation is unusual, but many sagacities seem in Dürer not to starve one another. St. Jerome and his beast of burden the lion, in the room with the bottle-glass window-lights, the "St. Eustachius," a small Turner-like water-color of the Tyrol in the Ashmolean, tempt one to have favorites, and the eye is promptly engaged by that sensitiveness to magnificence in apparel which gives us the knight's parti-colored clothing and pointed shoes, the "drowsing elegance of the sugar-bag hat," and the little hat "couched fast to the pate like an oyster." Dürer's gifts excited "the admiring courtesy of the Italians," we are told; and certain portraits seem to mirror and to gild in mirroring, Italy's almost finer than Oriental politeness. There is danger of extravagance in denoting as sacrosanct or devout, an art so robust as to include in it that which is neither, but Dürer's separately perfect media do somehow suggest the virtues which St. Jerome enumerates as constituting the "hous of cryste"—of which he says in conclusion: "And good perseueranunce nouryssheth theym." His mere journeyings are fervent—to the Dutch coast to look at a stranded whale that was washed to sea before he was able to arrive; to Bologna to learn as he says, "the secrets of the art of perspective which a man is willing to teach me," and in his several visits to Italy. The secrets of Dürer, however, are not easily invaded, the clearness and simplicity of his signature in the adjusted yet natural housing of the D beneath the medievally prominent A, being a subtlety compared with the juxtaposed curves of the modern monogram, the printing of letters backward, or the variously arranged inverting of duplicates.

The reliquary method of perpetuating magic is to be distrusted; nevertheless a living energy seemed still to reside in the wood blocks and engraving

*Over time, God has granted me diligence, a lesson I have learned well.

tools of Dürer's which were exhibited at the Metropolitan Museum some years ago and one values the effort of experts to recover mutilated originals, to repudiate "copies," and to recognize Dürer's many priorities.

Appreciation which is truly votive and not gapingly inquisitive, commits one to enlightenment if not to emulation, and recognition of the capacity for newness inclusive of oldness which seems in Dürer an apparitional yet normal miraculousness like a heraldic flame or separate fire in the air, could have its part in persuading us to think—with him—not too ill of "subtilty," "*ingenia*," and of "artwork which is altogether new in its shape."

PRINTS by Dürer and his contemporaries are now in exhibition in the print room of the New York Public Library and will remain till the autumn.

One welcomes additional reproductions of Dürer's woodcuts: *The Complete Woodcuts* edited by Dr. Willi Kurth with introduction by Campbell Dodgson (W. & G. Foyle, Ltd.); and of his engravings on copper: *The Masters of Engraving and Etching—Albrecht Dürer*, with introduction by Campbell Dodgson (The Medici Society).

The Dial, 85 (July 1928), 89–90.

• • •

> So when Ptolemy, Alexander's Favourite was hurt with a poisoned dart in a fight, and lay in grievous pain sick of it; Alexander sitting by him fell asleep, and saw a Dragon which his Mother Olympias kept, carrying a little root in his mouth, and shewing the place where it grew, saying it was of such vertue that it would cure Ptolemy: Alexander being awake, told his dream, and sent to seek that root (for the place was not far off) which having found, it cured, not only Ptolemy, but many other Souldiers which were hurt with those kind of darts.
>
> RICHARD SAUNDERS

THOMAS Heriot was pleased with the "greate hearbe in form of a Marigolde, about sixe foote in height" which we have in America. "Some take it to bee *Planta Solis*"; he says, "of the seeds herof they make both a kinde of bread and broth" and Nicholas Monardes published in his treatise on the medicinal uses of American plants, a picture of the sassafras tree, and its leaf, "used against all kinds of diseases."

In *The Divine Origin of the Craft of the Herbalist*[1] by Sir E. A. Wallis

Budge, there is much that is curious and important if one has an interest in magic, medicine, or the healing properties of herbs, "the unsatisfactory term magic" having been used originally to designate learning among Medes and Persians famed for their skill in working enchantments. Science is exonerated of credulity by the assertion that the herbalists' knowledge of medicine would have been greater but for their patients' "invincible love of magic" though the caduceus is retained symbolically, its serpents suggesting immortality in their power of shedding and renewing the skin. Sumerian, Egyptian, Babylonian, and Assyrian herbals are here shown to be the foundation of Greek herbals—disseminated also, by way of Arabic, through Asia, Turkestan, and China; and the antiquity of the craft, the nature of it, and the diversity of texts, are graphically suggested by prescriptions, plant lists, and plates, among which last a typographic leopard from Ethiopia is particularly comely; the following Egyptian herbalist's formula against baldness being included: to mix together fat of the lion, fat of the hippopotamus, fat of the crocodile, fat of the cat, fat of the serpent, and fat of the Nubian ibex. Early magic has many counterparts. In the "facility of his reformation" by the garland of roses, Apuleius' metamorphosis into an ass delightfully illustrates the plausibility of magic:

> I took Fotis by the hand, . . . and said: "I pray thee, . . . grant me some of this ointment . . . and I will ever hereafter be bound unto you by a mighty gift and obedient to your commandment, if you will but make that I be turned into a bird and stand, like Cupid with his wings, beside you my Venus." . . . And then I put off all my garments and greedily thrust my hand into the box and took out a good deal of ointment, and after that I had well rubbed every part and member of my body, I hovered with mine arms, and moved myself, looking still when I should be changed into a bird . . . ; and behold neither feathers did burgeon out nor appearance of wings but verily my hair did turn into ruggedness and my tender skin wore tough and hard; my fingers and toes leaving the number five grew together into hooves, and from the end of my back grew a great tail, . . . and so without all help (viewing every part of my poor body) I perceived that I was no bird, but a plain ass.

As one is made aware by Sir Wallis Budge, herb doctor and magician have from the earliest times accompanied each other, and it is not surprising that Apuleius should have given us both the *Golden Ass*[2] and a Herbarium.

Herbs and magic belong characteristically also to the North American Indian, and in his use of them as in other primitive practice, the sinister cannot be said to have quite strangled the good. Chief Standing Bear has provided, in his autobiography,[3] a much needed antidote to "white" superstition regarding "medicine," massacres, stealth, and various forms of "savage" diffidence. He admits certain superstitions, vicarious sacrifice by ordeal, and a tendency to retaliation, saying also without embarrassment, "The Spotted Tail Indians thought they would go after the Poncas. . . . They had no reason for bothering this tribe, but they just did not like them"; yet has imparted profound respect for primitive resourcefulness, loyalty, and domestic aestheticism. It is impossible not to be ashamed of our civilized ignorance in moving-picture and other representations of the Indian, for Chief Standing Bear finds that we prefer a pseudo-Indian life to the actual one and are indifferent when reasoned with. The conventionalized all-Greek living statuary of Ringling Brothers' "On the War Path," and "The First Americans" may be over-ambitious, but it is not really misleading.

In the American wing of The Metropolitan Museum there is a colonial bedspread in which the motive is Columbia on her triumphal car, drawn by leopards and acclaimed by Indians, under the legend, Where Liberty Dwells There is My Country. In view of the fact that about twenty-four dollars was paid for Manhattan and that we should like occupancy to be guardianship, one hopes that civilization may yet be a right substitute for primeval ecstatica.

[1] *The Divine Origin of the Craft of the Herbalist* by Sir E. A. Wallis Budge. Published at Culpepper House (London), by The Society of Herbalists.

[2] *The Golden Ass of Apuleius, Being the Metamorphoses of Lucius Apuleius*. An English Translation by W. Aldington (1566). Revised 1915–1927. With an Essay by Charles Whibley. Boni & Liveright.

[3] *My People the Sioux* by Luther Standing Bear. Edited by E. A. Brininstool. With Introduction by William S. Hart. Houghton Mifflin Company.

The Dial, 85 (August 1928), 178–80.

• • •

THOUGH tragedy in literature is not literature unless true to life, slayings and sluggings seem counterfeit—as tragedy even felonious—in newspaper reports based on facts, if advertised to provoke the same sensations that provoked the crime. Such futile particulars of murder as last January displaced notice of Mr. Hardy's death are fallacious compared with the verity of his own somber fictive presentations, with the spectral scourgings of conscience in Tolstoy's *The Power of Darkness*, or the impulsive sagacities of Maxim Gorki's pleasing little inferno, *The Lower Depths*. Aristotle, Gorki,

Hardy—all who know the truth underlying appearances—are agreed that "a probable impossibility is to be preferred to a thing improbable and yet possible." Among Maxim Gorki's triumphs of permanent fugacity none perhaps is more vivid than his group of lodgers in the cave-like room with its bunks, anvil and vise, smashed hat-box for making cap-visors, a trouser for cap material, a damaged samovar, a hunk of black bread, and so on: a baron, a market-woman, a cap-maker, a lock-smith, an actor, a lodging-house keeper, a pilgrim, a shoemaker, a policeman's uncle, two porters, tramps, supernumeraries, and others. The baron gives Nastiah a blow on the head with the book she is reading—*Disastrous Love.*

Say! You! "Disastrous Love!" Wake up!
Nastiah. "And this is a nobleman!"
Baron. "Do a little bit of sweeping for me—will you?"

The piece has been included in a selection of world tragedies[1] that Dr. R. M. Smith has chosen for college students—*Othello*, for instance, *Medea*, *The Cenci*, and *Ghosts*. In conjunction with certain philosophic dramas[2] in this series—*Job, Everyman, Prometheus Bound*, and *Prometheus Unbound*, it brings before us as was intended, "problems of life, death, and destiny" and strongly supports the conviction that life and death are conceivably more than living and dying. It metamorphoses experience into something beyond epicurean necessities and measures of satisfaction.

News is the reporter's prerogative and in many newspaper pronouncements we recognize the sense of polarity and a becoming aplomb. But the yield of murders and revived murders makes evident to us that for the press, temptation lies in violence. America's capacity for suspicion, and certain ill-advised smotherings and burgeonings have many counterparts. In a recent book,[3] the author speaks of having been arrested in Russia from one to three times a day successively for ten days. Nevertheless to condone frailty by comparison with yet greater frailty is not profitable. As Maxim Gorki's pilgrim reiterates, "Man is born to give strength," the immaterial strength to which he refers, being a power very different from that of the rhinoceros or the gorilla such as newspapers when roused to violence consent to employ.

[1] *Types of World Tragedy* edited by Robert Metcalf Smith. World Drama Series, Prentice-Hall.
[2] *Types of Philosophic Drama* edited by Robert Metcalf Smith. World Drama Series, Prentice-Hall.
[3] *Seeing Russia* by E. M. Newman. Funk and Wagnalls.

The Dial, 85 (September 1928), 269–70.

• • •

STRANGE things are said about good people and none stranger than remarks hazarded about geniuses as if they were boxers or champion live-stock. When one cannot appraise out of one's own experience, the temptation to blunder is minimized, but even when one can, appraisal seems chiefly useful as appraisal of the appraiser.

In the months which have passed since the death of Dame Ellen Terry, the irresponsibleness of some and the assumed responsibleness of others have suggested these acerbities; but the sense of benefit one has always experienced in the thought of her makes acerbities not the right word, for her generosity should mellow us toward the littleness of those who would make little of her uncommon gift and attainments—to say nothing of her sense of honor—not always associated with genius. She felt it "hateful" to be "compelled to break faith," "hated the idea of drawing a large salary and doing next to no work," and felt that "not until we have learned to be useful can we afford to do what we like." "The artist," she said, "must spend his life in incessant labor" and she notes in Henry Irving "a kind of fine temper, like the purest steel, produced by the perpetual fight against difficulties," his fortune "counted not in gold, but in years of scorned delights" and "deep melancholy." The axiom is not a favorite with artists, that "before you can be eccentric you must know where the circle is," but Miss Terry had the mystic's conviction that humility and common sense are the same thing. She recollects eagerly Mrs. Kean's sharp lessons in enunciation: "You must say *her* not *har*; it's *God*, not *Gud*; re*mon*strance, not re*mun*strance"; but she also notes that to take criticism in a slavish spirit is of little use and it is a picture of herself she gives us in bequeathing the instruction, pace "is not a question of swift utterance only, but of swift thinking."

Familiar as the word gratitude is, and Ellen Terry was incandescently grateful, its fire is not something to be learned like the "ardent exits" she studied to perfect. With her it was innately a part of that goodness without malice which speaks so unselfprotectively of our (America's) able architects, our scholarly critics, of our young girls each with a cast of the Winged Victory in her room, and of our Negro servants as "delightful," "so attractive," "so deft and gentle."

"Why the word 'theatrical' should have come to be used in a contemptuous sense," Miss Terry wrote, "I cannot understand"; nor can we, recalling the imagination and sensibility which some have brought to the theater. The sense of "life as imagination"—shared by her son, but first hers—constitutes a nimbus before which death retires. Imagination receives homage, but "Principalities and Powers and Possibilities," that "crowd of unseen forms," "those words which are never heard," "those figures which seldom shape themselves more definitely than a cloud's shadow," bequeath more than bays. In such presence, as a writer in this issue of *The Dial* reminds us

> Time is but a shadow
> Which forever passeth away.

Imagination, moreover, that is kind, travels far without occasion to carp, and despite the suddenness of certain "terrific" scenery which she did not quite like, Miss Terry thought America "a land of sunshine and light, of happiness, of faith in the future." We ourselves scarcely find it in harmony with the oldness of England. But not all of it is without usefulness—the modest value she bespoke for herself. One recalls her saying, "I *have* been a useful actress." A gallant bowsprit that leads when heavier vessels sink, she never spoke of being tired, though she says somewhere, "the long low lines of my Sussex marshland near Winchelsea give me rest." One instinctively envies the children who came to her garden of their own accord, but association so gentle was fitting; and those remote and deprived will cherish the lines well liked by Miss Terry herself, "e'en in our ashes burn our wonted fires."

The Dial, 85 (October 1928), 361–62.

• • •

A literary period would not be a period but for personality which makes it what it is and unaccountable charm can be imparted to it by a single mind— as in the instance of Goldsmith. In his father's home, "an old, half-rustic mansion, . . . overlooking a low tract occasionally flooded by the River Inny," "we were told that universal benevolence was what first cemented society"; he says, "we were taught to consider the wants of mankind as our own." The portrait of Lysippus in *The Bee* is a kind of desperate miniature of Goldsmith, his father, and his Uncle Contarine: "His generosity is such that it prevents a demand, and saves the receiver the trouble and the confusion of a request. His liberality also does not oblige more by its greatness than by his inimitable grace in giving. Sometimes he even distributes his bounties to strangers, and has been known to do good offices to those who professed themselves his enemies." Inclined to regard money lightly—as Goldsmith was—to

> . . . press the bashful stranger to his food
> And learn the luxury of doing good,

it is not strange that gallant execution should become on occasion, burlesque, pitifulness or domestic debacle.

Though he quivered under insult, a masqueraded mock melancholy put plumes on desperation and whereas a paraded sense of melancholy is unpersuasive, dejection not induced in the hope of response has the opposite effect, as in the remarks, "When once a man addicts himself to the sciences, or commences author, if he be not of the church, his friends lament him as lost," and "I resemble one of those animals that has been forced from its forest to gratify human curiosity. My earliest wish was to escape unheeded through life; but I have been set up for half-pence, to fret and scamper at the end of my chain." The humility of the apologia for *The Vicar of Wakefield* is the completeness of dignity: "There are an hundred faults in this thing, and an hundred things might be said to prove them beauties. But it is needless. A book may be amusing with numerous errors, or it may be very dull without a single absurdity. The hero of this piece unites in himself the three greatest characters upon earth; he is a priest, an husbandman, and the father of a family. He is drawn as ready to teach, and ready to obey; as simple in affluence, as majestic in adversity. In this age of opulence and refinement, whom can such a character please?"

Frequently doubting his own product—not that he did not think the thing good, but that he did not think people would think it so—he was freely encomiastic with respect to others and says of Voltaire, "When he was warmed in discourse, . . . it was rapture to hear him. His meager visage seemed insensibly to gather beauty: every muscle in it had meaning," and in dedicating *Mistakes of a Night* to Doctor Johnson: "By inscribing this slight performance to you, I do not mean so much to compliment you as myself. It may do me some honor to inform the public, that I have lived many years in intimacy with you. It may serve the interests of mankind also to inform them, that the greatest wit may be found in a character, without impairing the most unaffected piety."

Nor was respect mere formality. Willingness to sacrifice labor and "in deference to the judgment of a few friends, who think in a particular way," to revise or restore, was not a recollecting that he could write. To us Doctor Primrose is one of the diamond-set snuff-boxes of the curioso and the "long fight against the deuterogamy of the age" as well as other equally valuable irrelevant plausibilities have lost nothing with time.

Of eighteen of Goldsmith's essays now for the first time reprinted,[1] an especially pleasing one on South American Giants—was occasioned by a book published at Madrid, "a work, entitled *Giganthalogia*, by P. Joseph Tarrubias," and the editor's necessity to create pages "for his own perusal" is as unapparent in it as in some of his more famous unautographed writings. Approving of certain of the giants—a body consisting of about four hundred— he says, "the lowest soldier in the whole army was not under nine feet high; and the tallest was about eleven. Their features were regular, their limbs exactly proportioned; they had a sweetness and affability in their looks, and their speech was deep, clear, and sonorous. . . . They lived in a state of perfect equality among each other, and had people of ordinary stature to do the domestic offices of life."

The plays are plays not essays and the poems are "full of quality" as Professor Saintsbury says, "though not always of strictly poetical quality"; but in Goldsmith a miscellaneous tendency and a hopping, zigzag consistency are oddly expressive of his parti-colored being. Reflecting upon history and climate and race and poverty, and ranting—on paper—against the "hostilities" of a Scotch minuet performed "with a formality that approaches a despondence," we know that he distrusted "all honest jog-trot men who go on smoothly and dully"; but he was not kind to folly and could "wish that he might find men, when employed upon trifles, conscious that they are but trifles." He may have regarded as ephemera, the somewhat monstrous character of the fairy with the train fifteen yards long supported by porcupines, and the blue cat who showed the prince that "his passion for the white mouse was entirely fictitious, and not the genuine complexion of his soul"; but the eclipse of the sinister is always in Goldsmith an inversion of injury. Now a hundred years later, when publishers whose "valuable stock can only bear a winter perusal" and a "muster-master-general, or review of reviews" would admit that he had not employed himself upon trifles, his proffered skepticism, "let folly and dullness join to brand me" seems rather absurd. Avoiding the church and its black vestments by accident as much as by prudent decision, he seems to have been able to "moderate rage" and to have occupied in the world without realizing that he was so doing, a Samaritan and pastoral office.

[1] *New Essays by Oliver Goldsmith, Now First Collected and Edited with an Introduction and Notes by Ronald S. Crane.* Chicago University Press.

The Dial, 85 (November 1928), 450–53.

. . .

THERE will always be some who are in a hurry, and pleased to be shot from ship to land in an airplane so as to arrive in advance of the usual time. Equipment, however, material or academic, is not invariably a part of culture as Mr. Douglas Kennedy reminded those who saw the exhibition of English folk dancing at The Art Center last autumn. We have long been familiar with the valuable unimitativeness of folklore—the green men, dogs, horses, and other sincere impossibilities in varying guises which appear in sagas and ballads the world over—the sister that as "a machrel of the sea," every Saturday at noon, combs the hair of her brother, the Worm; and newest perhaps in the Danish version[1] the lover to be disenchanted by voluntary ordeal:

> You've plighted your word, and now be true
> Give hither your hand, my claw take you.
>
> The lady she gave the bird her hand,
> And free from feathers she saw him stand.

W. P. Ker noted that "strange excellence in the ballads," "not merely of repeating old motives, but of turning the substance of daily life into poetry." Folk dancing at any rate is a natural means of expression like language and presents itself as an antidote to shyness and those insidiously anti-social forms of considerateness which tend to impair innocence without conferring security. It is the aim of The English Folk Dance Society not so much to provide entertainment for the onlooker as to afford people means of entertaining themselves. Though no dancing could be more delightful to watch than that of Mr. Kennedy and his group. The spiral swirled attitudes as in certain kinds of ships' figure-head, the "speed and neatness," the "flashes of wit cropping up in the movements," were shapely and gracious, the terminal and divisional pauses seeming more deferentially courteous even than those of the minuet. The Morris dancing in its rhythmic complexity and patter-step, achieved an effect of mastery the more remarkable that the dancers were not a full complement, and suffered nothing apparently in the absence of box hats, wreaths, fluttering streamers, Tom-fool and She-male (a man dressed as a woman) as supplementary coquillage. It was obvious that Morris and Sword dances are not "for as many as will," but for men, and for those that can do them; the Fool's Dance by Mr. Kennedy alone was a particularly wise and unfatigued little whirligig of ability.

There is power in mystery and it is not disappointing not to know the origin of the Morris Dance or the significance of the handkerchief in either hand and to be aware merely that a good dancer should, as the Morris men said, feel the weight of his handkerchiefs. The "purpose" of wands, bells, blue and cerise ribbons tying the bells to the legs, and of miniature music, needs no explanation. Ensnared by the fineness of the airs and steps, one desires that it all be repeated and in certain places in England teams may be seen once a year on a particular day, "about teatime" as Mr. Kennedy suggests, since indigenous and rightful folk dancers appear *on* the day, not having engaged in self-distrustful preliminary practice.

Partly as novelty but also in itself, the drum and tabor (tabber) accompaniment perfected the grace of the scene and satisfies Henry Peacham's contention in *The Compleat Gentleman* that the musician is a second physician; that his art is a thing which "prolonge l'existence, guerit certaines maladies, rend inoffensive la piqûre de la tarentule, corrige les défauts de pronunciation et remedie au begaiement chez les enfants."*

To see fortunately and delicately executed movements is as true an introduction to the skill of music as one could have. Lost words and airs rediscovered by Cecil Sharp in the Appalachian mountain region repaid him for many endurances and are important for speed-ridden and to some extent coreless modern expertness, reaffirming our belief that delightful manners, conversation, and culture, can exist devoid of opportunity and advantages.

*"extends life, heals some illnesses, makes the tarantula's bite harmless, corrects pronunciation mistakes and overcomes stuttering in children."

[1] *Folklore in the English and Scottish Ballads* by Lowry Charles Wimberley. University of Chicago Press.

The Dial, 85 (December 1928), 541–42.

• • •

THE Dial Award this year has been proffered by the donors to Kenneth Burke.

It is difficult to think about art we are told, where there is a great deal of noise, or to talk of it to those who are inattentive. Mr. Burke has, however, without discovering a retreat for himself, devoted himself uninterruptedly to writing and to so good purpose that word of his service to literature will come to the reading public in no sense as news. Nor in his studies has one art starved another for music enjoyably and scientifically—enjoyably perhaps because scientifically—is present in his aesthetics. "The artist, as artist, is not a prophet," he remarked in a pamphlet some while since; "he does not change the mould of our lives: his moral contribution consists in the element of grace which he adds to the conditions of life wherein he finds himself." The opinion of the skeptic that the artist can thrive only under the most favorable conditions is often shared by the artist; but discipline under provocation, an integrity of confident expectation, the refusal to be warped by misadventure, are not infirm refutations.

Translating requires that one put at the service of something not one's own, the most sharpened and excellent tools in one's armory; that is to say, there is character rather than good fortune in translation of finish.

A creatively investigating interest in psychology can be felt in any aspect of Mr. Burke's writing; and richly, in those forms which people have a way of terming creative. As he has himself said, "The artist does not run counter to his age; rather, he refines the propensities of his age, formulating their aesthetic equivalent."

The Dial, 86 (January 1929), 90.

• • •

WHEN an artist is willing that the expressiveness of his work be overlooked by any but those who are interested enough to find it, he has freedom in which to realize without interference, conceptions which he personally values. But advertising, the opposite of such intensiveness, has its uses. One recalls Sir Philip Sidney's miniature of Edward Wotton's passion for horses: "no earthly thing bred such wonder to a prince as to be a good horseman; skill of government was but a *pedanteria* in comparison. . . . Then would he add . . . what a peerless beast the horse was . . . that if I had not been a piece of a logician before I came to him, I think he would have persuaded me to have wished myself a horse." Although one may not know much about occultism, one feels an involuntary indulgence toward Saunders' *Chiromancy* when Lilly says, "there is not in any one *Book* or *Volume* yet extant, in any Language of *Europe*, that comprehends so many rarities, so neatly couched, so judiciously Methodized, as are by our *Author* comprized in this his Labour. The *Author* for his pains, and the *Book* for its merits, I commend to this unthankful Age." Poetry of this kind persuades in one way if not in another, and makes a friend of the advocate if not of his client. And the miraculous need not be objectionable; for though one might not guess Messrs. Foyle's "output of school-books" to be "30 tons a week," one can believe it. Too great strain upon credulity results in inattention, however; when a masterpiece is desired that will "grip and burn like Nessus' magic shirt," we are not inspired to compete; and iteration is wasteful unless a first saying was so alluring that we welcome an encore, as in the announcement of Barnum's "two living whales, two living whales, two living whales."

The semi-confidential impartial enthusiasm of the pre-auction descriptive catalogue suggests a desirable mechanics of eulogy and the same kind of honor without exaggeration is seen occasionally in guide-books and travel bureau advertisements. Though somewhat unguarded and uncompactly eager in comparison with Karl Baedeker's contagious impassivity, certain handbooks[1] of the University Travel Department of The North German Lloyd Company pictorially and with characteristic abundance, are a little cyclorama of engaging remarkableness—medieval carvings and ecclesiastical treasures, luxurious crockery, boilers for the Europa, the domestic interior with the window for cactuses, the racing Ring at Nürnburg, and—by no means incompatible with combustion-chambers and cylinders—Dürer's design of the automatically movable carriage driven at the will of the occupants by a system of cog-wheels. There is mention of the German university with its "complete freedom and strenuous discipline," of the art of the placard, of the Farbenfreude of the booksellers in exhibiting novels that look like "birds, butterflies, and orchids"; of small towns, of great cities. And if one doesn't like cities, there are the mountains "so lonely, so easily reached."

The desire to see good things is in itself good when not degraded by inquisitiveness or predatoriness, and it is not just to regard as rapacity the advertiser's art of educating visualization.

[1] *Art and Germany* edited by Karl Kiessel and Ernst O. Thiele; *Passing Through Germany 1928–1929;* The Terramare Office, Wilhelmstrasse 23, Berlin SW 48.

The Dial, 86 (February 1929), 179–80.

• • •

THE English Singers' third visit to America has seemed as needful and their singing as comely as any random kind of strangeness sometimes is at first. The wiliness of their art and the innocence of their manner, unaided by musical instruments, have again emphasized the difference between preciosity and what is to be treasured.

We are tempted by these madrigals, folk-songs, and carols as recently sung, to infer that musical spontaneity is more spontaneous than verbal spontaneity; that words when separated from accompaniment miss the music more than the music when separated misses the words; and whereas some words are sufficient to themselves, others live only by association with the tune; but in a matter of enjoyment there is no need for weighing pleasures. In the "Corpus Christi," however, both musics assert themselves—the buried fire and almost tuneless murmur of the tune with its slow fast according tongues of discord, and the apparitional text:

> And in that hall there was a bed:
> It was hangèd with gold so red,
> And in that bed there lithe a knight.
> His woundes bleeding day and night.
> By that bedside there kneeleth a may,
> And she weepeth night and day;
> By that bed side there standeth a stone:
> *Corpus Christi* written thereon.

How complexity of rhythm can be made to seem natural, and words and music one, the English Singers have shown us; but an Elizabethan prevalence of musical proficiency—musical good will and an aptitude for it impromptu—is probably not common to all ages and has a connection with learning; there is more than fearlessness and the hope that strangers will like something that has never been published.

This company of six, in a co-ordinated sentience of ancient beauty with a never better accuracy, persuades us that there can now and then be an armistice in our sometimes pointless tumultuousness.

THE Countryman,[1] quarterly non-party review and miscellany of rural life and industry, discusses in its January issue, lack of imagination on the part of those who would preserve old cottages in which they don't have to live. There is a kind of pro-picturesque sentiment that is as false *The Countryman* contends, "as the satisfaction some of our ancestors had in imitation 'ruins' and 'hermitages' " and he recalls Thomas Hardy's feeling about the cast of mind of a certain man who " 'would talk about bishops' copes and mitres in an earnest, serious, anxious manner as if there were no tears or human misery beyond tears.' " Devotion to machinery and to motors is countenanced, and simple furniture is recommended. "Iron bedsteads of the period 1820–40 are works of art. . . . The Duke of Wellington and Napoleon both preferred iron bedsteads." *The Countryman*'s mind on the subject of fox-hunting is eloquently "without hypocrisy" and we in this country may care to apply to ourselves what is said about names that are taking, and headlines that are not—and the dreary way in which some "keep speaking of 'adults' and 'adolescents.' "

"Winning speech," "sensitiveness and vitality . . . and the appreciation of periods of reflection that mark the true countryman" are richly present in this publication.

[1] Edited and published by J. W. Robertson Scott at Idbury, Kingham, Oxford, England.

The Dial, 86 (March 1929), 269–70.

. . .

W E hear daily of the respective gains of peace and armament and of a desire for peace on the part of countries where blood is being shed, and of the vigor of America as the principal peace factory.

Prescriptions for complacently self-dependent quiescence meanwhile appear to be crowding one another; and complacency is not, as we know, an element of peace. There is an unscientific tendency not to recognize the debt to antecedent deprivations and sacrifices which have resulted for us in a life different from that of Nicobar islanders, or of East Africans seized by ghosts or wind spirits and known as the *wazi-wazi* (wind-witted) until freed by a "busy knave" girdled with lion-skins, snake-skins, necklets of claws, knuckle-bones, and little gourds.

War is pillage versus resistance and if illusions of magnitude could be transmuted into ideals of magnanimity, peace might be realized. In discussing contemporary architecture, Claude Bragdon sees the skyscraper a thief of air and sunlight—a symbol of "ruthless and tireless aggression on the part of the cunning and the strong." We may not adopt quickly all that he says of glyphs, the logarithmic spiral as the possible form of the universe, or of "spheres" as constituting a single hyper-sphere, but can understand that "the use and justification of sacrifice is that it shall accomplish that which without it could not be accomplished, that it shall diminish the sum total of suffering and even change it to its opposite." We need "the feminine ideal" as Mr. Bragdon puts it,[1] "(not the female)"; that is to say, "the compassional" not "the forceful," and willingness to work for "the establishment of a world-polity not founded upon fear and hate."

That magnanimity is more than a negative virtue is shown us by lands and ages other than our own. The Goodman of Paris,[2] who seems in reading, statecraft, observation, and travel to have been far from nearsighted, might or might not be apprehensive about our wild manner of attainment. "It is noteworthy, as I have heard tell," he says, "that the Queens of France after that they be wed, read never sealed letters, save such as be by the hand of their husband, as is said, and those read they all alone, and for the others they call company and bid them to be read by others before them, and say often that they know not to read letter or writing, save that of their husband." "You ought to give alms out of your own true possessions, buxomly, speedily, secretly, devoutly and humbly," he writes, and "have naught to do with folk who answer back and be arrogant, proud and scornful, or give foul answers, however great profit or advantage it seemeth to be and however cheaply they be minded to come; but do you graciously and quietly send them away from you and from your work." Besides a gravity contrasting with the aplomb of a generation which "like an acrobat" according to Mr. Bragdon, "perform each difficult and dangerous feat smiling," there is also a certain beauty of politeness as, after telling the stories of Lucrece and of Susanna, the Goodman says, "and they be given you rather for the tale, than for the teaching."

Where all demons are there may or may not be warfare, but there is pandemonium; the mere absence of armament is not necessarily peace. Milton was impressed by the fact that where all angels are there is not necessarily heaven, and we have seen contest result in cessation of warfare which is not peace—merely dearth of equipment. True non-materialism is not that, however, but itself a war on self-interest. Of those who would become "masters over time" Mr. Bragdon says, "each must pour out affection which is unrequited, for to be thrifty in love is to be vile; each must pay debts never in his life contracted, and redress wrongs he knows not of. To reconcile these conflicting and often opposite obligations—of the world and of the spirit—constitutes the real art of life, and to this each should address himself, paying all debts and spending only the surplus, be it of energy, money or time."

¹ *The New Image* by Claude Bragdon. Illustrated. Alfred A. Knopf.
² *The Goodman of Paris (Le Menagier de Paris): A Treatise on Moral and Domestic Economy by a Citizen of Paris (c. 1393) now first translated into English, with an Introduction and Notes by Eileen Power*. Harcourt, Brace and Company.

The Dial, 86 (April 1929), 359–60.

• • •

THE exhibition of Soviet Russian art and handicraft at the Grand Central Palace confirmed one's sense of Russia's strong feelings, composite geography, and separateness of expressions, despite her taste for abbreviated similarities such as U.S.S.R., AKHRR, ORS, and OST. Besides more evident pieces, there were a little drawing by D. I. Mitrokhin, some wood engravings by V. A. Favorsky of sheaves and reapers, a wispish slow-motion ink and brush study of boxers by A. A. Deyneka, also a pleasing one by him of a dancer, an accordion-player, and group of workmen with gourd-like heads, and intent, large yet dot-like eyes. As in the time of Turgenev, the country still has maple and birch; indigo cashmere shawls with red roses; fur objects piped with clipped fur of contrasting color; malachite, lapis lazuli, and other stones, among which was a sad, vigorously true marble alligator. Things could be bought, though not so easily as to aid thieving on the part of such as know better the possibilities of a thing than the unconsciously aesthetic makers know.

Naturalness and ability can apologize for the grandeur of a palace that is not grand, and as has been said by Mr. McBride, one had the feeling that in permitting the exhibition, the Soviet officials are really aiming at our good opinion.

EZRA Pound may proffer too readily Stendhal's remark that it takes eighty years for anything to reach the general public, and he is not afraid of repeating what he has said before; but a discussion by him in *The Herald-Tribune*— "How to Read, or Why"— is a lively, or better say a living, thing, and not undistinctive rhetorically in its dual method of emphasis by over- and by under-statement.

The field of comparative literature has, as Mr. Pound says, been full of redundance. The reader would "profit by an orderly arrangement of his perceptions" and should have "axes of reference by knowing the best of each kind of written thing," latitude being permitted persons inclined to substitute one best for another. "Literature incites humanity to continue living," says Mr. Pound; "it eases the mind of strain, and feeds it." By specific recommendations and in reviving "the feel of and the desire for exact descriptive terms" he does his part in "maintaining the health of thought"; and differences of trend need not, as he points out, bother bona fide appetite.

T H E gilded wagons and bellows-warbled, now high, now low, hollow music of the circus have again invited us to wander among the cages, stare at the sword-swallower and the pin-head, and surreptitiously touch kangaroo and camel. The purity of the new Garden affords a less likely background than the dingy tea-canister aspect of the old one, but the formidableness of cattle and keepers and the high cleverness of the virtuosi are not abating, even should only some of the names be new and some of the virtuosity be the same that has pleased us through several years.

Toulouse-Lautrec's, Seurat's, and Emanuel Faÿ's equestriennes, Mr. Jack Yeats' out-door circus man and spotted ponies, Benjamin Kopman's pagan god- or goddess-like roundabout of human four-footed persons, Charles Demuth's acrobats, Picasso's saltimbanques and harlequins, and Ernest Fiene's impersonally definite, silvery monotoned lithographs containing it all as it were a fern-leaf in agate, assert by implication that they have not been based on nothing. Where there is much to see, worth is in danger of being overlooked; moreover, the pain of seeing a bear ride a bicycle may outweigh the pleasure of seeing six little black dogs clown the maneuvers of Herman Hesse's six black stallions from Hungary. One does not admire so much the elephant's ability to beat a drum with a small cannon-ball attached to the tail, as the slack-rope drunkard's self-possession; the monkeys' uncontrol of their gazelle-hound wavy-tailed mounts; the utility of ostrich and sulky; the tumblers' fondness for meeting the feet with the hands and resting quadruped-wise, the stomach-side in the customary position of the back; the courtier-like equipoise and fairness of the acrobats standing in twos among the stanchions of the roof. Rashness and regality may not be teaching us anything; animals should not be taken from their proper surroundings, and in staging an act the bad taste of patrons should not be deferred to; but apparently this medicinally mingled feast of sweet and bitter is not poisonous; it is not all aconite.

The Dial, 86 (May 1929), 449–50.

. . .

BRAVURA as one of the attributes of the 17th century keeps rising into our vision from time to time like the bouquet of a fountain, its gaudy phases less richly than the more shadowy ones in Jeremy Taylor, Richard Hooker, or Sir Thomas Browne, or in such an inscription as we have on an Austrian executioner's sword[1] lately brought to America:

> Who takes it paying not the cost
> Will find it lost.
> That one will die before he ill shall lie.[2]

17th century portraits, heraldic emblems carved in the pavements and the little tabernacles within tabernacles in the aisles of cathedral churches, seem to extenuate superficialities of the age, and there were others besides Sir Thomas Browne to whom ashes were more than dust. But to many, mortality was without personal significance, and suffering was traded upon. A recent book[3] tells of a remedy for the Morow-Cure of the Gout and Agues of all sorts, Tertian, Quartan, and Quotidian; of *Coward's Comfort* drawn from the hearts of *Mandrakes* and *Tongues of Mermaids*, quoting a recipe in which gold—supposed to be coincident with immortality—was filed into dust, to be drunk in canary sack; and there was dependence as there had been a century earlier, in the fern—"a plant so strange that it hath the peculiar power of making persons invisible." The Lady Read had "cured multitudes defective in their sight, particularly several who were born blind." Thomas Rands had performed an excellent cure upon a Captain who had a cannon ball lodg'd in his little finger; likewise the carpenter of the same ship who had swallowed a handspike. Nathaniel Merry could save hands, arms, and legs from cutting off when order'd for amputation by the vulgar and had discovered a cure for the Dogmatical Incurables. Stage figures these personages now seem to us with their apparatus, monkeys, zanies, and Spanish gravity, irresponsibleness being an almost requisite accessory. And indifference to death as we have it in a collection of broadside elegies edited by Professor John W. Draper[4] is a discord of the epoch, equally definite. In the introductory pages resemblances are noted between the elegy, the ballad, the hymn, the pensive lyric, and other forms; and despite a kind of customary callousness there are some fossil flowers, odder and more delicately impressed than is easily compatible with the absent-minded pomposity of public poetry. In Jeremiah Rich's piece "On the death of the Right Honourable Iohn Warner, Late Lord Mayor of London," the rhyming suggests "The Song of Love and Death" in *The Idylls of the King:*

> Thus is our wealth but want, our flower fades, Our light is
> darkness, and our sun-shine shades.
>
> . . . .
>
> Thus is our glory grass, our bravery breath,
> Our light is darkness, and our life is death;

and we are again reminded of it by "The Humble Address of *Anthony Wildgoos*, Workman-Printer, in Divine Meditations on Death Made upon these Nine Words, Nothing more sure then Death, for all must Die"; each of the nine words being the initial word of a stanza.

>   Took away King *Herod* in his Pride,
>   Spar'd not *Hercules* for all his strength;
>   Struck Great *Alexander* that he dy'd;
> *Death*   Long spar'd *Adam*, yet he dy'd at length.
>   The Beggar and the King, the Low, the High;
>   *Nothing more sure then Death, for all must Dye.*
>
>   Scepters, Crowns, Imperial Diadems;
>   All the Beauties that on Earth do live:
>   Pleasures, Treasures, Jewels, costly Jems;
> *For*   All the Glory that the World can give,
>   Death will not spare his Dart, but still reply,
>   *You, and you, and you, and all must Dye.*

Lofty emotion is dealt a blow by expediency, but there is individuality in "A Rhetorical Rapture by Mr. Slater as Composed into A Funeral Oration At the Mournful Moving of His Highnes [Cromwell's] Stately Effigies from Somerset-House":

> Seventh *Henry's* Chappel may Thy *Corps* entombe,
> But for Thy Monuments the *World's* the room:
> Seventh *Henry's*, or *Cromwell's* Chappel, which you please
> Call it; or, to Them Both, *Chappel of Ease;*
> Or, *Honors Cabinet* or, *Valours Tent*
> To repose in, after the Day is spent,
> To rise at sound of Trump, clad *cap a pe*
> In bright Armour of *Immortalitie.*

The inch wide bands of black, pseudo-architectural embellishments, bones, trowels, darts, hour-glasses, skeletons, and portraits that appear as part of the typographic design of some of the broadsides, are worthier to see than the lines are worthy to read, but the 17th century bears scrutiny, and since sources are not easily accessible we thank the studious for permitting us the luxury of being curiosos in absentia.

[1] One of the Executioner's swords of a known castle, dated 1673, sold at auction by The American Art Association, Inc., in November, 1928.

[2] Wer kavft ed fa viel Wirt und
Find ed verlorn eird
Der stirpt ed er krank wirt.

[3] *The Quacks of Old London* by C. J. S. Thompson. J. B. Lippincott Company.

[4] *A Century of Broadside Elegies: being ninety English and ten Scotch broadsides illustrating the biography and manners of the seventeenth century.* Photographically reproduced and edited with an Introduction and Notes by John W. Draper. Ingpen & Grant.

The Dial, 86 (June 1929), 540–42.

BRIEFER MENTION

Memoirs of the Empress Eugénie, by Comte Fleury (Appleton), are not the enactment in daily life of a Watteau picture. The Empress regarded dress as she would regard the wheels of a coach—of necessity perfect, but being so of no further moment. Her one thought was the Empire; her ideal, "a tyrant of genius who would lead the people toward goodness and happiness without bothering them to know how he accomplished this end."

Comte Fleury combats the trend of social evolution in assuming that an aristocratic government could not but be better for France than a republic; and his view of Napoleon as the liberator of Italy does not impose itself on one with much power; but it is ironic that one who could strike a balance between French Catholic disapproval, the *amour propre* of the See of Rome, and the impetus of Italy toward political unity, should be a victim of the quibble with regard to the placing of a Hohenzollern prince on the throne of Spain. One cannot but agree with Comte Fleury in hating the Republic for declaring itself when one half the governing power was in England and the other at Wilhelmshöhe.

The Dial, 70 (January 1921), 107.

Medallions in Clay, by Richard Aldington (Knopf). We are told from time to time that the Greeks knew more about love than we do. If, today, we sometimes involuntarily confuse *eros* with *agape*, the Greeks were not open to this confusion and one knows to look in them for that in which they excelled—wit, the beauty of ritual, and the piercing quality of imagined satisfactions. Anyte of Tegea appears in this volume, less piercing, superlative, and "Homeric" than does Meleager, but we have occasionally in Meleager's Garland, as we have in the Latin poems of the Renaissance, supreme beauty—and, along with it, sensuality *in excelsis*. Those whom the translator designates as the unenlightened, will perhaps find Vitali's "Rome," Meleager's "Shipwrecked," and Anyte's "To Eros," the most beautiful poems in the book.

The Dial, 71 (July 1921), 120.

Motion Pictures in Education, by Don Carlos Ellis and Laura Thornborough (Crowell). One does not quarrel with the statement that "the more senses utilized in conveying knowledge, the better the result" and one conceives through the presentation of certain subjects in this book of practical information for teachers, the possibility of supplementing what seems to be poverty in the average child and adult, of knowledge by association. Although in the case of "films purporting to be historical and literary," one mistrusts a conception of the deluge in which a lion cub is a tiny replica of the lion which carries it, and a Solomon's Court with mural decorations which appear to be stenciled representations of Alaskan tribal spirits, one perceives the value of films which portray scenic wonders, plant and animal life, civic and domestic thrift, industrial processes, progress in mechanics and the evolution of commerce. The chapter, moreover, "How to Use Films in Teaching" with its insistence upon repetition and supplementary reading, upon exact preparation on the part of the teacher—with its pedagogic genius in exposition and the recapitulating quiz—is an enthralling demonstration of the author's facile assertion that "seeing is believing."

The Dial, 75 (September 1923), 302.

A Selection from the Poems of Michael Field, with a Preface by T. Sturge Moore (The Poetry Bookshop). Certain themes require that one should be overwhelmed, not merely pleased. Flaws and the lack of monumental genius detract from the high felicity of some of these poems. An amplifying of Sappho, moreover, which is not an "expansion of gold to airy thinness beat" is, one feels, a fault in judgment. But what flashes of ecstasy, what vibrations, what unstrained-for accuracy of feeling and of speech arrest one in the texture of this all but major poetry!

The Dial, 76 (February 1924), 200.

The Poems of Charles Cotton, edited by John Beresford (Boni & Liveright). Poetic afflatus which results in transport rather than induced hyperbole, is not found in these poems. We have in them as Coleridge says, "the milder muse"—even the mindless muse. An age of brilliance ought not to be commemorated in four hundred and twenty pages of conventional love, bucolic conviviality, and elaborate idleness. Nevertheless one considers with serious respect, the translator of Montaigne and the author with Izaak Walton of *The Compleat Angler* and it would be unfair to forget an occasional perfection.

The Dial, 76 (March 1924), 289.

Parson's Pleasure, by Christopher Morley (Doran). To speak of the "cider-colored eyes" and "naily paws" of one's dog and of maple seeds as "coat-hangers for a fairy's closet," is poetic. For one pestered by friends "to whom you daren't be rude," to befriend the convict, the foreigner, the literary lion-cub, is noble; but what Brobdingnagian ingenuousness or daring could lead this good man—a lover of "experienced proud words," whose library would make one love him for its sake alone—to proffer in verbiage such as "extuition," "hugeous," "enticive," "dolorobiliously," "inerasably," "pluperfectly," "inscrutables," "indignants and blasés,"—under the patron spirits of George Herbert, Thomas Fuller, Sir Thomas Browne, Oxford University, the Phi Beta Kappa Society of Harvard University, these addenda to Shakespeare in lame gosling prose, these "grams" and "taphs," these luckless jingles which are like nothing so much as those attempts at verse-making courageously extemporized in a game of forfeits?

The Dial, 76 (June 1924), 561.

Out of Silence and Other Poems, by Arthur Davison Ficke (Knopf). In these poems not "so great as to be prolific of greatness," one perceives a finely attuned ear not slavishly obeyed, a not warped if somewhat winter-starved worldly wisdom, an alert appreciation of the peeled willow-wand aspect of woman, and in its exactness, what is a sometimes exciting portrayal of the sea and the rock-bound coast.

The Dial, 77 (July 1924), 83.

Green Shoots, by Paul Morand, introduction by A. B. Walkley, preface by Marcel Proust, translated by H. I. Woolf (Seltzer). In these three portraits of women, we find not to be improved upon bits of actuality, and a graceful, seven-zephyred, corybantic suavity of interpretation which could be, in itself, impeccable—but does not M. Morand owe it to the docile reader to discriminate more pedagogically between fact and fiction? In the preface, Mr. Walkley is hospitably, undogmatically genial, and the *littérateur* will find in Marcel Proust's introduction, a comment on Flaubert, which he will prize.

Atlas and Beyond, by Elizabeth J. Coatsworth, woodcuts by Harry Cimino (Harper). Feeling for rhythm is apparent in these poems—the author's own, and feeling for that of others; frequently, however, instinctiveness vanishes, the insistent weightiness of enunciation which replaces it, not resulting in "spherical harmony." We have the enticing minutiae of appearance and of behavior, of the lower animals; in other of the verses, imagination which consistently, always opulently, and often contagiously, assembles the stage properties of resplendent visibility; pleasure in compelling as complements, symbols so contradictory as Pan's pipe and the crucifix; a clandestine thrill in the contemplation of forbidden fruit; and a bronze-breasted, steel-gauntleted voluptuousness which is not always alluring.

The Dial, 77 (August 1924), 171-72.

Harvest, by David Morton (Putnam). While neither piercing nor galvanic, with occasionally a conclusion which is not a climax and the recurrence as subject matter, of the moon, the spring of the year, and the pale beauty of woman, these sonnets exhibit genuine poetic sensibility, delicate imagination, and deft, sound execution.

The Middle Twenties, by John Farrar (Doran). Despite poems so impressive as "Lucile" and "Marguerite," one feels in this book, a lack of poetic machinery commensurate with the gravity of certain themes which the author has chosen, or has generously consented, to treat. The fanciful, Fourteenth-of-February arabesques upon jealousy and upon the marriage of Amaryllis, please most.

The Lost Flute of the Book of Franz Toussaint, translated by Gertrude Joerissen (Brentano). In this collection of Chinese lyrics, early and modern, the decoratively perfect poetic properties of the East are like the titles of the poems, themselves, dazzling. The subject matter of a number of the poems seems insufficient or unworthy, but there are certain masterpieces, and since the labor of translation has been undertaken with delight, the reader deplores an ingratitude which permits him to confiscate the meaning of words with which he quarrels.

The Dial, 77 (September 1924), 266.

Childhood in Verse and Prose: An Anthology, chosen by and with preface by Susan Miles (Oxford University Press). These selections of prose and verse, taken from the fourteenth and succeeding centuries, carefully indexed by source, author, and first line, command one's gratitude. Besides unknown, and certain unfamiliar masters, we have Herrick, Bunyan, Scott, Marjorie Fleming, Ruskin, Hardy, and W. H. Hudson to enchant us out of our hackneyed objection to the internecine character of anthologies; to dissipate our grievance that favorite pieces are not here, and our gloom because sorrow of and for children would seem, in this book, to preponderate over joy.

Heliodora and Other Poems, by H. D. (Houghton Mifflin). Accustomed as we are in modern poetry, to reminiscent rhythms and revised cultures, we cannot but participate in the triumph of an author who has achieved a tension, a balance, a mood and language which are Greek—without a trace of alien feeling. The perfect cadences and formal beauty of these poems, the Periclean world made for us here, of matter delicately sumptuous, are dazzling; "that flame, that flower (ice, spark, or jewel)," the "green, grey-green fastnesses of great deeps," the camellias, "the wind-indented snow," the "bright gloss of pearls," recalling in their vibrant emotion heightened by a chiseled severity of aspect, Pygmalion's statue "which understood my heart's quick sound."

Essays by Present-Day Writers, edited by Raymond Woodbury Pence (Macmillan). The compiler of these essays observes that "the essay of the present-day is preeminently the familiar essay." One has no quarrel with informal writing which enriches. In this book, however, one resists a cruel commingling of the work of certain gifted authors, with squibs—not essays—which evince a madness of bad taste not often known to man.

Poems, by Lady Margaret Sackville (Allen & Unwin). Despite a sometimes unselfprotective hazarding of thought which is slight, in forms which provoke comparison with metrical inventions of a sterner, wilder magic, we find in this book, certain conspicuously perfect poems, an alluring actuality, imaginative *esprit*, an elate chivalry, a stately completeness, and throughout—clear, energetic, prepossessing craftsmanship.

The Dial, 77 (October 1924), 347-48.

Religious Lyrics of the XIVth Century, edited by Carleton Brown (Oxford University Press). This resplendent collection of lyrics—to be followed by a collection of thirteenth century and one of fifteenth century lyrics—is a notable volume. That conciseness of word and intention which is characteristic of the highest poetry, a Latin glamour in certain instances, of cadence and of design, with mystical beauty, and the augmenting of knowledge by notes, glossary, and the scholarly arrangement of the poems, as here combined, signally illustrate in accordance with the editor's plan, the contribution of the fourteenth century to the development of the English lyric.

The Janitor's Boy and Other Poems, by Nathalia Crane (Seltzer). An occasional dead word, unevenness of rhetoric, and flaws of rhyme and rhythm are to be found in these poems by a child eleven years old. The work is not perfect; neither is it marred by self-conscious, missish assumptiveness. Its conspicuous quality is its vigor, manifested in resilient humor and sometimes captivating diction—the product, it would seem, of rich association and inheritance.

An Autobiography, by Anthony Trollope, with introduction by Michael Sadleir (Oxford University Press). This new edition in the World's Classics Series of Anthony Trollope's autobiography, with an expert, indeed exquisitely alert introduction by Michael Sadleir, is greatly welcome. In addition to unconsciously revealed secrets of authorship, and deliberate observations upon methods and purposes of novel writing, the chic wariness, "the pride," "the humility," the openness, the verbal harmony of the novels are well reflected in the autobiography—this "brisk and manly" record which is, in its contagious opposition to stupidity and cupidity, a model of self revelation.

The Dial, 77 (November 1924), 437–38.

House of Ghosts, by John Grimes, introduction by Vincent Starrett, decoratively interpreted by James Cady Ewell (Robert O. Ballou). A sensitive assertiveness, precise vision, and philosophic hardihood characterize these poems, the which while not evincing a superlatively trained mind nor faultless craftsmanship, are indubitably the product of high intelligence and literary gift. The book, fastidiously made and printed, is, in its inclusion of certain concentratedly felicitous compositions, not one of those indifferent excellences which one respects and does not read, but an instant and rewarding companion.

The Lowery Road, by L. A. G. Strong (Boni & Liveright). Although abounding in that which is ethically valuable, exhibiting now and then a vivid, gracious aspect of the natural world, or a facet of mental significance, these poems present unpoetic analogies and mixed symbolism which are disaffecting, a choice of subject too frequently superficial, and workmanship which is with few exceptions, conspicuously undisciplined.

Ariel: The Life of Shelley, by André Maurois; translated by Ella D'Arcy (Appleton). Impatience with this ultra traditional, heedlessly translated life of Shelley, is moderated by an occasional eloquently imaginative conceit, a sometimes acute adjective, and a number of justly tart comments upon human behavior. The narrative is firm, continuous, actual; wish to as one may, however, it is impossible to attribute to this Ariel of the biographer—"the Beauteous Harriet's 'doctrinaire husband' " "discussing some profound question or other"—capacity for artistry, elevation of spirit, or passion for thought.

The Dial, 77 (December 1924), 524–25.

Lazarillo of Tormes, His Life, Fortunes, Misadventures, translated and introduced by Mariano J. Lorente (Luce). Assumed in the introduction which informs rather than pleases, to have been the progenitor of the roguish novel, appearing we are told in 1553, this first Spanish picaresque tale, is in its delicate vagabond wiles of mood and speech, a delighting piece of extravagance—as curiously modern in its pliant dexterity as it is inalienably Spanish in flavor.

The Tattooed Countess, by Carl Van Vechten (Knopf). The presentableness of the lacquered boot, talent for detail, and a sometimes pleasing wit, appear in this would-be romantic novel with the aptly chosen title—to be taken figuratively and literally—of an American woman who, on returning to Iowa at fifty, as the widow of an Italian count, falls in love with a boy of twenty, proposes marriage to him, and is accepted. Our inability to be captivated or really moved by this without-a-touch-of-Paris, frantically-hungry-to-be-French protest against "village moral indecencies" and the cruelty of society to "the sensitive imaginative boy," is due somewhat to little affronting American banalities of speech, to obtrusively stiff bits of *papier mâché* dialogue, to the fact that certain attitudes of characters portrayed are not well dovetailed, to a manner of telling impaired by lack of stature and degraded by parentheses, to a moralistic instructiveness at odds with the author's religion of unmoral Epicureanism; to a blight which Mr. Van Vechten has placed upon the book, of just that dogged provincialism which he endeavors to exorcise.

The Tiger in the House, a new edition, by Carl Van Vechten (Knopf). In this book about "the domestic tiger," there is an almost painful rigor of insistence that the cat cannot be "owned"—that "he lives in homes because he chooses to do so"; a monotonously frequent use of the words mostly, mystery, puss, pussy; and an irrelevant excluding of the dog from a book about the cat; one's gratitude for research is put off by an unsifted air accompanying the trove; dismay is occasioned by finding the author in the *rôle* of mentor to Henry James and approving "the line that saves Shakespeare." One needs the cat's instinctiveness, patrician insulation, mastery of mechanics, and imperviousness to compulsion, in order to pick one's way nicely in and out of the dreary and the bright detail assembled. But one finds here and there, a sinuous quip, an image, a shred of chivalry or superstition salvaged from the past, which delight one; not to speak of "the grace, the idle charm, the magnificence, the essential mystery of the cat," by which one is hypnotically detained. Preceding an index, furthermore, one welcomes a first real bibliography of cats, annotated and arranged under subjects; and although to the captious "felinophile" some of the photographs and drawings of cats will be more rich than sympathetic, the most repining critic must prize with increasing fervor, on the cover of this book, the design of a medal struck in 1725, now in the French National Library.

Random Rhythms, by Rodney Blake (Publishers Press). The title by no means suggests the temper of this book, full of vehemence, impetuosity, outraged dignity, and ardor, as it is. Both manner and matter seem for the most part "wrong," but certain poems are well conceived and well constructed, and the author's irrepressible faith in romance and in human nature augurs well.

Secrets, by W. H. Davies (Harcourt Brace). The true poet visualizes an imaginary realness which is more real than actuality; therefore one feels defrauded when a gifted writer who arouses the highest expectation, deadens the pretty conceit with bathos, and permits narrowness of understanding to blur poetic vision.

The Sleeping Beauty, by Edith Sitwell (Knopf). An accomplished way-wardness of mood and execution; prismatic color; dramatic, narrative, and lyric power are apparent in this most moving and archly elfin poem. Despite an occasional end rhyme less persuasive than the adjacent dainty disso-nances, certain conceits which seem not of a piece with the poem's appro-priate, exquisitely multicolored "deceiving of expectation," and an insistent consciousness of the use of simile—despite infinitesimal infelicities—one must be *distrait* indeed, whom the force and the flavor of *The Sleeping Beauty* cannot enchant.

The Soul of Samuel Pepys, by Gamaliel Bradford (Houghton Mifflin). In this methodical, historically accurate, generously catholic "simplifying" of Pepys' Diary, Pepys is shown to have been "the average man"; he does not, however, transcendently emerge as the extraordinary diarist. One notes two, perhaps three, unforgettably characterizing flashes, but an ineffective, face-tious shrewdness and a stubborn adherence to ineptitudes of diction and of syntax smother the reader's proffered cordiality.

Casanova: An Appreciation, by Havelock Ellis, with Selections from the Mémoires (Luce). These three selections from the Mémoires of Casanova, collectively and separately prefaced as they are by Dr. Ellis' scientifically acute, aesthetically perfect appreciation, will go far toward persuading the reader that the ardently elastic Casanova, "delivering himself bound into the hands of the moralists" as Dr. Ellis chivalrously observes—this "con-summate master of the dignified relation of undignified experiences"—has left us a record which is valuable "as a mere story of adventure," as "a picture of the eighteenth century," and as "a veracious presentation of a certain human type."

Blake and Milton, by Denis Saurat (Dial Press). Concerned chiefly with their philosophy, this compact, vigilant, poetically brilliant exposition of "the resemblance in difference between Blake and Milton," illumines anew, the "harmonious world" of the one, the "wild and populous soul" of the other; the charm, the ordered philosophical equipoise of its logic, the ex-perienced, wiry, differentiating economy of presentation, completely persuading one of "a close relationship in their work brought about by their generous pride, their passionate temperament, their ardor for religion and art considered as one."

Literary Studies and Reviews, by Richard Aldington (Lincoln MacVeagh, Dial Press). In these studies of early French poets, of Landor, of Victor Hugo, of Remy de Gourmont, Marcel Proust, Madame du Deffand, T. S. Eliot, James Joyce—of varied types of writing and of writers—an assured, balanced carefulness, a pith, poetic irritability, self-protectiveness, and polish, are opposed throughout to that which is intellectually stupid or sensibly unpleasurable. One detects upon the finely wrought texture of these themes, an occasional reiterative adverb, as in the temper of the writing one feels a stubborn hardihood, an integral unpity; the author's to us most enriching genealogical genius for literary roots and relationships, strays perhaps in its willfully paternal mistrust of literary benefit from the influence of James Joyce; but we have here, an emotion, a stir, a bibliomania, a conviction of beauty, a valuable indocility, a witty practiced manner of thought which exemplifies the virtues which it lauds, a mind concerned not with what is merely "chic, but with what is really cultured."

The New Vision in the German Arts, by Herman S. Scheffauer (Huebsch). This book, while it is distinctly a salute to Germany in expositing with rich particularity German experiments in new aesthetic media, is not bound by a locality; the author's belief in the ideal of a triumphant beauty is contagious—a belief in this "expressionism" of which he writes, "which acts from within upon the external world"; his unpretentiously learned simplifying of the possibly arcane or unfamiliar, is exhilarating and his intelligent, imaginative, experienced, workmanlike triumphs of particularization as an interpreter, benefit the reader, per se.

The Dial, 78 (January 1925), 75–80.

Apples Here in My Basket, by Helen Hoyt (Harcourt, Brace). In a book which urgently proclaims with mongrel metrical inconsequence, the lordship of the flesh, it is a pleasure to find three well wrought poems, the content of which is movingly poetic.

The Dial, 78 (February 1925), 158.

Spring Thunder and Other Poems, by Mark Van Doren (Seltzer). Although the author temerariously thwarts the current of rhetorical emphasis, failing sometimes to create a tune of the kind which pertains to either prose or verse; although he assumes large license in making the adjective a noun, and at other times, a verb; in making nouns, verbs; and transitive verbs, intransitive; although he not infrequently couples with the "why and where," "far and high" manner of writing, a "midwife cat," "the mountain is me" vernacular, he nevertheless presents enticingly, the world of the weasel, the crow, and the chipmunk; depicts "the lantern on the snow," "behind each clod, a mouse's ear"; and in bringing to us eagerly the atmosphere of a loved place, the attitude of a loved human being, modifies our consciousness of a sometimes faulty taste in subject and in treatment.

Modern Essays: Second Series, selected by Christopher Morley (Harcourt, Brace). There are in this volume, a number of illuminated, signally great essays, "generous qualities of mind and temperament" being evinced by preface and biographical notes. However, an anthologist's "tenderness" so "cordial" as not to be literary is shown in the inclusion of certain minor, badly wrought essays.

Life of William Congreve, by Edmund Gosse, with a prefatory note by the biographer (Scribner). With a discovering and elegant adroitness as different from the sometimes dullness of biography as "a crystal is from a jelly-fish," Mr. Gosse has given us in this revised and enlarged edition of the memoir published in 1888, a corrected insight into Congreve's work, an enticing impression of his "friendliness," a vivid presentation of the Collier controversy, and a knowledge of early eighteenth century drama and theatrical production. He has pondered as a light upon his plays, Congreve's works as a novelist and as a poet, and has rescued from oblivion much that ought to have been preserved two hundred years ago. Admitting that Congreve "made a helot of himself by producing the worst specimen of the false ode on record," yet reviving in us, "the wild satiric garden of his drama" the consummate flower of which comedy is "not to be turned over but to be re-read until the psychological subtlety of the sentiment, the perfume of the delicately chosen phrases, the music of the sentences, have produced the full effect upon the nerves," Mr. Gosse has truly in this most complete life of "the greatest of our comic dramatists," been "patient to finish as well as spirited to sketch."

The Dial, 78 (March 1925), 247, 249–50.

The Chapbook: A Miscellany, 1924, with "Apology" (Poetry Bookshop, London). The Apologist's hope that the 1924 Chapbook may provide "entertainment sufficient for the moment," is much more than realized in "Doris's Dream Songs," by T. S. Eliot; in Voltaire's "Advice to a Reviewer," translated by Richard Aldington; in Sacheverell Sitwell's lines, "I sing, stone statue in chill water, never warmed by sun"; in Osbert Sitwell's Sicilian tiger-tamer "and her eighteen Ferocious Debutantes"; in a pen drawing by Paul Nash, in two pen portraits by McKnight Kauffer, in two woodcuts by John Nash and Eric Daglish, respectively. The poetaster's now almost universally prevailing vogue for deity with a small d, puzzles one; and the arithmetical balance of gratitude for Mr. Harold Monro's "Midnight Lamentation," is unsatisfactory—four stanzas being a gain and four, a loss.

A Far Land, by Martha Ostenso (Seltzer). Ever attentive as the reader of poetry must be—to the elf, the witch, the crow, the duck, the swan, the loon, the leprechaun, to "moonlight and mist," to hazel-tree, birch, briar, and hawthorne—he finds them sometimes deftly placed in these friendly verses. Harmonic inequalities of movement are disturbing and snared imagination starts at certain words and phrases; at "most everything," "gloamy," "ghost-rare," "shambly," "youngish," and "my mouth on the quiet of your dew sweet face."

Chills and Fever, by John Crowe Ransom (Knopf). Unrewarding dissonances, mountebank persiflage, mock medieval minstrelsy, and shreds of elegance disturbingly suggestive of now this, now that contemporary bard, deprive one of the faculty to diagnose this "dangerous" phenomenon to which one has exposed oneself.

Poems, by Lady Margaret Sackville (Lincoln MacVeagh, Dial Press). With the distinctness of the spinet and the rigor of the sermon, restrained without constraint, preserved when they tremble upon the brink of a banality by that sensibility which recoils from malapert insistence, these erect poems are consistently alluring in their respect for a freedom that must be permitted in the same measure in which it is enjoyed; as in their predilection for romance—for flagged paths and mignonette, for roses by the latticed window, for polished floors and peacocks of clipped yew.

The Gallants, by E. Barrington (Atlantic Monthly Press). One is enticed by the glamour of Elizabethan words and leisure, in Sir John Harrington's letters; and by the poetically just inequities of chivalry in Dame Petronille's twelfth century account of Henry II's relationship with Eleanor of Aquitaine and with Rosemonde de Clifford. In certain of these memorials to passion, however, letters and conversations imagined as authentic, seem presumptuous; the consuming flirtations of the Duke of Monmouth, the "shameless amours" of George IV "best forgot one and all," yet lovingly lingered over— suggesting by their content as by their manner of narration, the photodramatist's portrayal of love's violent duel between the vulnerable heart of woman and the voracious vagrancy of man.

The Dial, 78 (April 1925), 337–38.

Ducdame, by John Cowper Powys (Doubleday, Page). In this novel we may study the exaltation of physical consciousness as we have it in Rook Ashover for whose love three women simultaneously contend. Estranged from him by his detachment—by "an irresistible attraction" on his part "to the feminine body and mind with an absolute lack of emotional passion," which finds expression in the phenomenon of lovemaking rather than in the blasting power of love—we are not moved by the tragedy of his murder, even dramatically timed as it is to coincide with the birth of his son. By the precision of certain similes, by the black magic—the static flicker—of a proud and prompt imagination, by the author's passion for the "mysterious, inviolable" beauty of nature, we are genuinely moved.

Old English Towns, by William Andrews and Elsie M. Lang (T. Werner Laurie, London). Enriched by photographs, drawings, and by most alluring early engravings, by curious epitaphs, and manifold engaging items transcribed from civic monuments, taxation rolls, parish registers, from the Domesday Book, from Leland the antiquarian, from John Aubrey, and from The Venerable Bede, these historical accounts of the rise of forty-three English towns provide a wealth of information concerning customs and stirring episodes of old-time social life. Although the rhetoric of the recital— particularly that of Mr. Andrews—is a courageously unpanoplied accompaniment to the glittering pageantry of the matter recorded, the reader has not the hardihood to be ungrateful to authors whose research has provided from history and legend so much that is rewarding.

The Authors' Thames, by Gordon S. Maxwell, illustrated by Lucille Maxwell (Brentano). Provided with a chronological list of authors and painters, with a general and a topographical index, this book "about the Thames Valley lying between London and Windsor," enchants the errant bookworm with resplendent fragments of poetry, of humor, and of biography, culled from nineteen centuries of literary history. Although the crispness of the recital is sometimes lost in gratuitous climax and mild exposition, one is transported by the veracious presence of Elias Ashmole, Gay, Fuller, Pope, Walpole, Dr. Johnson, Fanny Burney, R. D. Blackmore, and a host of other literary luminaries.

The Dial, 78 (May 1925), 426, 428.

The Rhyming Dictionary of the English Language, by John Walker, revised and enlarged, with a preface and introduction to index of allowable rhymes, by Lawrence H. Dawson (Dutton). With Mr. Dawson's expository preface, an appended index to rhymes introduced by sagely careful comment, with cautionary asterisks, cross references, and Table of Divisions, *The Critical Pronouncing Dictionary* published by John Walker in 1775, comes to us enlarged and rewritten throughout. For these 54,000 words grouped as originally, in accordance with the reversed spelling of the word, not only "songsters," Sunday paper acrostic enthusiasts, and "schoolmasters" in search of derivatives, but fanatics of cadence, may well accord with Lord Byron and the New York Public Library, in offering the authors fervent thanks.

The Dial, 78 (June 1925), 522.

The Banquet and Other Poems, by Frances Fletcher (Dorrance). Presenting the paradox of the pond lily's whiteness blurred by shadows, the simplicity of the complex mood which is appreciative yet ardent in escape, aloof and alluring in their sleights of swift precision, these poems possess depth of experience, sensitiveness to thought, and power of observation, which are not contradicted by definite defects in thought and treatment.

Poetry from the Bible, edited by Lincoln MacVeagh (Lincoln MacVeagh; The Dial Press). As Mr. MacVeagh suggests, an anthology of the Bible is not the Bible. The twenty-fifth and the one-hundred-fourth psalms have in this instance been omitted, and sometimes disassociation from the grandeur of the setting detracts from the essential magnitude of what is quoted. One must in every case be sensible, however, of the splendor of the famous passages assembled here, of the careful choice of version, of now a metrical, and now a prose arrangement, of the compact magnificence of this small volume.

An Anthology of Pure Poetry, edited with an introduction by George Moore (Boni & Liveright). In accordance with Mr. Moore's definition of pure poetry as "something that the poet creates outside of his own personality," we have in this anthology—abstinent in purport and exquisite in content—beauty that cannot be encountered too often. Some of the best work of the poets here represented is not without what Mr. Moore has termed "subjective taint"; therefore, we must regard the anthologist's rigor as abundance, prefaced as it is by the poetically autobiographic prose of the introduction, which would in itself make the volume a valuable acquisition.

Ancient Rhetoric and Poetic, Interpreted from Representative Works by Charles Sears Baldwin (Macmillan). Concentrated pleasure as well as knowledge are to be found in this orderly and expertly compact book in which the author, "with complementary technical analysis of ancient achievement," has allowed Greek and Latin writers themselves to be his spokesmen, this "way" seeming "surest toward recovering inductively the ancient artistic experience." We are indebted to Dr. Baldwin for a bibliography at the head of each chapter, for a tabular index of Latin and Greek rhetorical terms, for a general index, for uniquely purposeful punctuation, for a retranslating of terms, for a "grave" and magnificently poetic translating of texts—and for memorable interpretations of Aristotle, Cicero, Virgil, Quintilian, Dio of Prusa, and others. It may surely be said of him as he says of Cicero, "Few men writing on style have shown in their own styles so much precision and charm."

John Donne: A Study in Discord, by Hugh I'Anson Fausset (Harcourt, Brace). Sometimes didactic, over-decorated, and carelessly familiar—as Walton's "too devout miniature" is not—this accurately denominated study in discord, strives with Freudian energy to commemorate a man "compact of sensuality and sublime longings, fury and fastidiousness, morbidity and rapture, the gracious and the grotesque"—a "Dionysus" who "played the man by acknowledging the beast."

The Dial, 79 (July 1925), 77–79.

A Reader's Guide Book, by May Lamberton Becker, with foreword by Henry Seidel Canby (Holt). These bibliographies with advice, and informative forays into ground other than that of reference books, present to the intellectually curious, cosmic riches. Certain omissions, and a sometimes too trustful hazarding of humor, of diction, and of critical approval, are negligible when compared with the alluring classified information afforded the inquirer, about writers and writing, printing, music, economics, education, history, biography, travel, plays, poetry, novels, and many other subjects; the author's ingenuity in making fiction an adjunct to the study of history, of art, of certain professions, of specificities and localities, projecting itself as by an extension Utopian scaling-ladder, far beyond the achievements of most library experts—to whom the book is graciously inscribed.

The Dial, 79 (August 1925), 176.

Poems for Youth: An American Anthology, compiled with preface and introduction by William Rose Benét (Dutton). Assuming the work of certain poets to be not within "the understandings of average young people in their late 'teens and early twenties," omitting John Burroughs' "My Own Shall Come to Me," and certain household favorites, Mr. Benét presents in this anthology many narrative poems of personal prowess, ballads, poems in dialect, certain masterpieces of emotion and description, and directs the reader's judgment with a biographical critical note upon each author.

Poems, by Ralph Hodgson (Macmillan). The device which in one instance dazzles—in another disappoints—and a manner sometimes perhaps too self-perpetuating, infinitesimally discount Mr. Hodgson's genius. Imaginatively contrived as conceived—deft, sudden, and sane like many of the creatures human and other which are embodied in them—these poems could, one feels, charm even the confirmed poet-hater.

The Dial, 79 (October 1925), 352.

The Thirteenth Caesar, and Other Poems, by Sacheverell Sitwell (Doran). Archaic treatment of the modern is deftly balanced by modern treatment of the archaic in these aesthetically intent, precipitate, by no means "easy" poems. Although impact and clarity are sometimes sacrificed to opulence of method and of content, the reader is obdurate who can resist the charm—in this cosmography of Mr. Sitwell's—of the "salamander, safe and breathing," the snow "sliding slow," "turtle shells" and "pearls," "the music of the waves' glass bodies," "the sapling grace and symmetry" of Greek statuary, "swans working with their webbed oars," and "dockyards full of boats a-building."

Miscellaneous Writings of Henry the Eighth, edited and with preface by Francis Macnamara (Golden Cockerel Press). Fastidiously printed, with an ingeniously irrelevant preface, with modernized spelling and in some instances, modernized grammar, these writings confirm one's suspicion that The Defender of the Faith or "Henry the hunter" as he styles himself, was, if a man of letters, essentially a man of love letters. "Green Groweth the Holly" and "Song VII"—"whoso loveth should love but one"—are perhaps with the letters to Anne Boleyn, Henry the Eighth's most "congruous" and royal writings.

The Dial, 79 (November 1925), 433–34.

New Writings by William Hazlitt, collected by P. P. Howe (Lincoln MacVeagh; Dial Press). One is grateful to Hazlitt's biographer for presenting with characteristically precise footnotes and an index, these new later writings in which, resist it as one may, one recognizes a spirit as authoritative as it is unbusinesslike. "Underlit by unquenchable fire," ironically and prepossessingly yet unjustly abusive in his miniature scholasticism, Hazlitt does persuade one, uniformly and with powerful inconsistency, that "all impediments in fancy's course are motives of more fancy."

Doodab, by Harold A. Loeb (Boni & Liveright). From this well-meaning, meaningless book which is not a novel or even a story, one infers that the typical unresourceful man has been discarded by his employers, turned adrift by his wife, and killed by a locomotive. Named in this instance, Henry

Doodab, he has dreamed self-exalting dreams of life in the jungle and has been killed; but he has never lived.

The Dial, 79 (December 1925), 516.

Replenishing Jessica, by Maxwell Bodenheim (Boni & Liveright). There is sometimes the illusion of good writing—if one can have good writing that is not good reading—in this disillusioned exposition of what women like and of what men know. Said to be of social position enviably remote, although besetting and beset by every kind of man but the morally and socially fastidious; said to be "wealthy, symmetrical, and fairly intelligent," although apparently without caste or culture—Jessica Maringold, married at last but soon divorced, proposes marriage to a mentally cowed, physically crippled, financially shattered museum attendant and is accepted.

Voices of the Stones, by A. E. (Macmillan). One whose "fancy soon forsakes all that is perfect to the eye," can often depict the material world as the materialist can not. Surely A. E. gives us the "perilous magic mountains" of actuality and those "ice-tinted mounds of quivering malachite" which are the sea, in words as "holy" as those in which he speaks of "eternity," "survival," "resurrection," and "the flame within the body's lamp."

Out of the Flame, by Osbert Sitwell (Doran). Equipoise of form and content encountered once or twice, and abundant sensibility, are insufficient compensation for lack of sentience and rigor of form, in these fox-trotting, sometimes ribald, unmirthfully satiric nursery-rhymes.

The Dial, 80 (January 1926), 68–70.

The Chapbook: A Miscellany, 1925, edited by Harold Monro (Jonathan Cape). An air of fervent fastidious personal eagerness, a general sense of animation behind the scenes, is palpable in *The Chapbook*. That thanks are partial is due perhaps to a feeling that the curtain has gone up too soon. Various readily proffered lines seem not secure and one involuntarily wishes that contributions by the same author might be adjacent. But wherever or however suddenly one might come upon them, the many well-inked woodcuts and pen drawings in this book would be enjoyed, and one is likely to read again, the poem by H. D., "The Lost Thrush" by Liam O'Flaherty, "A Note on Free Verse" by Richard Aldington, *two* poems by Harold Monro, and a poem called "Divers" by Peter Quennell.

Color, by Countee Cullen (Harpers). Despite a sometimes too easy grasp of colossal themes and a mechanics more limber than learned, these much crowned poems by a Negro poet are in certain respects impressive. One cannot evade the resoluteness of this author, to whom "primal clay" is not dirt and to whom "glory," in the evangelistic sense of the word, is not ridiculous. One is, moreover, content to be reminded that "the soul of Africa is winged with arrogance."

Thamyris or Is There a Future for Poetry? by R. C. Trevelyan (Dutton). Taking into its confidence the modern Thamyris is revolt against the past; this gently didactic little book assures us that we need not despair of poetry's "salvation"; that free verse is only by exception unprosaic; that modern poetry has not the emotional potency of performed ancient poetry; that one must not be impatient of rhetoric; that long lyrics, comic poetry, narrative poetry, philosophic poetry, the treatise, and the poetic satire, "have not been made our own."

Rider's California, with 28 maps and plans, compiled under the editorship of Fremont Rider by Frederic Taber Cooper (Macmillan). We have not in this remarkably able guide-book, the resplendent diction of Karl Baedeker; in certain instances one feels a need of explicitness greater than that afforded by the asterisk of commendation; the pronunciation of Spanish names has, wisely perhaps but unkindly, not been indicated—editorial rigor in this respect being emphasized by a multiplicity of such grieving American names as Shakespeare Rock, Ham Station, Rubicon Springs, Peanut, Dome Peak, Gibraltar Dam. We have, however, in the clear type of these carefully ordered pages, a genuine guide to California—a general and a circumstantial description, a history, a bibliography, and a conscientiously impartial appreciation of "a magnificent state."

The Dial, 80 (February 1926), 160–61, 163–64.

Episodes and Epistles, by W. L. (Seltzer). Despite seeming unceremony and certain distractingly far from established technical novelties which sometimes resound rightly from another lyre, one finds among these graphic poems—urban, suburban, sentimental, and descriptive—a sure, delightful rhythm, a thought, a feeling, a phase of experience, to which one cannot be indifferent.

In the American Grain, by William Carlos Williams (A. & C. Boni). Appraising in the name of beauty, Montezuma, Christopher Columbus, Ponce de Leon, Benjamin Franklin, Abraham Lincoln, Edgar Allan Poe, Aaron Burr, and others, Dr. Williams finds in these separate studies, interrelated proof of American aesthetic deprivedness, or is it depravity? "Morals are deformed in the name of PURITY"; he says, "till, in the confusion, almost nothing remains of the great American New World but a memory of the Indian." Unsubmissive to his pessimism and sometimes shocked by the short work which he makes of decorum, verbal and other, we wisely salute the here assembled phosphorescent findings of a search prosecuted "with antennae extended." In "The Discovery of the West Indies" and in "The Destruction of Tenochtitlan," in the giltheads, parrots, lizards, and wandlike naked people of the one, as in the eloquent minutiae of the other, we recognize a superbly poetic *orificeria* of meaning and of material—in the idols, the jasper, the birds of prey, the "lions and other animals of the cat kind," the wrought stone and wrought leather, the silver, the gold, and the courtyard "paved with handsome flags in the style of a chessboard."

The Dial, 80 (March 1926), 253.

Along the Wind, by Chard Powers Smith (Yale University Press). Significantly a part of the content of these poems, decorous uninsistence results technically in the sense of a not quite full orchestra. Equivocal progress, a faint last line, an unincisive transition is, however, noted rather than remembered. For the most part sonnets, these affecting poems *in memoriam* do in their sensitiveness and depth of reflection, achieve a kind of sober transcendence.

Scarlet and Mellow, by Alfred Kreymborg (Boni & Liveright). Simeon Scarlet and Montague Mellow, a radical poet and a conservative poet respectively, have provided co-operatively in this volume, "music," thoughts of town and country, and various respectfully romantic, unsubserviently accurate observations upon woman. They chide you for chiding them "for not being what they cannot be," so perhaps we must say that we wish they were at all times as profound as they are sometimes witty.

Thesaurus of English Words and Phrases, by Peter Mark Roget, enlarged by John Lewis Roget, newly revised and enlarged (1925) by Samuel Rommily Roget, M. A. (Longmans). Emended and enlarged, with a new and minutely comprehensive index, this present edition of Peter Mark Roget's *Thesaurus* constitutes, as originally, a classification of words by ideas—a verbally affiliated network of thought analogous to the laboratory scientist's classification of species in botany or zoology. Willing to seem redundant rather than to be insufficient, the authors of this favorite word-book have, without impairing the unity of the several categories, indicated necessary natural points of connection, and not ignoring "middle terms," have placed antithetic ideas in parallel columns—"convexity, flatness, concavity." Without ever sacrificing clearness to compactness, or the beneficiary's convenience to the benefactor's philosophy of arrangement, Mr. Samuel Rommily Roget, his father and grandfather, seem in this volume, to have perfected perfection. "Primus inter pares," they have, if one may borrow their own synonym for gilding, "borne away the bell."

The Dial, 80 (May 1926), 427–28, 431.

The Doom of Atlas and Other Poems, by William Jeffrey (Gowans and Gray). Any four poems—upon respectively, Atlas, Nature, Christ with Mary Magdalene, the cosmos prior to human life—may well seem less than august, and the four poems which comprise this book suffer from what seems an absence of epic afflatus. If, however, "frailsome," "tremulant," "ruth," and "wizard passion" are poetically unwary, power manifests itself in "the stinging scent of the eternal sea," "the cedar takes the storm within its boughs," a "thong drawn careless o'er the dew." There is an impression in these poems, of competence, of poetic body, of reserve power, of new eyes upon old themes, and one could not but approach with eagerness, other examples of this author's work.

The Dial, 80 (June 1926), 522.

The Verdict of Bridlegoose, by Llewelyn Powys (Harcourt, Brace). Reminding himself of Judge Bridlegoose in the "third book of Rabelais's Works," Mr. Powys tells in "simplicity" and "equity" of his coming from England to America, of living for a time in New York, of going for his health's sake to

San Francisco, of his return to New York, of an expedition to the Rocky Mountains, of a winter in the Catskills, of his departure from New York to live in England. Accurately divined by a quick, learnedly imaginative insight into the style and aspect of the living thing, his people seem animals, exteriorly presented; his animals seem human. In his delineation of the celebrity, we have many a "stroke." It must be admitted, however, that deferential, trouble-taking, judicial, and bold, as our appraiser is—commending the resources literal and figurative of the special person—he does somehow, sometimes fail to give us the writer, the thinker, the artist, which this special person is. That a verdict so literary and exquisitely graphic should seem ephemeral, may be accounted for perhaps by the fact that throughout, it is deliberately "instructive." Pedagogically to insist that sensuality is noisome, or pedagogically to insist, as here, that it is needed, is an aesthetic indiscretion, and inevitably justice operates. As truly in the work of one's favorite and most scholarly friends, as in the book of the mountebank, one can be reminded that "the wild beasts sent to devour St. Eufemia not only fawned upon her but 'joined their tayles together, and made of them a chair for her to sit on' and ate the judge who had directed the torture."

The Dial, 81 (July 1926), 84.

Roving through China, by Harry A. Franck (Century). In this "plain" account of people, of places, and of methods of travel in southern China— with many photographs—a seemingly experienced elasticity of judgment is, in matters not topical nor topographical, multifariously contradicted. The religious philosopher, the political scientist, the student of civilization would, in certain opinions diverge from this author: the *littérateur* would not accompany him. Mr. Franck is scientific as a wanderer if not as a thinker or as a writer. His itinerary is impressive and he is, if one may have in one's feet a science which one has not in one's head, an accomplished traveler.

The Dial, 81 (July 1926), 84-85.

A Manual of Style, with Specimens of Type (University of Chicago Press). Rules have been added, such as have become superfluous have been omitted, and new illustrative matter and also a simplifying and perfecting of exposition, emphasize the value of this eighth revised edition of the typographic rules of The University of Chicago Press. Besides a chapter on book structure, there is a section on "composition"—capitalization, punctuation, abbreviating, spelling, suggestions to the literary typographic novice; a glossary of terms; a list of printer's symbols; specimens of type; and *magna cum laude*, an executive zeal and power over subject-matter, which cannot but advantage and animate the reader, be or be he not, versed in the look and the logic of the printed page.

The Dial, 81 (August 1926), 176.

Chosen Poems, by Douglas Ainslie, with preface by G. K. Chesterton (Hogarth Press). Between moon-blue, sunset-green, and grey marbled boards of enticing frog-spawn-like appearance, these one hundred and sixty-eight pages of clear small type, constitute a beautiful and compact little book. In an ingenious introductory apologia for the small and rare, Mr. G. K. Chesterton says that Mr. Ainslie says that "the earth might be the smallest of the stars and yet be the best of the stars"—in short, the "Athens of the angels." And a poem such as "Trees" is truly Athenian. But in all those chosen lines about waterfalls and mountains, about Ariosto, and Diana, about that which is "calm and curious," about French history and Scotch history, about Buddha, and about Shakespeare, why should one have constantly to apologize to oneself; and to Mr. Ainslie, for having to do so? Why should there here, so often seem to be associated, of things aesthetic which are not to be associated? Why should the need for a nicer uniting of the grave and the colloquial, and a need for greater rhythmic selectiveness, perturb one so much?

A Boat of Glass, by Frances Fletcher (Dorrance). Liking the flowers, the icicles, "the forest's nave," and in the lines entitled "Adrift," "a boat of thin-spun glass," one wishes that each of the poems in this book, were technically shipshape.

Men, Women and Colleges, by Le Baron R. Briggs (Houghton Mifflin). We have in this small book, a discussion of liberalism, of the fallacy of "leading one's own life," a differentiating between college and university, a paper on "the life and the equipment of a teacher" and one upon the multiform value of college education. The book is small in the sense that Napoleon was a little corporal. Should literary wariness seem sometimes to retire before forensic efficiency one is upon every page the advanced victim of "accuracy with poetic truth," of a humorous and capturing discernment, of a subjecting moral effectiveness. One could not contemplate the doctrines here set forth, and wish to lurk or lean or look anywhere but in the eye of an illumined honor. Above the correct attitude and independent of time, these pages constitute an atmosphere which is, in early dust-cover parlance, "the genuine ozone of the peaks."

The Dial, 81 (September 1926), 263, 265.

Innocent Birds, by Theodore F. Powys (Knopf). As one proceeds through this bleak narrative, one is held, indeed bound, by the author's deliberately precise, untouched, resourcefully direct way of speaking. One ponders the detail of Dorsetshire, the "large rich ivy leaves," the "small yellow flowers," the "hedgerow grasses," the dock leaves, "a thorn bush that a golden cloud appeared to have set a match to," and even spotted pigs and spiders. As for the subject matter of the story, is one odd, unadjusted, absent minded, or crudely unadvantaged, in finding the interwoven tragedy of many feminine innocents, an enigmatically unobjective phantasm, unlike anything that has ever seemed real to one?

The Tremulous String, by Monk Gibbon (The Greyhound Press at Foulis Court). These poems recall to one, "the grass in the meadow," "the long grass about the ditches," "some tall flower not to be hidden by either." They commemorate "a face," "a head," "love also," and counsel lovers to "be patient, and not always pursuing." Should one in certain poems feel a lack of cumulative force or insufficient strictness, gentility of word and feeling are equally palpable—a rounding of the phrase with the thought and "beauty which is not touched by season."

Elizabethan Life in Town and Country, by M. St. Clare Byrne (Houghton Mifflin). Far from resulting in a "fancy picture," the facts here presented cannot but suggest in their compositely historical verisimilitude, the restored or hypothetically actual museum replica and one resists subconsciously, an effect of many genial adjectives. But thanks are legion, not only for the kind of book this is, but for its contents—its modest compactness, its reproduced engravings, and its much matter in fine print at the end. In the time of Elizabeth, "actuality" was truly cause for "wonder," and students of history could revive never too often—V-shaped doublets and melon-shaped, bom-basted breeches; twisted brickwork chimneys; "geese gaggling on the green"; gates "pestered with coaches"; the "huswife's" thread made of nettles, Elizabethan "moon-men" and rogues, hautboys and serpents, revels, children, universities, and wonder-books.

Historic Churches of the World, by Robert B. Ludy (Stratford Company). Persuasively illustrated and modestly unassumptive in its exposition of facts— in a sense not "written" at all—this reverent and comprehensive book by a United States army surgeon, presents many a heavenly and many a mundane example of architecture: Cologne Cathedral, York Minster, the Temple of Nikko, the Temple of Diana, the Mormon Temple, the Russian Orthodox Church of Sitka, "the smallest church in the world," the Cathedral of Mexico City, Old South Church—Newburyport, indeed so much as scarcely to admit of curiosity's alighting. Dr. Ludy has compiled "numerous interesting facts," which are just to his concept of the Church as more than a mere outward symbol.

Universal Indian Sign Language of the Plains Indians of North America, with Dictionary of Synonyms and Codification of Pictographic Word Symbols of the Ojibway and Sioux Nations, by William Tompkins (William Tompkins, San Diego, California). It is not rash to say that expert and amateur alike, would value the table of pictographs and the pictographic stories which have been included in this ethnologically weighty pamphlet. Drawing our attention to the distinction between pictographic painting upon bark, skin, pottery, or other paintable surface, and petroglyphs and petrographs, Mr. Tompkins presents also and primarily, as correlative with such findings, a codifying of Indian sign language. He shares with Mr. George Moore, an expert's if not a *littérateur's* prejudice against "the inroads of modern education," hopes that sign language will not fall into disuse, and justifies its practicability by reminding us that standardized traffic signals are in use by more than twenty million automobile drivers. He commends his work to the young person; a reviewer commends it to "men who go hunting"; we commend it to the poet, the logician, the ethnologist, and all who value an authentic plains atmosphere. Only the incurious could easily resist the critically discerned expressiveness of this graceful, truly aboriginal, first American language—a speech not borrowed from the deaf, and dependent upon no concomitant facial assistance. Arrested (crossed wrists): book (hands half open): bird (hands flapping at shoulders; small birds rapidly, large birds slowly).

The Dial, 81 (October 1926), 352–53, 355.

The New Standard Bible Dictionary, edited by Melanchthon W. Jacobus, Edward E. Nourse, and Andrew C. Zenos (Funk & Wagnalls). Based upon the American Standard text of the Bible, in marked contrast with, yet not contradicting early literalism, courageously definite in its exposition of disputed questions, *The New Standard Bible Dictionary* will be found by scholar and amateur alike, a usefully concise, unprejudiced, and authoritative work. In alphabetical order and correlated with that which is Biblical, moreover, "Disease and Medicine," "Exploration and Evacuation," and other extended articles upon subjects of outside interest, have been included in the volume.

The Dial, 82 (January 1927), 75.

Evolution in Modern Art, by Frank Rutter (Lincoln MacVeagh; The Dial Press). Mr. Rutter perceives in the public taste, a revived interest in design and reminds of the essential incompatibility between symbolism and representation. He writes of Impressionism; of Cézanne, Van Gogh, Gauguin, and Matisse as "the pillars of Post-Impressionism"; of Wyndham Lewis, W. P. Roberts, Mrs. Dod Proctor, Henry Lamb, and other British painters. His paragraphs upon Sir Francis Galton's enquiries into the faculty of visualization and the comparison from Hermann Bahr between the mind's eye and the bodily eye, set one thinking. As for the hopefully, painstakingly, lecturingly kindly manner of this history, one must not dwell upon it. Nice press-work and pleasing pictures are not—even conjointly—able to redeem a certain kind of haggard diction.

The Dial, 82 (February 1927), 166.

Twelve Modern Apostles and Their Creeds, with introduction by Dean Inge (Duffield). Written independently of the series and of each other, these contemporary creedal apologia constitute much useful comparative data and much tolerance. It is, one hazards, not a loss to be able to identify as Baptists—Defoe, Milton, Bunyan, the first President of Harvard, the John D. Rockefellers, Senior and Junior, David Lloyd George, and Secretary Hughes. As writing and as thought, however, the presentment of Unitarianism, that of Quakerism, and the book's firm preliminary pronouncement, seem most nearly hyper-physical. Dean Inge is, in this introductory essay, "outspoken" and commanding. In *Lay Thoughts of a Dean* (Putnam) he is not so homogeneous, not so august. Certain of these "strong convictions," literary, political, social, and religious, seem more fixed than strong. But one sees no occasion for carping or caricature—and surely no excuse for misquotation. Despite informal phrases such as "on the brain," and "let off steam," these essays are good reading. In parents and teachers, one is familiar with a certain narrowmindedness, a narrowmindedness of the great; but pre-eminently one associates with this author, that saying of his, "unworldliness based on knowledge of the world is the finest thing on earth."

The Dial, 82 (March 1927), 257.

Spanish Folk-songs of New Mexico, collected and transcribed by Mary R. Van Stone, with foreword by Alice Corbin (Ralph Fletcher Seymour). In these love songs, shepherd songs, and lenten hymns—with English words, Spanish words, and the music—we have a legacy of primitiveness authentically transmitted from person to person in the manner of ballad-descent; and we have in the foreword, besides information, a notably contagious presentment of southwesterly American primitive scenery—of men threshing wheat with goats, of black-shawled women, whitewashed walls, and candles in tin sconces, of *penitentes;* of burros laden with cedar, of music in the plaza; of the blind man with a guitar, leading to dance, wedding, or christening, the blind man with a fiddle. To translate verse into verse is not easy and it is apparently impossible to achieve perfect typographic and perfect musical presentment, but one wishes—one is indeed persuaded—not to find fault. A collection such as this, is greatly welcome.

The Dial, 82 (April 1927), 344.

The Psalms, translated by J. M. Powis Smith (University of Chicago Press). Such readers as could charge this translation of the Psalms with being less sonorous than the King James version, admit to caring for sound irrespective of meaning. With a desire to enlarge our understanding of "the thought and feeling of the original," Doctor Smith presents decisions of interpretation which must, by their scholarly exactness and stateliness of expression, command gratitude. Appended also are Textual Notes and comment upon the spirit and purpose of the Psalter.

Ideals of Conduct, by John Dashiell Stoops (Macmillan). We have in this book, a comparison of the old ethnic order of Hebrew life, with that of pre-Socratic Greece; a consideration of such moral detachment as is exemplified in Jeremiah and in Socrates; and an examination of Christian and of Socratic inner idealism as enriching objective organized interests. One covets for such books, an exquisite aesthetic simplicity, but would not dwell upon defects, welcoming as one does, the author's unselfish, thoughtful scrutiny of present problems of behavior and his conviction that private morality must include the interests of family, property, and state.

The Dial, 82 (June 1927), 527, 529.

Spring Night: A Review of Youth, by Edward Steese (Erskine MacDonald). Concerned with "immortality, the sadness of change, and the beauty of universities"—a sonnet-salutatory as it were, addressed to "imaginary hearers"—this sequence is not in the instance of every sonnet, so expertly harmonized as in "Honor the Aged"; nor so augustly projected as in "There bracken only." The book is unusual however and one wishes that it were universal, in the power that it manifests of substantiating to the reader "the inherent and potential nobility of man."

Notorious Literary Attacks, edited by and with introduction by Albert Mordell (Boni & Liveright). With editorially expedient perhaps, but perhaps also aesthetically injudicious omissions of material quoted in the original papers, fifteen attacks upon the work of nineteenth-century authors from Hazlitt to Stevenson, are here presented in the belief that one-time contemporary atrabiliar criticisms are part of literary history like military dispatches written in battle—that such opinions help us to understand an author, that we may see how books once considered immoral have become required reading for high-school girls, and that authors subjected to present abusiveness may be consoled. Uncleverness is not predominant in the review of Jane Eyre by Elizabeth Rigby or in Henley's autobiographically pertinacious objection to the Graham Balfour *Life of Stevenson*. To say that nothing so "bairnly is to be found in the Breviary of the Innocents" as certain parts of Tennyson, is innocuously hackneyed and Lord Morley's dislike of Swinburne's "snakes and fire, and blood and wine and brine," is not unliterary.

This book is on the whole, however, valuable as instruction rather than as writing. We perceive that there has since the time of Byron and Shelley, been a change in literary manners and are forcibly persuaded by it, of the tediously ineffective dullness of published personal invective.

The Dial, 83 (July 1927), 77, 79.

Hans Christian Andersen: The True Story of My Life, translated by Mary Howitt, with preface by Hanna Astrup Larsen (American Scandinavian Foundation). As originally written for the German edition of his works in 1846, this memoir is valuable as preserving to us the times and the aspect of many favorite persons—Goethe, Heine, the Brothers Grimm, Rachel, and others; as an account of travel "in which the most remarkable transition takes place from naked cliffs to grassy islands," in which there are "wandering gypsies," "wailing birds," and "deep solitude," with once "an Æolean harp made fast to the mast." But chiefly it is rare as making us acquainted with one of those men—as he said of his benefactor, Collin—"who do more than they promise"; a bachelor, poor, "morbidly sensitive and good-natured to a fault," who found that homage "scorched the roots of pride rather than nourished them"; whose being was, as he said of another, "penetrated with the great truths of religion, and the poetry which lies in the quiet circumstances of life."

The Dial, 83 (August 1927), 176.

The Homeland of English Authors, by Ernest H. Rann (Dutton). Unharmed by what seems an equal friendliness to greatness and to greater greatness; despite the intrusion also, of such phrases as "another proposition" and "relics galore," one delights in the natural, living presence of characters real and imaginary as one encounters them in this book. Self-effacingly helpful, specific in reference, and expertly selective, Mr. Rann has contrived that those of whom he speaks, should speak to us themselves—Dickens, of Gad's Hill; George Eliot, of Griff House; Hardy, of Boscastle and Maumbury Ring; Fitzgerald, of "a Maid servant who as she curtsies of a morning lets fall the tea-pot, etc." It would be folly not to be at the trouble to undertake a pilgrimage so rewarding.

The Dial, 83 (September 1927), 266.

Dream Tapestry, by Joseph Kling (Samuel A. Jacobs). A poetic commentary in twenty-two chapters is not easy to write and is not always easy to read. To this one, however, upon book-stores, art-galleries, architecture, politeness, dignity, ease, contours, colors, poverty, "Need," "Moneygrubbing," "beautiful lights," "black depths," and much else, one is not indifferent, for evinced in it throughout, are sincerity, shrewdness, and not a little fortitude.

Palmerston, by Philip Guedalla (Putnam). A scientifically spangled Houdini-Caruso of the archives in his employment of detail operatically as accompaniment to a general progress, Mr. Guedalla has demonstrated that "the Life of Palmerston was the life of England and to a large extent, of Europe in the last sixteen years of the Eighteenth and the first sixty-five years of the Nineteenth Centuries." He has endeavored to present a Palmerston "more cosmopolitan" than "the traditional effigy"—"more assiduous in the performance of his public duties," and more "Liberal." We thank him for having read so prodigiously as he has. Vividness is not, however, invariably synonymous with good taste, and our real debt to Mr. Guedalla is for an assembled wealth of particulars rather than for vividness through implication, or for authentic impersonal reverence.

The Dial, 83 (October 1927), 354–55.

Why Do They Like It? by E. L. Black, with foreword by Dorothy Richardson (Pool, Territet, Switzerland). The author—about fifteen years old—protests in this book, against "games he hated, played by fellows he hated, of a school he hated": against unsanitary food, pseudo-instruction, and "this fagging business worse than anything" he "had ever dreamed of." Injustice to children has not the effect of making children just, and Mr. Black's condemnation of teachers and parents is a very sweeping one. But aesthetic justice is sometimes to be met with in these pages—certain specimens of conversation having even to the jaded eye of maturity, verisimilitude and charm as exhibiting masculine juvenile psychology.

Book Reviewing, by Wayne Gard (Knopf). In this handbook the author quotes a number of editorial concepts of the ideal review, reprints typical reviews, makes suggestions for editing a book-page, discusses the beginnings of criticism, and critical methods, and provides an alphabetical conspectus of the market. He cautions the reviewer not to be guided in the choice of books for review, by their literary prominence, binding, or price-mark; nor to review them without having read them and observes that "one who sits in judgment certainly cannot afford to be caught napping in elementary matters." He has not been "indolent," but certain implications and opinions surprise the hardened reviewer and his verbal technique is rather unlucky.

The Dial, 83 (November 1927), 445, 447.

Up the Years from Bloomsbury: An Autobiography, by George Arliss (Little, Brown). To those readers, to whom Mr. Arliss as actor, wears the halo of infallibility, his writing will scarcely seem secular. "Colubrine" and "subtle, unselfish, gifted, merry, facete, and juvenile," he embodies—despite himself as self-effacing witness—the virtues we are accustomed to associate with the church rather than with the theater; a uniting of the serpent and the dove, which in these unsainted times is conspicuous.

The Dial, 84 (January 1928), 72.

Mrs. Leicester's School, by Charles and Mary Lamb, with illustrations by Winifred Green (Dutton). In these ten stories which purport to have been told by school-girls for the entertainment of school-companions on the first evening of arrival at school, we have that novelty in naturalness, height in humility, and humor in gravity, which are peculiarly Charles Lamb's. Should specifically the excellences which we have in mind be Mary Lamb's, the piecing is so perfect and so sensitively uninsistent that anonymity again seems like a signature.

The Dial, 84 (March 1928), 251.

The Wheel in Midsummer, by Janet Lewis (The Lone Gull, Lynn, Massachusetts). Extensile, hair-fine sensibility informs these poems, and their subject matter—safely imperceptible to the profane—is to be reverenced; "violets minute and scarce where the great ants climb," "dear among the withered asters," "fish paler than stones," "the badger's children creeping sideways out," "sunlight and daylight fading upon the air like sound."

Guide-Posts to Chinese Painting, by Louise Wallace Hackney, edited by Dr. Paul Pelliot (Houghton Mifflin). That a delighted consideration of art should be less than delightful; that as writing and as thinking it should be occidentally "prompt" is in this survey compensated for by illustrations such as "Winter Landscape," "Narcissus," a "Ming Ancestral Portrait"; and one is as attentive as the author could wish one to be, to the "ideals and methods" of Chinese painting, to "influences and beliefs reflected in it," and the influence exerted by it. Any lover of beauty may well be grateful to a book which commemorates the blade of grass as model for the study of the straight line, the skill of calligraphers, with "hog's hair on finely woven silk," "methods of treating mountain wrinkles," "tones of ink to 'give color,' " the thought of genii, winged tigers, and Emperor crossing " 'weak waters' on a 'bridge made of turtles,' " or a theme so romantic as that of Yang Kuei-fei "going, 'lily pale, between tall avenues of spears to die.' "

The Dial, 84 (April 1928), 344-45.

Min-Yo: Folk-Songs of Japan, selected, translated, and with introduction by Iwao Matsuhara (Shin-Sei Do, Tokyo). These songs—with introductory classification and a word as to composition—are presented in three versions; English, Japanese, and an English phonetic equivalent. Certain songs are, as English rhyme, not quite satisfactory, but the collection as a whole leads one to reflect that compression, mastery of the single tone, of the muted tone, of silence, are cardinal accomplishments.

Disraeli: A Picture of the Victorian Age, by André Maurois, translated from the French by Hamish Miles (Appleton). Adjustingly and as he feels justly M. Maurois has set his garland above "this sad and clever face"; if it is not a saint's halo, and M. Maurois says not, it is a species of crown. We are glad to have been acquainted before with those not congenial to M. Maurois' temperament—Gladstone, Sir Robert Peel, and the Earl of Derby—but we rejoice that our old favorite, who was possessed not only of charm but of greatness, should be fortunate in his biographer. The entertainingly and perfectly fused excellences of the Life are indelible. "Wizardry and power," "gratitude," the "symbol of what can be accomplished, in a cold and hostile universe, by a long youthfulness of heart"—these are Disraeli.

The Dial, 84 (May 1928), 435, 437.

The Bare Hills, by Yvor Winters (Four Seas). Nature's hieroglyphics of the visibly significant can be man's testament to suffering—to the arrogance, the humility, the pain, the pleasure, the discipline, the undiscipline of existence—and these poems acutely convey understanding, or to be exact, apperception, of the sharpened sensoriness of one who can eat bread "as if it were rock," whose cumulative eloquence, "trapped and morose" at times, recedes in geometric inverse ratio to its imperativeness; who does yet see sacramentally, "a fern ascending," "a last year's leaf turned up in silence," "the streets paved with the moon smooth to the heels." For Mr. Winters "the harvest falls . . . with a sound of fire in leaves"; "sunrise is set as if reflected from a violin hung in the trees"; "the hairy cows . . . move here and there with caution."

Fugitives: An Anthology of Verse (Harcourt, Brace). Including for the most part more than a single poem by each of the eleven authors represented, this anthology is judiciously persuasive. Throughout the collection, however, one is conscious of a prevailing attitude—of equivalences shall one say— of thought and feeling which make one wish that feeling were an easier thing to exposit and that contemporary vernacular were less hydra-headed, ostrich-natured, insatiate, and in the manner of the Indian *fakir* on the bed of spikes, relentless toward itself.

An Essay on Conversation, by Henry W. Taft (Macmillan). To the science of this matter Mr. Taft has applied the wisdom of Addison, Montaigne, Doctor Johnson, Doctor Mahaffy, Macaulay, Lord Chesterfield, Lamb, Hazlitt, Thoreau, Emerson, and others. He implies that tactful persons are more nearly equipped to prevail in conversation than "a race of contenders" and would welcome, with Doctor Johnson, opportunity for friendly interchange of thought "where suspicion is banished by experience, and emulation by benevolence; where every man speaks with no other restraint than unwillingness to offend, and hears with no other disposition than desire to be pleased." For so kindly a book one craves an invulnerable verbal mechanics unmarred by stock phrases and rhetorical "inaction"; but as trustworthy and conversible readers, we must accord our benefactor appreciation, not mere mechanical appraisal.

The Dial, 84 (June 1928), 522–23.

Poems, by Clinch Calkins (Knopf). Although a voluptuous defiance, pontifical not discursive, weights them and hauteur sometimes pervades too unhaughty a fabric, these poems are poems. Trueness is key, resilient verbal antitheses, "small birds swinging aloft on the precarious leaf" and here, and other small things that in poetics are not small.

A Letter to a Friend, Anonymous (Open Court). To this personal record of religious experience, the student of life and religion could not be indifferent. It is perhaps irrelevant to admit that the literary method might not in itself be consoling to readers of perversely Ashmolean temper. The desire for spiritual equilibrium is universal, however, and many have doubtless verged upon the feeling expressed by the person to whom this Letter was written: "The gods put winds about our heads and hurdles before our feet, and our bodies and souls crack and break. What becomes of the pain in the heart, no one has offered to suggest."

The Dial, 85 (August 1928), 172, 174.

The Temptation of Anthony and Other Poems, by Isidor Schneider (Boni & Liveright). One is held by the richness of the confession, "We search like rivers for a level and we find the greater torment of the sea." It is odd that where real strength and beauty are to be found, there should be images in excess of effectiveness, ambiguity, misplaced emphasis, and subversion rather than flight. One seems surrounded by unnecessarily intimate whelplike things: pre-imagist circumlocution, post-Joyce agglutination, the "hath done" style, "allwheres" selfconscious frolic—"a wink and a tear." From persons who have encountered injustice we expect tolerance not reproaches, and magnanimity not defiance. But as Mr. Schneider says, "the melancholy of the sun is its question, intent eye, inflaming the sky with its search."

Present-Day Russia, by Ivy Lee (Macmillan). A hurried account of a tenday visit to Russia is not necessarily a magazine of aesthetic ammunition, but is in this instance effective, systematic, and most acceptable to non-excursive herbivora. It is easier to read of the mountain which is Russia than to be the Mohammed that Mr. Lee has bravely been. In what is here told of marriage laws, espionage, art, trade relations, the press, and much else, he conveys a lively sense of conditions in the Soviet Utopia.

The Dial, 85 (September 1928), 266, 268.

English Verse, chosen and arranged by W. Peacock, Vol. I, The Early Lyrics to Shakespeare (Oxford University Press). In the preface to this first of five volumes to be issued as a companion work to the Oxford Selections of English Prose, the anthologist reminds us that " 'the best is the best though a hundred judges have declared it so,' " and if one misses this or that—if Skelton's lines on Phyllyp Sparowe seem a shade better than those on the sparrow and the cat, and nothing is better than Henryson's taill of the lyoun and the mous, it is evident to the reader that "skillful might gaue many sparkes of blisse." The irresistible attractiveness of Chaucer, Shakespeare, and intervening authors, could not be suggested, one feels, with more bouquet-like enticement than here.

The Dial, 85 (November 1928), 442.

The Mysteriousness of Marriage, by Jeremy Taylor, with illustrations from drawings by Denis Tegetmeier (Francis Walterson, Abergavenny, South Wales). That such good authorship and beautiful bookmaking should be defaced with comic illustrations is confusing. The contrast, in this instance, of practice with preaching scarcely seems "salutary"—unbecoming though it is for a dial to discourage interest in contemporary virtuosity or in drawings so able as those which Mr. Walterson has taken the trouble to procure.

Contemporary British Literature, by John Matthews Manly and Edith Rickert (Harcourt, Brace). This manual for the student of current tendencies in literature, with its biographical data, bibliographies, study outlines, selected reviews, and suggestions for reading, is valuable in itself, and not less so as a demonstration in method. One can understand how not all British authors and not "even the most important notices of individual books" could be included, for "among the scores of striking successes it is hard to find a dozen, much less a score, of authors who have anything of permanent value to contribute to literature, and of these the greater part are not the best known." It is not at once apparent to one, however, why there should not be mention of Gordon Craig, Charles Whibley, George Saintsbury, John Eglinton, Llewelyn Powys, Percy Lubbock, Logan Pearsall Smith, or Roger Fry.

The Dial, 85 (December 1928), 538–39.

The First Harvest, by Mary Leighton, with two illustrations by John S. Sargent (Four Seas Company). To retell the story of Adam and Eve is permissible, however prone "book-takers" are to think Ralph Hodgson, Milton, and the King James translators the best tellers; and if Eve has been portrayed by Blake, Dürer, Botticelli, and some five or six sculptors, there is perhaps the more reason why Sargent should also be moved to depict her. Of statement verbal or linear in this account of the Garden, that which recurs to one as having been least anticipated is, " 'The threat of ill—what *is* to die—?' The snake replied from rocky shelf: 'To cast thy form, but not thyself.' "

Annie Besant, by Geoffrey West (Representative Women Series, Viking Press). By this portrait of "a propagandist militant of the apostolic variety," we are reminded that social, political, and religious enlightenment owe more than they may well be conscious of, to this fearless solitary pilgrim who for almost eighty years has fought "on the side of the angels" and been "attacked most bitterly by the godly." So spare, emphatic, and reasoned a life is in itself a pleasure; but our debt is primarily to the sharp sense it gives of a uniquely able woman—a person full of energy, self-discipline, and confident, exalted soberness.

The Dial, 86 (January 1929), 77, 79.

The Lost Lyrist, by Elizabeth Hollister Frost (Harper's). These poems reflect one's sense of nature's unimplicated aspect when one's primary sensation is of "pain, that puts out brighter pain," and an absorbed somnambulistic instinct for tracing perceptibly what is unperceived by any but one's self. The reader doubts the poetic rightness of certain impulsive comparisons of the temporal with the eternal, but is aware of the assembling eye, of a sometimes engagingly unanticipated lyric succinctness, and is deeply impressed by the inquiring note of loneliness.

Alger: A Biography without a Hero, by Herbert R. Mayes (Macy-Masius). We cannot be sure that "Alger is a name better known than Dickens or Tolstoy or Balzac or Hawthorne" or that an author who "accepted Henry James as a master stylist" had "a mediocre mind" or that hand to mouth, slang to hand writing about a man who was not a "hero" helps a defeated author or present reader. We perceive, moreover, that Horatio Alger's 119 times repeated theme of Rough and Ready, Frank and Fearless, Do and Dare, Sink or Swim, by no means rivals in interest the story of his own career, were his "sense of the fine things of life" but conveyed to us seriously, not waggishly and wordishly.

The Dial, 86 (February 1929), 164, 167.

Hedylus, by H. D. (Houghton Mifflin). We have in this book sharp renderings of exterior beauty. Hedyle an Athenian hetaira is, with her son, resident at a Greek court, and of their life we are given a single day—a drama of filial-parental conflicting sensibilities which attains its climax in Hedylus' self-assertive flight from his mother and from the court. One has a sense of adjectives and italics and "manner," which one cannot think of as characteristic of H. D., but the fervor and "exact fantasy of visualization"—and the beauty in print and arrangement—seem hers.

The Dial, 86 (March 1929), 264.

Traveling Standing Still, by Genevieve Taggard (Knopf). Despite an occasionally informal limerick quality and contradictions of the spiritual by the mundane, one admires in these poems a felicity of motion, a lyric contour, and an ardent poring upon Nature; in short, a whorl of aesthetic contemplation that is serious and affecting.

Arachne, by Amos Niven Wilder (Yale University Press). These sensitive and at the same time powerful perceptions of the visible and of the invisible, are hampered by an effect of verbal over-accouterment; and occasional lapses from the poetic deter, indeed smite, the reader; yet a humble, even penitent consciousness of having been admitted to that which is timeless must be acknowledged. Depth of outlook upon life is so rare, that appraisal of it seems ill-adjudged and in these poems regality of concept is its own advocate.

The Dial, 86 (April 1929), 345–46.

Mist: A Tragicomic Novel, by Miguel de Unamuno, translated from the Spanish by Warner Fite (Knopf). Ingenuity can be tiresome and literature perhaps tends to seem customary. To certain of one's moods at any rate, effects are not right; but Cervantes' "genial caricature of literary baroquism" has been lasting, and in Unamuno's *nivola,* Mist, there are things that cannot easily be brushed away: Augusto's mother and his mother's hand, "a hand made, not for grasping, but only for perching, like the foot of a dove—upon the shoulder of her husband," the game of chess, Dona Ermelinda and "the accident of the fall of the canary," Don Augusto's impassioned detachment; "I have always thought that there is nothing more—more—how shall I put it?—nothing more cynical than innocence." The story is not formidable (Augusto Pérez—deluded by a music teacher and eluded by a laundress—consults Unamuno and is told that he must die, for Unamuno does not know what to do with him); and confidences, as in *Mist,* between author and the hero threaten illusion, but in this intensive yet impersonal unfolding of personality, one learns something about one's self, as well as about romance. "Confusionist, indefinitionist" art of this kind is like the piano, of no service, merely serving "to fill the fireside with harmony and keep it from being an ash-pit."

The Hamlet of A. MacLeish (Houghton Mifflin). "No man living but has seen the king his father's ghost" and "Thou wouldst not think / How ill all's here about my heart!" constitute the theme of this poem, of which so great a portion is unprincely and unhistrionic that one tends boorishly to reiterate the query, "Why must I always / Stoop from this decent silence to this praise / That makes a posture of my hurt?" But eloquence transcends confusion, and poetry is to be encountered here.

The Dial, 86 (May 1929), 435–36.

Contemporary British Literature, by John M. Manly and Edith Rickert (Harcourt, Brace). One is under obligation to those who are able to provide in small compass, information so comprehensive as is given in this survey (revised) of types and schools of writing in contemporary British literature, with biographical data, bibliographies, reading-lists, and recommended studies and reviews. Compression requires succinctness and it would seem that experts have the right to be didactic; nevertheless, one mourns the absence of such authors as Charles Whibley, George Saintsbury, John Eglinton, and Logan Pearsall Smith.

The Dial, 86 (June 1929), 528.

The good fortune of The Oxford University Press—that is to say, its high ability—in making re-editions seem necessary, is again exemplified in *The Autobiography of Leigh Hunt* with introduction by Edmund Blunden. That Leigh Hunt "takes his place among the mystics as well as the men of letters" needs to be said, and we may well be brought anew into the "radiant pleasure of his notions."

England from Wordsworth to Dickens, by R. W. King (Harcourt, Brace). This anthology of English verse and prose, in minuteness like a scene viewed through a little glass-covered aperture in an Easter-egg, is a picture of England and of English character between 1784 and 1837, in specimens of writing that one would value for their intrinsic richness; and political, economic, cultural, and social aspects of a country, as seen in debates, dinners, dress, plays, vehicles, Mayings, boxing-matches, and university life, are not a dull peep-show.

The Dial, 86 (July 1929), 632.

III. THE MIDDLE YEARS
1931-1947

EXPERIENCED SIMPLICITY

UNEMPHASIZED rhymes, a flattened rhetoric, and retreating verse patterns are likely to be sincerer than is convenient to the reader; but earlier work by Mr. Ross, not here included, presents some of these themes in more fluent guise, and these poems—American pieces and a series entitled *Myth*—are evidently disciplines in the art of poetic exactitude. A scientist has been studying

> The mystery
> of measured matter
> with the aid
> of crucible,
> or test-tube held
> above the flame.

What may appear sometimes to be unwariness, is deliberate—like the unwariness of the stick insect and the thorn beetle—making us realize that we have been permitted, rather than invited, to observe. We see

> something of
> what quality may mark us off
> from older Europe—
> something "North American"—

"skyscrapers," "pistons," "pulleys and shafting moving together," "a whirling saw," a "laboratory," and in the sequestered brilliance of Canada, "rolling streams," "falling water," "a rocky bay," "the clear expanse of lake and air." We see the poplar leaves, "whitish-surfaced," and

> in the deep shadow
> of the pine, . . .

Review of *Laconics*, by W. W. E. Ross (Overbrook Press).

> . . . .
> the ghostly glimmering
> of the gum.

Science's method of attaining to originality by way of veracity is pleasing, and it is here enhanced by the considering conscience which feels as well as sees; which asks in looking at factories:

> Are these things
> designed for men?
> Or men for these?
> Or are men things?—

which is not too self-justifying with regard to a fish "pulled from the lake," that had

> . . . wandered to and fro . . .
> . . . .
> among mysterious
> recesses
> there in the semi-
> light of the water.

The artist's tendency is always to be seeking better explicitness and simpler simplicities, and the studious imagination that Mr. Ross has gives pleasure, besides suggesting a method.

Poetry, 38 (August 1931), 280–81.

A MACHINERY OF SATISFACTION

> What seas what shores what grey rocks and what islands
> What water lapping the bow
> And scent of pine and the woodthrush singing through the fog
> What images return
> O my daughter.

This inquiry, without question mark, is the setting of *Marina*. It is a decision that is to animal existence a query: death is not death. The theme is frustration and frustration is pain. To the eye of resolution

> Those who sharpen the tooth of the dog, meaning
> Death
> Those who glitter with the glory of the hummingbird, meaning
> Death
> Those who sit in the stye of contentment, meaning
> Death
> Those who suffer the ecstasy of the animals, meaning
> Death
> Are become unsubstantial.

T. S. Eliot is occupied with essence and instrument, and his choice of imagery has been various. This time it is the ship, "granite islands" and "woodthrush calling through the fog." Not sumptuous grossness but a burnished hedonism is renounced. Those who naively proffer consolation put the author beyond their reach, in initiate solitude. Although solitude is to T. S. Eliot, we infer, not "a monarchy of death," each has his private desperations; a poem may mean one thing to the author and another to the reader. What matters here is that we have, for both author and reader, a machinery of satisfaction that is powerfully affecting, intrinsically and by association. The method is a main part of the pleasure: lean cartography; reiteration with compactness; emphasis by word pattern rather than by punctuation; the conjoining of opposites to produce irony; a counterfeiting verbally of the systole, diastole, of sensation—of what the eye sees and the mind feels; the movement within the movement of differentiated kindred sounds, recalling the transcendent beauty and ability, in *Ash Wednesday*, of the lines:

> One who moves in the time between sleep and waking, wearing
> White light folded, sheathed about her, folded.
> The new years walk, restoring
> Through a bright cloud of tears, the years, restoring
> With a new verse the ancient rhyme.

As part of the revising of conventionality in presentment, there is the embedded rhyme, evincing dissatisfaction with bald rhyme. This hiding, qualifying, and emphasizing of rhyme to an adjusted tempo is acutely a pleasure besides

---

Review of *Marina*, by T. S. Eliot (No. 29 of *The Ariel Poems*, Faber & Faber).

being a clue to feeling that is the source, as in *Ash Wednesday*, of harmonic contour like the sailing descent of the eagle.

Marina is not for those who read inquisitively, as a compliment to the author, or to find material for the lecture platform. Apocalyptic declaration is uncompliant to parody. If charged by chameleon logic and unstudious didactism with creating a vogue for torment, Mr. Eliot can afford not to be incommoded, knowing that his work is the testament of one "having to construct something upon which to rejoice."

Poetry, 38 (September 1931), 337–39.

THE CANTOS

THESE Cantos are the epic of the farings of a literary mind.

The ghost of Homer sings. His words have the sound of the sea and the cadence of actual speech. *And So-shu churned in the sea, So-shu also.*[1] In Canto III we have an ideograph for the Far East, consisting of two parts:

> Green veins in the turquoise,
> Or, the gray steps lead up under the cedars.

The Cantos are concerned with *books, arms*, and *men of unusual genius*. They imply that there is nothing like the word-melody of the Greek; we have that of Latin also—Virgil and Ovid. One's ear can learn from the Latin something of quantity. " 'Not by the eagles only was Rome measured. / Wherever the Roman speech was, there was Rome.' / Wherever the speech crept, there was mastery." The Cantos imply that there is pleasure to be had from Propertius and Catullus, that Catullus is very winning; it is plain that in liking him, one has something of his attitude of mind. "Can we know Ovid," Mr. Pound asks in his "Notes on Elizabethan Classicists," "until we find him in Golding? . . . is not a new beauty created, an old beauty doubled when the over-change is well done?" On returning to Paris after seven years, *Knocking at empty rooms, seeking for buried beauty*, Mr. Pound is told by *A strange concierge, in place of the gouty-footed*, that the friend he asks about is dead. For the attar of friendship of one long dead

---

Review of *A Draft of XXX Cantos*, by Ezra Pound (Hours Press).

> Dry casques of departed locusts
> speaking a shell of speech . . .

are not a substitute. Golding afforded "reality and particularization"; whereas Paris is a thing of *Words like the locust-shells, moved by no inner being;* and Mr. Pound thinks for a moment of the scarlet-curtain simile in the "Flight from Hippomenes" in Ovid's *Metamorphoses,* translated by Golding,[2] and murmurs, *The scarlet curtain throws a less scarlet shadow.* This Paris Canto— VII—is one of the best; the eleven last lines—memorable, stately.

It is apparent that the Latin line is quantitative. If poetics allure, the Cantos will also show that in Provençal minstrelsy we encounter a fascinating precision; the delicacy and exactness of Arnaut Daniel, whose invention, the sestina form, is "like a thin sheet of flame folding and infolding upon itself." In this tongue—you read it in manuscripts rather than in books— is to be found pattern. And the Cantos show how the troubadours not only sang poems but *were* poems. Usually they were in love, with My Lady Battle if with no other, and were often successful, for in singing of love one sometimes finds it—especially when the *canzos* are good ones. And there were jealous husbands. Miguel de la Tour is most pleasing to Mr. Pound in what he says of Piere de Maensac, who carried off the wife of Bernart de Tierci. "The husband, in the manner of the golden Menelaus, demanded her much," and there was *Troy* in *Auvergnat.* But it happened often that the minstrel was thrown into prison or put himself there, like Bernart de Ventadorn, who sang of the lark and who "ended his days in the monastery of Dalon." In this connection, disparity in station, under which people suffer and are patient, is regrettable; Madonna Biancha Visconti was married by her uncle to a peasant; and the troubadours oftener than not were frustrated in love; they were poor and were usually more gifted than the men whose appurtenance they were. But things are sometimes reversed, as when a man of title falls in love with a tirewoman. And not always are people to be balked, as we see in the case of this Pedro the persistent, who came to reign, murdered the murderers of the tirewoman, and married the dug-up corpse. Pedro's ghost sings in Canto III and again in XXX.

Mr. Pound brings to his reading, master-appreciation; and his gratitude takes two forms; he thanks the book and tells where you may see it. "Any man who would read Arnaut and the troubadours owes great thanks to Emil Levy of Freiburg," he says in *Instigations,* "for his long work and his little dictionary (*Petit Dictionnaire Provençal-Français,* Karl Winter's Universitätsbuchhandlung, Heidelberg)." He sings of this in Canto XX—of the old man who at about *6:30 /in the evening, . . . trailed half way across Freiburg / before dinner, to see the two strips of copy.*

And as those who love books know, the place in which one read a book or talked of it partakes of its virtue in recollection; so for Mr. Pound the cedars and new-mown hay and far-off nightingale at Freiburg have the glamour of Provence. He says (Canto XX):

> You would be happy for the smell of that place And never
> tired of being there, either alone
> Or accompanied.

And he intimates that no lover of books will do himself the disservice of overlooking Lope de Vega, his "matchless buoyancy, freshness," "atmosphere of earliest morning," "like that hour before the summer dawn, when the bracing cool of the night still grips the air," his "sprightly spirit of impertinence," his tenderness. In Canto III is echoed from the joke from the *Cid* about the gold—the two chests of sand "covered with vermillion leather" and pawned with the proviso that "they be not disturbed for a year"; and there are echoes of the slumber song that speaks of angels a-flying.

As for Dante, even the mind most unsparing of itself will not easily get all that is to be got from him. Books and arms. Either is not necessarily a part of the other any more than the books from the London Library that were taken to the late war by T. E. Hulme and were buried by a shell in a dugout. But we enjoy Homer, Virgil, Dante, and what they had to say about war. And arms are mentioned in the *Chanson de Roland* and in Shakespeare. And we enjoy the Cantos in which Mr. Pound sings of the wars between cities in an Italy of unsanitary dungeons and great painting, and what he says of diplomatic greed as disgusting and also comic; and like what he says of wigglings, split fees, tips, and self-interest:

> Sigismundo, ally, come through an enemy force,
> To patch up some sort of treaty, passes one gate
> And they shut it before they open the next gate, and he says:
> "Now you have me,
>   Caught like a hen in a coop."

Speaking of Italy, we find in Canto XXVI a picture of Mr. Pound outside St. Mark's on one of his first visits to Venice, of which visit he says:

> And
> I came here in my youth
>   and lay there under the crocodile
> By the column. . . .

To one looking up at it, it is small, like the silhouette of a lizard, this bronze crocodile, souvenir of Venetian acquisitiveness.

> And at night they sang in the gondolas
> And in the barche with lanthorns;
> The prows rose silver on silver
> taking light in the darkness.

To return to fighting, "Dante fought at Campaldino, 'in the front rank,' " and "saw further military service," and other men of literary genius have survived war. Canto XVI alludes to Lord Byron, who once bore arms for Greece, though the canto alludes to him as wrapped in scarlet and resembling a funeral; not dead, merely drunk. But the drunkenness that is war! War such as this last:

> And Henri Gaudier went to it,
> and they killed him

Why cannot money and life go for beauty instead of for war and intellectual oppression? This question is asked more than once by the Cantos. Books and arms. Under the head of arms, as you will have noticed, come daggers— like Pedro's and Giovanni Malatesta's sword that slew Paolo, the beautiful. Books, arms, men. To Dante antiquity was not a figment; nor is it to Mr. Pound any more than Mme. Curie is a figment, or the man he knew in Manhattan,

> 24 E. 47th, when I met him,
> Doing job printing.

Men of unusual genius, *Both of ancient times and our own.* Of our own (Canto VII), Henry James

> Moves before me, phantom with weighted motion,
> *Grave incessu,* drinking the tone of things,
> And the old voice lifts itself
> weaving an endless sentence.

And there was an exemplary American, favorable to music.

> "Could you," wrote Mr. Jefferson
> "Find me a gardener
> Who can play the french horn?"

And the singer curses his country for being *Midas lacking a Pan!* To cite passages is to pull one quill from a porcupine. Mr. Pound took two thousand and more pages to say it in prose, and he sings it in a hundred-forty-two. The book is concerned with beauty. You must read it yourself; it has a power that is mind and is music; it comes with the impact of centuries and with the impact of yesterday. Amid the swarming madness of excellence, there is the chirping of "the young phoenix broods," the Chinese music, the slender bird-note that gives one no peace. "Great poets," Mr. Pound says, "seldom make bricks without straw. They pile up all the excellences they can beg, borrow, or steal from their predecessors and contemporaries and then set their own inimitable light atop the mountain." Of the Cantos, then, what is the master-quality? Scholastically, it is "concentrating the past on the present," as T. S. Eliot says; rhetorically, it is certitude; musically, it is range with an unerring ear. Note Cantos XIII, XVII, XXI, and XXX. And in all this "wealth of motive," this "*largesse,*" this "intelligence," are there no flaws? Does every passage in this symphony "relieve, refresh, revive the mind of the reader—at reasonable intervals—with some form of ecstasy, by some splendor of thought, some presentation of sheer beauty, some lightning turn of phrase?" Not invariably. The "words affect modernity," says William Carlos Williams, "with too much violence (at times)—a straining after slang effects. . . . You cannot *easily* switch from Orteum to Peoria without violence (to the language). These images too greatly infest the Cantos."

Unprudery is overemphasized and secularity persists, refuted though this charge is by the prose praise of Dante: "His work is of that sort of art which is a key to the deeper understanding of nature and the beauty of the world and of the spirit"; "for the praise of that part of his worth which is fiber rather than surface, my mind is not yet ripe, nor is my pen skilled." Most of us have not the tongues of the spirit, but those who have, tell us that, by comparison, knowledge of the spirit of tongues is as insignificant as are the clothes worn by one in infancy. We share Mr. Pound's diffidence.

T. S. Eliot suspects Ezra Pound's philosophy of being antiquated. William Carlos Williams finds his "versification *still* patterned after classic meters"; and, apropos of "feminolatry," is not the view of woman expressed by the Cantos older-fashioned than that of Siam and Abyssinia? knowledge of the femaleness of *chaos,* of the *octopus,* of *Our mulberry leaf, woman,* appertaining more to Turkey than to a Roger Ascham? Nevertheless Mr. Pound likes the denouement of *Aucassin and Nicolette,* and in comparing *Romeo and Juliet* with De Vega's *Castelvines y Monteses,* sees "absolutely no necessity for the general slaughter at the end of Shakespeare's play." He addresses the lutanists in their own tongue (Canto VIII):

"Ye spirits who of olde were in this land
Each under Love, and shaken,
Go with your lutes, awaken
The summer within her mind,
Who hath not Helen for peer,
Yseut nor Batsabe."

But, a practical man in these matters, he sees the need for antidotes to "inebriation from the *Vita Nuova*"; namely, Sir James Fraser and Remy de Gourmont; one no longer mistakes the singer's habilement for his heart any more than one acquainted with the prose of James Joyce would find the bloom on the poems in *Chamber Music* artless.

What about Cantos XIV and XV? Let us hope that "Disgust with the sordid is but another expression of a sensitiveness to the finer thing."

Petty annoyances are magnified; when one is a beginner, tribulation worketh impatience.

Stock oaths, and the result is ennui, as with the stock adjective.

An annoyance by no means petty is the lack of an index.

And since the Cantos are scrupulous against half-truth and against *what had been thought for too long*—ought they not to suggest to those who have accepted Calvin by hearsay—or heresy—that one must make a distinction between Calvin the theologian and Calvin the man of letters? Or is Mr. Pound indifferent to wit from that quarter—as sailors in the Baltic are said not to shave when the wind is favorable?

Those who object to the Cantos' obscurity—who prefer the earlier poems—are like the victims of Calvin who have not read him. It may be true that the author's revisions make it harder, not easier, for hurried readers; but flame kindles to the eye that contemplates it. Besides, these *are* the earlier poems. A critic that would have us "establish axes of reference by knowing the *best of each kind of written thing*" has persisted to success; is saying something "in such a way that one cannot re-say it more effectively." Note the affinity with material commonly called sentimental, which in most writers becomes sickly and banal, and in the Cantos is kept keen and alive; and the tactility with which Mr. Pound enables us to relive antiquity: *Da Gamma wore striped pants in Africa.* And he sets it "to paint" so that we may *see* what he says. The pale backgrounds are by Leonardo da Vinci; there are faces with the *eyes of Picasso;* the walls are by Mantegna. The yellow in Canto XVII, of the fawn and the broom, and the cerise grasshopper-wing, gain perhaps by contrast with a prevailing tendency, in the Cantos, to blue. *Malachite, green clear, and blue clear, blue-gray glass of the wave, Glare azure, Black snout of a porpoise.* The dramatist's eye that sees this and *Cosimo's red leather note book* and the *big green account book* and the lion whelps *vivos et piloses living and hairy, waves . . . holding their form / No light reaching through them,*

> And the waters richer than glass,
> Bronze gold, the blaze over the silver,
> Dye-pots in the torch-light,

finds the mechanistic world also "full of enchantments," "not only the light in the electric bulb, but the thought of the current hidden in the air," "and the rose that his magnet makes in the iron filings." And added to imagination is the idiosyncratic force of the words—the terseness in which some reflower and some are new. Of Mr. Pound and words, Dr. Williams says, "He has taken them up—if it may be risked—alertly, swiftly, but with feeling for the delicate living quality in them, not disinfecting, scraping them, but careful of the life." The skill that in the prose has been incomparably expert in epitomizing what others have bungled, shows us that "you can be wholly precise in representing a vagueness." This ambidextrous precision, born of integrity and intrepidity, is the poet's revenge upon those "who refuse to say what they think, if they do think," who are like those who see nothing the matter with bad surgery. And allied with veracity are translatorly qualities that nourish ingenuity in the possessor of them: a so unmixed zeal for essence that no assaying of merits in rendering is a trouble; an independence that will not subscribe to superstition—to the notion, for instance, that a text written in Greek is of necessity better than a text written in Latin. Even Homer can be put characteristically into Latin. *Andreas Divus* "plucked from a Paris stall" "gave him in Latin," *In officina Wecheli,* 1538,

> Caught up his cadence, word and syllable:
> "Down to the ships we went, set mast and sail,
> Black keep and beasts for bloody sacrifice,
> Weeping we went."

And the English of Golding's Ovid is as good as the Latin. "A master may be continually expanding his own tongue, rendering it fit to bear some charge hitherto borne only by some other alien tongue"; yet as Fontenelle said to Erasmus, "If before being vain of a thing" men "should try to assure themselves that it really belonged to them, there would be little vanity in the world."

The new in Mr. Pound, as in any author, hides itself from the dull and is accentuated for the quick. Certain implements in use by James Joyce are approved: the pun, the phonetic photography of dialect, propriety with vibrating edge of impropriety, the wry jest—'Helion t' 'Helion. "All artists who discover anything . . . must, in the course of things, . . . push certain experiments beyond the right curve of their art," Mr. Pound says, and some would say, the facing in many directions as of a quadriga drawn by centaurs, which we meet in the Cantos, puts strain on bipedal understanding; there is love of risk; but the experienced grafting of literature upon music is here very remarkable—the resonance of color, allusions, and tongues sounding one through the other as in symphonic instrumentation. Even if one understood nothing, one would enjoy the musicianship.

> Thus the book of the mandates:
>
> Feb. 1422.
>
> We desire that you our factors give to Zohanne of Rimini
> our servant, six lire marchesini,
> for the three prizes he has won racing our barbarisci,
> at the rate we have agreed on. The races he has won
> are the Modena, the San Petronio at Bologna
> and the last race at San Zorzo.
>
> (Signed) Parisina Marchesa

Mr. Pound says, "Everyone has been annoyed by the difficulty of indicating the *exact* tone and rhythm with which one's verse is to be read," but in the "capripedal" counterpoint of the above little fugue à la gigue he has put it beyond our power to stumble. And there is discovery in the staccato sound of the conclusion to Canto XXX, in the patterning of the "y" in "thirty" on the "i" in *mori:*

> Il Papa Mori.
>
> Explicit canto
> XXX

The master-quality throughout the Cantos is decision:

> SIGISMUNDUS HIC EGO SUM
> MALATESTA, FILIUS PANDULPHI, REX PRODITORUM

But however explicit the accents in the line, the fabric on which the pattern is focused is indispensable to accuracy. There is the effect sometimes, as in the medieval dance, of a wheel spun one way and then the other; there is the sense of a horse rushing toward one and turning, unexpectedly rampant; one has stepped back but need not have moved. Note the luster of a subtle slowing exactly calculated (Canto V):

> Fades the light from the sea, and many things
> "Are set abroad and brought to mind of thee."

"The music of rhymes depends upon their arrangement, not on their multiplicity." We are aware in the Cantos of the skill of an ear with a faculty for rhyme in its most developed arrangements, but, like that of a Greek, against the vulgarity of rhyme; a mind aware of instruments—aware of "the circular bars of the Arabs, divided, like unjust mince pies, from the center to circumference," and of "the beautiful irregularities of the human voice." Whatever the training, however, "a man's rhythm" "will be, in the end, his own, uncounterfeiting, uncounterfeitable"; and in Canto XIII, in the symbolic discussion of the art of poetics, what is said is illustrated by the manner of saying:

> And Tseu-lou said, "I would put the defences in order,"
> And Khieu said, "If I were lord of a province
> I would put it in better order than it is."
> And Tchi said, "I would prefer a small mountain temple,
> With order in the observances,
>   with a suitable performance of the ritual,"
> . . . .
> And Kung said, "They have all answered correctly,
> That is to say, each in his nature."
> . . . .
> And Kung said, and wrote on the bo leaves:
>   "If a man have not order within him
> He cannot spread order about him;
>   . . . .
>   "Anyone can run to excesses,
> It is easy to shoot past the mark,
> It is hard to stand firm in the middle."

There is no easy way if you are to be a great artist; and the nature of one, in achieving his art, is different from the nature of another.

Mr. Pound, in the prose that he writes, has formulated his own commentary upon the Cantos. They are an armorial coat of attitudes to things that have happened in books and in life; they are not a shield but a coat worn by a man, as in the days when heraldry was beginning. He serves under Beauty, with the motto, Τό Καλόν. "Ordinary people," he says in his turtle poem, "touch me not." His art is his turtle-shell or snail house; it is all one animal moving together, and

> Who seeks him must be worse than blind,
> He and his house are so combined,
> If finding it he fails to find
> its master.[3]

[1] Material quoted from the Cantos appears in Italic or is indented; from other work, in double quotation marks.

[2] "As when a scarlet curtain streyned against a playstred wall
   Doth cast like shadowe, making it seeme ruddye there-with all."

[3] "The Snail" by Cowper.

Poetry, 39 (October 1931), 37–56; *Predilections; A Marianne Moore Reader*.

IN SATURATED SOLUTION

O N E is wary of new novels. Instead of the originality and "flawless prose" that have pleased a reviewer, one finds usually the opposite. But in *Hester Craddock*, Alyse Gregory's third novel, there is originality; and the writing is so good that it is not necessary that it should be flawless.

Hester Craddock, Nelly, and their brother, Wilfred, live in Dorset, near the chalk cliffs by the sea. Not far from them is the cottage of Edwin Pallant, a litterateur, whose frequent companion is Halmath Tryan, a painter. The two men fall in love with Nelly, the two women fall in love with Tryan, and Hester kills herself by an intentional misstep from the head of the cliff, allowing it to be inferred that the fall was an accident.

A main debt to the author is, perhaps, the feeling one has of experiencing the region depicted, the sense of place being implicit in the writing rather than in the result of definite description. We feel the immensity of the six-hundred-foot cliff with its green mat of close, brilliant turf sloping back to the "low-lying cup of pasture lands"; this green over the white cliff, repeated as it were in the floor of the sea that kept changing "in color from glaucous to jade green and from jade green to a milky white." More personally typical

---

Review of *Hester Craddock*, by Alyse Gregory (Longmans, Green and Company).

is the Pallant cottage embedded in the downs and showing only the peak, its submerged character emphasized by the impression from inside, of "tall grasses waving backward and forward in the square opening of the window" as if a "tropical plant were growing on the sill." Saturation of effect is contributed by incident like that in which the arriving visitor "took out his pipe as if he intended to stay." Connotative detail evokes mood: the two walking-sticks that immediately after Hester had set them in the corner, "came clattering down at her feet," and the sitting-room that without Nelly's care "looked damp and uninviting and almost as if some disaster had taken place in the house."

The story is centered in three phases of sex antagonism: that between man and woman; that between a man and a man; and that between a woman and a woman. And there are multiplied instances of "negativeness." Hester fixates on the consciousness of inferiority that has been strengthened by Edwin Pallant's remark when she had irritated him: "You shut out the light wherever you go." She becomes the prey of self-deception, suspicion, fear, jealousy, and of an all-inclusive sense of guilt in the thought that it is within her power to neglect to the point of death Nelly, who is critically ill. The physical as a determining principle of attraction is shown in the voracity of the question reiterated by Pallant, when Hester had evaded it: "And your sister, Nelly, is she pretty?" and in Hester's thinking eventually, "how unattractive Pallant looked." He is a hunchback.

We are shown man's willingness to think of women as "a lot of dangerous, witless shrews," and woman's contempt for his contempt; Hester's sense of her brother's unworth, for instance, when he dismissed her "with that look of superiority with which the logical regard the completely irrational." We have also, as the accompaniment of unopposed neuroses, a reversing of sex attitudes. Hester intrudes upon Tryan. Her insistence is that of a seagull losing and retrieving a scrap of fish. The result is studied politeness on his part, and on hers, obduracy proportionate with the weakness of her position.

Under the characterizations, mental and physical, there is impassioned observation of emotion. Hester is the dominant figure—"tall and ungainly . . . impetuous and heedless," conscious of her "conspicuous teeth and awkward body." With the understanding that she is to meet Tryan, the painter, she has been invited by Pallant to come to his cottage to tea and has promised to bring her sister, who has not met Pallant. Having failed to speak to her sister of the plan, she is asked by Pallant when she appears at the door, if her sister is not coming. "She had to go to the village," says Hester. "The words were spoken vivaciously as if she suspected the presence of an invisible listener." But reciprocally, Pallant had not invited Tryan. The embattled unease of her nature is typified by the answer she makes

Pallant on a later occasion when he asks why she has come: "I came because I thought it was fitting." " 'Fitting?' he inquired." And there is Wilfred, nominally an invalid. "He spoke with weary, well-bred precision as if he suffered from every one's stupidity but his own." Opposed to his deadness are the vigor and naturalness of Tryan; also, in contrast with Wilfred's faded irony, a fastidious colloquialism that is most pleasing.

Hester is foil to Nelly, who is patient and beautiful, and Pallant, foil to Tryan. In this characterization of Pallant we have a very unusual thing, the successful enactment of the difficult role of brilliance and unexpectedness. In his attentive manner when addressed and in the seductive simplicity of his answers, in the plausibility of his dialects, we perceive a type seldom realized outside French thinking.

Some are not interested in sex pathology; there are exacting readers who may complain of a tendency to adjective and adverb mannerism, to inadvertent rhymes, and to certain wordings, but one is carried beyond small deterrents. The casual reader will be enticed by the clear picture, the pulsating quiver of life, the swiftness of the current which bears it, and the natural yet somewhat reserved audacity of repartee, for the story itself is sufficient.

The book is essentially for those interested in literary secrets of manipulation; one feels in it the presence of an important mind.

New York Herald Tribune Books, 8 November 1931, p. 21.

IF A MAN DIE

THE *Coming Forth by Day of Osiris Jones* is, as the introductory note implies, a Book of the Dead; or more exactly, a Dead Man's Book. It is the deceased man's justification of himself by charms, rubrics, and acclamation, that in the *psychostasia*—the weighing of the heart against the feather of truth—he may come forth into the day with the similitude of a god and perform such transformations as his heart may desire. It is as Osiris the god of the underworld that terrestrial man presents himself in his book of transcripts from the magic texts, since Osiris, overcome by Set the Liar and reconstituted by eating the eye of Horus, was the first to be delivered from

---

Review of *The Coming Forth by Day of Osiris Jones* and *Preludes for Memnon*, by Conrad Aiken (Charles Scribner's Sons).

the Devourer and be adjudged "true of voice," his individuality perfect, his soul divine, his words exquisite.

In his coming forth, Osiris Jones desires that he may have rest, food, continuance. Since childhood, only in dreams has he been The Resting One. There must be food for the body, for the mind, for the soul: for the table, such as anyone that he might marry would provide, including vegetables one might raise for diversion. It would seem that to the author of *Discordants* marriage is a sacrament. "Bread I broke with you was more than bread." But in the case of Osiris Jones it is more difficult to determine to exactly which food category marriage is regarded as belonging. Food for the mind, books; for the spirit, a knowledge of the Absolute. As for continuance, if intellectual children and the love of God are to take the place of progeny in the tribal sense of the term, these substitutes must be good ones.

In his critical writings Mr. Aiken has been honest; he has not influenced doubtful material to make an author appear to advantage, and in the trying of his own conscience he is equally honest. The questions asked are three: must the illusions of childhood end with childhood? must one let love alone? are books one's only friend? His answer is: "I was a rash man in my time." But the heart need merely balance the beam, not counterbalance it.

In *The Coming Forth by Day of Osiris Jones,* which is psycho-realistic poetic drama intentionally distorted, the arrangement is that of the disrelated chapter of a funerary roll or grave-book; and as on a late dynastic roll or on one of the Empire there were sometimes illustrations, there arise here—not consecutively—favorite thoughts or might one say vignettes, and certain sensations prominent to the consciousness of Osiris Jones.

I. A magic of white is upon him—of grave clothes, of ivory, or a rose coming to pieces in the hands, of magnolias, of jasmine, of camellias, of pale lamplight, or "White-waved water," of snow, of fog, of clouds, of dunes, of white flesh, of "the white street of pain." II. His "veins are streets,"— "a room, a house, a street, a town"—the "hot asphalt" of Broad Street; the house, "red brick, with nine rooms," the asphalt walk in a park, an avenue with a bench, a street outside a theater, by a subway entrance, beside a graveyard. "Millions of men rush through me," he says. "Which, in this terrible multitude, is I?" III. He is, it seems, a scribe with a reed pen, palette, and ink—a young poet. He says an artist is one who knows "the effect of what he is doing": sensibility can be accreted, he says, and by a slow process poetry can be "extended to embrace all that man is capable of feeling and perceiving." IV. The Confession of the Secret Self. Peter Jones was deceptively candid; it now appears that he is generous, magnanimous, tender, sad, greedy, cautious, a fool, somewhat vain, not sure of himself, not mawkish nor callous nor illogical. Ambition. V. deals with murder.

a. Unintentional, with "love abruptly ended." Murder is of the mind the text says. To hurt a person is to murder the person. If the person is querulous, a slip of the tongue, an accidental coldness, a quarrelsome eye, can be fatal. b. One can murder art by trying too hard. A friend of Osiris Jones is seen engaged in this kind of murder and Osiris Jones is saying, "What cannot be captured, . . . it is no use killing. Brutality is no substitute for magic." VI. The sun disc directing its rays upon a childhood. The words are "yes for no"; "the always lost but always known," and we see the sun. a. On a palmetto leaf and on a certain kind of head that smiles in a certain side-long way. b. On death. VII. is of Death. a. Osiris Jones is seen shrinking from the sight of death with the sun on it, and compelled to look at it. When a friend has died of spinal cancer one is permanently saddened. b. is a dream of second death. The mind, "the core of anguish, underground," has been uprooted and the tree of hope turned on its side: the dead lies in full view; a crowd gathers; a schoolboy derides red hair; an undergraduate, the cut of the trousers; a man who is sometimes usher at church weddings, asks if his friends were "ladies" and if they read the proper books. The con-spicuous thing here is the "disparateness of flesh and word, . . . wisdom's dishevelment, the purpose lamed, / and purposeless the footsteps eastward aimed." VIII. Music said: a. "your heart is beating, your will is strong / you are walking in a hall of clouds / your hand is cunning and the gods are young." b. is "mortal music" by which one is overwhelmed, drugged, and left for dead. As it sounds, two faces appear—the face of one's mother; and a face though kind, which is associated with an Arthurian name and unmercy, which sees one "sinking / depe depe and deeper darkly down and drown / drenched and despatched and drunk with more than ether." IX. is the vindication of the consciousness by the books it has written. Fame is saying to a Narcissus-like figure with chapeleted hair, "I know thee and I know thy name, and know / the names of all those gods who dwell with thee." The dead is now to be on an equality with Shakespeare.

Funerary models have been placed in the tomb: a nursery in which there are Bible tales and fairy tales and tales from Shakespeare, "and footsteps pause behind the door—"; a father's office; schoolroom "desks, all carved with names"; a school hospital; a drawing room; a ballroom; a room in a city hospital; a creaking stateroom with "a majesty of waves / washing the heart, a memory but a night / in which at last a single face is bright." There are funerary models of costumes—cradle clothes, "a bonnet of angora," "six sailor blouses," "a black velvet jacket," "white flannels," "a dress suit," "a raincoat," a green "tweed hat bought in England," and sundry felts. Un-disguised baby-wear in a Kuniyoshi painting is permitted and Beau Nash's tab collars and mushroom tucks relieve the half-caste motley of cigarette and cosmetic advertisements in a theater program, but one hesitates before certain poetic implications of the Osiris Jones funerary wardrobe.

"It is the poet's office," Mr. Aiken says, "to delight with beauty and to amaze with understanding," and since Peter Jones was a poet, the comments, speeches, and inscriptions, chosen by him for his grave-book ought to be good ones and some of them are, as where the Face is withdrawn,

> diffused, and more diffused, till music speaks
> under a hundred lights, with violins.

And the timbre and intervals of the cricket, in the "Landscape with Figures," show the poet to be the scientist:

> zeek . . . zeek . . . zeek
> seek . . . seek . . . seek . . .seek
> seek . . . see . . . seek . . . see. . . .

He listens.

The nature of the material requires that there be almost as much space as there is text.

> The pauses in the music are not music,
> Although they make the music what it is.

Even so, the text is heavily leaded. One is not always sure whether the note is that of singing or speaking. There is occasionally a quarter-tone jamming of sound that is not unequivocally that. "Orion" as an end-word after "time" seems not so much a variant as another variety. One debates the wisdom of certain joints and conclusions. When the manner is that of prose, as in the medical report, an air of conscious adaptiveness combats interest. But the directive note is unmistakable, and the contrasting strains echo through one another as the elements of an acrostic answer simultaneously in all places.

In the Osiris Jones the souls must come forth; and in the Preludes, Memnon symbolizes the burdened sensibility; literally the Amenhotep III colossus at Luxor, cut from a single block of stone, in which a fissure was made by an earthquake—the god who "sang the day before the daybreak came" and reminded the Greeks of Memnon, Aurora's son slain at Troy, waiting in darkness for the dawn, his mother.

Like Osiris Jones, the Memnon is broken. He is not interested in dynasties nor the stoop of the vulture nor the presentation crocodile nor the yacht nor the harper who pats his mouth with his hand to make a warbling sound. He is asking, IF A MAN DIE SHALL HE LIVE AGAIN? and what Buddha and Confucius and Christ have said about this, and what would make mortality's instinct for continuance valid and everlasting? Christ said the attitude of mind which prevailed in childhood could, if duplicated, be attended by the same illusions: humility by hopefulness; receptiveness by abundance— virtue being a form for which humanity is appropriate matter, not a thing to be vain of. If one's hands are accomplished they are not one's hands but the hands of humanity.

But the Memnon finds that whether one is arrogant or is matter of fact about one's self, frustration is the concomitant of maturity. He resists the "causeless melancholy that comes with rain," he touches "the cold treble" of the piano. How is it "other men could live so simply" and "go unscathed?" Or "do they lie?" He sees and can say pain is "the somber note that gives the chord its power," but what he reflects upon is the fashion pain has of returning to what pained it. He tends to curse both "The visitor who comes and sits too long, / Angels who come too seldom." He was born when the sun was at the meridian and it is dark "in his strange world."

The sense of strangeness, may we say, is an illusion. Those with keen perceptions may suffer more than others, but the same sufferings and desperations are common to each and in almost the same way. One goes into a friend's study. The books, prints, convenient desk, make one feel that one could work in such a place. Others have a similar impression of one's own surroundings—that seem to one at times like a subway at the rush hour, or a way-station on a cinder-bank. Sensibility—or is it self-pity—transmitted from childhood—infects any air and can retain in any surroundings the message from the S-4: "Is there no hope?"; the impact of Sir Walter Scott's debt: the recollection of a bird fascinated by a snake.

One encounters also in the Preludes, that polygon of frustration, woman: the meager intense poison of the spider, the bat that turns and clings to you however you may turn, the octopus with arms that reach out to you from all directions, the sea that drops from under you or pounds you from above. This is woman—"literalness," "abysmal nothingness," "staleness," the untaught "tendency to italics." Some feel their own sex to be more inane than the other, some the other to be more inane than their own. Some find both inane. It is not possible to differentiate in favor of either, according to Professor Papez' collection of brains at Cornell. They are, as it were, alligators. If one wishes to look upon Mrs. Thrale, Lady Waller, and the Countess of Pembroke, as exceptions, and upon Socrates as the rule, one may. There are, however, men and women who feel themselves unworthy of the devotion bestowed on them by over-burdened, self-indulgent highly endowed members of the other sex; and for the management of difficult persons there is a technique. Woman's beauty is carrion or not depending on the way it is worn. Love is more important than being in love, as memories of childhood testify; but even for the lesser things there are preservatives. If by some miracle of felicity a man is unselfish and his wife is unselfish, no technical harmonizing of marriage is required. But usually if a marriage is to stand, a technique in maintaining it must be known to the less selfish of the two. If husband and wife are equal in selfish ferocity, the marriage, of course, cannot stand. One may have for woman's humiliating battery of fascinations, "Gehenna's smile." One may wish to let love alone. As instances of impersonalism, there are Sir Isaac Newton, Washington Irving, Henry James, and Lord Balfour. Mr. Aiken says, "Must I / . . . Renounce my food, hating mankind and all / Because this lizard's eye has . . . *looked* at me? / Absurd! It is an indigestion merely. / . . . Or too much looking at the moon, too little / Upon the sun. The print I read's too small: I will get larger books, with larger margins. / I will cut down the tree that shades my window. I will go to music. . . ."

But music is aconite. In enjoyment there is frustration; and, obversely, in what is ascetic. "I sit in my chair and work and work," Mr. Aiken says; "Add, subtract / Divide or subdivide with verbs and adverbs" as the therapists say one should, and the room is far from luxurious; while a man with a mediocre brain and ornamental family, lives on his father's dower. To wonder if the "feminine keen eye" that one no longer pleases, would admire the accomplished arithmetic if it saw it, makes matters no better. Art, however, is not an overture to a neighbor. One's work would not be the potent and accomplished thing it is, if it were done for any reason but to fulfill the instinct for technical mastery. What scientist thinks of being thanked for what he does? It is a pleasure to be so gifted that one's work is important as science is important. There is no pleasure subtler than the sensation of being a good workman; and in work there is the sense of consanguinity— unconscious as a rule but sometimes conscious. Shakespeare "moulded and melted / The things he loved and hated, lest he melt / His own heart's tallow." There were doubtless compensating presences, but his real consanguinities were posthumous. They were not William Holgrave, someone else, or Anne Hathaway. And all die—Hardy, Conrad, Rimbaud, Verlaine. "Cheops and Jones indifferent grass will cover." But "dust cannot hold what shines beyond the dust."

The terrestrial mind makes ascriptions of praise to the terrestrial mind and is damned by them, reiterating the negative confession of Osiris Jones; or like Memnon, protesting the verdict. To the skeptic, the ritual of the feather and conscience is not convenient. The lurking sense of an adhered-to attitude on the part of those who regard themselves as religious, stands in the way of what they might do for one. When we get away from the mystical, however, we put ourselves under the power of nature and nature is cruel. Sir Thomas Browne felt that he spoke as a physician when he said the pulse is not the main indication of life and that unless we are part of the "inextinguishable core" of life there is no warmth for flesh to stimulate, "no heat under the Tropick; nor any light, though I dwelt in the body of the Sun." Ask a servant for something, and you will presently get it, but God is not a servant. Man, when not making complaint to man, usually overlooks the fact that he is asking a supernatural question and expecting a mortal answer. Furthermore, it is not possible to prepare for a crisis in the middle of a crisis. To start a large turbine you cannot throw steam into the drum; the inertia is too great; you run it by means of a small engine until it has been stepped up to the point at which steam can be added. If you desire a certain result, you must put a train of circumstances in motion that will bring it about; in this way, and in this way only, will you be able to defy Satan or the Devourer or the Fissured Mind when it puts its hand on your throat and tells you you were meant to die and not to live.

Misgiving is in itself, however, an evidence of subterranean power. The Preludes are full of this power and of a music correspondingly rich. In them one forgets the snare-drum multiplicity of undergraduate adverbs in the early prose. Banality and cheapness are damped out; and there is no trace of doggerel, thought to be exact, the clash of the symphony drowns it.

The musical principle of restatement after contrast, exemplified in the Osiris Jones and in previous work, is here justified. The unrhymed pattern is as much an "algebra of enchantment" as the rhymed:

> Angelic power, divinity, destruction,
> Perfect in itself—the sword is heartshaped,
> The word is bloodshaped, the flower is a coffin,
> The world is everlasting. . . .

There is the sense of "a surf of leaves, when the wind blows"; or of mid-ocean when "Rain with a shrill seethe sings on the lapsing waves."

It is a wound in air. It is last year.

A use of vowels such as this, is performance. Only the chiseled pianissimo of experience could set as a chord at the end of the XVth Prelude, "See that the heart that dreamed this thing be safe." And in Prelude XV, one recognizes the characteristically irreproachable diminuendo by dactyl:

> Dead hand, you touched the heart of time, you knew
> Whispers of silence, the mute path of God;
> Hot chaos knew with its rank arteries,
> And anguish, with its blood. . . .

Mr. Aiken is an artist.

Reminiscently speaking, at the suggestion of *Wake* Editions, he was the perfect reviewer, Diogenes' one honest man, fearing only to displease himself; determined before pronouncing, to have read everything pertaining to the subject in question, and by the subject; punctual and explicit; what he presented was the complete thing, no as-if pronunciamento for gradual emendation. "Reliable," as I had been told when provided with a list of reviewers by *The Dial*.

Hound and Horn, 5 (January–March 1932), 313–20; *Wake*, No. 11 (1956), 50–56.

CHARLOTTE BRONTË

MR. BENSON wishes, in his life of Charlotte Brontë, to give us a portrait "in the round." That his Piltdown regressive excites surprise rather than pleasure, and represents a departure from the genial verisimilitude of other portraiture by him, need not change one's regard for him nor estrange one from Charlotte Brontë.

A Scotland Yard aptitude for clues is not negligible in biography, and Mr. Benson bristles with accuracies. It is curious to note the portentous significance found by him in the fact that a line by Charlotte Brontë which was, for Swinburne, the epitome of her genius, was not by her. She had taken it "verbatim from one of Mr. Brontë's poems." We are glad, however, to be persuaded that Branwell Brontë did not deteriorate so early as is generally thought, and that he had a part in the writing of *Wuthering Heights*. And we agree with Mr. Benson that Mrs. Gaskell sacrificed individuality by omitting the letters concerning Miss Celia Amelia—the Rev. William Weightman. Mr. Benson evidently thinks Charlotte Brontë's regard for M. Heger is more than regard, a disgrace; and he attaches guilty importance to

Review of *Charlotte Brontë*, by E. F. Benson (Longmans Green, and Co.).

Mrs. Gaskell's "suppressions" in this connection—risked in the belief that they "would never be disclosed. The odds in her favor were enormous," says Mr. Benson, "but the hundred-to-one chance went against her." A suggestion, however, gives as strong an impression as an assertion, and we could not fail to infer from such extracts as Mrs. Gaskell gave, and from the novels, an emotional cataclysm; also that it was one-sided. If Charlotte Brontë could speak now, one feels that she would wish to be without certain faults Mr. Benson enumerates; and would wish to take back the look which Branwell says "struck him like a blow in the mouth"; but one dares to think it possible that, reviewing her second Brussels visit, which she mistrusted in advance, she might have the courage to let it remain.

Charlotte Brontë's father, Patrick Brunty, peasant schoolmaster, was a person of easy conscience when he usurped "the noble surname" Brontë, Mr. Benson thinks; though to the dull conscience of some it is like the kiss requested of Anna by the circuit-rider in Hardy's story. It would do her no harm and it would do him a great deal of good. And Currer Bell's referring to "my brothers" and receiving a letter addressed "C. Brontë, Esq.," are to her biographer, cheating. If "longing to be considered male was indeed an obsession with her," it is also true, as Mr. Benson says, "it was no use wishing anything of the sort."

Did Charlotte Brontë as "a burglar" discover Emily's poems, and deliberately sacrifice their sale by letting them be "sandwiched" between worthless ones? Mr. Benson says she called men "coarse." No word could be plainer of interpretation apparently, nor in her use of it is psychologically more complex. Also, she exemplifies, though not in its flower, the Celtic tendency to express affection disguised as abuse as in the comment: "Man is, indeed, an amazing piece of mechanism when you see, so to speak, the full weakness of what he calls his strength."

Mr. Benson's synopsis of *Jane Eyre* makes one pause. Beside his iron-maiden *et seq.*, his asterisk of commendation does not wholly suggest an authoress "pale with the secret war of feeling"—the scene, indoors or out, assisting the mood; "the falling fir-cones," the "quiet dust" on mirrors and "darkly-polished old mahogany" in the red room. This self-taught author "followed no one," as Professor Saintsbury says, "and many have followed her." Nevertheless, the implied question—would her novel be at once accepted now—is of interest, for the school-taught man adds schooling to what the self-taught man teaches himself.

In explaining Mr. Brontë's seeming lack of hospitality, "Charlotte wrote just the letter that would have made Jane Austen's eyes twinkle," Mr. Benson thinks. Perhaps so, for the urbanities of Bath and compelled facilities of Yorkshire were no more like, than a master-confectioner's product of fine-bolted flour is like, the roots and kernel of the wheat that makes the flour. And our disadvantaging advantages in these days make it all but impossible for us to know the peculiar weight of the last straw. The over-serious letter, however, might not have made Cowper's eyes twinkle—nor Lamb's. As for Charlotte Brontë being "incapable of appreciating" Miss Austen, Mr. Benson no doubt, is in the main, right; yet one recalls the remark: "She does her business of delineating the surface lives of genteel English people curiously well. There is a Chinese fidelity, a miniature delicacy in the painting."

A novelist "all to bits with the strain of her accomplished work," able to give her fiancé "a good wigging" and "resounding smacks" to uncongenial reviewers, suggests Bret Harte's re-strike of Mr. Rawjester and Miss Mix. We do value, however, the allusion to her literary instinct as flame, "kindled, after long ash-covered smouldering," and the narrative becomes intent when it visualizes the intentness of the three sisters:

> . . . as in the darkness of the hive the unseen and furious industry of the bees generates the curtains of wax on which are built the honey-cells, so in the dining-room of the sequestered parsonage and round the kitchen fire the weaving of dreams and the exercise of imagination were their passionate preoccupations.

This halcyon moment of enjoyment—in contemplating the bees—prompts civility, and we think of the rule in yachting, "Give room at marks." *Up and Down. Our Family Affairs.* . . . We recall, in *Up and Down*, the memorable words, referring to pleasure, there are so many things one doesn't want. We delay over these books, and agree with Gertrude Stein "it is very difficult in quarreling to be certain in either one what the other one is remembering." Then, over-sanguine—returning to Charlotte Brontë—to love, honor, and be gay, in the narrow shaft of sunlight, her marriage—we find her satirically presented. Is one to protest it, or be rammed, or give room?

The Criterion, 11 (July 1932), 716–19.

VICTORIOUS DEFEATS

THIS book is a study in vision. Dr. Van Doren for the sake of perspective has taken, in epitome, five generations. Their ways and the ways of those

---

A Review of *Jonathan Gentry,* by Mark Van Doren (Albert & Charles Boni).

with whom they have to do, give rise to self-searching. Is society blind? Half blind? What is sight? The author shows us Jonathan Gentry and his fellow pioneers on a river boat or ark they had built. The miscellaneous twenty-two found in their company a gentleman of the old world, so different from themselves that even their children stared at him. The fellow-travelers might drift; the man might look like a statue; but we are made aware of life; and of the tragedy in it—for those who see as well as for those who do not. But for those who do not, with the tragedy there is nothingness. In part two of this chronicle, the time of the Civil War, there is again a man who sees, Jonathan Gentry Third, for whom joy at home is as enticing as the sorrow was great that drove his grandfather from home. Again the multitude, doing, sheeplike, the same things that are done by those who have a deathless motive. And again tragedy; but not nothingness. Of two brothers, one returns to the homestead, one lies on the battlefield. Finally, two brothers of the present time—a Joseph Gentry and Jonathan Gentry Fifth. They return from college; one to an office; the other to the farm. Jonathan Gentry's wife classmate of both, liking the city, turns to the brother in vain, and is impelled to suicide. But defeat is not defeat for those who see. Fraternity is here cemented by defeat, as in childhood it was typified by the associated letters on the mail-box, "J. & J."

To write unemotionally of this book is to do it injustice. In depth of presentation it is the longed-for contrast to historical unveracity on the screen. It should be studied by lecturers and others who self-defensively rail at Puritanism. It is a narrative poem, each of its three parts—*Ohio River, Civil War,* and *Foreclosure*—being followed by a summarizing lyric: boat song, soldier's song, wise fool's commentary on master and mistress. And there are songs throughout. Power as verse and narrative will seem to some impaired by the vernacular of colloquialism employed and by difficulties of rhythm, but to the unwillful eye it has verity; and the author's unclouded accuracy in perception of detail—such as the spiraling vultures, the light on the face of the sheep a man was driving, the river that "followed and flowed and flowed and followed, and stopped in eddies only to go again"— one has reason to envy and is bound to salute.

Poetry, 40 (July 1932), 222–24.

EMILY DICKINSON

To the 1894 edition of these *Letters*, phrases, sentences, and complete letters added in this 1931 edition and listed in an appendix, make more distinct the lineaments that had conveyed the same impression originally, with curious exactness. Comparing omissions with inclusions, one notes reticence: a determination to cover from the voracity of the wolfish, a seclusive, wholly non-notorious personality; an absence of legend; and care lest philistine interest in what is fine be injudiciously taxed. A significant group of the letters as first issued is here significantly augmented—that to Mr. C. H. Clark and his brother concerning the Reverend Charles Wadsworth. Though innocence is invulnerable to betrayal or curiosity, one objects to sharing emotion that was intended only for another, and we are glad that if Emily Dickinson's notable secret has not perfectly the aspect of a secret, it is revealed by herself rather than by "so enabled a man" as the twentieth-century critic. The fitting of the poems "into the sequence where they belong" remains to be done, Mrs. Todd says, and several "groups of unpublished letters now known to exist are not included." One notes her exactness in omitting *The* from her title.

You can't say to people, my sensibilities are finer than yours and where I feed you may not; and apart from literary significance, the letters are important as expressing a friendship. In search and research, in divining dates and scripts, by consultation with persons, that she might somewhat perpetuate the magnificent entity Emily Dickinson was; in sensibility that has not suppressed, and in candor that has not victimized, Mrs. Todd has been more than the usual editor. Not many years after they were issued, the 1894 two-volume "*Letters* were being bound in one volume, and sold for twenty-five cents a copy," a circumstance which rivals in irony the stealing of a Bible from a church pew.

If we care about the poems, we value the connection in which certain poems and sayings originated. The chief importance of the letters for us, however, is in their establishing the wholesomeness of the life. They are full of enthusiasm. The effect of the whole personality is in the phrase, from a letter to the Misses Norcross, "Now children, when you are cutting the loaf . . . ," and in the lines to Miss Whitney: "You speak of 'disillusion.' That is one of the few subjects on which I am an infidel." Professor Whicher sees in the poems "the same instinct of sound workmanship that made the

---

Review of *Letters of Emily Dickinson,* edited by Mabel Loomis Todd (Harper & Brothers).

Yankee clipper, the Connecticut clock, and the New England doorway objects of beauty," and there is in the letters another phase of that exciting realness.

Though she needed a more than partial response to her work, the process of "interiorization," as Mr. Trueblood puts it, was not a dark one. She understood the sudden experience of unvaluable leisure by which death is able to make one "homeless at home." "The heart wants what it wants, or else it does not care," she said; and death in its several forms—betrayal, separateness of dwelling, the sense of one's inadequacy, and physical death— she expresses in such a way one does not see how it could be expressed better. "I wish I was somebody else," she said after Leonard Humphrey's death, and after her father's, I "forget what I am doing, . . . wondering where he is." To free or to protect was her necessity, and not to be able to break the fetters mental or actual that are too strong for mortality was her discipline. "The seeing pain one can't relieve makes a demon of one," she said. But she was full of gratitude. To be able to give is to be willing to receive and she did not scorn gifts, even a Christmas gift.

She was not a recluse, nor was her work, in her thought of it, something eternally sealed. Acquiescing in deferred publication she said, "My barefoot rank is better," because she valued her work too much to hurt it if greater stature for it could be ensured by delay. Mrs. Todd refers to Emerson's remark, " 'Now and then a man exquisitely made can live alone,' " and to Bacon's version of the thought, " 'Whosoever is delighted in Solitude is either a Wilde Beast or a God.' " She presents Emily Dickinson as that rare thing, the truly unartificial spirit—flashing like an animal, with strength or dismay. One resents the cavil that makes idiosyncrasy out of individuality, asking why Emily Dickinson should sit in the dim hall to listen to Mrs. Todd's music. Music coming from under a window has many times been enhanced by its separateness; and though to converse athwart a door is not usual, it seems more un-useful to discuss such a preference than it would be to analyze the beam of light that brings personality, even in death, out of seclusion.

A portrait of Emily Dickinson that we prize is the description of her magic effect upon children, by Martha Dickinson Bianchi in the introduction to *The Single Hound*; and the Dickinson setting given her in *The Life and Letters of Emily Dickinson* is a companion piece to it: the New England town with its black firs in the days when "Amherst College and Amherst were one"; when Emily Dickinson's father walked to and from his office wearing "a black beaver hat glossy beyond compare with that of any young beau"; when sometimes at an evening party, quoting *Amherst Sixty Years Ago*, by S. G. Dickinson, there were solos by Lavinia Dickinson or by a paradoxically retiring "Basso, of profundity beyond all known musical necessity"; when souvenirs of Palestine sent by a missionary were shown—cloisonné coffee-cups and lentils, "husks—such as-the-swine-did-eat."

Emily Dickinson was reason's pupil but her technique was intuitive, and in that matter she was "wayward." Study which she bestowed on her poems related only to a choice of words that would sharpen the meaning, we are told. Her appeal to Mr. Higginson for instruction, though sincere, was actually for a commission authorizing her to proceed. As Mr. Trueblood has noted, "What she said seems always said with the choicest originality." Whittier, Bryant, and Thoreau were choice; and to some extent Emerson. Hawthorne was a bear but great. All of these except Whittier seem less choice than their neighbor—"Myself the only kangaroo among the beauty" she called herself, not realizing the pinnacle of favor to which her words of dejection were to be raised.

An element of the Chinese taste was part of this choiceness, in its daring associations of the prismatically true; the gamboge and pink and cochineal of the poems; the oleander blossom tied with black ribbon; the dandelion with scarlet; the rowan spray with white.

In both poems and letters one sometimes rejects an attitude or a phrase; and from a eulogy of flaws or misfortunes the mind dissents. Although the behavior of an ear that lives on sound is as sudden as the rush of the canoe toward the rapid, the swerve to a pun or the quoting of a familiar phrase in a new connection—even by so justified a person as Emily Dickinson—gives one a start. Against near rhyme or no rhyme where rhyme is required, complaint seems general. But Emily Dickinson was a person of power and could have overcome, had she wished to, any less than satisfactory feature of her lines. The self-concealing pronoun ("Had we the art, like you, to endow so many by simply recovering our health . . ."), independence of the subjunctive, and many another select defect, are, for the select critic, attractions.

To some, her Japanesely fantastic reverence for tree, insect, and toadstool is not interesting; many who are "helped" by a brave note, do not admire the plucked string; by some the note of rapture is not caught; and by the self-sufficient, Emily Dickinson has been accused of vanity. A certain buoyancy that creates an effect of inconsequent bravado—a sense of drama with which we may not be quite at home—was for her a part of that expansion of breath necessary to existence, and unless it is conceited for the hummingbird or the osprey to not behave like a chicken, one does not find her conceited.

She was not usual, but her need was the universal human one, never disguised. She saw no comfort in refusing to question that about which she wished most to be sure. "Are you certain there is another life? When over-whelmed to know," she said, "I fear that few are sure." And later:

> The spirit lasts, but in what mode—
> Below, the body speaks,
> But as the spirit furnishes—
> Apart it never talks.
> The music in the violin
> Does not emerge alone
> But arm in arm with touch, yet touch
> Alone is not a tune.
> The spirit lurks within the flesh
> Like tides within the sea
> That makes the water live; estranged
> What would the either be?

She had "a habit of discounting disappointment by anticipating it." The frankness with which in a letter—as above—she speaks verse as if it were prose, to the one to whom she writes, is strange. In these days of composite intellect and mock-modest impersonalism, this nakedness is striking. If our capacity for suffering is the necessary antithesis of our capacity for joy, we would—with Emily Dickinson—not wish to have it less. "Though I think I bend," she said, "something straightens me." The heart is like a house. It has to have scaffolding and then it stands alone. She exemplifies to Professor Whicher "that quality in New England character which enables it to invert suffering into a kind of joy"; and despite doctrinaire reassurances—from the kind of modern ego for which suffering is unholy and uneasiness ex-cusable—one feels that she suffered, and also that she shared the prerog-atives she attributed to her cousins when she said their home symbolized to her "peace, sunshine, books."

It was hers to make words convey "more than the sum of their meanings laid end to end"; and to attain splendor of implication without prefatory statement, for her conciseness was as extreme as her largess. How justly Mrs. Todd insists that her picture should have a plain frame. In studying the letters one seems to feel an anxiety lifted, the apparently opposed but united honor compelled by conscience—Emily Dickinson's openness and her friend's reticence—constituting the sense of a super-identity and of violence rebuffed. One owes much to Emily Dickinson and her friend, who have somehow enabled one, through these pages, to forget the ruses and dust-obscured emulations of ambitious biography.

Poetry, 41 (January 1933), 219–26.

WORDS FOR MUSIC PERHAPS

WHILE aware of his "international fame, his personal charm and authority, his devotion to culture, his theater, his share in the management of the State," one thinks of Mr. Yeats as a poet driven by the moon "to the edges of the sea"—as one whose poetry is "a flight into fairyland from the real world and a summons to that flight." Poetry is for him metaphor enriched by emotion that has "passed through the centuries" and he has "the minutely appropriate words necessary to embody those fine changes of feeling which enthrall the attention" whether he is discerning something in another or giving it for the first time. In speaking of Samuel Ferguson he sets the jewel by removing it when he recalls from Cougal of the Mire, "the stiffened mantle of the giant specter Mananan Mac Lir, striking against his calves with as loud a noise as the mainsail of a ship makes 'when with the coil of all its ropes, it beats the sounding mast.' " He tells of an old man whose "face was almost as fleshless as the foot of a bird." The flamingo "ruffles with his bill the minnowed water," and there is no end to the beauties one might separate out from Mr. Yeats' abundance, his daring, his self-knowledge and harmony of mind. "A miserable man," he says, "may think well, and express himself with great vehemence, but he cannot make beautiful things, for Aphrodite never rises from any but a tide of joy."

In defiance of Ireland, Swift knew this; and in defiance of unprosperity, Goldsmith knew it. Some of Goldsmith's joy and a great deal of Blake's, some of Shelley's and some of Spenser's, are in the rhythms of Mr. Yeats' early poetry, but we now have the elements of the song subdued to a harmony like this:

> "She will change," I cried,
> "Into a withered crone."
> . . . .
> "Uplift those eyes and throw
> Those glances unafraid:
> She would as bravely show
> Did all the fabric fade;
> No withered crone I saw
> Before the world was made."
>
> Abashed by that report
> For the earth cannot lie,

Review of *The Winding Stair*, by W. B. Yeats (The Fountain Press); *Words for Music Perhaps and Other Poems*, by W. B. Yeats (The Cuala Press).

> I knelt in the dirt;
> And all shall bend the knee
> To my offended heart
> Until it pardon me.

Among the reeds of *Words for Music Perhaps*, under the guise of Folly—Crazy Jane and Tom the Fool—Mr. Yeats hides his Leda's egg of greatest wisdom, it would seem to me. He ever associates himself with water—with the sea, the mirroring lake, or the jet "that falls again where it had risen." We may say of him as he says of Blake, "it is as though the spray of an inexhaustible fountain of beauty was blown into our faces." He now makes in his own way that, in Spenser, which as a young man he imitated:

> Scattered on the level grass
> Or winding through the grove
> Plato there and Minos pass,
> There stately Pythagoras
> And all the choir of love.

"Art is a monotony in external things for the sake of an interior variety," Mr. Yeats says, and he admires in the Noh players "the impression not of undulation but of continuous straight lines"—"a swift or a slow movement and a long or a short stillness." Used as he is to the romantic tradition and his own work, he instinctively asks when he comes on the verse of our modern unromantic poets, "What are all those fish that lie gasping on the strand?"

In this which we love so well, is there nothing to wish away? Like Arthur Symons, Mr. Yeats is, in his prose, overtaken sometimes by the pursuing wave of his own delicacy; he "borrows from himself" (Prof. Rhys); and (John Eglinton) it is always as if he were strung up to an audience. Occasionally, in the midst of thought that with care one is just able to follow, a meaning seems mild. There are moments when Mr. Yeats is like anybody else; when, in his verse, sadness looks like cynicism; when the stanza is perhaps too neat; is summary; the rhymed line, unduly firm—despatched-dealt-with-and-buried-from-sight—lending a touch of disdain that seems to apply to the reader rather than to the thing written of. "The test of poetry," however, "is not in reason but delight." In *The Winding Stair* Mr. Yeats says:

> What matter if a blind man drink his drop?
> What matter if the ditches are impure?
> What matter if I live it all once more?
> Endure that toil of growing up;

> The ignominy of boyhood; the distress
> Of boyhood changing into man;
> The unfinished man and his pain
> Brought face to face with his own clumsiness;

and he is, for me, the one author whose failures—if they are that—subtract themselves as one comes to them and do not in memory remain to mar the fortunate cloak of invisibility. If, moreover, from one's bog of incompetence and hindrance one is at any time tempted to think harshly of him in his tower, one may well recall what he says about the death of Henley's daughter; or read those retrospective words in which, having been a trouble to parents, grandparents, and himself, he wonders if he is to make a success of his life.

Harmonies of key and chord mingled, as in the verse, and the elaborately woven yet unconcealed insistent beauty of the prose, are answer. The life from which they arise has not become a crusade against the traducer, but continues to be a quest, and though homage is for God only, one is—with Ezra Pound—desirous that "the fine things should not always seem to go on in a corner."

Poetry, 42 (April 1933), 40–44.

MODERN THOUGHTS IN DISGUISE

I N magazines favorable to innovation, Mr. W. W. E. Ross is conspicuously one of the writers of this day. It is therefore not surprising that these sixty-nine sonnets (privately printed) should have freshness, responsibility, and authenticity of locality. They are about the oak, the pine, the lake, the river, the Indian, injustice, the supernatural, death, art, the Muses. In being proffered, some of them as imitative of Dante and of Italians before him, their modesty is appropriate but only conduces to an augmented conspicuousness. It is plainly "one of the writers of this day" who gives us sonnets "*1*" and "*2,*" "*To the English Language,*" and no one could have made the following sonnet without having "boldly faced the difficulties that to verse belong":

> Prometheus, bound in adamantine chains
> To the grim rock stark-lifting from the sea,

Review of *Sonnets*, by E. R. (Hugh Heaton Publishing Co.).

Watching with eyes that wandered ceaselessly
The sea and sky, the sky and sea; whose pains
Not yet become a torment in his veins
Were still sufficient, while in tension he
Awaited the strong hand of deity,
Expectant of some increase to his pains,—
Bound as he was, his eyes were growing dim;
Discouraged, he relaxed the effort vain
Of rude rebellion on that fatal day,—
When, like the dolphins in their lively train,
Gliding toward the rock in bright array,
The sea-nymphs sang encouragement to him.

There is present the Spenser-Sidney-Milton-Wordsworth elegance, and an ingenuity with dactyls which recalls the Melic poets. To so staggering a roster of consanguinities with an occasional defect, one may demur, but poetry with the unforced note is rare; and if in matter and spirit the book is not valuable, this writer is far afield.

Poetry, 42 (May 1933), 114–15.

SWEENEY AGONISTES

I N *Sweeney Agonistes* Mr. Eliot comes to us as the men of the neighboring tribes came to Joshua under a camouflage of frayed garments, with moldy bread in the wallet. But the point is not camouflaged. Mortal and sardonic victims though we are in this conflict called experience, we may regard our victimage with calmness, the book says; not because we don't know that our limitations of correctness are tedious to a society which has its funny side to us, as we have our slightly morbid side to it, but because there is a moment for Orestes, for Ophelia, for Everyman, when the ego and the figure it cuts, the favors you get from it, the good cheer and customary encomium, are as the insulting wigwaggery of the music-halls.

Everyman is played by Pereira, an efficiently inconspicuous, decent, studious chap. Well, not so decent, since he pays the rent for Doris and Dusty, who are an unremarkable, balky, card-cutting pair of girls whose names symbolize society's exasperating unanimity of selfishness. Shake-

---

Review of *Sweeney Agonistes*, by T. S. Eliot (Faber & Faber).

speare's "lecherous as a monkey" is rather strong, but in a world of buncombe and the fidgets, where you love-a me, I love-a you, "One live as two," "Two live as three"—and there is no privacy under the bamboo tree, the pair of given names go well with the surnames of a laidly, shallow set of heroes from America, London, Ireland, Canada, who became intimate at the time they "did" their "bit" and "got the Hun on the run." There is, as the author intended, an effect of Aristophanic melodrama about this London flat in which the visitors play with the idea of South Sea languor and luxury—work annihilated, personality negatived, and conscience suppressed; a monkey to milk the goat and pass the cocktails—woman in the cannibal-pot or at hand to serve.

It is correct and unnotorious for the race to perpetuate itself; committing adultery and disclaiming obligation is the suicide of personality, and the free spirit wearies of clarity in such matters. The Furies pursuing Orestes are abler casuists than the King of Clubs and Queen of Hearts of Dusty and Doris. "They are hunting me down," he said.

A stark crime would not be so difficult to commit as the mood of moral conflict is difficult to satisfy. One is dead in being born unless one's debts are forgiven; and equipoise makes an idiot of one. The automatic machinery of behavior undoes itself backwards, putting sinister emphasis on wrong things, and no emphasis on the right ones.

> If he was alive then the milkman wasn't
> and the rent-collector wasn't
> And if they were alive then he was dead.
> . . . .
> Death or life or life or death—
> Death is life and life is death.

Is one to become a saint or go mad?—remain mad, we should say. "The soul cannot be possessed of the divine union until it has divested itself of the love of created beings," St. John of the Cross says; as all saints have said. If one chooses God as the friend of the spirit, does not the coffin become the most appropriate friend for the body? "Cheer him up? Well here again that don't apply," says Sweeney. "But I gotta use words when I talk to you." This plucky reproach has in it the core of the drama. In their graveyard of sick love which is no love, which is loneliness without solitude, the girls can't understand what Pereira has to do with it and that it is a lucky eclecticism which cuts him off from what the Krumpackers and Horsfalls call a good time. A man should not think himself a poor fish or go mad, Sweeney maintains, because two girls are blockheads. He should answer a question as often as they ask it and put in as good an evening as possible with them. If by saying, "I gotta use words when I talk to you," he insults them and they don't know they've been insulted, they, not he, should go mad.

When the spirit expands and the animal part of one sinks, one is not sardonic, and the bleak lesson here set forth is not uncheerful to those who are serious in the desire to satisfy justice. The cheer resides in an admitting that it is normal to be abnormal. When one is not the only one who thinks that, one is freed of a certain tension.

Mr. Eliot is not showy nor hard, and is capable at times of too much patience; but here the truculent commonplace of the vernacular obscures care of arrangement, and the deliberate concise rhythm that is characteristic of him seems less intentional than it is. Upon scrutiny, however, the effect of an unhoodwinked self-control is apparent. The high time half a dozen people of unfastidious personality can seem to be having together, is juxtaposed with the successful flight of the pursued son of Agamemnon, and it is implied, perhaps, that "he who wonders shall reign, he who reigns shall have rest." One is obliged to say "perhaps"—since Sweeney in conflict is not synonymous with Sweeney victorious.

Poetry, 42 (May 1933), 106–9.

THE WARDEN

THIS is the fiftieth anniversary of Anthony Trollope's death, and one welcomes the reissue of his characteristic novel, *The Warden*. It comes to us by the effort of Mr. E. F. Stevens of the Pratt Library, Brooklyn, New York— printed at The Lakeside Press, Chicago, under the supervision of Mr. W. A. Kittredge. Mr. Stevens says, "Where copyrights expire or do not exist . . . there is set a free carnival of indiscriminate reprinting which, in endeavoring to make books inexpensive and accessible, often makes them contemptible." He is "confident that books can be worthy of the writings they embody," and says with William Morris, "my work is . . . to bring before people's eyes the thing my heart is filled with." His edition has the endorsement of Anthony Trollope's family whom he visited in Minchinhampton; and profits, should there be any, will go to that family. It is the first effort, moreover, to reverse wrongs of which Anthony Trollope was

---

Review of *The Warden*, by Anthony Trollope (Pratt Institute Free Library).

helplessly conscious; Miss Trollope making the assertion that her grand-father's entire life of authorship had been harassed by American piracy.

It has not been selected as the best novel Trollope wrote or his best-liked novel, but as a protest against poor clothes for worthy books. When Mr. Yeats was in America recently, someone asked him what last-century novels of Irish life to read, and he answered Anthony Trollope's; and there are many not essentially interested in Irish life who give these novels current importance. Thomas Hardy has a more etched, Henry James, a more emerald-encrusted effect than Trollope; but all three have that verisimilitude which outshines life and seems more urgent than what is going on about one at the moment. Like Bach and Prokofieff, they have with it power of sustaining the mode which they set for themselves at the beginning of the composition; and as part of this skill, a fitness of expression like the sense of balance in the gondolier or the peacock. Trollope says of the Rectory of Plumstead Episcopy, it

> was not without ample consideration that those thick, dark, costly carpets were put down; those embossed, but sombre papers hung up; those heavy curtains draped so as to half exclude the light of the sun. Nor were these old-fashioned chairs, bought at a price far exceeding that now given for more modern goods, without a purpose. The breakfast service on the table was equally costly and equally plain. The apparent object had been to spend money without obtaining brilliancy or splendor. The urn was of thick and solid silver, as were also the teapot, coffee-pot, cream ewer and sugar bowl; the cups were old, dim dragon china, worth about a pound apiece, but very despicable in the eyes of the uninitiated.

There is the marshaling for effect, the self-confident spark at the center, in every potent novel—a force in comparison with which decorum or indecorum is incidental. Jane Austen shocks by sandstorm-like propriety of presentation; the effect of Mary Butts' unretouched negatives of raw nerves is quietly, darkly affecting; in the mere dying of Emily Hotspur—Trollope—or of Thomas Mann's Joachim, there is tension; some of our unsparingly terrific novels and plays that are spoken of in review as mystical or spiritual, are merely labored. Trollope has always the bones of a story, but does not trust to suspense for interest. Often, as one recalls, he places a synopsis before the reader, as before relating his experiences an explorer sometimes presents a map. Lady Dumbello, Sir Raffle Buffle, Mr. Bullbean, the livings of Eiderdown and Goosegorge, are accessory but of a significant gusto. To *The Warden*, as indeed to any novel by Trollope, George Moore's not quite proven remark applies—the ability to manufacture small talk is the sign manual of the great writer.

The Criterion, 12 (July 1933), 711–12.

A PENGUIN IN MOSCOW

OUT of "plain downright honest curiosity: that very greatest of all the virtues," a penguin-Dante visits Moscow—"panacea Negation haven of all (in life's name) Deathworshipers"—and has written a droll book. In his "enormous dream" about the proletarian fable, the main proficiency is the spry-slow suave quaintly-toddling selfsufficient imperviousness to weather. "Eros wins; always: . . . ecstasy, triumph, immeasurable yes and beautiful explosion. . . ." That is to say the book is a large poem. "The whole thing marvelously whirls and this total supreme whirl is made of subsidiary, differently timed yet perfectly intermeshing, whirlings." "(if he had been playing a fiddle i had / been dancing" may express it; though with dancing, various arts, sports, and sciences, are entwined—drama, painting, taxidermy, logic, interior decoration, ballistics, tailoring, landscape gardening, tumbling, music, poetry, wire-walking, flying, swimming, fencing, calligraphy, typography, and the art of the cartoon.

Style is for Mr. Cummings "translating"; it is a self-demonstrating aptitude for technique, as a seal that has been swimming right-side-up turns over and swims on its back for a time—"killing nears in droves and slaying almosts massacring myriads of notquites": "the worm knocks loud," "sit / the bum said"—with numerous finds in the realm of unconscious bourgeois obnoxiousness: "eye buleev money rules thith woyl"—. . . "wen uh man's gud thad bright gole thing in his fist, he's strong." This pluck-the-duck, scale-the-fish 15th century appetite for aliveness equivalent to a million trillion musical light years, results in some effects which are as much better than those in *The Enormous Room* (the germ for these) as *Viva* is an improved vagueness and judicious anonymity over most of what preceded. And the typography, one should add, is not something superimposed on the meaning but the author's mental handwriting. There courageous innocently penguineyed comrade capitalist Cummings gets the best of strong publisher and boorish public.

Review of *Eimi*, by E. E. Cummings (Covici, Friede, Inc.).

To the hoop poem in *Viva* there are various companion effects—not to mention "and off away offoffoff rolls andAnDaNd wonderfully I wibble-Awabbling circle a wheel A—" Examine "silversaying-fish," "& so at twilight," "toward a sunset I turn my face," "did you ever keep caterpillars,"

a
n
d
   here
a flapping dove
           —A
-light
     ing
      (low.

Yes, "the tragedy of life always hasn't been and . . . isn't that some people are poor and others rich, some hungry and others not hungry, some weak and others strong. The tragedy is and always will be that most people are unable to express themselves."

One does not like to praise, then take away the praise—and will not; but there are a few queries. (a) Not to be confused with Virgil's necessary artificial argot of politeness, the sharkskin papillae pebble-pattern of the Italian garden-walk, undesirably changes now and then to polished white mosaic: "Not only has Turk been up; he's been doing"; (b) a Saint Sebastian—as our Dante probably knows—may be hid by too many arrows of awareness; (c) a tag is perhaps too much a certain kind of tag for a' that it is used by a poet; (d) one is never going to be able to score words as one scores sounds, "condefusionpair" being not hard on the brain but awkward for it; (e) the book should have an index though it may be like suggesting that the kangaroo pouch accommodate a grown kangaroo; (f) which freedom wears best? that of a leprechaun a leopard a leper a hyperholiest priest of Benares, or of the mystic for whom leprosy becomes negligible? Mr. Cummings' obscenities are dear to him, somewhat as Esau's hairiness is associated with good hunting, but one thing is certain: if an otherwise divine burlesque is a bouquet that has a stench, a chair that was a garbage-pail—then a grin, a smirk, a smile are synonymous; B is not for Beatrice but for bunk, and i am not Dante.

But—possibly—perhaps "the hole point" is not that Odessa has "the best mud in the world."

"Birdlike and boy," "defunct," "dwarfish," "chipmunk lion," "mr/ cricket" and mr crab (the 5-year vermin), Comrade Can't, and "So do I" recall Mr. Civility, Pickthank, and Cutpurse, and this to some extent children's story, by an author whose kindness to comrade stunned, equals America, has traits in common with Hashimura Togo, Ezra Pound, Gertrude Stein, T. S. Eliot, and the Guls Hornbook; the consanguinity with James Joyce being the nostalgic note, quite as much as a similarity in harmonics; cf. "the tide's acute weaving murmur" and "my blueveined child."

Tyrannies fall "by the hand of Poietes." But magnanimity is greater than valor; that Mr. Cummings has well learned this lesson appears in his summary of those wasmen which Virgil showed him, among whom And How—"weed of dogma flourishes"—with no airhole for I am: "This is a tragic time" and Russians are "artists because giving is their nature, their self, what they wish to do and what they can be. Take this fellow; the Russian who gave me his bed—. . . If he'd had three beds or five beds he'd have given three beds or five beds."

The publishers say *Eimi* is a novel; but in penguin, "pour l'artiste, voir c'est concevoir, et concevoir, c'est composer" "little capcom Kem-min-kz" says Cézanne says.

Poetry, 42 (August 1933), 277–81.

FICTION OR NATURE?

MADCHEN in Uniform shown in America last winter set our studios an example in photography and somewhat reinstated the plausibility of emotion but Hollywood has the bad luck to be outstarred by its whereabouts: eucalyptus-trees, calico horses with pale eyes, bits of sea-coast with cormorants or pelicans, or rolling hills with shadows. George Arliss is neutralized by the dogville-comedy aspect of his support and Greta Garbo is shabbied by luxury. Plucked eyebrows, reinforced eyelashes, a slouch, do not improve an already fortunate equipment. (If Henry James and John Gay, Dr. Mensendieck and a sea-lion, could but make some suggestions.) And for G. G. a foil is needed like Carlyle Blackwell whom "certain adults still able to totter about the streets on a fine day" will remember; tried and true Lochinvars of the studios are a strong handicap.

No; we do not like "loveing pictures. We like any kind but love." Brooklyn shares this repugnance—expressed by Birmingham children to their city enquiry committee, 1931—but nature films would not here come last in the category of choices; nor films of other countries. *Bring 'Em Back Alive*, with Frank Buck (the man) between showings, held the attention; also the Martin

Johnson's *Congorilla:* the crocodiles and the great prehistoric bulrush-and-palm hippopotamus scene with twitching ears, submergings, and unanimous yawnings—not to mention peculiarities of narrative, and contrasts in racial sensibility. (The pigmy drops his staff so that Mr. J. may measure him; is in doubt about the propriety of recovering it; withdraws in embarrassment from refined white obliviousness.) And other studies in "native bravado."

In *Seeing Europe on a Budget*—the Burton Holmes lecture with motion pictures by Andre La Varre—black and white sheep of varying sizes and the Magyar shepherd in full-length natural fleece mantle, were a hit; also Hungarian pigs fed from both sides of the trough, the momentum of the drove resulting in an occasional pig chairing; a flock of ducks entering a pond on a glide so smooth the transition from running to floating was undetectable. Part of this travelogue was the white marble Spanish Riding School of Vienna filmed by Bryson Jones; followed by ski-jumping and miscellaneous skill on steep slopes. Leap and landing were here so well pieced and the detail contributing to equilibrium—on new snow—when leaping gullies and circling obstructions was so neat that by comparison, the average newsreel version is like a jig-saw puzzle before the piece begins. Lacking the technical merits of the Burton Holmes, and not to be compared in style with the Shippee-Johnson pictures of Peru, was *I Am From Siam* photographed by Karl Robilov—a record under difficulties, of the cremation ceremonies of the late King Rama VI of Siam and of the coronation of King Prajadipok. Sunday supplements gave an idea of the samovar-like grandeur of the glassy gold mountain of the coronation (ascended behind a curtain) but did not suggest the nervousness of the occasion as the conscientious potentate accepted one by one the symbols of office and placed the crown on his head, none lesser than a crowned head being fit to touch a king's head, and the strewing—in benediction—of gold flowers from a little gold bowl. Nor could anything but motion suggest the pompous inability of the elephants to be stereotyped, the top-heaviness of the three-tiered parasols, the wiriness and blood of the horses. Following the aristocratic portion of the film, the popular portion: a motley of sports, habits, and occupations: the swarming halloween skirmish of figures on stilts with animal heads, the foot-ball game played with a tennis-ball—goaled through napkin rings; convoy of the little white elephant to the temple of purification, through streets lined with banana-trees to simulate jungle. (Shown with the foregoing, the desperate and blast-worthy *Puss in Boots.*)

The Mystic Land of Peru by Robert Shippee, co-leader and geologist of the Shippee-Johnson Expedition to the Peruvian Andes. Lieut. George R. Johnson being chief photographer of the Expedition. Plain and piebald llamas; stray dogs; mules reluctantly crossing a grass suspension bridge of the kind Pizarro saw—as though walking on a hammock—with grandly designed backdrop of dim peaks and clear mountain-side—a remnant of civilization in the Lost Valley of the Colca, marching to music from souvenir bugles, flutes, and drums, played by home-folk-deserters from the army—with a ceremonial head to the procession, of tin pans of silver mounted on sticks. The photographic moment in it all, no doubt is bread-making on the mountain side, by a native woman—beginning with elephant trunk-like motion of the body strangely continued: a back view in which the feet are revealed winnowing grain—bare feet below a long dress. There are the crescentic sand-dunes on La Joya Pampa—175 feet from tip to tip—blown along in formations sixty feet a year by trade winds; walls of oblong rock staggered in modern fashion, with here and there a block weighing 200 tons; harvest-field cross of wheat; pottery simulating animal forms; the characteristic straw hat of the Inca, with turned-up brim; striped ponchos; and so on.

Carveth Wells' *This Strange Animal World*—a little crude as to narrative—for the Northwest Scientific Expedition of Perth, West Australia, on a voyage with motion-picture camera to the northwest coast—showed the best Australian opossums ever seen by this (Brooklyn) Barnum—a gray one and an albino; the best merino champion ram; also an alligator-dance, tribal women and a few dogs looking on, the alligator: a line of twenty men diminishing in height from the first to the end of the line, standing on spread legs, beneath which trellis a man wriggles on hands and feet from the tail forward and out through the head. Mr. Wells' giant clams (of the kind said to amputate legs and never let go) were not so vivid as Captain Hurley's shown here some years back; nor were the coral-beds, zebroid fish, sponges, etc., so sharp as Captain Hurley's. The wild kangaroos in flight, undulating like the rapids of a dangerous stream, as they crossed the ditches and scrub, were impressive; also a momentary but hyper-clever close-up of the flying opossum's leg-to-leg membranes; and the above-referred-to opossums: the gray one on hind legs in a eucalyptus tree, plucking a branch, retiring along the tree; swinging head down as it ate of the foliage, suspended by tail, by tail only, then up again—weaving around, back of, and through, a clump of vertical twigs, in serpent loops and eights without standing-place or space to squeeze through. The platypus on land, with dry coat of furrier's beaver—was a best thing; as was the echidna disappearing in such a way as to produce no mound of accumulating earth—mere surface convulsions.

In *Alaska*, motion pictures of Aniakchak crater—Father Hubbard's sea-gulls, salmons, and hair seals, were of interest—especially the seagulls, flat to the lee of a storm-wave, widely spaced, with head to the wind. Shafts of iceberg breaking from the mass emphasized the deceptiveness of the telephoto lens—as did Mr. Shippee's sanddunes—the scale being as much altered as the area of Russia would be diminished in a dime-sized map of Europe. Father Hubbard is important but his filming is less lovable than that of Amos O. Burg (in Alaska and South America) and that of Captain Stanley Osborne (in Australia).

The kings of the season probably were Dr. Bailey, Dr. Ditmars, and Captain Knight. In Dr. A. M. Bailey's and Mr. Robert J. Niedrock's bird and small mammal studies for their library of nature films at the Chicago Academy of Sciences—with enticing commentary by Dr. Bailey—there is not a dull foot. Last year, *Camera Shooting in Southern Marshes*. This year, *In Haunts of the Golden Eagle*, tests with turned duck-eggs—pointed ends out and round ends in, and with avocet eggs, indicate that the duck-eggs point in by intention, and that a bird will brood in an all-clutch imposture. Dipper-birds (i. e., water-ousels)—new to the motion-picture camera—were shown running in and out of their tunnel-shaped nest on a darkly shaded ledge, spattered at intervals by drops from a heavy torrent; and an albinistic prairie falcon and nest (prairie form of the duck-hawk) now filmed for the first time. This falcon, and Mr. Wells' white captive opossum, suggest that the charm of whiteness varies—albino crows and rattlesnakes seeming belittled by their oddness, the white elephant being not a success and deserving added sympathy by reason of its prominence. One can imagine no more sumptuous effect, however, than the coat of this falcon tossed by the gale but undisordered—the hard legs, flattened head, and glass-black eye, setting it off. The sensation of these five reels perhaps was the continuous very close close-up of a long-eared (i.e., rabbit) owl—tiger-striping on red-amber body-color—among well-twigged branches of a tree like the tamarack, with a shaft of evening sun slanting down from Mt. Evans; both eyes flaming yellow but the eye in shadow, round with round pupil; the one toward the sun—iris and pupil—narrowed to a vertical oval. The great horned owl and nest were shown and various lesser owls; the mammalogist of the party "making a trip every morning to the nests of the owls and in this way collecting mammals he could secure in no other way." Recalling, though not precisely of course, Captain Knight's merlin's nest with a jackdaw walking about it looking for scraps of meat, and Carveth Wells' Australian eyrie from which a native was coming away with eagle's food for himself.

Dr. Bailey's golden eagle eyrie on a narrow shelf of rock at the summit of a bleached pinnacle striped by transverse erosions, without vegetation or neighboring peaks was more "terrible" than Captain C. W. R. Knight's Scotch eyrie scenes—though no partial study can rival a life history such as Captain Knight showed, of male and female eaglet in *The Filming of the Golden Eagle*, 1929. It is difficult not to write a bookful on work such as this; the shadings into unsatisfactoriness and the supreme peaks of attainment, but of the present film, *The Romance of the Golden Eagle,* one must be content to mention a few rarities only: an Ailsa Crag gannet, in slow motion, leaving the nest; the razor-bill steering itself with its feet, one on either side like little black masons' trowels; the suggestion of power in the interacting arcs of the wings braking the momentum of the eagle as it pitches, on the ground, feet forward; "the pass" or transfer in air, of the frog or mouse that he has in his feet, by the male marsh-hawk to the female as she flies toward him before he reaches the nest; the tame raven with "beak rather like a pair of pliers"; tame owl turning its head first one way and then the other, from a point in the circle around to the point from which it started without moving shoulders or body; two young cuckoos so tall the foster robins must "hover in the air to hand over the ration." Captain Knight's interpretation of terms used in falconry, by examples of their use by Shakespeare should be embodied in a book; as should the steps in training a falcon, given in *The Filming of the Golden Eagle.*

In *Strange Animals I Have Known,* Dr. R. L. Ditmars, Curator of Reptiles and Mammals at the Bronx Zoological Park, presents a series of parallels in protection; comparing the anthropoid apes "with a more lowly type like the beaver," with insects, crabs, clams, cuttlefish, sea-hares, and the like. He made the pictures "with various cameras" and "machinery such as used in dramatic studios, some less complicated than that, and some more complicated." The study of beavers is of curious interest and represents seven years' work but does not smite the mind aesthetically as the insects do, and the triangular very black front of an armadillo's head; "certain pallid forms on desert sand which in a way is like snow"; or the giant anteater lapping milk with a tongue like a surveyor's tape for length, its "mouth so small that when yawning it would barely admit the tip of one's little finger"—a royally exotic animal with its white-edged isosceles triangle from the shoulder down the foreleg, a black patch on each shin, and heavy tail of upcurving fountaining fringe. The platypus moving about in water like a salamander, with pin-tipped claws connected by delicate black webs like internal membranes, was informing. An echidna gathering, with what resembled an anteater's tongue, a colony of white winged-ants from a fallen tree, should be mentioned—and a horned toad defined by white paper slipped behind the points of its collar. The manifestations of protection in marine creatures, photographed through the co-operation of the Biological Station in Naples and the Oceanographic Museum at Monaco—with equipment presented to Dr. Ditmars by the Prince of Monaco—have this advantage over the Williamson pictures, and Dr. Beebe's—the activity of the creatures is recorded under characteristic conditions, not under the stimulus of excitement or at temperatures inimical to them. It might be added, however, that photography, like the lie detector of the criminal court, reveals agitation which the eye fails to see—especially evident in Dr. Ditmars' horned toads when touched, in Captain Osborne's invaluable tuateras, and the Carveth Wells newly hatched turned-over turtle.

To say that Dr. J. Sibley Watson has completed the filming of *Lot in Sodom* on which he has been working for some years, with Mrs. Watson in a principal role and music by Louis Siegel, Rochester composer—is by this time not a violation of secrecy. Mr. Herbert Ives' most recent demonstration of his depth movie-device is also an item in American progress: photographing an object as seen in a curved mirror and recording it on a sensitized plate with convex ridges from top to bottom, back and front.

Close Up, 10 (September 1933), 260–65.

THE POEM AND THE PRINT

"THE Poet is chiefly distinguished from other men by a greater promptness to think and feel without immediate external excitement." This familiar statement by Wordsworth is satisfactory to us in the West, but "think and feel" do not quite characteristically express the East. Nevertheless, "Japanese poets have their own literary danger," Yoné Noguchi says. "There is nothing more sad for art than the time when simplicity . . . degenerates into exaggeration" . . . but "suppose you stand at Miidera Temple gate high upon the hill lapped and again lapped by the slow water." "Our poems, when they are good, are a thing most perfect and audacious." "Isolated, swift, and discontinuous," these lyrics "strangely generalized with the key-note of simplicity" can "express a rare moment when emotion awakes, and still more wonderful . . . the rarer moment when that emotion suddenly subsides." Sometimes to the western mind damaged by intellectual power, Japanese Uta-poems or Hokku-poems are disturbing because they are not disturbing, but the Japanese mind "makes them perfect and whole" and Mr. Noguchi tells of his visit to the poet, Yeiki Kilkakudo, when conversation was "the beauty of the shadow, when it stamped the dustless mats as a strange-shaped ageless pine tree."

Moreover, there do not seem to be times when the eastern poet is a contradiction of himself, bustling and utilitarian. In addition to being useful

---

Review of *The Ukiyoye Primitives*, by Yoné Noguchi (privately published).

to the judge of prints, Mr. Noguchi's recent book, *The Ukiyoye Primitives*, is a synonym of uncommercial research and irrepressible fantasy. Skepticism of complacent attributions, and a maintaining of obscurity for which conjecture would not be a good substitute, are praise which early art cannot well forego; yet essentially and conspicuously such a book as this belongs to poetry. The note is struck as by a bird and you are asked to let it vibrate.

Mr. Noguchi's Japanese-English is a renovated language of unimpaired connotation. Its diverting redundance curiously defies eastern conciseness and western notions of austerity, presenting as it were the counterpart of non-western format, in the serried pages like the lamellae of the mushroom, not meant to be cut—quadrangularly sewn—the book in its case; the case in a box. Having retired into sober shadow, however, the connoisseur of cricket music or of "a willow tinged with blue," springs out leopard-like and explicit, to say, "this print is one section of one oblong sheet which, when divided equally, becomes four pictures"; "that Kiyomasu the Second was as good as Kiyonobu the Second means that the former was as bad as the latter"; or "it is true that our failure to appreciate the Ukiyoye prints was one of the saddest things we ever committed." The biographic epitomes, beginning with Moronobu—1650—and extending to polychromy—1765, show the evolution of the print as the battles in a historical romance compel a sense of the period, and even without the confirming illustrations, suggest the spirit of Japanese decoration. Recalling the primacy of the Greek nude, Mr. Noguchi says the reason "we did not venture to find the highest symbol of art in the human form, should be discovered in social ethics . . . which taught us how to transform life's falsehood into a hyperbole of superficial arabesque beauty." "In Kyoto, the peaceful metropolis many hundred years old with the nobles and court ladies, in lacquer-cap and vermilion skirt, Sukenobu Nishikawa spent his mind dreaming how to create the beautiful woman figures which, having neither peculiarity nor exaggeration of characterizing, easily distinguished themselves in sweet atmosphere. . . . And see again what an elastic art, something like a chamois-skin, is hidden under the seeming absence of strength." In Kiyomasu the First—showing Danjuro the Second in the role of *Wait a While*—"half beast, half man," "the triple combination of the persimmon yellow in the outer garment, the fresh green in the clothes, and the carnation rouge that is shaded in the face, is beautiful indeed." How masculine! The dressmaker has much to do with the success of personality, and in his treatment of the prints, Mr. Noguchi as artist exerts the pitiless domination of a Poiret. One cannot but recall here, in what he says of the print, what he said of the poem. His requirement of the one being moderation, of the other a completing mood of reverie; Toyonobu's actor Kikugoro Onoye, and the inscription at the side, illustrating each, the other:

Two swords are heavy,
Long sleeves are heavy—
. . . heavy on one's sense
Is the autumnal shower.

Candidly detached, the presentation is a triumph of verbal physics like the equilibrium of the tower of tables which the Japanese tumbler interposes upward between himself and a second tumbler, and subtracts again, tossing the folded brother safe to the ground.

Poetry, 43 (November 1933), 92–95.

LOT IN SODOM

L O T in Sodom, derived from the Book of Genesis—and not a talkie—is the best art film I have seen. Directed and photographed by J. Sibley Watson, Jr., and Melville Webber; with music by Louis Siegel.[1]

You have wafts of cloud; a temple surrounded by buildings set together at various angles—grayed and unified in El Greco perspective (an air view) and one of the best pictorial effects in the film; a glittering vertebrae of fire—the tree of life; Lot's house with plaster walls, thick doors, and small windows; a market-place and the men who vexed Lot day by day. Lot in profile, like a fresco, stands reading; turns his back to you and is the bowed, intense, darkly caparisoned, overclothed, powerful, helpless Jew—talking, gesticulating, resisting. (Played by Frank Haak, and not without lapses.) Lot's wife (Hildegarde Watson) is perhaps insurmountably the lissom nymph, and fair, as companion figure to so grief-stricken and striking a piece of archaeology as Lot; but rapt, listening premonitoriness of face and attitudes throughout, are right; and as part of the pause before the destruction, the figure running down steps with garments fluttering aside, is a dramatic ace. With it, the daughter (Dorothea Haus) is well harmonized. The film is a thing of great strength and one has no wish, nor a very good chance, to pick flaws; but to an imagination based on the Child's Bible, the men of Sodom do not look quite so responsibly sinister as they might, nor fully oriental. High points are Lot's House—Morning, with the blur of waving candle-flame on the undulating coarse-weave curtain; the glass-black blood quivering along a prostrate body; the glistening elaborate lily with snake-spots; the tortoise-shell spotted pallor of the snake with beady eyes. Of the Angel—

first appearance (Lewis Whitbeck, Jr.), the real face, in its fixity, against suggested wings, achieves genuine splendor.

As I was coming out of the playhouse I overheard an incorrigible movie-unenthusiast say, "It has richness of imagination enough to last you a year and makes you want to see a film every week." I agree. The painting-and-poetry—an atmosphere of the preface to *The Wings of a Dove*, of the later bloodcurdling poems of James Joyce, of E. E. Cummings' elephant-arabesques at their unlabeled truculent best—is very nearly too exciting for a patron of the old newsreel. One salvages from the commercial ragbag a good bisection or strange-angle shot, but there, even a *cum laude* creates no spinal chill, being intellectually unself-realized. Here, the camera work, with a correlating of poetic influences—the Blake designs in the fire, the Pascin, Giotto, Doré, and Joseph Stella treatment—shows us wherein slow motion, distortion, the sliding track, can be more legitimate than the face to face stage-set. Personality coalescing with a piece of stone, the obliterating cloud of doves, "the silver cord" and other historic color, are incontrovertibly conclusive for the art of the film.

An illusion of quiescence of which one is scarcely conscious should be mentioned—that of not looking at just another motion-picture-house Derby dash for the post. (Sensation of this kind, imparted by tested sensibility, could be of interest to those who have been studying the effect of motion-pictures on the sleep of children.) This principle, of control contributing to the impression obliquely, again prevails in the chanted lines by Lot's wife, against the body of the orchestra—somewhat as the recorded nightingale song is drowned by the orchestra in Respighi's *The Pines of Rome*.

And the beauty which is on the head of the fat valley shall be a fading
flower
And the stream thereof shall be turned to pitch.
From generation to generation it shall lie waste; none shall pass through it
forever and ever.
And he shall stretch out upon it the line of confusion and the stones of
emptiness.
The mirth of the tabret ceaseth.
The song of them that rejoice endeth.
The joy of the harp ceaseth.

(Isaiah)

Speech would be meaningless by comparison with the harrowing flute for the writhing combatants, and the harp melody for the angel; the music is not the national anthem nor a passing band; it tells the story. As you know better than anyone else does, how to open your combination safe, a civilization that has reached an extreme of culture, is going to have pleasure, will have it and is meting out justice to any man that interferes. But the pleasure is not joy, it is strangling horror—the serpent that thrusts forward rigid—and does not know it ever was anything else. We see luxury extinguished and hauteur collapse—with gaiety waning into anguish, fire, ashes, dust.

¹ Movie Makers says, "In this latest film, Dr. Watson and Mr. Webber have used a technique similar to that of *The Fall of the House of Usher* but differing from the latter in that it is smoother and more thoroughly controlled. In the new film, they have achieved far greater photographic beauty—a beauty of mobile forms of light and shade that is, at times, bewildering in intensity. Movie Makers hopes that wider recognition will be given these two experimentalists for certainly nothing in the professional field ever has approached the subtlety of their technique."

Close Up, 10 (December 1933), 318–19.

THE HAWK AND THE BUTTERFLY

"I do not think men change much in their deepest thought," Mr. Yeats says, and his books are each the other, as oak-leaf missal-thrush nests are like preceding ones; as also the birch-bark-and-cobweb nest of the blue-headed vireo recurs and is different from its predecessors and from other birds' nests.

None perhaps so well as Mr. Yeats, has known to "choose from among his ideas those which belong to his life" and to poetry. When a child he pursued tortoise-shell and peacock butterflies with his net, and knew of a rare moth found only in one place—brought to Ireland from Italy in a bale of silk. Of the herring-fishers he says, "the dropping of their nets into the luminous sea and the drawing of them up has remained with me as a dominant image,"—and he is in his soul identified with " 'Ben Bulben, famous for hawks' "—"the mountain in whose side the white door swings open at nightfall to loose the gay rabble of faery"; with the tower of "the old square castle, Ballylee" also, and its "little river and great stepping-stones"; with "a deep pool where an otter hurried away under a grey boulder, . . . and many fish came up out of the dark water at early morning 'to taste the fresh water coming down from the hills.' " Ballylee is in the Barony of Kiltartan and is haunted by "Mary Himes" who "died there sixty years ago," of whom an old woman said to Mr. Yeats, "I never saw anybody so handsome as she was and I never will till I die. . . . As many as eleven men asked her in marriage in one day, but she wouldn't have any of them. . . . She was poor, but her clothes every day were the same as Sunday, she had such neatness. . . ."

Blue belongs to the church; also to the poet, and it is not a surprise to find in the work of an author who lives in Ireland "the stars and the deep blue they swim in," the blue hem embroidered with roses, "tombs of lapis lazuli," the blue-eyed hawk, unicorns with aquamarine eyes, and a "low blue hill flooded with evening light." Mr. Yeats speaks of having a ring on which are a hawk and a butterfly—"the straight line of logic" and "the zigzag of imagination"; and often becomes the symbol—that is to say, is "the sign of a moral thing"—and is his mask, which he defines as "that which is one and toward which one moves."

Sir William Drummond thought one's device should not be so obscure as to require a Sphinx to interpret it, yet should be somewhat retired from the capacity of the vulgar. In this instance the zigzag of the butterfly becomes a geometry of spiritual activity. For Blake, and for W. B. Yeats, "the imagination is the man himself." Further back are Plotinus; Heraclitus; Ma'aseh Bersith and the problem of the beginning; and Ma'aseh Merkabah, the Seat of the Divine Element in Creation. This tree or pyramid of minds resting on a concept of Unity of Being, is the antithetical self's philosophy for which the symbol is three; it is philosophy that is science and science that is art—a trinity which repeats the heaven, hell, and purgatory, of the church; the salt, sulphur, and mercury of alchemy; Cornelius Agrippa's view of nature as threefold; the sun, moon, and person beneath of astrology. "Quiet is the condition of vision"—of the saint in his cell; of the tide under the moon; of the artist's trance. This indivisible triangle is thus a unity of being like Dante's in the Convito, "where all the nature murmurs if a single note be touched."

We are warned by Mr. Yeats that in our speaking of his doctrines we may be talking about what no longer exists; but the poems exist and should he now ignore the tinge on them of disclaimed speculation he nevertheless must pardon our thinking about what he formerly may have thought.

For the antithetical self he found the gyroscope a prototype. ("Michael Robartes called the universe a great egg that turns inside out perpetually without breaking its shell.") It is "choice forced by conflict"; the world of the mind being accounted for by an interior power acting toward the center; and the external world, by an activity directed toward the periphery. "Every new logical development of the objective energy intensifies in an exact correspondence a counter-energy, or rather adds to an always deepening unanalyzable longing." "Recalling the philosophy of the Judwalis and of Giraldus," Mr. Yeats says, "I found myself on the third antinomy of Immanuel

Kant, . . . but I restate it. Every action of man declares the soul's ultimate, particular freedom, and the soul's disappearance in God; declares that reality is a congeries of being and a single being; nor is this antinomy an appearance imposed on us by the form of thought but life itself which turns, now here, now there, a whirling and a bitterness." It is the gyre of the owl, of the dancer, of "the snail's elaborate whorl," it is "the track of the whirling zodiac," the country "where swans fly round coupled with golden chains"; it is "the winding stair" of one's "life." It is " 'The things below are as the things above' of the Emerald Tablet of Hermes!" It is Jacob Boehme's: humility does not consist in fear but in dignity, and Blake's: "I grow stronger and stronger as this foolish body decays." "All things are from antithesis" the poems say—"out of hell or down from heaven. We cannot have unmixed emotions. There is always something in our enemy that we like, and in our sweetheart that we dislike. It is the entanglement of moods which makes us old"—"yes and no"; "maybe and perhaps." As opposed to "those intuitions of coming power which every creator feels," "the dark powers cling about us day and night, like bats upon an old tree." From Leda's egg hatched Love and War and Mr. Yeats wonders to what extent the hatred of Synge and James Joyce for Ireland, is love. For himself he reiterates Ruysbroeck: "I must rejoice, I must rejoice without ceasing, even if the world should shudder at my joy!" Youth for him was two halves; suffering submissiveness and that mustered-up self-sovereignty which presents itself as a bulwark and turns the wave to spray. In his work, woman is pitied and pitiless—a concept which one will always resist. Nevertheless—as in Pliny, a medicine—"the Imperishable Rose of Beauty" which can cure "the crime of being born," is also to Yeats the instinctive feminine personality. His implication that one's knowledge of beauty should be stronger than one's sense of revenge, and that we must forgive in ourselves those internal injuries inflicted by choice as we forgive the more ostentatious wounds made by the daggers of enemies, we are able to accept.

"What greater task falls to a man than to help other men with all he knows and has," Oedipus asks of Teresias. "Aye, and what worse task than to be wise and suffer for it," Teresias answers. Possessed of self knowledge, Mr. Yeats says with the player, "My strength is in my truth." His candor is perhaps more severe toward himself than toward an enemy. He remembers being told as a boy, that he had reined his pony in at the same time he had struck it with the whip. "I have felt in certain early work of my own which I have long abandoned," he says, "and here and there in the work of others of my generation, a slight, sentimental sensuality which is disagreeable," and in *Stories of Michael Robartes and His Friends,* he refers to "an inaccurate, obscure, incomplete book called 'A Vision.' " As for courage of the easier sort, when he must, he tells a clergyman that he is ignorant, a fine gentleman that he is a tyrant, a literary man that he "has put half the world's classics in prison"; knowing the while that certain "houses with trout-streams will not ask him for a visit." "There still is not any society," he says, "where a man is heard by the right ears, but never overheard by the wrong, and where he speaks his whole mind gaily, and is not the cautious husband of a part." With controlled politeness which is slightly intimidating, he is susceptible to irritation; notices the "badly rolled shabby umbrella," chickens among the cobbles, a grimy fan-light, "the dead phrases in a leading article."

"But one cannot, perhaps, love or believe at all if one does not love or believe a little too much," and when he says, in *Ideas of Good and Evil*, "if our painters of Highland cattle and moss-covered barns were to care enough for their country to care for what makes it different from other countries they might discover their very selves," he admits that he is "moved by some touch of fanaticism." One recalls his remark that Moses was not of use to his people till he had slain an Egyptian, and John Eglinton's allusion to Mr. Yeats' "platonic hatred of England," and "tendency to make Irish literature include the Irish part in English literature." Love of country, love of the unseen, and much to be reformed are synonyms for Ireland; but Mr. Yeats feels that a man serves his country best by having "a point of view not made for the crowd's sake but for self-expression," and despite much that needs reforming, he has set himself to cast an enchantment on Ireland so great that she will look like a queen and be ever young.

"The poet binds with a spell his own mind when he would enchant the minds of others," he says; and for him this enchantment has resulted in poetry that is music, drama that is poetry, and prose that is "like the spoken word." Drama, he feels, is a thing of "logic," "imagination," and "beautiful words"—"simplicity of setting" "giving depth of color" as "the lack of color in a statue fixes the attention on the form." "Speech" should be "rhythmical" and "sung words" should be "intelligible." "My ears are only comfortable," he says, "when the singer sings as if mere speech had taken fire." But in the professional actor he finds a menace to his ideal, since "it is certainly impossible to speak with perfect expression after you have been a bagpipes for many years." If plays are to succeed, an audience also has responsibility, and Professor Rhys is a playgoer of the kind needed when he says of *The Pot of Broth* which he heard read without actors or scenery, "It left us all laughing and saying an Irish comedy should be listened to and never explained." The naturalistic turn which the Abbey plays have taken cannot quite fulfill the original idea for the Abbey Theatre. However, in resisting "the despotism of fact" as "the tumbler who unrolls his carpet in the way of a marching army," Mr. Yeats has not been harmed, and sustains his conviction that "we should write out our thoughts in as nearly as possible the language we thought them in."

The Westminster Magazine, 23 (Spring 1934), 63–66.

HENRY JAMES AS A
CHARACTERISTIC AMERICAN

To say that "the superlative American" and the characteristic American are not the same thing perhaps defrauds anticipation, yet one must admit that it is not in the accepted sense that Henry James was "big" and did things in a big way. But he possessed the instinct to amass and reiterate, and is the rediscerned Small Boy who had from the first seen Europe as a verification of what in its native surroundings his "supersensitive nostril" fitfully detected and liked. Often he is those elements in American life— as locality and as character—which he recurrently studied and to which he never tired of assigning a meaning.

Underlying any variant of Americanism in Henry James' work is the doctrine, embodied as advice to Christopher Newman, "Don't try to be anyone else"; if you triumph, "let it then be all you." The native Madame de Mauves says to Euphemia, "You seem to me so all of a piece that I am afraid that if I advise you, I shall spoil you," and Hawthorne was dear to Henry James because he "proved to what use American matter could be put by an American hand. . . . An American could be an artist, one of the finest, without 'going outside' about it . . . ; quite, in fact, as if Hawthorne had become one just by being American enough."

An air of rurality, as of Moses Primrose at the fair, struck Henry James in his compatriots, and a garment worn in his own childhood revealed "that we were somehow *queer*." Thackeray, he says, "though he laid on my shoulder the hand of benevolence, bent on my native costume the spectacles of wonder." On his return from Europe, James marveled at the hats men wore, but it is hard to be certain that the knowledge-seeking American in Europe is quite so unconsciously a bumpkin as Henry James depicts him. When Newman has said, "I began to earn my living when I was almost a baby," and Madame de Bellegarde says, "You began to earn your living in the cradle?" the retort, "Well, madam, I'm not absolutely convinced I *had* a cradle," savors of the connoisseur. Since, however, it is over-difficult for Henry James, in portrayals of us, not to be portraying himself, there is even in his rendering of the callow American a tightening of the consciousness that hampers his portrayal of immaturity.

"I am not a scoffer," the fellow countryman says to Theobald, the American painter, and if it were a question of being either evasive or ridiculous, James would prefer to seem ridiculous. His respectful humility toward emotion is brave, and in diffidence, reserve, and strong feeling, he reminds one of Whittier, another literary bachelor whom the most ardent sadist has not been able to soil. We remember his sense of responsibility for the United States during the World War, and his saying of the Civil War, in *Notes of a Son and Brother*, "the drama of the War . . . had become a habit for us without ceasing to be a strain. I am sure I thought more things under that head . . . than I thought in all other connections together." What is said in the same book on the death of Mary Temple, the cousin who so greatly "had a sense for verity of character and play of life in others," is an instance of reverent, and almost reverend, feeling that would defend him against the charge of casualness in anything, if ever one were inclined to make it. It is not the artist, but responsibility for living and for family, that wonders here about the death and has about "those we have seen beaten, this sense that it was not for nothing they missed the ampler experience . . . since dire as their defeat may have been, we don't see them . . . at peace with victory." Things for Henry James glow, flush, glimmer, vibrate, shine, hum, bristle, reverberate. Joy, bliss, ecstasies, intoxication, a sense of trembling in every limb, a shattering first glimpse, a hanging on the prolonged silence of an editor; and as a child at Mr. Burton's small theater in Chambers Street, his wondering, not if the curtain would rise, but "if one could exist till then"; the bonfires of his imagination, his pleasure in the "tender sea-green" or "rustling rose-color" of a seriously best dress, are too live to countenance his fear that he was giving us "an inch of canvas and an acre of embroidery."

Idealism which was willing to make sacrifices for its self-preservation was always an element in the conjuring wand of Henry James. He felt about the later America "like one who has seen a ghost in his safe old house." Of "Independence Hall . . . and its dignity not to be uttered, . . . spreading staircase and long-drawn upper gallery, . . . one of those rare precincts of the past against which the present has kept beating in vain," he says, "nothing . . . would induce me to revisit . . . the object I so fondly evoke." He would not risk disturbing his recollections of *The Wonder-Book* and *Tanglewood Tales* by rereading them, and Dickens "always remained better than the taste of overhauling him." The aura is more than the thing. New Hampshire in September was "so *delicately* Arcadian, like . . . an old legend, an old love-story in fifteen volumes," and "Newport, . . . the dainty isle of Aquidneck," and "its perpetually embayed promontories of mossy rock," had "ingenuous old-time distinction . . . too latent and too modest for notation." Exasperated by the later superficiality of New York's determination "to blight the superstition of rest," he termed the public libraries "mast-heads on which spent birds sometimes alight in the expanses of the ocean," and thought Washington Irving's Sunnyside, with its "deep, long lane, winding, embanked, overarched, such an old-world lane as one scarce ever meets in America, . . . easy for everything but rushing about and being rushed at." The "fatal and sacred" enjoyment of England "buried in the soil of our primary culture" leads him to regard London as "the great distributing heart of our traditional life"; to say of Oxford, "No other spot in Europe extorts from our barbarous hearts so passionate an admiration"; and for the two Americans in "hedgy Worcestershire" beneath an "English sky bursting into a storm of light or melting into a drizzle of silver, . . . nothing was wanting; the shaggy, mouse-colored donkey, nosing the turf, . . . the towering ploughman with his white smock-frock, puckered on chest and back." "We greeted these things," one says, "as children greet the loved pictures in a story-book, lost and mourned and found again . . . a gray, gray tower, a huge black yew, a cluster of village graves, with crooked headstones. . . . My companion was overcome. . . . How it makes a Sunday where it stands!"

Henry James' warmth is clearly of our doting native variety. "Europe had been romantic years before, because she was different from America," he said, "wherefore America would now be romantic because she was different from Europe." His imagination had always included Europe; he had not been estranged by travel nor changed by any "love-philtre or fear-philtre" intenser than those he had received in New York, Newport, or our American Cambridge. "Culture as I hold, is a matter of attitude quite as much as of opportunity," he said in *Notes of a Son and Brother*, and "one's supreme relation, as one had always put it, was one's relation to one's country." In alluding to "our barbarous hearts" he had, of course, no thought of being taken at his word—any more than Mrs. Cleve did when abusing America—and even in the disillusions attendant upon return to this country, he betrayed a parentally local satisfaction in the way American girls dressed.

Nationally and internationally "the sensitive citizen," he felt that patriotism was a matter of knowing a country by getting the clue. Our understanding of human relations has grown—more perhaps than we realize in the last twenty years; and when Henry James disappoints us by retaining the Northerner's feeling about the Confederate, we must not make him directly contemporary, any more than we dispute his spelling "peanut" with a hyphen. He had had no contact with the South, and all the bother-taking Henry James needed for doing justice to feeling was opportunity to feel.

"Great things . . . have been done by solitary workers," he said, "but with double the pains they would have cost if they had been produced in more genial circumstances." Education for him, in a large sense, was conversation. Speaking of Cambridge, he said, "When the Norton woods, nearby, massed themselves in scarlet and orange, and when to penetrate and mount a stair and knock at a door, and, enjoying response, then sink into a window-bench and inhale at once the vague golden November and the thick suggestion of the room where nascent 'thought' had again and again piped or wailed, was to taste as I had never done before, the poetry of the prime initiation and of associated growth."

We observe in the memoirs, treasured American types: "silent Vander-pool, . . . incorruptibly and exquisitely dumb," who looked so as if he came from 'good people,' . . . the very finest flower of shyness, . . . a true welter of modesty, not a grain of it anything stiffer—"; "the ardent and delicate and firm John May"—student at Harvard; and there was Robert Temple, a cousin, "with a mind almost elegantly impudent, . . . as if we had owed him to Thackeray"; and Mary Temple, " 'natural' to an effect of perfect felicity, . . . all straightness and charming tossed head, with long light and yet almost sliding steps and a large light postponing laugh." There was "a widowed grandmother who dispensed an hospitality seemingly as joyless as it was certainly boundless," and Uncle Albert, a kinsman who was " 'Mr.' to his own wife . . . his hair bristling up almost in short-horn fashion at the sides," with "long, slightly equine countenance, his eyebrows ever elevated as in the curiosity of alarm."

A child is not a student of "history and custom, . . . manners and types"; but to say that Henry James as a child was "a-throb" with the instinct for meanings barely suggests the formidable paraphernalia which he was even then gathering. It is in "the waste of time, of passion, of curiosity, of contact—that true initiation resides," he said later; and no scene, strange accent, no adventure—experienced or vicarious—was irrelevant. When older, he alluded to "the maidenly letters" of Emerson; but in New York, Emerson had been strange and wonderful to the child he had invited "to draw near to him, off the hearth-rug." He was "an apparition sinuously and elegantly slim, . . . commanding a tone alien to any we had heard round about"; and the schoolmate Louis De Coppet, in "his French treatment of certain of our native local names, Ohio and Iowa for instance, which he rendered . . . O-ee-oh and Ee-o-wah, . . . opened vistas." He said, "There hung about the Wards, to my sense, that atmosphere of apples and nuts . . . and jack-knives and 'squrruls,' of domestic Bible-reading and attendance at 'evening lecture,' of the fear of parental discipline and the cultivated art of dodging it, combined with great personal toughness and hardihood"; and there was

" 'Stiffy' Norcom . . . whom we supposed gorgeous. . . . (Divided I was, I recall, between the dread and the glory of being so greeted, 'Well, Stiffy—!' as a penalty for the least attempt at personal adornment.)"

"You cannot make a man feel low," his Christopher Newman says, "unless you can make him feel base," and "a good conscience" is a pebble with which Henry James is extremely fond of arming his Davids. Longmore's "truth-telling eyes," are that in him which puzzled and tormented the Baron. "They judged him, they mocked him, they eluded him, they threatened him, they triumphed over him, they treated him as no pair of eyes had ever treated him." In every photograph of Henry James that we have, the thing that arrests one is a kind of terrible truthfulness. We feel also, in the letters and memoirs, that "almost indescribable naturalness" which disappears in the fancy writing of his imitators. If good-nature and reciprocity are American traits, Henry James was a characteristic American—too much one when he patiently suffered unsuitable persons to write to him, call on him, and give him their "work." Politeness in him was "more than a form of luxurious egotism" and was in keeping with the self-effacing determination to remain a devotee of devotees to George Eliot "for his own wanton joy," though unwittingly requested to "take away, please, away, away!" two books he had written. (Mrs. Greville had lent the books as introductory, previous to her calling with Henry James on the Leweses, but no connection was noticed between books and visitor.) The same ardor appears in the account of his meeting with Dickens. He speaks of "the extremely handsome face . . . which met my dumb homage with a straight inscrutability. . . . It hadn't been the least important that we should have shaken hands or exchanged platitudes. . . . It was as if I had carried off my strange treasure just exactly from under the merciless military eye—placed there on guard of the secret. All of which I recount for illustration of the force of action, unless I call it passion, that may reside in a single pulse of time."

Henry James belongs to "the race which has the credit of knowing best, at home and abroad, how to make itself comfortable," but there was in him an ascetic strain, which caused him to make Longmore think with disgust of the Baron's friend, who "filled the air with the odor of heliotrope"; and Eugene Pickering's American friend found "something painful in the spectacle of absolute enthralment, even to an excellent cause." Freedom, yes. The confidant, in comparing himself compassionately with the Eugene of their schooldays, says, "I could go out to play alone, I could button my jacket myself, and sit up till I was sleepy." Yet the I of the original had not "been exposed on breezy uplands under the she-wolf of competition," and there was not about him "the impertinent odor of trade." Some persons have grudged Henry James his freedom and have called it leisure; but as Theobald, the American painter, said of art, "If we work for her, we must often pause." Of *The Tragic Muse*, James said in a letter, "I took long and patient and careful trouble which no creature will recognize"; and we may declare of him as he did of John La Farge, "one was . . . never to have seen a subtler mind or a more generously wasteful passion, in other words a sincerer one." Reverting to the past of his own life, he was overpowered by "the personal image unextinct" and said, "It presents itself, I feel, beyond reason and yet if I turn from it the ease is less."

There was in him "the rapture of observation," but more unequivocally even than that, affection for family and country. "I was to live to go back with wonder and admiration," he says, "to the quantity of secreted thought in our daily medium, the quality of intellectual passion, the force of cogitation and aspiration, as to the explanation both of a thousand surface incoherences and a thousand felicities." Family was the setting for his country, and the town was all but synonymous with family; as would appear in what is said of "the family-party smallness of old New York, those happy limits that could make us all care . . . for the same thing at once." It "is always a matter of winter twilight, firelight, lamplight." "We were surely all gentle and generous together, floating in such a clean light social order, sweetly proof against ennui." "The social scheme, as we knew it, was, in its careless charity, worthy of the golden age . . . the fruits dropped right upon the board to which we flocked together, the least of us and the greatest"; "our parents . . . never caring much for things we couldn't care for and generally holding that what was good to them would be also good for their children." A father is a safe symbol of patriotism when one can remember him as "genially alert and expert"—when "human fellowship" is "the expression that was perhaps oftenest on his lips and his pen." "We need never fear not to be good enough," Henry James says, "if only we were social enough," and he recalls his mother as so participatingly unremote that he can say, "I think we almost contested her being separate enough to be proud of us—it was too like our being proud of ourselves." Love is the thing more written about than anything else, and in the mistaken sense of greed. Henry James seems to have been haunted by awareness that rapacity destroys what it is successful in acquiring. He feels a need "to see the other side as well as his own, to feel what his adversary feels"; to be an American is not for him "just to glow belligerently with one's country." Some complain of his transferred citizenship as a loss; but when we consider the trend of his fiction and his uncomplacent denouements, we have no scruple about insisting that he was American; not if the American is, as he thought, "intrinsically and

actively ample, . . . reaching westward, southward, anywhere, everywhere,"
with a mind "incapable of the shut door in any direction."

Hound and Horn, 7 (April–May 1934), 363–72; *Predilections; A Marianne
Moore Reader.*

A DRAFT OF XXX CANTOS

"IT is a disgraceful thing," Ezra Pound says, "for a man's work not to show
steady growth and increasing fineness from first to last," and anyone alert
to the creative struggle will recognize in the *Cantos* under later treatment
as compared with earlier drafts, the rise of the storm-wave of literary security
and the tautness obtained by conscious renunciation.

We have in them "the usual subjects of conversation between intelligent
men"—"books, arms . . . men of unusual genius, both of ancient times and
our own"—arranged in the style of the grasshopper-wing for contrast, half
the fold against the other half, the rarefied effect against a grayer one. Mr.
Pound admits that he can see, as Aristotle did, a connection sometimes
where others do not: between books and war, for instance. It is implied that
if we were literally in communication, at home and internationally, we should
be armed against "new shambles"; against "one war after another," started
by men "who couldn't put up a good hen-roost." And, obversely, "if Ar-
mageddon has taught us anything it should have taught us to abominate the
half-truth, and the tellers of the half-truth in literature." The *Cantos* are
both a poring upon excellence and a protest against "the tyranny of the
unimaginative." They are against "the vermin who quote accepted opinion,"
against historians who ought to have "left blanks in their writings for what
they didn't know"; and are for work charged with realness—for "verity of
feeling" that releases us from "the bonds of blatant actuality."

"The heart is the form," as is said in the East—in this case the rhythm
which is a firm piloting of rebellious fluency; the quality of sustained emphasis, as of a cargo being shrewdly steered to the edge of the quai:

> Under the plumes, with the flakes and small wads of color
> Showering from the balconies
> With the sheets spread from windows

Review of *A Draft of XXX Cantos,* by Ezra Pound (Faber & Faber).

> with leaves and small branches pinned on them,
> Arras hung from the railings; out of the dust,
> With pheasant tails upright on their forelocks,
>   The small white horses, the
> Twelve girls riding in order, green satin in pannier'd habits;
> Under the baldachino, silver'd with heavy stitches,
> Biancha Visconti, with Sforza,
> The peasant's son and the duchess.

"Every age yields its crop of pleasant singers," Mr. Pound says, "who write poetry free from the cruder faults," and in the *Cantos* the quiver of feeling is not conveyed by "rhyming mountain with fountain and beauty with duty"; though in the present evolved method the skill of the more apparent method remains. The edges of the rhetoric and of sound are well "luted," as in good lacquer-work, and the body throughout is ennobled by insinuated rhyme effects and a craftily regulated tempo:

> *Di cui* in the which he, Francesco. . . .

One notices the accelerated light final rhyme (lie), the delayed long syllable (grass),

> The filigree hiding the gothic,
>   with a touch of rhetoric in the whole
> And the old sarcophagi,
>   such as lie, smothered in grass, by San Vitale;

the undozing ease of

> And hither came Selvo, doge
>   that first mosaic'd San Marco,
> And his wife that would touch food but with forks,
> Sed aureis furculis, that is
>   with small golden prongs
> Bringing in, thus, the vice of luxuria.

There is many a spectacular concealment, or musical ruse should one say, in the patterns presented of slang, foreign speech, and numerals—an ability borrowed as it were from "the churn, the loom, the spinning-wheel, the oars": "Malatesta de Malatestis ad Magnificum Dominum Patremque suum, etc." about the gift of the bay pony. We have in some of these metrical effects a wisdom as remarkable as anything since Bach.

To the motion of the verse is added descriptive exactness which is, like the good ear, another indication of "maximum efficiency":

> The gulls broad out their wings,
>   nipping between the splay feathers;
> . . . .
> Gold, gold, a sheaf of hair,
>   thick like a wheat swath;

and "the old woman from Kansas . . . stiff as a cigar-store Indian from the Bowery . . . this ligneous solidity . . . that indestructible female. . . ."

Mr. Pound has spent his life putting effort and impudence into what people refuse to take time to enjoy or evaluate: in demonstrating "the *virtu* of books worth reading"; in saying by example, that "the thing that matters in art is a sort of energy"; that "an intensity amounting to genius" enters into the practice of one's art, and that great art is able to overcome "the fret of contemporaneousness." Horror of primness is not a crime, "unvarnished natural speech" is a medicine, and it is probably true that "no method is justified until it has been carried too far." But when an author says read what you enjoy and enjoy what you read, one asks in turn, can a man expect to be regarded as a thing of superlatives and absolutes when he dwells on worthlessness as in the imprecatory cantos, forsaking his own counsel which is good! One may vanquish a detractor by ignoring him ("he could have found the correction where he assumed the fault"); or may "turn to and build." And one may embarrass with humor, which is in the *Cantos* a not uningenious phase of dogma. At least we infer that an allusion to easy science, namely easy art, which "elected a Monsieur Brisset who held that man is descended from frogs," is not a compliment; and that the lines about "sucking pigs, pigs, pigs, small pigs, porkers throughout all Portugal" is more than mere decoration. But rather than blunt the point of his wedge, a writer is sometimes willing to seem various things that he is not; and Mr. Pound is "vitally interesting." His feeling for verse above prose—that for prose "a much greater amount of language is needed than for poetry"—is like Schonberg's statement: "My greatest desire is to compress the most substance into the least possible space," and Stravinsky's trick of ending a composition with the recoil of a good ski-jumper accepting a spill. Furthermore, as art grows, it deviates. "I know of no case when an author has developed at all without at least temporarily sacrificing one or several of his initial merits," Mr. Pound says. In the *Cantos* the "singing quality" has somewhat been sacrificed to "weight"—to "organ base." The automatic looser statement of primary impulse penetrates better than the perfected one of conscious improvement and the undevout reader might perhaps see the water better in the following lines of prose criticism: "the cross run of the beat and the word, as of a stiff wind cutting the ripple-tops of bright water," than in: "the blue-grey glass of the wave tents them" and "a tin flash in the sun-dazzle." But the day is coming when spareness will seem natural.

The test for the *Cantos* is not obstinate continuous probing but a rereading after the interval of a year or years; "rhythmic vitality" needs no advocate but time. "The great book and the firm book" can persuade resisters that "good art never bores one," that art is a joyous thing.

The Criterion, 13 (April 1934), 482–85.

"THINGS OTHERS NEVER NOTICE"

STRUGGLE is a main force in William Carlos Williams. And the breathless budding of thought from thought is one of the results and charms of the pressure configured. With an abandon born of inner security, Dr. Williams somewhere nicknames his chains of incontrovertibly logical apparent non-sequiturs, rigmarole; and a consciousness of life and intrepidity is charac-teristically present in "Stop: Go—"

> a green truck
> dragging a concrete mixer
> passes
> in the street—
> the clatter and true sound
> of verse—

Disliking the tawdriness of unnecessary explanation, the detracting com-pulsory connective, stock speech of any kind, he sets the words down, "each note secure in its own posture—singularly woven." "The senseless unar-rangement of wild things," which he imitates, makes some kinds of correct writing look rather foolish; and as illustrating that combination of energy and composure which is the expertness of the artist, he has never drawn a clearer self-portrait than "Birds and Flowers":

Review of *Collected Poems, 1921–1931*, by William Carlos Williams, with a preface by Wallace Stevens (Objectivist Press).

What have I done
to drive you away? It is
winter, true enough, but

this day I love you.
This day
there is no time at all

more than in under
my ribs where anatomists
say the heart is—

And just today you
will not have me. Well,
tomorrow it may be snowing—

I'll keep after you, your
repulse of me is no more
than a rebuff to the weather—

If we make a desert of
ourselves—we make
a desert. . . .

William Carlos Williams objects to urbanity—to sleek and natty effects—and this is a good sign if not always a good thing. Yet usually nothing could better the dashing shrewdness of the pattern as he develops it and cuts it off at the acutely right point.

With the bee's sense of polarity he searches for a flower, and that flower is representation. Likenesses here are not reminders of the object, they are it, as in "Struggle of Wings":

And there's the river with thin ice upon it
fanning out half over the black
water, the free middlewater racing under its
ripples that move crosswise on the stream.

He is drugged with romance—"O unlit candle with the soft white plume"—but, like the bee, is neither a waif nor a fool. Argus-eyed, energetic, insatiate, compassionate, undeceived, he says in "Immortal,"

Yes, there is one thing braver than all flowers;
. . . .
And thy name, lovely One, is Ignorance.

Wide-eyed resignation of this kind helps some to be cynical, but it makes Dr. Williams considerate; sorry for the tethered bull, the circus sea-elephant, for the organ-grinder, "sour-faced," "needing a shave."

He ponders "the justice of poverty / its shame, its dirt" and pities the artist's hindered energy as it patiently does what it ought to do, and the poem read by critics who have no inkling of what it's about. But the pathos is incidental. The "ability to be drunk with a sudden realization of value in things others never notice" can metamorphose our detestable reasonableness and offset a whole planetary system of deadness. "The burning liquor of the moonlight" makes provable things mild by comparison. The poem often is about nothing that we wish to give our attention to, but if it is something he wishes our attention for, what is urgent for him becomes urgent for us. His uncompromising conscientiousness sometimes seems misplaced; he is at times almost insultingly specific, but there is in him—and this must be our consolation—that dissatisfied expanding energy, the emotion, the *ergo* of the medieval dialectician, the "therefore" which is the distinguishing mark of the artist.

Various poems that are not here again suggest the bee—and a too eclectic disposing of the honey.

Dr. Williams does not compromise, and Wallace Stevens is another resister whose way of saying what he says is as important as what is said. Mr. Stevens' presentation of the book refreshes a grievance—the scarcity of prose about verse from him, one of the few persons who should have something to say. But poetry in America has not died, so long as these two "young sycamores" are able to stand the winters that we have, and the inhabitants.

Poetry, 44 (May 1934), 103–6; *Predilections*.

ARCHAICALLY NEW

I N trying to reveal the clash of elements that we are—the intellectual, the animal; the blunt, the ingenious; the impudent, the imaginative—one dare not be dogmatic. We are a many-foliaged tree against the moon; a wave penetrated by the sun. Some authors do not muse within themselves; they "think"—like the vegetable-shredder which cuts into the life of a thing.

A comment accompanying three poems by Elizabeth Bishop, "The Reprimand," "The Map," and "Three Valentines."

Miss Bishop is not one of these frettingly intensive machines. Yet the rational considering quality in her work is its strength—assisted by unwordiness, uncontorted intentionalness, the flicker of impudence, the natural unforced ending.

Mere mysteriousness is useless; the enigma must be clear to the author, not necessarily to us.

> Such curious Love, in constant innocence,
>   Though ill at ease,

has the right air, and so has this:

> —Sure of my love, and Love; uncertain of identity.

The specific is judiciously interspersed with generality, and the permitted clue to idiosyncrasy has a becoming evasiveness. We are willing to be apprised of a secret—indeed glad to be—but technique must be cold, sober, conscious of self-justifying ability. Some feminine poets of the present day seem to have grown horns and to like to be frightful and dainty by turns; but distorted propriety suggests effeteness. One would rather disguise than travesty emotion; give away a nice thing than sell it; dismember a garment of rich aesthetic construction than degrade it to the utilitarian offices of the boneyard. One notices the deferences and vigilances in Miss Bishop's writing, and the debt to Donne and Gerard Hopkins. We look at imitation askance; but like the shell which the hermit-crab selects for itself, it has value—the avowed humility, and the protection. Miss Bishop's ungrudged self-expenditure should also be noticed—automatic, apparently, as part of the nature. Too much cannot be said for this phase of self-respect.

We cannot ever be wholly original; we adopt a thought from a group of notes in the song of a bird, from a foreigner's way of pronouncing English, from the weave in a suit of clothes. Our best and newest thoughts about color have been known to past ages. Nevertheless an indebted thing does not interest us unless there is originality underneath it. Here, the equivalence for rhyme, achieved by the coming back again to the same word, has originality; and one feels the sincerity, the proportionateness, and the wisdom of superiority to snobbery—the selectiveness.

One asks a great deal of an author—that he should not be haphazard but considered in his mechanics, that he should not induce you to be interested in what is restrictedly private but that there should be the self-portrait; that he should pierce you to the marrow without revolting you. Miss Bishop's sparrows ("Valentine I") are not revolting, merely disaffecting. It is difficult, moreover, not to allow vigilance to fluctuate; an adjective or an "and" easily eludes one, and a mere shadow of the unintentionally mechanical deflects interest. Some phrases in these pieces of Miss Bishop's work are less live than others, but her methodically oblique, intent way of working is auspicious; one is made aware of the kind of refraction that is peculiar to works of art, that is in accordance with a good which is communicated not purveyed.

In *Trial Balances*, ed. Ann Winslow. New York: Macmillan, 1935, pp. 82–83.

IDEAS OF ORDER

POETRY is an unintelligible unmistakable vernacular like the language of the animals—a system of communication whereby a fox with a turkey too heavy for it to carry, reappears shortly with another fox to share the booty, and Wallace Stevens is a practiced hand at this kind of open cypher. With compactness beyond compare and the *forte agitatio* competence of the concert room, he shows one how not to call joy satisfaction, and how one may be the epic one indites and yet be anonymous; how one may have "mighty Fortitudo, frantic bass" while maintaining one's native rareness in peace. Art is here shown to be a thing of proprieties, of mounting "the thickest man on the thickest stallion-back"; yet a congruence of opposites as in the titles, "Sad Strains of a Gay Waltz," and "A Fish-scale Sunrise." Meditation for the fatalist is a surrender to "the morphology of regret"—a drowning in one's welter of woes, dangers, risks, obstacles to inclination. Poetry viewed morphologically is "a finikin thing of air," "a few words tuned and tuned and tuned and tuned"; and "the function of the poet" is "sound to stuff the ear"; or—rather—it is "particles of order, a single majesty"; it is "our unfinished spirits realized more sharply in more furious selves." Art is both "rage for order" and "rage against chaos." It is a classifying, a botanizing, a voracity of contemplation. "The actual is a deft beneficence."

These thirty-three poems, composed since the enlarged edition of *Harmonium* appeared, present various conclusions about art as order. They are a series of guarded definitions but also the unembarrassing souvenirs of a man and

> . . . the time when he stood alone,
> When to be and delight to be seemed to be one.

Review of *Ideas of Order*, by Wallace Stevens (Alcestis Press).

In the untrite transitions, the as if sentimental unsentimentality, the meditativeness not for appraisal, with hints taken from the birds, as in Brahms, they recall Brahms; his dexterousness, but also his self-relish and technique of evasion as in the incident of the lion-huntress who was inquiring for the celebrated Herr Brahms: "You will find him yonder, on the other side of the hill, this is his brother."

Wallace Stevens can be as serious as the starving-times of the first settlers, and he can be Daumier caricaturing the photographer, making a time exposure watch in hand, above the title, *Patience is an Attribute of the Donkey*. The pieces are marvels of finish, and they are a dashing to oblivion of that sort of impropriety wherein "the chronicle of affected homage foxed so many books." They are "moodiest nothings"; "the trees are wooden, the grass is thin"; and they are

> . . . Evening, when the measure skips a beat
> And then another, one by one, and all
> To a seething minor swiftly modulate.

Mr. Stevens alludes to "the eccentric" as "the base of design," "the revealing aberration"; and employs noticeably in such a poem as "Sailing After Lunch," the principle of dispersal common to music; that is to say, a building up of the theme piecemeal in such a way that there is no possibility of disappointment at the end. But ease accompanies the transpositions and pauses; it is indeed a self-weighted momentum as when he says of the eagle,

> Describe with deepened voice
> And noble imagery
> His slowly-falling round
> Down to the fishy sea.

An air of "merely circulating" disguises material of the dizziest: swans, winter stars; that "body wholly body," the sea; "roses, noble in autumn, yet nobler than autumn"; "the mythy goober kahn"; "peanut people"; "rouged fruits"; "the vermillion pear"; "a casino in a wood"; "this tufted rock"; "the heroic height"; "tableau tinted and towering"; the fairy-tale we wished might exist; in short, everything ghostly yet undeniable.

Serenity in sophistication is a triumph, like the behavior of birds. The poet in fact is the migration mechanism of sensibility, and a medicine for the soul. That exact portrayal is intoxicating, that realism need not restrict itself to grossness, that music is "an accord of repetitions" is evident to one who examines *Ideas of Order;* and the altitude of performance makes the wild boars of philistinism who rush about interfering with experts, negligible. In America where the dearth of rareness is conspicuous, those who recognize it feel compelled to acknowledgment; yet such a thing as a book notice seems at best an advertisement of one's inability to avoid bluntness.

The Criterion, 15 (January 1936), 307–9.

IF I AM WORTHY, THERE IS NO DANGER

IN this drama of the death of Becket, Archbishop of Canterbury, we have in *Part I*, powers invisibly moving that in *Part II* culminate in the murder of the Archbishop; his sermon on Christmas Day standing as an interlude between the two parts. The women's chorus of Canterbury's poor bespeaks the apprehensiveness of the people, tremulous at the thought of business and private peace interfered with. And the priests, concerned for the Church, the Archbishop and themselves, aware that "Had the King been greater, or had he been weaker, Things had perhaps been different for Thomas," ask "What peace can be found / To grow between the hammer and the anvil?" It is difficult even today for conscience to know how justifiably inexorable the King might be, or how morally compelled to inflexibility the Archbishop was.

Four tempters appear to Thomas; the first advocating easy compliance; the second churchly authority:

> Disarm the ruffian, strengthen the laws,
> Rule for the good of the better cause.

The third advises that he be one with the people, ignoring the King; and the fourth, "the right deed for the wrong reason," martyrdom and fame through sanctity—the apex of seduction, "Dreams to damnation."

The historical re-realizing of the character of Becket is a literary *tour de force*. Wickedness is less troubling to those who are immersed in it than it is to a man like Job whose one thought is to serve and obey. It is easier to be faithful than it is to have faith, and to act with courage than to suffer with patience; but the mere martyr becomes the saint when he is able to say, as Becket does to the dismayed priest, "I am not in danger; only near

Review of *Murder in the Cathedral*, by T. S. Eliot (Harcourt Brace & Co.).

to death." The profiteer is reluctant to think of duty, or evil, or of the law of God. It is only a Samson of incorruptibility who is driven to exclaim, "Can I neither act nor suffer without perdition?" The saints are daily taken to task for beliefs which they never have held, and Mr. Eliot's Becket is not the last martyr to cry out,

> I give my life
> To the Law of God above the Law of Man.
> Those who do not the same,
> How should they know what I do?

One may merely mention the appropriateness of verse to subject matter and the consequent varying rhythms; the unforced suitability and modesty of presentation; the evidence that originality is not a thing sealed and incapable of enlargement, but that an author may write newly while continuing the decorums and abilities of the past; touches reminiscent of early idiosyncrasy, as

> . . . Sometimes at your prayers,
> Sometimes hesitating at the angles of stairs,

or "the dark green light from a cloud on a withered tree"; accuracies such as "the evasive flank of the fish," "the western seas gnaw at the coast of Iona"; and the self-contamination of the four tempters as they declare life to be "a cheat and a disappointment. . . ."

> The Catherine wheel, the pantomime cat,
> The prizes given at the children's party,
> The prize awarded for the English Essay,
> The scholar's degree, the statesman's decoration.

Mr. Eliot is sarcastic but not sardonic; we are made to realize that egregiousness is not primitive more than it is modern, and that we are ourselves satirized in the murderers' attitude to their deed; the Second Knight being "awfully sorry" and at pains to assure the public that "*we* are not getting a penny out of this"; another alluding to the balderdash of his companion as "his very subtle reasoning," and hazarding the further subtlety that the Archbishop had used every means of provocation, had determined upon death by martyrdom, and could not but receive the verdict, "Suicide while of Unsound Mind."

Mr. Eliot steps so reverently on the solemn ground he has essayed, that austerity assumes the dignity of philosophy and the didacticism of the verities incorporated in the play becomes impersonal and persuasive.

Poetry, 47 (February 1936), 279–81.

"IT IS NOT FORBIDDEN TO THINK"

THE *Collected Poems* of T. S. Eliot, complete except for *Murder in the Cathedral,* are chronological through 1930, and two tendencies mark them all: the instinct for order and a "contempt for sham." "I am not sure," Mr. Eliot says in "The Uses of Poetry," "that we can judge and enjoy a man's poetry while leaving wholly out of account all the things for which he cared deeply, and on behalf of which he turned his poetry to account." He detests a conscience, a politics, a rhetoric, that is neither one thing nor the other. For him hell is hell in its awareness of heaven; good is good in its distinctness from evil; precision is precision as triumphing over vagueness. In *The Rock* he says, "Our age is an age of moderate virtue / And of moderate vice." Among Peter the Hermit's "hearers were a few good men, / Many who were evil, / And most who were neither."

Although, as a critic, Mr. Eliot manifests at times an almost combative sincerity, by doing his fighting in prose he is perhaps the more free to do his feeling in verse. But in his verse, judgment indeed remains awake. His inability to elude "the Demon of Thought" appears in Prufrock's decision:

> Oh, do not ask, "What is it?"
> Let us go and make our visit.

and in the self-satire of "Lines for Cuscuscaraway and Mirza Murad Ali Beg":

> How unpleasant to meet Mr. Eliot!
> With his features of clerical cut,
> . . . .
> And his conversation, so nicely
> Restricted to What Precisely
> And If and Perhaps and But.

Review of *Collected Poems,* by T. S. Eliot (Harcourt, Brace & Co.).

One sees in this collected work, conscience—directed toward "things that other people have desired," asking, "are these things right or wrong"—and an art which from the beginning has tended toward drama. We have in *The Waste Land* a stage for a fortune-teller, for a game of chess, for a sermon, for music of various kinds, for death by drowning and death from thirst; finally for a boat responding gaily "to the hand, expert with sail and oar," and for a premonition of Peace. "T. S. Eliot forged the first link between . . . psychological and historical discoveries of his period and his period's poetry," Louise Bogan says; "far from being a poem of despair," *The Waste Land* "projects a picture of mankind at its highest point of ascetic control—St. Augustine, Buddha—as well as mankind at its lowest point of spiritual stupor, ignorance, and squalor."

In *Ash Wednesday* and later, Mr. Eliot is not warily considering "matters that with myself I too much discuss / Too much explain"; he is *in* them, and *Ash Wednesday* is perhaps the poem of the book—a summit, both as content, in its unself-justifying humility, and technically, in the lengthened phrase and gathered force of enmeshed rhymes.

Mr. Eliot's aptitude for mythology and theology sometimes pays us the compliment of expecting our reading to be more thorough than it is; but correspondences of allusion provide an unmistakable logic of preference: for stillness, intellectual beauty, spiritual exaltation, the white dress, "the glory of the humming-bird," childhood, and wholeness of personality—in contrast with noise, evasiveness, aimlessness, fog, scattered bones, broken pride, rats, draughts under the door, distortion, "the style of contentment." Horror, which is unbelief, is the opposite of ecstasy; and wholeness, which is the condition of ecstasy, is to be "accepted and accepting." That is to say, we are of a world in which light and darkness, "appearance and reality," "is and seem," are ineludable alternatives.

Words of special meaning recur with the force of a theme: "hidden," "the pattern," and "form." Fire, the devourer, is a purifier; and as God's light is for man, the sun is life for the natural world. Concepts and images are toothed together so that one poem rests on another and is part of what came earlier; the musical theme at times being separated by a stanza as the argument sometimes is continued from the preceding poem—"O hidden" in "Difficulties of a Statesman" completing the "O hidden" in "Triumphal March."

The period including *Ash Wednesday*, concerned with "The infirm glory of the positive hour," is succeeded by the affirmative one to which *Murder in the Cathedral* belongs, and "Burnt Norton" ("And do not call it fixity," "The detail of the pattern is movement."):

> We move above the moving tree
> In light upon the figured leaf
> And hear upon the sodden floor
> Below, the boarhound and the boar
> Pursue their pattern as before
> But reconciled among the stars.

In "Usk," Mr. Eliot depicts the *via media* of self-discipline:

> Where the roads dip and where the roads rise
> Seek only there
> Where the gray light meets the green air
> The hermit's chapel, the pilgrim's prayer.

One notices here the compacting of visible, invisible, indoors, and outdoors; and that in these later poems statement becomes simpler, the rhythm more complex.

Mr. Eliot has tried "to write poetry which should be essentially poetry, with nothing poetic about it, poetry standing naked in its bare bones, or . . . so transparent that in reading it we are intent on what the poem *points at* and not on the poetry." He has not evaded "the deepest terrors and desires," depths of "degradation," and heights of "exaltation," or disguised the fact that he has "walked in hell" and "been rapt to heaven."

Those who have power to renounce life are those who have it; one who attains equilibrium in spite of opposition to himself from within, is stronger than if there had been no opposition to overcome; and in art, freedom evolving from a liberated constraint is more significant than if it had not by nature been cramped. Skepticism, also constraint, are part of Mr. Eliot's temperament. Art, however, if concealing the artist, exhibits his "angel"; like the unanticipated florescence of fireworks as they expand with the felicitous momentum of "unbroke horses"; and this effect of power we have in "Cape Ann"—denominated a minor poem:

> O quick quick quick, quick hear the song-sparrow,
> Swamp-sparrow, fox-sparrow, vesper-sparrow
> At dawn and dusk. . . .

Another unemphasized triumph of tempo and terseness, we have in "Lines for an Old Man":

> The tiger in the tiger-pit
> Is not more irritable than I.

> The whipping tail is not more still
> Than when I smell the enemy
> Writhing in the essential blood
> Or dangling from the friendly tree.
> When I lay bare the tooth of wit
> The hissing over the archèd tongue
> Is more affectionate than hate,
> More bitter than the love of youth,
> And inaccessible by the young.
> Reflected from my golden eye
> The dullard knows that he is mad.
> Tell me if I am not glad!

In the above lines we have an effect—have we not?—of order without pedantry, and of terseness that is synonymous with a hatred of sham.

The Nation, 142 (27 May 1936), 680–81; *Predilections; A Marianne Moore Reader*.

NOT SEEN ON A COOK'S TOUR

THIS account of the experiences of a postal courier, a captain in the American Army, assigned to the Vienna-Warsaw-Budapest-Paris mail route, with headquarters in Paris, is of value as reflecting the period of economic exhaustion in Europe after the Armistice, and as telling something of an American Army service which few of us know much about. For the Society of Silver Greyhounds it will revive memories of luxury, deprivation and difficulty; and for the Cook-Baedeker conducted and restricted civilian it has various novelties to offer: a glimpse of the palace in Trieste once occupied by Maximilian of Mexico; an all-red town containing a stone lion with a red tongue; empty frames in the Royal Art Museum in Vienna, with placards reading, "Unlawfully removed by the Italian Armistice Commission"—the same being contradictorily alluded to in a catalogue as "Acquired from Venice, 1815"; and "Acquired from Venice, 1838"; the not often seen interior of the Imperial Palace with its hundreds of clocks—one of which the face was "about half the size of a dime"; one needed to be wound "every

Review of *The Course of the Silver Greyhound*, by C. Alison Scully (G. P. Putnam's Sons).

two years only"; and one of silver and tortoise-shell. "As it ticked, an Emperor Francis I and a Maria Theresa appeared on the face, followed by courtiers bearing crowns on satin cushions; then came a Spirit of Evil with a serpent in its hand, which was driven off by somewhat perky blows from the club of a Ministering Angel, after which Cherubim blowing trumpets descended from the heavens and . . . an Angel wrote in letters of gold, 'Vivant Francesco et Maria.' " At a Czechoslovak ball, "Hamburger steak seemed to be the favorite dish; rather odd for a ball, I thought," the author says. He recognized Mr. and Mrs. Paderewski at the opera in Warsaw, and on a railway platform where their train was delayed as they were going to the Peace Conference, handing food from a small supply of their own, to men, women and children, who were begging. On departing for America with "forty-five mail sacks, all full," he was given for conveyance a plaster bust of General Pershing wrapped in brown paper. He encountered a fearsome hotel room in which it seemed best to lay the mail pouch on the pillow and clothing on the pouch before attempting to sleep. After being ferried across the River March by means of a rope attached to a stake, his automobile subsided in mud. He "squirmed through barbed wire" into a nest of hostile Red Guards who detained him for the night. One of them came into the room without knocking, but "merely wanted me to carry a letter to his brother in Chicago."

Touristry and hazards to life make good reading, but it is the manner of the book which is striking; for while enemy barricades and worst hotels in the world have been mentioned in other war-books, one here gains the impression that our country may after all be bedrock in the ideal sense. A lawyer by vocation and the author of certain professional studies, Captain Scully seems not to attach great importance to this memoir. But the method of understatement as bringing out the ludicrous, the calm view of meretricious glamour, the feeling against war, the effect conveyed of true valor and efficiency, the grateful tribute to Prof. Philip Marshall Brown for the part taken by him in "preventing bloodshed and lawlessness" afford a specimen of American feeling which one hopes is not unique. One is at a loss for anything fine enough to say about it.

Brooklyn Daily Eagle, 14 June 1936, p. 12C.

POETRY IS NOT AN OPIATE

THE words poetic and fatuous ought not to be synonyms; and to encounter a mind which is against mock society, mock poetry, mock justice, mock spirituality—against any form of enslavement—is a benefit. There is something very satisfactory about the peculiar energy with which the author of this book pronounces such words as spade, toad, beast, plant. He is full of unlooked-for happily fantastic metaphor—"spider . . . very like a larch tree; you hemlock fanged with boughs"; "The Turtle bursts not, but pulls its six limbs in—head, legs, and tail." There is unlooked-for wording that is not so happy; and one wonders if Mr. Wheelright means by injustice what one means by it oneself; for his originality, creativeness, urgency, voracity of imagination and varied reading, make his philosophy difficult to assort. It is like a fish too strong for what has caught it but too restricted not to be hampered by the net.

Mr. Wheelright says the uses of poetry are to sound, show, teach; and pedagogically he is not timid. He says, "Many uncanonical sayings of Jesus are consistent with Gospel sayings; and this uncanonical wisdom . . . recovers for systematic Christianity moral qualities which Quietists now leave to Skeptics." "Forty Days"—concerning "doubt as the arena of faith"—recalls these remarks. "Each Apostle" certainly did "carry his own death with him to the center of men's will—that is to say, the city of God on earth."

As for the prerogative of poetry to show what might not have been perceived, exactly observed detail is a main strength of this book, and "North Atlantic Passage"—setting forth the contradictoriness and splendor of the sea—abounds in it. "Bottle-glass," "bubbles," "pearl in platinum," are coordinated with spray "clustered like bullets"; and "scalloped whitecaps"

> climbing never, always mounting,
> slipping always, never sinking,

qualify the statement, "This tumult flattens to pewter." Saying the opposite of what we thought was being said, strengthens the sense of exhilarating chaos; and throughout the book there is this aptitude for inversion. Mr. Wheelright says of the machinery of discourse and interrogation, in "Forty

---

Review of *Rock and Shell: Poems 1923–1933*, by John Wheelright (Bruce Humphries).

Days," "within these sections answers are given out before the questions to call them forth, and consequences are told in advance of their causes." In certain pieces, he has Blake's pellucid-aphoristic method; and has it instinctively. "Any Friend to Any Friend" is constructed with spiderlike care; and one offers as an instance of compact articulation, "Canal Street":

> Venice, whose streets are wavering reflections . . .
> . . . your seed-pod domes have scattered
> seeds of dome-capped towers over our cities
> constructed of still flames, whose streets are shade.

The author hopes his heavy poems are fine in structure like a rock, and light ones firm in structure like a shell. Readers with imagination will not grudge him his title, for there is here that which is strong and that which is fine; not completely and invariably the latter; for he can be daring to his own disadvantage; but if there is such a thing as modern American poetry, these poems are part of it.

Brooklyn Daily Eagle, 12 July 1936, p. 11C.

PERSPICUOUS OPACITY

GERTRUDE Stein has a theory that the American has been influenced by the expansiveness of the country and the circumstance that there are great areas of flat land where one sees few birds, flowers, or animals. There are no nightingales, she says, and the eagle is not the characteristic bird it once was; whereas "the mocking-birds . . . have spread . . . and perhaps they will be all over, the national bird of the United States"—one ambiguous significance which she makes unequivocal. We owe very much to Thornton Wilder for giving us the clue to the meanings in the book, since the mind resists a language it is not used to. Realizing the laziness of the ordinary reader, Mr. Wilder explains that Miss Stein, as a result of thinking about masterpieces of literature, found that in them the emergencies of the Human

---

Review of *The Geographical History of America, or The Relation of Human Nature to the Human Mind,* by Gertrude Stein, with an introduction by Thornton Wilder (Random House).

Mind were dependent upon the geographical situations in which the authors lived—flat land conducing to the ability to escape from identity, hilly land conducing to the specific and the insistent. The Human Mind and Human Nature, as he says, are here "invented terms" of a "private language,"— the Human Mind being selfless and without identity, Human Nature insisting on itself as personality; and "it cost pain to express and think these things." Therefore sadness and tears are mentioned as connected with Human Nature and the exterior trudging we do, as opposed to felicity and the operations of the Human Mind. When an author writes as if he were alone, without thought of an audience, "for an audience never does prove to you that you are you," it is this which makes a masterpiece. "Anyone who writes anything is talking to themselves," not conversing, "and that is what Shakespeare always has done, he makes them say what he wants said," and is "everlastingly interesting."

Miss Stein likes naturalness. "Nothing I like more," she says, "than when a dog barks in his sleep"; and in giving lectures here, her attitude to pretense was calculated to make those who overanalyze a piece of straight thinking seem like the milliner's assistant in *Punch* who asks a dull patron, "Would Modom entertain a feather?" She says, "I like to look about me," "I love writing and reading." In looking about her she has detected things; in science, "well they never are right about anything"; excitement "has to do with politics and propaganda and government and being here and there and society"; the electioneering politician "has no personality but a persistence of insistence in a narrow range of ideas" and is not exciting; whereas science is exciting and so is writing. Miss Stein says, "I wish writing need not sound so like writing," and sometimes she has made it sound like writing that one does not see at first what is meant. Looking harder, one is abashed not to have understood instantly; as water may not seem transparent to the observer but has a perspicuous opacity in which the fish swims with ease. For example, "There is no doubt of what is a master-piece but is there any doubt what a master-piece is."

To like reading and writing is to like words. The root meaning, as contrasted with the meaning in use, is like the triple painting on projecting lamellae, which—according as one stands in front, at the right, or at the left—shows a different picture: "In China china is not china it is an earthen ware. In China there is no need of China because in china china is china." Definitions are pleasurable, and words can fall sweetly on the ear:

> I like a play of so and so.
> Loho Leho.
> Leho is the name of a Breton.

"Winning is a description of a charming person," and "the thing about numbers that is important is that any of them have a pretty name. . . . Numbers have such pretty names in any language."

It is a feat of writing to make the rhythm of a sentence unmistakable without punctuation: for example, "When they said reading made easy reading without tears and someone sent me such a beautiful copy of that," or "No one knowing me knows me. And I am I I." In a real writer's experimenting there can be an effect of originality as one can achieve a kind of Venetian needlepoint by fitting into each other two pieces of a hackneyed pattern of peasant edging.

The Geographical History of America is offered as a detective story—"a detective story of how to write," making use of the political situation in the United States, with allusions to the two Roosevelts and the two Napoleons—and is not propaganda, which is platitude. A detective story is a conundrum, and this one has "content without form" and is "without a beginning and a middle and an end"—Chapter I following Chapter II, and Chapter III following Chapter II. The repeatings and regressions are, as Thornton Wilder says, sometimes for emphasis, sometimes a method of connecting passages, sometimes a musical refrain, sometimes playful. And, one adds, sometimes a little inconsiderate and unaccommodating and in being willing to be so, partake of Human Nature rather than of the Human Mind. And "nobody need be triumphant about that." But the book is a triumph, and all of us, that is to say a great many of us, would do well to read it.

The Nation, 143 (24 October 1936), 484–85.

COURAGE, RIGHT AND WRONG

"THE fertile periods of literature are those of philological innovation," James Laughlin says; and in his stating of the purpose of *New Directions* he is informed, modest, open, and orderly. But modesty in the other sense does not mark the story by him, "A Natural History." There is talent in it, and in his poem "The Cat and Dog at Love's Door"; and prudery in itself is a

---

Review of *New Directions in Prose and Poetry*, edited by James Laughlin IV (New Directions); *New Writing II: Autumn 1936*, edited by John Lehman (The Bodley Head); *The New Caravan*, edited by Alfred Kreymborg, Lewis Mumford, and Paul Rosenfeld (W. W. Norton and Company).

kind of obscenity. But it is not prudery to regret that this young patriot, helping to lead us out of the wilderness, in company with the editors of the other two books under discussion, should like them have courage of the wrong sort as well as of the right. The conspicuous item in *New Directions* is the self-reflexive essay by Jean Cocteau subtitled "The Painter Chirico," in which the author reciting as it were with eyes closed, exhibits a macabre irony and counterfeits cadaverousness with health in a way not short of wonderful. The translation by Olga Rudge is also of interest—showing that gifted intuition transcends small errors. John Wheelwright, critic and poet, contributes four "Elegies" of wirily obdurate rhythm. One sees by the cautiously exerted strength and effect of ulterior brilliance in "The Gentleman of Shalott" and two other poems by her that Elizabeth Bishop is serious and a writer. One suspects that Mary Barnard too, somewhat leanly represented by three poems, has a "future." Woodrow Wilson said we must have peace without victory, and Wallace Stevens writes sternly these days on the subject of peace *with* victory. He contributes to *New Directions* a group of poems distinct as usual in sound and substance, and to *The New Caravan* a poem about a triumphal statue of "gawky plaster," in a world in which covetousness is replacing patriotism, and Minerva's owl, the quaint citizen of Athens, is becoming a murderer. Kay Boyle, represented by three one-page stories, has a suicidal desire to be revenged on fate for having withheld something that she wishes; but even without it has a weapon which deserves a magnificent edge. Ezra Pound's wry wit and successfully unique use of italics appear in a tiny "Canto"—useful for comparison with his flock of imitators. We have a straight look from William Carlos Williams as contributor of a prose episode called "A Face of Stone"; and he has seldom done better than in his poem, "Perpetuum Mobile: The City." Miss Stein also is present.

New Writing, a bi-annual magazine in book form, "aims at providing an outlet" for writers whose work is held in question by "established magazines." Like *New Directions*, this book does not threaten to founder through fear of prudery, but there are in it examples of deep insight and superior writing. George Orwell's "Shooting an Elephant," which indelibly pictures mob power, is not only penetrating but unforgettable: "They had not shown much interest in the elephant when he was merely ravaging their homes, but it was different now that he was going to be shot." "When the white man turns tyrant it is his own freedom that he destroys." Mulk Raj Anand—contributor to *Life and Letters Today* and author of possibly the best condensed history of Persian painting that we have—has the turn of mind and the wording of a poet; creative inaccuracies of phraseology which are accuracies of meaning, impossible to any native American or Englishman; a mastering of dialect, that is to say, which preserves traces of foreignness, as in the plural for the singular, "she had touched the edges of prosperity." He has high humor and fine content: the converting of handicap into power. Martin Freedgood's "Good Nigger" and Leslie Halward's "Boss" are graphic and memorable.

The New Caravan set out to be "a collection of recent America's real and organic thoughts," and one hopes that Sheldon Cheney, writing of "The Art Theater Twenty Years After," is typically and organically American and may everlastingly be so. "A few of us . . . believe," he says, "that the theater can be so potent . . . that it may be one of the agencies changing social environment," but "what room is there for conviction, for faith, when an author is writing . . . about the petty personal activities of unimportant faithless people?" In the work of certain co-contributors he is confronted by the very thing which he begs us to overcome—a diseased and selfish insufficiency; and when editors muddy the purity of criticism by the demure implication that we further art by presenting refuse to which cold-hearted publishers are inhospitable, the impurity under the guise of purity is doubly a reproach. Mr. Cheney, however, is not the only sound soul which the *Caravan* values. Ruth Lechlitner's group of poems has authority; "Song of Starlings" especially, in the rhythmic force of gravity which precedes the last stanza; and her biographical note is a model of trustworthy sensibility and firm technique. There are two poems by Anne Porter which reflect character; as in turn, her biographical note approximates poetry. E. E. Cummings is represented by an expert biographical note rather than by his somewhat self-concealing two pages in the body of the book. To Conrad Aiken, Socrates' Greece and our cathedrals are equally shadows; social goodwill is hypocrisy, home life is lifeless. Stanley Burnshaw, on the other hand, says defeat is not defeat, and in "The Driving Song" bids you "Trust the dim light that drives / The torrents of your blood." Marsden Hartley, chivalrous and shrewd—a painter writing about painters—has in two reminiscences given us what one hopes is part of a book. He speaks of the hands of Charles Demuth, "Chinese in character," that seemed "to be living a life of their own"; of his paintings, "harmonious, possibly to excess" but reflecting "a master of the comic insinuation"; and in the other memoir— Albert P. Ryder—says, "A great spirit was among us, finding, despite the thirteen cents a day, that he could live copiously in that world of greater experience in which . . . the only immoral act is not to do one's best work. . . . Be humble before the deep purpose of the universe, Ryder would seem to be always saying." Emjo Bashee in his play about the masses has constructed an apparent monotony which is a rivet-driver of impact at every point. Clarkson Crane and Ernest Brace are close observers. One applauds Paul Corey's description of the tractor-binder needle "flashing over the straw like a snake striking," and Philip Stevenson's ball-game lines: "When a batter slowed his swing for a curve or speeded it for a fast straight one, timed it right, met it square, and cracked it on a line for a hit—well—." The professional balance and ripely humorous humanitarianism of this latter story do a great deal for the *Caravan*. In his play, *The Dead Are Free*, Alfred Kreymborg says "gabbling women gobble time"; and Edna Bryner in her story, "Prelude and Fugue," also coins an aphorism: "Scoop away the scum and the water is still stagnant." This story has energy, verisimilitude, and charm, despite a few touches which if true to life ought not to be, and an aesthetic courage which gives the writing at times a rococo, insisted-upon effect. Eva Goldbeck's soliloquy, "There Was No Time," is keenly applicable to all of us but in relation to the author's subsequent death seems sociologically both a dagger and a ghost.

Judged by our experimental writing, we are suffering today from unchastity, sadism, blasphemy, and rainsoaked foppishness; and since warnings to editors are not heeded, one would like to ask of one's fellow-writers, Is publication always better for one's talent than temporarily thwarted ambition? And since we can no longer depend upon the chivalry of editors to protect us against appearing at our worst, must we not achieve our own rigor?

The Nation, 143 (5 December 1936), 672–74.

A VEIN OF ANTHRACITE

A D A M , as depicted by any artist, has that artist's psychology, and William Carlos Williams' Adam is "a demon, fighting for the fire it needed to breathe"; self-repugnant at times, because of docilities in which instinct does not concur. This Adam is an exile who "never had but the one home." For him

> driven—
> out of Paradise—to taste
> the death that duty brings
> so daintily, so mincingly,
> with such a noble air—
> . . . .
> never would

Review of *Adam and Eve in the City*, by William Carlos Williams (Alcestis Press).

> peace come as the sun comes
> in the hot islands.

And he is tempted "to escape and leap into chaos." As Wallace Stevens says, "poets are never of the world in which they live." But does Dr. Williams realize—would he admit, one wonders—that every one is an exile? Possibly; for he is honest, prompt to submit his premise, serious to the point of bitterness, compassionate; ruled by affection and the compulsion to usefulness.

Temperament does not change and Dr. Williams is not becoming sociological, hostile to war or vivid against injustice; he was always all of these. But he does seem, with time, wiser and juster; and more completely the poet. In this collection his previous lines about "pinkflowered and coral-flowered peachtrees in the bare backyard of the old Negro with white hair" have been reset to advantage; his end rhymes and inner rhymes ("inevitable end / never wincing—never to unbend—" and

> with shells and hurricanes—
> the smells)

are those of the confirmed artist. The welded ease of his compositions resembles the linked self-propelled momentum of sprocket and chain; his respect for rhythm as personality being seen in his unwillingness to substitute meter of his own for the rocking-horse rhythm of the Lupercio de Argensola poems translated by him here; this Spanish group being of interest as showing Dr. Williams in an infrequent role.

Besides "Adam," and the translations, we have a poem entitled "Eve" (to the author's mother), one "To the Memory of Charles Demuth," lines "To an Elder Poet" (Emily Dickinson), a kind of interior-exterior retrospect of life, "Perpetuum Mobile: The City," and certain short pieces among which "To a Wood Thrush" well symbolizes the author's attitude to art; the collection as a whole being dedicated "To My Wife." Dedications, like more literal gifts, often lack effectiveness apart from the offerer's consciousness of having offered them; but this tribute, as some know, is far other than a becomingly kind perfunctoriness. One feels a great sincerity also in "The Crimson Cyclamen," the poem to Charles Demuth mentioned above; for in continuing the nature of the man it is not merely a supreme verbal flower-portrait but inherently a memorial; the harmony of the composition expanding with sharpened diminishments like the stag's antlered crown.

Dr. Williams is not a lugubrious poet; his work is occasionally even comic; and it is, all of it, made from what we have and are; it is American.

Anthracite coal did not sell at first; people wanted bituminous, and had to learn with time that anthracite is cleaner and burns longer. In the same way, Dr. Williams is substituting good fuel for the more transitory. The compressed fire in his work makes one think of the blaze in the blacksmith's forge, permeating dull iron until the metal gradually shows a clear red. It makes one sure that it is possible for the artist to use suffering and not be effaced by it. It, in all solemnity, enforces the Apostle's assertion, tribulation worketh patience; and patience experience; and experience, hope.

Brooklyn Daily Eagle, 20 December 1936, p. 15C.

IN MEMORY OF HARRIET MONROE

T H E aura of a friend who has died seems to abash the harshness of attempted acknowledgement, but if one may speak of Miss Monroe as if to praise, I think of her valor, her goodness to us all, her imperviousness to plebian behavior, her affection, the subordinatingly humorous trace of indulgence— one would not call it scorn—in her attitude to suggestions bearing on literary self-protectiveness, her independence of being squired or attended upon. I recall her matter-of-fact "Oh, I don't think anything of rain," and on another occasion—the day before her departure for Mexico some years back, at her hotel, in a room of frigid temperature, when she had consented to rest while talking to me, "I don't believe I need a cover. Oh, if you like; I'm not used to having anyone *cover* me." I recall when she spoke, and read from her work, at the Brooklyn Institute, her somewhat skeptical proffer of literary experience and opinion, her deep uninsisted-upon eloquence as she read *The Pine at Timber-line*; and despite her own belief in her mind—one dislikes the term "muse"—her air of alone-ness, her self-reliant and winning incredulity that it should be liked so very much as it was by us who heard her. Her fearless battle for art—and in art—was present for me there in a conspicuous though disclaimed laurel, and I can but reverently anticipate a continuously increasing expression of praise and gratitude for Miss Monroe from countless ones whose tribute would have astonished her.

Poetry, 49 (December 1936), 155–56.

CONJURIES THAT ENDURE

FOR some of us, Wallace Stevens is America's chief conjurer—as bold a virtuoso and one with as cunning a rhetoric as we have produced. He has naturally in some quarters been rebuked for his skill; writers cannot excel at their work without being, like the dogs in *Coriolanus*, "as often beat for their barking / As therefore kept to do so." But like Handel in the patterned correspondences of the Sonata No. 1, he has not been rivaled:

> The body dies; the body's beauty lives.
> So evenings die, in their green going,
> A wave, interminably flowing.

IIis repercussive harmonics, set off by the small compass of the poem, "prove" mathematically, and suggest a linguist creating several languages within a single language. The plaster temporariness of subterfuge is, he says,

> Like a word in the mind that sticks at artichoke
> And remains inarticulate, . . .

And besides the multiplying of "h's," a characteristically ironic use of scale should be noted, in "Bantams in Pine-Woods":

> Chieftain Iffucan of Azcan in caftan
> Of tan with henna hackles, halt!

The playfulness of such rhymings as "Scaramouche" and "barouche" is just right. But best of all, the bravura. Upon the general marine volume of statement is set a parachute-spinnaker of verbiage which looms out like half a cantaloupe and gives the body of the theme the air of a fabled argosy advancing.

Not infrequently Wallace Stevens' "noble accents and lucid, inescapable rhythms" point to the universal parent, Shakespeare. A novice of texts, if required to name author or century of the line, "These choirs of welcome choir for me farewell," might pay Wallace Stevens a high compliment; and the continuing of a word through several lines, as where we see the leaves

---

Review of *Owl's Clover*, by Wallace Stevens (Alcestis Press), and *Ideas of Order*, by Wallace Stevens (Alfred A. Knopf).

> Turning in the wind,
> Turning as the flames
> Turned in the fire,

is cousin to the pun of Elizabethan drama. We feel in the detached method of implication the influence of Plato, and an awareness, if not the influence of T. S. Eliot. Better say each has influenced the other, with "Sunday Morning" and the Prufrock-like lines in "Le Monocle de Mon Oncle" in mind,

> Shall I uncrumple this much-crumpled thing?
> . . . .
> For it has come that thus I greet the spring

and the Peter Quince-like rhythmic contour of T. S. Eliot's "La Figlia che Piange." Each has an almost too acute concept of "the revenge of music," of a smiling, Voltaire-like, self-directed pain, which, as John L. Sweeney says, "gores itself on its own horns." Each is engaged in a similar, very differently expressed search for that which will endure.

We are able here to see the salutary effect of insisting that a piece of writing please the writer himself before it pleases anyone else; and how a poet may be a wall of incorruptibleness against violating the essential aura of contributory vagueness. Such heights of the romantic are intimated by mere titles; one might hesitate to make trial of the content lest it seem bathos; but Wallace Stevens is a delicate apothecary of savors and precipitates, and no hauteurs are violated. His method of hints and disguises should have Mercury as consultant-magician, for in the guise of "a dark rabbi," an ogre, a traveler, a comedian, an old woman, he deceives us as the god misled the aged couple in the myth.

To manner and harmonics is added an exultant grasp of spectacle that is a veritable refuge of "blessed mornings, meet for the young alligator"; an equivalence for jungle beauty, arctic beauty, marine beauty, meridian, hot-house, consciously urban or unconsciously natural beauty—which might be alarming were it not for its persistent foil of dissatisfaction. This frugally unified opulence, epitomized by the "green vine angering for life"—in *Owl's Clover* by the thought of exploited Africa, "The Greenest Continent," where "memory moves on leopards' feet"—has been perfected stroke by stroke since the period of "the magenta Judas-tree," "the indigo glass in the grass," "oceans in obsidian," the white of "frogs," of "clays," and in "withered reeds"; until now, tropic pinks and yellows, avocado and Kuniyoshi cabou-chon emerald-greens, the blent but violent excellence of alianthus silk-moths and metallic breast-feathers—as open and unpretending as Rousseau's "Snake-

Charmer" and "Sleeping Gypsy"—combine in an impression of incandescence like that of the night-blooming cereus.

Despite this awareness of the world of sense, one notices the frequent recurrence of the word "heaven." In each clime the author visits, and under each disguise, the dilemma of tested hope confronts him. In *Owl's Clover*, "the search for a tranquil belief" and the protest against the actualities of experience become a protest against the death of world hope; against the unorder of this "age of concentric mobs." Those who dare to forget that "As the man the state, not as the state the man," who divert "the dream of heaven from heaven to the future, as a god," are indeed the carnivorous owl with African greenness for its repast. The land of "ploughmen, peacocks, doves," of Leonardo da Vinci, has been "Combating bushmen for a patch of gourds, / Loosing black slaves to make black infantry"; "the widow of Madrid / Weeps in Segovia"; in Moscow, in all Europe, "Always everything / That is dead except what ought to be"; aeroplanes which counterfeit "the bee's drone" and have the powers of "the scorpion" are our "seraphim." Mr. Stevens' book is the sable requiem for all this. But requiem is not the word when anyone hates lust for power and ignorance of power as the author of this book does. So long as we are ashamed of the ironic feast, and of our marble victories—horses or men—which will break unless they are first broken by us, there is hope for the world. As R. P. Blackmur has said, "The poems rise like a tide." They embody hope that in being frustrated becomes fortitude; and they prove to us that the testament to emotion is not volubility. Refusal to speak results here in an eloquence by which we are convinced that America has in Wallace Stevens at least one artist whom professionalism will never demolish.

Poetry, 49 (February 1937), 268–72; *Predilections*.

ICHOR OF IMAGINATION

IN *The Infernal Machine*, Jean Cocteau is as he was in *Orphée*, a " 'fantaisiste' on a known theme." Fulfilling the prediction of the oracle, as in Sophocles, Oedipus kills his father Laius (by accident, not knowing the victim), thwarts the Sphinx (the devourer of the young men of Thebes), is

Review of *The Infernal Machine*, by Jean Cocteau, in the English version by Carl Wildman (Oxford University Press).

rewarded by marriage with Jocasta (queen, his own unrecognized mother) and, having been made aware of his guilt, puts out his own eyes. "He solves riddles, becomes king and an object of affection, is envied of all, yet suffers a desperate end; never call a man happy until you have read the last chapter" is the summary by Sophocles, and with it one compares *The Infernal Machine* by Cocteau, also Carl Wildman's statement in the introduction: Cocteau "has dived with the greatest ease into the heart of the legend and brought back the almost sacred characters stiff with glory, brought them back to life, humanized them." Act I lacks contagion, but the play does gradually compel in the reader an author-forgotten, participating suspense.

A potent device in fiction or drama is that in which one character describes another to that other, unaware that he addresses the person of whom he speaks. Of this principle, inherent in the original *Oedipus*, Cocteau has made the most; as in Jocasta's remark, "What a courteous young man! He must have been taken care of by a very kind mother, very kind"; and where, misconceiving the recoil of awareness with which Jocasta recognizes scars on his feet, Oedipus says they were "from the hunt, I think." This principle is extended by Cocteau in the encounter of the Theban matron with the young girl in white, whom she warns against the Sphinx. Sophocles' device of the corroborating shepherd who confirms Oedipus to himself is matched by Cocteau in the episode of the talisman returned to Oedipus by Teresias— the belt Oedipus had given the Sphinx, saying, "This will bring you to me when I have killed the beast." It is a good moment in Act I in which Laius' ghost calls to Jocasta and the soldiers—undiscerned by them while they commiserate with one another on its non-appearing; and there is drama in the mockery of Oedipus by Anubis, in the nightmare—Anubis repeating the words Oedipus had naively spoken to the Sphinx, "Thanks to my unhappy childhood. . . ."

"Logic forces us to appear to men in the shape in which they imagine us; otherwise they would see only emptiness," Anubis is made to say—a statement of which the invisible ghost of Laius is an illustration; also a clue to the mind of Jean Cocteau himself. The extra character, Anubis—death's orderly—is an invention especially characteristic of Cocteau—cognate to Azrael and Raphael, death's assistants in *Orphée*, in which play "darkness has been shown in broad daylight," Mr. Wildman says. And always it is as the poet we must think of Cocteau—the person who says, "a thing can rarely at the same time be and seem true," who says he is "incapable of writing a play for or against anything"; and warns one that "it is not the poet's role to produce cumbersome proofs." M. Cocteau does not spread his cloak on the mud, he does not make promises, and his temperament permeates all his concepts; he is fervent. His ardor, voracity of presentment, inexhaustible fund of metaphor, and fastidious apperceptiveness seem rivaled only by that of the animals.

Aphorism is one of the kindlier phases of poetic autocracy—used from time to time in *The Infernal Machine*. Creon says, "The most secret of secrets are betrayed one day or another to the determined seeker," and the Soldier says, "A word of advice: let princes deal with princes, phantoms with phantoms, and soldiers with soldiers." But going beyond mere incisiveness, M. Cocteau sometimes imparts to a word a lovable neatness, such as we have in Aristophanes, where he speaks of the man who whiled away the time making frogs from fruit skins. We have it in Corbière and in E. E. Cummings; and in Clarence Day, where "L'hippopotame" is introduced as the Biblical behemoth.

Cocteau's vituperative tendency toward contentiousness appears in the Soldier's banter; and, as Mr. Wildman notes, in the Sphinx. Still more marked—as an asset, however—is the tendency to incantation. One sees it in Le Grand Ecart, in the Narcissus passage, where the river "cares nothing about the nymphs or the trees it reflects—longing only for the sea"; and in the Sphinx's self-characterization: "A judge is not so unalterable, an insect so voracious, a bird so carnivorous, the egg so nocturnal, a Chinese executioner so ingenious, the heart so unpredictable, the prestidigitator so deft, the star so portentous, the snake sliming its prey so intent . . . I speak, I work, I wind, I unwind, I calculate, I muse, I weave, I winnow, I knit, I plait. . . ."

The author has invested the play with modern emotion and, reveling in verisimilitude, causes Jocasta to say to Oedipus as she lifts him from the nightmare, "Don't make yourself heavy, help me." Oedipus, vivid and panting, arrests the eye, Jocasta half infatuates, the Sphinx—symbolizing the machinery of the gods' injustice—inspires fear, though her femininity and emphasized claws point to a crotchet on M. Cocteau's part. He appears to have an unfeminist yet not wholly detached attitude to woman; Jocasta being, like the Sphinx, "of the sex disturbing to heroes." Burdensome yet seductive, she asks, "Am I so old then?" and adds, "Women say things to be contradicted. They always hope it isn't true."

At the end of the play, instead of a somber dimming of personality, as in the Greek, there is an allusion to "glory," as completing the destiny of Oedipus. *Ought* horror to be believed?

Aware that imagination with Jean Cocteau is no appurtenance but an ichor, as it was shown to be in *Le Sang d'un Poète*, one has, nevertheless, the sense of something submerged and estranged, of a somnambulist with feet tied, of a musical instrument in a museum, that should be sounding; of valor in a fairy tale, changed by hostile enchantment into a frog or a carp that cannot leave its pool or well. In myth there is a principle of penalty: Snow White must not open the door of the dwarfs' house when the peddler knocks, Pandora must not open the box, Perseus must not look at the Gorgon except in his shield; and M. Cocteau, in refusing to be answerable to any morality but his own, is in the Greek sense impious and unnatural. But he is a very fine inhabitant of the world in which ichor is imagination, in which magic imparts itself to whatever he writes.

The Nation, 144 (6 February 1937), 158–59; *Predilections*.

THE FARM SHOW

CHOOSING a cluster of saplings not far from the show-ring, and having fastened the bridles of their horses each to a sizable trunk, they walked towards the livestock, noting the motley of exhibitors, farmhands, and non-descripts, rustic or fashionable, that loitered in an apparently bustling congestion.

Jersey heifers were being judged, shining strands like the hair of a Sieglinda that formed the lock at the end of the tail, striking the ankles of the animal at each step. The much waiting and deliberateness of the comparisons gave ample opportunity to notice the clamshell wrinkles about the eyes, line within line; the clipped-rabbit texture of the dewlaps seamed by longitudinal wrinkles, the hairs from opposing directions coming together in a ridge down the tail; the oiled hoofs and small devil-horn points on the forehead, polished to the texture of agate.

The animals continued to stand, tame but uncomprehending—in their eyes the accidental arch effect of wonder characteristic of cows. As the final entry was led in, slate-grey tinged with speckles on the shoulders, a man in a blue denim suit and farm hat remarked to an old fellow leaning on a knobbed stick: "Carrying a little more meat than the others, but I don't like the color." The judge stood off to consider, passed his hand along the back of now this one, now that; or stooped to examine the milk-veins.

Then came some bulls, locomotive-like forms with peg legs and faces like a chopping-block. Venturing a glance in Alec's direction, the old man moved a step nearer and said: "I don't see much in classed cattle; and I don't think much of grafting. I used to grow 'cots in California—Red Royals and White Royals; Big Royals and Little Royals. Grafting's all foolishness; it don't make them any better, but you have to do it for the trade. I've had pretty good success with vegetables, though; and flowers. You interested in flowers?"

Alec: "Some. Yes, I like flowers; I think they're very nice."

Old Fellow: "I've done a little scientific hybridizing. From five dollars' worth of seed I sold a hundred and forty dollars' worth of squash. It takes about seven years to perfect a type. It's not hard to do; it just takes time. I got the Boston Marrow and it took me five years to eliminate the green. About the *biggest* thing I ever raised was a castor-oil plant."

Nat (narrowing his eyes into an expression of simulated curiosity): "Did the beans yield much oil?"

Old Fellow (coming closer): "How's that? A castor-*oil* plant—*Ricinis Zanzibarensis*. The leaf measured fifty-two inches across. I made an oval flower-bed and I had that in the middle; then around that I had cannas; gladi-ole-as next, and next them red and white foliage-plants; and round the outside, geraniums—though I don't like the smell of them."

Alec: "I know more about straw than I do about flowers—though not any too much about that either. They've improved the mechanical strength but they don't seem to be doing much for the chemical strength."

Old Man (reverently attentive): "Yes, a sappy straw can't hold up a heavy head of grain. Six-foot straw is going to lie down if it gets wet."

Alec withdrew, impinging on Nat. "Suppose we have a look at the swine." There were Berkshires, Durocs, and Mule-foots, housed under roofed pens; also a much-heralded assortment of hybrids derived from four breeds— Poland China, Duroc Jersey, Chester White, and Yorkshire—said to come in larger litters, to wean earlier, grow faster, and cost less to feed than the pure-breds.

Nat: "Ever seen the old Apricot before?"

Alec: "I may have. He's all right," (leaning down and silking an ear of one of the Mule-foots). "You never felt a sweeter thing."

Nat: "Didn't you see that sign as we came in? 'Visitors must not touch the animals.' "

Alec: "Well, these are neighbors; they belong just down the road from us. I wouldn't want to hurt their feelings by acting as if they were pigs."

Nat: "They have certain pig marks about them."

Alec: "Silk ears, I suppose you mean."

Nat: "What's the difference between pigs, hogs, and swine?"

Alec: "Hogs are pork on the hoof; pigs are young hogs; and all are swine."

Nat: "True. Of course."

In a building, with specimen apples and varieties of corn, were samples of hay and alfalfa below fine-print bulletins on the wall, concerning grasses, harvesting, and the control of disease. Noticing a man, who was addressing six or seven people, catch up a handful of hay from a bin, Alec said: "He's talking about sun-drying and vitamins; see if he isn't," and they heard, handsomely enunciated as they came nearer, "This artificially dried alfalfa on a ten-pound per day ration increases milk production by two-thirds of a quart to one quart of milk per cow each day. To the value of this increase of milk should be added the saving in the cost of the grain ration, which may be cut down due to the high protein content of the alfalfa." Adjacent was the drier itself and a paddle-wheel-like arrangement for letting in the chopped hay in regular amounts, and a blower which fanned the dried hay into storage.

An observer taking a pinch of hay from the bin under discussion remarked: "Smells like tobacco." Manufacturers' representatives were expatiating on the advantage of storing feed in this or that type of silo. There were specimen grains under glass, sacks of fertilizer in rows, salesmen presenting poultry-feed and cracked oyster-shell. Nearby, two tree-surgeons, advocates of contrasting methods, stood conversing between their respective exhibits. Making a partial survey of the machinery, but disliking to leave without so much as a sight of the horses, Alec and his guest crowded through a compartment choked with handlers and owners who stood admiring "the matchless conformation at the ground" of a champion Percheron. The bobbins stood up stiffly along the ridge of the neck; and the bun of a tail was tied with blue yarn, projecting whiskers of clipped wheat-straw having been bound into the whole. With casual listeners worming past him a man of resourceful eye—custodian of the great Percheron—was insisting: "If the horse is to go barefoot, it should have plenty of horn; but if it's going to work on hard-surfaced roads . . ." Alec said to Nat: "Do you want to stay and hear about shoes and hoof-oils?"

Nat: "No. I guess Zenophon and the Army Manual will suffice for my needs."

On returning to the copse to get their mounts it seemed that all was as it should be, except the horses, in moving to avoid the sun, had wound the reins around the tree-trunks. A sense of sylvan remoteness was all-pervasive—in the dropping of an acorn, the scurry of a chipmunk over a log, the faint aroma of drying leaves, and with instinctively prolonged deliberateness they were approaching the exit when a touring-car that was being eased gently over the inequalities of the dusty road caused them to back out of the way. A man in a Panama hat and light homespun suit was driving the car and with him was a girl, erectly wiry, also in light clothes and wide white hat. Alec, suddenly under constraint, with an unnaturalness which even the awkwardness of his horse did not cover, smiled, waiting. Then, his manner changing, he called out pleasantly: "Hello, Camelford! Henrietta! Come ahead, we're big-hearted. You first." Camelford, acknowledging the pleasantry with a nod toward the stock-pens, said: "Anything here worth bothering about?" Alec twisted round and rested his palm on the horse's back, so he faced Camelford directly. "A lot; some merino rams and an immense porker with curling tusks. You don't want to miss him, even if you don't see anything else."

Camelford: "The world is full of them." And starting the car, he moved on.

Nat: "Funny, I thought for a minute that was Eloise with him."

Alec (recessively): "So did I."

Nat, suddenly curious, inspected Alec, willing to penetrate his recovered aplomb. Resistance to propinquity is love's apologia, and the more unimplicated the behavior, the blinder the involvement. But Alec, pricked to naturalness and the sense that hospitality had been dormant, said: "You know Henrietta Camelford, don't you? Didn't you meet her at Emily's the other day?"

Nat: "Yes, and before that; about fifteen times. No matter how often I see her, she never knows me, and I have to be introduced over again; but I don't mind keeping on."

Alec: "Scared of you, probably."

Nat: "I wonder? . . . You know, the authentic queen bee is industriously buzzed about—in my experience—"

Alec (startled and turning on Nat): "What queen bee?" With glances of mutual vigilance but with unimplicated goodwill, they looked ahead again, and the horses proceeded in unison.

Life and Letters To-Day, 16 (Spring 1937), 57–60.

FAME CAN BE MODEST

How Writers Write is of interest not that celebrated authors "have frankly divulged the devices of which they make use" but that they bring us into the workshop and maintain an attitude of studious enquiry.

One wishes that Ellen Glasgow's sanity, moral courage, and contagious spontaneity, were not marred by inadvertent triviality. John P. Waters' observations on the decline of the essay are too concave a mirror to be helpful;

Review of *How Writers Write: Essays by Contemporary Authors*, edited by Nellie S. Tillett (Crowell).

but humor is as the individual takes it. Virginia Woolf's "Letter to a Young Poet" might also come under the head of humor, but either as words of advice, "And for heaven's sake, publish nothing before you are 30" is frightening. In the Montaigne library-motto quoted by Elizabeth Drew, we have almost a substantive for the man himself: "I do not understand; I pause; I examine"; and the statement that "Lamb writes in a mood of comedy, Hazlitt in one of disillusion" also is valuable. But like Mrs. Woolf, Miss Drew is intimidating when she says, "Addison is a very dull writer." Moreover, she herself has not been proof against the mildew of the stock phrase. Writing is like living, better taught by example than by precept; and William Ellery Leonard defeats his purpose as though bewitched. To six authors however, without cavil, and to Miss Tillett for emphasizing them to us, we are much indebted.

Both writer and reader should find support in the sense of struggle and responsibility communicated by Joseph Conrad's preface to *The Nigger of the Narcissus* here reprinted; and incentive in his advice "to go undeterred by faltering, weariness or reproach."

Somerset Maugham puts at the disposal of the apprentice valuable conclusions. In drawing character, he says it is well to have a living model but "nothing is so unwise as to put in a work of fiction a person drawn line by line from life. . . . He never convinces." Again, "The writer whose creative faculty has been moved by something peculiar in a person . . . falsifies his idea if he attempts to describe that person other than as he sees him. . . . If he sees him tall, tall he must remain."

Paul Green's chapter on folk drama, in its conversational method, and use of the weather as prototype of mental fertility, is in itself a subject for study. His obligingly precise answering of somewhat awkwardly searching questions is notable.

In "Writing for the Movies," Philip Wylie's at times consciously uneffeminate manner is not just the bone for the literary starved dog, but it has marrow.

There is much to be learned from the industrious method, generous explicitness, firmness, honesty, and true humor of "How I Write Biography," by Harold Nicholson. "Never write a biography," he says, "about any one whom you personally dislike or from whose mental and topical atmosphere you are sundered either by prejudice or lack of knowledge. . . . Distaste may not cause [you] to violate the canons of truth and personality, but it will certainly induce [you] to violate the canons of art."

Mrs. Wharton's literary behavior, if one may be permitted the phrase, her uninflated accuracies, sudden sensibilities of statement, her feeling that the artist cannot ask too much of himself and must be prepared to pardon the public's "lack of imaginative response to his effort" is a true guide, not so much toward becoming famous, as toward an essential discernment of values. Admitting flaws, such as the too mundane phrase in context that is reduced and aware, *A Backward Glance*, from which the present pages are taken, steadies fortitude, demonstrates the worth of self-discipline, and revives confidence in charm made profitable by sincerity.

Brooklyn Daily Eagle, 18 April 1937, p. 15C.

THE DIAL: A RETROSPECT

A s growth-rings in the cross section of a tree present a differentiated record of experience, successive editorial modifications of a magazine adjoin rather than merge; but the later *Dial* shared, or thought it shared, certain objectives of its predecessors.[1] It is that *Dial* which I know best, and when asked about it recollections spring up, of manuscripts, letters, people.

I think of the compacted pleasantness of those days at 152 West Thirteenth Street; of the three-story brick building with carpeted stairs, fireplace and white-mantelpiece rooms, business office in the first story front parlor, and in gold-leaf block letters, THE DIAL, on the windows to the right of the brownstone steps leading to the front door. There was the flower-crier in summer, with his slowly moving wagon of pansies, petunias, ageratum; of a man with straw-*ber*-ies for sale; or a certain fishman with pushcart-scales, and staccato refrain so unvaryingly imperative, summer or winter, that Kenneth Burke's parenthetic remark comes back to me—"I think if he stopped to sell a fish my heart would skip a beat."

I recall a visiting editor's incredulity when I said, "To me it's a revel," after being asked if I did not find reading manuscript tiresome—manuscripts meaning the requested, the volunteered, and the recommended; that third and sometimes uneasy entrant inducing a wish, not infrequently, that the roles of sponsor and author might be interchanged, as when in a letter of introduction a (Persian, I think) typographic neighbor wrote us, "In the country where I came from, the people say: 'Ham Liyarat, Ham Tujarat'— Both pilgrimage and business, and so it is. Miss Z would like to have you see some of her poems."

Before being associated with *The Dial* editorially, I had been a subscriber, and still feel the impact of such writing as the W. B. Yeats reminiscences— "Four Years," "More Memories," and "An Autobiographic Fragment"; Paul

Valéry's "An Evening with M. Teste"; Mary Butts' "Speed the Plow"; D. H. Lawrence's sketches, "Rex" and "Adolph." I recall the aplomb of "Thus to Revisit," by Ford Madox Ford and the instructively mannerless manner of W. C. Blum's pages on Rimbaud; the photograph of Rimbaud as a child, reproduced next the translation of *A Season in Hell;* and Julien Benda's statement in *Belphegor,* "The problem of art is to discipline emotion without losing it." There was the continually surprising work of E. E. Cummings; William Carlos Williams' insurrectious brio; the exciting unconformity of the "Bantams in Pine-Woods" poems by Wallace Stevens. Thomas Mann's "German Letter" was for us a commentary on his fiction, as Ezra Pound's "Paris Letter" and T. S. Eliot's "London Letter" italicized their poetry. I recall the strong look of H. D.'s "Helios" on the page, and my grateful skepticism in receiving her suggestion that I offer work also.

Among the pictures, as intensives on the text, were three verdure-tapestry-like woodcuts by Galanis; Rousseau's lion among lotuses; "The Philosophers" by Stuart Davis; Adolph Dehn's "Viennese Coffee House"; and Kuniyoshi's curious "Heifer"—the forehead with a star on it of separated whorled strokes like propeller fins; Ernest Fiene, Charles Sheeler, Arthur Dove, John Marin, Georgia O'Keeffe, Max Weber, Carl Sprinchorn, the Zorachs, and Bertram Hartmann; Wyndham Lewis, Brancusi, Lachaise, Elie Nadelman, Picasso and Chirico, Cocteau line drawings, and Seurat's "Circus."

Such titles as "Sense and Insensibility," "Engineering with Words," "The American Shyness"; and the advertising—especially some lines "Against the Faux Bon" and "technique" in lieu of "genius"—seemed to say, "We like to do this and can do it better than anyone else could"; and I was self-warned to remain remote from so much rightness; finding also in Alyse Gregory's delicately lethal honesty something apart from the stodgy world of mere routine.

There was for us of the staff, whatever the impression outside, a constant atmosphere of excited triumph; and from editor or publisher, inherent fireworks of parenthetic wit too good to print.

In analyzing D. H. Lawrence's social logic, one usually disagrees with him, but I remember the start of pleasure with which I came on his evocation of violets, in the introduction to his *Pansies:* "Pensées, like pansies, have their roots in the earth, and in the perfume there stirs still the faint grim scent of under-earth. Certainly in pansy-scent and in violet-scent it is so; the blue of the morning mingled with the corrosive smoulder of the ground." Typical of W. B. Yeats' wisely unaccommodating intensity was his article on "The Death of Synge": "Synge was the rushing up of buried fire, an explosion of all that had been denied or refused, a furious impartiality, indifferent turbulent sorrow. Like Burns' his work was to say all that people did not want to have said."

And there were our at times elusive foreign correspondents: commenting from Germany, Thomas Mann; from Italy, Raffello Piccoli; from Madrid, Ortega y Gasset; from Vienna, Hugo von Hofmannsthal; from Dublin, John Eglinton; from London, Raymond Mortimer;[2] from Paris, Paul Morand;[3] from Russia, Maxim Gorki—the foregoing "active." And Bela Belazs (Hungary) and Otaker Fisher (Prague)—"inactive." Those were days when, as Robert Herring has said, things were opening out, not closing in.

I recall the explicit manual of duties with which the office was provided; and despite occasional editorial remonstrance, the inviolateness—to us— of our "contributing editor-critics," Gilbert Seldes (The Theatre); Henry McBride (Modern Art); Paul Rosenfeld and later Kenneth Burke (Music). Even recklessly against the false good, they surely did represent *The Dial* in "encouraging a tolerance for fresh experiments and opening the way for a fresh understanding of them."

Rivaling manuscript in significance were the letters; indivisible as art in some instances from their authors' published work. The effect of vacuum silence and naturalness in a note or two from D. H. Lawrence belongs for me with Mabel Dodge Luhan's statement, " 'Inessentials' seemed deadly to him who knew how to savor a piece of crusty bread on the side of a hill."

11 Feb 1929

> c/o Signor G. Orioli
> 6 Lungarno Corsini
> Florence Italy

Dear Marianne Moore

. . . I should have liked to see you in New York—but how was I to know you would like to see me!—many people don't. . . . We are staying here in Bandol near Marseille a little longer, then going back to Italy—so will you write me there, if you get the poems. And many greetings.—

Regarding my statement about the Pensées: there are lines in the book, that are the outcome of certain hurts and I am not saying that in every case the lines themselves leave no shadow of hurt. . . .

18 April 1929
Dear Marianne Moore
. . . I like the little group you chose—some of my favorites. . . . I think I shall withdraw that introduction from the book form—so you just keep any part of it you wish, & use it with your group of poems, as you wish. . . .

I knew some of the poems would offend you. But then some part of life must offend you too, and even beauty has its thorns and its nettle-stings and its poppy-poison. Nothing is without offense, & nothing should be: if it is part of life, & not merely an abstraction.

We must stay in this island a while, but my address is best c/ G. Orioli.

All good wishes

D. H. Lawrence

And from Paul Valéry in a reply to a letter about his *Introduction to the Method of Leonardo da Vinci: Note and Digression, Part I:* ". . . I am very pleased to hear you have found some spiritual refreshment in a work which so many readers feel a little too much hard and bitter tasted for common sense. But lucidity and will of lucidity lead their passionate liver in crystal abysses deeper than old Erebus. . . ."

Besides humor in our correspondence, there was satire as in A. E.'s reply to a suggestion that it was a long time since he had sent us work, "Hawks should not prey upon Hawks." And an ostensible formality of our own, concocted by Kenneth Burke, recurs to me—the answer to an advertising manager who complained that if books which had received long reviews and unanimous approbation elsewhere were to be damned at *The Dial* by brief notices and faint praise, might they not be damned somewhat more promptly? To this complaint from an acquaintance of Mr. Burke's who had not foreseen that someone he knew might be answering it, Mr. Burke said, "Why not give *The Dial* credit? As you have said, under our silence the book went through five editions. Now that we have spoken there may never be a sixth. Further, we are happy to learn that whereas we had feared that our 'Briefer Mention' was a week or two late, the continued success of the book has kept our comment green. We are, you might say, reviewing a reprint—a courtesy not all gazettes will afford you. . . . And are you, after all, so sure that a book benefits by having the reviews all let off at once like something gone wrong in the arsenal, followed by an eternity of charred silence!"

And we were not without academic loyalty in the guise of reproof, one complainant who had been writing some very good verse taking us to task about a review which he considered "unfair to the author" in being "nothing but a warped summary" and "dangerous" as "a bad piece of work . . . sponsored by a magazine of *The Dial*'s reputation." Almost simultaneously with the complaint we received a letter from the ill-treated author, who said in conclusion, "And may i tell you how much i was pleased with A. A. A.'s review of— —? Quite apart from the fact that it was kind, it seemed to me an almost miraculous 'summing-up.' I have always wondered if A. A. A. was a nom de plume. Will you extend my thanks to him or her?"

Occasional inadvertencies, moreover, at the expense of the acting editor, were not wanting—sundry inquiries requesting the attention of the "Active Editor"; a letter from one of our Spanish contributors beginning, "My respectable Miss"; and, resulting from statements about *The Dial* Award as acknowledging a contribution to "letters," offers to provide any sort of letters we required.

It was an office truism that a manuscript returned with a printed card had been read as carefully as a manuscript returned with a letter. But occasionally there was the compliment of anger, from those whose grievances were imaginary as from those whose grudges were real. Some were so incurious in their reading as to accuse us of anti-Semitism, or hid salt between pages to test the intensiveness of our reading. But not all "contributors who were not allowed to contribute" bit the hand that had not fed them. One to whom Alyse Gregory had given advice replied that before submitting work to *The Dial* he had not known there was such a thing as editorial reciprocity, that he had rejection slips enough "to paper the Washington Monument inside and out"; that at last, however, as a result of *The Dial*'s encouragement, he was appearing regularly in the XYZ (a fiction magazine of robust circulation). And I recall the generous disappointment of a writer whose work had elicited suggestions, when we returned to him a check that he had thought might be "used for a reckless meal."

Misunderstandings were with us in most instances, like skepticism that "doubts in order to believe"; and anything in the way of ill-wishing fulminations was constantly neutralized by over-justice from other quarters; by such stringence against encroachment as Raymond Mortimer's, when he wondered if certain requested work might not be done more to our liking by someone else, and by his patience when *Dial* work of his was reprinted without his permission; by Gilbert Seldes' magnanimity toward a minor phase of collaboration, and L. A. G. Strong's willingness to believe that editorial crochets are not all of the devil; by Yvor Winters' conscientious resistances and tincture of editorial virus; by such quixotry as Professor Saintsbury's hesitating to incorporate in an article on Poe material that Andrew Lang had not published, saying that once an article had been declined, he did not care to offer it "to the most different of editors"; by Professor Charles Sears Baldwin's acquiescent addendum in omitting a touch of underlining humor, "You are not only good friends but good critics."

To some contributors—as to some non-contributors—*The Dial*, and I in particular, may have seemed quarrelsome, and it is regrettable that manners should be subordinated to matter. Mishaps and anomalies, however, but served to emphasize for me the untoxic soundness of most writers. And today, previous victims of mine have to dread from me, as pre-empting the privilege of the last word, nothing more than solicitude that all of us may write better.

I think of Mr. McBride—his punctuality and his punctuation, each comma placed with unaccidental permanence, and the comfortable equability of his pitiless ultimatums. One does not lose that sense of "creeping up on the French," of music, of poetry, of fiction, of society sparkle, that came with his visits to the office. He did not "specialize in frights," nor in defamation, nor nurse grudges; and too reverent to speak in religious accents often, could not trust himself to dwell on personal losses, sentiment with him was so intense.

Gaston Lachaise's stubbornness and naturalness were a work of art above even the most important sculpture. Admitting to an undiminishing sense of burden that made frivolities or time-killings a sort of poison to him, he was as deliberate as if under a spell. I remember his saying with almost primitive-tribal moroseness, "But I believe in a large amount of work"; as on another occasion, "Cats. I could learn a million of things from cats." And there was, *when* there was, E. E. Cummings, the really successful avoider of compromise, of scarecrow insincerity, of rubber-stamp hundred-per-cent deadness.

I think of Charles Sheeler coping with the difficulty of photographing for reproduction Lachaise's polished brass head of Scofield Thayer, mounted on glass—glitteringly complicated from any angle—and have never seen anything effected with less ado or greater care; these scientifically businesslike proceedings reminding one of the wonderfully mastered Bucks County barn and winding stair turn.

Decorum, generosity, and genially decorative improvements to the proof-sheets were matched in Gordon Craig by an unsubservience justifying the surname "crag" as synonym for Craig. I recall Ezra Pound's precision as translator of Boris de Schloezer—reinforced by an almost horrendous explicitness on returned proofs. But nothing supplants in recollection the undozing linguistics and scholarly resourcefulness of Ellen Thayer as assistant editor; occasional untender accusations from authors, of stupidity or neglect of revisions, being found invariably to be reversible.

Padraic Colum's clemency and afflatus were not confined to the printed page, and upon his visits to the office, routine atmosphere was transformed into one of discovery. And John Cowper Powys, inalienable verbalist and student of strangeness, inventor of the term "fairy cardinal" for Padraic Colum, seemed himself a supernatural being; so good a Samaritan, any other phase of endowment was almost an overplus. As Mrs. Watson said of his conversation, "He is so intense, you don't know whether he's talking or listening." And his brother Llewelyn's dislike of "a naturalist with an umbrella," of shams and pickthank science, come back to one in connection with his gift for metaphor; also, to one who has known the shallows of a tree-bordered stream, his phrase, "the cider-colored reaches of The Stour." And though suicidally kind to victims of injustice, he was as aloof from the world of non-books as a fish without eyes.

Above all, for an inflexible morality against the "nearly good"; for a non-exploiting helpfulness to art and the artist, for living the doctrine that "a love of letters knows no frontiers," Scofield Thayer and Dr. Watson are the indestructible symbol. One recalls their support of James Joyce when *The Little Review* was censored for publishing *Ulysses*. "Our insistence that *The Dial*'s award is not a prize is frequently taken to be a characteristic pedantry on our part," they said, but "a prize is something to be competed for, an award is given—given to afford the recipient an opportunity to do what he wishes and out of that to enrich and develop his work." Nor was a gift ever more complete and without victimizing involvements.

As it was Abraham Lincoln's ideal to lift "artificial weights from all shoulders . . . and afford all an unfettered start," so here. And since in lifting weights money has its part, contributions were paid for on acceptance; for prose, two cents a word; for verse, twenty dollars a page or part of a page; for reviews termed Briefer Mentions, two dollars each. There were not special prices for special contributors—a phase of chivalry toward beginners that certain of them suspiciously disbelieved in. Any writing or translating by the editors was done without payment, Dr. Watson's participation, under the name W. C. Blum, being contrived with "quietness amounting to scandal." And payment was computed in amounts that are multiples of five. For example, as stated in our manual of procedure: "If a manuscript counts up to $15.98 or $16.01 or $18.01, the writer should be paid $20.00; and if same is more than $90.00 it should be computed in multiples of ten."

Writing is an undertaking for the modest. Those of us employed at *The Dial* felt that the devisers of the organization we represented could do better than what we were trying to do, and we shall ever feel their strength of purpose toward straightness, spontaneity, and usefulness. "If," as has been said, "*The Dial* had rough seas to navigate because it chose to sail uncharted zones, structure was the better tested"; and I think happily of the days when I was part of it.

[1] *The Dial*, founded in 1840 with Margaret Fuller as editor, Emerson as next editor, and Oliver Wendell Holmes, Hawthorne, and others as contributors, was discontinued after four years. In 1880 it was re-established by Francis F. Browne of Chicago, but in 1917 there was a change in editorial policy. The publication offices were moved to New York, and as a fortnightly with socially humanitarian emphasis, it was varyingly edited,

first by George Bernard Conlin, then by Robert Morss Lovett, with Thorstein Veblen, Helen Marot, Randolph Bourne, Van Wyck Brooks, Harold Stearns, and others as contributing editors. In 1920 it was refashioned and brought out as a non-political monthly by Scofield Thayer, editor, and J. S. Watson, president, with Lincoln MacVeagh as treasurer—and was entitled *The Dial*, The Dial Publishing Company Inc. being the full title of the company, as it had been of the fortnightly *Dial*. The Dial Press, it might be noted, was not synonymous with it but a separate organization. Then, after having Stewart Mitchell as managing editor, followed by—though not always with the same title—Gilbert Seldes, Alyse Gregory, Kenneth Burke, and Marianne Moore, it was discontinued with the July issue, 1929.

² Succeeding T. S. Eliot.
³ Succeeding Ezra Pound.

Life and Letters To-Day, 27 (December 1940), 175–83 and 28 (January 1941), 3–9; *Partisan Review*, 9 (January–February 1942), 52–58; *Predilections*.

TO UNMASK THE DEVIL

THIS time W. H. Auden has given us a poem entitled "New Year Letter," in octosyllabic couplets with an occasional triplet—addressed to Elizabeth Mayer; "Notes to the Letter," a group of poems entitled "The Quest," a "Prologue" and an "Epilogue." In "This *aide-mémoire*. . . . This private minute for a friend," he has as in the "Letter to Byron," chosen a form "large enough to swim in," and in it discusses our quest for freedom; we being—as epitomized by Montaigne on the title-page—"double in ourselves, so that what we believe we disbelieve, and cannot rid ourselves of what we condemn." The Double Man asks

> Who built the Prison State?
> Free-men hiding from their fate.
> Will wars never cease?
> Not while they leave themselves in peace.

"We wage the war we are," Mr. Auden says; and having not waged it well, we find ourselves waging the other kind of war also; from Spain to Siberia, from Ethiopia to Iceland; irresponsibleness having brought about "The Asiatic cry of pain," "The Jew wrecked in the German cell, / Flat

Review of *The Double Man*, by W. H. Auden (Random House).

Poland frozen into hell." We are in this "coma of waiting, just breathing," because of our acedia or moral torpor, and

> . . . true democracy begins
> With free confession of our sins.

"Dante . . . showed us what evil is: not . . . Deeds that must be punished, but our lack of faith." For "volunteers," it is "the penitential way that forces our wills to be freed," . . . "hell's fire" being "the pain to which we go / If we refuse to suffer";

> . . . each determined nature must
> Regard that nature as a trust.

When liberty has been recognized as "a gift with which to serve, enlighten, and enrich," then man is not in danger of being "captured by his liberty": girls are not "married off to typewriters," children are not "inherited by slums"; and instead of terror, pride, and hate, we have faith, humility, and love. Just now, however, "with swimming heads and hands that shake," we watch the devil attempting to destroy the root of freedom,—that "absence of all dualities," that grows from "the roots of all togetherness," for "no man by himself has life's solution." "The Prince that Lies" he who

> . . . controls
> The moral asymmetric souls,
> The either-ors, the mongrel halves,

"knows the bored will not unmask him"—the cynics who in disillusion, as observed by Hans Kohn, "desert their ideals," defending themselves to us with the logic of frogs under a stork king, explaining that a creature with legs so much longer than theirs, ought to be able to see further than they.

W. H. Auden, however, is not bored, nor is his imagination tired, and he has attacked the devil with a complexly deadly weapon of magnificent clarity. "The great schismatic" "hidden in his hocus-pocus," has "the gift of double focus," but is here unmasked;

> . . . torn between conflicting needs.
> He's doomed to fail if he succeeds.
> . . . .
> If love has been annihilated,
> There's only hate left to be hated.

Understanding his art as "The fencing wit of an informal style," Mr. Auden has not taken a leaf from Pope, he has devised the needful complement whereby things forgot are henceforth known; and with the apparently effortless continuity of the whale or porpoise in motion, evolves suddenness of thought or treatment, changes at will from English to Latin, Greek, or a modern language, instead of naming things, presents them; and has throughout as the crowning ornament of his work, paradox at its compactest. Since the "New Year Letter" incorporates rather than indicates, the plodding reader might gain time by reading the "Notes" before reading the "Letter." As an enemy of primness, Mr. Auden sometimes requires that we enjoy "the Janus of a joke" at our own expense as when he relegates the feminine to Laocoön status,

> *Das Weibliche** that bids us come
> To find what we're escaping from.

He is laughing at us also when he rhymes "ideas" with "careers" and "delta" with "skelter." "Industry's whosoever will, let him come," is another matter. To use the temptations in the wilderness or the Christian symbols, blood or cross, as handy apparatus of trade, is soul-diminishing. And as is here made impossible to forget—to be low is not to be lowly.

One is sorry that there has been pain to be covered with "a worldly smile," that injustice has helped the discerning of a distinction between tribulation and temptation; that we are all "the living dead" beneath selfishness and ingratitude; furthermore, that few have seen Jesus and so many "Judas the Abyss." Persuading us to "the positive" rather than "the negative ways through Time," and showing the cure for either tribulation or temptation to be humility, Mr. Auden's New Year thoughts

> Convict our pride of its offense
> In all things, even penitence.

For we have here, despite much about the devil, a poem of love and things of heaven, with a momentum of which Buxtehude's or Bach's ordered beauty need not be ashamed, the melodic entirety being something to marvel at; and all, with the succinctness of prose.

Decision, 1 (May 1941), 70–71.

* The feminine

COMPACTNESS COMPACTED

W O M E N are not noted for terseness, but Louise Bogan's art is compactness compacted. Emotion with her, as she has said of certain fiction, is "itself form, the kernel which builds outward form from inward intensity." She uses a kind of forged rhetoric that nevertheless seems inevitable. It is almost a formula with her to omit the instinctive comma of self-defensive explanation, for example, "Our lives through we have trod the ground." Her titles are right poetically, with no subserviences for torpid minds to catch at; the lines entitled "Knowledge," for instance, being really about love. And there is fire in the brazier—the thinker in the poet. "Fifteenth Farewell" says:

> I erred, when I thought loneliness the wide
> Scent of mown grass over forsaken fields,
> Or any shadow isolation yields.
> Loneliness was the heart within your side.

One is struck by her restraint—an unusual courtesy in this day of bombast. The triumph of what purports to be surrender, in the "Poem in Prose," should be studied entire.

Miss Bogan is a workman, in prose or in verse. Anodynes are intolerable to her. She refuses to be deceived or self-deceived. Her work is not mannered. There are in it thoughts about the disunities of "the single mirrored against the single," about the devouring gorgon romantic love, toward which, as toward wine, unfaith is renewal; thoughts about the solace and futilities of being brave; about the mind as a refuge—"crafty knight" that is itself "Prey to an end not evident to craft"; about grudges; about no longer treating memory "as rich stuff . . . in a cedarn dark, . . . as eggs under the wings," but as

> Rubble in gardens, it and stones alike,
> That any spade may strike.

We read of "The hate that bruises, though the heart is braced"; of "one note rage can understand"; of "chastity's futility" and "pain's effrontery"; of "memory's false measure." No Uncle Remus phase of nature, this about the crows and the woman whose prototype is the briar patch: "She is a stem

---

Review of *Poems and New Poems*, by Louise Bogan (Charles Scribner's Sons).

long hardened, / A weed that no scythe mows." Could the uninsisted-on surgery of exposition be stricter than the term "red" for winter grass, or evoke the contorted furor of flame better than by saying the fire ceased its "thresh?" We have "The lilac like a heart" (preceded by the word "leaves"); "See now the stretched hawk fly"; "Horses in half-ploughed fields / Make earth they walk upon a changing color." Most delicate of all,

> . . . we heard the cock
> Shout its unplaceable cry, the axe's sound
> Delay a moment after the axe's stroke.

Music here is not someone's idol, but experience. There are real rhymes, the rhyme with vowel cognates, and consonant resonances so perfect one is not inclined to wonder whether the sound is a vowel or a consonant—as in "The Crossed Apple":

> . . . this side is red without a dapple,
> And this side's hue
> Is clear and snowy. It's a lovely apple.
> It is for you.

In "fed with fire" we have expert use of the enhancing exception to the end-stopped line:

> And spiny fruits up through the earth are fed
> With fire;

Best of all is the embodied climax with unforced subsiding cadence, as in the song about

> The stone—the deaf, the blind—
> That sees the birds in flock
> Steer narrowed to the wind.

When a tune plagues the ear, the best way to be rid of it is to let it forth unhindered. This Miss Bogan has done with a W. H. Auden progression, "Evening in the Sanitarium"; with G. M. Hopkins in "Feuer-Nacht"; Ezra Pound in "The Sleeping Fury"; W. B. Yeats in "Betrothed"; W. C. Williams in "Zone." All through, there is a certain residual, securely equated seventeenth-century firmness, as in the spectacular competence of "Animal, Vegetable, and Mineral."

What of the implications? For mortal rage and immortal injury, are there or are there not medicines? Job and Hamlet insisted that we dare not let ourselves be snared into hating hatefulness; to do this would be to take our own lives. Harmed, let us say, through our generosity—if we consent to have pity on our illusions and others' absence of illusion, to condone the fact that "no fine body ever can be meat and drink to anyone"—is it true that pain will exchange its role and become servant instead of master? Or is it merely a conveniently unexpunged superstition?

Those who have seemed to know most about eternity feel that this side of eternity is a small part of life. We are told, if we do wrong that grace may abound, it does not abound. We need not be told that life is never going to be free from trouble and that there are no substitutes for the dead; but it is a fact as well as a mystery that weakness is power, that handicap is proficiency, that the scar is a credential, that indignation is no adversary for gratitude, or heroism for joy. There are medicines.

The Nation, 153 (15 November 1941), 486; *Predilections.*

WHO SEEKS SHALL FIND

DEPTH is not the fashion, and even the well-disposed reader may startle at certain paradoxical avowals in these bravely deep poems by José Garcia Villa. A new poet, "a young native of the Philippines," this author; and his work is for the most part new to print, but final wisdom encountered in poem after poem merely serves to emphasize the disparity between tumult and stature.

Mr. Villa thinks of a poem as musical, slender, secret, wise, humble, and rapt; with Deity housing that "hidden voltage" in it which only fire may safely touch. In some of the poems a new rhyming—"a principle of reversed consonance never used in English poetry before, nor in any poetry"—substitutes for the crudeness of rhyme a more gently weighted, more richly textured effect:

> It's a mastery of death   (a)
> And that's Love. It's the bequeathèd (a)

Review of *Have Come, Am Here,* by José Garcia Villa (The Viking Press).

> Mind of Christ. It's I, it's Love   (b)
> What the great deaths reveal.   (b)

Here d-followed-by-th in the word "death" rhymes with th-followed-by-d in the word "bequeathèd," and the l-followed-by-v of "Love," is rhymed with the v-followed-by-l of "reveal." The delicacy with force of such writing reminds one of the colors of black ink from a hogs'-hair brush in the hand of a Chinese master. "The antique ant" is a drawing; the watermelon, yellow strawberry, giraffe, and leopard poems are, in effect, paintings; nor could reticence be more eloquent than in the poems beginning "And if the heart cannot love" and "She has gone."

"It is easy to become obscure if one says too little of too personal an experience," Charles Mauron says in another connection; and surely tenderness devoid of mawkishness is a thing which personality makes difficult. But only the purblind would dissect a rose to determine its fragrance, or a poem to discover its secret; for a poem deprived of its mystery would no longer be a poem. And mystery is different from obscurity. So Mr. Villa is with great effect, at times, "deliberately aiming just beside the mark"; as when he says, "Sir, there's a tower of fire in me / Binding me with terrible strength," or:

> The wind shines
>   The sun blows:
> . . . .
> The birds bloom,
>   The flowers fly:
> The bees sing,
>   The birds sting!

Some of Mr. Villa's marvels suggest similar ones.

> Dared my groveling bloodscape,
> It to a dazzling diamond made

and various reiterated sighs and mortal groans are not unconscious of G. M. Hopkins. E. E. Cummings, who would consider it blasphemy to interfere with another's poem, has none the less provided subsequent palmers and templars with a certain antecedent courage in the matter of odd diction. Mr. Villa's uncapitalized "am so very am / and speak so very speak"; his "Angelity" and "instancy" and "deinstance" have a kind of two-twilled authority; nor should Mr. Cummings deprecate Poem 13 on the ground that it has no title, or for other reasons.

There is a one that createth me,
He that of me is my sun my sum
My father and my only child:—
Behold—we do wander, wonder
Which of us is the uplifted candle,
Which of us will read, will rede
The image of our living shadow;
O there's a Third of us will live,
There's a Third of us will dive
Out of the Light, out of the Wooed,
Into eternity dazzling dark;
O but here shall turn, shall spring
The word young, young, blue-eyed yet,
Slender as an infant fawn and
Whole without death's antlers yet.

The lyric beginning "Always did I want more God" is beautifully made: the wording is so natural one does not at first perceive the fugue-like recurrence of God, rood, blood, yield, field, distilled. Nor has Mr. Villa been indifferent to those illumined wayfarers, Dante, Spenser, and Blake, who adjure us to "speak with moderation; but think with great fierceness."

Amid the mysteries of the poems about divinity, the principle of reversed consonance has been extended to content, with a result that is indeed strange, and deadly to self-esteem. Though severe responsibility is imposed by the statement

> The shadow of a great man
> Is always Christ,

it is not conventional to say "Christ progresses from me," or "Greatly imagine me, my God." But is it not true that "God is messageless" unless one listens? Is it not true that God has been cast out unless we "permit him to be of our Own Blood?" John Bunyan could have understood José Villa's statement, "I saw myself reflected / In the great eye of the grave," and could have accepted the confession that with "the Nativity of Everness" "My human eyes" become "God's lens / Through which I see—all of Love."

Since Mr. Villa does not disguise exaltation, one must not feign to be unimplicated. And would not Everyman—however camouflaged from himself—be glad to believe that God is present and is accessible to personality?

> How shines my dark-world
> Upon the sun! and gives it
> Light . . .

is humility's paradox. It truly constrains us to admit that transfiguration is not incompatible with intimacy and that what one seeks one shall find.

The Nation, 155 (17 October 1942), 394.

SOME POEMS OF FRIEDRICH HÖLDERLIN

FOR some of us it is not so much that Hölderlin is forgotten as that we have not known him, and James Laughlin has done us a service in issuing these twelve early lyrics with a translation by Frederic Prokosch,—the German facing the English. Even before turning to the poems, one is benefited by the reflected attitude of Mr. Prokosch in the biographical note,—his deep unintrusive gratitude lending verity to the statement that Hölderlin's worship of nature and passion for Hellas are penetrating and affirmative.

Hölderlin was born in 1770 and died in 1843. That his last thirty-six years of life were clouded by incurable—though harmless—madness, is in poignant contrast with the impression his work gives, of self-discipline, reverence, and exaltation.

Use of the Greek long syllable followed by three short syllables—"a place for all my grief"—indicates the ardor without bluster of Hölderlin's mind, and Mr. Prokosch in his version achieves the same modest directness. An indeed remarkable continuity, the eight stanzas "To Nature," as approximating the German, in accent, syllable, and rhyme:

> Often I lay lost in senseless grieving
> And the world's own fulness gathered me,
> As a river, after endless weaving,
> Winds at last into the open sea;
> I would hurl myself from the exhausting
> Solitude of time and come
> To the embrace of the everlasting,
> Like a pilgrim to his father's home.

There is an impassioned humility in the run-over ending, as where "gray" is separated from "clouds"—in the German—and "my" from "eyes." For these Mr. Prokosch provides an equivalent, if not the actual verbal transcript:

Review of *Some Poems of Friedrich Hölderlin*, translated by Frederic Prokosch (New Directions).

> . . . on
> The dusky clouds.
>
> . . . .
>
> More clearly, more serenely, happy
> One, . . .

We note also—in the lines "To Nature"—the modesty of the unindented rhymes.

The vibrant honesty of the work provokes an eager loyalty of disagreement. In the stanzas entitled "Man,"

> . . . and soon he is fully grown; the beasts
> Avoid him, knowing man for a different kind,

might one risk the more informal

> . . . and he is soon full grown; avoided by the
> Animals, who know that man is different?

Though the weighting of phrases in the two languages does not correspond exactly, something seems lost by altering the order of words in English from the order in German, and

> Stillness of ether I understood,
> But the words of man never

suggests this possibility:

> I understood the soundless air
> Human speech I could not grasp.

Sometimes one cannot have both the desirable word and the desirable rhyme, as where "Stoppelfeld" is not translated stubblefield because "gone" requires as rhyme "field of stone."

German word-masonry, with its accompanying sound harmony, defies translation, as Mr. Prokosch observes in his foreword. How talented his

> . . . and deep
> To the current falls the brook: . . .

for

> . . . in dem Strom
> Tief fallt der Bach, . . .

and

> . . . in the
> Saintly sobering water

for

> Ins heilignuchterne Wasser.

Agree or disagree, one is benefited; this is a valuable presentation—a Jacob's ladder for the heart that is not hard. Here is nature worship that we cannot resent; or to speak more exactly, the forces of nature embodying worship as set forth in the New Testament. At any stage of growth, "the heart desires too much"; but for Hölderlin, nature was not an intensive on nothing; it "made golden . . . a life of poverty." His nobility and capacity for renunciation met suffering as their proving-ground.

The initial lines of "Patmos" are in themselves a psalm of life:

> Near, near and
> Difficult to grasp is the Almighty.
> Where the danger lies, there
> Likewise lies the salvation.
> In darkness dwell
> The eagles. . . .

The interpenetrating of literal and figurative,—"the massed summits" of the Alps, the peaks of existence, the dazzle of purity, the gulfs impassable to frail personality however close-gathered, the bridge disproportionate to the torrent, the thought of living water, the words "faithful" and "wings," with their overtone of "O that I had the wings of a dove,"—is incalculably magnificent. And the background is the foreground in its combined consciousness of Acts 17:27, Rev. 1:15 and 17 and Isaiah 40:31: Near is the Lord "if haply we may find him." "And when I saw him, I fell at his feet as dead, and his voice as the sound of many waters saying, . . . I am he that liveth"; "they shall mount up with wings as eagles, they shall run, and not be weary; and they shall walk, and not faint."

Accent, 3 (Summer 1943), 247–48.

"WE WILL WALK LIKE THE TAPIR"

"SAVAGE" and "brutal" are false terms, the brute is so often the man. In a documentary-film close-up, some years ago, of an elephant trimming a turf-bordered walk, the fingertip of the trunk was shown plucking off grass to an edge of better than humanly sheared precision. The elephant that piles teak scans the result from a distance, and if a timber projects too far, returns and pushes it into place with his head. Here at home, as the press seems to enjoy reminding us, the army is being reinforced by paratroop dogs and patrol dogs.

In the September, 1927, issue of the *Forum*, in an article entitled "Can Man Keep Savage Virtues," Dr. Herbert J. Spinden says, "Brutality is hardly a proper character of savages or even of brutes. . . . Real people of the wilds are timid and retiring creatures, for all their sturdiness of bone and muscle"; and in the same article he speaks of a museum exploration trip in Honduras, made with the help of Paya Indians. Despite his "ignorance of the first arts of life," he says they were willing to aid him—seven of them, besides a woman with a baby—poling their way up the Plantain River in two boats hollowed out of mahogany logs. Having several specimens of worked stone to carry, they came to a deep pool in the creek with precipitous walls on either side. The stones were lashed to poles and could perhaps have been dragged through the water by means of ropes, but saying, "We will walk like the tapir," they tramped into the pool, and across, in water three or four feet over their heads. Dr. Spinden preferred to climb the rocky wall rather than go through the water, but before beginning the climb he handed his watch to an Indian, explaining that it was to be kept dry. "The Indian wrapped the timepiece in a leaf and putting the little package in his mouth dived to the other side." The woman was taking home a large grinding stone that weighed at least seventy-five pounds, and with the child slung in front carried the stone on her back the eight miles out to the river, helped by the men only at the deep pool.

A recent lecture by Dr. Spinden—"Many-Sided Latin America" was the title—augmented the view set forth in the "Savage Virtues" article, especially certain comments on Columbus as discoverer of the discoverers of America—the Indians, namely, who brought him the first pineapples he had eaten and excited wonder by "sleeping in a strange net they called a hammock." Then in answer to questions touching on the superiority hobgoblin, Dr. Spinden said anthropologists "think there is little difference between the highly skilled people of every race. The man with skill has a flair," that is all; or should one say, that is everything. "The difference is between the best members of a group and the worst members of the group, and the trouble comes from the people who haven't quite so much superiority as they think they have." (This feeling about flair would seem to be related to Amédée Ozenfant's thought that "talent in art is the innate awareness of what is great." Nor is Henry McBride playing cat's-cradle with us, one suspects, when he says he has the answer to a question young painters incline to ask. They wish to know what makes painting great, and the answer is easy— greatness of character.)

One of the most eloquent phases of savage resourcefulness is thrift, involving as it does responsibility to nature. "The actual use is a technique"— Dr. Spinden's good-neighbor discussion again—"but back of it is a discipline." When the Indian caught a salmon and threw head and backbone into the river to generate new salmon, "it was unscientific, but as emotional restraint against waste it was magnificent." After removing a plant, the Indian was careful to drop a seed in the hole, and it is humbling to realize that no species of animal or growing thing was exterminated in America till the coming of our savage selves.

In England paper, metals, rags, *and bones* are salvaged. One pays a fine for throwing away a used bus ticket that could have been conserved as waste paper, and the grocer is not expected to furnish a bag with what he sells but to put it into the basket or shopping bag brought by the purchaser. If inadvertent waste is dismaying, intentional waste is treason; one does not like to be told by a fastidious, supposedly educated person that if we process our cans, "forty people who are paid to remove the paper from cans will lose their jobs." Self-interested waste, moreover, as part of chain advertising, is now a curious porcupine quill in the torso of slumbering civic indifference. Launched in rapid succession from widely separated cities, stout packets of order blanks and data with illustrations importune us to buy nuts, fruits, garden tools, magazines, electric appliances, dishes, or wearing apparel; and in answer to a request that one's name be removed from such and such a list, one is told it is not the firm's intention to burden anyone with an unwanted volume of mail, but that it is impossible to remove names on request, since circulars are mailed to addresses rented from others who have compiled them!

We could bear it if cosmetics that resemble house paint when worn, bugaboo perfumes, circus-wagon shoes, and lapel ornaments of the weather-vane variety could be converted into munitions. If uncompact printing and non-acute, speciously luxurious publishing could see themselves in a Joyce distorting mirror of energetic economy, alas, "Suffoclose! Shikespower! Seu-dodanto! Anonymoses!"

Morale, Professor Henry Wyman Holmes tries to persuade us in his book

The Road to Courage, implies something "over and above one's own advantage." What if the promoters of mother-father-brother-day spirit, and of commercialized sacred days of the calendar, should take to heart General MacArthur's words about Corregidor and commemorating an anniversary? "Until we claim again the ghastly remnants of its last gaunt garrison we can but stand humble supplicants before Almighty God. There lies our Holy Grail." Surely we are not fit to live if we have not that indomitable feeling of being strong in defeat; if we are not, as Eugene Ginsberg puts it, under "command of the dead"—if they cannot "sinew us to victory"; if we do not "see them when we are most gay" and "feel them when we are most free."

"Be gentle and you can be bold" is an ancient Chinese saying; "be frugal and you can be liberal; if you are a leader, you have learned self-restraint." W. H. Hudson was unwilling to extol the bees for building their wonderful hexagons, since they were merely following instinct; but we are not bees, and when we undertake to be workmanly it is different; the most scientifically self-interested effort cannot effeminize one who walks like the tapir and works like the elephant.

The Nation, 156 (19 June 1943), 866–67.

THE PAST RECAPTURED

THIS deep and strange book—the story of Sebastião Manrique, a seventeenth-century Augustinian friar and his journey to Arakan on the Bay of Bengal, land of the Mahamuni, or great image of Buddha—is really a study of church and state, with applications private and political, for twentieth-century behavior.

"Strengthened by 'the stimulus of pressures,' the Portuguese irruption into Asia was a continuation of the crusade against the Moors," says Mr. Collis—this interpretation recalling Sir Francis Bacon's observation that civil wars are like the heat of fever; foreign wars are like the heat of exercise.

In this account, based on Manrique's "Travels," published in 1649 and other true sources, "Golden Goa," on the west coast of India, is depicted as gruesome Goa, with its "fidalgos, slaves, murders, adulteries, poisonings and ignorance"; of a piece with "the spectral hall" in the black stone palace

Review of *The Land of the Great Image*, by Maurice Collis (Alfred A. Knopf).

of the Inquisition, which "selected its victims and concocted a process afterward," in the manner of the Gestapo.

A main and significant emphasis is placed on private and political defeat through "pride, idleness, luxury and vice." With power of becoming "invisible, invulnerable to hurt by men or spirits," King Thiri-thu-dhamma "surrendered to paranoia, a sign that he would not long remain on his throne." "A Buddhist king who, forgetting the compassion and sanity of the Eightfold Path, opened his mind to the evil suggestions of a wizard and murdered his subjects to obtain occult powers, had lain down with monsters, and because he had looked into the abyss, the abyss looked into him." That self-ensorceled sixteenth-century king became a prototype of twentieth-century Japan. A Buddhist nation has "conceived . . . the task of rescuing Asia . . . from being divided . . . among the . . . nations of the West," "discarding for the moment" the "Buddhist way of virtue" in order to make herself "invulnerable and invisible, " and has "looked to secret weapons" . . . at "a moment when the nations of Europe fell upon one another."

Mr. Collis draws attention to the fact that "the British invaded Burma in 1825 by the same route they have taken today"; and as we follow Friar Manrique's journey to Arakan, through "mountains full of tigers"—"the track hard to find"—the trees infested with ants, through country in which "three hundred inches of rain may fall between May and October," our Allied fliers' defiance of the monsoon cannot but be in our minds.

As a study of "the Brahmic vision"—defined in terms other than Emerson's—this book is unforgettable. It is also one to which no curioso could be indifferent. With uncanny verisimilitude, it demonstrates how the power of suggestion may be augmented by "tattooing in squares"; by "hearing *taran*" (chance remarks); by vibrations from the great Yattara bell—"not sounded as a warning but as an occult offensive." A vanished world is made graphic in its reverences, costumes and generosities. We see a pair of newly captured young elephants "taking up sugar-cane in their trunks in a glad greedy way," and "elephants endorsed with towers" in a coronation procession; Manrique observing, "There is no animal which better graces a parade than an elephant, with its stately walk and lofty mien. Here were four hundred elephants, each decked till it was a pageant in itself, an ambling treasury of color. . . . And the elephants differed in character. . . . Yet fierce or mellow, they were equally disciplined, as they came on, two by two"—"dancers . . . crying out their names . . . the Victorious, the Master of Thunder, the Van Lord. And the great beasts were as tame as dogs . . . an expression of indulgence on their antediluvian masks."

A Dublin-born Oxford civil servant sent to Burma in 1912 and there for twenty-one years, Mr. Collis retired in 1936 by reason of his close sympathy with the Burmese. How, "under the present wave of belief in right conduct," he asks, "will America comport herself when paramount in Asia?" And shall we indeed have that dreamed-of universal state which in the sixteenth century, Goa and Rome were unable to achieve?

The New Republic, 109 (27 September 1943), 431–32.

THERE IS A WAR THAT NEVER ENDS

WALLACE STEVENS protects himself so well against profanation that one does not instantly see the force of what he is saying, but with discernment focused the effect is startling; and it is a happy circumstance that we have *Notes toward a Supreme Fiction* not long after *Parts of a World*, for they are interrelated roots of the same tree.

Mr. Stevens has chosen "clouds" for "pedagogues." His "imagination's Latin"—compounded "of speech, paint, and music"—enables us to "see the sun again with an ignorant eye" as "A voluminous master folded in his fire," "Washed in the remotest cleanliness of a heaven / That has expelled us and our images." It is

> As if the waves at last were never broken,
> As if the language suddenly, with ease,
> Said things it had laboriously spoken.

"Logos and logic . . . / And every latent double in the word," bring "the strong exhilaration / Of what we feel from what we think . . . / . . . a pure power." A poet does not speak language but mediates it, as the lion's power lies in his paws; he knows what it is "to have the ant of the self changed to an ox," "young ox," "lion," "stout dog," "bow-legged bear."

> It is a thing to have,
> A lion, an ox in his breast,
> To feel it breathing there,

to know that the "impossible possible" of imagination is so much stronger than reason that the part is equal to the whole. The poet—

Review of *Parts of a World*, by Wallace Stevens (Alfred A. Knopf), and *Notes toward a Supreme Fiction*, by Wallace Stevens (Cummington Press).

> He is like a man
> In the body of a violent beast.
> Its muscles are his own . . .

> The lion sleeps in the sun.
> Its nose on its paws.
> It can kill a man.

Delight "lies in flawed words and stubborn sounds," Mr. Stevens says; or, as the metaphoric ox apis might say, "bull words," "aphonies." "Words add to the senses. . . / Are the eye grown larger, more intense" and make fact what we want it to be. In this cosmos of reverie, a diamond is of poor worth as compared with the value to infinity of "words for the / Dazzle of mica," as gold was without value to the Incas but a delight to them because it was "the color of their revered Sun."

It is made evident, however, that imagination and the imaginer are different from images and imagers, from the nature-loving Narcissus who sees only himself in every pool, from "the strongly heightened effigy" which is but "a setting for geraniums." The eye of the imaginer is "the center of a circle, spread / To the final full"; in it, "the part is the equal of the whole," "a self that touches all edges." And to this mind's eye in the circle, the holy health of the pines is derived from their color as much as from their resin.

> . . . The blue-green pines
> Deepen the feelings to inhuman depths.

> These are the forest. This health is holy,

Mr. Stevens says. Where he alludes to spruce trees and historic markers, we find that wording can be painting and that we are face to face with Maine's imperishable portrait: "everywhere spruce trees bury soldiers," and "Everywhere spruce trees bury spruce trees." The gulls "are flying / In light blue air over dark blue sea" that "flows / In sapphire, round the sun-bleached stones." Another major canvas is the one in *Notes toward a Supreme Fiction* about "a face of slate" with "vines around the throat":

> A lasting visage in a lasting bush,
> A face of stone in an unending red,
> Red-emerald, red-slitted-blue, a face of slate,
> . . . .
> Red-in-red repetitions never going

> Away, a little rusty, a little rouged
> A little roughened and ruder, a crown
>
> The eye could not escape, a red renown . . .
> Blowing itself upon the tedious ear.
> An effulgence faded, dull cornelian
>
> Too venerably used. . . .

"The elephant-colorings of tires," children "in pauvred colors," "the blue bushes," "the purple odor, the abundant bloom," the "red blue, red purple" lilacs that appear in these pages, are surely "paint."

Besides being speech and paint, the poems are music. Wallace Stevens is as susceptible to sound as objects were to Midas' golden touch. But he does not sophisticate his music. He listens to that of the bumblebee and the sea. Reverie is not a diplomatic occasion in Liberia. It must have "a music constant" like "the central humming of the sea." "It must give pleasure"— like "summer with its azure-doubled crimsons," like "The blue sun in his red cockade,

> Taller than any eye could see,
> Older than any man could be.

"Two things of opposite nature seem to depend on one another, the imagined on the real," Mr. Stevens says; we have "winter and spring," "morning and afternoon," "North and South," "sun and rain, a plural like two lovers."

Willingness to baffle the crass reader sometimes baffles the right one. That is to say, interrupted soliloquy can amount to disrupted logic. Yet delayed progression is wonderfully demonstrated here, as in the "profane parade": "a-rub, a rub-rub," "hip-hip," "hurrah, hip / Hip, hip, hurrah."

For the Connoisseur of Chaos, a "great disorder is an order"—"the eye, the ear, all things together," like "a repetition on one string." As for the "anti-master man" with "eye touched," "ear so magnified by thunder, parts, and all these things together were the truth"; so with Canon Asprin, "Beneath . . . the surface of / His eye and audible in the mountain of / His ear, . . . " "It was not a choice

> Between, but of. He chose to include the things
> That in each other are included, the whole,
> The complicate, the amassing harmony.

This "anti-master man" seems to be a kind of supernatural "skeleton" or "Nabob of bones" for whom

> . . . The cataracts
> As facts fall like rejuvenating rain,
> Fall down through nakedness to nakedness,
> To the auroral creature musing in the mind.

He feels that if one is to be "erudite in happiness," unnecessary learning must be left out—"anti-ideas and counter-ideas," "reason's click-clack and its applied enflashings." On arrival from Guatemala "at the Waldorf, . . . wild country of the soul," he is again among "men remoter than mountains." A now "chromatic florid Lady Lowzen in glittering seven-colored changes," who had been "Flora MacMort . . . in her ancestral hells, . . . skins the real from the unreal." Whereas *eligo*—I choose—is "the moon Blanche"; is truth, "the star, the vivid thing in the air that never changes."

The "ancestral hells" have something in common with James Joyce. Ezra Pound might, conceivably, address the "Academy of Fine Ideas" as "My beards"; and life on the battleship *Masculine*—"the captain drafted rules of the world, Regulae mundi, as apprentice of Descartes"—puts the stamp of its approval on certain Pound cantos. Like Shakespeare and the aforementioned authors, Mr. Stevens is not a prudish man, and since he feels that he is sufficiently restrained, perhaps we should allow comic relief to be offset by the larger meanings.

"To meditate the highest man . . . creates . . . what unisons create in music."

> . . .—Can we live on dry descriptions,
> Feel everything starving except the belly
> And nourish ourselves on crumbs of whimsy?

he asks. This highest man "is not a person" but "his breast is greatness." He is "the familiar man," the hero who "rejects false empire" and is "complete in himself despite the negations of existence." His affirming freedom of the mind is involved in "war that never ends." He and the soldier are one. Mr. Stevens has summarized it in *The Noble Rider and the Sound of Words,* where he says that "as a wave is a force and not the water of which it is composed, which is never the same, so nobility is a force. . . . It is a violence from within that protects us from a violence without. It is the imagination pressing back against the pressure of reality." In the final poem of *Notes toward a Supreme Fiction,* the violence from without is summarized— the soldier who is preserving that freedom of soul which gives rise to the violence within. Surely this is "the bread of faithful speech" for soldiers in the "war that never ends."

Kenyon Review, 5 (Winter 1943), 144–47; *Predilections*.

AN ACCURACY OF ABUNDANCE

JOHN STEUART CURRY was born in Kansas in 1897 and is now Artist in Residence at the University of Wisconsin. His native state, the sunflower state, is geographically the center of America, and as noted by Reginald Marsh, the Hereford bull "Ajax" completed as an oil in 1940—is "good beef" and is also John Curry. The bull has "the solid weight of sculpture," "the mass is insistent"; "as he grazes he leans," head sideward to tear the grass, his legs planted with a certain "deadly earnestness."

Mr. Curry's factual understanding of animals is daringly honest; as portrayed in the "hip slouch" of a tired horse, the sitting crouch of a frightened horse, in "The Stallion" "as he prances forth from the runway into the arena." Curry has always had an admiration for hogs, we are told, and this admiration has a counterpart in his respect for elephants. "With an elephant's as with a pig's eyes," he says, "you don't see the eye at first," "then suddenly you become conscious of its gleaming presence in the shadow of the ear."

Animals are eternity not less than subjects of a different kind; yet Mr. Curry's symbolic demands for national repentance should in themselves be enough to make him glad to have been born. "The trembling terror of the fugitive," his feet prehensilely flattened like bark to the tree; John Brown towering above "free-soil and pro-slavery forces," "a man who, when the nation was stagnating and threatening to disintegrate, pointed the way to renewed strength"—there with a vengeance, we have "the shock of vital subject matter." We have it also in the drawing "Corn Stalks," in which the plant's hard-veined, stiffly fluting ribbons seem a portrait of Mr. Curry's statement, "My whole life was made up of sensations. I used to go out in the garden and pull tomato vines to pieces so that I could smell them."

His biographer calls him "a factual romanticist"—poetry being fact plus imagination, or as Wallace Stevens puts it, "an accuracy of abundance." The brown thrasher fronting the sun from the well-furnished osage-orange

---

Review of *John Steuart Curry's Pageant of America*, by Laurence E. Schmeckebier (American Artists Group).

bough is the farm's Magnificat. "Flora" is both a person and spring; "Chris L. Christensen" is a friend to art and the genius of agricultural research. "Love Is Like a Bird"—like "two lovers swinging through the air in the dove-shaped gondola of a rickety Ferris Wheel"; love has a "stocky cylindrical form" with sow's ears, biting at a snake in defense of hapless young; love is like a coffin in "The Return of Private Davis." One does not envy Mr. Curry the life he has led, but one envies him the heart for such a life, his patience with fakes, failures, and victims; his courage, reverence, compassion, humility, his will to storm the stars. Struggle has been his release— exteriorized in man's conflict with emotion (the "religious" subjects), with the "elements" (tornado and flood scenes), with "beasts," and with man ("battle scenes and athletic contests").

Artist in Residence has a pleasing sound; this one, however, has been and in feeling is a farmer, to whom as to the seaman weather is more than weather; it is life and death. And besides the twister, the flood, lightning, and erosion, there are the plagues—"the parched earth," the "dust storm," "the blazing sun" before which "floats the cloud of hoppers." Mr. Curry feels that painting should be true to "the still small voice" of "birth, training, environment, and faith." He has worked to achieve "solid form, controlled movement, and clear space," the subject "so organized that it fits into a design that gives it authority"; as where a predominating form arranges the lesser mass—the awning of the merry-go-round, for example, in the crowd at the "State Fair." There are moments when the needful technique ceases to operate: when the paint has a worked-with look ("The Light of the World"), or the line strays ("Performing Tiger"). No one, however, could be more conscious than John Curry of what he regards as his "seemingly insurmountable shortcomings." He is indefatigable like the badger, and Paris for him was not a luxury but a place in which to learn to draw; when he felt that he could achieve better results by using oil with tempera, he changed to that method; his working note, "Wrinkles go at right angles to muscles," savors of mastery, nor is it pulling the heavens down about his ears to say that in his "Stallion" the white of the eye, the white bobbins, and white underglaze conduce to a Piero della Francesca clear splendor of actuality. But he has said in words as with pigment, "Great art is within you," "There is no borrowed coat of perfect fit"; and Professor Schmeckebier's generous diminishings of the immortal great to advantage him result in automatic resistance. "Ruben's" for "Reubens' " "pig's" for "pigs'," and faulty indexing might be charged to bad proofreading. As writing, however, the pull of the meaning in one direction is against the pull of the phrase in another, the unnecessary word blurs what would have been clearer without it, and even supposing Professor Schmeckebier to be foreign, his wording throughout the book is dangerously inexact.

"Kansas," Mr. Jewell says, "has found her Homer"; but Mr. Curry is modest. Jealousy and animosity are not in him. He thinks of painting as something that can be enjoyed "here and now by you and you." He feels that America's intensity need not always be a "tragic prelude." He thinks of the artist as a self-devoted servant, not a hireling. Surely, as one who would be "more completely than ever a servant of the people," he has found freedom.

The Nation, 157 (11 December 1943), 708–9.

ANNA PAVLOVA

"To enter the School of the Imperial Ballet is to enter a convent whence frivolity is banned, and where merciless discipline reigns," Pavlova tells us in the autobiographic miniature entitled *Pages of My Life*. In keeping with that statement was her ability to regard genius as a trust, concerning which vanity would be impossible. "My successes," she said, are "due to my ceaseless labor and to the merits of my teachers." And yet, whereas the impression of security she gave could have been the result of an exacting discipline, for there have been virtuosi whose dancing was flawless, she was compelling because of spiritual force that did not need to be mystery, she so affectionately informed her technique with poetry.

Something of this we see in the photograph of her taken at the age of twelve—in the erectness of the head; the absolutely horizontal brows indicating power of self-denial; eyes dense with imagination and sombered by solicitude; hair severely competent; the dress, dainty more than proud. "We were poor—very poor indeed, . . . my father having died two years after my birth," she says of childhood days with her mother in the country. "Bareheaded, and clad in an old cotton frock, I often would explore the woods close by the cottage. I enjoyed the mysterious aspect of the cloisterlike alleys under the fir trees," and "at times I wove myself a wreath of wildflowers and imagined myself to be the Beauty asleep in her enchanted castle."

Here are contrasts, romance unharmed by poverty and dreams that were ardor, recognizable in the very titles of parts danced in later years: the Butterfly, the Dragonfly, the Snowflake, Crystal Clear Spring, Fleur de Lys'

Friend, Giselle "the newborn fairy, daughter of the breeze." And as the memoir tells further on, "In countries abroad, it was said there was 'something novel' in my dancing. Yet what I had done was merely to subordinate its physical elements to a psychological concept: over the matter-of-fact aspects of dancing—that is, dancing *per se*—I have attempted to throw a spiritual veil of poetry. . . ." So above all, it is affection for beauty that is unmistakable—reverie which was reverence. At even her "first motion," wrote René Jean, "she seems about to embrace the whole world"; world being a term precise in more than the immediate sense, for in her dancing with persons, remoteness marked her every attitude. It is the uncontaminated innocence of her fervor that is really her portrait in the pose in which she is protectingly entwined with an actual swan—guarding and adoring what is almost a menace. Again the paradox of spirit contradictory with fact, in the *Autumn Bacchanal*—her fingers resting as a leaf might have come to rest; as the Dragonfly, she inclines the point of the left wing toward her head by the merest incurving touch of the fingers from below, as if there were on it silver-dust or dew that must not be disturbed, while controlling the right wing by curving it over the wrist, with thumb and finger meeting upon the firmly held edge, though just within it. These truthful hands, the most sincere, the least greedy imaginable, are indeed "like priests, a sacerdotal gravity impressed upon their features"; yet, as noticed by Cyril Beaumont, they "were a little large for her arms, and the fingers inclined to be thick"; so the illusion of grace, though not accidental, must have been a concomitant of her subconscious fire; her expression, Mr. Beaumont continues, being as "changeable as the very face of nature; her body responding to the mood of a dance as a tuning-fork vibrates to a blow." And in the fervent reminiscences of her by Victor Dandré, her husband, we find that, losing patience with the lack of individuality in her dancers, she would say to them, "Why do you go about expressing nothing? Cry when you want to cry and laugh when you want to laugh."

Her feet, remarkable for the power of the ankle, their high arch, and "toes of steel," made her *pizzacati* on tiptoe and steadily held pauses possible; but not easy, as noted by Mr. Dandré, since her long main toe, by which the whole weight of her body had to be borne, did not provide the squared support of the more level toes of the somewhat typically thickset virtuoso. Yet "when standing on one toe, she could change her entire balance," André Olivéroff says, "by moving the muscles of her instep. This may seem a small thing, but it was one of the many that contributed to her dancing the perpetual slight novelty that made it impossible for an instant to tire of watching her."

Theodore Stier, musical director of her performances for sixteen years, says, "She is, I think, the most sincere woman it ever has been my good fortune to meet, sincere with herself as with others"; and this doubly un-deceived honesty was matched by logic. She did not admire Degas, because he had delineated attitudes not movement; and when inventing three social dances—the Pavlovana, the Gavotte Renaissance (not to be confused with the *Gavotte Pavlova*), and the Czarina Waltz—she took precaution that every step and pose should be within the ability of the average dancer. Her utter straightness of spirit was matched by an incapacity for subterfuge that is all but spectacular; as when in speaking of stage fright she admitted that each time before an appearance she was subject to it, and "this emotion," she said, "instead of decreasing with time, becomes stronger and stronger. For I am increasingly conscious of . . . my responsibilities."

"Her feet are light as wings, her rhythm speaks of dreams," has been said by many in many ways; but if dreams are to transform us, there must be power behind them, and in Pavlova the unself-sparing dynamo, will power, by which she was to be incommoded and to incommode others, made itself felt when she was not more than eight. To celebrate Christmas, she was— for the first time—on her way to the Maryinsky Theatre with her mother, and, inquiring what they were to see, was told, "You are going to enter fairyland." "When we left the theater," she says, "I was living in a dream. I kept thinking of the day when I should make my first appearance on the stage, in the part of the Sleeping Beauty." Begging to be allowed to enter the School of the Imperial Ballet, and refused by her mother, she then says, "It was only a few days later, wondering at my firmness of purpose, that she complied with my desire and took me to see the Director of the School." Deferred by him until she was ten, since no child might be admitted earlier, she persevered after two years in persuading her mother to request admittance again, and was accepted. However tiring a journey it might have been, "it was rare for her to go to her hotel in a town where she was to appear, before visiting the theater," Mr. Stier says, and in the draftiness of a darkened stage, she would practice while others rested. At rehearsal she was a "re-lentless taskmaster," we are told. Mr. Dandré says, "She was firm because she knew she was right." The word "firm" again;

ANNA PAVLOVA

THE INCOMPARABLE

PRIMA BALLERINA ASSOLUTA

stamped in violet on the back of one of her St. Petersburg photographs, is, one feels, part of the likeness.

Will power has its less noble concomitant, willfulness, and although Pavlova could not be convinced on occasion, that she was mistaken in giving aid to an impostor she pitied, or that she should desist from an over-impetuosity that she might repent of, she "did not know the meaning of the word cynicism." "Better thrice imposed on," she said, "than turn the empty away; . . . it is so easy to forgive people who must find it hard to forgive themselves." Willful and will-powerful though she was, however, a modest deference of attitude was so natural to her that it marked her as all but one with the snowdrops and wildflowers she loved. Ever accurate, when wishing to make clear that the term ballerina is not used in speaking of a dancer who is merely one of the ballet, she uses the passive voice: "I left the Ballet School at the age of sixteen and shortly afterwards was permitted to style myself Première Danseuse, which is an official title. . . . Later I was granted the title Ballerina, which but four other dancers of the present time have received." Here again, a persuasion of contrasts: undogmatic decisiveness, strength of foot with lightness of body; technical proficiency with poetic feeling; aloofness and simplicity in one who had chosen as her art that most exposed form of self-expression, dancing. It is said that "she proceeded intelligently, calmly, prudently," and that as she stood on tiptoe, the sole of her foot was "an absolute vertical"—a proof of "adequate training." Yet with the focused power there was an elfin quality of suddenness as incalculable as the fire in a prism, suggested by the darting descent to one knee, in *The Dragonfly*. "When she was excited about anything," André Olivéroff says, "she had a way of clenching her hand and pressing it to her mouth, glancing sideways as though in search of a possible adventure." May not this propensity to bewitchment explain the fact that she found irksome some of the portraits of her that others admire? and that she would try, as she entered the theater, not to see her simulacrum, flaunted to attract patronage? Nothing is so striking as the disparity between her many likenesses; and nothing so eludes portraiture as ecstasy.

In dancing we have the rhythms of music made visible; also color and design; and if the result is to be more than acrobacy, power of dramatic expression, Pavlova was virtuoso of each: of slender form and aerial buoyancy, with strength of foot, perfect technique, which it was ever her study to "repair," and interpretive power whereby she "acted the dancing and danced the acting."

Through its harmonized symmetries, style combines "the ability to disengage and coordinate elements"; and in her attitudes, as in the timing of steps, Pavlova possessed it. She was balanced harmony, in her thinking and in her motions. Having begun the brief account of her life with the forest, she concluded with it: "The wind rustles through the branches of the fir trees in the forest opposite my veranda, the forest through which as a child

I longed to rove. The stars shine in the evening gloom. I have come to the end of these few recollections."

So with pictorial symmetry. In the photograph taken at Ivy House, of her seated on the grass beside the chair of Maestro Cecchetti, her teacher of dancing, the descending line of the propped forearm, of her dress and other hand, of ankle and foot, continues to the grass with the naturalness of a streamer of seaweed—a stately serpentine which imparts to the seated figure the ease of a standing one. Again, in the photograph in which she is seated on the wide steps of a building in Italy—her hands on her sunshade which rests on her lap—the middle finger and little finger of each hand, higher than the finger between, adhere to classic formula but with the spontaneous curve of the iris petal.

It seems to have been an idiosyncrasy of Pavlova's that one hand should copy rather than match the other, as in the Aimé Stevens portrait, in which the hands, holding a string of jade and lifted as though to feel the rain, tend both in the same direction, from left to right (Pavlova's right), instead of diverging equilaterally with the oppositeness of horns. In *Spring Flowers*, the right foot turning left is imitated by the left foot's half-moon curve to the left. *Giselle*—hands reaching forward, feet (tiptoe) in lyrelike verticals—is all of a piece. Everything moves together, like a fish leaping a weir; the tiny butterfly wings seen in silhouette, weighting the space above the level skirt that in soaring out repeats the airy horizontal of the arms. And as with the swan curves of *Giselle*, so with the perfectly consolidated verticals in the *Gavotte*, *The Dragonfly*, and *The Swan*. Balance is master.

Harmony of design would be lacking were it not for what does not show— the devoted effort that made it possible. "The Dancer," Pavlova said, "must practice her exercises every day." She "must feel so at ease so far as technique is concerned, that when on the stage she need devote to it not a thought and may concentrate upon expression, upon the feelings which must give life to the dances she is performing."

Observers said, "It is as though some internal power impels the arabesque"; "even when engaged in extreme feats of virtuosity and bravura, she preserves spontaneity and ease." "I was essentially a lyric dancer," she says,—in the Provençal sense of dance as a song, a *ballada*. She did not make the Italian mistake of introducing school exercises in her dancing, and "never was interested in purposeless virtuosity"; would not, had she been able, have cared to be a circus virtuoso, suspended by teeth and wrist, revolving in a blur for half an hour. "When she danced," Mr. Beaumont says, "the hands seemed delicate and the fingers tapering. . . . She turned pirouettes with an elegant ease, and though she rarely did more than two or three, she executed them with such a brio that they had the effect of half-a-dozen."

"The stage is like a magnifying glass. Everything tends toward exaggeration," and as in music sensibility does not misuse the pedal, so with Pavlova; humor, esprit, a sense of style— also a moral quality—made it impossible for her to show off, to be hard, to be dull; the same thing that in life made her self-controlled rather than a prison to what she prized. "Her dancing," says Mr. Beaumont, quoting "a French writer," was " '*la danse de toujours, dansée comme jamais*'—the dance of everyday as never danced before"; and speaking of the "Gavotte danced to 'The Glow-worm' music, by Paul Lincke, nothing could be more ordinary from the viewpoint of both choreography and music, yet she made it into a delicious miniature of the Merveilleuse period."

Although rhythm is the repetition of a sound or effect at regulated intervals, independence of rhythm is essential, and Pavlova never contented herself with literalities; her inventions—the trill on tiptoe, the long pause on tiptoe, and the impulsive pirouette—being temperament's enlarging of accepted convention. "Her hands possess a life of their own," it was said. In the little finger apart from the fourth, one deduces independence; in its double curve, poetic feeling; in the slightly squared fingertips, originality—qualities which seem to have something in common with a similar freedom in the dancing of Nijinsky, and with the stateliness of Greta Garbo. One recalls, moreover, in connection with the independent fingers, Pavlova's choosing to appear at the Palace Theatre in London and at the Hippodrome in New York. She indeed was, as has been remarked by someone, "a teaching."

A special aspect of her independence was what Lincoln Kirstein calls the "openness" of her dancing, as in the Gavotte she advanced with the swirling grace of a flag. Mr. Olivéroff says, "I have sometimes felt that I would rather see her walk out on the stage to take a curtain call than see her dance *Swan* or *Papillon*"; throwing light on her own statement, "Whatever a person does or refrains from doing out of fear, is bad." Moreover, Mr. Beaumont says, "As the microphone amplifies the slightest sound, so her least movement held the attention of the audience," and we can understand how "she was never so successful in her ballet as in her *soli* and *pas de deux*"; how "the ballet, being a composite work, . . . fell apart with Pavlova and her partner executing *soli* or *pas de deux;* the others coming on at intervals when it was necessary for the principals to rest."

Fairyland! It may be ecstasy but it is a land of pathos, and although Pavlova's parts were poetry, there were in most instances symbols of grief: Giselle, a Wili of the moonlight who must at dawn return underground from the world of light and love; La Péri, Servant of the Pure, who "realized that yon flower of life (the scarlet lotus) was not for her"; Crystal Clear Spring, the Ghost King's daughter, who warns her sisters not to open the door to the stranger, that if they disobey they must die, then chooses to die with them; Esmerelda, the forsaken gypsy who must dance at the festivities in honor of her betrayer; the Dying Rose, the Swan.

Does imagination care to look upon a sculptured fairy, a live or any demonstrable creature of the moonlight? What could constitute a greater threat to illusion than the impersonated quiver of a dragonfly, or be less like a swan than the two little wings arising unbiologically from the waist? It would seem that Pavlova was obliged to overcome her roles, and for the most part her costumes, for which she needed an Omar Kiam with a sense of structural continuity, and novelty that does without novelty; though one must make an exception: the Gavotte, as portrayed in Malvina Hoffman's wax statuette. Mordkin's gladiator-like torso might identify itself with his roles, whereas Pavlova was, theoretically, always at a disadvantage. Is the motion-picture of her Death of the Swan entirely becoming to her? Photographs of her dances taken even at the good moment fail, one feels, of the effect she had in life; and "those who never saw her dance may ask what she did that made her so wonderful. It is not so much what she did," Mr. Beaumont says, "as how she did it"; and one suspects that she so intently thought the illusion she wished to create that it made her illusive—hands and feet obeying imagination in a way that compensated for any flaw. She had power, moreover, for a most unusual reason—she did not project as valuable the personality from which she could not escape. Of her Dying Swan, Mr. Beaumont says, "The emotion transferred was so over-powering that it seemed a mockery to applaud when the dance came to an end." This impression is corroborated by others; Andrei Levensohn's summary of that dance (the translation is here slightly altered) being a lament as well as a description: "Arms folded, on tiptoe, she dreamily and slowly circles the stage. By even, gliding motions of the hands, returning to the background whence she emerged, she seems to strive toward the horizon, as though a moment more and she will fly—exploring the confines of space with her soul. The tension gradually relaxes and she sinks to earth, arms moving faintly as in pain. Then faltering with irregular steps toward the edge of the stage—leg bones a-quiver like the strings of a harp—by one swift forward-gliding motion of the right foot to earth, she sinks on the left knee—the aerial creature struggling against earthly bonds, and there, transfixed by pain, she dies."

"I imagined," she said, ". . . I dreamed that I was a Ballerina and spent my whole life dancing, like a butterfly"; but her dance of the swan was a rite—arms folded crusader-like, in the sign of the cross—"the rhythms disintegrating" symbolically, as in Giselle's dancing they disintegrated under madness, literally undoing her earthly joy. "Pavlova was simple, simple as a child is simple," André Olivéroff says, "and yet there was a great tenderness about her, sadder than a child's and more peaceful." Why should one so innocent, so natural, so ardent, be sad? If "self-control is the essential condition of conveying emotion," and giving is giving up, we still cannot feel that renunciation made Pavlova sad; may it have been that for lives that one loves there are things that even love cannot do?

Of herself as she stood on the balcony of her hotel in Stockholm she said, "I bowed from time to time; and suddenly they began to sing. . . . I sought vainly for a way of expressing my gratitude. But even after I had thrown my roses and lilies and violets and lilacs to them they seemed loath to withdraw." And "in Belgium, following a brief season in Liège," as recalled by Mr. Stier, "when we went to settle with the various newspapers in which the performances had been advertised, to our astonishment, they refused to accept payment. Pavlova has done so much for the national appreciation of art, they explained, that 'we cannot bring ourselves to accept money from her.' "

"How rare it is," she said to André Olivéroff, "to find an artist who combines passion with intellect, who dances always with a mind and a body both trained, and with a heart that is on fire. Of the two, if I had to say, I would always choose the heart. But that alone is not enough. You must have both." In giving happiness, she truly "had created her crown of glory and placed it upon her brows." That which is able to change the heart proves itself.

Partial Chronology

Anna (Matveyevna) Pavlova was born February 16, 1882, in St. Petersburg, but her name day was January 30th.

She made her debut at the Maryinsky Theatre, January 1, 1899, and became Prima Ballerina in 1901.

In 1907, with Adolph Bolm as partner, she went on tour with a company— Helsingfors, Stockholm, Copenhagen, Prague, Berlin.

In 1909 she danced in two performances with the Diaghilev Company during their Paris season, crossed to London, to dance at a party given by Lady Londesborough in honor of King Edward VII and Queen Alexandra.

In 1910 she purchased Ivy House, North East Road, Hampstead, just outside London.

In 1911 she returned to the Palace Theatre, bringing *La Nuit*, *Papillon*, and various ballets.

In 1912, 1913, 1914, she returned to London. "Jealousies, desertions, unpunctualities and demands for leaves of absence on the part of her

Russian dancers made it necessary to replace certain of them, until finally the entire ballet was British." "Then," says Theodore Stier, "began an era of peace for Pavlova such as she had not thought possible."

From 1914 onward she made extended tours over the world.

In 1920 an Orphan Home for twenty refugee children from Russia was founded by her, in the rue Chemin de Fer, Paris. This was her fondest charity and in preference to receiving a birthday gift it became her custom to request of her company that they give to her for her orphans what might have been contributed toward a gift for herself.

In January 1931 she died in Holland, of pleurisy. While en route to the Hague via the Riviera, to begin a tour, after a sleepless night in a train that had stood on a siding all night, she caught cold—recorded thus reverently by Mr. Beaumont: "Hardly settled in the Hotel des Indes, she fell ill; the flame that was her life, flickered, burnt low, and half an hour after midnight on Friday, January 23, went out."

Dance Index 3 (March 1944), 47–52; *Predilections*.

ONE TIMES ONE

"ONE'S not half two. Its two are halves of one": Mr. Cummings says. So *1 x 1* is a merging of two things in a "sunlight of oneness," "one thou"; and "beginning a whole verbal adventure," this onederful book is primarily a compliment to friendship.

It is a book of wisdom that knowledge cannot contradict; of mind that is heart because it is alive; of wealth that is nothing but joy. Its axioms are also inventions: "as yes is to if, love is to yes," for instance; and

> all ignorance toboggans into know
> and trudges up to ignorance again:

Ignorance that has become know is to Mr. Cummings a monster; and nothing could say how valuable he is in slaying this "collective pseudobeast" in its

> . . . scienti
> fic land of supernod

Review of *1 x 1*, by E. E. Cummings (Henry Holt and Company).

where freedom is compulsory
and only man is god

It is useless to search in a book by E. E. Cummings for explanations, reasons, becauses, dead words, or dead ways. His poems, furthermore, are not encumbered with punctuation; you are expected to feel the commas and the periods. The dislocating of letters that are usually conjoined in a syllable or word is not a madness of the printer but impassioned feeling that hazards its life for the sake of emphasis. For E. E. Cummings, the parts of speech are living creatures that alter and grow. Disliking "all dull nouns," he concocts new ones that are phenomena of courage and mobility. Nouns become adjectives; and adverbs, adjectives. His hero and heroine are "mythical guests of Is"; truth is "whereless," and "there's nothing as something as one."

"I am abnormally fond of that precision which creates movement," he says, and we see how a sensibility of crystalline explicitness can achieve, without using the word, a poem about a kite and have it resplendent art:

o by the by
has anybody seen
little you-i
who stood on a green
hill and threw
his wish at blue

with a swoop and a dart
out flew his wish
(it dived like a fish
but climbed like a dream)
throbbing like a heart
singing like a flame

blue took it my
far beyond far
and high beyond high
bluer took it your
but bluest took it our
away beyond where

what a wonderful thing
is the end of a string
(murmurs little you-i
as the hill becomes nil)

> and will somebody tell
> me why people let go

The ambidextrous compactness of the Joyce pun is one of poetry's best weapons and is instinctive with E. E. Cummings, as where he tells how nonentity and "the general menedgerr" "smoked a robert burns cigerr to the god of things like they err." The word "huge" in this book, and certain lines—for example, you "whose moving is more april than the year"—remind one of earlier work by E. E. Cummings. If, however, one's individuality was not a mistake from the first, it should not be a crime to maintain it; and there are here poems that have a fortified expressiveness beyond any earlier best love poems. Like that painting in the Cummings exhibition at the American-British Art Center entitled "Paris Roofs, rue de la Bûcherie," Poem XXXIX, containing the line "Swoop (shrill collective myth) into thy grave," is as positive as a zebra and as tender as the new moon.

This is the E. E. Cummings book of masterpieces. It will provoke imitation, but mastery is inimitable—such as we have in "the apples are (yes they're gravensteins)"; in "plato // told him"; and in "what if a much of a which of a wind." Indeed, in all the rest; for endeavoring to choose, there is nothing to omit. Nothing? The reader who is so childish as to hope that a book of wonders could be wonderful throughout will encounter obscenity and be disheartened. Obscenity as a protest is better than obscenity as praise, but there is—between the mechanics of power in a spark of feeling and the mechanics of power in a speck of obscenity—an ocean of difference, and it does not seem sagacious of either to mistake itself for the other. As for indignities—if one may ask admiration consciously to ignore and unconsciously to admire—this writing is an apex of positiveness and of indivisible, undismemberable joy. It is a thing of furious nuclear integrities; it need not argue with hate and fear, because it has annihilated them; "everybody never breathed quite so many kinds of yes)." When it appears to ask a question—

> i've come to ask you if there isn't a
> new moon outside your window saying if
> that's all, just if

—it has the answer to life's riddle. It is reiterating:

> death, as men call him, ends what they call men
> —but beauty is more now than dying's when

The paintings "have the purities of mushrooms blooming in darkness," says Mr. McBride, throwing light on the poetry's secret of beatitude, for poetry is a flowering and its truth is "a cry of a whole of a soul," not dogma; it is a positiveness that is joy, that we have in birdsongs and should have in ourselves; it is a "cry of alive with a trill like until" and is a poet's secret, "for his joy is more than joy." Defined by this book in what it says of life in general, "such is a poet and shall be and is."

The Nation, 158 (1 April 1944), 394; *Predilections*.

FEELING AND PRECISION

FEELING at its deepest—as we all have reason to know—tends to be inarticulate. If it does manage to be articulate, it is likely to seem overcondensed, so that the author is resisted as being enigmatic or disobliging or arrogant.

One of New York's more painstaking magazines asked me, at the suggestion of a contributor, to analyze my sentence structure, and my instinctive reply might have seemed dictatorial: you don't devise a rhythm, the rhythm is the person, and the sentence but a radiograph of personality. The following principles, however, are aids to composition by which I try, myself, to be guided: if a long sentence with dependent clauses seems obscure, one can break it into shorter units by imagining into what phrases it would fall as conversation; in the second place, expanded explanation tends to spoil the lion's leap—an awkwardness which is surely brought home to one in conversation; and in the third place, we must be as clear as our natural reticence allows us to be.

William Carlos Williams, commenting on his poem "The Red Wheelbarrow," said, "The rhythm though no more than a fragment, denotes a certain unquenchable exaltation"; and Wallace Stevens, referring to poetry under the metaphor of the lion says, "It can kill a man." Yet the lion's leap would be mitigated almost to harmlessness if the lion were clawless, so precision is both impact and exactitude, as with surgery; and also in music, the conductor's signal, as I am reminded by a friend, which "begins far back of the beat, so that you don't see when the down beat comes. To have started such a long distance ahead makes it possible to be exact. Whereas you can't be exact by being restrained." When writing with maximum impact, the writer seems under compulsion to set down an unbearable accuracy; and in connection with precision as we see it in metaphor, I think of Gerard Hopkins and his description of the dark center in the eye of a peacock feather as "the color of the grape where the flag is turned back"; also his saying about some lambs he had seen frolicking in a field, "It was as though it was the ground that tossed them"; at all events, precision is a thing of the imagination; and it is a matter of diction, of diction that is virile because galvanized against inertia. In Louis Ginsberg's poem "Command of the Dead," the final stanza reads:

> And so they live in all our works
> And sinew us to victory.
> We see them when we most are gay;
> We feel them when we most are free.

The natural order for the two mosts would be

> We see them when we are most gay;
> We feel them when we are most free

but that would mean, being at our gayest makes us think of them, and being free makes us feel them—gross inaccuracy since these "mosts" are the essence of compassion.

"Fighting Faith Saves the World," an inadvertent ambiguity, as the title for a review of *Journey Among Warriors* by Eve Curie, seems to mean, fight faith and the world is saved; whereas to say, a fighting faith saves the world, would safeguard the meaning.

Explicitness being the enemy of brevity, an instance of difficult descriptive matter accurately presented is that passage in the Book of Daniel (X: 9, 10, 11) where the writer says: "Then was I in a deep sleep on my face, and my face toward the ground. And, behold, an hand touched me, which set me upon my knees and upon the palms of my hands. And I stood trembling." Think what *we* might have done with the problem if we had been asked to describe how someone was wakened and, gradually turning over, got up off the ground.

Instinctively we employ antithesis as an aid to precision, and in Arthur Waley's translation from the Chinese one notices the many paired meanings—"left and right"; "waking and sleeping"; "one embroiders with silk, an inch a day; of plain sewing one can do more than five feet." Anyone with contemporary pride thinks of W. H. Auden in connection with antithesis, as in *The Double Man* (the *New Year Letter*) he says of the devil:

> For, torn between conflicting needs,
> He's doomed to fail if he succeeds,

. . . .
If love has been annihilated
There's only hate left to be hated.

Nor can we forget Socrates' answer: "I would rather die having spoken in my manner than speak in your manner and live." And there is that very dainty instance of antithesis in Thomas Watson's and William Byrd's madrigal, "A Gratification unto Master John Case":

Let Enuy barke against the starres,
Let Folly sayle which way she please,
with him I wish my dayes to spend, . . .
whose quill hath stoode fayre Musickes frend,
chief end to peace, chief port of ease.

When we think we don't like art it is because it is artificial art. "Mere technical display," as Plato says, "is a beastly noise"—in contrast with art, which is "a spiritual magnetism" or "fascination" or "conjuring of the soul."

Voltaire objected to those who said in enigmas what others had said naturally, and we agree; yet we must have the courage of our peculiarities. What would become of Ogden Nash, his benign vocabulary and fearless rhymes, if he wrote only in accordance with the principles set forth by our manuals of composition?

I love the Baby Giant Panda
I'd welcome one to my veranda.
I never worry, wondering maybe
Whether it isn't Giant Baby;
I leave such matters to the scientists—
The Giant Baby—and Baby Giantists.
I simply want a veranda, and a
Giant Baby Giant Panda.

This, it seems to me, is not so far removed from George Wither's motto: "I grow and wither both together."

Feeling has departed from anything that has on it the touch of affectation, and William Rose Benét, in his preface to the *Collected Poems of Ford Madox Ford*, says: "Whether or not there is such a thing as poetic afflatus there are certain moments that must be seized upon, when more precise language than at any other time, is ready to hand for the expression of spontaneous feeling." My own fondness for the unaccented rhyme derives, I think, from an instinctive effort to ensure naturalness. "Even elate and fearsome rightness like Shakespeare's is only preserved from the offense of being 'poetic' by his well-nested effects of helpless naturalness."[1]

Chaucer and Henryson, it seems to me, are the perfection of naturalness in their apparently artless art of conveying emotion intact. In "Orpheus and Eurydice," Henryson tells how Tantalus stood in a flood that rose "aboif his chin"; yet

> quhen he gaipit thair wald no drop cum In;
> . . . .
> Thus gat he nocht his thrist [to slake] no[r] mend.
>
> Befoir his face ane naple hang also,
> fast at his mowth upoun a twynid [threid],
> quhen he gaipit, It rollit to and fro,
> and fled, as it refusit him to feid.
> Quhen orpheus thus saw him suffir neid,
> he tuk his harp and fast on it can clink;
> The wattir stud, and tantalus gat a drink.

One notices the wholesomeness of the uncapitalized beginnings of lines, and the gusto of invention, with climax proceeding out of climax, which is the mark of feeling.

We call climax a device, but is it not the natural result of strong feeling? It is, moreover, a pyramid that can rest either on its point or in its base, witty anticlimax being one of Ludwig Bemelmans' best enticements, as when he says of the twelve little girls, in his story *Madeline*:

> They smiled at the good
> and frowned at the bad
> and sometimes they were very sad.

Intentional anticlimax as a department of surprise is a subject by itself; indeed, an art, "bearing," as Longinus says, "the stamp of vehement emotion like a ship before a veering wind," both as content and as sound; but especially as sound, in the use of which the poet becomes a kind of hypnotist—recalling Kenneth Burke's statement that "the hypnotist has a way out and a way in."

Concealed rhyme and the interiorized climax usually please me better than the open rhyme and the insisted-on climax, and we can readily understand Dr. Johnson's objection to rigmarole, in his takeoff on the ballad:

> I put my hat upon my head,
> And went into the Strand,

> And there I saw another man,
> With his hat in his hand.

"Weak rhythm" of the kind that "enables an audience to foresee the ending and keep time with their feet," disapproved by Longinus, has its subtle opposite in E. E. Cummings' lines about Gravenstein apples—"wall" and "fall," "round," "sound," and "ground," worked into a hastening tempo:

> But over a (see just
> over this) wall
> the red and the round
> (they're Gravensteins) fall
> with a kind of a blind
> big sound on the ground

And the intensity of Henry Treece's "Prayer in Time of War" so shapes the lines that it scarcely occurs to one to notice whether they are rhymed or not:

> Black Angel, come you down! Oh Purge of God,
> By shroud of pestilence make pure the mind,
> Strike dead the running panther of desire
> That in despair the poem put on wings,
> That letting out the viper from the veins
> Man rock the mountain with his two bare hands!

With regard to unwarinesses that defeat precision, excess is the common substitute for energy. We have it in our semi-academic, too conscious adverbs—awfully, terribly, frightfully, infinitely, tremendously; in the word "stunning," the phrase "knows his Aristotle," or his Picasso, or whatever it may be; whereas we have a contrastingly energetic usefulness in John Crowe Ransom's term "particularistic," where he says T. S. Eliot "is the most particularistic critic that English poetry and English criticism have met with." Similarly with Dr. Johnson's "encomiastick," in the statement that Dryden's account of Shakespeare "may stand as a perpetual model of encomiastick criticism."

It is curious to see how we have ruined the word "fearful" as meaning full of fear. Thomas Nashe says of his compatriot Barnes—quoting Campion—"hee bragd when he was in France, he slue ten men, when (fearful cowbaby), he never heard a piece shot off but he fell on his face."

One recalls, as a pleasing antidote to jargon, Wyndham Lewis' magazine *The Tyro*, which defined a tyro as "an elementary person, an elemental usually known in journalism as the veriesttyro." "Very," when it doesn't mean true, is a word from which we are rightly estranged, though there are times when it seems necessary to the illusion of conversation or to steady the rhythm; and a child's overstatement of surprise upon receiving a gift— a playhouse—seems valuable, like foreign-language idiom—"This is the most glorious and terrific thing that ever came into this house"; but Sir Francis Bacon was probably right when he said, "Hyperbole is comely only in love."

I have an objection to the word "and" as a connective between adjectives— "he is a crude and intolerant thinker." But note the use of "and" as an ornament in the sonnet (66) in which Shakespeare is enumerating the many things of which he is tired:

> And art made tongue-tied by authority,
> And folly (doctor-like) controlling skill,
> And simple truth miscall'd simplicity,
> And captive good attending captain ill.

Defending Plato against the charge of "allegorical bombast" in his eulogy of man's anatomy and the provision whereby the heart "might throb against a yielding surface and get no damage," Longinus asks, "Which is better, in poetry and in prose, . . . grandeur with a few flaws or mediocrity that is impeccable?" And unmistakably Ezra Pound's instinct against preciosity is part of his instinct for precision and accounts for his "freedom of motion" in saying what he has to say "like a bolt from a catapult"—not that the catapult is to us invariably a messenger of comfort. One of his best accuracies, it seems to me, is the word "general" in the sentence in which he praises "the general effect" of Ford Madox Ford's poem "On Heaven"—avoiding the temptation to be spuriously specific; and although Henry James was probably so susceptible to emotion as to be obliged to seem unemotional, it is a kind of painter's accuracy for Ezra Pound to say of him as a writer, "Emotions to Henry James were more or less things that other people had, that one didn't go into."

Fear of insufficiency is synonymous with insufficiency, and fear of incorrectness makes for rigidity. Indeed, any concern about how well one's work is going to be received seems to mildew effectiveness. T. S. Eliot attributes Bishop Andrewes' precision to "the pure motive," and the fact that when he "takes a word and derives the world from it, . . . he is wholly in his subject, unaware of anything else." Mr. McBride, in the New York Sun, once said of Rembrandt and his etching "The Three Crosses": "It was as though Rembrandt was talking to himself, without any expectation that the print would be seen or understood by others. He saw these things and so testified."

This same rapt quality we have in Bach's *Art of the Fugue*—his intensively private soliloquizing continuity that ends, "Behold I Stand before Thy Throne." We feel it in the titles of some of his works, even in translation—"Behold from Heaven to Earth I Come."

Professor Maritain, when lecturing on scholasticism and immortality, spoke of those suffering in concentration camps, "unseen by any star, unheard by any ear," and the almost terrifying solicitude with which he spoke made one know that belief is stronger even than the struggle to survive. And what he said so unconsciously was poetry. So art is but an expression of our needs; is feeling, modified by the writer's moral and technical insights.

[1] Quoting myself, in *Contemporary Poetry*, Summer 1943.

Sewanee Review, 52 (Autumn 1944), 499–507; *Predilections*.

WHO HAS RESCUED WHOM

ABUNDANCE, for Christopher Smart, was not hampered by fear of surfeit, one suspects, when he was writing "A Song to David," and the all but defiantly reiterative prolonging of the poem seems natural because the thinking was feeling. "Behold the Jew"—a recent prize poem in England—is also a poem of praise, a fiery testament of love that leaves one with a sense of rapture.

Naming some of "the mighty" who have been earth's best ornament, the author exclaims, "Oh world, . . . Behold / how many and how bright the Jews!" Nor is the heroic Jew exceptional, she says. Judas Maccabaeus and the soldier "in khaki ere his turn," "donating blood," then life itself, are alike. It is indeed self-evident that Jews have a money sense. "When they break a thing they pay"; and when they owe nothing, they give. Jews who give enormously are, Mrs. Jackson perceives, not unlike the small shop-keepers she has known, and the tailor who "threw the buttons in," three expensive mohair buttons; the club members who "dug down deep" for a certain caretaker and for victims he had never seen. "No strings trailed from such givings. He / gave fully, freely, silently." Recalling "Anna Marks" whom every charm enshrined, Mrs. Jackson says, "I will assay and prove the Jew / as I weigh other nations—by / the hearts I know, the hearts I knew."

Review of *Behold the Jew*, by Ada Jackson (Macmillan).

Then what of "the slaughter camps; the piteous vans / where souls must choke their way to God." And that particular tone of voice for the Jew, used by "my kind," my freedom-loving Gentile kind; what of it? "If I keep silence all these things / are done of me and in my name," Ada Jackson says. Even now—("While you read they die, they died").

As poetry, the crippling death of Anna Marks perhaps has an effect of over-tragic imbalance, and one would prefer a neater wording for the sentence, "God hath with / lesser tools than we / worked miracles / for all to see." But what neatness of articulation as part of an instinctive music, in the allusion to *baum* and *stein* and *brunnen*—"names that are rock and tree and well—/ of judges and of counsellors / and captains over Israel." How eloquent reiteration can be, as an element of compactness: "Praise God for death," . . . and "all the loveliness you knew / befouled and lost and trodden down, / for that you were a Jew, a Jew—." There is expert allusiveness throughout the poem, especially where the simile of the mustard seed heightens David's towering slenderness above the prostrate body of Goliath:

> There was a day
> when warriors paled
> and armies shook,
> and a young lad
> stooped down and took
> five little pebbles
> from the brook—.

Some do not believe that all nations are of one blood, and shrink from the un-fascist minister who says the star of David is not the enemy of the star of Bethlehem, that "we cannot have love in our hearts for one star and hatred in our hearts for the other star." And "while you read they die, they died"; they, by way of whom all our moral advantages have come. If we yet rescue them—those who are alive to be rescued—we are still in debt and need to ask ourselves who would have rescued whom.

The New Republic, 111 (16 October 1944), 499–500.

BALLET DES ELEPHANTS

THE Elephant Ballet directed by George Balanchine—eighteenth display in the Ringling Bros.-Barnum & Bailey Circus, 1942—was the result of an idea picked up by John Ringling North in Budapest before the war. It comprised a Corps de Ballet and a Corps des Elephants featuring Modoc (in center ring) and Vanessa, a Hindoo première ballerina. The music was by Stravinsky, and Walter McClain, Ringling Superintendent of elephants, collaborating with Mr. Balanchine, "taught the elephants their routine."

Routine is the carefully right word, since an elephant is graceful when doing things it could do if not taught to do them, and is enhanced by a skirt as the grace of a venerable live oak would be enhanced by a skirt. And although as actors or workers, "in ring or in harness," of the sixteen hundred troupers in the circus, "the most obliging and even-tempered creatures on the lot" are said to be the elephants, it is "when they lay aside the buskin" that they have it on. Their deliberate way of kneeling, on slowsliding forelegs— like a cat's yawning stretch or a ship's slide into the water—is fine ballet; the pageant of fifty elephants with lights dimmed for the closing feature, gave an effect of rocks with traces of snow in the fissures that, with the overwhelming sameness of the all-pink whirling nymphs and their fifty rigid garlands, became a gigantically perfect monotone. The garlands—of appleblossoms or wild roses—were presently laid aside, and if memory does not deceive me, each nymph, with an elephant as partner, made a stair of the elephant's knee, pulling hard on the ear to gain the summit, and sat—arm lifted—on the bandeau worn by the elephant.

Then, flitting from the shadow to join the principal elephant, came a fairy in powder blue with the constantly interested impetus of the paisano-bird. Her steps were not a novelty as she semi-circled the elephant—were in fact, a summary of maneuvers already performed by the ballet. Her momentum was the surprise. A Javanese dancer's hinged hands and feet moving at right angles to the bone, give a similar impression, making the usual dancer by comparison a trifle unnatural; as though a man were impersonating a woman or a boy were waving at someone from the top of a freight-car. Swirled aloft on the elephant's trunk, Vanessa with a confidence in his skill that was unanimity, had the security of a newt in the fork of a tree,—the spiral of the elephant's trunk repeating the spirals of the dancing: a moment of magnificence.

Dance Index, 5 (June 1946), 145.

PAUL ROSENFELD (1890–1946)

PAUL ROSENFELD was an artist. In his performances one finds "a level of reality deeper than that upon which they were launched"; his experiences have not been "made by fear to conform with preconceived theories." Now to be thus "strong in oneself is to be strong in one's relationships. A give and take is effected, that feeds the powers"; powers that have afforded us "a great panorama of conclusions upon the contemporary scene." The mind which has harbored this greater than great Noah's ark of acknowledgments was characterized by an early compliment to it in the *Nation* as "courageous, clear, and biased."

Biased. Biased by imagination; a poet, as we see in Paul Rosenfeld's mechanisms of verbal invention. Mass epithet would not do; sensibility exacted poetry; John Marin was "a timothy among the grasses"; *The Enormous Room* had a "brindled style"; "love and aversion" were "darts of light on a flowing stream; wave-caps cast up and annihilated again by a silently rolling ocean." The author of a first novel "tuned his fiddle like a tavern minstrel, and out of the little rocking or running design rises the protagonist solidifying from the rhythm as heroes solidified from mist."

Matching the ardor of this method, there was in Paul Rosenfeld a republicanism of respect for that *ignis fatuus*, liberty; a vision of spiritual fitness without visa; of "inner healing" for white America's black victims, those "splintered souls" whose "elasticity of young rubber is weakened and threatened and torn." Although a bachelor, Paul Rosenfeld valued "woman," as Margaret Naumberg, Gertrude Stein, my timid self, and many another have testified. He understood children, their "infantine works and little houses"; their way of "cooking a meal without the friction of personalities," since "the end irradiates the means."

He said, "The artist is no lily-leaning wishful willowy waning sentimentalist," but "a man of stomach," producing "hard form which reveals itself the larger the more it is heard." "Heard" suggests music, and in this regard there is an Amazon to explore; an Amazon that was a river, "flowing and branching throughout a continent."

In objectifying what poets, novelists, educators, painters, photographers, sculptors had given him, Paul Rosenfeld poignantly exemplified his conviction that enrichment involves responsibility. He toiled to benefit his benefactors; or to put it exactly, to benefit benefaction; to justify justice. It is not merely D. H. Lawrence, E. E. Cummings, Gaston Lachaise, Nodier, El Greco, Marsden Hartley, Mozart, or Stravinsky, whom he craved to burnish, but painting, writing, music.

Nor was critical rectitude in Paul Rosenfeld something apart from more prosaic manifestations of conscience. "Michelangelo," he said, "does not stand entirely besmirched for having ceased work on the Medici tombs in order to fortify Florence against brutal Emperor and treacherous Pope." Paul Rosenfeld cared for what becomes of us. "America," he said, "must learn to subordinate itself to a religious feeling, a sense of the whole life, or be dragged down into the slime."

Flamboyant generalities are the refuge of the lazy, things that sound well; but in this instance *are* well. Paul Rosenfeld in his impassioned and varied books was a poet. He was a scientist of music; a musician; the rescuer of Tristram and Iseult from the half-scholarship of judicious translating (Bédier); "contented," "refreshed," "rejoicing," "gladdened" by his multifariousness of gratitude—a figure best praised by his own myriad chivalries, drudgeries, and masteries. When everything has its price, and more than price, and anyone is venal, what a thing is the interested mind with the disinterested motive. Here it is. We have had it in Paul Rosenfeld, a son of consolation, a son of imagination, a man of deeds.

The Nation, 163 (17 August 1946), 192; *A Marianne Moore Reader*.

A MODEST EXPERT

ELIZABETH BISHOP is spectacular in being unspectacular. Why has no one ever thought of this, one asks oneself; why not be accurate and modest? Miss Bishop's mechanics of presentation with its underlying knowledges, moreover, reduces critical cold blood to cautious self-inquiry.

The adornments are structural, as with alliteration, contrast, and the reiterated word as a substitute for rhyme. And rhyme, when used, outshines restraint. Miss Bishop says, "icebergs behoove the soul," "being self-made from elements least visible . . . fleshed, fair, erected indivisible"; and of "snow-fort" "sand-fort" Paris at 7 a.m.,

> . . . It is like introspection
> to stare inside, or retrospection,
> a star inside a rectangle, a recollection.

Review of *North & South*, by Elizabeth Bishop (Houghton Mifflin Company).

One notes the difficult rhyme-schemes of "Roosters," sustained through many stanzas:

> St. Peter's sin was . . .
> . . . . . .
> of spirit, Peter's
> falling, beneath the flares
> among the "servants and officers."

Among the many musicianly strategies is an expert disposition of pauses; and the near-rhymes are impeccable, as in "Wading at Wellfleet,"

> the sea is "all a case of knives."

> Lying so close, they catch the sun,
> the spokes directed at the shin.

One has here a verisimilitude that avoids embarrassingly direct descriptiveness; when journeying from the "Country to the City," for instance: "flocks of shining wires seem to be flying sidewise"; and direct description is neat, never loose, as when the asphalt is said to be "watermelon-striped, light-dry, dark-wet," after the water-wagon's "hissing, snowy fan" has passed. We find that enumerative description—one of Miss Bishop's specialties—can be easy and compact:

> Now can you see the monument? It is of wood
> built somewhat like a box. No. Built
> like several boxes in descending sizes
> one above the other.
> Each is turned half-way round so that
> its corners point toward the sides
> of the one below and the angles alternate.

The wake of the barge is foliage with "Mercury-veins on the giant leaves," always the accurate word; and sensation, yet more difficult to capture than appearance, is objectified mysteriously well:

> Alone on the railroad track
>   I walked with pounding heart.
> The ties were too close together
>   or maybe too far apart.

Miss Bishop does not avoid "fearful pleasantries," and in "The Fish," as in the subject of the poem, one is not glad of the creature's every perquisite; but the poem dominates recollection; "Anaphora" does; and "The Weed" has so somber an authority, surrealism should take a course in it.

Dignity has been sacrificed to exactness in the word "neatly": "The mangrove island with bright green leaves edged neatly with bird-droppings like illuminations in silver"; and in "Songs for a Colored Singer," where impulsiveness is the verbal machinery, has every phrase the feel of the rest of the words—the auxiliary verb "will" for instance? "And if I protest Le Roy will answer with a frown." Like Pyramus and Thisbe, however, ardor in art finds a way, and apostrophe *s* is the deft spelling for "is": "All we got for his dollars and cents / 's a pile of bottles by the fence." The omission of three poems which appeared in *Trial Balances* is a loss—"The Reprimand," and "Valentines I and II."

Art which "cuts its facets from within" can mitigate suffering, can even be an instrument of happiness; as also forgiveness, symbolized in Miss Bishop's meditation on St. Peter by the cock, seems essential to happiness. Reinhold Niebuhr recently drew attention in *The Nation* to the fact that the cure for international incompatibilities is not diplomacy but contrition. Nor is it permissible to select the wrongs for which to be contrite; we are contrite; we won't be happy till we are sorry. Miss Bishop's speculation, also, concerning faith—religious faith—is a carefully plumbed depth in this small-large book of beautifully formulated aesthetic-moral mathematics. The unbeliever is not ridiculed; but is not anything that is adamant, self-ironized?

> . . . Up here
> I tower through the sky
> For the marble wings on my tower-top fly.

With poetry as with homiletics, tentativeness can be more positive than positiveness; and in *North & South*, a much instructed persuasiveness is emphasized by uninsistence. At last we have a prize book that has no creditable mannerisms. At last we have someone who knows, who is not didactic.

The Nation, 163 (28 September 1946), 354.

MR. AUDEN'S "BAROQUE ECLOGUE"

THIS baroque eclogue is so baroque it will be read trembling by those who have noticed how contagious Mr. Auden's innovations are, but it can well afford a suspicious air, since it is his most significant piece of work.

On All Soul's Night, the night of the day of prayer for those in purgatory, four strangers drinking at a bar gradually become acquainted: a tired old widower named Quant, employed as a shipping clerk near the Battery. His mind is full of mythology, like unclaimed luggage, and he thinks he sees an eternal Utopia, whereas it is Eternal Life. Malin, a Canadian medical intelligence officer on leave, thinks he is in search of a good time, but it is goodness. Rosetta, someone's "shadowy she," forever dreaming of her true love, is seeking what Professor Maritain has called gospel love. Born in England, "a couth land," she is now buyer for a large department store in big, empty, noisy America. Emble, a Midwestern college sophomore who had enlisted in the Navy, harbors the illusion that his unease is unique.

The four have an inescapable bond. Their Zion is a doomed Sodom, a tired Gomorrah, a crime accusing all. As Rosetta said, "Lies and lethargies police the world in its periods of peace. What pain taught is soon forgotten. We celebrate what ought to happen as if it were done; are blinded by our boasts. Then back they come, the fears that we fear."

Thinking, at the bar as well as drinking, Quant, Malin, Emble and Rosetta take a mental journey through time, by pairs that interchange, through the seven supperless ages of anguish and the seven stages of suffering. Canoeing through an arcadia in which they encounter the Platonic myth, Emble says to Quant, "Pleasant my companion, but I pine for another," and Quant says, "Our canoe makes no noise. The waterway winds as it wants to through the hush. O, fortunate fluid her fingers caress."

Night is drawing nigh, shadows of the evening steal across the sky (the bartender is turning out the lights). Fantasy now takes on actuality and emotion is personalized. Rosetta suggests that they come to her apartment for a snack and a nightcap. Emble asks Rosetta to dance, and takes the hero's leap into love; Malin builds an altar of sandwiches, and Quant, in new barbarian style, pouring out the dregs of his glass on the carpet as a libation, invokes the local spirits. After seeing Malin and Quant to the elevator, Rosetta the romantic—miles from mother, marriage or any workable world—returns to find Emble, the king of comeliness, on her bed in a

Review of *The Age of Anxiety: A Baroque Eclogue*, by W. H. Auden (Random House).

drunken snore. Dreams have not descended into conduct. Alcohol, lust, fatigue, and the longing to be good, had induced a euphoric state in which it seemed as if it were only some trifling error, improper diet, inadequate schooling or an outmoded moral code which was keeping mankind from the millennial Earthly Paradise. Just a little more effort, perhaps merely the right terms in which to describe it, and surely absolute pleasure must immediately descend upon the astonished armies of the world and abolish forever all their hate and suffering.

We have in this eclogue a morality play showing us the route to hope and health; a deep and fearless piece of work, matched by a mechanics of consummate virtuosity. Mr. Auden is not ashamed of seeming to have done some reading. A wicket gate and the journey through significances recall Bunyan. Bible rhythms and truths abound, as in "Long is the way, slow the going, and few are faithful to the end." "Mosses set in motion to overrun the earth" and "Fair my far, when far ago. / Like waterwheels wishes spun / Radiant robes: but the robes tore" suggest Joyce. "Shilly and Shally the Shepherd Kings, whose sheep nibble nightshade, / Greetings from the great misguided dead," "Hide me, haunt me, in hills to be seen, my visible verb, my very dear," and innumerable alliterative counterparts recall Piers Plowman. "Many have perished, more will" (perished?) would be wrong in an amateur but perhaps is permissible in a master.

Mr. Auden has made progress arresting by placing at the end of a line an adjective, a preposition or an O—a unique form of emphasis, consistently agile in these pages. The rhythms are so firm as to survive prose presentation, and bits of self-burlesque should not blind one to the fact that we have in W. H. Auden a master musician of rhythm and note, unable to be dull, in fact an enchanter, under the magic of indigenous gusto.

The eclogue having ended, there is that dangerous thing, an epilogue, for which, however, Mr. Auden, in his fearsome explicitness, deserves our thanks, together with the reward humility guarantees. "Denial like a friend," he says, "confirms the Self-So, which is the same at all times, which condescended to suffer death, scorned on a scaffold. In our anguish we struggle to elude Him, to lie to Him, our minds insisting on their own disorder as their own punishment, made in our unbelief, waiting unawares for His World to come."

In Mr. Auden's *The Double Man*, the world was at war and we were "in a coma, just breathing, lest the devil destroy the root of freedom." For victims of terror, pride, and hate, there was but one hope, contrition. Now that we have freedom, and peace of mind is being destroyed by lust and fear, since freedom is boredom and we will not make effort, who is well, witty, glad, or good?

Strengths such as love and faith are a reverently attained secret, not to be thrust on the reluctant; when we love only ourselves, however, and have faith only in self, Mr. Auden says, we are lost!

> Well may he appear dejected
> Who must be self-resurrected
> From the ruin he has wrought.

Soiled souls tasting of untruth, self-judged we sit, sad haunters of Perhaps. We cannot forgive ourselves; yet *The Age of Anxiety* assures us that fear and lust have, in faith and purity, a cure so potent we need never know panic or be defeated by Self.

The New York Times Book Review, 27 July 1947, pp. 5, 29.

IV. THE LATER YEARS
1948-1968

A VIRTUOSO OF MAKE-BELIEVE

THE magazine, *Time*, has spoken of "the ferocious fancy latent" in T. S. Eliot's "cat poems." It is tame praise, to substitute query for characterization and postulate triumphs which could not surpass fact; yet does not Mr. Eliot appear to be, in discreet ways, a novelist? Observe in *The Naming of Cats*, would-be familiarity at an impasse; the maneuver, "O Cat"; the overture, Strassbourg Pie or potted grouse; the awaited denouement:

> And so in time you reach your aim
> And finally call him by his *NAME*.

"The doings of the Borgias," Mr. Eliot says, "need to be told by a writer, not by a Dryasdust"; when he refers to a contemporary as having "laid about him in uncompromising fashion," a poet who takes things hard, is lent the flavor of Dumas. He feels magic to be "a natural human preoccupation." One cannot have failed to note his interest in thrillers—"supernatural thrillers," "inverted thrillers," and "flesh-creepers." He ponders "the maladies of contemporary society" and commends to the attention, pages "which describe with frightful clarity the deterioration and damnation of a human soul"; then elsewhere with commensurate urgency devises a hero: "Only the mind of a boy who has seen destruction come to the quiet families of an ordinary town could give a local habitation and a name to war's impersonal terror." Raconteur-like indeed, the suggested effect of frustration where a writer is shown withheld from his task by the tyranny of circumstance— "unemployed, starving, . . . thinking interminably of scenes for which he had a feeling but no pen." Nor is the gusto feigned—note the comma after "And"—with which mere romance is recalled to us: "And, at night there is the ball. We see the glittering uniforms; . . . the Skorokhods, the Cossacks, the Court Arabs. Camellias and orange-trees stand in the center of the supper-tables . . . we look out on the ice floes of the Neva, until the ball ends brilliantly as it began. . . . Nostalgic and intoxicating . . . this evening's entertainment *à la Russe*."

The intensities suggested by the foregoing excerpts from sources too varied to catalogue, point to any of several possibilities; a tale of sampans, pullaways and junks; a kerbside inn-tale of "suspense heightened till all the characters are drawn within its tense circle"; a "classical haunting," or "a modern dilemma expressing a permanent problem."

Another query; since we have in the author of the *Practical Cats*, a virtuoso of make-believe, perhaps we have as well—my persistent suspicion—a master of the anonymous. May we not already have been carried past our destination on the railway, absorbed in a *roman à clef* by Mr. Mistoffelees, the cat who could never be caught?

In *T. S. Eliot: A Symposium*, compiled by Richard Marsh and Tambimuttu. Chicago: Henry Regnery Co., 1948, pp. 179–80.

M. CAREY THOMAS OF BRYN MAWR

CAREY THOMAS was a Quaker with "an almost Renaissance imagination." She "gloried in combat and movement" and "never wasted energy in vain regret," was "critical of praise," adept in reprimand. She had a passion for "joining in and setting things straight." "Slovenly enunciation irritated her." As a child she resented "having to listen in Bible class to a young woman preaching about simplicity, who must have spent an hour or two arranging 'the horrible little curls' that adorned her head." Longing to go to Vassar, she said, "There is one thing I can do and that is study"; and exhilarated by preparatory subjects, "I wish the air were pure oxygen, and then as it says in our chemistry, our life would sweep through its fevered burning course in a few hours and we would live in a perfect delirium of excitement and would die vibrating with passion, for anything would be better than this lazy sluggish life." She was undeterred by "the awful amount of drudgery a first-rate education" involves, remarking in later life, "I cannot remember a time when I did not read at every available moment." Each succeeding phase of study seemed more interesting than the last. Of Wordsworth's *The Prelude* she said, "He spoke right to me. I was almost frightened as I found thought after thought there that had come to me so often"; and

---

Review of *Carey Thomas of Bryn Mawr*, by Edith Finch (Harper).

on discovering *Jane Eyre,* "My throat was parched . . . and cheeks fairly scorched. Oh, though I dare say it isn't a good book, yet it seems to me as if it were something worth while to write something that should have the power to excite and intensely interest to such a degree." She was an irrepressible traveler, delighted in "horrid crags," "fir-clad ravines," "tall spires," and "dusky aisles touched with motes of color from stained windows." A rebel against ambiguous morality, she deplored over-concreteness in religion, yet could say of Leonardo da Vinci's sketch for the head of Christ and the *Last Supper* itself, "One bows before them as by magnetism and immediately one's past becomes a poor undeveloped thing because they have been wanting to it and one's future full of longing without them." Unself-protective if a cause required her to be, she was not afraid of failure; though so honest against herself as to say upon falling in love, "I never came to anything before, I could not partially at least manage."

This account of frustration upon frustration and crusade after crusade to free the mind from legal and other barriers, extends in significance far beyond Quakerism, family, and period. Sobered by obstruction, with forces knit by the injustices of convention, Carey Thomas avowed what in life she contradicted: "Secrecy and guile are the only refuge of a down-trodden sex." The victim of gossip because she had discussed a scholastic matter with a German student on what her landlady termed "the betrothal sofa," she thence behaved as she had in the Cornell "elegant garden of young men," "not only with decorum but marked decorum" and said years after, "Bryn Mawr need not be the less guarded because it is good."

The quest for a degree, from Leipzig to Göttingen to Zurich, seems a fantasy of anachronism. When raising the Women's Fund to establish the Johns Hopkins medical school, Carey Thomas and four of her friends—"The Ladies" as they were called—stipulated that women be admitted on an equality with men and that entrance requirements should not be less rigid than those prescribed by the committee. Miss Thomas, chairman, referring to herself and Miss Gwinn, said, "My father almost wept . . . that two young women should take such a position"; Doctor Welch remarking to Doctor Osler, "We are lucky to get in as professors, for I am sure that neither you nor I could ever get in as students."

Any who have thought of Carey Thomas as ipso facto Bryn Mawr, will find it difficult to realize what handicap "the shrine of womanhood" once constituted, and that a woman who was virtual administrator and dean of a college was made president officially by a majority of but one vote; then only after years of "wary foresight in holding back and driving forward at the right moments," was grudgingly elected to the board of trustees.

Mr. Blackmur says that writing nowadays lacks the positiveness which derives from conviction. Carey Thomas had it, conversationally and in her literature course—living in another world from that of "half happiness," "half love," and "the little little poems that were being written." By her "clarity," her "assurance of values, she impelled others to-ward . . . discriminations"; had the "power of gauging under what circumstances special capabilities might flower most fully," "spared no pains to push and prune," and in faculty selections was willing to give every chance to a candidate in whom she saw promise—"even though he saw little in himself," an insight confirmed by the continual loss of professors to larger colleges. Her name is—understandably—associated with education, the points she made in 1901 nearly coinciding with those made by the "Harvard Committee on the objectives of a general education in a free society" in 1945.

Again Miss Finch is, in her relentless justice, a Vermeer of circumstance and idiosyncrasy when she says of Carey Thomas, "the conflict between deliberate and natural behavior" made her "a little *farouche.*" "She had no use for usual chitchat. Compelled to suffer it, the warmth of her manner chilled to bare civility, the heavy eyelids drooped . . . , her face became a mask of controlled impatience and distaste." One perceives, moreover, that as a disdainer of casuistry, Miss Finch believes in Carey Thomas and means it when she attributes an appearance of "despotism and double-dealing" in her to "real open-mindedness" and "lapse of memory." Miss Gwinn is not less a personality than a type, in "the calculated impression" she made "of knowing all the answers had she chosen to give them," and of finding "struggling conversationalists a little dull."

This is portraiture, verisimilitude in personality matched by verity of setting. Student days in Germany come to life in the " 'regally cultivated' Grüneissen sisters, three maiden ladies of whom Fraülein Mathilde had 'read every one' of the five hundred books on art that comprised their father's library," and "knew almost every picture in existence painted by an Old Master"; she also painted, though "given no chance to train her talent or see the originals." At Leipzig, fellow students "often opened doors for the two expatriates from Baltimore—though sometimes hesitated, then passed through determinedly first, themselves"; yet as Carey Thomas said in her journal, "after a year they seemed to have developed 'a sort of contemptuous affection for us.' " Apparently subordinate descriptive statements having startling precision, as where at Cornell Carey Thomas' parents "plodded about the campus on its hill above the town, appraised the fine old trees and the still rather new-looking halls." Bryn Mawr, equally, is unmistakable in "the autumn smell of dry and burning leaves"; in the busts of the emperors on their golden oak pedestals in Taylor Hall, and in what is said of the Bible "on the square block of the speaker's desk at morning chapel, with Carey Thomas swiftly mounting the platform . . . " then "reading some great passage."

We have here an instance of that difficult but, as Mr. Saintsbury considered, best method of exhibiting a personality—direct quoting; the whole thing so neatly compacted that even a summary of building expansion is not dull. The book is a performance, as biography and as the portrait of one who was for woman an impassioned emancipator.

Hudson Review, 1 (Autumn 1948), 433–35; *A Marianne Moore Reader*.

HIGH THINKING IN BOSTON

AT Miss Gifford's, a boarding-house in the South End of Boston, such subjects were discussed as Chinese poetry, the title-page of a Dutch Bible, Seurat's "La Grande Jatte," Thoreau, and fear of daisies.

The heroine's irresistible, because unintentional, charm seems a counterpart to the method of the book itself, in which modesty lends force to the preoccupations of a modern conscience. " 'Now patience; and remember patience is the great thing, and above all else we must avoid anything like being or becoming out of patience.' " This maxim from Joyce, adopted by Miss Gifford's most individual boarder, underwrites a conviction that "without suffering we do not advance"; that "we lose the blessings of Love by refusing to conform to the law of Love." To both private and to public maladjustment, moreover, an identical logic applies: "There is a lot to worry about and one can make one's self sick or decide to be sane." In Miss Gifford's, "a slight tendency toward melodrama" corrects itself by calling itself that; and we are enticed by verisimilitude and originalities of characterization.

Miss Jones has the art of metaphor, as when she says of Miss Ambler, "She studied her mottled hands as if they were botanical specimens." More important than verisimilitudes of the eye, we have complicated insights expressed compactly, as in the delineating of a young man, a Boston decorator with whom Miss Gifford sometimes took counsel concerning her charges. "He thought what a relief it was when a woman's smile was devoid of intention to stress her charm."

Conspicuous by reason of contrasting accuracies, a verb or epithet in *Miss*

Review of *Miss Gifford's*, by Kathrine Jones (Exposition Press).

Gifford's occasionally stand out as an anachronism, hazarded one almost feels as a certificate of independence; indeed one is ill who cavils at a straightforward story which clearly implies that malady and world malady can be cured if the individual will humbly endeavor to rule not the world but his own spirit. Profundities need not be a bore; and presented with the light touch, by a serious mind, can be, as here, a prism of fascination.

The Saturday Review of Literature, 31 (6 November 1948), 28.

HUMILITY, CONCENTRATION, AND GUSTO

IN times like these we are tempted to disregard anything that has not a direct bearing on freedom; or should I say, an obvious bearing, for what is more persuasive than poetry, though as Robert Frost says, it works obliquely and delicately. Commander King-Hall, in his book *Total Victory*, is really saying that the pen is the sword when he says the object of war is to persuade the enemy to change his mind.

Three foremost aids to persuasion which occur to me are humility, concentration, and gusto. Our lack of humility, together with anxiety, has perhaps stood in the way of initial liking for Caesar's *Commentaries*, which now seem to me masterpieces. I was originally like the Hill School boy to whom I referred in one of my pieces of verse, who translated *summa diligentia* (with all speed): Caesar crossed the Alps on the top of a diligence.

In Caxton, humility seems to be a judicious modesty, which is rather different from humility. Nevertheless, could anything be more persuasive than the preface to his *Aeneid*, where he says, "Some desired me to use olde and homely termes . . . and some the most curyous termes that I could fynde. And thus between playn, rude and curyous, I stand abasshed"? Daniel Berkeley Updike has always seemed to me a phenomenon of eloquence because of the quiet objectiveness of his writing. And what he says of printing applies equally to poetry. It is true, is it not, that "style does not depend on decoration but on simplicity and proportion"? Nor can we dignify confusion by calling it baroque. Here, I may say, I am preaching to myself, since, when I am as complete as I like to be, I seem unable to get an effect plain enough.

We don't want war, but it does conduce to humility; as someone said in the foreword to an exhibition catalogue of his work, "With what shall the artist arm himself save with his humility?" Humility, indeed, is armor, for it realizes that it is impossible to be original, in the sense of doing something that has never been thought of before. Originality is in any case a by-product of sincerity; that is to say, of feeling that is honest and accordingly rejects anything that might cloud the impression, such as unnecessary commas, modifying clauses, or delayed predicates.

Concentration avoids adverbial intensives such as "definitely," "positively," or "absolutely." As for commas, nothing can be more stultifying than needlessly overaccentuated pauses. Defoe, speaking in so low a key that there is a fascination about the mere understatement, is for me one of the most persuasive of writers. For instance, in the passage about the pickpocket in *The Life of Colonel Jacque,* he has the Colonel say to the pickpocket, "Must we have it all? Must a man have none of it again, that lost it?" But persuasiveness has not died with Defoe; E. E. Cummings' "little man in a hurry" (254, *No Thanks*) has not a comma in it, but by the careful ordering of the words there is not an equivocal emphasis:

> little man
> (in a hurry
> full of an
> important worry)
> halt stop forget relax
>
> wait

And James Laughlin, the author of *Some Natural Things,* is eminent in this respect, his "Above the City" being an instance of inherent emphasis:

> You know our office on the 18th
> floor of the Salmon Tower looks
>   right out on the
>
> Empire State & it just happened
> we were finishing up some
>   late invoices on
>
> a new book that Saturday morning
> when a bomber roared through the
>   mist and crashed
>
> flames poured from the windows
> into the drifting clouds & sirens
>   screamed down in

> the streets below it was unearthly
> but you know the strangest thing
> we realized that
>
> none of us were much surprised be-
> cause we'd always known that those
> two Paragons of
>
> progress sooner or later would per-
> form before our eyes this demon-
> stration of their
> true relationship.

Concentration—indispensable to persuasion—may feel to itself crystal clear, yet be through its very compression the opposite, and William Empson's attitude to ambiguity does not extenuate defeat. Graham Greene once said, in reviewing a play of Gorki's, "Confusion is really the plot. A meat-merchant and a miller are introduced, whom one never succeeds in identifying even in the end." I myself, however, would rather be told too little than too much. The question then arises, How obscure may one be? And I suppose one should not be consciously obscure at all. In any case, a poem is a concentrate and has, as W. H. Auden says, "an immediate meaning and a possible meaning; as in the line,

> Or wedg'd whole ages in a Bodkin's eye

where you have forever in microscopic space; and when George Herbert says,

> I gave to Hope a watch of mine,
> But he an anchor gave to me,

the watch suggests both the brevity of life and the longness of it; and an anchor makes you secure but holds you back."

I am prepossessed by the impassioned explicitness of the Federal Reserve Board of New York's letter regarding certain counterfeits, described by the Secret Service:

> $20 FEDERAL RESERVE NOTE . . . faint crayon marks have been used to simulate genuine fibre. . . . In the Treasury Seal, magnification reveals that a green dot immediately under the center of the arm of the balance

scales blends with the arm whereas it should be distinctly separate. Also, the left end of the right-hand scale pan extends beyond the point where the left chain touches the pan. In the genuine, the pan ends where it touches the chain. The serial numbers are thicker than the genuine, and the prefix letter "G" is sufficiently defective to be mistaken for a "C" at first glance, . . . the letters "ry" in "Secretary" are joined together. In "Treasury" there is a tiny black dot just above the first downstroke in the letter "u." The back of the note, although of good workmanship, is printed in a green much darker than that used for genuine currency.

December 13, 1948.   Alfred M. Olsen, Cashier

I am tempted to dwell on the infectiousness of such matters, but shall return to verse. You remember, in Edward Lear's "The Owl and the Pussy-Cat," they said:

> "Dear Pig, are you willing to sell for a shilling
> Your ring?" Said the Piggy, "I will."

The word "piggy" is altered from "Pig" to "Piggy" to fit the rhythm but is, even so, a virtue as contributing gusto; and I never tire of Leigh Hunt's lines about the fighting lions: "A wind went with their paws." Continuing with cats, T. S. Eliot's account of "Mungojerrie and Rumpelteazer," "a very notorious couple of cats," is, like its companion pieces, a study in gusto throughout:

> If a tile or two came loose on the roof,
> Which presently ceased to be waterproof,
> . . . .
> Or after supper one of the girls
> Suddenly missed her Woolworth pearls:
> Then the family would say: "It's that horrible cat!
>   It was Mungojerrie—or Rumpleteazer!"
> —And most of the time they left it at that.

The words "By you" constitute a yet more persuasive instance of gusto, in T. S. Eliot's tribute to Walter de la Mare upon Mr. de la Mare's seventy-fifth birthday:

> When the nocturnal traveler can arouse
> No sleeper by his call; or when by chance
> An empty face peers from an empty house,

By whom: and by what means, was this designed?
The whispered incantation which allows
Free passage to the phantoms of the mind?

By you; by those deceptive cadences
Wherewith the common measure is refined;
By conscious art practiced with natural ease;

By the delicate invisible web you wove—
An inexplicable mystery of sound.

Dr. Maurice Bowra, pausing upon the query, Can we have poetry without emotion? seemed to think not; however, suggested that it is not overperverse to regard Cowper's "The Snail" as a thing of gusto although the poem has been dismissed as mere description:

Give but his horns the slightest touch,
His self-collective power is such,
He shrinks into his house with much
  Displeasure.

Where'er he dwells, he dwells alone.
Except himself, has chattels none,
Well satisfied to be his own
  Whole treasure.

Thus hermit-like his life he leads,
Nor partner of his banquet needs,
And if he meets one, only feeds
  The faster.

Who seeks him must be worse than blind,
He and his house are so combined,
If finding it, he fails to find,
  Its master.

Together with the helpless sincerity which precipitates a poem, there is that domination of phrase referred to by Christopher Smart as "impression." "Impression," he says, "is the gift of Almighty God, by which genius is empowered to throw an emphasis upon a word in such wise that it cannot escape any reader of good sense." Gusto, in Smart, authorized as oddities what in someone else might seem effrontery; the line in Psalm 147, for instance, about Jehovah: "He deals the beasts their food."

> To everything that moves and lives,
> Foot, fin, or feather, meat He gives,
> He deals the beasts their food.

And in "A Song to David":

> Strong is the lion—like a coal
> His eyeball—like a bastion's mole,
> His chest against the foes:
> . . . .
> But stronger still, in earth and air
> And in the sea, the man of pray'r,
> And far beneath the tide;
> And in the seat to faith assign'd
> Where ask is have, where seek is find,
> Where knock is open wide.

With regard to emphasis in Biblical speech, there is a curious unalterableness about the statement by the Apostle James: The flower "falleth and the grace of the fashion of it perisheth." Substitute, "the grace of its fashion perisheth," and overconscious correctness is weaker than the actual version, in which eloquence escapes grandiloquence by virtue of gusto.

Spenser is reprehended for coining words to suit the rhyme, but gusto in even the least felicitous of his defiances convicts the objecter of captiousness, I think, as in *The Shepheards Calender* (the "Chase After Love")— the part about "the swayne with spotted winges, like Peacocks trayne"— the impulsive intimacy of the word "pumies" substituted for a repetition of pumie stones brings the whole thing to life:

> I levelde againe
> And shott at him with might and maine,
> As thicke as it had hayled.
> So long I shott, that al was spent;
> Tho pumie stones I hastly hent
> And threwe; but nought availed:
> He was so wimble and so wight,
> From bough to bough he lepped light,
> And oft the pumies latched.

In any matter pertaining to writing, we should remember that major value outweighs minor defects, and have considerable patience with modifications of form, such as the embodied climax and subsiding last line. Wallace

Stevens is particularly scrupulous against injuring an effect to make it fit a stated mode, and has

> . . . iceberg settings satirize
> . . . .
> The demon that cannot be himself.

Beaumarchais, in saying, "A thing too silly to be said can be sung," was just being picturesque, but recordings of poetry convince one that naturalness is indispensable. One can, however, be careful that similar tones do not confuse the ear, such as "some" and "sun," "injustice" with "and justice"; the natural wording of uninhibited urgency, at its best, seeming really to write the poem in pauses, as in Walter de la Mare's lines about the beautiful lady, the epitaph:

> Here lies a most beautiful lady,
> Light of step and heart was she;
> I think she was the most beautiful lady
> That ever was in the West Country.

All of which is to say that gusto thrives on freedom, and freedom in art, as in life, is the result of a discipline imposed by ourselves. Moreover, any writer overwhelmingly honest about pleasing himself is almost sure to please others. You recall Ezra Pound's remark? "The great writer is always the plodder; it's the ephemeral writer that has to get on with the job." In a certain account by Padraic Colum of Irish storytelling, "Hindered characters," he remarked parenthetically, "seldom have mothers in Irish stories, but they all have grandmothers"—a statement borrowed by me for something I was about to write. The words have to come in just that order or they aren't pithy. Indeed, in Mr. Colum's telling of the story of Earl Gerald, gusto as objectified made the unbelievable doings of an enchanter excitingly circumstantial.

To summarize: Humility is an indispensable ally, enabling concentration to heighten gusto. There are always objectors, but we must not be too sensitive about not being liked or not being printed. David Low, the cartoonist, when carped at, said, "Ah, well—." But he has never compromised; he goes right on doing what idiosyncrasy tells him to do. The thing is to see the vision and not deny it; to care and admit that we do.

Grolier Club Gazette, 2 (May 1949), 289–300; *Predilections; A Marianne Moore Reader*.

E. McKNIGHT KAUFFER

E. McKNIGHT KAUFFER is a very great artist. Instinctiveness, imagination, and "the sense of artistic difficulty" with him, have interacted till we have an objectified logic of sensibility as inescapable as the colors refracted from a prism. Mr. Kauffer's posters, book-jackets, and illustrations, partake of one attitude which is affirmative in all directions, so that here if nowhere else in the world, "street art" is art. Shadows are as arresting as objects; numerals and letters are so rare in themselves that opposing angles, contrasting sizes, and basic parallels, are of consummate elegance—the only kind of eloquence not intrusive. This language of blacks and grays is color in the sense that Chinese brush masterpieces are color. Literal color, moreover, rivals the acetylene blues of the cotinga and the tones in the beak of a toucan. We have here a poetry of synonyms like "the immediate meaning and possible meaning" of poetry, as where a Mexican hat has the form of a plane, the heroism of helplessness is symbolized by a Greek child, and "the medieval tower is half castle and half castle in the air."

E. McKnight Kauffer is a parable of uncompromise—a master of illusion, focusing scrutiny upon the crease and curl of a Stetson, or on the firm solidity of a winter apple, verifying Democritus' axiom, "Compression is the first grace of style."

"What is to be feared more than death?" the man asked; the sage replied "Disillusion." Here, actually, we have a product in which unfalsified impulse safeguards illusion.

In the American British Art Gallery's *Drawings for the Ballet and the Original Illustrations for Edgar Allan Poe by E. McKnight Kauffer*. New York: The Gallery, Batsford House, 1949, p. [2].

"THE WORLD IMAGINED . . . SINCE WE ARE POOR"

THE imagination is "a roamer," Wallace Stevens says, and poetry is "a page from the tale that it tells"; this time, of "Hans by a drift-fire" near "a steamer foundered in ice," "opening the door of his mind" to the aurora

---

Review of *The Auroras of Autumn*, by Wallace Stevens (Alfred A. Knopf).

borealis—to "flames." "The scholar of one candle sees an arctic effulgence flaring on the frame of everything he is, and he feels afraid" but is at ease in "a shelter of the mind with supernatural preludes of its own" to enchant and hypnotize. "The stars are putting on their glittering belts. They throw around their shoulders cloaks that flash. . . ." Thus happiness of the in-centric surmounts a poverty of the ex-centric. This is "the center, the sat-isfaction" which "increases the aspects of experience"—where disembodied converse is "too fragile, too immediate for any speech." The poison in the meditations of the serpent in the ferns is "that we should disbelieve" that there is a starry serpent in the heavens on which to fix the grateful mind.

Thus poetry substitutes for poverty, abundance, a spiritual happiness in which the intangible is more real than the visible and earth is innocent; "not a guilty dream" but a "holiness" in which we are awake as peacefully as if we lay asleep. For the beggar "in a bad time," feeling is frozen.

> What has he that becomes his heart's strong core?
> He has his poverty and nothing more.
> His poverty becomes his heart's strong core. . . .

Yet from illusion's paradise of permanent realization, the self sees "new stars . . . a foot across" come out; becomes someone

> On his gold horse striding like a conjured beast,
> Miraculous in its panache and swish.

Amid grandeur of this sort, surrounded by the "imagination's mercies," one knows the difference between the grand and the grandiose; is safe from "harangue," "ado," and "the ambitious page." Poetry is a "permanence of impermanence," a text obscurely concise perhaps, but nutritive, like the nursery-rhyme: "when the rain raineth and the goose winketh, little wotteth the gosling what the goose thinketh." That is to say, the child is sane, however many times he asks "what is it?" whereas the adult succumbs to an "enfantillage" of intrusiveness and asks you who you are. Safety from verbal myopia as said, is solitude in which "the bouquet is quirked and queered by lavishings of the will to see." The real is made more acute by an unreal; illusiveness is an intangible region in which images flit, for metaphor is a "flit-er" that reflects itself in verisimilitudes of a mirror,—a thing of magic surely, where "It blows a glassy brightness on the fire and makes flame flame." "The pines that were fans and fragrances emerge"; we see "wheat rapturous in the wind," and—objectified to perfection—the fixity in motion of the stream:

> The river kept flowing and never the same way twice,
> Through many places as if it stood still in one.

The "ultimate poem" truly is "far beyond the rhetorician's touch": is as reliable as the bird, the waterfall, "these locusts by day, these crickets by night." It creates an illusion of peace. Peace—

> This is that figure stationed at our end,
> Always in brilliance, fatal, final, formed
> Out of our lives to keep us in our death,
> . . . .
> . . . a king as candle by our beds
> In a robe that is our glory as he guards.

The Hans of these Auroras of Autumn, speaks in a variety of dainty modes; dispersing rhyme as where at intervals, "is," "exists," and "visible," contrast with one another. Sometimes the flexible chain of sound recalls the self-initiated balance of the pendulum, it has such ease:

> Life fixed him wondering on the stair of glass,
> With its attentive eye.

Besides the proprieties of rhyme and of casual statement as in the above lines about the beggar and his heart's strong core, we have un-rhyme with the effect of rhyme:

> blue as of a secret place,
> in the anonymous color of the universe;

and alliterative effects such as "a sovereign, a souvenir, a sign"; "the fidgets of a fire"; "from finikins to fine finikins, edgings and inchings of final form"; the f's taking us back to

> Chieftain Iffucan of Azcan in caftan
> Of tan with henna hackles, halt!—

an effect of tones and pauses matching La Fontaine's Thrysis urging the fish to forsake Naiads for Annette (*Book X:* Fable X):

> Ne craignez point, d'entrer au prison de la belle.
> Ce n'est qu'à nous, qu'elle est cruelle.*

In combining spectacularly quiet verbal harmonies—as follows—with a modestly precise authoritativeness, Wallace Stevens is the La Fontaine of our day:

> Eulalia, I lounged on the hospital porch,
> On the east, sister and nun, and opened wide
> A parasol which I had found, against
> The sun.

One notices further similarities as when La Fontaine differentiates expertly, becomes demure, and says, "I leave it to the authorities"; and Mr. Stevens sets down that the poet "mumbles," writing with the utmost nicety what for us is "the durable, the classic, the incontestable." The vulgarity of poetry is an insisting upon the subsidiary as major; whereas the interior thing is its glory. Sensibility imposes silence which the imagination transmutes into eloquence and then, for the spiritual mariner, however northern, stranded, or chilled, there is society in solitude. Indeed "If it should be true that reality exists / In the mind," one has it all—"the heavens, the hells, the worlds, the longed-for lands," "the invisible tree which may hold a serpent whose venom and whose wisdom will be one." This "force of illusions" underlies whatever Mr. Stevens has written:

> That's it. The lover writes, the believer hears,
> The poet mumbles and the painter sees,
> Each one, his fated eccentricity.

It is "the spirit's speech," "a disused ambit of the spirit's way," "a gorgeous fortitude," the "tidal undulation" in this tale of Hans—a brilliant book, as Padraic Colum said recently—*Auroras of Autumn*—embodying the thinking of a lifetime.

Poetry New York, No. 4 (1951), 7–9.

---

*You need not shrink from the creel you will presently fill, / Since you are not mortals Love can kill (M. M. translation).

EVERY SHADOW A FRIEND

THIS treatise *On the Making of Gardens*, first issued in England in 1909, is notable as an exposition of its subject and no less as a portrait of the impassioned mind—of its author as poet and moralist, "regarding his surroundings with analytic attention." Sir Francis Bacon's "Essay on Gardens" at last has a counterpart. Poetic implacability was never seen to better advantage than in the style of Sir George Sitwell, in which nicety is barbed with a kind of decorous ferocity, as when he says, "Forgery in art is not a crime unless it fails to deceive." Metaphor so merges with context as scarcely to be distinguishable from it—in the statement, say, that "architecture, the most useful of the arts, belongs to the passerby."

The glory of the book, however, is in its originality of emphasis—upon the Campagna ruins, for instance, lost at the horizon in a gleam of the sea, though "not like the sea, which is dreadful because it remembers not." "We must be ready," Sir George says, "to learn all that science can teach us concerning the laws of presentment." "When setting himself to anything," we are told in the Introduction by Sir Osbert Sitwell, "no pain was spared, either to himself or to others." "He particularly liked to alter the levels at which full-grown trees were standing," Sir Osbert says. "Two old yew trees in front of the dining-room windows at Renishaw were regularly heightened and lowered." Engineering zeal in any case is seen to have its verbal prototype. It is "the passion for ideality" which has excluded such words as "very" and "extremely" from these pages of consummate elegance. The secret of burnished writing is strong intention. The man is the style.

In garden-making the great secret of success, it would seem, is "the profound platitude that we should abandon the struggle to make nature beautiful round the house and should rather move the house to where nature is beautiful"; "the garden should be in sympathy with both . . . 'as if one were stepping from one room to another' "; and "like every other work of art, it should have a climax." It should be "presented with economy of the recipient's attention"—"without features which disturb or detract," since "if a picture be complete, everything that is added is something taken away."

The guiding principle of garden-makers of the Italian Renaissance, Sir George Sitwell says, was imagination. "We learn from them the value of contrast," and "if care has been taken to make the expectation less than the reality, we shall have the added thrill of wonder." At the Villa Mondragone,

---

Review of *On the Making of Gardens*, by Sir George Sitwell, with an introduction by Sir Osbert Sitwell (Charles Scribner's Sons).

for instance, there is "a little iron balcony"; after "gloom and confinement as you step out upon it the boundless view takes your breath away." Inversely, while "all the landscape seems to swoon in a white haze of heat," one may have the contrast of unexpected shade in "the deep refreshing green of an avenue of cypresses half a millennium old."

In their mastery of "the water-art," Sir George likens the great Italians to "a sultan with his jewels or Turner playing with light," "prisoning the blue of the sea," "green of chrysoprase," or "the rainbow in a crystal spray." His imparting of technicalities is explicitness itself, as when he says, "The delicious softness of the grass, gives at the first footstep a release from care, which should be proffered close to the house and if possible at a center of beauty."

Sir George Sitwell shows us in this glittering treatise how to look at what we see; his stately observations are applicable to small as well as to great gardens; and throughout, an inescapable lesson is afforded us—that discipline results in freedom. "If the scheme has no air of permanence," we are told, "if it preaches the uncertainty of life and the uselessness of effort— the cup of beauty it offers will be tainted with sadness." "In a garden, a new character is put upon the individual. Instead of life's double face, every shadow is a friend."

"The garden is inimical to all evil passions; it stands for efficiency, for patience in labor, for strength in adversity, for the power to forgive." "In the garden of the Bamboo Grove, Buddha taught the conquest of self, and in the Garden of Sorrows, a greater teacher was found." Gardens are thus seen to be "a background for life"—"not for refreshment alone" but "for the unbending of a bow that it may shoot the stronger."

The New York Times Book Review, 19 August 1951, pp. 7, 20; *Predilections*.

IMPACT, MORAL AND TECHNICAL; INDEPENDENCE VERSUS EXHIBITIONISM; AND CONCERNING CONTAGION

PROFESSOR Levin talks about the owl of wisdom and I was going to ask if you would condone my simplicities. If I was so gifted as to be able to say what Stephen Spender said last night about the continuing principle in poetry beyond its intrinsic terms, that is what I would like to say. Now is there such a thing, I would like to ask, as intrinsic attraction that can surmount indifference to technique? I doubt it. Rigor here is essential, and not the mortuary kind, but the studious kind, can be our salvation.

I was to talk about words, and about how one can hold people's attention. I feel that the clue to contagion is to take a clinical view of our clumsiness, and that subject-matter that takes possession of us—that interests us— affords us the patience to work at the weak spots. As Bernard de Voto, in his recent book on fiction, says: "We will always choose the novice to the superior person and a first-rate technician who is a second-rate person." As for the superior person, I don't mean Gibbon and Lord Chesterfield. Mr. Ransom is a help there, where he says that the human creature is doomed to constitutional fear, to worry and anxiety which are out of relation to his many actual masters. But he has a means of deliverance, his talent for affection. That is most fortifying.

I have of late been trying to translate La Fontaine's fables. All I can say about my efforts is that I am trying for expression that is reliable, and I feel that the principles essential to efficient translation have a bearing on writing in general. One tries to avoid dead phrases and dependent clauses; and the active voice is more arresting and stronger than the passive voice; and this is my mania—the natural order of words, the subject, the predicate, and the object. I think that Dudley Fitts and Robert Fitzgerald in the *Antigone* are most remarkable in this respect. That passage on man:

> The storm gray sea yields to his prow,
> The huge crests bear him high.
> O fate of man, working both good and evil!
> When the laws are kept, how proudly his city stands!
> When the laws are broken, what of his city then?
> Never may the antarctic man find rest at my heart;
> Never be it said that my thoughts are his thoughts.

Dante Gabriel Rossetti, in translating from Francesco de Barberino concerning *Caution*, says:

> Wouldst thou protect thy son from sorrow
>   having some sin before he can begin?
> Wouldst guard thy house, one door have and
>   no more?
> With seven orchard walls be free of fruit to all.

I fell into a trap there; that did not seem to me very satisfactory, so for myself I altered it:

> . . . give of thy fruits all.

which is certainly damaging, and doesn't bear out the meaning at all; so I of course re-established the translation as it is:

> . . . be free of fruit to all.

Now the precepts cited, are deduced from various authors: Rossetti, Ezra Pound, and others. Ezra Pound makes a point of the natural order of words, and I find that he breaks that rule over and over again because it is necessary—which shows that we dare not be mechanistic about these things. This is Rossetti, at the conclusion of one of the Cavalcanti sonnets—

> Alas, my soul within my heart does pine and sigh.
> And drowned in bitter tears those sighs depart.
> And then there seems a presence in the mind
> As of a lady's thoughtful countenance
> Come to behold the death of this poor heart.

That has wonderful ease to my mind; and I suppose it is more than just that; but I think what really attracts me to these verses is their naturalness. Professor Levin has been examining my La Fontaine, and when in desperation I said "forsooth" or "erstwhile" or "whilst," in a very small hand he wrote in the margin, "Do you really like this?" No, I do not.

The first requisite of a translation, it seems to me, is that it should not sound like a translation. That similacrum of spontaneity can be a fascinating thing indeed. Hannah Josephson in her translation of Stendhal's *Memoirs of Self-Examination* gets it surprisingly at some points: where he says of Philippe de Ségur "the beast has courage." That sounds to me quite as if it might have been written in English. Now this sort of verisimilitude drives home the fact that the intention matters supremely. There is no room for furious virtuosity. A master axiom for all writing, I feel, is that of Confucius: "When you have done justice to the meaning, stop." That implies restraint, that discipline is essential. I listened eagerly to what Mr. Viereck said about obscurity last night, and now I can plead guilty there. I have a very special fondness for writing that is obscure, that does not quite succeed, because of the author's intuitive restraint. All that I can say is that one must be as clear as one's natural reticence allows one to be.

It is a commonplace that we are the most eloquent by reason of the not said. This is especially true of rhythm, the pattern of the pauses in a piece of verse—but I am still talking about contagion, and making what one is trying to say effective. Terseness and that simultaneous double meaning of the pun have been irresistible to writers always: to the metaphysical poets, to James Joyce and William Empson, and to ourselves. La Fontaine is interesting in this respect, I think. He goes out of date and ahead of it. I consider him out of date where he says:

> He'd sing from break of day till the sun would disappear,
>   Like a seraph; any there
> Admired as the clear arpeggios would sink
>   Deeper than the seven sages think.

That "deeper" is literal, without the shimmer of the unsaid, and the word "light" is literal where the milkmaid is counting her eggs before they are hatched, "and her head grew light as her summer attire," when she thought of all she would get for the milk she would sell. Now he succeeds, to my mind, when he says that "the court belle adjusts her artificial fly-freckle," intensifying her complexion by a little patch before she goes forth to conquer; and where the ant says to the fly, "but flies are spies and sure to be hung"— playing on the word *mouche* with which the word "patch" is identical, and it is so compact that it is a desperation because we are not often able to achieve such simultaneity ourselves. Robert Bridges insisted that words be in keeping—or, might we say, deliberately out of keeping.

Rhythm and rhyme, of course, are magic and mesmerizing; and Stendhal speaks of the inane sing-song of the Alexandrine; the inane is one of the most useful expedients in the world, however, when the author knows the inane from the spirited, can profit by it and not fight himself from two directions. La Fontaine says of the hag and the "web" spinners, "An old hag had two maids spinning flax she prepared, so artfully the Fates would not dare to compare their webs with the maids' more concealed artistry, and each day the old hag was industriously supplying her spinners with more and more flax." And then again by his demureness, this mischief in the midst of apparent sobriety, he says in "Love and Folly," where Love was handicapped after Folly blinded him:

> Unless perhaps a service was done,
> Let lovers say, a lonely man has no criterion.

Well, writing is difficult—at least it is for me. As Katherine Anne Porter said the other evening, quoting Lewis Carroll's "Reeling and writhing and fainting in coils," "our salvation is urgency. That saves us." I was also interested in Wallace Fowlie's statement that Paul Valéry thought writing poetry is a bending of the will to all kinds of constraint. Somebody asked me if I was going to say something about why I dislike poetry. I say it with all my heart: I fear and dread it, and we are estranged from it by much that passes for virtuosity—that is affectation or exhibitionism—and then talent comes to the rescue, and we forget about what we think and automatically we are helplessly interested. But here instinct outdoes intellect, for the rhythm is the person. And rhythm is added when W. H. Auden says, in his birthday verses to John Rettger:

> I'm not such an idiot
> As to claim the power
> To peer into the vistas
>   Of your future, still
> I'm prepared to guess you
> Have not found your life as
> Easy as your sister's
>   And you never will.

Now verbal bravura is not a thing to be carefully acquired, but we can be careful of substituting exhibitionism for bravura. I bordered on it very much myself when I was going to say that that remark of Mr. Ransom's is like my new magnesium stepladder. A neighbor came in and called it "outstanding." When someone asked Bernard Shaw how he would spend his birthday, he said, "I shall rise, dress, feed, undress and go to bed." I think that word feed is a little overemphatic. Particularization, here, affords the positive aspect of this phase of the matter.

The chairman of English at Brooklyn College, when I gave a talk there, said that their lectures were highly schematized, but that I afforded an interesting contrast. I trembled to realize that I had, and I tremble again. My observations cannot be regularized, but I might summarize them by saying that I believe verbal felicity is the fruit of ardor, of diligence, and of refusing to be false.

In *Harvard Summer School Conference on The Defense of Poetry*. Cambridge: Harvard University, 1951, pp. 71-76.

IN HARALD'S SERVICE

FREEDOM is the hero of *The Fourteenth of October* and Wulf, the Saxon boy who is the chief character, is a wolf of uncompromise. The author's undeceived eye for beauty and her passion for moral beauty have produced a Bayeux tapestry, pertinent to the thought of a free world—fraught with precepts which could save us. A gallant book.

Wulf—hostage of the Danes—is brought from them by Rollo the Norman to tend his dogs, and is carried into exile. He escapes with Rafe, a half-Saxon man-at-arms, to Rafe's village in South Britain and, later, with a band of others they set forth to join King Harald's army.

As scientific habitat groups re-create a species—entirely free from the plaster-of-paris facsimile effect in this instance—the story of Wulf revives Norman Conquest days and the defeat of Harald at Hastings on the 14th of October, 1066—an arrow through his helmet as we have known; but we have not known the dress, occupations, and landscape as here.

This account by Bryher—an Englishwoman whose name derives from one of the Scilly Isles off Cornwall—has the temperate objectiveness of Freeman's *Norman Conquest*. It has the urgency of G. A. Henty's *Wulf the Saxon*, and is further animated by two factors which make interest in the Battle of Hastings one's own: the poetic eye and deep philosophical insight. And the power of implication, insured by compactness, lends *The Fourteenth of October* emotional verisimilitude considerably greater than that of *The Golden Warrior* by Hope Muntz.

"The first real departure in the historical novel since Sir Walter Scott," Horace Gregory says; indeed compared with Bryher's kind of fictional history, previous chronological historical statement seems pallid. Wulf was told how, on the eve of battle, "a harper began" and presently "the whole army was chanting the story of the race, the staves, the staves rising and falling in the rhythm of axe swings." We see the Normans "ride forward, perfectly

Review of *The Fourteenth of October*, by Bryher (Pantheon Books).

spaced, as quietly as if they were hunting." "Just before darkness," the "cove was flecked with points of oyster light." Forebodings were heard. "It is the Doom." "If we held together. . . ." "That, people will never do, they are too selfish."

Wulf deplores apathy, "the clutch of habit," and the sense of "possessions as important." He says, "The people blame Harald but they would not follow him; there is blood guilt on them . . . ; do everything the same way always; make no changes, hunt the stranger." This is a warning identical with General Eisenhower's plea for "selfless leadership at all levels of society. . . . If only the people of the West have the wisdom to make a complete break with many things of the past and show a willingness to do something new . . . can they avoid disaster."

The New York Times Book Review, 27 April 1952, p. 4.

VIBRANT TALE OF THE JACOBEAN THEATER REANIMATES HISTORY

"WHAT goes on here?" What about all this probity and mouse-colored velvet? one is inclined to inquire, like Margaret O'Brien's friend, the criminal, in *Lost Angel*; brought up short here after serving as an unwilling testing ground for rough and ready fiction.

What goes on is somber enough. Told that his father had died of the plague, even before warned of his illness, James Sands is apprenticed to Awsten Phillips. "Nobody could ever replace Awsten"—incomparable as actor and master. Awsten dies of a fever, after apprenticing Sands to Sly, who leads him as a page to Beaumont, the dramatist—Francis Beaumont the brilliant, the perceptive yet "remotest of men"—to the player's boy a kind of god. " 'Flatterer!' Mr. Beaumont said and tapped me lightly on the shoulder." For Beaumont, himself, life was

> . . . but the giving over of a game
> That must be lost.

He had written his own epitaph. Then Ralegh—"the wisest captain we ever had, clapped into the Tower . . . . If it had not been for the ships, the

---

Review of *The Player's Boy*, by Bryher (Pantheon Books).

King would have had neither realm nor riches to inherit.' " 'They are bringing him out. . . . And then Sir Walter will kneel and thank God for his mercy and the King for his clemency.' . . . There was a terrible silence. The people swayed. I could not move my arms. 'God have mercy on him' people whimpered who had not lifted a hand to save him." Executed before Westminster Hall at ten in the morning. " 'Disperse, disperse,' the Guard were using their staves. The bell of their far-off cries tolled not for a man but for a nation."

Much may happen in life that cannot happen in a novel, and one does not like it that so gallant a tale should be so sad. Sands is trapped and murdered in revenge for having drawn his dagger and frustrated thugs of snatching ten pounds. Tragedy, yes; but tragedy with an application: It is attitude rather than circumstances of which life consists. Life has point "if one may better what is wrong"—or try to better it. Sad but dainty reading this, for the author has a gifted eye and a satiric one. She is hard-headed and a poet. She "pours everything into the moment"—never permitting the moment, however, to obscure basic verisimilitude. For the player's boy, "it was the dark Thames. (Oh, here it was not silver.)" "The rain thundered on the roof, with an occasional wilder shower threshing through the regular beat." Time "never ran in a straight scythe-cut. . . . It lay like the grass at haying time . . . stem and flowers upside down together." We have the Indies caught to perfection by the sea-captain's nephew who "used to climb to the masthead and look down at the flying fish trimble tremble between the waves." And we have a knight's manor-house in Kent where Beaumont is presenting and acting a preliminary version of his Bellario—with a fat squire remarking, "I'd as soon hunt otters, till my boots were full of water, than sit on a stool for hours, listening to a tale I cannot follow."

Fidelity sums it up. Only an unparalleled degree of scruple, historic imagination, and tireless interworking of sources, could have produced this vibrant simulation of a period—of regression following the reign of Elizabeth; an even stricter example of history reanimated, than *The Fourteenth of October*, the author's account of the Battle of Hastings.

New York Herald Tribune Review of Books, 24 May 1953, p. 4.

OVERRUN BY BARBARIANS

I N *Roman Wall* Bryher has written a story of 265 A.D., with philosophical implications important for ourselves in a world not unlike that of the Roman Empire as barbarians overran the frontier. Prominent in the story are Valerius, a Roman officer; Valodius, governor of Aventicum, and Demetrius, a Greek, trader. Valerius, his sister Julia, her ward Veria, and a young Helvetian as farm boy, live at Orba in a once handsome Alpine villa on a slope above fertile meadows. They are under threat of invasion by Alemanni and when another outpost falls, take refuge in a nearby town.

It is possible to be grateful to a man, Bryher says, yet dislike him, and her work makes plain that it is possible to be a woman and see faults in women. We have in Julia, the austere householder, "a woman of injured moods," in whose presence one is uncomfortable; whereas Fabula, the wife of a commander under whom Valerius had served, was a person "so merciful and majestic" one felt awkward in her presence for the opposite reason.

Inwrought with the tale are some of the great secrets of philosophy: many promises mean broken promises; there is strength in forgiveness; the art of arts is simplicity. As in all Bryher's work, her eye is on the object and we see it too—"the dogs chasing mice as the men moved forward with their scythes." We see "fires everywhere, villas flaming" as Aventicum falls; then Plinius with "cloak around his mouth, pushing his way through the cloudy air as if he were swimming under water." Despite an exactitude that avoids preciosity, there is this flaw in the realism of the book: Bryher attributes to nearly all her characters an equally keen eye in the appreciation of nature.

As in her two previous historical novels—*The Fourteenth of October* (an account of the Battle of Hastings), and her novel of Elizabethan times, *The Player's Boy*—Bryher is here asking a question: Why must we pay with our lives for lessons we could learn from the past? She is insisting: be resolute, face the cause of your peril and say to the cowardly, "God will be with me, I do not have to pretend to be indifferent when I am trembling all over."

Aventicum is sacked by Alemanni, and the inhabitants are set wandering because "Rome condoned certain deeds and spared the individual at the expense of the race." "It was common practice to trap herdsmen and sell them beyond the Rhine." "Beatings were administered that were meant for somebody else." Slavery, bribes and gambling were taken for granted. The governor complained that he had to give up a third of his income to pay the worst gladiators ever to step into an arena; and he had a peace party to deal

Review of *Roman Wall*, by Bryher (Pantheon Books).

with, initiated by a man with a large warehouse. "The people would not work, they would not pray." "There was constant talk about invasion; nobody now was certain as to who was emperor of what. Most roads got mended, trade went on, yet he could not deny the change. Something had happened; it was as if a sentry had been asked to keep one watch too many and his fiber had snapped."

As history reanimated, Bryher's *Roman Wall* is remarkable. A man of imagination and a good soldier, Valerius is satisfactory as hero; the real hero of the book is the mind that does not deceive itself.

The New York Times Book Review, 16 May 1954, p. 5.

WHAT SO WISE AS SIMPLICITY!

F O R Rossini's *Cinderella—La Cenerentola*—as performed by the New York City Opera, a huge cerise curtain drawn to a central pucker, with a border of heavy gold fringe, strikes a note to which everything that follows conforms. This setting by Rouben Ter-Arutunian is adapted from a Pollock Theatre— that boldly colored but exquisitely constructed and ingeniously operated nineteenth century miniature stage. Pollock Theatres are equipped with toy-sized replicas of actual productions; Mr. Ter-Arutunian's principal source was a reproduction of the *Cinderella* staged at Covent Garden in 1830, but he has borrowed elements from other Pollock sets.

La Cenerentola had its premiere in Rome, January 25, 1817; was sung in Italian in New York from 1826 on; was first performed in English in 1831. One June 23, 1852, Madame Alboni, one of the greatest voices of the era, sang an aria from *La Cenerentola* at her debut concert. On December 27, she opened her season of opera at the Broadway Theatre with a performance of the complete work, with Sangiovanni and Barili. Walt Whitman, who had a passion for coloratura singing, was in the audience. In 1934, the opera was directed in London by Otto Erhardt who also staged the City Center production. (Conchita Supervia, Spanish mezzo-soprano, took the part of Cinderella in the 1934 production, becoming for a time the virtual proprietor of the role.)

The City Center staging gives us the traditional Cinderella of the brothers

---

Review of Rossini's *La Cenerentola*, as performed by the New York City Opera.

Grimm, on her knees by the fire, with dust-brush and bellows, ruby sea-horses in the Park fountain, the gold coach, the clock at ten minutes to one. A prince must marry at once or be disinherited; to ensure a true choice, he is impersonated by his servant Dandini—who wears, though with a pro-tectingly ambiguous suspicion of burlesque, the Order of the Garter and an unmistakably royal cape of crimson velvet that swings and swirls. At the end, the Prince-in-disguise becomes himself—royalty somewhat stiffly at-tired with a pale blue ribbon against white satin. And, like Cinderella, he wears a crown of diamonds set in old-time upright imperial points.

Slight alterations of plot in no way detract from the charm of the story or interfere with its force as a parable. Don Ramiro, Prince of Salerno, dis-patches Alidoro, court philosopher and tutor to the Prince, to discover and adjudge all marriageable girls in the kingdom. Alidoro comes as a beggar to the palace of Don Magnifico—a baron whose fortunes are in disrepair, like his palace. Wrecked by a passion for ostentation, Magnifico has squan-dered the dowry of his daughter, Angelina, and she, as Cinderella, is now kept in servitude by her father and step-sisters, Clorinda and Tisbe. Ali-doro—equivalent here of the fairy-godmother with a wand—is hospitably received by Cinderella after being rebuffed by the step-sisters. He provides her with attire for the ball at the palace, where Dandini lays bare the mercenary incivility of the sisters as they fawn upon him and scorn Prince Ramiro, whom they take for a groom. In this version, Cinderella gives the Prince one of two diamond bracelets; the one she keeps identifies her later, when the Prince finds her drudging for Don Magnifico.

The enticements of the story have an irresistible replica in the music—vibrant, spectacular, robust, modest, melodious, personal, grand and witty by turns. Joseph Rosenstock, who conducts *La Cenerentola*, has both fire and taste in his muted effects, his management of the undulating, precisely-paced diminuendo, the escorting innuendoes of the bass drum; he makes picturesque to an extreme the flute and the piano alone.

One wishing to acquire a language, should encounter an endearing story told in that tongue, as here where this best of fairy tales is sung in Italian. "Condone it; pardon my simplicity," Cinderella pleads when she suddenly comes upon the Prince and lets the cup she was bringing drop and shat-ter. . . . "*Scusate—perdonate alla mia semplicità.*" Stunned by high graces in a servant, the Prince soliloquizes, "What innocence! What candor! (*Che innocenza! che candore!*)."

Enunciatory triumphs of orchestra and word glorify the production all along, leaving an impression of spontaneous brio, especially as the Prince muses on the glittering bracelet, his clue by which to find the giver: "I shall find her; yes, I swear it! (*Sì, ritrovarla, io giuro!*)" What "body" we have in the voice of Don Magnifico as he expounds his dream of civic eminence—of shining as "the rarest of donkeys—a very beautiful donkey—yet one of great dignity (*un belissimo somaro, ma solenne*)." "Then suddenly, oh what a portent! Hundreds of feathers sprouted from my shoulders and, whoosh, I launch away in flight."

> Quando a un tratto, o che portente!
> Su le spalle a cento a cento
> Gli spuntarono le penne,
> Ed in alto, scùi, vòlò!

When Don Ramiro chooses Cinderella, the dream is blasted for father and step-daughters; Tisbe protests, "A hard pill to swallow (*La pillola e un poco dure*)." Such humor in diction is matched by virtuosities of behavior—as in Dandini's caricoles and one-leg pirouette.

A fable of fortunes reversed! Hauteur defeated by humility, strategy by sincerity and love, malevolence by kindness. What so wise as simplicity!

Center: A Magazine of the Performing Arts, 1 (April–May 1954), 21–22.

A BOLD VIRTUOSO

IN reviewing *Harmonium*—reprinted in 1931—Horace Gregory said, "All voices fall to a whisper and the expression of the face is indicated in the lifting of the eyebrow."[1] This is the perfect description of Wallace Stevens.

"Poetry is an unofficial view of being," Mr. Stevens says, and of our own today, "it wears a deliberately commonplace costume. . . . We do not write in the rhythm of *The Lady of the Lake*, any more than General Eisenhower would wear the armor of Agamemnon." Crispin

> . . . gripped more closely the essential prose
> As being, in a world so falsified,
> The one integrity for him, the one
> Discovery still possible to make,
> To which all poems were incident, unless
> That prose should wear a poem's guise at last.

The poet commits himself to that one integrity: antipathy to falsity. But "the imagination always makes use of the familiar," Mr. Stevens says, "to produce the unfamiliar," and "a deliberately commonplace costume" clothes themes far from commonplace, as we see in this metaphor of the shawl ("Final Soliloquy of the Interior Paramour"):

> Light the first light of evening, as in a room
> In which we rest and, for small reason, think
> The world imagined is the ultimate good.
> . . . .
> Within a single thing, a single shawl
> Wrapped tightly round us, since we are poor, a warmth
> A light, a power, the miraculous influence.

A single shawl—Imagination's—is wrapped tightly round us since we are poor. Wallace Stevens embeds his secrets, inventing disguises which assure him freedom to speak out; and poverty is one of his favorites. In "Page from a Tale" (*The Auroras of Autumn*), Hans is poor and chilly—Hans "by his drift-fire" near "a steamer . . . foundered in the ice," warmed by fires of his imagining; "a beggar in a bad time" "opening the door of his mind" to the aurora borealis, "to flames." "The scholar of one candle sees an arctic effulgence flaring on the frame of everything he is, and feels afraid," but is at ease in "a shelter of the mind." "The stars are putting on their glittering belts. They throw around their shoulders cloaks that flash." Thus happiness of the in-centric surmounts a poverty of the ex-centric. For poverty, poetry substitutes a spiritual happiness in which the intangible is more real than the visible and earth is innocent, "not a guilty dream" but a "holiness, in which we are awake as peacefully as if we lay asleep. One sees "new stars . . . a foot across" come out; becomes someone ("In the Element of Antagonisms")

> On his gold horse striding, like a conjured beast,
> Miraculous in its panache and swish.

Amid grandeurs of this sort, surrounded by the imagination's "mercies," one knows the difference between the grand and the grandiose. With a metaphysician, an ogre, a grammarian, a nomad, an eel, as disguise for intensity, one is safe from "harangue," "ado," and the ambitious page.

Mr. Stevens carries to an extreme the art of understatement. Notice in the nun and the sunshade, i. e., "Certain Phenomena of Sound," Part III (*Transport to Summer*), the art of velvet emphasis, suspended till scarcely detectable:

> Eulalia, I lounged on the hospital porch,
> On the east, sister and nun, and opened wide

A parasol, which I had found, against
The sun. The interior of a parasol,
Is a kind of blank which one sees.
So seeing, I beheld you walking, white,
Gold-shined by sun, perceiving as I saw
That of that light Eulalia was the name.
Then I, Semiramide, dark-syllabled,
Contrasting our two names, considered speech.

In Professor Gustave Cohen's *La Grande Clarté du Moyen-Age*, we have:

Buona pulcella fu Eulalia
Belle avret corps, bellezour anima.
"Sage pucelle fut Eulalie
Bel avait corps, mais plus belle avait l'âme."*

Whereas for the nun on the hospital porch, personality is focused on speech.
Names are part of Wallace Stevens' "persistent euphony"—a term used by
William James in a letter to Henri Bergson, quoted by Wallace Stevens in
his "Figure of the Youth as a Virile Poet." It is surely appropriate to "Le
Monocle de Mon Oncle" (*Harmonium*):

A deep up-pouring from some saltier well
Within me, bursts the watery syllable.

The many water metaphors in the work of Wallace Stevens are striking
evidence, moreover, of his affinity—say, synonymity—with rhythm. In "That
Which Cannot be Fixed" (*Transport to Summer*) he says:

. . . there is

A beating and a beating in the center of
The sea, a strength that tumbles everywhere,

and in "This Solitude of Cataracts" (*Auroras of Autumn*), the river "kept
flowing and never the same way twice, flowing / Through many places, as
if it stood still in one"—a master description of the uniformity in variety of
flowing water. We find unrhymed lines that have the effect of rhyme:

*A virtuous maiden was Eulalia
 Beautiful of body, more beautiful of soul.
 "A wise maiden was Eulalia
 Her body had great beauty, but her soul had even more."

> blue as of a secret place
> in the anonymous color of the universe;

but even without rhyme, Mr. Stevens is a master of sound, as in "the icy Elysée"; "a sovereign, a souvenir, a sign"; "the fidgets of a fire"; "from finikins to find finikin, edgings and inchings of final form." We have "shawl" and "shell," "swell" and "shawl"; "hill" and "sail"—in "Continual Conversation with a Silent Man" (*Transport to Summer*):

> The broken cartwheel on the hill.

> As if, in the presence of the sea,
> We dried our nets and mended sail.

The compacted spontaneity with pauses, counterpoint, and euphony of "Certain Phenomena of Sound"—already quoted—match La Fontaine: " . . . sister and nun," I "opened wide / A parasol, which I had found, against / The sun."

Together with the infallible mastery of pause and tone, there is in Wallace Stevens a certain demureness of statement, as when—setting down what he has to say with the neatest kind of precision—he says, "the poet mumbles"; much as La Fontaine affects impartiality, ponders the practice of predecessors, and submits preference to "the authorities"; or says of Cupid blinded by Folly, "but perhaps a service was done. / Let lovers say; a lonely man has no criterion." Surely the term that Pierre Schneider applies to La Fontaine applies to Wallace Stevens, a "melomane." In his treatise "Le Paradis et l'Habitant," Mr. Schneider says of La Fontaine, his "speech is a golden thread of words" leading us into gardens of Versailles where the grass is soft and thick and the waters against walls of green "are lost in crystal geometry that never ends." "His prose is not less poetic than his poetry," Mr. Schneider says. The same may be said of Wallace Stevens' essay, "Figure of the Youth as a Virile Poet," where he speaks of a place in which it would be pleasant to spend a holiday, where he imagines "a rock that sparkles, a blue sea that lashes, and hemlocks in which the sun can merely fumble."

[1] *New York Herald Tribune*, September 27, 1931.

From a series of commentaries on selected contemporary poets, Bryn Mawr, 1952; *Predilections*.

"TEACH, STIR THE MIND, AFFORD ENJOYMENT"

O U R debt to Ezra Pound is prodigious for the effort he has made to share what he knows about writing and, in particular, about rhythm and melody; most of all, for his insistence on liveness as opposed to deadness. "Make it new," he says. "Art is a joyous thing." He recalls "that sense of sudden growth we experience in the presence of the greatest works of art." The ode to "Hugh Selwyn Mauberley" applies of course to himself:

> For three years, out of key with his time,
> He strove to resuscitate the dead art
> Of poetry; to maintain "the sublime"
> In the old sense. . . .

And, above all, it is the art of letters in America that he has wished to resuscitate. He says in "Cantico del Sole":

> The thought of what America would be like
> If the classics had a wide circulation
> Troubles my sleep. . . .

America's imperviousness to culture irks him; but he is never as indignant as he is elated.

Instruction should be painless, he says, and his precept for writers is an epitome of himself: teach, stir the mind, afford enjoyment. (Cicero's *Ut doceat, ut moveat, ut delectet.*[1]) Dudley Fitts grants him his wish and says, "The Pound letters are weirdly written; they are nevertheless a treatise on creative writing, treasure-trove, *corpus aureum, mina de oro.* . . . The vivacity of these letters is enchanting." Hugh Kenner says, "The whole key to Pound, the basis of his Cantos, his music, his economics and everything else, is the concern for exact definition"—a passion shared by T. S. Eliot, Mr. Kenner adds—"a quality which neither has defined." What is it? a neatening or cleancutness, to begin with, as caesura is cutting at the end (*caedo,* cut off). For Dante, it was making you see the thing that he sees, Mr. Pound says; and, speaking of Rimbaud, says there is "such firmness of coloring and such certitude." Mr. Pound admires Chinese codifyings and for many a year has been ordering, epitomizing, and urging explicitness, as when he listed "A Few Don'ts" for Imagists:

Direct treatment, economy of words; compose in the sequence of the musical phrase rather than that of the metronome.

The true poet is most easily distinguished from the false when he trusts himself to the simplest expression and writes without adjectives.

No dead words or phrases.

A thought should be expressed in verse as least as well as it could be expressed in prose. Great literature is language charged with meaning to the utmost possible degree. There is no easy way out.

Mr. Pound differentiates poetry as

logopoeia (music of words),
melopoeia (music of sound)—the music of rhymes, he says, depends upon
    their arrangement, not only on their multiplicity—and
phanopoeia (casting images on the imagination).

Under the last head, one recalls the statement by Dante that Beatrice walked above herself—*come una crana*. Confucius says the fish moves on winglike foot; and Prior, in his life of Edmund Burke, says Burke "had a peculiarity in his gait that made him look as if he had two left legs." Affirming Coleridge's statement that "Our admiration of a great poet is for a continuous undercurrent of feeling everywhere present, but seldom anywhere a separate excitement," Mr. Pound says Dante "has gone living through Hell and the words of his lament sob as branches beaten by the wind."

What is poetry? Dante said, "a song is a composition of words set to music." As for free verse, "it is *not* prose," Mr. Pound says. It is what we have "when the thing builds up a rhythm more beautiful than that of set meters"—as here:

The birds flutter to rest in my tree,
    and I think I have heard them saying,
"It is not that there are no other men—,
But we like this fellow the best. . . ."

In Dante, "we have blending and lengthening of the sounds, heavy beats, running and light beats," Mr. Pound says. "Don't make each line stop dead at the end. Let the beginning of the next line catch the rise of the rhythm wave, unless you want a longish definite pause." For example, the lines from "Envoi" in "Mauberley," when he speaks of "her graces":

I would bid them live
As roses might, in magic amber laid,

Red overwrought with orange and all made
One substance and one color
Braving time.

This is the way in which to cement sound and thought. In "Mauberley," also note the identical rhymes in close sequence without conspicuousness, of "Medallion":

The face-oval beneath the glaze,
Bright in its suave bounding-line, as,
Beneath half-watt rays,
The eyes turn topaz.

"Words," T. S. Eliot says, "are perhaps the hardest medium of all material of art. One must simultaneously express visual beauty, beauty of sound, and communicate a grammatical statement." We have in "her" a mundane word, but note the use of it in the Portrait, from "La Mère Inconnue" (*Exultations*):

Nay! For I have seen the purplest shadows stand
Always with reverent chere that looked on her,
Silence himself is grown her worshipper
And ever doth attend her in that land
Wherein she reigneth, wherefore let there stir
Naught but the softest voices, praising her.

Again, from Ezra Pound's translation of Guido Cavalcanti: "A Bernardo da Bologna,"

And in that Court where Love himself fableth
Telling of beauties he hath seen; he saith:
This pagan and lovely woman hath in her
All strange adornments that ever were.

William Carlos Williams is right. "Pound is not 'all poetry.' . . . But he has an ear that is unsurpassable." "Some poems," Mr. Pound himself says, "have form as a tree has form and some as water poured into a vase." He also says, quoting Arnold Dolmetsch and Mace, "Mark not the beat too much"—a precept essential to light rhyme and surprises within the line; but inapplicable to satire, as in W. S. Gilbert's *Pirates of Penzance*—the policemen:

> And yet when someone's near
> We manage to appear
> As unsusceptible to fear
> As anybody here.

"The churn, the loom, the spinning-wheel, the oars," Mr. Pound says, "are bases for distinctive rhythm which can never denigrate into the monotony of mere iambs and trochees"; and one notices in "Nel Biancheggiar" the accenting of "dies," in "but dies not quite":

> I feel the dusky softness whirr
> Of color, as upon a dulcimer
> . . . .
> As when the living music swoons
> But dies not quite. . . .

One notes in "Guido Invites You Thus" (*Exultations*) the placing of the pauses and quickened "flames of an altar fire":

> Lo, I have known thy heart and its desire;
> Life, all of it, my sea, and all men's streams
> Are fused in it as flames of an altar fire!

And "A Prologue" (*Canzoni*) has the same exactitude in variety:

> Shepherds and kings, with lambs and frankincense
> Go and atone for mankind's ignorance:
> Make ye soft savor from your ruddy myrrh.
> Lo, how God's son is turned God's almoner.

Unending emphasis is laid by Ezra Pound on honesty—on voicing one's own opinion. He is indignant that "trout should be submerged by eels." The function of literature, he says, is "to incite humanity to continue living; to ease the mind of strain; to feed it" (Canto XXV):

> What we thought had been thought for too long;
> . . . .
> We have gathered a sieve full of water.
> . . . .
> The dead words, keeping form.

We suffer from

Noble forms lacking life
. . . .

The dead concepts, never the solid; . . .

As for comprehension of what is set forth, the poet has a right to expect the reader, at least in a measure, to be able to complete the poetic statement; and Ezra Pound never spoils his effects by over-exposition. He alludes as follows to the drowning of a Borgia:

The bust outlasts the shrine;
The coin, Tiberius.
. . . .
John Borgia is bathed
at last. And the cloak floated.

"As for *Cathay*, it must be pointed out," T. S. Eliot says, "that Mr. Pound is the inventor of Chinese poetry of our time"; and seeing a connection between the following incident and "the upper middlebrow press," Hugh Kenner recalls that when Charles Münch offered Bach to the regiment, the commandant said, "Here, none of that mathematical music." One ventures, commits one's self, and if readers are not pleased, one can perhaps please one's self and earn that slender right to persevere.

"A poet's work," Mr. Eliot says, "may proceed along two lines of an imaginary graph; one of the lines being his conscious and continuous effort in technical excellence," and the other "his normal human course of development. Now and then the two lines may converge at a high peak, so that we get a masterpiece. That is to say, an accumulation of experience has crystallized to form material of art, and years of work in technique have prepared an adequate medium; and something results in which medium and material, form and content, are indistinguishable."

In *The Great Digest and Unwobbling Pivot* of Confucius, as in his *Analects*, Ezra Pound has had a theme of major import. *The Great Digest* makes emphatic this lesson: He who can rule himself can govern others; he who can govern others can rule the kingdom and families of the Empire.

The men of old disciplined themselves.
Having attained self-discipline they set their houses in order.
Having order in their own homes, they brought good government
to their own state.
When their states were well governed, the empire was brought
into equilibrium.

We have in the *Digest*, content that is energetic, novel, and deep: "If there be a knife of resentment in the heart or enduring rancor, the mind will not attain precision; under suspicion and fear it will not form sound judgment, nor will it, dazzled by love's delight nor in sorrow and anxiety, come to precision." As for money, "Ill got, ill go." When others have ability, if a man "shoves them aside, he can be called a real pest." "The archer when he misses the bullseye, turns and seeks the cause of error in himself." There must be no rationalizing. "Abandon every clandestine egoism to realize the true root." Of the golden rule, there are many variants in the *Analects:* "Tze-kung asked if there was a single principle that you could practice through life to the end. He said sympathy; what you don't want, don't inflict on another" (Book Fifteen, XXIII). "Require the solid of yourself, the trifle of others" (Book Fifteen, XIV). "The proper man brings men's excellence to focus, not their evil qualities" (Book Twelve, XVI). "I am not worried that others do not know me; I am worried by my incapacity" (Book Fourteen, XXXII). Tze-chang asked Kung-tze about maturity. Kung-tze said: To be able to practice five things would humanize the whole empire—sobriety (*serenitas*), magnanimity, sticking by one's word, promptitude (in attention to detail), kindliness (*caritas*). As for "the problem of style. Effect your meaning. Then stop" (Book Fifteen, XL).

In "Salvationists," Mr. Pound says:

> Come, my songs, let us speak of perfection—
> We shall get ourselves rather disliked.

We shall get ourselves disliked and very much liked, because the zest for perfection communicates its excitement to others.

[1] See Kenneth Burke's "The Language of Poetry, 'Dramatically' Considered," paper written for a symbolism seminar conducted in 1952–53 by the Institute for Religious and Social Studies, New York (*Chicago Review*, Fall 1954): "We would spin this discussion from Cicero's terms for the 'three offices of the orator.' (See *Orator, De Oratore*, and St. Augustine's use of this analysis of Christian persuasion in his *De Doctrina Christiana*.) First office: to teach or inform (*docere*). Second office: to please (*delectare*). Third office: to move or 'bend' (*movere, flectare*)."

From a series of commentaries on selected contemporary poets, Bryn Mawr, 1952; *Predilections; A Marianne Moore Reader*.

RETICENT CANDOR

THAT T. S. Eliot and Wallace Stevens have certain qualities in common perhaps is obvious—in reticent candor and emphasis by understatement. Speaking as from ambush, they mistrust rhetoric—taking T. S. Eliot's definition of the word, in his "Rhetoric and Poetic Drama," as "any adornment or inflation of speech which is not used for a particular effect but for general impressiveness." Of "omnivorous perspicacity,"[1] each has been concerned from the first with the art and use of poetry, and has continued to be a poet. And although too much importance should not be attached to this, the following passages are of interest, it seems to me, as revealing consanguinities of taste and rhythm; in T. S. Eliot's "La Figlia che Piange":

> So I would have had him leave,
> So I would have had her stand and grieve,

and Wallace Stevens' "Peter Quince at the Clavier":

> So evenings die, in their green going,
> A wave, interminably flowing.
> . . . .
> So maidens die, to the auroral
> Celebration of a maiden's choral.

Reviewing *The Waste Land,* Conrad Aiken said, "T. S. Eliot's net is wide and the meshes are small. . . ";[2] especially wide and small as prose bearing on poetry. In "The Music of Poetry," Mr. Eliot says, "Poetry must give pleasure";[3] "find the possibilities of your own idiom"; "poetry must not stray too far from the ordinary language we use and hear"—principles in keeping with the following statements quoted by Mr. Eliot from W. P. Ker: "the end of scholarship is understanding," and "the end of understanding is enjoyment," "enjoyment disciplined by taste."

T. S. Eliot's concern with language has been evident all along—as when he says in "A Talk on Dante," "The whole study and practice of Dante seems to me, to teach that the poet should be the servant of his language, rather than the master of it." And "To pass on to posterity one's own language, more highly developed, more refined, and more precise than it was before one wrote it, that is the highest achievement of the poet as poet. . . . Dante seems to me," he says, "to have a place in Italian literature which in this respect, only Shakespeare has in ours. They gave body to the soul of the

language, conforming themselves to what they deemed its possibilities."
Furthermore, "In developing the language, enriching the meaning of words
and showing how much words can do," Mr. Eliot says, the poet "is making
possible a much greater range of emotion and perception for other men
because he gives them the speech in which more can be expressed." Then,
"The kind of debt that I owe to Dante is the kind that goes on accumulating. . . . Of Jules Laforgue, for instance, I can say that he was the first . . . to
teach me the poetic possibilities of my own idiom of speech. . . . I think
that from Baudelaire I learned first, a precedent for the poetical possibilities,
never developed by any poet writing in my own language, of the more sordid
aspects of the modern metropolis, of the possibility of fusion between the
sordidly realistic and the phantasmagoric, the possibility of the juxtaposition
of the matter-of-fact and the fantastic . . . and that the source of new poetry
might be found in what has been regarded [as] the intractably unpoetic. . . . One has other debts, innumerable debts," he says, "to poets of
another kind. . . . There are those who remain in one's mind as having set
the standard for a particular poetic virtue, as Villon for honesty, and Sappho
for having fixed a particular emotion in the right and the minimum number
of words"[4]—the words "poetic" and "minimum," explicit as if italicized.

To quote what is in print seems unnecessary, and manner is scarcely a
subject for commentary; yet something is to be learned, I think, from a
reticent candor in which openness tempts participation, and places experience at our service—as in the above-mentioned commentary, "A Talk on
Dante"; as in "Poetry and Drama" (the Theodore Spencer Memorial Lecture);
and in the retrospect of Ezra Pound that appeared in the September 1946
issue of *Poetry*.

In "Poetry and Drama," helpfully confidential again, Mr. Eliot asks if
poetic drama has anything potentially to offer that prose can not. "No play
should be written in verse," he says, "for which prose is dramatically adequate." "The audience should be too intent upon the play to be wholly
conscious of the medium," and "the difference is not so great as we might
think between prose and verse." "Prose on the stage," he says, "is as artificial
as verse," the reason for using verse being that "even the pedestrian parts
of a verse play have an effect upon the hearers without their being conscious
of it." "If you were hearing *Hamlet* for the first time," Mr. Eliot says, "without
knowing anything about the play, I do not think it would occur to you to
ask whether the speakers were speaking in verse or prose." For example,
the opening lines:

> Bernardo: Who's there?
> Francisco: Nay, answer me: stand and unfold yourself.

Bernardo: Long live the king!

. . . .

Francisco: Not a mouse stirring.
Bernardo: Well, good night.[5]

Then of his own "intentions, failures and partial success," Mr. Eliot says that *"Murder in the Cathedral* was produced for an audience of those serious people who go to 'festivals' and expect to have to put up with poetry—though some were not quite prepared for what they got." "The style," he says, "had to be neutral, committed neither to the present nor to the past. As for the versification . . . what I kept in mind was the versification of *Everyman*"; despite its only "negative merit in my opinion," it "succeeded in avoiding what had to be avoided. . . . What I should hope might be achieved is that the audience should find . . . that it is saying to itself: 'I could talk in poetry too!' " "I was determined in my next play," he says, "to take the theme of contemporary life. *The Family Reunion* was the result. Here my first concern was . . . to find a rhythm in which the stresses could be made to come where we should naturally put them. . . . What I worked out is substantially what I have continued to employ: a line of varying length and varying number of syllables, with a caesura and three stresses. The caesura and the stresses may come at different places . . . the only rule being that there must be one stress on one side of the caesura and two on the other. . . . I soon saw that I had given my attention to versification at the expense of plot and character." Then the Furies. "We put them on the stage. They looked like uninvited guests from a fancy-dress ball. . . . We concealed them behind gauze. We made them dimmer, and they looked like shrubbery just outside the window"; diagnosis followed in the same vein of candor, by, "My hero now strikes me as an unsufferable prig." Next: "You will understand . . . some of the errors that I endeavored to avoid in designing *The Cocktail Party*. To begin with, no chorus, and no ghosts. . . . As for the verse, I laid down for myself the ascetic rule to avoid poetry which could not stand the test of dramatic utility: with such success, indeed, that it is perhaps an open question whether there is any poetry in the play at all." Then, as flatly objective, "I am aware that the last act of my play only just escapes, if indeed it does escape, the accusation of being not a last act but an epilogue." "I have, I believe," he says in conclusion, "been animated by a better motive than egoism. I have wished to put on record for what it may be worth to others, some account of the difficulties I have encountered and the weaknesses I have had to overcome, and the mistakes into which I have fallen." Now this kind of candor seems to me not short of sensational—as technical exposition to which carefully accurate informality lends persuasiveness.

The retrospect of Ezra Pound's London years shares the (to me, useful) tone of the Spencer lecture; I detect no difference between it and conversation. Mr. Eliot is speaking here of 1908 and of Ezra Pound as suggesting "a usable contemporary form of speech at a time of stagnation." He says, "Browning was more of a hindrance than a help for he had gone some way, but not far enough in discovering a contemporary idiom. . . . The question was still: where do we go from Swinburne? and the answer appeared to be, nowhere." One notes the adjectives, numerous without heaviness: "Pound was then living in a small dark flat in Kensington. In the largest room he cooked, by artificial light; in the lightest but smallest room, which was inconveniently triangular, he did his work and received visitors. [He gave the impression of being transient,] due, not only to his restless energy—in which it was difficult to distinguish the energy from the restlessness and fidgets . . . but to a kind of resistance against growing into any environment. . . . For a time, he found London, and then Paris, the best center for his attempts to revitalize poetry. But though young English writers, and young writers of any nationality, could count on his support if they excited his interest, the future of American letters was what concerned him most."

"No poet, furthermore was, without self-depreciation, more unassuming about his own achievement in poetry," Mr. Eliot says. "The arrogance which some people have found in him is really something else. . . . [He] would go to any lengths of generosity and kindness; from inviting constantly to dinner, a struggling author whom he suspected of being under-fed, or giving away clothing (though his shoes and underwear were almost the only garments which resembled those of other men sufficiently to be worn by them), to trying to find jobs, collect subsidies, get work published and then get it criticized and praised."

Pound's critical writing, Mr. Eliot goes on to say, "forms a corpus of poetic doctrine. . . . The opinion has been voiced that Pound's reputation will rest upon his criticism and not upon his poetry. I disagree. It is on his total work for literature that he must be judged: on his poetry, *and* his criticism, *and* his influence at a turning point in literature. In any case, his criticism takes its significance from the fact that it is the writing of a poet about poetry; it must be read in the light of his own poetry, as well as of poetry by other men whom he championed. . . . You cannot wholly understand Aristotle's doctrine of tragedy without reference to the remains of the Attic drama upon which Aristotle's generalizations are founded." And bearing upon this, Mr. Eliot quotes Ezra Pound as saying that "theoretically criticism tries to . . . serve as a gunsight, but that the man who formulates any forward reach of co-ordinating principle is the man who produces the demonstration. . . . They proceed as two feet of one biped."

"I know that one of the temptations against which I have to be on guard," Mr. Eliot says, "is trying to re-write somebody's poem in the way which I should have written it myself. Pound never did that: he tried first to understand what one was attempting to do, and then tried to help one do it in one's own way." As part of the definiteness with openness which aids this commentary, we have the following aside: "In the Cantos there is an increasing defect of communication. . . . I am incidentally annoyed, myself, by occasional use of the peculiar orthography which characterizes Pound's correspondence and by lines written in what he supposes to be Yankee dialect. But the craftsman up to this moment . . . has never failed." (One notices "moment" as replacing the usual, less intent word "time.")

"Pound's 'erudition,' " Mr. Eliot says, "has been both exaggerated and . . . underestimated: for it has been judged chiefly by scholars who did not understand poetry, and by poets who have had little scholarship." (Apropos here, Dr. Tenney Frank's statement to students at Bryn Mawr in connection with Ezra Pound's "Homage to Sextus Propertius": anyone might render a line impeccably; few can communicate appetite for the thing and present content with the brio with which Ezra Pound presents it.)

"Pound's great contribution to the work of other poets," Mr. Eliot says, "is his insistence upon the immensity of the amount of *conscious* labor to be performed by the poet; and his invaluable suggestions for the kind of training the poet should give himself—study of form, metric and vocabulary in the poetry of divers literature, and study of good prose. . . . He also provides an example of devotion to 'the art of poetry' which I can only parallel in our time by the example of Valéry, and to some extent that of Yeats: and to mention these names is to give some impression of Pound's importance as an exponent of the art of poetry" at a time when

> The "age demanded" chiefly a mould in plaster
> Made with no loss of time,
> A prose kinema, not, not assuredly, alabaster
> Or the "sculpture" of rhyme.

As Ezra Pound, J. V. Healy says, followed T. E. Hulme's precept, that language "should endeavor to arrest you, and to make you continuously see a physical thing, and prevent your gliding through an abstract process," I would say that T. S. Eliot has not glided through an abstract process in formulating the three discourses just cited—exposition consonant in vividness with his best use of metaphor—"the seabell's perpetual angelus" and the lines about standing at the "stern of the drumming liner, watching the furrow that widens behind us."

Of poetry, current at Oxford, W. H. Auden says in the *Letter to Lord Byron*, "Eliot spoke the still unspoken word," and in the tribute by him "To T. S. Eliot on His Sixtieth Birthday," 1948, says:

> . . . it was you
> Who, not speechless from shock but finding the right
> Language for thirst and fear, did much to
> Prevent a panic.

The effect of Mr. Eliot's confidences, elucidations, and precepts, I would say, is to disgust us with affectation; to encourage respect for spiritual humility; and to encourage us to do our ardent undeviating best with the medium in which we work.

[1] Hugh Kenner in another connection (*Hudson Review*, Autumn 1949).

[2] *New Republic*, February 7, 1923.

[3] During World War II, George Dillon was stationed in Paris and, writing to *Poetry* (issue of October 1945), said: "The other night I went to hear T. S. Eliot's lecture on the poet's role in society. . . . The little Salle des Centraux in the rue Jean-Goujon (Champs-Elysées neighborhood) . . . was packed with the most miscellaneous gathering. . . . Finally Paul Valéry stepped to the platform. . . . After Valéry's introduction, Eliot stood to acknowledge the applause, then sat down, in French fashion, to give his talk. . . . He made a few remarks in English, expressing his emotion at being once more, and at such a time, in Paris. . . . Then . . . he read his lecture in French—I was interested to note, with an almost perfect French *rhythm*. His lecture elaborated the distinction between the apparent role and the true role of the poet, stressing the idea that *a writer who is read by a small number* over a long period may have a more important social function than one who enjoys great popularity over a limited period; also, that the people who do not even know the names of their great national poets are not the less profoundly influenced by what they have written. . . . He emphasized his belief that poetry must give pleasure or it cannot do good. Good poetry is that which is '*capable de donner du plaisir aux honnêtes gens.*' The part of his lecture which the French seemed to enjoy most was his definition of the two kinds of bad poet—the '*faux mauvais,*' those who have a spurt of writing poetry in their youth, and the '*vrais mauvais,*' those who keep on writing it."

[4] *Kenyon Review*, Spring 1952.

[5] Lindsay Anderson says of Marcel Pagnol's *Amlé*, performed in the courtyard of the thirteenth-century Château of the Roi René at Anger: "The outstanding virtue of Pagnol's translation (never played before) is its directness, its lucidity, its consistent sense of the dramatic. . . . Warmer, more vital than Gide, the author of *Marius* has given his version [of *Hamlet*] the impact of contemporary theatrical speech. . . . In its new language, the lyric drama seems to reveal its contours afresh" (*The Observer*, July 4, 1954).

From a series of commentaries on contemporary poets, Bryn Mawr, 1952; *Predilections; A Marianne Moore Reader*.

W. H. AUDEN

WE surely have in W. H. Auden—in his prose and verse—stature in diversity. It is instructive, moreover, to see in him the abilities he admires in others—the "capacity for drawing general conclusions," mentioned by him as "the extraordinary, perhaps unique merit" of de Tocqueville; and together with clinical attention to cause and effect, a gift for the conspectus. After speaking of de Tocqueville as a counterrevolutionary—i. e., one who has no wish to return to the condition which preceded revolution—he says, "The body knows nothing of freedom, only of necessities; these are the same for all bodies," and "insofar as we are bodies, we are revolutionaries; insofar, however, as we are also souls and minds, we are or ought to be *counter*-revolutionaries." He feels that "The books of de Tocqueville belong together with Thucydides, the Seventh Epistle of Plato, and the plays of Shakespeare, in the small group of the indispensable."

Mr. Auden embodies in his work many gratitudes. His *New Year Letter*, addressed to Elizabeth Mayer—"This *aide-mémoire* / This private minute to a friend"—constitutes a veritable reading list of those to whom he feels a debt, and—an even better compliment—he has adopted various of their idiosyncrasies, as in the dedication to *Another Time* he recalls Blake's

> Till I Will be overthrown
> Every eye must weep alone.

In the *New Year Letter*, he says that Blake

> . . . even as a child would pet
> The tigers Voltaire never met,

he feels that he has a debt to young Rimbaud,

> Skillful, intolerant and quick,
> Who strangled an old rhetoric,

and he says,

> There DRYDEN sits with modest smile,
> The master of the middle style.

If by the middle style he means the circumspectly audacious, he too is possessed of it.

He directs a warm glance toward Catullus,

> Conscious CATULLUS who made all
> His gutter-language musical.

Nor is Mr. Auden himself too fettered to use "who," "he," "the," or "which," as an end rhyme. He sees Voltaire facing him "like a sentinel." He says, "Yes, the fight against the false and the unfair was always worth it." He feels a debt to

> HARDY whose Dorset gave much joy
> To one unsocial English boy,

and Shakespeare? One is

> . . . warned by a great sonneteer
> Not to sell cheap what is most dear.

"Only by those who reverence it, can life be mastered." There is a suggestion of *Murder in the Cathedral* about that; as about the following reflection from *A Christmas Oratorio*, "The Temptation of St. Joseph":

> Sin fractures the Vision, not the Fact; for
> The Exceptional is always usual
>   And the Usual exceptional.
> To choose what is difficult all one's days
> As if it were easy, that is faith. Joseph, praise.

Mr. Auden has a fondness for the seven-syllable-line rhythm,

> Now the ragged vagrants creep
> Into crooked holes to sleep;

the rhythm of

> Where the bee sucks, there suck I:
> In a cowslip's bell I lie . . .

and "Shame the eager with ironic praise" recalls Pope.

We infer approval of Ogden Nash in "a stranded fish to be kind to" and "had he a mind to"; again, in "Are You There?":

> Each lover has some theory of his own
> About the difference between the ache
> Of being with his love and being alone.

Appreciative of others he can afford to be. He could never sound as much like others as others sound like him. His collected poems, moreover, constitute, as Louise Bogan says, "the most minute dissection of the spiritual illness of our day that any modern poet, not excluding T. S. Eliot, has given us." He is a notable instance of the poet whose scientific predilections do not make him less than a poet—who says to himself, I must know. In "The Walking Tour," he speaks of how

> The future shall fulfil a surer vow
> . . . .
> Not swooping at the surface still like gulls
> But with prolonged drowning shall develop gills.

Commenting on Maria Edgeworth's Letters, Cecilia Townsend says, "Without sorrow, the spirit dwindles."[1] "Why are people neurotic?" Mr. Auden asks. "Because they refuse to accept suffering." And in one of his Cornelia Street Dialogues with Howard Griffin, he says, "suffering plays a greater part than knowledge" in our acts of the will. One can say, "I should do this. Will I do it? A part of the mind looks on; a part decides. Also one must not discount Grace." Mr. Griffin says: "You mean supernatural intervention— the light that appeared to Saul on the road to Damascus?" Mr. Auden: "Not really supernatural. . . . It may be perfectly natural. It depends on intensification of normal powers of sensitivity and contemplation."

In an address to the Grolier Club (October 24, 1946), Mr. Auden said, "Without an exception, the characters in Henry James are concerned with moral choices. The Beast in the Jungle is . . . the shrinking of the subject's sovereign will from decisive choice. . . . The interest itself is in the freedom of the will. Deny this freedom . . . and your interest vanishes." We have a debt to Mr. Auden for this emphasis put on "denial of free will and moral responsibility" as "a recent feature of our novels." Why must we "see ourselves," he asks, "as a society of helpless victims, shady characters and displaced persons, . . . as heroes without honor or history—heroes who succumb so monotonously to temptation that they cannot truly be said to be tempted at all?" The thought of choice as compulsory is central to everything that he writes. "Of what happens when men refuse to accept the necessity of choosing and are terrified of or careless about their freedom, we now have only too clear a proof," he said in 1941. "The will, decision, and the consequences—there is no separating them." His "Star of the Nativity" (A Christmas Oratorio) says:

> Descend into the fosse of Tribulation,
> Take the cold hand of Terror for a guide;

. . . .
But, as the huge deformed head rears to kill,
Answer its craving with a clear I Will;

"In War Time" makes emphatic

The right to fail that is worth dying for.

Home is

A sort of honor, not a building site,
Wherever we are, when, if we choose, we might
Be somewhere else, yet trust that we have chosen right.

And we have in the Notes to Part III of the *New Year Letter:*

I'm only lost until I see
I'm lost because I want to be.

We must make "free confession of our sins." Humility, alas, can border on humiliation. In the *New Year Letter*, alluding to great predecessors, he asks, "Who . . .

Is not perpetually afraid
That he's unworthy of his trade,
. . . .
Who ever rose to read aloud
Before that quiet attentive crowd
And did not falter as he read,
Stammer, sit down, and hang his head?

"Cogitation," he says, "is always a specific historic act, accompanied by hope and fear."

How hard it is to set aside
Terror, concupiscence and pride.

Sin, fear, lust, pride. "The basis of pride," Mr. Auden says in "Dialogue I," is to be found in "lack of security, anxiety, and defiance; . . . says pride can be defined as a form of despair." And in the *New Year Letter* he says to the Devil:

You have no positive existence,
Are only a recurrent state
Of fear and faithlessness and hate,
That takes on from becoming me
A legal personality
. . . .
We hoped; we waited for the day
The State would wither clean away,
. . . .
Meanwhile at least the layman knows
That none are lost so soon as those
. . . .
Afraid to be themselves, or ask
What acts are proper to their task,
And that a tiny trace of fear
Is lethal in man's atmosphere.

Aware that Aladdin has the magic lamp that "Can be a sesame to light," he says:

Poor cheated Mephistopheles,
Who think you're doing as you please
In telling us by doing ill
To prove that we possess free will.

We have this metaphor of missed logic again in *The Rake's Progress*, where Nick Shadow leads Tom astray by suggesting that he is freed by disregarding passion and reason and marrying a freak. Choice is open to us each, and in *The Sea and the Mirror*, Alonso says:

Learn from your dreams what you lack,
. . . .
Believe your pain: praise the scorching rocks
For their desiccation of your lust,
Thank the bitter treatment of the tide
For its dissolution of your pride,
That the whirlwind may arrange your will
And the deluge release it to find
The spring in the desert, the fruitful
Island in the sea, where flesh and mind
Are delivered from mistrust.

Similarly, Sebastian says:

> O blessed be bleak Exposure on whose sword,
> Caught unawares, we prick ourselves alive!
> . . . .
> The sword we suffer is the guarded crown.

In his preface to *The Sea and the Mirror*, Mr. Auden quotes Emily Brontë:

> And am I wrong to worship where
> Faith cannot doubt nor Hope despair
> Since my own soul can grant my prayer?
> Speak, God of Visions, plead for me
> And tell why I have chosen thee.

"Happiness does not depend," he says, "on power but on love." "The person must begin by learning to be objective about his Subjectivity"; so that "love is able to take the place of hate." And in *A Christmas Oratorio*:

> The choice to love is open till we die.
> . . . .
> O Living Love replacing phantasy.

The patriot may then ("Epithalamion," *Collected Shorter Poems*)

> Feel in each conative act
> Such joy as Dante felt
> When, a total failure in
> An inferior city, he,
> Dreaming out his anger, saw
> All the scattered leaves of fact
>   Bound by love.

"The Meditation of Simeon" (*A Christmas Oratorio*) would have us see "the tragic conflict of Virtue with Necessity" as "no longer confined to the Exceptional Hero. Every invalid is Roland defending the narrow pass against hopeless odds; every stenographer is Brunhilde refusing to renounce her lover's ring which came into existence" through the power of renunciation; and, redefining the hero, Mr. Auden's introduction to the brothers Grimm says: "The third son who marries the princess and inherits the kingdom is not a superman with exceptional natural gifts." He "succeeds not through his own merit, but through the assistance of Divine Grace. His contribution is, first, a humility which admits that he cannot succeed without Grace;

secondly, a faith which believes that Grace will help him, so that when the old beggar asks for his last penny, that is, when humanly speaking he is dooming himself to fail, he can give it away; and lastly, a willingness . . . to accept suffering. . . . From tale after tale we learn, not that wishing is a substitute for action, but that wishes for good and evil are terribly real and not to be indulged in with impunity." But, in the "Journey to Iceland," Mr. Auden asks:

> "Where is the homage? when
>   Shall justice be done? O who is against me?
>   Why am I always alone?"

"Aloneness is man's real condition," he says; and as for justice, "The artist does not want to be accepted by others, he wants to accept his experience of life, which he cannot do until he has translated his welter of impressions into an order; the public approval he desires is not for himself but for his works, to reassure him that the sense he believes he has made of experience is indeed sense and not a self-delusion."[2]

"Lonely we were though never left alone," he says. We see loneliness "sniffing the herb of childhood" and finding home a place "where shops have names" and "crops grow ripe"; and "In Praise of Limestone" (*Nones*) he reminds himself of

> . . . rounded slopes
> With their surface fragrance of thyme and beneath
> A secret system of caves and conduits; . . .

indeed says,

> . . . when I try to imagine a faultless love
> Or the life to come, what I hear is the murmur
> Of underground streams, what I see is a limestone landscape.

In the essay on Henry James—already referred to—he also says, "It is sometimes necessary for sons to leave the family hearth; it may well be necessary at least for intellectuals to leave their country as it is for children to leave their homes, not to get away from them, but to re-create them"; adding, however, that "those who become expatriate out of hatred for their homeland are as bound to the past as those who hate their parents." Having, like James, left the family hearth, an exile—"to keep the silences at bay"— must "cage / His pacing manias in a worldly smile" ("Vocation," *The Double Man*). It is not, however, a case of wishing nothing to be hard.

"A problem which is too easy," Mr. Auden says, "is as unattractive as a problem which is senseless or impossible. In playing a game, the excitement lies not in winning but in just-winning, and just-losing is almost as good as winning, and the same surely is true for thinking." Alluding to superficial or hasty persons, he says in "Our Bias":

> How wrong they are in being always right.
> . . . .
> For they, it seems, care only for success:
> While we choose words according to their sound
> And judge a problem by its awkwardness.

"A favorite game of my youth," he says, "was building dams; the whole afternoon was spent in building up what in the end was destroyed in a few seconds."

As offsetting the tribulations of life and a sense of injustice, one recalls Wallace Stevens' emphasis on the imagination as delivering us from our "bassesse." This, poetry should do; and W. H. Auden quotes Professor R. G. Collingwood as saying, "Art is not magic, but a mirror in which others may become conscious of what their own feelings really are. It mirrors defects and it mirrors escape"—affirmed in "The Composer" (*Collected Shorter Poems*):

> You alone, alone, O imaginary song,
> Are able to say an existence is wrong
> And pour out your forgiveness like a wine.

Thinking of W. H. Auden the person, one recalls the *Letter to Lord Byron:*

> But indecision broke off with a clean-cut end
>   One afternoon in March at half-past three
> When walking in a ploughed field with a friend;
>   Kicking a little stone, he turned to me
>   And said, "Tell me, do you write poetry?"
> I never had, and said so, but I knew
> That very moment what I wished to do.

"He dramatizes everything he touches," Louise Bogan says—as in "Under Which Lyre" (*Nones*),

> Our intellectual marines,
> Landing in little magazines
> Capture a trend. . . .

He sees "The bug whose view is baulked by grass," and our discarded acts

> Like torn gloves, rusted kettles,
> Abandoned branchlines, worn lop-sided
> Grindstones buried in nettles.

The recitative to *Night Mail*—the British documentary film on the nonstop express from London to Edinburgh—is drama without a break:

> As it rushes by the farmhouse no one wakes
> But a jug in a bedroom gently shakes.

Poets are musicians, and Mr. Auden's "In Praise of Limestone" says that one's "greatest comfort is music," "Which can be made anywhere and is invisible"; unlike

> The beasts who repeat themselves, or a thing like water
> Or stone whose conduct can be predicted. . . .

A poet is susceptible to "elegance, art, fascination," and words demonstrate the appetite for them which made them possible:

> Altogether elsewhere, vast
> Herds of reindeer move across
> Miles and miles of golden moss,
> Silently and very fast.

That Mr. Auden is a virtuoso of rhythms we see in Ariel's refrain, "I," to Caliban ("Postscript," *The Sea and the Mirror*) rivaling in attraction Herbert's "Heaven's Echo":

> Weep no more but pity me,
> Fleet persistent shadow cast
> By your lameness, caught at last,
> Helplessly in love with you,
> Elegance, art, fascination
>   Fascinated by
>   Drab mortality;
> Spare me a humiliation
>   To your faults be true:
> I can sing as you reply
>   . . . I [Echo by the Prompter]

And the next verse ends:

> I will sing if you will cry
>   . . . I

And the last verse:

> What we shall become,
> One evaporating sigh.
>   . . . I

Urgency of a different sort we have in "Many Happy Returns (For John Rettger)":

> I'm not such an idiot
> As to claim the power
> To peer into the vistas
>   Of your future, still
> I'm prepared to guess you
> Have not found your life as
> Easy as your sister's
>   And you never will.

"One Circumlocution" (*Nones*) masters the art of rapt celerity:

> Speak well of moonlight on a winding stair,
> Of light-boned children under great green oaks;
> The wonder, yes, but death should not be there.

Could the skill of the pauses be better, in "To You Simply"?

> Fate is not late,
> Nor the speech rewritten,
> Nor one word forgotten,
> Said at the start
> About heart,
> By heart, for heart.

And, superlatively accomplished, there is Poem XI in *Songs and Other Musical Pieces:*

> Lay your sleeping head, my love,
> Human on my faithless arm;

Time and fevers burn away
Individual beauty from
Thoughtful children, and the grave
Proves the child ephemeral:

The emphasis on "from" corroborates an impression that Mr. Auden is exceptional, if not alone, in imparting propriety to words separated from the words to which they belong. He has notably, moreover, a faculty for keeping a refrain from falling flat, as where in *A Christmas Oratorio* the Wise Men say, "Love is more serious than Philosophy"; reinforcing interior rhymes, we have intermittently the variant on "y" as a refrain—apathy, deny; tyranny, occupy; certainty, anarchy, spontaneity, enemy, energy, die; phantasy, by, and "Time is our choice of How to love and Why"—a device of great dignity.

As preface to his *Collected Poetry*, Mr. Auden says: "In the eyes of every author, I fancy, his own past work falls into four classes. First, the pure rubbish which he regrets ever having conceived; second—for him the most painful—the good ideas which his incompetence or impatience prevented from coming to much ('The Orators' seems to me such a case of the fair notion fatally injured); third, the pieces he has nothing against except their lack of importance; these must inevitably form the bulk of any collection since, were he to limit it to the fourth class alone, to those poems for which he is honestly grateful, his volume would be too depressingly slim."

Destined for the last category, surely, is *The Double Man*—particularly its *New Year Letter*, written in octosyllabic couplets with an occasional triplet, a diagnosis of the spiritual illness of our day and a landmark in literature. Here, as in the *Letter to Lord Byron*, Mr. Auden has chosen a form "large enough to swim in," and in it discusses our quest for freedom; we being— as epitomized by Montaigne on the title page—"double in ourselves, so that what we believe we disbelieve, and cannot rid ourselves of what we condemn." The Double Man asks (*New Year Letter* and Notes):

Who built the Prison State?
Free-men hiding from their fate.
Will wars never cease?
Not while they leave themselves in peace.

Therefore:

The situation of our time
Surrounds us like a baffling crime.
. . . .

> Yet where the force has been cut down
> To one inspector dressed in brown,
> He makes the murderer whom he pleases
> And all investigation ceases.

"Peace will never be won," Mr. Dulles insists, "if men reserve for war their greatest effort"; as "we wage the war we are," Mr. Auden says; and not having waged it well, find ourselves waging the other kind also; from Spain to Siberia, from Ethiopia to Iceland; irresponsibleness having brought about

> The Asiatic cry of pain,
> . . . .
> The Jew wrecked in the German cell,
> Flat Poland frozen into hell.

We are in a "coma of waiting, just breathing," because of our acedia or moral torpor,

> And all that we can always say
> Is: true democracy begins
> With free confession of our sins.

"Dante . . . showed us what evil is; not . . . deeds that must be punished, but our lack of faith." For "volunteers," it is "the penitential way that forces our wills to be freed," hell's fire being "the pan to which we go if we refuse to suffer."

When liberty has been recognized as "a gift with which to serve, enlighten, and enrich," then man is not in danger of being "captured by his liberty"; girls are not "married off to typewriters," children are not "inherited by slums"; and instead of terror, pride, and hate, we have faith, humility, and love. Just now, however, "with swimming heads and hands that shake," we watch the devil trying to destroy the root of freedom—that "absence of all dualities" that grows from "the roots of all togetherness," for "no man by himself has life's solution." "The Prince that Lies," he who

> . . . controls
> The moral asymmetric souls
> The either-ors, the mongrel halves
> Who find truth in a mirror, laughs.

He "knows the bored will not unmask him." Mr. Auden is not bored and has here met the devil with a deadly and magnificent clarity. "The great schismatic . . . hidden in his hocus-pocus" has "the gift of double focus," but

> . . . torn between conflicting needs,
> He's doomed to fail if he succeeds,
> . . . .
> If love has been annihilated
> There's only hate left to be hated.

Understanding his art as "The fencing wit of an informal style," Mr. Auden has taken a leaf from Pope and devised the needful complement whereby things forgot are henceforth known; and with the apparently effortless continuity of the whale or porpoise in motion, he evolves constantly entertaining treatment, resorting to varied terminology—Greek, Latin, English, or other—presenting what he has to say, with that crowning attraction, as he uses it, paradox at its compactest.

An enemy to primness, Mr. Auden sometimes requires that we enjoy "the Janus of a joke" at our expense, as when he relegates the feminine to Laocoön status:

> Das weibliche that bids us come
> To find what we're escaping from.

And he is laughing at us also when he rhymes "ideas" with "careers," "delta" with "skelter," and "Madonnas" with "honors."

It is sad that we should be "the living dead" beneath selfishness and ingratitude; that "few have seen Jesus," and so many "Judas the Abyss." Persuading us to "show an affirming flame" rather than "the negative way through Time," and to believe that the cure for either tribulation or temptation is humility, these New Year thoughts

> Convict our pride of its offence
> In all things, even penitence.

For we have here, despite much about the devil, a poem of love and things of heaven—with a momentum of which Buxtehude or Bach need not be ashamed, the melodic entirety being something at which to marvel.

Inconvenienced, aided, attacked, or at large; a wave-worn Ulysses, a Jerome among his documents; a misinterpreted librettist; or a publisher's emissary insistently offered at luncheon a dish of efts, Mr. Auden continues resolute. He has a mission. Kimon Friar says, "There is an impersonality, it seems to me, . . . at the very center of Auden's style and thinking, a veritable Ark of the Lord in which may be housed the Holy Spirit or—to the unbaptized eye—state the matter in accordance with your nature."[3] Education and tribulation certainly have not been wasted on Mr. Auden. His leaf does not wither; his technical proficiencies deepen. In "The Shield of Achilles," he says he saw

> a ragged urchin, aimless and alone,—who'd never heard
> of any world where promises are kept,
> or one could weep because another wept.

Even a tinge of "greed" makes him "very ill indeed." His studies of Henry James and of Poe show to what heights of liberality he can rise. As a champion of justice, he will always have a champion in the pages he has penned; and as the Orpheus of our mountains, lakes, and plains, will always have his animals.

[1] *The Spectator*, October 3, 1932.

[2] *Partisan Review*, April 1950, reviewing *The Paradox of Oscar Wilde* by George Woodcock. To Oscar Wilde, Mr. Auden says, "Writing was a bore because it was only a means of becoming known and invited out, a preliminary to the serious job of spellbinding."

[3] *Poetry*, May 1944.

From a series of commentaries on selected contemporary poets, Bryn Mawr, 1952; *Predilections*.

WHAT THERE IS TO SEE AT THE ZOO

THE peacock spreads his tail, and the nearly circular eyes at regular intervals in the fan are a sight at which to marvel—forming a lacework of white on more delicate white if the peacock is a white one; of indigo, lighter blue, emerald and fawn if the peacock is blue and green.

Look at a tiger. The light and dark of his stripes and the black edge encircling the white patch on his ear help him to look like the jungle with flecks of sun on it. In the way of color, we rarely see a blacker black than tiger stripes, unless it is the black body down of the blue bird of paradise.

Tiger stripes have a merely comparative symmetry beside the almost exact symmetry of a Grevy's zebra. The small lines on one side of the zebra's face precisely match those on the other side, and the small sock stripes on one front leg are an exact duplicate of those on the other front leg.

Although a young giraffe is also an example of "marking," it is even more impressive as a study in harmony and of similarities that are not monotony— of sycamore-tree white, beside amber and topaz yellow fading into cream. The giraffe's tongue is violet; his eyes are a glossy cider brown. No wonder Thomas Bewick (pronounced Buick, like the car), whose woodcuts of birds and animals are among the best we have, said, "If I were a painter, I would go to nature for all my patterns."

Such colors and contrasts educate the eye and stir the imagination. They also demonstrate something of man's and the animals' power of adaptation to environment, since differing surroundings result in differences of appearance and behavior.

The giraffe grows to the height of certain trees that it may reach its leafy food. David Fleay, an authority on Australian wild life, tells us that the lyrebird "has a very large eye that it may see [grubs] in the dim light of the tree-fern gullies in which it lives." Certain chameleons have an eye that revolves in its socket, as some searchlights turn on a revolving swivel, in order to look forward and back.

The bodies of sea lions, frogs, and eels are streamlined so that they can slip through the water with the least possible effort. Living almost entirely in the water, an alligator is shaped like a boat and propels itself by its tail as if it were feathering a sculling oar.

The elephant has an inconsequential tail, but its long nose, or trunk, has the uses of a hand as well as the power of a battering-ram. It can pull down branches for food or push flat the trees that block its progress through the jungle. Helen Fischer, in her photo series "The Educated Elephants of Thailand," shows how "up and onto the waiting truck, an elephant maneuvers a heavy log as easily as we would a piece of kindling." Then "after work, it wades and splashes in a cool stream."

An elephant can use its trunk to draw up water and shower its back or to hose an intruder. With the finger at the end of its trunk, the elephant can pluck grass that has overgrown a paved walk, leaving a line as even as if sheared by man. It can pick up a coin and reach it up to the rider on its back—its mahout (ma-howt', as he is called in India). What prettier sight is there than the parabola described by a elephant's trunk as it spirals a banana into its mouth?

A certain gorilla at the Central Park Zoo in New York sometimes takes a standing leap to her broad trapeze. She sits there, swinging violently for a time, and then suddenly drops without a jar—indeed, descends as lightly as a feather might float to the ground. Walking through the monkey house at the Bronx Zoo, we stop before the cage of an orangutan as he jumps to his lead-pipe trapeze with half an orange in one hand and a handful of straw in the other. He tucks the wisp of hay under his neck and, lying on his back as contentedly as if at rest in a hammock, sucks at the orange from time to time—an exhibition of equilibrium that is difficult to account for.

The gorilla's master feat—the standing leap to a swing the height of her head—is matched by the pigeon when it flies at full speed, stops short, pauses and without a detour flies back in the direction from which it came. At dusk, four or five impalas will timidly emerge from their shelter, then bound through the air, in a succession of twenty-foot leaps, to the end of their runway. Perhaps Clement Moore had seen or heard of impalas and was thinking of them when, in *A Visit from St. Nicholas*, he wrote of Santa Claus' reindeer skimming the housetops.

The swimmer has a valuable lesson in muscular control as he watches a sea lion round the curve of its pool, corkscrewing in a spiral as it changes from the usual position to swim upside down. Hardening-up exercises in military training, with obstacles to surmount and ditches to clear, involve skills neatly mastered by animals. In the wilds, bands of gibbons swing from tree to tree as army trainees swing by ropes or work along the bars of a jungle-gym.

Animals are "propelled by muscles that move their bones as levers, up and down or from side to side." The ways in which the movements of their muscles vary provide an ever fascinating sight. The motions of animals are so rapid that we really need the aid of an expert such as James Gray to analyze them for us. In his book *The Motions of Animals*, Mr. Gray says that the bear—a browser, not a runner—rests on the entire foot when walking. The horse and the deer—built for speed—rest on tiptoe (the hoof); the hock never touches the ground.

An essential rule of safe living is well illustrated by animals: work when you work, play when you play, and rest when you rest. Watch two young bears wrestling, rolling, pushing and attacking. One tires, climbs to a broad rock and stretches out full length on its paws. The other stands up, strains forward till it can reach with its mouth the ear of the bear on the rock and keeps tugging at the ear as though dragging a hassock forward by the ear. The rester gets up, comes down and once more both are tumbling, capsized and capsizing.

There is nothing more concentrated than the perseverance with which a duck preens its feathers or a cat washes its fur. The duck spreads oil on its feathers with its beak from a small sac above the tail. The feathers then lie smooth and waterproof, reminding us that we too must take time to care for our bodies and equipment. For as much as fifteen minutes at a time, a leopard will, without digressing to another area, wash a small patch of fur that is not sleek enough to satisfy it. It may then leap to its shelf, a board suspended by rods from the ceiling of the cage. Dangling a foreleg and a hindleg on either side of the shelf, its tail hanging motionless, the leopard will close its eyes and rest.

Patience on the part of animals is self-evident. In studying, photographing or rearing young animals, human beings also need patience. We have in Helen Martini a thrilling example of what may be done for young animals by a human being. Mrs. Martini has reared two sets of tiger cubs, a lion cub and various other baby animals for the Bronx Zoo.

The zoo shows us that privacy is a fundamental need of all animals. For considerable periods, animals in the zoo will remain out of sight in the quiet of their dens or houses. Glass, recently installed in certain parts of the snake house at the Bronx Zoo makes it possible to see in from the outside, but not out from the inside.

We are the guests of science when we enter a zoo; and, in accepting privileges, we incur obligations. Animals are masters of earth, air and water, brought from their natural surroundings to benefit us. It is short-sighted, as well as ungrateful, to frighten them or to feed them if we are told that feeding will harm them. If we stop to think, we will always respect chains, gates, wires or barriers of any kind that are installed to protect the animals and to keep the zoo a museum of living marvels for our pleasure and instruction.

The Book of Knowledge 1955 Annual. New York: Grolier Society, 1955, pp. 33–36.

THE WONDERFUL WINTER

IT was a wonderful winter for Robin—for young Sir Robert Wakefield— because of desperations averted, because Shakespeare had just written *Romeo and Juliet,* was acting in it, and because a part in it was found for Robin himself.

Intended for young people, we have in this factual fantasy a winter's tale that can be treasure to readers of any age: real persons made more real by legitimately imagined incident, uninsistently delicate humor, and philo-

---

Review of *The Wonderful Winter,* by Marchette Chute (Dutton).

sophical insights which apply to ourselves and embody principles which suggest solutions for world problems today.

Brought up in Suffolk by three humorless aunts, at the mercy of a new tutor "whose lips smiled when his eyes did not," an orphan in a dull house, Robin was standing by the river one evening, "saw a faint ripple, the ripple became a splash, and he found himself master of a spaniel. 'Oh, dog!' he said softly." He had never had a pet, though once when harvesters had orphaned eight little field mice, he had found their nest that had hung on a thistle and "if allowed, might have raised the whole family." With the dog hid in his doublet, he was discovered by his tutor and presently overheard his Aunt Isabella say, "it must be disposed of in the morning." Escaping with it before dawn, he made his way toward London, spent one night in the woods, and the next in the van of a carter to whom he had given his one piece of money for a lift. Then, faint with hunger, in the van in which he had slept, as he waited for the carter to return from the inn at which they had stopped, he was discovered by a maid who brought him a buttered bun with chicken in it—the most wonderful gift he had ever received. By the time the van reached London, the carter had mellowed and gave him a penny that he might climb to the top of St. Paul's. "He had a penny and was going to see all London"—a comment embodying the key thought of the book. From St. Paul's, two round wooden buildings with thatched roofs could be seen—theaters he was told, "the haunt of actors, thieves and vagrants." A boy who had not yet found work was a vagrant.

With Ruff, his spaniel beside him, Robin slept under a bookstall in St. Paul's churchyard; the next morning, found a field in which Ruff could run about, but had a skirmish with a thief, who followed, who was gaining on them and had a knife. To escape, Robin joined a queue, behind a young girl whose farthingale partly hid him. A man shaking a box of coins was saying, "One and all, a penny apiece." Robin stared; the young girl said, "He is with me; I am paying for both"; and he was in a theater—that den of iniquity against which he had been warned by his guide at St. Paul's. "It looked wonderful."

When the play was over, the thief was waiting but Robin escaped into the building again, up a side staircase to a kind of store-room; and among weapons, gilt crowns, upright coffins and other objects asleep on a bed that "must have been designed for a race of giants" he was found by two of the players he had been watching, John Heminges and an older man—could it be true—"Mr. Shakespeare." They were discussing expenses and the possible purchase of a bed for Juliet. "I am very fond of Dick. I am very fond of the whole Burbage family," the older man was saying. "But I never knew a group of people with such a well-developed gift for spending money."

Taken home for the night by John Heminges, Robin was asked by Mrs. Heminges, "Did you enjoy the play?" "It was wonderful," he said. "He wished he could see Mr. Shakespeare again. He would have liked to thank Mr. Heminges too, who worried about money and yet was willing to house and feed a strange boy." Somewhat later, since he could fence and had a knowledge of music, he was asked by Mr. Heminges if he might like to work at the theater in return for room and board. "He said. 'Sir,' and stopped helplessly. 'Sir, it would be wonderful.' " "That night his head was full of dreams about being an actor; he thought it would probably be as an apprentice or serving boy" but "they might wish him to take the part of a knight with gilt armor and a jeweled sword." The next day he was given a heavy bundle tied with cord—a woman's dress. Women's parts were taken by men or boys, who must not only walk but dance, in pleated petticoats and a far- thingale held out by hoops of cane or bone. A boy had played the part of the queen in the play about King Henry. "Stricken," Robin "groped with the problem"; but he was no longer a vagrant, no longer made conscious that he was an orphan, he had friends—besides the Heminges family, Augustine Phillips of the theater company, and Thomas Pope, instructor of apprentices and custodian of script—a dragon of vigilance lest someone steal and print the author's sole copy. Mr. Pope "had never married, which he said was no misfortune, but he adopted a succession of children because he liked to have them round the house." Then there was "Dr. Gerarde, the herbalist, who seemed to have a passion for growing whatever was wrong for the climate." And, befriended by Shakespeare, Robin was guided by him to the Royal Exchange, lent fifteen shillings—then three more—having asked advice about a present for Mrs. Heminges and been shown a chain which was the very thing but expensive. He had first admired a little dagger, which he relinquished as too masculine—only to receive it upon his de- parture for Suffolk, a gift from Shakespeare and the theater company. He was returning home to help his aunts with the farm, hoping to apply expe- dients discovered by Dr. Gerarde for improving the soil.

The winter had been wonderful because patience under injustice becomes fortitude, because good will invites friendship; and because Robin had a capacity for ecstasy. What to others might seem of no great importance, to him could be cause for wonder.

Marchette Chute has a genius for reviving the past, for presenting the essential picture with self-effacement that becomes an intensive. She is, moreover, an expert observer of human behavior and of nature, as when Robin learns a lesson from nerves out of control—noticing that "a rabbit will break for open country when if it had stayed under cover it would have been safe." He thought he could explain why martins always nest on the north side in building against a wall. "They can only do a little at a time and must wait for each section to harden; if they worked on the south side, heat would crack the clay." When he is learning to dance the lavolta and the capriole, hampered by the huge skirt that his woman's part required, Mrs. Heminges tells him "it is really a matter of rhythm, like using a scythe in long grass. An experienced mower lets the scythe do the work"; as in dueling, "with a long rapier in one hand for attack and a dagger in the other for defense, if the actor cringed, it would seem to the audience that he had been struck. It was a game of illusion."

The Wonderful Winter is a masterpiece of compression, like the following account of Romeo's and Juliet's cumulative misfortunes: "Mercutio had been killed." Tybalt had been "determined to bully him" . . . and "Romeo fought to avenge his dead friend," . . . ran under Tybalt's guard "and killed him. But then things were worse than ever because Tybalt was Juliet's cousin. . . . Juliet's father tried to force her to marry another man and she drank a potion so her family would think she was dead. She was too young to have so much trouble." Robin "was glad of course that the play was a success. But the young lovers were dead, and nothing would bring them to life again. Even when Robin saw Mr. Burbage, still in Romeo's costume, bury his hot face in a tankard of ale it made no difference; . . . family pride had killed the two most beautiful people Robin had ever seen."

Miss Chute is here, as in her *Shakespeare of London*, our firmly, unostentatiously great benefactor, writing in the same spirit in which John Heminges and Henry Condell, who outlived Shakespeare and others of his Company, brought out the first Folio of plays, "not for money or fame but only to keep the memory of so worthy a friend and fellow alive as was our Shakespeare."

The Book Parade, No. 225 (1956), 2–4.

WHAT MAKES A COLLEGE?

A T the time Bryn Mawr was founded, two questions were being debated, we are told by Cornelia Meigs in her history of the College: Had women a right to demand admittance to institutions set up for men, and had they the capacity to make full use of the advantages afforded? Cornell, "where any

Review of *What Makes a College? A History of Bryn Mawr*, by Cornelia Meigs (Macmillan).

person might find instruction in any subject study," was an answer to the first question and Miss Meigs' history of Bryn Mawr surely answers the second.

"Among Quakers, women had always been given the right of leadership. Where was preparation for opportunity of such importance?"

"Joseph Wright Taylor, a Quaker gentleman and doctor of medicine, with a growing knowledge of contemporary education and a powerful spirit of rebellion against narrowness," had attended an educational conference in Baltimore, called by Francis King and James Carey Thomas. Later as a guest in the home of James Carey Thomas and Mary Whitall Thomas, Dr. Taylor was afforded food for thought by a conversation with their daughter, Martha Carey Thomas, a Senior at Cornell, home for the Christmas vacation. Carey Thomas "did not believe that women would be allowed to teach anywhere but at women's colleges."

The Society of Friends was toiling to win freedom for the enslaved and afford them a knowledge of how to use it. Education among Friends was synonymous with vision, and signified "something to give humanity"; it meant, furthermore, "advancement of learning, not merely passing on the sum of learning already accumulated"; it meant research and conditions which make research possible. "At the Baltimore educational conference, women's education had not been mentioned," and, restive under the conviction that women suffered injustice, Dr. Taylor provided in his will (made in 1877) a fund to be devoted to the founding of a college for women—Bryn Mawr. A conventional, unbigoted bachelor, desirous that daughters should not be denied educational opportunities "so freely offered to young men," liberal and considerate, he was sure that a religiously enlightened life was the happiest, and those requested to serve as trustees of Bryn Mawr shared his convictions. (Instructors appointed were, preferably to be Quakers and "the Christian life of the students was to be cared for according to Quaker principles" but "should it be impractical to carry out any of the above provisions literally," Dr. Taylor said, "my Executors and Trustees are to use their discretion." The following words in a letter to the Trustees of Bryn Mawr—"May Grace, Mercy and Peace be the reward of all who shall labor in this work is the prayer of your friend, Joseph Wright Taylor"—embody, it seems to me, both the Quaker mind and a portrait of Joseph Taylor himself.)

As the Society of Friends toiled to end slavery, Dr. Taylor toiled for the liberation of the soul and the intellect. Unwilling, when building plans were being discussed, to delegate responsibility, he visited Mount Holyoke, Smith, and Wellesley. Francis King, Dr. James Carey Thomas (Trustees) and Addison Hutton (architect), "went with him." President Seelye of Smith reported that Vassar and Wellesley had made the mistake of omitting closets—"The young Ladies were not satisfied with wardrobes"—too late to save Merion, closetless for fifty years.

After ground had been broken for an administration building—named Taylor Hall despite modest objection on the part of the donor—Dr. Taylor, that he might oversee progress, "would ride every day, from Woodland to Burlington, leave his horse with a friend, take a train to Camden, hurry to the ferry landing to cross the Delaware, hurry up the other bank and get a streetcar across Philadelphia, and hurry to the train for Bryn Mawr"—worth recounting, one feels as indicative of Joseph Wright Taylor's unself-sparing zeal.

"What makes a College?" Miss Meigs asks readers "to come to a decision. The founder can never be duplicated," she says, "his reward, in lieu of gratitude," being "some grain of himself and his idea, in later accomplishment; of his spirit and vision, persisting in trustees, successive presidents, teachers, donors, and students." James E. Rhoads, intimate friend of Dr. Taylor, Bryn Mawr's first President, and President of its first Board of Trustees, indeed shared the spirit of the founder. A doctor of medicine who had been obliged to give up practice because of ill health, he had, as Editor of the *Friends Review*, devoted his energies to improving prison conditions, to securing just treatment for Indians, and employment for freedmen. He also took a vigorous part in the founding of Hampton Institute—a man who had managed "to see fifty patients in a day—troubled suddenly by the thought that he was making an undue amount of money ($4,000 a year) by the relief of suffering." For his son, the late Charles J. Rhoads, as well—ever a help, and when unable to help, never willing to complicate matters, we are told by Miss McBride—a trustee since 1907 and Chairman of the board until his death in January of this year, only a way of life could be sufficient tribute.

When James E. Rhoads was made president in March, 1884, M. Carey Thomas ("she was almost 27"), had written to the Trustees, "I felt that I might without presumption, and in case no one better fit should be found, offer myself as a candidate for the presidency." It was the task of James Rhoads to write to her that the Board had selected him as president and her to be his assistant with the title, Dean of the Faculty. "The true welfare of the college was a subject that lay nearest our thoughts," she replied, "and I feel that in the future, it will be a constant pleasure to be able to work with thee in promoting its success."

Miss Meigs's account of M. Carey Thomas is drama, a parable of genius for leadership, a tribute which is at the same time objective appraisal. Miss Thomas suffered constant obstruction. At Cornell she had earned an A.B. in two years. Refused a Ph.D. by Göttingen, by Leipzig, after three years' residence—having been unaware that the University did not grant women degrees—and again by Göttingen, she was granted the degree by Zurich, *summa cum laude* in 1882. Dr. Rhoads retired at the age of 65, convinced that Carey Thomas was the person to succeed him. She was inducted as President, however, only after Miss Garrett had stipulated that $10,000 would be provided annually on condition that the presidency be offered Miss Thomas (a proposal made without consulting Miss Thomas), an inducement reinforced by a circular letter to the Trustees from Dr. James Carey Thomas (father of Miss Thomas)—saying, "If she were a man you would appoint her without hesitation!" She was in 1902 made a member of the Board of Trustees only after "a whirlwind building-fund campaign" to supplement $25,000 given by Mr. Rockefeller (a sum completed just in time for Commencement). "She had a total disregard for obstacles, clutching at the veriest straws if they seemed to drift in the direction of fulfillment," Miss Meigs says. A yet more notable less conspicuous trait than her indomitableness, was her co-operativeness under defeat—as in her letter to Dr. Rhoads concerning the presidency. Years later when the question of relationship between faculty and administration arose (during her own presidency)—with regard to the making and terminating of faculty appointments, it was voted that the Faculty be given a vote and place on the Board of Trustees. She acquiesced, "rendering the College her largest service," Miss Meigs says, "the generosity of her surrender obviating a hundred difficult moments." "She was positive, even dictatorial," Miss Meigs says, but "she could change her mind." She changed it after resisting the alumnae's suggestion that they be represented on the Board of Trustees, and again changed it during a session of the Bryn Mawr Summer School for Women Workers in Industry—persuaded after conversation with a buttonhole-maker, at luncheon, that Labor rather than professional educators knew how to govern Labor. She capitulated also, when it was found advisable to replace formal language examinations, "Orals," by written ones. She also relinquished the Bryn Mawr unique entrance examinations on which she had insisted, convinced that it was desirable "to integrate Bryn Mawr methods with the field of education as a whole," a pioneering example of functioning through the group. She could make each group independent, with its word to contribute, and all groups work together.

Above all, Miss Thomas stands out on these pages, as the disinterested servant and benefactor of Bryn Mawr, "with a passion for excellence," as Rufus Jones said. Her disinterested adherence to what she deemed scholastically best for the College could not be better illustrated than in her decision to retire in 1922, at the age of 65. "She did not hesitate. She could recollect . . . having seen, in universities in Germany and Switzerland, a Department's usefulness paralyzed as all waited for an aged incumbent to die. She determined that this should not happen at Bryn Mawr." "Forcible in argument, unconsciously rough-shod, broadly constructive," she declared at Bryn Mawr's 50th anniversary, "Women have not even yet been given the full rewards of deserving scholarship; we must push on until they have complete recognition and high employment."

In 1922, succeeding Miss Thomas as President, Marion Edwards Park "was the very epitome of conscientiousness and fair play," Miss Meigs says. Amid Labor and Communist troubles in the Summer School, "whose sessions had for 18 years been carried on with glowing success," Miss Park said, "This generation must relearn loyalty to an idea." And in stating that students came "to prepare themselves, not be taught," she inaugurated a new approach to education. "You would go to her for advice," Frances Browne says, "and come away feeling that you had yourself reached the decision."

During Miss Park's administration, for the double major system of individually paired subjects, a central subject with "allies" was substituted. Miss Park took the initiative in establishing the three-college co-operation of Bryn Mawr, Haverford, and Swarthmore. She was, as the faculty said, "a great liberal."

Made President in 1942, Katharine E. McBride has served and stabilized the College through a period more difficult for students and faculty than any that Bryn Mawr has known. In her inaugural address, she said, "Peril does not undermine them"—a statement applicable to herself and, one hopes, to Bryn Mawr. Mr. Charles J. Rhoads spoke of her high scholastic achievement, of a "quality of mind and spirit tangible but indescribable—of her unflagging enterprise." The *College News* said, "She is both wise and young." How do justice to her way of meeting crises precipitated by war? and her deciding of questions for which there was no precedent? Whereas "in the middle and later nineteenth century, to have studied in Germany was the mark of professional efficiency, refugee scholars were now made welcome at Bryn Mawr"— among then, Dr. Erich Frank, an authority in the field of religion, "with honest humbleness and enormous sweep of mind," Emmy Noether, and Evan Fiesel—a student of Etruscan inscriptions and language.

Members of the faculty were released for service during and after the war years. For Mlle. Brée's work in France, the Croix de Guerre was bestowed on her. When pressure of war made the introduction of Russian essential, Bettina Linn of the English Department supplemented earlier work with a summer of study at Harvard, and carried on classes in Russian. Elizabeth Gray Vining came to lecture and said, "We must have students from Japan again." Into a difficult situation—with diminished Faculty and resources, came the G.I. Bill of Rights, and masculine figures were seen reading at desks in the Library. Discerning in the Youth Movement in Germany, its insidious undermining of natural integrity, Miss McBride welcomed an opportunity to afford education of which the results were both "wise and productive."

When in 1944, "a group voiced the idea that self-government in itself was an anomaly and an anachronism," she met the crisis by reminding the group that a "self-government association had a responsibility to the College as a whole, not just to individuals, not even just to the student body." "Her administration is thirteen years old. It has moved smoothly, in part as the result of her gift for organization, and her knowledge of the human side of every situation"; she is accessible to everyone. "Based on reason, her leadership," as Mr. Rhoads foresaw, "has been one of brilliant enterprise."

Enterprise on the part of the Alumnae should be illustrated by more than abstract statements—Evangeline Andrews' suggestion, for instance, that May Day revels should be attempted, to provide funds for a Students' Building. Alumnae drives for endowment, under the direction of Caroline McCormick Slade, so inspired the Trustees with confidence in the fulfilling of Alumnae plans that in 1947 faculty salaries were raised, for which the Alumnae had undertaken to provide funds by 1948. Nor was such fundraising mere money-getting, but an expression of vision and of devotion to what began with James E. Rhoads.

In keeping with Dr. Taylor's high goal and Miss Thomas' determination that Bryn Mawr teaching should be at a high level, the College was first in giving science courses for freshmen and a survey course in English literature; first to give a course in economics, politics and history; in not making attendance at chapel compulsory; in establishing a model school where children might learn house-management and to lead, not dominate—The Phebe Anna Thorne Model School, in connection with which Miss McBride and Frances Browne have our gratitude; in establishing the already-mentioned Summer School for Women Workers in Industry.

Miss Meigs presents Bryn Mawr and Bryn Mawr personalities with vigilance, insight and delicacy. Alluding to Commencements and the need for a students' building, she revives, to the life, Taylor Hall's utilitarian gold oak and prosaic aspect—"with half the spectators in a back room where they could hear nothing, the rigorous architecture only slightly softened by the tremendous ropes of daisies which the Sophomore Class had been working on till two in the morning of Commencement Day. 'How excellent it is to think of all those daisies having been removed from the fields,' the owner of an estate was heard to exclaim."

With great skill she tells of Dr. James E. Rhoads' death. He had walked through heavy snow to the train. The train came and went. He still sat on the bench on which he had been sitting when the station-master had first noticed him. He had died.

Chivalry to the chivalrous, furthermore, marks Miss Meigs' account throughout:—to Carola Woerishoffer; to the Julius Goldman family; to the parents of an English Bryn Mawr student, donors of a scholarship at Oxford, representing funds intended for their daughter's education at Bryn Mawr, a fund they had been unable during the war to transmit. Of Howard Goodhart, Miss Meigs says, "No one will ever know the sum of his gifts large and small, the special salaries underwritten, books and dissertations published for those who could ill afford publication—a kind of giving continued in his manner and with his spirit, by Phyllis Goodhart Gordan and her husband."

Sensibility makes this book a phenomenon among memoirs, and the reading of it an ennobling experience.

Bryn Mawr Alumnae Bulletin, 26 (Spring 1956), 2–4.

SELECTED CRITICISM

THIS writing has fiber. The subject matter, reprinted from various sources, is arranged chronologically except as it has been regrouped for clarity. Miss Bogan's first book of poems was published in 1923; and in 1924 her first book review, in the *New Republic.* Her contributing of verse criticism to *The New Yorker* began in 1931, "at first as 'omnibus reviews' which covered the year's books at six-month intervals. From 1937 her *New Yorker* reviews have appeared as a regular subdepartment of 'Books' under the heading 'Verse.' "

An extensive survey, this; which includes besides Emerson, Emily Dickinson[1]—and her father "who stepped like Cromwell when he went to gather kindling"—Thoreau, "wholesome Thoreau-like Robert Frost," Henry James, Hardy, G. M. Hopkins, W. B. Yeats; also, as coloring their respective periods, Wyndham Lewis, Ezra Pound, T. S. Eliot, Wallace Stevens, E. E. Cummings, W. C. Williams and others; Edmund Wilson and R. P. Blackmur (as critics), Gide's *Journals,* Colette, Virginia Woolf, Robert Graves, and poets 1944–1955.

As the precursors of modernism in literature, mingled sensibilities, tendencies, and inter-related experiments are accounted for by Miss Bogan and brought into sequence. "The population after the Cuban war," she says, "was infatuated with power . . . an era of gilt wicker furniture, hand-painted

---

Review of *Selected Criticism—Prose, Poetry,* by Louise Bogan (Noonday Press).

china, lace curtains, and 'sofa cushions,' " of "the pulp magazine" and "a taste for 'sordid elegance,' " "attacked by Thorstein Veblen and others from the left." "American realism finally broke through": we had Dreiser's novels, " 'disguised autobiographies' " and free verse. Wagner and Villiers de L'Isle-Adam, Debussy and Mallarmé, post-impressionist "anatomizing of nature" and the Armory show in 1913, are correlated. We have Gertrude Stein in Paris, Imagist poetry in England and America, and "the novel as a Luciferian universe in the hands of Joyce."

"With an eye to virtues rather than defects," Miss Bogan does not overbear; she has no literary nephews, her pronouncements are terse, rendered with laboratory detachment. Unmistakable emphasis is placed on two capacities as indispensable to achievement—instinctiveness and "coming to terms with one's self"—instinctiveness as contrasted with Henry James' Mona Brigstock who was "all will." Goethe's central power is seen as "interpretive imagination," an interior compulsion linked with integrity. In *The Family Reunion*, "an integration," Miss Bogan sees T. S. Eliot "in complete control of himself." Was Joyce in *Finnegans Wake*, she asks, "the farceur" or have we here, "immaturity transcending suffering?"—a query one connects with Henry James' observation in discussing Turgenev's fiction: "The great question as to a poet or novelist is, how does he feel about life? What in the last analysis is his philosophy? This is the most interesting thing their works offer us. Details are interesting in proportion as they contribute to make it clear."

These compact, unequivocal studies are set off by a kind of dry humor-incognito which is idiosyncratically eloquent. Henry James "really was a great poet and profound psychologist," Miss Bogan says. "He has been thought genteel when he had become the sharpest critic of gentility, a dull expatriate when his books flashed with incisive American wit." "He must be approached as one approaches music," she says. "He continuously shifts between development and theme, never stops, never errs." She affirms Rilke's conviction that "we must adhere to difficulty if we would make any claim to having a part in life" and feels that we have in Rilke "one of the strongest antidotes to the powers of darkness"; "often exhausted, often afraid, often in flight but capable of growth and solitude—he stands as an example of integrity held through and beyond change."

The combination of open writing, unstereotyped insights, and daring, is most attractive, as when Miss Bogan says, "Yeats and Pound achieved modernity. Eliot was modern from the start." We have Ezra Pound, "whom," Miss Bogan says, "time will in the end surely honor," delineated in his statement, "I am trying to use not an inch rule but a balance"; and perhaps with his tendency to diatribe in mind, she says, "Pound's ideal reader is a person who has experienced real discomfort at being shut up in a railway train, lecture hall, or concert room, with well-modulated voices expressing careful, well-bred opinions on the subject of the arts." Contradictions presented by W. B. Yeats are set forth: his august statement, "We are artists who are servants not of any cause but of mere nature" and his "lifelong struggle against the inertia of his nation"; "his variety of stress and subtlety of meaning"; his vehemence: "how hard is that purification from insincerity, vanity, malignance, arrogance, which is the discovery of style."

W. H. Auden is especially well observed. "He gives humanity a hard unprejudiced stare," Miss Bogan says—but is capable of gaiety which can even be "hilarity." "He points up and freshens the language," "describes with great originality the power drives of succeeding eras," and in *Poets of the English Language*, has participated, with Norman Pearson, in "a peculiarly modern achievement." His "lack of hatred, his fight against intellectual stupidity as well as outer horror" are noted; certain speeches in *The Sea and the Mirror: A Commentary on Shakespeare's The Tempest*, as constituting "a little museum of form: terza rima, followed by a sestina, a sonnet, and a ballade." We have in Mr. Auden, Miss Bogan feels, "a poet, one of whose urges always will be to transcend himself." Paul Valéry is portrayed at a stroke. While discerning his gifts,—"that he continually denies them," Miss Bogan says, "lends to his work a faint continual tone of sophistry." And nothing said about Joyce seems to me sounder than this accounting for the effect on us of *Finnegans Wake*—its "miraculous virtuosity of language maintained through a thousand variations in its attack on every known patois—the whole resting on Bruno's theory of knowledge through opposites and Vico's theory of psychic recurrence." This "private language" of mixed meanings, "related to 'the puzlator' of Panurge," to the language of "Lear," "Carroll," and Mother Goose, is summed up by Miss Bogan in H. W. Fowler's definition of the pun as "a jocular or suggestive use of similarity between words or a word's different senses—'For a burning wood is come to dance insane.' " "*The Letters of Rainer Maria Rilke* and the study of Gide's *Journals* reveal the bristling amateur who fears to be soft"—show what philosophy that is equity can be; and typical of the whole temper of the book—Miss Bogan says of Yvor Winters, a writer "very nearly without listeners, let alone friends and admirers, his interest appears limited only because he has made choices, proof of probity and distilled power in unlikely times. These facts should delight us."

A fascinating book, abounding in important insights such as, "Loose form must have beneath, a groundswell of energy." "If one hates anything too long . . . one forgets what it is one could love"; the advice of W. B. Yeats that we "write our thoughts as nearly as possible in the language we thought them in." And we are warned against "stubborn avant-gardism when no real need for a restless forward movement any longer exists; the moment comes," Miss Bogan says, "for a consolidation of resources, for interpretation rather then exploration."

One has here mastery of material and associative creative insight—a conspectus of the transition from fettered to new writing—"from minor to major art"; to precision and "a transcending of the self through difficulty." The book rises above literariness, moreover, and fortifies courage, in practicing a principle which is surely Confucian; implying that one need not demand fair treatment, but rather, see that one's treatment of others is fair.

[1] As summarizing Emily Dickinson, Miss Bogan's review of the three-volume *Poems of Emily Dickinson*, edited by Thomas Johnson (*New Yorker*, October 8, 1955), seems the natural apex of these studies—a masterly critique.

Poetry London-New York, 1 (March–April 1956), 36–39; *A Marianne Moore Reader*.

BEOWULF

THE art of Winifred Macpherson, whose pen name is Bryher, is an archeology of the imagination, bringing to life circumstantially as fiction certain aspects of history. *The Fourteenth of October* reanimated the Battle of Hastings, *The Player's Boy* the Elizabethan stage, *Roman Wall* the days of Rome's crumbling empire.

Her new book *Beowulf* depicts the blackout, food-rationing, and prosaicheroic life in London during the Second World War. Miss Selina Tippett and Angelina, her partner, served teas. Angelina did the buying, although "her heart was really with the courses that she was taking to improve, as she said, 'the future of us women.' " She "had always been what the French called an amateur of meetings. It gave her such an illusion of travel to hurry off, sometimes before supper, to a hall in some unheard of suburb of London." With inapropos prowess, since the rent was yet unpaid, she returned one day with an almost life-size plaster bulldog whom she named "Beowulf"— prototype of the hero who slew Grendel, the dragon—bound "to triumph," as Caedmon tells us, "or in foe's clutch fastened, fall in battle."

Horatio Rashleigh, one of Selina's two lodgers, was a painter, whose ships had "made gay 'First Steps to History Part II,' a calendar, even a jigsaw

Review of *Beowulf*, by Bryher (Pantheon Books).

puzzle." His phrase, "with Whitehall's permission" describes him, as he handed over his book for "the usual thing," a few ounces of tea. Unlike him, Colonel Ferguson "preferred to shop as expeditiously as possible . . . still fuming over yesterday's interview. . . . There were years of work in him still if he could only get a job. 'I don't understand, sir, why you returned to London,' the official had said. 'You have been domiciled abroad ever since you left India and you are well over military age.' Colonel Ferguson had not even troubled to reply, 'To offer my services.' . . . A piece of parachute silk fluttered from a branch near the circle of a new crater. . . . How pay the rent with all customers gone to the country? . . . Selina supposed she must restrict cakes, one to a customer," whereas "she felt that life ought to be generous, wildly generous. . . . She looked sadly at the meagre row; there was something stinted and miserly about it. It was not the bombs that distressed her, awful as the noise was, so much as the lack of loaded trays to make up for the horrors of the night. She hated ration cards, less because she wasted more food herself than because they were a symbol of some poverty of spirit. They reminded her of vegetarian teachers with cramped ideas. If Angelina would only eat more, she would be less restless and talk less strangely. How detestable the propaganda of the Food Ministry was, with the emphasis upon oatmeal and raw carrots; were they not fighting for an England of sirloins of beef and mountains of cheddar cheese?"

She saw poor Mr. Rashleigh trotting up the street in his worn-out overcoat. "She was thankful that Angelina was not there to see him. 'That dreadful old man,' [Angelina] would say, rapping the desk with her pencil. 'But, Angelina, we can't turn him out, he has nowhere to go.' She dreaded seeing again the contemptuous shrug of her partner's shoulders. 'In a properly organized Britain there would be places for such people,' Angelina would say." During a raid she had no sooner compelled Mr. Rashleigh to leave his room and grope his way to the shelter than "half the sky seemed to explode. . . . the planes seemed at chimney level. . . . Occupants of the shelter and their Lido of beds and chairs had been flung like a trampled ant heap onto the floor." The tea shop had been hit by an incendiary bomb— "one of them centuries" as Ruby, the waitress, called them.

Like the Colonel's return, Bryher's work is always an offer of services. *Beowulf* is not only a close-up of war but a documentary of insights, of national temperament, of primness and patriotism, sarcasm and compassion, of hospitality and heroism, a miniaturama of all the folk who stood firm.

The Saturday Review of Literature, 39 (1 September 1956), 11.

OF MIRACLES AND KINGS

A s certain French, German, Irish and other folk tales are household treasure, a guide to their sources with indication of variants is not merely of interest, it is enthralling. In the instance of the Sources of Commentary appended by Paul Delarue to his *Borzoi Book of French Folk Tales* ("as countrymen and villagers have re-told them") it is surely so. The selections comprise: Tales of the Supernatural: among them, "The White Dove" (Perrault's "Bluebeard") of which "there are thirty-eight variants in French"; "The Lost Children" allied to Hansel and Gretel (Grimm), and "The Old Woman in the Well," thought to have been based by Perrault on oral tradition but derived by him from "Les enchantments de l'éloquence ou les effets de la douceur" (*Oeuvres meslées*, 1695, by Mlle. Lhéritier), the tale of two sisters contrastingly endowed by a fairy—one, so amiable that her words are attended by showers of precious stones; one, so surly that toads fall when she speaks.

Animal Tales: "The Mole of Jarnages" typifies "the theme of unsuccessful punishment," as when an animal is put back in its own element (an eel, drowned; a crow, thrown from a cliff, and a kin to Brer Rabbit thrown into the briar-patch).

Humorous Stories: "The Miraculous Doctor" who accidentally amuses and so cures by laughter a princess who had swallowed a fishbone; and "The Shepherd Who Got the King's Daughter," the formula of improbability capped by "lies" progressively greater and greater.

As for "best" tales, what is meant? The most poetic, most unusual, best told? "La Ramée and the Phantom," of these stories, perhaps says most in few words; also meets M. Delarue's requirement that "ambiance"—the original atmosphere of a story—be preserved in the retelling. La Ramée, a soldier, would rather serve the devil seven years than enlist for another year with a captain who will not promote him, leaves and is given a pair of scissors by a woman winnowing wheat, who says, "Do not defend yourself. The Phantom will try to smother you. Lean down then and clip its nails"; La Ramée obeys; the phantom becomes a princess and he, the king's heir.

When we impart distinctiveness to ordinary talk, William Archer says, still keeping it ordinary, we have literature. At all events, the diction in a

---

Review of *The Borzoi Book of French Folk Tales*, selected and edited by Paul Delarue, translated from the French by Austin E. Fife, illustrated by Warren Chappell (Alfred A. Knopf).

story of charm should match the material; as with Andrew Lang's version of the Grimms' tales, Mary Mian's translation of *A Treasury of French Folk Tales* by Henri Pourrat; Padraic Colum's "The Girl Who Sat by the Ashes." Any translator who has staggered about among English equivalents for oral French naturalness should, in chivalry, make allowance for an oversight or two, a felicity dulled by repetition, or idiom translated literally. Here one has to admit that with no pains spared every page is painful.

Can one say, "The surly sister receives the disgrace of casting forth a frog?" "The dog escapes before the eyes of the consternated boy?" "He came out of the church . . . and acted brave before the people?" "The king had been thinking of marrying his three daughters?" But M. Delarue—the very embodiment of nicety, vigilance, and fire—can survive deadly damage. As an expert of "oral tellings" by nursemaids, artisans, field-hands, and servants, he deplores "sophisticated reworkings" and zealously exposes "contaminants." His fervor and sense of ethnographic suitability themselves become a focus of human interest, as of scientific admiration, when he reports the following loss to France of a text ("The Old Woman in the Well"). "The manuscript of this version prevalent in langue d'oc," he says, "was purchased by the Morgan Library . . . for a sum the Bibliothèque Nationale was unable to match. I was authorized, however, to consult it, and to note the variants before its departure for America."

M. Delarue finds tales of all countries, European, Asiatic, to be part of a common fabric: "There are very pretty versions in all European, Asiatic and North African countries, and an American Chinese scholar, Jameson, has recently made known to us a Chinese Cinderella of the ninth century who gets her golden slippers not from a fairy but from a marvelous fish and who loses one of them not in escaping from a ball but on coming back from a festival in a neighboring region. . . . It is known that the Cinderella of Perrault has sisters with white skin, brown skin, yellow skin and black skin, under many skies, and yet they are quite recognizable in spite of their costumes and their various names. Adaptations to extremely different milieus and embellishments added by storytellers of all countries reveal, underneath, a common fabric."

But the variants acquire characteristics special to the country in which found: the German tale full of mysterious adventure in somber woods inhabited by dwarfs, giants, and talking animals, as Irish tales abound in enchanters, combats and fairies. Mediterranean tales reflect sea and sun; femininity sometimes being found in roles usually taken by men, as when a princess rescues a prince, cast by an enchanter into continuous sleep. In France, the supernatural is subordinated to logic and action and Bluebeard is a country squire, not that French folk tales, we are assured, have been "despoiled of their poetry."

Vice President since 1951 of the Société d'Ethnographie Française, M. Delarue has been made director of a massive undertaking—the assembling of the best supernatural tales of the provinces of France—three volumes of which have been published with others to follow (Editions Erasme, 31 quai de Bourbon, Paris 10).

Paul Delarue is a phenomenon of scientific responsibility, with a passion for results, and long may he live—a spur to curiosity which might prove but an irony were it not for his ethnographic insight, poetic sensibility and gift for the practical.

The New York Times Book Review, 11 November 1956, p. 5.

A GRAMMARIAN OF MOTIVES

KENNETH BURKE is a philosopher and a satirist—a humorist of the somatic kind, whose self-styled "flat tire of satire" has been indispensable to the lingual, political, moral, and poetic apparatus which has carried him to an enviable destination—the expert's. He feels that "eye, hand, and mental keenness" should be "busied for the good of the many" ("Plea of the People," page 58). "We would be men of good will," he says.

> To be strong in hate or to rot in wretchedness—
> Do not force us to this choice that is no choice.

In his "Neo-Hippocratic Oath," although he "cannot offer cures for stony hearts," he "swears that he will try not to belittle the work of those who would," and if he "comes upon unsavory private matters," he "will keep them to himself except insofar as he noises them abroad to everyone / as observations about everyone" ("Moments," page 8). In his technique of persuasion, he is a philosopher of opposites. He is not "launching an attack; nor does he suffer a sense of defeat." "Each principle advocated is matched

---

Review of *Book of Moments: Poems 1915-1954*, by Kenneth Burke (Hermes Publications).

by an opposite principle." "The connoisseur will be will-less ("Counter-Statement"). The artist "must recognize the validity of contraries," he says. On the title page of his *Moments* he quotes Emerson's statement, "Our moods do not believe in each other." He is in agreement with Thomas Mann that "the problematical is the proper sphere of art." Concur and one "will find moral indignation impossible."

His "Moments" "treat of love, politics, and kindred conundrums," he says, and as if to match the philosophy of opposites he says they "are somewhat irresponsible in their way of canceling out one another." Whatever else they do, they illustrate Plato's antithesis that if we think in universals, we feel in particulars. They are records of experience—"Delight, Promise, Victory, Regret, Apprehension, Arrival, Crossing, Departure, Loneliness, Sorrow, Despair, etc." and are reinforced at the back of the book by several pages of "Flowerishes"—dicta "which emerge these days somewhat dizzily," Mr. Burke says, and as print, flower in circles, serpentines, comet-tails, dotted lines, back to back and turning corners; some light and some in darkface. Here are two: "Must it always be wishful thinking? Can't it sometimes be thoughtful wishing?" "Draw out the time—and one part of an eddy going downstream might seem all your life to be going upstream."

In *Counter-Statement* (1931), discussing form "emotional and technical," "a work has form," Mr. Burke said, "insofar as one part leads a reader to anticipate another part and be gratified by the sequence." "Neglect organic progression and our emotions remain static." Alluding to virtues and diseases of form, he mentioned hypertrophy of information as a disease of form, said of Proust that whereas "a single page is astonishing, he becomes wearisome after extended reading"; noted also that "Shakespeare's style approaches mannerism insofar as it over-emphasizes metaphor." Eloquence, he said, consists in "matching the important with the important," and "by innovation is not meant something new but an emphasis to which the public is not accustomed." "A rhythm," he said, "is a promise which the poet makes the reader and in proportion as the reader comes to rely upon this promise, he falls into a state of general surrender which makes him more likely to accept, without resistance, the rest of the poet's material." His to me master-maxim is this: "Truth in art is not discovery of facts or addition to knowledge, it is the exercise of propriety."

With the foregoing aids to composition in mind, how does Mr. Burke come off poetically? He has in his "Problem of Moments"—if I am reliable—a masterpiece:

> I knew a man who would be wonder-wise,
> Having been born with both myopic eyes

Scratched in again.
—a symbol of "the motionless pursuit of us by pain," this man.

Note squirrel on log, how pert, now in, now out—
But classicists find either too much drought
Or too much rain.

(Wise, eyes, again
Absolute, pursuit, pain
Out drought, rain)

Here we have balance, compression, crescendo, and neatly articulated, impeccably accelerated rhyme, with each stanza punctuated by a rhymeword, the same words grouped in the same order, as climax of the final stanza. "Star-Fire" is expert counterpoint: "Fly-things sing-sit / On grow-things. . . . Hallo-la hella-lo!" There are many phases of Joyce inter-cross-ings: "As I lurk look from Look-Out." Mr. Burke is a master of the mellow-sardonic enforced by alliteration, as in his salute to alcohol: "ALKY, ME LOVE . . . Always there was something or other / Just couldn't stand it"; not of the mellow-sardonic only but of the mellow: as "Dozing" then "awaking to the cosmic roar"

Of the sea
(the onrushing, perpetual sea),

He never saw the sea so jammed with water.

Is not this "exposition," this picture of "Jack's Bandbox"?

The cover of this box is made secure
By a small catch of wire which, when released,
Permits the lid to open with a snap

And this an intrinsic pearl?

Beat the devil, beat the devil, beat the devil,
Beat the devil, beat the devil, beat the . . .

(Hear the train
Drive steadily on
Towards nowhere)

Alert to the practice of others, moreover, Mr. Burke reveals a strong liking for William Carlos Williams ("The Wrens Are Back"); pleasure in E. E. Cummings ("Frigate Jones") "With hands like feet, and feet in turn like legs / It was his job to lightly step on eggs"; in Wallace Stevens ("From Outside"):

> He could have called this place a bog; quaking
> With life, made cheap by multitude, . . .

and in the rhetoric of the Bible.

Complaints? With Rabelais and Joyce to brother him, Mr. Burke is sometimes coarse. Might he not recall that "the reader has certain categorical expectations that crave propriety?" that "self-expression of the artist is not distinguished by the uttering of emotion but by the evocation of emotion?" The theology in Mr. Burke's suggestions for a "Modernist Sermon," as in his "Lines in the Spirit of Negative Theology," is certainly negative. Led to expect some kind of counter-statement, we find "prayer" a mere figure of speech ("Invective and Prayer," "Dialectician's Prayer," "Industrialist's Prayer"). Looking elsewhere, we can say that solemnity and humility dominate "Night Piece," in which Mr. Burke says:

> I have stood on the edge of the jumping-off place
>
> Waiting
> have looked down
>
> To see still stars at the bottom of a lake
> Looked out
> Upon a dark riddle within;

and in "Faustkunde," nowhere implies a somewhere—a constancy at least:

> In bed, one thinks of fearsome things.

"When up, one laughs and calls himself a devil." Here, one seems to have both shells of the clam, the seeker for truth, the self-misled—and something alive within. Eternity is made the focus of these reflections,

> Wahrend in dem Wogen, der Ewigkeit er wiegt.*

*While he rocks in the waves of eternity.

Well; if it is not faith, it is poetry: "in dem Wogen er wiegt."

"A capacity is a command to act in a certain way," Mr. Burke says; and, fortunately for us, he has been impelled to think and to teach. A philosopher, a grammarian of motives, a methodologist and precisionist, an authority on language who "uses logic not merely to convince but because he loves logic," he has "felt as opportunity what others feel as a menace" and "taken a professional interest in his difficulties"; is an artist. His "new precisions offer new possibilities of development" and his original theorems do not stale. A poet in what he says and in knowing how what is said has been said, he has—Coleridge-fashion—doubled roles and planted two harvests, so that in each we have the best strengths of both.

Poetry London-New York, 1 (Winter 1956), 47–52; *A Marianne Moore Reader.*

LITTLE NEW ENGLAND

THIS initiate unperfunctory booklet commemorates an exhibition of "privately owned previously unrecorded material" from six New England states; the basis of the selection having been merit as art and "the importance of the sitter in history." Oliver Hazard Perry (Commodore and diplomat), Mrs. Perry; Nathaniel and Mrs. Nathaniel Bowditch; Major General Ira Allen, Noah Webster, Gilbert Stuart, Thomas Motley (father of Father of John L. Motley the historian), and other select personalities, are represented. (One new to the field need not be at a loss, since besides other New England collections listed, reference is made to Harry Wehle's *American Miniatures,* New York, 1927, and for devotees, to Paul Revere's *Day Book.*)

A miniature or "portrait in little," as defined by Mrs. Parker, can be very dull. Here, however, one has mood, character, command of the medium, and a number of studies which are notable. The medium—watercolor on ivory—with a few exceptions as specified, is in itself of interest, presupposing a material to which few painters are sensitive. A technique, moreover, which involves an infinitude of tiny brush-strokes has become an archaism to any but miniaturists of India and Iran.

That the portrait of John Singleton Copley of himself is "the first positively dated American miniature" and Copley's ability to give his work a three-

---

Review of *New England Miniatures, 1750–1850,* by Barbara Neville Parker (Boston Museum of Fine Arts).

dimensional quality, make him predominant—an impression surely justified by the self-portrait, the miniature of Mrs. Samuel Waldo, and the commanding portrait of Samuel Fayerweather; despite the fact, as Mrs. Parker says, that he apparently painted few miniatures after the 1760's when he became established as a painter of portraits in oil. Miss Sarah Goodridge, Edward Bone Malbone and John Trumbull, are, one perceives, integral to the collection. That Malbone "was sensitive to ivory as a medium which lends itself to portraying flesh-tones," is evident in his *Martha H. Babcock*, her pallor, ebony hair and dark eyes heightened by horizontals of turquoise; also in the Museum's using with great exactitude as an appliqué in color on the cover of the booklet, his oval locket-miniature, bordered by pearls, of an unidentified young woman. He is represented also by a landscape of rocks and smooth water. Any landscape, however, fairly or not, suffers comparison with a sublimity such as Asher Durand's *Kindred Spirits* (William Cullen Bryant and Thomas Cole conversing on a projecting shelf of rock, beneath foliage shading a ravine and brook from a waterfall) or the Isaac Oliver miniature of Sir Philip Sidney—in the collection at Windsor—the figure in velvet, and serpentine-striped gold jerkin, seated on a hassock of turf which encircles a great lime in full leaf, against a garden perspective of formal beds and architecture.

An absorbing characterization—perhaps the feature of the exhibition— is Sarah Goodridge's portrait of Gilbert Stuart, of which George Mason, his biographer, is quoted in the booklet as saying that when Stuart "saw himself looking 'like a fool' in the miniature he had permitted a New York artist to paint, he was unwilling to be handed down to posterity thus represented, so asked Miss Sarah Goodridge to paint him. When she had developed the head, she wished to add more to it but he would not allow her lest she injure the likeness." John Trumbull's *Christopher Gore* is impressive; Trumbull, working with oil on wood—distinguished by his ability to individualize and also present likeness in association as exemplified by his signers to the Declaration of Independence, a canvas but 30 inches wide (not in this collection). Endearing as subject and as treatment, is Mrs. Timothy Greene in silhouette, her cap-ruffle held in by a wide glossy ribbon (artist unknown). In the unknown man by Williams, 1810, we have a man of feeling by a man of feeling—drawn with a pencil of Ingreslike sensibility—the straight gaze, hair tending to curl, double-breasted coat, double-button-holed lapels and voluminous neckerchief, delineated with relish. Another triumph is *John Durrie Reading*, by John H. Durrie, his son. Delicate steel-rimmed spectacles which cast a shadow, and a left hand firming the page, remind one of Charles Peale's *The Lamplight Portrait* of James Peale.

The many instances in which "Artist Unknown" is substituted for a signature, stir speculation with regard to thirst, on the part of some, for pre-eminence. Is impassioned performance able to look with and at its own eye simultaneously? In any event, study of this collection induces mellowness toward "the portrait in little"; toward initiates of art research, toward the nature of what it is the artist does for us, and toward institutions which take trouble about it.

Art News, 56 (September 1957), 33, 63.

SELECTED WRITINGS OF
JUAN RAMON JIMENEZ

SPAIN has had in Miguel de Unamuno, "a David against the Philistines," Juan Ramon Jimenez says (in an essay included in this volume) and himself is a David—with sensibility as the stone in his shepherd's scrip. Born in 1881 in Moguer, Andalusia, he made a first trip to the United States in 1916, to marry Zenobia Camprubi who, after their engagement in Madrid, had come to New York to visit relatives. A person of rare mind, studious and idealistic like Juan Ramon, she was shall one say, "another himself," enheartening him and aiding him—indeed assisting him in making a translation of the entire work of Tagore. In 1956, she died, three days after the award of the Nobel Prize to Señor Jimenez had been announced. He now lives in Puerto Rico.

Dr. Florit's undogmatic affectionate survey of this book, and the choices of verse and prose made by him in consultation with the author, afford the newcomer a real sense of what is there. It is not as with many an introduction, so adulatory as to defeat its purpose. It would profit by scrutiny of certain wordings; but as biography and as providing a chronology personally lived, it is indispensable. One is very much its debtor.

The book presents a man's work but also his person in its essence. The prose work appears in English here for the first time: the prose sketches of small events, sensitively visioned, the portraits of contemporaries, the extensive essays on great issues of today, the ideas of which, one infers, some were his own reasons for his voluntary exile from his native land. Here one

---

Review of *The Selected Writings of Juan Ramon Jimenez*, edited by Eugenio Florit, translated by H. R. Hays (Farrar Straus & Cudahy).

becomes aware of a man of stern beliefs who has triumphed in holding to truth and beauty and to a life close to God.

Until the Nobel Prize focused attention upon his work, he was perhaps best known for *Platero and I*, the series of poem monologues with Platero, his donkey, as audience: begun in 1907, the whole has now been translated (and recently published) by Eloise Roach and beautifully, although H. R. Hays (in twelve selections from the work in this volume) sometimes has for a word of hers, a more natural one. These delicately unstereotyped, and at the same time, elate miniatures, are typical of the whole man: they should charm anyone. Señor Jimenez was, to begin with, a painter and sees with the eye for romance, of a Corot or a Turner—lemon-yellows of sunset touched with wine; and Platero's eyes as mirrors of black glass above the pink, gold, or blue flowers which he is nosing in the meadow. As master rides to church the farmhands in their Sunday clothes stop to look: "There is steel in him. Steel and quicksilver."

The work selected from Señor Jimenez' "Anthologies" and from his critical work, constitute a "spiritual history" which seems to fall into three periods, of which the first might be termed The Experiencing; the second, one of intellectual enrichment and technical development, in which he perfects and polishes an originality already basic. These years of "nonconformity" and insistence upon "essence" include poems which border on surrealism, apostrophize mutability, and "Memory, blind buzzing bee of bitterness"; also poems which allude to travel from Philadelphia to New York, recall the Hudson, Broadway at night. This period is dominated by images in which nature as Rachel Frank in her essay in the issue of *Poetry* devoted to Jimenez (July 1953) says of pantheism, "has a life of its own as if it were a person." "I heard the trees talking. I heard them talking about me . . ." Señor Jimenez says, "and how could I disappoint them?" All his creative advance, he says, has tended toward the idea of God, and in his later work or third period, "the divine becomes for him concrete, a consciousness unique, just, universal, of beauty within and outside us."

Mallarmé-like in the instinctiveness of his symbolism, he says to The Solitary Poplar as a symbol of Spain to be commiserated, "Terrible, sad, ardent, solitary Spanish people." The Wheatear is for him a symbol of poetry; "its closepacked treasure is spilled, / then from its cradle or tomb, the earth / . . . it springs into finer ears, fuller, firmer, taller . . . the one form which lifts the soul to / the unattainable, oh poetry, infinite, aureate, upright."

Señor Jimenez is a virtuoso of sound and cadence. A master of accent and of the unmonotonous refrain, varying by a touch what is repeated, not allowing it to become flat—an effect which recalls T. S. Eliot's "Triumphal

March": "Stone, bronze, bronze, stone, steel, stone," and certain of the Pound Cantos.

With regard to word-use, sound and order, felicities in the original must be a translator's despair. As H. R. Hays says in his introductory Note, "Spanish is much richer than English in feminine endings and abounds in rippling syllables for which the English has but monosyllables," but Mr. Hays is a fine and sensitive translator and has for the most part surmounted his difficulties.

What an author admires in other authors throws light on himself and surely applies to Señor Jimenez in his characterization of Adolfo Becquer as "individual, authentic, recondite, precise." Of Francisco Giner, called by some, "little Don Francis," Señor Jimenez says, "No, no, he was nothing like that . . . a spiritualized inferno."

We use the term literature as including poetry. Señor Jimenez uses it in a derogatory sense, as meaning conscious rather than instinctive, pretentious, literal. "Literature can be rich in metaphor," he says, "but there is a profounder profundity." "Poetry is institution—not written but realized. . . . Poetry is always natural, the antithesis of pretentiousness" and when using "rigid forms converts them into flexible ones. . . . Poetry can only become difficult when its rhetoric is not of the spirit."

As recurring motifs in Señor Jimenez' thought, we have a pre-occupation with the sea, with the dream, with eternity; and with death—regarded not as a defeat but as a triumph of the permanent over the temporal, a deliverance from the dominance of the perishable. Señor Jimenez feels that in art and in life, "to be ever new one must be so by instinct for the spiritual" and think of life as "a continual becoming"—"like surf or waves forever new that do not leave the sea or the shore." The work is rich in aphorisms, two of which are a kind of self-portrait: "The assassin of life is haste: Don't run, go slow. It is only to yourself you have to go."

Characteristic of Señor Jimenez' mature work is his "Animal of Depth," in which as in his "The Wheatear," the soul born to be erect says, "I am not I, I am he who walks at my side without seeing him. He who pardons gently when I am hating. He who walks where I am not. He who shall stand erect when I am dead":—surely a feat to capture in words, so elusive an entity as the nature of the soul.

"Fantasy is a characteristic of man, who dreams by means of the will," Señor Jimenez says; and "the poet is the greatest enemy of the false." "In living his dream, he will integrate a better society."

Bulletin of the Marboro Book Club, 3, No. 33 (1958), 2–4.

ROBERT ANDREW PARKER

ROBERT ANDREW PARKER is one of the most accurate and at the same time most unliteral of painters. He combines the mystical and the actual: he works both in an abstract and in a realistic way, without contradictions. One or two of his paintings—a kind of private calligraphy—little upward-tending lines of real writing like a school of fish—approximate a signature or a family cipher.

His subjects include animals, persons—individually and en masse; trees, isolated and thickset; architecture, ships, troop movements, the sea; an ink drawing of an elm by a stone wall between meadows. A work such as *Sleeping Dog* is the whole thing in essence: simplicity that is not the product of a simple mind but of the single eye—of rapt, genuine, undeprecatory love for the subject. The dog's pairs of legs curve out parallel, his solid cylinder of tail laid in the same direction as the legs, and the eye seen as a diagonal slit in the nondescript pallor of whitish skin; they focus thought on treatment, not just on the dog. A cursive ease in the lines suggests a Rembrandt-like relish for the implement in hand; better yet, there is a look of emotion synonymous with susceptibility to happiness. Entwined in a Beethoven-like Lost Groschen of rhythms, the chalk-gray and dead-grass tones of *Celery and Eggs, No. 2*, have resulted in eminence—are something elate. The rigidly similar forms, in dark blue, of the audience in *Mario and the Magician* perfectly state the suspense in Thomas Mann's sinister story that one has never known how to define.

His Holiness Pope Pius XI's cloak of even, celestially flawless violet lined with ermine, against a black ground, is a triumph of texture, with tinges of lemon defining the four conjoined ridges of the Papal cap. Similar in his satiric tendency and feeling for tones, Robert Parker is finer than Charles Demuth—goes further—but his wide swaths of paint with a big brush and washes of clear color touched by some speck or splinter of paint—say, magenta or indigo—spreading just far enough, are surely in the same category with the Demuth cerise cyclamen and illustrations for Henry James. Mr. Parker is not afraid of sweet-pea pink for the face of a soldier in khaki or for the dress of a lady with orange-gold hair. He has plenty of aplomb in his juxtaposings of rust, blood red, shrimp pink and vermilion. In marine blues, blue that could be mistaken for black, faded denim, sapphire-green and—thinking of *Oarsmen*—a Giotto-background blue or telephone-pole-insulator aquamarine, Mr. Parker is a specialist. Here the design of the men and boat is integrated with the sea as seeds are set in a melon—the men braced by resistance to the mounding weight of deep water; the crisscross of the oars, uninterferingly superimposed on the vastness of a sea without sky. Payne's gray is another specialty of Mr. Parker's, as in the etched-over *Head of a Lady*, and in the fainter gray scene but explicit turrets and rig of the cruiser, *Admiral Hipper*.

Mr. Parker is a fantasist of great precision in his studies of troop movements, seen in the *Invasion of an Island*, from the "Gyoncho" series—and in the balanced color-pattern dominated by white, of *East Yorkshire Yeomanry Disembarking from H. M. S. Cressy*—its caraway-seed multitudes pouring down the ship's sides in streams like sand in an hourglass, the sea choked with landing boats repeated to infinity. For this science of tea-leaf-like multitudes there is an antecedent, if not a counterpart, in the swarm-populous, seed-compact, arc- or circle-designed battle scenes in central Greece painted by Panaghiotes Zograpos (1836–40) for General Makryannis (reproductions in *Eikones*, April 1956). As multitudinous, although unaware of the Greek scenes, Mr. Parker manages to be epic without being archaic. His *October, 1917* is intensely his own. A platoon, sabers up, seen from the side, reduplicates identical-identical-identical boots that are as black as the men's tunics are flaming vermilion—with an effect resembling the leaves of a partly open book standing upright.

We have here masterpieces of construction plus texture, together with a passion for accuracies of behavior, as where, in the semi-frowning fixity of the eyes, in his portrait of Mrs. Parker, the artist has caught her expression of pleasing unselfconscious naturalness. Warren Hennrich, moreover, has for his "Field Exercises" (*Wake* magazine, June, 1945) the perfect illustration in Robert Parker's *The Retreat from Caporetto* and its deadly uniformity of faces smothered by their helmets:

> Harmonious men
> In harmonious masses
>
> Suspend at attention
> Bright, gleaming cuirasses,
>
> And then march away
> In monotonous classes.
>
> They follow the outline
> Of bordering grasses,
>
> Anonymous men
> In anonymous masses.

Mr. Parker has an eye: typified by the waiting horse down on one haunch, by the flick-back of the hoof of a horse in motion, or the tremendous force of a rearing movement. *Hussar, 1900, South Africa,* with raised saber, launching forward, the down-darting definiteness of the tapered boot, and counterpoint of galloping hoofs, almost rivals *The Attack, No. 1,* and its unified chaos. The excitement here is not all in sabers and furious action. Humor lurks in the beach scenes of distorted perspective; in the slightly over-curled-in claws and rumpled topknot of the *Fairy Shrimp* trundling along like a feather duster; in *Ugly Animal,* and *Another Dog.*

On no account should Mr. Parker's capacity for grandeur be underestimated—it is embodied in *An Imaginary Monument to a Lancer, No. 1,* and its reverie-at-dusk aspect; and in two rather similar equestrian statues, grand without being accidentally ironic—the rider in one, silhouetted against a glare of magenta fire; the other, massive above an ascending burst of yellowish fire.

Robert Parker is thirty—tall, slender and meditative—born in Norfolk, Virginia. He is unmistakably American, typical—perhaps say, reliable—in the sense so pleasing to Henry James. That his likings and proficiencies should range wide and that, so young, he should have depth and stature unvitiated by egotism, seems remarkable. He is in a sense like Sir Thomas Browne, for whom small things could be great things—someone exceptional—*vir amplissimus.*

Arts, 32 (April 1958), 48–49.

IF I WERE SIXTEEN TODAY

WHEN I was sixteen—in fact thirteen—I felt as old as I have ever felt since; and what I wish I could have been when sixteen is exactly what I am trying to do now, to know that to be hindered is to succeed. If one cannot strike when the iron is hot, one can strike *till* the iron is hot (Lyman Abbott).

With every reason to feel confident—except that we were in straitened circumstances financially (my mother, brother, and I)—I felt insecure, and took a day at a time, not because I knew it was best but because I had to. I regarded myself as a wall-flower; I did not like my face, and not many of my clothes. I was an introvert.

However, I experienced society vicariously, my brother was not introspective, or brooding, or too diffident; he abounded in invitations. He did not exalt "the power of life to renew itself"; he exemplified it. He did not foresee his own later warning to a boy who had completed preparatory-school work, whose mania was dancing. "Remember, every girl has one question: 'Is he going to marry me?' and every man: 'How safe am I?' "

I received the present of a bicycle—a maroon Reading Standard. Was I delighted? Not at all. I would have to learn to ride; riding itself was work. Little did I anticipate sweeping down smooth roads lined by tassels of waving locust-blossoms, or pausing on a little bridge over a brook to drop leaves and see them whirled away as minnows veered or hung motionless.

If I could alter my attitude retroactively, I would say as my brother says, "Be confident; burn your bridges behind you. . . . You may have to get tough in a good cause. A bear has paws and teeth and sometimes has to use them." And, taking the advice of James Stern in a *Times Book Review* section, beware of "the uncertain approach"; of objecting to what you object to "in no small degree"; of belonging to a school which the late George Orwell once described as "that of the not ungreen grass."

I would, if I could, let little things be little things—would be less susceptible to embarrassment. David Seabury says, "When you are saying, 'I can't be calm, I can't be calm,' you *can* be calm." Don't relive bad moments, or *revive them for others*, or be expecting more of them. To postponers, I would say, DO IT NOW; and to firebrands of impatience, ROME WAS NOT BUILT IN A DAY. "Superiority" is at the opposite pole from insight. Fashion can make you ridiculous; style, which is yours to control individually, can make you attractive—a near siren. What of chastity? It confers a particular strength. Until recently, I took it for granted—like avoiding *"any drugs."*

Instead of hating an over-heavy curriculum and applying jest about the army—"the incompetent teaching the indifferent the irrelevant," I would give thought to the why rather than merely the what of my subjects. Progressive forms in mathematics have unity-structure. You may not like arithmetic; my aplomb suffers a trifle when a bank teller says, "Yes; it's all right; I just changed a 6 to a 7." Arithmetic demands of memory a very exact kind of co-ordination; and in school, I found geometry a relief; Smith's advanced algebra, easier than arithmetic; it exerted a certain fascination. Caesar's Commentaries are—it is true—unostentatiously skillful, not traps for a drudge. Xenophon on dogs and in his treatise on horsemanship, is an expert.

1. Whatever you do, put all you have into it.

2. Go to the trouble of asking, "What good does it do?" "Why Portuguese? I may never use it."

3. Give "culture" the benefit of the doubt; don't look on art as effeminate, and museums as "the most tiring form of recreation there is."

4. I would, like Sir Winston, refuse to let a betrayal rob me of trust in my fellow man.

5. One should above all, learn to be silent, to listen; to make possible promptings from on high. Suppose you "don't believe in God." Talk to someone very wise, who believed in God, did not, and then found that he did. The cure for loneliness is solitude. Think about this saying by Martin Buber: "The free man believes in destiny and that it has need of him." Destiny, not fate.

And lastly, ponder Solomon's wish: when God appeared to him in a dream and asked, "What wouldst thou that I give unto thee?" Solomon did not say fame, power, riches, but an understanding mind, and the rest was added.

World Week, 33 (7 November 1958), 16–17.

SUBJECT, PREDICATE, OBJECT

OF poetry, I once said, "I, too, dislike it"; and say it again of anything mannered, dictatorial, disparaging, or calculated to reduce to the ranks what offends one. I have been accused of substituting appreciation for criticism, and justly, since there is nothing I dislike more than the exposé or any kind of revenge. Like Ezra Pound, I prefer the straightforward order of words, "subject, predicate, object"; in reverse order only for emphasis, as when Pope says:

> Men must be taught as if you taught them not,
> And things unknown proposed as things forgot.

Dazzled, speechless—an alchemist without implements—one thinks of poetry as divine fire, a perquisite of the gods. When under the spell of admiration or gratitude, I have hazarded a line, it never occurred to me that anyone might think I imagined myself a poet. As said previously, if what I write is called poetry it is because there is no other category in which to put it.

Nor is writing exactly a pastime—although when I was reading H. T. Parker's music page in the *Boston Evening Transcript*, in what it is not speaking too strongly to call an ecstasy of admiration, to be writing in emulation, anything at all for a newspaper, was a pleasure: no more at that time than woman's suffrage party notes, composed and contributed at intervals to the *Carlisle Evening Sentinel*.

I am reminded somewhat of myself by Arnold Toynbee's recital of his spiritual debts—indebtedness to his mother for awakening in him an interest in history, "to Gibbon for showing what an historian can do"; to "people, institutions . . . pictures, languages, and books" as exciting his "curiosity." Curiosity; and books. I think books are chiefly responsible for my doggedly self-determined efforts to write; books and verisimilitude; I like to describe things. I well understand the entrapped author[1] of an autobiography in three volumes, who says he rewrote the first volume some twenty-six times "before I got it to sound the way I talk."

"Sweet speech does no harm—none at all," La Fontaine says of the song that saved the life of the swan mistaken by the cook for a goose. But what simple statement, in either prose or verse, really is simple? Wariness is essential where an inaccurate word would give an impression more exact than could be given by a verifiably accurate term. One is rewarded for knowing the way and compelling a resistful un-English-speaking taxi-driver to take it when he says upon arrival—dumbfounded and gratified—"Ah, we did not suffer any lights."

It is for himself that the writer writes, charmed or exasperated to participate; eluded, arrested, enticed by felicities. The result? Consolation, rapture, to be achieving a likeness of the thing visualized. One may hang back or launch away. "With sails flapping, one gets nowhere. With everything sheeted down, one can go round the world"—an analogy said to have been applied by Woodrow Wilson to freedom.

Combine with charmed words certain rhythms, and the mind is helplessly haunted. In his poem, "The Small," Theodore Roethke says:

> A wind moves through the grass,
> Then all is as it was.

And from the following lines by Alberto de Lacerda (translated), one's imagination easily extends from the tiger to the sea, and beyond:

> The tiger that walks in her gestures
> Has the insolent grace of the ships.

Form is synonymous with content—must be—and Louis Dudek is perhaps right in saying, "The sound of the poem heard by the inner ear is the ideal sound"; surely right in saying, "The art of poetry is the art of singular form." Poetry readings have this value, they assist one to avoid blurred diction. It should not be possible for the listener to mistake "fate" for "faith"—in "like a bulwark against fate." The five-line stanzas in my *Collected Poems* warn one to write prose or short-line verse only, since my carried-over long lines make me look like the fanciest, most witless rebel against common sense. Overruns certainly belong at the right—not left—of the page.

Translations suit no one; even so, I still feel that translated verse should have the motion of the original. La Fontaine says of the adder that it lunged at its rescuer:

> L'insecte sautillant cherche à réunir,
> Mais il ne put y parvenir.

In

> The pestilent thirds writhed together to rear,
> But of course no longer adhere

the word "insect," so pleasing, is sacrificed; but "r," important as sound, ends the line.

Poetry is the Mogul's dream: to be intensively toiling at what is a pleasure; La Fontaine's indolence being, as the most innocent observer must realize, a mere metaphor. As for the hobgoblin obscurity, it need never entail compromise. It should mean that one may fail and start again, never mutilate an auspicious premise. The objective is architecture, not demolition; grudges flower less well than gratitudes. To shape, to shear, compress, and delineate; to "add a hue to the spectrum of another's mind" as Mark Van Doren has enhanced the poems of Thomas Hardy, should make it difficult for anyone to dislike poetry!

[1] "the entrapped author": Alexander King.

The Christian Science Monitor, 24 December 1958, p. 7; *Tell Me, Tell Me*.

IDIOSYNCRASY AND TECHNIQUE

I. Technique

IN his inaugural lecture as Professor of Poetry at Oxford,[1] Mr. Auden said, "There is only one thing that all poetry must do; it must praise all it can for

Inaugurating the Ewing Lectures at the University of California, October 3 and 5, 1956.

being as for happening." He also said, "Every poem is rooted in imaginative awe." These statements answer, or imply an answer, to the question: Why does one write?

I was startled, indeed horrified, when a writing class in which I have an interest was asked, "Is it for money or for fame?" as though it must be one or the other—and writing were not for some a felicity, if not a species of intellectual self-preservation. Gorgeously remunerated as I am for being here, it would seem both hypocritical and inappropriate to feign that a love of letters renders money irrelevant. Still, may I say, and with emphasis, that I do not write for money *or* fame. To earn a living is needful, but it can be done in routine ways. One writes because one has a burning desire to objectify what it is indispensable to one's happiness to express; a statement which is not at variance with the fact that Sir Walter Scott, driven by a fanatically sensitive conscience, shortened his life writing to pay what was not a personal debt. And Anthony Trollope, while writing to earn a living, at the same time was writing what he very much loved to write.

Amplifying the impression which Bernard Shaw, as music critic, himself gives of his "veracity, catholicity, and pugnacity,"[2] Hesketh Pearson says of him as stage manager of his plays, "No author could be more modest than Shaw. He did not regard his text as sacrosanct. He laughed over his own lines as if they were jokes by somebody else and never could repeat them accurately. Once, when an actor apologized for misquoting a passage, he remarked, 'What you said is better than what I wrote. If you can always misquote so well, keep on misquoting—but remember to give the right cues!' "[3] Writing was resilience. Resilience was an adventure. Is it part of the adventure to revise what one wrote? Professor Ewing has suggested that something be said about this. My own revisions are usually the result of impatience with unkempt diction and lapses in logic; together with an awareness that for most defects, to delete is the instantaneous cure.

The rhythms of the King James Version of the Bible stand forever as writing, although certain emendations as to meaning seem obligatory. The King James Epistle of Paul to the Philippians, 3:20, reads: "For our conversation is in heaven"; the Revised Standard Version reads: "We are a heavenly body"; each a mistranslation, according to Dr. Alvin E. Magary, who feels that Dr. Moffat got it right: " 'We are a colony of heaven'—a Roman outpost as it were, in which people conformed their lives to the life of Rome—an interpretation which makes sense as applied to Christianity"; Dr. Magary also emphasizes that the beatitude, blessed are the meek, should have no connotation of subservience, since if rendered more strictly, the word would be, not the meek, but the "begging."

The revisions by Henry James of his novels, are evidently in part the result of an insistent desire to do justice to first intention. Reverting to pronouncements on Milton and Goethe made previously, T. S. Eliot seems to feel that after-judgment can not merely be taken for granted, and when accepting the Goethe Prize in 1954 he said, "As one's reading is extended [one begins] to develop that critical ability, that power of self-criticism without which the poet will do not more than repeat himself. . . "; then further on: "To understand what Wisdom is, is to be wise oneself: and I have only the degree of understanding that can be obtained by a man who knows that he is not wise, yet has some faith that he is wiser than he was twenty years ago. I say twenty years ago, because I am under the distressing necessity of quoting a sentence I printed in 1939. It is this:

> Of Goethe perhaps it is truer to say that he dabbled in both philosophy and poetry and made no great success at either; his true role was that of a man of the world and a sage, a la Rochefoucauld, a La Bruyère, a Vauvenargues."

Mr. Eliot says he ". . . never re-read the passage in which this sentence is buried [and had] discovered it not so long ago in Mr. Michael Hamburger's introduction to his edition and translation of the text of Holderlin's poems." He then goes on to say of Goethe, "It may be that there are areas of wisdom that he did not penetrate: but I am more interested in trying to understand the wisdom he possessed than to define its limitations. When a man is a good deal wiser than oneself, one does not complain that he is no wiser than he is."[4]

Since writing is not only an art but a trade embodying principles attested by experience, we would do well not to forget that it is an expedient for making one's self understood and that what is said should at least have the air of having meant something to the person who wrote it—as is the case with Gertrude Stein and James Joyce. Stewart Sherman one time devised a piece of jargon which he offered as indistinguishable from work by Gertrude Stein, which gave itself away at once as lacking any private air of interest. If I may venture to say again what I have already said when obscurity was deplored, one should be as clear as one's natural reticence allows one to be. Laurence Binyon, reflecting on the state of letters after completing his Dante, said: "How indulgent we are to infirmity of structure . . ."[5] and structural infirmity truly has, under surrealism, become a kind of horticultural verbal blight threatening firmness to the core; a situation met long ago in *The Classic Anthology Defined by Confucius:*

> Enjoy the good yet sink not in excess.
> True scholar stands by his steadfastness.[6]

. . . .
Lamb-skin for suavity, trimmed and ornate,
But a good soldier who will get things straight.[7]

In attaining this noble firmness, one must have clarity, and clarity depends on precision; not that intentional ambiguity cannot be an art. Reinhold Niebuhr is not famed as easy reading, but is at times a study in precision as when he says, "The self does not realize itself most fully when self-realization is its conscious aim"; and of conscience says, "We will define it provisionally at least as capacity to view itself and judge obligation in contrast with inclination."[8] It is not "the purpose [but] the function of roots to absorb water," Dr. Edmund Sinnott notes in his book *The Biology of the Spirit*, in which he discusses the self-regulating properties of protoplasm—digressing, with a shade of outrage, to deplore untidiness in the use of terms. One is corrected when referring to certain African tribes for saying they worship the devil; they propitiate the devil; and if precise, one weeds text of adjective, adverbs, and unnecessary punctuation. As an instance of such concision, we have Mr. Francis Watson's account of Edward Arnold, "the traveler, linguist, and semi-mystic, with whom Matthew Arnold did not like to be confused."[9] Informing us that Edwin Arnold had been married three times and that two of his wives had died—a lack-luster kind of statement which few of us perhaps would avoid—Mr. Watson says, "after being twice bereaved, he found a third wife from Japan, a land whose culture he extolled in articles. . . ." Paramount as a rule for any kind of writing—scientific, commercial, informal, prose or verse—we dare not be dull. Finding Akira Kurosawa's film *The Magnificent Seven* too reiterative, Bosley Crowther says that "the director shows so many shots of horses' feet tromping in the mud that we wonder if those horses have heads."[10]

In his "Advice to a Young Critic" (Golding Bright),[11] Bernard Shaw says, "Never strike an attitude, national, moral, or critical"—an axiom he did not observe too fanatically if judged by the telegram he is said to have sent to an actress with a leading part in one of his plays: ". . . wonderful, marvelous, superb . . ." to which the actress replied, "Undeserving such praise"; and he: "I meant the play"; and she: "So did I."

I have a mania for straight writing—however circuitous I may be in what I myself say of plants, animals, or places; and although one may reverse the order of words for emphasis, it should not be to rescue a rhyme. There are exceptions, of course, as when Mr. Oliver Warner, speaking of Captain Cook, the explorer, in commending the remarkable drawings made by members of the Captain's staff, says: "None of Cook's artists worked to preconceived notions. They drew what they saw and wonderful it was."[12] To say "and it was wonderful" would have been very flat. We have literature, William Archer said, when we impart distinctiveness to ordinary talk and make it still seem ordinary.

Like dullness, implausibility obscures the point; so, familiar though we are with "Fenimore Cooper's Literary Offenses," by Mark Twain,[13] allow me to quote a line or two. "It is a rule of literary art in the domain of fiction," Mark Twain says, "that always the reader shall be able to tell the corpses from the others. But this detail often has been overlooked in the *Deerslayer* tale. [Cooper] bends 'a sapling' to the form of an arch over [a] narrow passage, and conceals six Indians in its foliage." Then, " . . . one of his acute Indian experts, Chingachgook (pronounced Chicago, I think) has lost the trail of a person he is tracking . . . turned a running stream out of its course, and there, in the slush of its old bed, were that person's moccasin-tracks. . . ." Even the laws of nature take a vacation when Cooper is practicing "the delicate art of the forest."

What has been said pertains to technique (*teknikos* from the Greek, akin to *tekto:* to produce or bring forth—as art, especially the useful arts). And, indeed if technique is of no interest to a writer, I doubt that the writer is an artist.

What do I mean by straight writing, I have been asked. I mean, in part, writing that is not mannered, overconscious, or at war with common sense, as when a reviewer of *The Evolution of Cambridge Publishing*, by S. C. Roberts, refers to "a demure account of Cambridge's flirtation with the *Encyclopaedia Britannica.*"[14] At the risk of seeming to find every virtue in certain authors and these authors in a certain few books or critiques, let me contrast with the unreal manner, W. D. Howells' *My Mark Twain* and a similar uninfected retrospect by the Duke of Windsor. "Of all the literary men I have known," Howells says of Mark Twain, "he was the most unliterary in his make and manner. . . . His style was what we know, for good or for bad, but his manner, if I may difference the two, was as entirely his own as if no one had ever written before. [He] despised the avoidance of repetitions out of fear of tautology. If a word served his turn better than a substitute, he would use it as many times on a page as he chose. . . . [There] never was a more biddable man in things you could show him a reason for. . . . If you wanted a thing changed, very good, he changed it; if you suggested that a word or a sentence or a paragraph had better be struck out, very good, he struck it out. His proof sheets came back each with a veritable 'mush of concession,' as Emerson says." "He was always reading some vital book . . . which gave him life at first hand," Howells continues. "It is in vain that I try to give a notion of the intensity with which he compassed the whole world. . . ."

The other instance of straight writing to which I referred is "My Garden," by the Duke of Windsor.[15] Prosperity and royalty are always under suspicion. "Of course they had help," people say. "Someone must have written it for them"; as they said of the shepherd made judge, in the fable of the shepherd and the King, ". . . *he* is given the credit; we did the work; he has amassed riches; we are poor."[16] So let me say, I have in the following narrative an impression of individuality, conviction, and verbal selectiveness.

"I think my deep enjoyment of gardening must be latent," the Duke begins. "At least it was not inherited. . . . The gardens at Sandringham and Windsor . . . made a fine show in summertime [a word with flavor, for me], but people did not really live with them. A garden is a mood, as Rousseau said, and my mood was one of intimacy, not splendor." Of his present gardening at The Mill, not far from Paris, he says, ". . . French gardens can be remarkably beautiful things. They look like continuations of the Savonnerie of Aubusson carpets in the great chateaus rolled outside the windows onto the lawns, perfectly patterned and mathematically precise. . . . I wanted an English type of garden, which means green grass and seemingly casual arrangement of flowers, and here I had the perfect framework." Commenting on one of the color photographs which supplement the account, he says, "The main entrance to the property has an old covered gateway with ancient oak doors and a cobbled drive which leads to the main building. There is a big sundial above the front door, put there when The Mill was restored about 1732. In the foreground is Trooper, one of our four Pugs." Technically an oversight, perhaps—the f-o-r-e ground and f-o-u-r pugs in close proximity—this clash lends authenticity, has the charm of not too conscious writing. Unmistakably all along, the article embodies a zeal for the subject, a deep affection for flowers as seen in the complaint, "The mildest stonemason turns scourge when it comes to plant life." The piece smiles, whereas saturninity is a bad omen. "We do not praise God by dispraising man."[17]

II. Idiosyncrasy

In considering technique, I tried to say that writing can be affirmative and that we must, as Dr. Nathan Scott says, "reject the attitude of philosophic distrust." The writer should have "a sense of upthrusting vitality and self-discovery"[18] without thinking about the impression made, except as one needs to make oneself understood.

We are suffering from too much sarcasm, I feel. Any touch of unfeigned gusto in our smart press is accompanied by an arch word implying, "Now to me, of course, this is a bit asinine." Denigration, indeed, is to me so disaffecting that when I was asked to write something for the Columbia

Chapter of Phi Beta Kappa Class Day exercises, I felt that I should not let my sense of incapacity as an orator hinder me from saying what I feel about the mildew of disrespect and leave appreciation to Mr. Auden, to salute "literary marines landing in little magazines." I then realized that what I was so urgent to emphasize is reduced in the First Psalm to a sentence: Blessed is the man who does not sit in the seat of the scoffer.

Odd as it may seem that a few words of overwhelming urgency should be a mosaic of quotations, why paraphrase what for maximum impact should be quoted verbatim? I borrowed, at all events, Ambassador Conant's title *The Citadel of Learning*, taken for his book from Stalin: "[Facing us] stands the citadel of learning. This citadel we must capture at any price. This citadel must be taken by our youth, if they wish to be the builders of a new life, if they wish, in fact, to take the place of the old guard."[19]

Blessed is the man

who does not sit in the seat of the scoffer—
   the man who does not denigrate, depreciate, denunciate;
     who is not "characteristically intemperate,"
who does not "excuse, retreat, equivocate; and will be heard."
(Ah, Giorgione! there are those who mongrelize
   and those who heighten anything they touch; although it may well be
     that if Giorgione's self-portrait were not said to be he,
it might not take my fancy. Blessed the geniuses who know

that egomania is not a duty.)
   "Diversity, controversy; tolerance"—in that "citadel
     of learning" we have a fort that ought to armor us well.
Blessed is the man who "takes the risk of a decision"—asks

himself the question: "Would it solve the problem?
   Is it right as I see it? Is it in the best interests of all?"
     Alas. Ulysses' companions are now political—
living self-indulgently until the moral sense is drowned,

having lost all power of comparison,
   thinking license emancipates one, "slaves whom they themselves have
     bound."
   Brazen authors, downright soiled and downright spoiled as if sound
and exceptional, are the old quasi-modish counterfeit,

mitin-proofing conscience against character.
   Affronted by "private lives and public shame," blessed is the author

who favors what the supercilious do not favor—
who will not comply. Blessed, the unaccommodating man.

Blessed the man whose faith is different
    from possessiveness—of a kind not framed by "things which do appear"—
        who will not visualize defeat, too intent to cower;
whose illumined eye has seen the shaft that gilds the sultan's tower.

I had written these lines about denigration as treason, and was assembling advice for some students of verse, when I found that Rolfe Humphries, in his little treatise entitled "Writing the Lyric,"[20] has thrown light on the use of consonants. "Take the letter *s*," he says, "one of the most insidious sounds in the language, one which will creep in, in a sibilant reptilian fashion like the original serpent in the garden, and if you are not careful, not only drive you out of Paradise, but hiss you off the stage; . . . see if you can write a quatrain without using it at all." Pondering my "Blessed is the man who does not sit in the seat of the scoffer," I could only say that another's expertise might save one considerable awkwardness. Initiate John Barry came to my rescue by citing the *Aeneid* (II,8):

Et iam nox umida caelo
praecipitat suadentque cadentia sidera somnos.*

Convinced that denigration is baneful, one readily sanctions the attack prompted by affection. In fact nothing is more entertaining than the fraternal accolade in reverse; as when *The London News Chronicle* of November 16, 1954, published a cartoon, and lines entitled "Winniehaha,"[21] concerning Mr. Churchill—Prime Minister then—after a cousin of his, Captain Lionel Leslie, had referred to the drop of Indian blood inherited by Sir Winston through his grandmother, Clara Jerome. The complimentary cast of the sally—a parody of Longfellow's *Hiawatha*—which was written before Mr. Churchill had been knighted, when the date of his retirement was a subject of speculation, is apparent from even a line or two:

In the center of the village
In the wigwam of the wise ones,
Where the head men of the nation
Come to talk in solemn council,
Squats the old chief, Winniehaha,

---

*And now the night calls dew down from heaven
    And the falling stars urge us to sleep.

> Also known as Sitting Bulldog; . . .
> Some there are with minds that wander
> From the purpose of the powwow;
> Minds that wonder will he give us
> Just an inkling, to be candid,
> Of the date of his retirement?
> Not that we would wish to rush him,
> Wish to rush old Winniehaha,
> Rush our splendid Sitting Bulldog
> From the headship of the head men
> In the center of the village,
> In the wigwam of the wise ones.
> Still, it's just a bit unsettling
> Not to know when Winniehaha
> Will give place to handsome Pinstripe.
> Will he tell us? Will he tell us?

In connection with personality, it is a curiosity of literature how often what one says of another seems descriptive of one's self. Would-be statesmen who spike their utterances with malice should bear this in mind and take fright as they drive home the moral of The Lion, The Wolf, and the Fox: "Slander flies home faster than rumor of good one has done."[22] In any case, Sir Winston Churchill's pronouncement on Alfred the Great does seem appropriate to himself—his own defeats, triumphs, and hardihood: "This sublime power to rise above the whole force of circumstances, to remain unbiased by the extremes of victory or defeat, to greet returning fortune with a cool eye, to have faith in men after repeated betrayals, raises Alfred far above the turmoil of barbaric wars to his pinnacle of deathless glory."[23]

Walter de la Mare found "prose worthy of the name of literature . . . tinged with that erratic and unique factor, the personal . . ." reminding one of the statement by Mr. F. O. Matthiessen, in his study of Sarah Orne Jewett, that "style means that the author has fused his material and his technique with the distinctive quality of his personality . . ." and of the word "idiolect" used by Professor Harry Levin as meaning "the language of a speaker or writer who has an inflection of his own." In saying there is no substitute for content, one is partly saying there is no substitute for individuality—that which is peculiar to the person (the Greek *idioma*). One also recalls the remark by Henry James: "a thing's being one's own will double the use of it." Discoveries in art, certainly, are personal before they are general.

Goya—in *The Taste of Our Times* series,[24] reviewed by Pierre Gassier somewhat as follows—should afford us creative impetus. After surviving a lethal threat, severe illness at Cadiz in 1792, Goya was left with his right side paralyzed, with dizzy spells, a buzzing in his head, and partial blindness. He recovered, only to find himself irremediably deaf. On returning to Madrid, he began work at once, painted eleven pictures for the Academy of San Fernando, and sent them with a letter to the director, Don Berbardo Iriarte. "In order to occupy an imagination mortified by the contemplation of my sufferings," he said, "and recover, partially at all events, the expenses incurred by illness, I fell to painting a set of pictures in which I have given observation a place usually denied it in works made to order, in which little scope is left for fancy and invention." Fancy and invention—not made to order—perfectly describe the work; the *Burial of the Sardine*, say: a careening throng in which one can identify a bear's mask and paws, a black monster wearing a horned hood, a huge turquoise quadracorne, a goblin mouth on a sepia fish-tailed banner, and twin dancers in filmy gowns with pink satin bows in their hair. Pieter Bruegel, the Elder, an observer as careful and as populous as Goya, "crossed the Alps and traveled the length of Italy, returning in 1555 to paint as though Michelangelo had never existed," so powerful was predilective intention.[25] In a television interview after receiving the National Book Award for *Ten North Frederick*, John O'Hara was asked if he might not have to find, as a background for fiction, something different from small-town life in Pennsylvania, to which he replied, "There is in one room in one day of one man's life, material for a lifetime." The artist does not—as we sometimes hear—"seek fresh sources of inspiration." A subject to which he is susceptible entices him to it; as we see in the epics of Marko Marulíc (1450–1524), the fifth centenary of whose birth Yugoslavia has celebrated, in honor of his Latin epic *Judita* (1501), enhanced by woodcuts such as *The Muster at Dubrovnic:* trumpeters, men at arms in an elephant-castle; dog; king, queen, and attendants. The New York Yugoslav Information Center says, "What is important is that in following the classics, Marulíc did not transplant . . . mechanically . . . but depended on his own poetic abilities," his novelty consisting in "comparisons taken from his own field of experience, in language abounding in speech forms of the people." An author, that is to say, is a fashioner of words, stamps them with his own personality, and wears the raiment he has made, in his own way.

Psychoanalysis can do some harm "taking things to pieces that it cannot put together again," as Mr. Whit Burnett said in a discourse entitled "Secrets of Creativeness." It has also been of true service, sharpening our faculties and combating complacence. Mr. Burnett drew attention to the biography of Dr. Freud by Ernest Jones, and to what is said there of genius as being not a quality but qualitative—a combination of attributes which differs with the person—three of which are honesty, a sense of the really significant, and the power of concentration.

Curiosity seems to me connected with this sense of significance. Thoreau, you may recall, demurred when commended for originality and said that it was curiosity: "I am curiosity from top to toe." I think I detect curiosity in the work of Sybille Bedford—in her novel *A Legacy*—in the statement, ". . . no one in the house was supposed to handle *used* [banknotes]. Everybody was paid straight off the press. The problem of change was not envisaged"; sententiousness in the writing, being offset by the unstereotyped juxtaposing of a word or two such as querulous and placid. Grandma Merz, for instance, "was a short bundle of a woman swaddled in stuffs and folds . . . stuck with brooches of rather gray diamonds. Her face was a round, large, indeterminate expanse . . . with features that escaped attention and an expression that was at once querulous and placid."[26] In Marguerite Yourcenar's "Author's Note" to her *Memoirs of Hadrian*[27]—a study which does "border on the domain of fiction and sometimes of poetry," as has been said—one sees what concentration editorially can be. And Paul Delarue's "Sources and Commentary" appended to the *Borzoi Book of French Folk Tales*[28] are similarly impressive—besides affording an exciting knowledge of variants. In "The White Dove" (the story of Bluebeard, abridged by Perrault), the ninth victim's pretexts for delay become specific—in this early version—"to put on my petticoat, my wedding-gown, my cap, my bouquet." And we learn that "The Ass's Skin," enshrined for us by La Fontaine in "The Power of the Fable,"[29] is the "Story of Goldilocks," and of Madame d'Aulnoy's "Beauty and the Beast" (1698). The presentment here of obscure minutiae, demonstrating that tales of all nations have a common fabric, makes the most artful of detective stories seem tame.

Creative secrets, are they secrets? Impassioned interest in life, that burns its bridges behind it and will not contemplate defeat, is one, I would say. Discouragement is a form of temptation; but paranoia is not optimism. In an essay entitled "Solitude" (the theme chosen by the *Figaro* for an essay contest), Maxime Bennebon, a boy of seventeen, visualizes "Michelangelo's *Moses*, head in hands, the attitude of the child who prays with eyes closed; of the pianist—his back to the audience; they must be alone that they may offer what is most treasurable, themselves."

The master secret may be steadfastness, that of Nehemiah, Artaxerxes' cupbearer, as it was of the three youths in the fiery furnace, who would not bow down to the image which the king had set up. "Why is thy countenance sad, seeing that thou are not sick?" the King asked. Nehemiah requested that he be allowed to rebuild the wall of Jerusalem and the King granted his request; gave him leave of absence and a letter to the keeper of the forest that he might have timber for the gates of the palace—subject to sarcasm while building, such as Sanballet's, "If a fox go up, he shall break down their wall." Summoned four times to a colloquy, Nehemiah sent word: "I am doing a great work and I cannot come down." Then when warned that he would be slain, he said, "Should such a man as I flee?" "So the wall was finished."[30] A result which is sensational is implemented by what to the craftsman was private and unsensational. Tyrone Guthrie, in connection with the theater, made a statement which sums up what I have been trying to say about idiosyncrasy and technique: "It is one of the paradoxes of art that a work can only be universal if it is rooted in a part of its creator which is most privately and particularly himself."[31]

Thomas Mann, fending off eulogy, rendered a service when he said, "Praise will never subdue skepticism." We fail in some degree—and know that we do, if we are competent; but can prevail; and the following attributes, applied by a London journal to Victor Gollancz, the author and publisher, I adopt as a prescription: we can in the end prevail, if our attachment to art is sufficiently deep; "unpriggish, subtle, perceptive, and consuming."[32]

[1] *Making, Knowing and Judging: An Inaugural Lecture by W. H. Auden Delivered before the University of Oxford on 11 June 1956* (Oxford at the Clarendon Press).

[2] Michael Tippett, "An Irish Basset-Horn," *The Listener*, July 26, 1956.

[3] Hesketh Pearson, "Bernard Shaw as Producer," *The Listener*, August 16, 1956.

[4] "Discourse in Praise of Wisdom," reentitled "Goethe as the Sage."

[5] *The Dalhousie Review*, January 1943.

[6] Translated by Ezra Pound (Cambridge: Harvard University Press, 1954), p. 55.

[7] *Ibid.*, p. 80.

[8] *The Self and the Dramas of History* (New York: Scribner, 1955).

[9] "Edwin Arnold and 'The Light of Asia,' " *The Listener*, June 14, 1956.

[10] *The New York Times*, November 20, 1957.

[11] *The Listener*, June 14, 1956.

[12] "In Honor of James Cook," *The Listener*, June 14, 1956.

[13] *The Shock of Recognition*, edited by Edmund Wilson (New York: Doubleday, 1943).

[14] Unsigned review in *The Times Literary Supplement*, London, March 2, 1956.

[15] *Life*, July 16, 1956.

[16] *The Fables of La Fontaine*, translated by Marianne Moore (New York: Viking, 1954), Book Ten, IX.

[17] Dr. Alvin E. Magary.

[18] Maxwell Geismar, *The Nation*, April 14, 1956.

[19] As "freely translated" by Charles Poore, reviewing James B. Conant, *The Citadel of Learning* (New Haven: Yale University Press, 1956), in the *New York Times*, April 7, 1956.

[20] In *Writers on Writing*, edited by Herschel Brickell (New York: Doubleday, 1949).

[21] Anonymous. Reprinted in the *New York Times*, November 17, 1954.

[22] *The Fables of La Fontaine*, Book Eight, III.

[23] *A History of the English-Speaking Peoples*, Vol. I: *The Birth of Britain* (New York: Dodd, Mead, 1956).

[24] "Essay on Prose," *The National and English Review* (in three sections, concluded in March 1955), quoted by *Arts* (New York).

[25] Fritz Grossmann, *The Paintings of Bruegel* (New York: Phaidon Press, 1955).

[26] Sybille Bedford, *A Legacy* (New York: Simon and Schuster, 1957).

[27] Translated from the French by Grace Frick (New York: Farrar, Straus and Young, 1954).

[28] Translated by Austin E. Fife (New York: Knopf, 1956).

[29] *The Fables of La Fontaine*, Book Eight, IV: "The moment The Ass's Skin commences, Away with appearances; I am enraptured, really am."

[30] Nehemiah 2, 4, and 6.

[31] *The New York Times Magazine*, November 27, 1955.

[32] *The Observer*, March 11, 1956.

Idiosyncrasy and Technique. Berkeley: University of California Press, 1958; *A Marianne Moore Reader*.

EDITH SITWELL, VIRTUOSO

GREAT in far greater ways, Dame Edith Sitwell is a virtuoso of rhythm and accent. She has given me immense pleasure, intensifying my interest in rhythm, and has also encouraged me in my rhythmic eccentricities. I can scarcely read the Bible without forsaking content for rhythm, as where the Apostle Paul speaks of the shipwreck on Malta and says, "when the ship could no longer bear up into the wind, we let her drive"—a better rhythm than "and were driven."

Façade, Dame Edith—or Miss Sitwell as she was then—insists, was but apprenticeship; of virtuoso quality with wit, one observes, as in "The Higher Sensualism" when Queen Circe said,

> "Young man, I will buy
> Your plumaged coat for my pig to try—
>
> Then with angels he'll go a'dancing hence
> From sensuality into sense!"

"I used to practice writing," Dame Edith says, "as a pianist practices music." She says that she would take a waltz or a polka or the music of the barrel organ beneath her window and translate it into words, as she has done in this phrase from "Country Dance":

> But Silenus
> Has seen us.

Dame Edith then considered the long line and its possibilities. William Carlos Williams has said in his book, *I Wanted to Write a Poem*, "I found I could not use the long line because of my nervous nature." An adagio, moreover, "is hard to sustain at concert pitch," as the *Times Literary Supplement* noted. We have it, however, when Edith Sitwell writes

> archipelagoes
> Of stars and young thin moons from great wings falling
> As ripples widen.

How pleasing, the dactyls, *porphyry, basilica, Babylon;* and *babioun* (*babioun* borrowed from Ben Jonson, as she says). How neat, the rhyme "Noctambulo" with "folio":

> The public scribe, Noctambulo
> Where moonlight, cold as blades of grass
> Echoes upon deserted walls,
> Turning his dusty folio;

and this: "old Bacchantes black with wine, / Whose very hair has changed into a vine." We have something of the self-impelled ease of Leslie Brooke's "Johnny Crow's Party":

> The snake
> Got entangled
> With the rake.
> The sheep
> Fell asleep
> And the armadillo
> Used him as a pillow.

Dame Edith's irregularities in set meter are hyper-skillful, as in creating a pause after *any* in "anybody": "Mary Stuart to James Bothwell" (Casket Letter No. 2):

> Leaving you, I was sundered like the sea!
> Departed from the place where I left my heart
> I was as small as any body may be.

That is to say, with the accent on *body*.

There is no melody in Pope, Dame Edith says, because there is no irregularity. "To have melody, there must be variations in the outward structure." An expert of the condensed phrase, she also says, "I try to make my images exact"; and does, in "sundered"; and by inventing "donkey's-hide grass" for the beast of the attorney:

> O'er donkey's-hide grass the attorney
> Still continues on his journey.

In the opening lines of "The Sleeping Beauty," the incantatory effect of the whole passage is a metaphor creating a sense of deep, mysterious, fairy-world remoteness:

> When we come to that dark house,
> Never sound of wave shall rouse
> The bird that sings within the blood
> Of those who sleep in that deep wood.

Katherine Anne Porter—reminded of Lully, Rameau, Monteverdi, and Purcell, "of old courtly music, weddings, christenings, great crystal-lighted banquets, in sweet-smelling gardens under the full moon"—is detained by the luster and admires the studiousness; says, "There is no finer sight than to see an artist growing great." Dame Edith's father, Sir George, said, "Edith will commit suicide when she finds she cannot write poetry." Need for this has not arisen.

One cannot be a virtuoso without being combated—an injustice prevalent in all the arts—noted by Mr. Henry McBride, art critic for *The Dial* and the *New York Sun*. He says, "One may judge the vitality of an artist by the extent to which he is resisted." Dame Edith recalls that lines of hers once received "a mingling of bouquets and brickbats—with a strong predominance of brickbats"; yet invariably, as *The New Statesman and Nation* said (June 23, 1954), "losing every battle, she won the campaign"; in fact, "emerged more majestic, more unaccountably modern than ever."

In *Façade* she said she found it necessary to find heightened expression for the heightened speed of our time. However, she added, "in spite of the fact that the rhythms which I practised in *Façade* were heightened, concentrated, and frequently more violent than those of the poets who had preceded us immediately, it was supposed by many that I had *discarded* rhythm. But we must not complain if the patterns in our mundane works are not perceived by the unobservant"—the allusion being to Bishop Burnet, who had found fault with the constellations and said, if only the stars had been composed "according to the rules of art and symmetry!"

Some may regard as arbitrary a word of Dame Edith's or find a statement too "oracular." In her choice of words, she is, to *herself*, always justified. "Neatness of execution is essential to sublimity," she says; improving De Quincey by considering language an "incarnation" of thought rather than "the *dress* of thought," and is instructively "neat" in revising her own work, as when substituting a general term for a specific in *Metamorphosis:*

> When first the dew with golden foot
> Makes tremble every leaf and strawberry root.

This is made to read in the second version of 1946:

> Here once in Spring, the dew with golden foot
> Made tremble every leaf and hidden root.

When she presents other authors—Christopher Smart in her early three-volume anthology—and when in *The Book of the Winter* she selects examples from Herrick, Blake, and Donne, her wand is tipped with a diamond. Of compiling *The Book of the Winter* she said, "I was not concerned with producing a hodge-podge of everything. . . . One of the greatest difficulties encountered in making an anthology of this kind is to resign oneself to omissions . . . many beauties because they pulled the pattern out of shape." From Donne, it is not verse that is quoted but this from a sermon preached by Donne in April 1629: "The root of all is God, but it is not the way to receive fruits to dig at the root but to reach to the boughs," and we have for Dylan Thomas a justly comprehensive apologia: "His love for those who have received no mercies from life is great." Fire and novelty mark *The Book of the Winter*—in Sir Thomas Browne's "Of Crystals and Icicles"; and in this apparition or vision from *I Live under a Black Sun*—Dame Edith's novel: "A figure would shine through the night, circling swiftly as if it were a swallow, or floating, a black swan on the wide water-black marble pavements. . . . Rag Castle after rag castle, the world of beggars was swept along, and night fell upon the two nations, the rich and the poor, who alone inhabit the earth"—prototypes of Lazarus and Dives made emphatic in later work. Tom O'Bedlam (anonymous), quoted in part, perhaps epitomizes the contagion of the whole anthology:

> While I do sing,
> "Any food, and feeding,
> Feeding, drink, or clothing,"
> Come dame or maid
> Be not afraid
> Poor Tom will injure nothing.

> The meek, the wise, the gentle
> Me handle, touch, and spare not;
> But those that cross
> Tom Rhinoceros
> Do what the panther dare not.
> . . . .
> With an host of furious fancies,
> Whereof I am commander,
> With a burning Speare, and a horse of aire,
> To the wildernesse I wander.

In his introduction to Paul Valéry's *The Art of Poetry*, Mr. Eliot includes a postscriptlike speculation: "How poetry is related to life, Valéry does not say"—connected in my own mind with Edith Sitwell's self-descriptive comment: "The behavior of the world affects our beliefs and incites the mind to tumult to speak as a Cassandra or as an elegist." Reflecting current preoccupation, Robert Frost answers the query, why write: "It is what every poem is about—how the spirit is to surmount the pressure upon us of the material world." In our battle, Dame Edith bears aid. As for interest taken by the poet in his fellow human being, she says, "He is a brother speaking to a brother . . . supporting his brother's flagging footsteps"; and—overpowered by a sense of "the Universal Cain, of brother as murderer of brother, of the chaingang sentenced to ninety-nine years"—says, "I come to testify." Of this testimony W. B. Yeats said, "Something absent from all literature was back again, passion ennobled by intensity, by endurance, by wisdom."

> "With what are these on fire?" she asks, "with passion, Hate,
> Infatuation, and old age, and death
> With sorrow, longing, and with laboring breath."

Summarizing her work in 1955, *Time* said, "she writes for the sake of sound, of color, and from an awareness of God and regard for man." For her "all great poetry is dipped in the dyes of the heart"; and, perhaps quoting Whitman, she says, "All things are in the clime of man's forgiveness"; saying of ideals she would reach, "How far I am from these no one could see more clearly than I. Technically, I would come to a vital language—each word possessing an infinite power of germination, spiritually give holiness to each common day." In her humility and compassion she cages conviction.

In *Four Poets on Poetry*, edited by Don Cameron Allen. Baltimore: Johns Hopkins Press, 1960, pp. 76–82; *A Marianne Moore Reader*.

TO "INFUSE BELIEF"

In *Gate to the Sea*, the gate is Paestum and the story—of the 4th century B.C.—parallels harrowing accounts in our own day: escape by plane, by sea, by plodding through enemy woods in snow almost waist-deep. Lykos, a Greek slave, and Harmonia, a priestess of Hera, attempt escape from foreign oppressors, Lucanian conquerors who have forbidden hereditary employment, observance of sacred rites, and the use by Greeks of even their own language.

As Lykos, Harmonia, and a few friends steal toward the sea at night they are detected before they can reach the small boat in which—all but overtaken—they row out to the ship which means freedom. Bryher's[1] previous novels have, each, revived an incident in history symbolic of free spirits overpowered but unconquered: the Battle of Hastings, the execution of Raleigh, the fall of Rome, the London blitz. Of them all, *Gate to the Sea* seems the most vivid and expertly absorbing—a masterpiece.

The statement by Paul Valéry that "poetry is to prose as dancing is to walking," is one upon which T. S. Eliot pauses, since some prose is poetry. We certainly have the poetry of heightened prose in Bryher's work; as in *Gate to the Sea* the Greek coast is typified by brevity such as this: "The path ended suddenly in the middle of a dune"; and the sea is for me ideally personified in: "She clung to the seat [of the boat] as they soared up and forward . . . rode down into a hollow, rolled again, and rose upon a shieldlike surface of blue sea. . . ." The personalities are made to matter; the pulse of the predicament beats in the mind. Best of all, patriotism and ancient piety here "infuse belief." Bryher is an invigorator. Faith, virtue, and freedom are her Ulysses—her Odyssey—enhanced by Paestum's scarred columns and porches, her pines and their shadows, as photographed by Islay de Courcy Lyons.

[1] A. W. Bryher—Sir John Ellerman's daughter—has, as a writer and as a citizen, adopted the name Bryher. She lives in Switzerland.

Poetry, 93 (February 1959), 320; *A Marianne Moore Reader*.

Review of *Gate to the Sea*, by Bryher (Pantheon, 1958).

"SENHORA HELENA"

My Life as a Little Girl was published in 1942—primarily to amuse family and friends and now a Brazilian classic. It continually rivals poetry; furthermore is "one of those rare stories that combines worldly success and a happy ending," its translator says; in its universal-personal insights is irresistible.

"Helena Morley" (a pseudonym) had, as ancestor, an English doctor who was for a time a member of a gold-mining affiliate of the São João del Rey Mining Company and remained in Brazil for reasons of health, settled in Diamantina, and married a Brazilian lady. "Senhora Helena," now a favorite in Rio de Janeiro society, is the wife of Dr. Augusto Mario Caldeira Brant, President of the Bank of Brazil, at whose suggestion the Diary was published.

In Diamantina, a center for gold and diamond mining, the Diary depicts life as lived by the Morleys and their many relatives. That a translator should share the qualities of work translated, Miss Bishop exemplifies in her gift for fantasy, her use of words and hyper-precise eye. The attitude to life revealed by the Diary, Helena's apperceptiveness, and innate accuracy, seem a double portrait; the exactness of observation in the introduction being an extension, in manner, of Miss Bishop's verse and other writing, as when she differentiates between marbleized or painted window-frames to imitate stone, and stone ones painted to imitate grained wood; again, in the description of rain-pipe funnels "flaring like trumpets," sometimes with "tin petals or feathers down them and around the mouth . . . repeated in tiles set edgewise up the ridges of the roofs, dragonlike and very 'Chinese.' " And it would be hard to find a process more accurately described than this, of panning for diamonds in a stream by the road: "A small quantity of gravel in the wide round sieve is held just beneath the surface of the water, swirled around and around and lifted out" and, "with the gesture of a quick-fingered housewife turning out a cake," the panner "turned the whole thing upside down on the ground, intact. He put on his horn-rimmed glasses, lowered himself to his knees in the wet mud, and stared, passing a long wooden knife over the gravel from side to side"—"the simplest of all forms of diamond 'mining.' " "One sometimes gets the impression that the greater part of the town, black and white, 'rich' and poor, when it hasn't found a diamond lately, gets along by making sweets and pastries, brooms and cigarettes and

---

Review of *The Diary of "Helena Morley,"* translated and edited, with a preface and introduction by Elizabeth Bishop (Farrar, Straus and Cudahy).

selling to each other. . . ." "Black beans instead of the bread of other countries seem to be equated with life itself."

The personality of Helena Morley would be hard to match. Besides an ardor synonymous with affection, she "steps in and out of superstition" as Miss Bishop says, "reason, belief, and disbelief, without much adolescent worrying. She would never for a moment doubt that the church is a good thing." "I admire good and holy people," she says, "but I can't possibly stop being the way I am." A main part of being the way she was, was compassion. On a night during the family's summer outing, when all were kept awake by a crying baby, Helena says, "To let her cry with pain, and then to beat her. I couldn't stand it. . . . I didn't even have to stay with her half an hour"—provoking a remonstrance from Mrs. Morley: "This girl, this mania of not being able to hear a baby cry without wanting to comfort it. She'll be the death of me." In recording the incident, Helena says, "I think if this little girl had been white, mama wouldn't have minded." On any page of the Diary we encounter similar "fire"; as here: "I don't have a corner to do my lessons in. So, with the help of God, I found something simply wonderful. I went to pick mulberries and climbed the tree to the very top. What a discovery. The mulberry was so overgrown with a vine that it looked like a mattress. I'd tell grandma that I was going to study under the mulberry-tree and then I'd climb up and stay on top looking at the view which is perfectly beautiful." Again, "José Rabela spends his time weighing vultures in the scales, in order to invent a flying-machine. Wouldn't that be wonderful! . . . I feel envious when I see the vultures soaring up so high." Not everything was wonderful. Of visiting the dentist, Helena says, "It is more nauseating than finding a toad in one's bed. He can't say a thing without a diminutive. 'Will you do me the favor of opening your little mouth?' . . . 'little mouth, little ache, little tooth.' I almost fainted in the chair, I disliked him so much." The Diary has tone. With regard to having a post-office, Helena says, "Wouldn't it be better . . . if they put in street lamps for us so that on dark nights we wouldn't have to walk slowly for fear of falling over a cow. And water pipes. . . . Nobody's going to die without a letter, but the water has killed lots of people who might have been living today." Then of submerged problems, "All year long, mama struggles with him [papa] to go to confession." "I suffered a great deal because of grandfather and don't want to suffer now too because of papa. My grandfather was not buried in the church because he was a Protestant. 'Any ground God made is holy ground,' he said." Alert to every pretext favorable to satire, Helena says, "Joas de Assis suffers from a strange complaint, he's so sorry for everyone, no matter who," and "Everybody says father is a good husband and yet nobody says mama is a good wife." She tells how, when a *caldeirão* is found (a pocket of diamonds), a slave falls on his knees, exclaiming, "My Lord and Heavenly Father, if this wealth endangers my soul, let it vanish." Charmed observation and reflexive ingenuity never pall. Helena's susceptibility to personality and commensurate candor constantly leave one with a sense of originality that nothing could impair. In an agony of diffidence because of having withheld at confession the sin of having thought a priest "homely," she is told that she should confess it, and to the same priest from whom she had withheld it; then admits, "But the priest is you, Father."

Being able to observe imagination in action here is like opening a watch and studying the continuous uninterfering operation of wheels amid wheels. We see, furthermore, as Miss Bishop says, "that happiness does not consist in worldly goods but in a peaceful home, in family affection,—things that fortune cannot bring and often takes away." And "it happened, that is the charm and the point of *Minha Vida de Menina*."

Poetry, 94 (July 1959), 247–49; *A Marianne Moore Reader*.

MUSIC AND SCRUPULOUS ART IN BABETTE DEUTSCH'S POEMS

BABETTE DEUTSCH, a teacher and a very special one as shown in her *Poetry Handbook*, is a craftsman, originator and translator. Unquestionably she appears in these "New and Selected Poems" as the artist she is. The new poems, furthermore, which open the book, seem an intensive on her previous work. The title poem, "Coming of Age," in characterizing the four elements, says: Earth to "her slave," mankind,

> still . . . gives him what so long she gave;
> All countries, and a grave.

"Water is clothed with terror"—the counterpart of "war." And

> There is one rages deeper, flies higher—
> In the deeps, in the vault, in the veins, there is fire.

Review of *Coming of Age: New and Selected Poems*, by Babette Deutsch (Indiana University Press).

"Of all things flying / she is the nurse," of "the kite, the sparrow," "song, cry, or curse, / And uttered verse." The "elements surround, support us"; "it is as if the darkness / Found speech" and "the ignorant heart, / That in despair first learns how to rejoice."

Miss Deutsch has a gift for verisimilitude as has been evident from the first, and here epitomizes Goya's *Disasters of War* in the phrase: THIS I SAW. The suspension bridge is magic wrought as by a spider engineer: "The spans fanned out, three spokes of a tireless wheel," "Like the hairs of a headless harp."

Direct statement, "music," and careful structure, attest the work of a craftsman; and as artful as it is scrupulous is Miss Deutsch's translation— implied translation—of Christian Morgenstern's "Night Song of the Fish," a peak of comeliness in its alternating of long feet and short.

Among the earlier poems, one must quote at least a line or two of "Quandary":

> There is no shelter anywhere
> For her whose wonder, like a hare
> Bursts through the briars of despair,
> And bleeds and leaps away.
> . . . .
> How to sustain the miracle
> Of being, that like a muted bell,
> Or like some ocean-breathing shell,
> Quivers, intense and still?

And indispensable in any collection of Miss Deutsch's work, is "Homage to John Skelton," "the Tudor's tutor":

> Your name is Parrot: "a bird of Paradise?"
> . . . .
> Tutor us, John Skelton, who whetted your beak
> On the bars of your cage, tell us how to speak.
> . . . .
> For our gardens, our graves, for the tower, for the dive?
> While your lessons flourish, English is alive.

Few can celebrate poetry, in poetry, as poetically in these lines entitled, "The Poem":

> The saint from Africa called every thing
> A word, the world being a poem by God,

> Each evil tuned to make a splendor sing.
> Ordered by God
> With opposites that praise His fingering.

Of translations included here, we have Rilke's natural—cemented by intensity emotional and verbal—"You are the Future":

> You are the deep epitome of things,
> That keeps its being secret with locked lip,
> And shows itself to others otherwise:
> To the ship, a haven—to the land, a ship.

"Put Out My Eyes," by Rilke, has also an indivisibly beautiful continuity—puzzled as one is by the abruptly strange verb "Slam."

In the Russian poetry—translated with the help of Dr. Yarmolinsky—Mayokovsky's "A Most Extraordinary Adventure" communicates brio and flavor, ignorant of Russian though one may be. One can understand the attraction Mayokovsky had for Pasternak, as one perceives Pasternak's positiveness and incapability of affectation in such lines as these in "If Only When I Made My Debut":

> But age is pagan Rome, demanding
> No balderdash, no measured breath,
> No fine feigned parody of dying,
> But really being done to death.

and "We're Few":

> We used to be people. We're epochs.
> Pell-mell we rush caravanwise
> As the tundra to groans of the tender
> And tension of pistons and ties.

If the briars of despair ever were a quandary for compassionate, dexterous, knowledgeable Miss Deutsch, they seem but a figure of speech as one contemplates her depth, range, straightness, and commanding stature as a poet.

New York Herald Tribune Book Review, 12 July 1959, p. 3.

ABRAHAM LINCOLN AND
THE ART OF THE WORD

"I dislike an oath which requires a man to swear he *has* not done wrong. It rejects the Christian principle of forgiveness on terms of repentance. I think it is enough if the man does no wrong hereafter."[1] It was Abraham Lincoln who said this—his controlled impetuosity exemplifying excellences both of the technician and of the poet.

The malcontent attacks greatness by disparaging it—by libels on efficiency, interpreting needful silence as lack of initiative, by distortion, by ridicule. "As a general rule," Lincoln said, "I abstain from reading attacks upon myself, wishing not to be provoked by that to which I cannot promptly offer an answer." Expert in rebuttal, however, as in strategy, he often won juries and disinterested observers alike, by anecdote or humorous implication that made argument unnecessary. His use of words became a perfected instrument, acquired by an education largely self-attained—" 'picked up,' " he said, "under pressure of necessity." That the books read became part of him is apparent in phrases influenced by the Bible, Shakespeare, *The Pilgrim's Progress*, *Robinson Crusoe*, Burns, Blackstone's *Commentaries;* and not least, by some books of Euclid—read and "nearly mastered," as he says, after he had become a member of Congress. The largeness of the life entered into the writing, as with a passion he strove to persuade his hearers of what he believed, his adroit, ingenious mentality framing an art which, if it is not to be designated poetry, we may call a "grasp of eternal grace"— in both senses, figurative and literal. Nor was he unaware of having effected what mattered, as we realize by his determined effort, when a first attempt failed, to obtain from the *Chicago Press and Tribune* "a set of the late debates (if they may be so called)" he wrote, "between Douglas and myself . . . two copies of each number . . . in order to lay one away in the raw and to put the other in a scrapbook." One notes that he did not neglect to say, "if any debate is on *both* sides of one sheet, it will take two sets to make one scrapbook."

Of persuasive expedients, those most constant with Lincoln are antithesis, reiteration, satire, metaphor; above all *the meaning*, clear and unadorned. A determination "to express his ideas in simple terms became his ruling passion," his every word natural, impelled by ardor. In his address at the Wisconsin Agricultural Fair, he said—regarding competitive awards about to be made—"exultations and mortifications . . . are but temporary; the victor shall soon be vanquished, if he relax in his exertion; and . . . the vanquished this year may be the victor next, in spite of all competition." At the Baltimore Sanitary Fair of 1864, in an address conspicuously combining antithesis with reiteration, he said, "The world has never had a good definition of liberty. . . . We all declare for liberty; but in using the same *word* we do not all mean the same *thing*. With some the word may mean for each man to do as he pleases with himself, and the product of his labor; while with others the same word may mean for some men to do as they please with other men, and the product of other men's labor. Here are two, not only different, but incompatible things, called by the same name—liberty. . . . The shepherd drives the wolf from the sheep's throat, for which the sheep thanks the shepherd as a *liberator*, while the wolf denounces him for the same act as the destroyer of liberty, especially as the sheep was a black one." In Lincoln's use of italics, one perceives that he is not substituting emphasis for precision but is impersonating speech. In declining an invitation to the Jefferson birthday dinner of 1859, he wrote, "The principles of Jefferson are the axioms of a free society. One dashingly calls them 'glittering generalities'; another bluntly calls them 'self-evident lies.' " And in combating repeal of the Missouri Compromise (which would have ended slavery), he said, "Repeal the Missouri Compromise—repeal all compromises—repeal the Declaration of Independence—repeal all history—you cannot repeal human nature."

Crystalline logic indeed was to be his passion. He wrote to James Conkling, "You desire peace; and you blame me that we do not have it. But how can we attain it? There are but three conceivable ways. First, force of arms. . . . Are you for it? . . . A second way is to give up the Union. Are you for it? If you are, you should say so plainly. If not for force, nor yet for dissolution, Compromise. I am against that. I do not believe any compromise is now possible." And to General Schurz he said, "You think I could do better; therefore you blame me. I think I could not do better, therefore I blame you for blaming me."

Unsurpassed in satire, Lincoln said that Judge Douglas, in his interpretation of the Declaration of Independence, offered "the arguments that kings have made for enslaving the people in all ages of the world. They always bestrode the necks of the people, not that they wanted to do it, but that the people were better off for being ridden." Of slavery as an institution he said, "Slavery is strikingly peculiar in this, that it is the only good thing which no man seeks the good of for *himself*."

Metaphor is a force, indeed magnet, among Lincoln's arts of the word. Urgent that the new government of Louisiana be affirmed, he said, "If we reject it, we in effect say, 'You are worthless. We will neither help nor be helped by you.' To the blacks we say, 'This cup of liberty which these, your old masters, hold to your lips, we will dash from you, . . . discouraging and paralyzing both white and black. . . . If on the contrary, we recognize and sustain the new government, we are supporting its efforts to this end, to make it, to us, in your language, a Union of hearts and hands as well as of states.' " Passionate that the Union be saved, he uses a metaphor yet stronger than the cup of liberty. He says, "By general law, life, *and* limb must be protected; yet often a limb must be amputated to save a life; but a life is never wisely given to save a limb. . . . I could not feel that, . . . to save slavery, . . . I should permit the wreck of government, country, and con-stitution altogether."

Diligence underlay these verbal expedients—one can scarcely call them devices—so rapt Lincoln was in what he cared about. He had a genius for words but it was through diligence that he became a master of them—affording hope to the most awkward of us. To Isham Reavis he wrote, "If you are resolutely determined to make a lawyer of yourself, the thing is half done already. It is a small matter whether you read *with* anybody or not. . . . It is of no consequence to be in a large town. . . . I read at New Salem, which never had three hundred people living in it. The *books* and your *capacity* for understanding them, are just the same in all places."

Diligence was basic. Upon hearing that George Latham, his son Robert's classmate at the Phillips Exeter Academy, had failed entrance examinations to Harvard, Lincoln wrote, "having made the attempt you *must* succeed in it. '*Must*' is the word . . . you *can* not fail if you resolutely determine that you *will* not." This intensity we see heightened in Lincoln's torment of anxiety, during the war, that the struggle be ended. "The subject is on my mind day and night," he said. During August, 1862, in a letter to Colonel Haupt on the 29th, he begged, "What news from the direction of Manassas?" On that same day to General McClellan he wrote, "What news from the direction of Manassas Junction?" On August 30th, to General Banks, "Please tell me what news?" and again "What news?" on August 30th to Colonel Haupt. The result was a man wearing down under continuous desperation when General Meade, unable to conclude the war at Gettysburg, allowed the Confederate forces to retreat south.

In speeches and in letters, Lincoln made articulate an indomitable ideal—that what the framers of the Constitution embodied in it be preserved—"and that something is the principle of 'Liberty for all,' that clears the *path* for all—gives *hope* to all—and by consequence *enterprise* and *industry* to all." Inflexible when sure he was right—as in his reply to Isaac Schermerhorn, who was dissatisfied with the management of the war, he said, "This is not a question of sentiment or taste but one of physical force which may be measured and estimated as horse-power and Steam-power are measured and estimated. . . . Throw it away and the Union goes with it."

There is much to learn from Lincoln's respect for words taken separately, as when he said, "It seems to me very important that the statute laws should be made as plain and intelligible as possible, and be reduced to as small compass as may consist with the fullness and precision of the will of the legislature and the perspicuity of its language." He was "determined to be so clear," he said, "that no honest man can misunderstand me, and no dishonest one can successfully misrepresent me." Exasperated to have been misquoted, he deplored "a specious and fantastic arrangement of words, by which a man can prove a horse-chestnut to be a chestnut horse." Consulted regarding a more perfect edition of his Cooper Institute speech, he said, "Of course I would not object, but would be pleased rather . . . but I do not wish the sense changed or modified, to a hair's breadth. Striking out 'upon' leaves the sense too general and incomplete. . . . The words 'quite,' 'as,' and 'or,' on the same page, I wish retained." Of Stephen Douglas he said, "Cannot the Judge perceive the difference between a purpose and an expectation? I have often expressed an expectation to die but I have never expressed a *wish* to die." The Declaration of Independence he made stronger by saying, "I think the authors of that notable instrument intended to include *all* men but they did not intend to declare all men were equal *in all respects.*" And to quibblers, after the surrender of the South, he replied, "whether the seceded states, so-called, are in the Union or out of it, the question is bad . . . a pernicious abstraction!" Indelible even upon a feeble memory— we recall the phrase, "With malice toward none and charity for all," and in the second inaugural address, "Let us strive on to finish the work we are in." We are *in.* Lincoln understood in the use of emphasis that one must be *natural.* Instead of using the word "confidential" in a letter to A. H. Stephens, he wrote in italics at the head of the page, *"For your eye only."* The result of this intensified particularity was such that in his so-called Lost Speech of 1856, which unified the Republican party, "newspapermen forgot paper and pad . . . to sit enraptured," and instead of taking down his eulogy of Henry Clay, "dropped their pens and sat as under enchantment from near the beginning, to quite the end."

Lincoln attained not force only, but cadence, the melodic propriety of poetry in fact, as in the Farewell Address from Springfield he refers to "the weight of responsibility on George Washington"; then says of "that Divine being without which I cannot succeed, with that assistance, I cannot fail." Consider also the stateliness of the three cannots in the Gettysburg Address: "We cannot dedicate—we cannot consecrate—we cannot hallow—this ground.

The brave men, living and dead, who struggled here, have consecrated it far above our poor power to add or detract. The world will little note nor long remember what we may say here, but it can never forget what they did here." Editors attempting to improve Lincoln's punctuation by replacing dashes with commas, should refrain—the dash, as well known, signifying prudence.

With consummate reverence for God, with insight that illumined his every procedure as a lawyer, that was alive in his every decision as a President with civilian command of an army at bay, Lincoln was notable in his manner of proffering consolation; studiously avoiding insult when relieving an officer of his command; instantaneous with praise. To General Grant—made commander of the Union army after his brilliant flanking maneuver at Vicksburg—he said, "As the country trusts you, so, under God, it will sustain you." To Grant "alone" he ascribed credit for terminating the war. Constrained almost to ferocity by the sense of fairness, he begs recognition for "black men who can remember that with silent tongues, and clenched teeth, and steady eye and well-poised bayonet, they have helped mankind to this consummation" (preserving the Union). He managed to take time to retrieve the property of a barber, a Negro, who had not recorded the deed to land he owned. Emphasizing by vivid addendum his request for promotion of a "brave drummer-boy" who "had accompanied his division under heavy fire," Lincoln said, "he should have his chance." For "a poor widow whose son was serving a long sentence without pay—recommending the son for re-enlistment with pay—he wrote, "she says she cannot get it acted on. Please do it." In constant disfavor with officers in charge of penalties, he said, "Must I shoot a simple soldier boy who deserts while I must not touch a hair of the wily agitator who induces him to desert? To silence the agitator and save the boy is not only constitutional but withal a great mercy." Of Captain McKnabb, dismissed on the charge of being a disunionist, Lincoln wrote, "He wishes to show that the charge is false. Fair play is a jewel. Give him a chance if you can." Afflicted by self-obsessed factions in Missouri, where private grievances should have been settled locally, he summarized the matter: "I have exhausted my wits and nearly my patience in efforts to convince both [sides] that the evils they charged on the others are inherent. I am well satisfied that the preventing of the remedial raid into Missouri was the only safe way to avoid an indiscriminate massacre, including probably more innocent than guilty. Instead of condemning, I therefore approve what I understand General Schofield did in that respect. . . . Few things have been so grateful to my anxious feeling as when . . . the local force in Missouri aided General Schofield to so promptly send a large force to the relief of General Grant then investing Vicksburg and menaced by General Johnston. . . . My feeling obliges nobody to follow me and I trust obliges me to follow nobody."

With regard to presidential appointments, it was in 1849, during Zachary Taylor's administration, that Lincoln said, "I take the responsibility. In that phrase were the 'Samson's locks' of General Jackson, and we dare not disregard the lessons of experience"—lessons underlying the principle which he put into practice when appointing Governor Chase Secretary of the Treasury. Pressed, in fact persecuted, to appoint General Cameron, he said, "It seems to me not only highly proper but a *necessity* that Governor Chase shall take that place. His ability, firmness, and purity of character produce the propriety." Purity of character—the phrase is an epitome of Lincoln. To a young man considering law as a career, he said, "There is a vague popular belief that lawyers are necessarily dishonest. If you cannot be an honest lawyer, resolve to be honest without being a lawyer." Deploring bombast, yet tactful, he opposed investigating the Bank of Illinois: "No, Sir, it is the *politician* who is first to sound the alarm (which, by the way, is a false one). It is he, who, by these unholy means, is endeavoring to blow up a storm that he may ride upon and direct it. . . . I say this with the greater freedom, because, being a politician, none can regard it as personal." Firm in resisting pressure, he was equally strong in exerting it, as when he wrote to "Secretary Seward & Secretary Chase" jointly, "You have respectively tendered me your resignations . . . but, after most anxious consideration, my deliberate judgment is, that the public interest does not admit of it. I therefore have to request that you will resume the duties of your departments respectively. Your Obt. Servt."

In faithfulness to a trust, in saving our constitutional freedom and opportunity for all, declaring that "no grievance is a fit object of redress by mob violence," made disconsolate by what he termed "a conspiracy" to "nationalize slavery," Lincoln—dogged by chronic fatigue—was a monumental contradiction of that conspiracy. An architect of justice, determined and destined to win his "case," he did not cease until he had demonstrated the mightiness of his "proposition." It is a Euclid of the heart.

[1] Quotations from Lincoln are taken from Earl S. Miers and Paul M. Angle, editors, *The Living Lincoln* (New Brunswick, N.J.: Rutgers University Press, 1955); and from Roy P. Basler, editor, *Abraham Lincoln: His Speeches and Writings* (New York: World, 1946).

In *Lincoln for the Ages*, edited by Ralph G. Newman. Garden City, N.Y.: Doubleday, 1960, pp. 378–83; *A Marianne Moore Reader*.

THE WAYS OUR POETS HAVE TAKEN IN FIFTEEN YEARS SINCE THE WAR

"In the years since the war, American poetry has entered upon a singularly rich period," Mr. Allen says and specifies three main groups: older contemporaries—W. C. Williams, Ezra Pound, Wallace Stevens, for instance; a contemporary group—Robert Lowell, Elizabeth Bishop, and others; and a third group now emerging (1945–1960)—the contributors to this anthology—"allied to modern jazz and abstract expressionist painting," a new generation who "have already created their own tradition," the editor says, "their own press and their public." Of the new group, many have been students of Charles Olson at Black Mountain College, share his views and have taken his verse as a model. He believes in a "loosened convention," "open form," and "composition by field," as he calls it. His "Song 4," from *The Songs of Maximus*, has a good climax:

> I know a house made of mud & wattles,
> I know a dress just sewed
>   (saw the wind
> blow its cotton
> against her body
> from the ankle
>   so!
> it was Nike

Robert Duncan, adopting Charles Olson's "open form," has imagination and is careful about cadence. In "Food for Fire, Food for Thought," he says,

> We trace faces in clouds: they drift apart.
> Palaces of air. The sun dying down sets them on fire . . .
> You have carried a branch of tomorrow into the room.
> Its fragrance had awakened me. No . . .
>   It was the sound of a fire on the hearth
>   Leapd up where you bankd it
> . . . sparks of delight . . .
> *If you look you will see the salamander—*
>   to the very elements that attend us,
>   fairies of the fire, the radiant crawling. . . .

Review of *The New American Poetry: 1945–1960,* edited by Donald M. Allen (Grove Press).

Denise Levertov has her own way of saying things in "Scenes from the Life of the Peppertree"; and in "Pleasures" *is* a pleasure when she says,

> I like the juicy stem of grass that grows
> within the coarser leaf folded round, . . .

With Robert Creeley's statement,

> . . . The unsure
> egoist is not
> good for himself

any would agree; and James Broughton also "thinks," has something to say about the self—about not mistaking "greed for need / and your sentence of death as a book of love." Edward Dorn—controlling the accent nicely— perfectly depicts a scene by "The Rick of Green Wood":

> . . . in the november
> air, in the world, that was getting colder
> as we stood there in the woodyard talking
> pleasantly, of the green wood and the dry.

Lawrence Ferlinghetti knows how to expand a metaphor; says

> the poet like an acrobat
>   climbs on rime
> to a high wire of his own making . . .
> performing entrechats
>   and slight-of-foot tricks
> and other high theatrics
>   and all without mistaking
> any thing
>   for what it may not be

Jack Spicer is not indifferent to T. S. Eliot and is not hackneyed, his specialty being the firefly flash of insight, lightening with dry detachment, as here:

> Poetry, almost blind like a camera
> Is alive in sight only for a second. Click,

the accents suiting the sense. Runovers, I think, might as well end the line naturally; but Lew Welch in his "Chicago Poem" has a runover of which the emphasis succeeds.

I lived here nearly 5 years before I could
meet the middle western day with anything like
Dignity . . . .

Welch is an observer, speaks of "The Goggled men / doing strong things
in / Showers of steel-spark" and he saw a fish, a Blue Gill

Lifted from its northern lake like a tropical. Jewel at its ear
belly gold so bright you'd swear he had a
Light in there . . . color fading with his life a small
    green fish . . . .

What he says about the "planet" on which we live, moreover, is applicable
to poetry:

. . . The trouble is
always and only with what we build on top of it.
    There's nobody else to blame.

To insert an apostrophe could scarcely slow Richard Duerden's word "seas"
too much in his apt lines about "the seas dark face. / Who'd call it lit, by
the moon?" But in the way of discarded punctuation, "the seas dark face"
is far outdone by Kirby Doyle's "Strange," a two-page sentence with *no*
punctuation.

Jack Kerouac is not for prudish persons. His "146th Chorus" (I almost
said Canto, and he does find it hard to get away from the manner of Pound's
Analects and Cantos) has unity, a tune, and the feel of the mountains. Allen
Ginsberg, quoting himself, has been "shopping for images in the poetic
super-market" and can foul the nest in a way to marvel at, but it is an
innocent enough picture of himself which he provides when he "sat down
under the huge shade of a Southern Pacific locomotive"; that he "found
minds unable to receive love because not knowing the self as lovely" is a
thoughtful statement. Gregory Corso has vehemence. His "Uccello" rings
true:

how I dream to join such battle!
a silver man on a black horse with red standard and striped
lance never to die but to be endless
    a golden prince of pictorial war

He takes a resilient view of "Marriage" and has a pithy piece, "But I Do Not Need Kindness." James Schuyler in his "Salute" has set down what is evidently in his own special vein—treasure for us as well, about gathering

> . . . one
> of each kind of clover,
> daisy, paintbrush that
> grew in that field. . . .

He says "February" was

> green and wet
> while the sky turns violet . . .
> I can't get over
> how it all works in together . . .

and in "Freely Espousing" he likes

> the tonic resonance of
> pill when used as in
> "she is a pill"

Frank O'Hara does not labor a simile: "It's as if I were carrying a horse on my shoulders / and I couldn't see his face . . ."; and his "Why I Am Not a Painter"—about Mike's painting called SARDINES—is one of the book's rewards for authors out of context. John Ashbery's "Instruction Manual" also is a pleasure, a documentary with structure and content. There is for me a haunting allusiveness about Gilbert Sorrentino's "The Zoo": "*Goliathus goliathus*, the one banana / peeling beetle in the U S A, . . . is dead. / 'Wrapped in his native grasses,' . . . "

In his "Statement on Poetics," Mr. Olson advocates open form or "composition by field," projective or field composition being offered as an improvement on inherited or "non-projective" form. Inherited non-projective form can be projective, I would say, and projective form may be weedy and colorless like suckers from an un-sunned tuber. Kenneth Burke's observation in *Counter-Statement*, it seems to me, applies both to the "field" and to the "library": "a work may be said to have form in so far as one part leads a reader to anticipate another part and be gratified by the result." Elsewhere, "Great artists feel as opportunity what others feel as a menace. This ability does not, I believe, derive from exceptional strength; it probably arises purely from professional interest the artist may take in his difficulties." As a composer's directions influence the performer's interpretation, punctuation aids precision, and precision is the glory of the craftsman; syntax being equivalent to the staff in music, without which interpretation would surely overtax the performer. (Intentional ambiguity and inadvertent ambiguity, need it be said, are not the same, the perfect analogy for intentional ambiguity being Rousseau's "Rendezvous in the Forest," in which the illusion is the more precise by the fact that the adjoining horses—the dapple and the black—are so merged as to be almost indistinguishable.)

Willa Cather, as quoted by Malcolm Cowley, says, " 'The artist's real problem is not how to change his material but how to simplify it, finding what conventions of form and what detail one can do without and yet preserve the spirit of the whole—so that all one has suppressed is there to the reader's consciousness as much as if it were in type on the page.' " It might be said here that the adjective "damn," the earmark of incompetence as an emphatic, operates in reverse—equivalent to: "spare diagnosis; this is no writer." "Anaemia and incompetence," also, deplored by Mr. Olson, are not present when the writer is able to compel the reader to put the accent where the writer wishes it put.

With regard to content: Good content, as Samuel Butler said, is usually matched by good treatment, and poets specializing in "organs and feelings"— severed from culture and literature, dogged by redundance and stench— have a stiff task. By comparison with the vocabularies of science, which are creative, in fact enthralling, exhibitionist content—invaded by the diction of drug-vendors and victims, sex addicts and civic parasites—becomes poetically inoperative. "Imagination can be forced," as Alfred Kazin said, "but it cannot be simulated."

Niceties of composition perhaps are inapplicable; but from the title, *The New American Poetry*, the article should be omitted, since various new poets are not included—Daniel Hoffman, Robert Bagg, George Starbuck; also striking of late as a poet in prose, Jean Garrigue; and it seems literalistic not to include Mr. I. A. Richards, technically "new" and of great attraction.

New York Herald Tribune Book Review, 26 June 1960, pp. 1, 11; *A Marianne Moore Reader*.

BROOKLYN FROM CLINTON HILL

Decorum marked life on Clinton Hill in the autumn of 1929 when my mother and I came to Brooklyn to live. An atmosphere of privacy with a touch of diffidence prevailed, as when a neighbor in a furred jacket, veil, and gloves would emerge from a four-story house to shop at grocer's or meat-market. Anonymity, without social or professional duties after a life of pressure in New York, we found congenial.

It was not unusual in those days, toward teatime, to catch a glimpse of a maid with starched cap and apron, adjusting accessories on a silver tray, in a certain particularly correct house of which the parlor-windows were screened by a Gauguin-green miscellany of glossy leaves—elephant-ear-sharp and rounder—amid ferns and tiny palms from the sill up, more than ever a grateful sight by contrast with starker windows.

"A city of churches," Brooklyn might also be called a city of trees. The wide leaves and violet blossoms of the catalpa lent an air of leisure to an occasional side- or back-yard. A linden at our corner diffused in spring just enough perfume, not too much; in autumn dropping its seeds, two on a stem from the center of each leaf, like the clustered bullet-tassels or fringe ornamenting Swedish wound wire silver buttons.

One year a scarlet tanager from a migrating flock chose as refuge to which it returned through several days, a nearby white magnolia in bloom—bouquet with removable jewel. Best of all there were the massive branches of elms with the anatomy of oaks, in Washington Park, emerging black after a shower through a mist of incipient emerald leaves.

One can scarcely refer to the Hill without mention of Dr. S. Parkes Cadman, who was pastor of the Central Congregational Church on Hancock Street. Dr. Cadman's counsel in *The New York Herald Tribune* was read by everyone and fascinatingly sane in its treatment of mighty topics—imaginatively inconclusive at need, as when suggesting that a chance of happiness is better if we want to do something than if we want to have something. A revolutionary force in the neighborhood also, is the Lafayette Avenue Presbyterian Church, its pastor since 1959, George Litch Knight, possessing momentum such that he and his congregation—compositely white, Negro, Puerto Rican, and Japanese (two uniquely rare sisters)—have renovated not only the building but in part its surroundings; mercury lights along South Oxford Street replacing the sinister shade cast by close-growing maples, enabling one to emerge from the subway without a police whistle, should stop-and-start patrons of some tavern inquire fictitiously for hospital or political headquarters.

Another landmark is the First Presbyterian Church on Henry Street—its pews having the original doors—a gallery, organ loft and air of simplicity with authority. In Dr. Phillips Packer Elliott, it has had a pastor for whom the term "a divine" is no archaism. His fraternal Presbyterial aid to other churches, sermons, and series of biographic studies—Great Preachers of the Past—make him one of the great preachers of the present. Following his sudden death on August 2, 1961, his "depth of compassion, humility, intellectual integrity, Christian commitment and ecclesiastical statesmanship are possessed by few religious leaders," the Reverend D. M. Potter, Executive Director of the Protestant Council, said in *The New York Times* of August 3. Students of "period," detained by Cuyler Gore, a tiny triangle of grass and elms between Fulton Street and Greene Avenue (named for Theodore Ledyard Cuyler, first pastor of the Lafayette Avenue Church)—find meat in Dr. Elliott's conspectus of Dr. Cuyler—a Matthew Arnold with sideburns and Victorian gravity who, as a Princeton senior of twenty, about to embark on a kind of grand tour, wrote to Wordsworth, Carlyle, and Dickens, requesting appointments with them and as Dr. Elliott observes, "heard from them afterward." Of his published writings, *How to Write a Sermon* (best undertaken "before the sun has reached its meridian"), *Straight to the Point, Reminiscences of a Long Life,* and other work, so excited his interest that my grandfather added them to his library in Missouri and when urged by his congregation to take vacation, said he needed none, merely wished to visit Brooklyn sometime and hear Dr. Cuyler preach in the Lafayette Avenue church. Visitors on the Heights do not leave usually without seeing Henry Ward Beecher's Plymouth Church of the Pilgrims on Orange Street near Willow. The plantation aspect of the building with columns and portico at street level beside a parallelogram of shaven grass afford a parable in sculpture of Dr. Beecher "selling slaves out of slavery"—a result literally of disrupting the service and directing ushers to "Pass the baskets." Dr. Beecher in bronze as in life—a slave at his feet with shoulder encircled by an angel of consolation at the rear of the green beside the church, stands out as on a stage.

Abraham Lincoln, upon first coming to Brooklyn, heard an impassioned abolitionist sermon by Dr. Beecher; and in 1865 "came once more to Orange Street." His "landau was seen to draw up at the corner of Columbia Heights and Pierpont Street," where "standing up and looking down at the Harbor" he is *said* to have said, "There may be more beautiful views in the world, but I have never seen them."

Brooklyn abounds in schools—Erasmus Hall, justifiably incorporating the name Erasmus, maintains an eminence in classics matching the severest college standards; and there is the Packer Collegiate Institute. Search the world over, you could not find a saner elegance, teaching more initiate, equipment more modern, together with a deep reverence for bequeathed value. Its rare book collection, oak-paneled chapel, shadowy organ, and gowned choir bring to life for me a linen-backed child's book I once had, *The Robin's Christmas Eve*. With beak parted to sing, scarlet breast lighted by a shaft of sun aslant the nave from painted windows, the robin shown resting on a church pillar wound with thick-berried holly.

Louis Zukofsky's anthology, *A Test for Poetry*, exhilarated me when it came out. It wears well and in his courses for engineers at the Polytechnic Institute on Livingstone Street not far from the Packer Institute, Mr. Zukofsky expertly presents poetry, composition, and American literature. The Brooklyn Technical High School for boys affords handsome confirmation that it is technical; its cast brass zodiac, sunk in the entrance floor, not having been worn away by the burnishing of countless feet. However, I was surprised to find that some who walk on it day by day have never noticed it. Their technical interests, however, do not seem to blind students to an interest in English, to Emil Gilels, "Cage and Cowell," or to Carlos Surinac's *Tientos* and Sylvia Marlowe—evaluated in neat clippings on a classroom bulletin board.

For its library school and prowess in design (engineering and aesthetic) Pratt Institute, renowned in the neighborhood and throughout the country, is an apex in performance, like its flagpole—clean-cut from the angled circular stone bench at its base to the gilded pineapple at the top. Pratt Institute Free Library, no longer open to the public, was for me on coming to Brooklyn a veritable desert rescue. The row of new accessions near the circulation desk went to one's head, new books appearing almost simultaneously with the advertising. In the stacks, related items in a subject often became more important than the original quest. And sometimes one came on startling finds acquired from private library dispersals. Stairs of polished oak, wide and easy, to the Periodical Room on the second floor, admit one to a room aired and maintained with unlapsing vigilance; newspapers in the racks, *Litell's Weekly* (cinnamon-covered), *The Yale Review*—obdurate against my timidly persistent product—with, richly counteracting the thought of its cruelty, *The Illustrated London News* on stout glossy paper, and *Natural History*, in a copy of which I found Dr. Robert Hatt's pangolins with text and camera studies, vivid substitute for their reclusive behavior and scaly integument.

At the foot of Clinton Hill, the Brooklyn Institute of Arts and Sciences (Arts without an "s" originally) has a telescope on the roof, large enough to attract the initiate who confer with initiates, while gapers expecting high-powered lenses to make brightness brighter, stand dejected upon finding the blaze of Sirius a hesitant glow. In the structure of the building itself certain materials intrinsically seem to me a feature: the interlacing Italian-Irish designs of the ground-floor concourse—related in period to the ground-floor mosaics in the Plaza Hotel in Manhattan. Then, for some stonemason, a triumph: the unpieced aspect of the staircase—satin-smooth oyster-gray marble with massive hand-rail—a deeply-grooved extension of the wall, with which it is continuous.

One winter, I attended so many presentations in lecture room or auditorium that I was pitied at home for not being able to sleep in the building—on certain days absent morning, afternoon, and evening. If one takes time for a thing, one should get as much of it as possible, I felt, so I usually sat in a front row. One evening I was so near the lecturer's "material," selected from the Staten Island Zoo snake house by the curator, Mr. Kauffield, to supplement his theme that snakes are an asset, as barely to be missed by a red racer which shot from the chromium tree which accommodated harmless snakes, into the lap of a boy in the first row, an incipient herpetologist evidently; or did the snake know him?

Daniel Gregory Mason, lecturing in that same room with piano to illustrate, converted me to Brahms, not a favorite with me, demonstrating the principle of restatement after contrast and the function of ornament, enlivening the series with such anecdotes as that of the woman who rushed up to Brahms with the impassioned inquiry, "Is this the great Brahms?" he replying, "His brother; you will find him over that hill." In the auditorium, Thornton Wilder in *one* evening characterized biography, poetry, fiction, and drama. George Russell, the Irish poet, A.E.—impressively unexaggerated in his attitude to dreams and extrasensory phenomena—told of visualizing from Dublin a certain house in New York, both street and number, associated with a man's death; the details verified by word received later.

In 1937, February 16, Stravinsky, in an all-Stravinsky program, no doubt exemplified the principle of restatement after contrast—primarily for me, I confess, rapt preoccupation with nicety of attack, fire, and tempo, projected concentratedly and unthreatened, in a manner so intent as to disable judgment. I can hear him still—a puzzle in the perfection of hoarded intentionalness.

For anyone with "a passion for actuality" there are times when the camera seems preferable to any other medium; or so I felt in 1896, enthralled by Lyman Howe Travelogues at the Opera House in Carlisle, Pennsylvania. As sequel to lantern-slides, cosmoscope, and stereopticon, Brooklyn Institute movies were Aladdin's magic. The documentary I should most like to see again is *Night Mail* with W. H. Auden's recitative dramatizing the mail-train's non-stop run from London to Scotland: the natural with the technical—steam from locomotive and fog on the meadow—a concentrate; the literal giving point to the figurative:

> In the farm she passes no one wakes,
> But a jug in a bedroom gently shakes.

The Brooklyn Museum, although representative, is not so vast as to justify the impression that gathered art can be the most lethal form of exhilaration.

It has "the" Peruvian double-fish-motive textile, a closely woven parallelogram with widely spaced pairs of fish in pale thread on maroon; almost an entire floor devoted to finely jointed carapaces by Japanese armorers. There are costumes, including a French mull Empress Josephine long dress with high waist, embroidered in a tiny flower-cluster design, appropriate to a Leghorn hat with pale-blue streamers in a Turgenev picnic-scene by a waterfall. Not only is art primitive, early, and modern, exhibited by the Museum, it has a class in painting taught by William von Kienbusch, whose own work, naturalistic or abstract, has plenty of drive.

Beyond Prospect Park's knolls, elms, lake, and bridle paths is the Zoo, ideally compact yet varied. One summer day when I was there, a Brahma zebu with hump and pale velour ears which it allowed to be felt, stood out of doors near wide-meshed fencing which enclosed a yard with a tree, not far from the small cats. Among them an ocelot with matching stencil of horned-owl richness paraded coldly; next a typically inquisitive ring-tailed coatimundi. Launched from their shelter like stones from a sling, in twenty- or thirty-foot arcs, a herd of impala soared down a run bordering meadow grass where two young bears were playing, hugging and staggering till, forced to a stand-still, one climbed a slab of rock and lay down.

Opposite the Zoo, the Botanic Garden, with willows and birds by a brook, is yellow in spring with forsythia, Brooklyn's flower symbolizing "unity and brotherhood." The Garden has rock plants, a wild-flower garden, plots for children, pools of tropical and hardy water lilies, Japanese cherries, a rose-garden beautifully divided by narrow grass paths, and a fragrance-garden for the blind, built up so that it may be touched.

The Bridge—a word associated with fantasy, a sense of leisure, shade under willows or at sunset, a pair of Chinese herdmen "enjoying the breeze in a fishing-boat"—is in Brooklyn synonymous with endurance—sacrifice; first by John H. Roebling, whose death resulted from a foot crushed by an incoming ferry when he was surveying for the bridge; with death for his son, Washington A. Roebling, who suffered caisson bends; and with heroism on the part of Mrs. Washington Roebling, who mastered calculus and engineering with one objective, the completing of the bridge. It was opened May 24, 1883—a notable triumph—memorialized by the cables ("Roebling cable"), towers, and centrally fixed arcs of filament united by stress, refined till diaphanous when seen from the Manhattan Bridge, silhouetted either by sun or the moon.

Another memorial—stirring for humanitarian and personal reasons, the Quaker passion for rescue—is the plaque in Squibb Park at the end of Middagh Street, to Edward Robinson Squibb, fiery Quaker and idealist with a passion for art and a technical capacity with the drive of a Polaris missile. (*Doctor Squibb: The Life and Times of a Rugged Idealist* by Lawrence G. Blochman—an enthralling story. Simon and Schuster, 1958.)

The name Squibb a hundred years ago meant "ether" and the most reliable ether mask; becoming associated with toothpaste and vitamins twenty years and more after Dr. Squibb's death. As a Quaker, since he would not be killing people but making them well—logic adduced by an aunt—Dr. Squibb felt that he could serve as a doctor in the Navy.

Doctor Squibb was outraged that patients with smallpox had died by reason of inefficient vaccine, his indignation mounting upon finding drugs wormy, decayed, or adulterated with chalk, bark, some even with plaster of Paris, and he resolved to obtain an appropriation for a laboratory that would manufacture pure drugs of uniform strength. Impeded for years by legislators who hesitated, and closed the fist, restricting funds as they do today for use as folly dictates, he began the laboratory himself—unwilling to patent his discoveries, saying they were "for those who needed them." He probably would disapprove of the cerise neon "Squibb" in magnified capitals on the building at Furman Street and the River; yet would most certainly approve of George S. Squibb, his great-grandson—one of the firm's experts—present with Miss Margaret Squibb and city dignitaries at the dedicating of the plaque in Squibb Park on September 23, 1959. The Park, antiseptically airy, has a kind of seaside bleached look.

Seth Low—born in Brooklyn in 1859—was its mayor from 1882 to 1886, President of Columbia, 1890 to 1901, moved the College to Morningside Heights, then resigned to become Mayor of New York on the fusion ticket; improved City finances, made essential changes in City departments as he had made significant changes in education. An annoyed citizen of that day could scarcely have said as has been said by one today, concerning the city's chief financier, "His ingratitude cannot disguise his ineptitude." Professor W. E. Hocking lived on Grace Court "Street"; W. H. Auden on Monroe Place; Jennie Jerome, the mother of Winston Churchill, on Henry Street; Grace Court—from Henry Street to the Esplanade—being one of our retreats for select persons, free from urban vexations, in autumn aglow with the artificial sunlight of falling leaves drying in tones of pale cadmium under Imperial trees of Japan.

In the Navy Yard, "westerly of the disbursing office (building 121), the Intelligent Whale may be seen"—said to be the first United States submarine, thirty feet long and about nine deep—to be propelled by hand at four knots—an evolution of Bushnell's Turtle, begun in New Jersey by Cornelius Bushnell, November 2, 1863, and completed in 1864 by a builder named Halstead. In a preliminary test of the Whale persevering Mr. Halstead nearly lost his life. The whale was condemned in 1872.

The *Monitor*—an iron-clad of wood like the *Merrimac*—was begun at Greenpoint, Brooklyn, in 1861 by John Ericsson and completed in 1862, defeating the *Merrimac* at Hampton Roads—changing the entire course of naval construction.

The Battle of Brooklyn is commemorated by the 1776–1951 heliotrope three-cent stamp: "Washington Saves His Army at Brooklyn," a figure on a white horse—arm raised—above the Bay dotted with sails. The designer of this stamp—now that a five-cent violet stamp is imminent—is commended to the Bureau of Printing and Engraving; also the behavior of the issue, which could not have given rise to Ogden Nash's recent complaint, rhyming with calf: "the perforations on sheets of stamps are optical delusions; if you believe that they are real you come up with either half a stamp or a stamp and a half." (Three sheets of *Washington Saves His Army* . . . —now gone—which matched a present of M. T. Bird violet, Crane single-sheet laid paper, accidentally but efficiently, I thought, emphasized history.)

Among Brooklyn Streets,[1] the names Ocean, Surf, Mermaid, and Half Moon are self-explanatory. The origin of Willow Street is less obvious, although at No. 27 there is still one remaining willow, all curves and angles as though by Harunobu. (Willow became official, it is *said*, when a Miss Middagh, undetected, substituted for the name "Jones" shingles on which she had painstakingly inscribed "Willow.") Across the street from 27, its frame house of coldish lizard blue and side yard with the willow, the last house on the street is a stately one of red brick. The rectangular doorstep is reached by six steps, the first three rising in a curve prettily emphasized by the swirl of the railing. In Brooklyn a wreath, square knot, or part of a chaplet sometimes ornaments the keystone above a white door; but on Willow Street the doors are black or green, their brass knobs complementing the old-style italic numeral in gold leaf on glass above the door. The numeral is usually repeated, one above the left and one above the right double door with a gold dot between. Unlike any other, the upper third of one door is divisioned in small squares with glass above, the lace behind the glass being of the same design as that of the parlor curtains—a needlework tracery of flowers and vines on transparent net. Dr. Squibb lived on Columbia Heights, facing the end of Clark Street. After distilling pure ether, he "had turned his attention to chloroform, then to money." That is to say, he built two houses just alike, connected by a tunnel—one for himself, one for his two sons. His house has been demolished; the other stands—a kind of severe mansion of pale brick, now occupied by Jehovah's Witnesses.

Originally I knew Montague Street as housing a valuable branch of the Public Library; and as headquarters for the Dodgers at 115. There is an eminent stationer on the street, McDonough and Company, where, from concealment, a clerk invariably emerges with an eye for the fretful itinerant— swift to produce an Esterbrook numbered list, Norma pencil, non-curl carbon paper, or other product. Your dog may wait inside but not among the merchandise. Brooklyn has, in a Womrath's nearby, a really literary bookstore, the young saleswoman being a bookman who knows what the wanted thing is and where to find it—a paperbook, an art study or small expensive book of poetry among hardbacks, a greeting card (Swiss flowers or cats-in-costume) well apart from the books and of grown-up nature—like rice, wheat, or cornchecks from Checkerboard Square.

Of the several florists, all meriting a compliment, E. Frank, with many fresh flowers in small space, is willing to provide a gardenia not made offensive by silver sparkles, starched net, or cotton-backed ribbon.

Brooklyn is susceptible to the lure of steel—stainless, unfortunately— but one of its *objets d'art* with Herculean potentialities is the vault of the Williamsburg Bank on Hanson Place: a Mosler safe, with the look of Cartier platinum and the burnish of a watch interior, its luster maintained year after year without a flaw.

Someone should delineate the Hill, the Heights, the center—doing justice to landmarks and losses. I like living here. Brooklyn has given me pleasure, has helped to educate me; has afforded me, in fact, the kind of tame excitement on which I thrive.

[1] Pierpont Street was named for Hezekiah Pierpont, grandson of a founder of Yale; and Montague Street is said to have been named by Harry Evelyn Montague (son of Hezekiah) for the family of Lady Mary Montague, a cousin, when the voyaging branch left to come to America. Clark Street commemorates James S. Clark, who joined Adrian Van Sinderen, Hezekiah Pierpont, and Adam Judall to found—in the basement of the Apprentice Library at Cranberry and Henry Streets—the Brooklyn Savings Bank, "a secure place of deposit for the savings of tradesmen, laborers, minors and servants." The managers, they said "disclaim personal emolument in any form whatever"; and they did not accept deposits from the hyper-prosperous. The cornerstone of the Apprentice Library was laid by Lafayette, whom Lafayette Avenue commemorates, on which the Institute stands. Orange, Cranberry, and Pineapple Streets were named, *perhaps*, by the Hicks family—farmers and grocers—for their merchandise from Cape Cod and the West Indies. Remsen Street was named for Henry Remsen, President of the Bank of Manhattan.

TO THE MEMORY OF A VIENNESE FRIEND

PETER ALTENBERG, singular man, died in Vienna in 1919, and Alexander King, as a memorial to this friend and mentor, has translated and illustrated with line drawings and two paintings, episodes related by him. "An attorney," Alexander King says, "without studying law, physician without studying medicine, book-seller who sells no books, a lover who never married . . . even a poet who writes no poetry"; a writer "who invented no clever endings," for whom "simple occurrences of the day—filtered through the mesh of acute observation"—became for the reader "nutritive spiritual fare." To such as Altenberg, "the shimmer on a horse's skin" could give acute joy, and "the snake was an ever ready springboard of fantasy, although he never saw one"; with a reverence for human relationships, he was a person who had no patience with dreariness and self-righteousness; "a passionate Anglophile" as a reader of Shakespeare; "a passionate Americanophile" as a reader of Emerson and Mark Twain. To the underdog of any aspect he could say, "Neither you nor any one else is a part of a mass"; could say "when people come around to live honestly they will be able to do very well without alcohol, a desperate means of eking out our complicated insufficiencies"; asking, "whom does Don Juan flitting from flower to flower actually cheat? Himself."

Among these evocations, one finds two of an ideality and tenderness which one can associate in tone with the author's and translator's compatriots, Mozart, Schubert and Rilke: one, "The Servant"—" '. . . it's nice being here, isn't it?' I said. 'Every one loves you . . . .' 'Yes,' she said"—a young girl, slender and of grave manner. "I said: 'What do you do evenings. . . ? Doesn't Jackie go to sleep around eight o'clock?' 'I would sometimes like to read the newspapers, but I sleep in the same room with the child and I am afraid the light might disturb him.' " The sequel: a screen to put around the bed and a lamp for the table. As companion-piece: "My Brother Georg"— "solidly as a sheet of steel and yet as unobtrusively as a spider web . . . as if he had assumed early in life a sacred mission to defend me against a hostile world, and even against myself; and although he himself was always involved in the disheartening struggle for existence, he never stinted time or thought or money in my behalf." Rarefying the evocation of "My Brother Georg" (upper right corner) an Austrian hat with chamois mount is depicted, and beneath it an alpenstock—in strokes of Ingreslike fidelity without a

---

Review of *Alexander King Presents Peter Altenberg's Evocations of Love*, with illustrations by Alexander King (Simon and Schuster).

stumble. Other drawings to be scrutinized: a birthday bouquet—an individualized miscellany of daisies large and small, minute adders' tongues and calla lilies, fragile inventions surrounded by ferns so delicate as to need the mutual support of proximity, lilies-of-the-valley with speary leaves in a juglike pitcher; on a beach, dwarfing the shell-gatherer, a spiny murex and a spotted mollusc; the end-paper drawing of a pair in a Victoria—a man, head bare and hat on knee, with a lady—the coachman's whiplash, unwound and trailing, beneath the leafless branches of a budding elm.

So exemplary an impression may have been given by the foregoing detail that objections must be stated—praise and indictment simultaneously of author and translator. One is puzzled. In television, conversation and in books, in the evocations and translations of them, Altenberg and King are hardly distinguishable from each other. Each trembles for inadvertent damage to treasures of the child's mind surrounded by the preoccupied grown-up world. Should chivalry not tremble for possible treasure in the minds of those older than children? That a scene is set in Vienna by no means compensates for an affront dealt one by the courage of too much nudity on the part of waitresses conveying champagne to clothed patrons. We do not wear the mire with the lily. As further complaint: in conversation we overstate; in poetry we do not. *Incredible, fabulous, rapturous*, used more than once in a lifetime, lose force. True, spontaneity matters more than correctness at times, and idioms in one language are not identical with those in another. Be this as it may be, one is seized by an impulse on behalf of a man whose aspect is one of commanding dignity, to regulate certain departures from careful usage: to omit "else" from "never let anyone else but me wait on him"; to omit "up" from "I leave it up to the reader"; to substitute "so" for "that" in "but it isn't that simple"; replace with "frequent," "hang out" used as a verb. Is this officious assistance? But one takes an interest. And also seizes upon a touch of injustice (in this book by "a man who was wholly without condescension,")—an attack even if included as irony. "What does an editor know of life and art? the algebra of existence?—that is why they are editors in the first place." *Some* epitomize the genius they attract, do they not?

A generality as comprehending captious inquiry: is it not possible to be savory in a situation which is *not* savory? Yes. Is it self-righteous to complain that acute observation might be yet more acute? Go farther? One does not know. Is it possible to triumph vicariously—and with all one's heart—in chivalry's achieving after a lifetime a long-contemplated tribute? It is.

New York Herald Tribune Book Review, 30 October 1960, p. 11.

FOREWORD TO
A MARIANNE MOORE READER

PUBLISHED: it is enough. The magazine was discontinued. The edition was small. One paragraph needs restating. Newspaper cuts on the fold or disintegrates. When was it published, and where? "The title was 'Words and . . .' something else. Could you say what it was?" I have forgotten. Happened upon years later, it seems to have been "Words and Modes of Expression." What became of "Tedium and Integrity," the unfinished manuscript of which there was no duplicate? A housekeeper is needed to assort the untidiness. For whom? A curioso or just for the author? In that case "as safe at the publisher's as if chained to the shelves of Bodley," Lamb said, smiling.

Verse: prose: a specimen or so of translation for those on whom completeness would weigh as a leg-iron. How would it seem to me if someone else had written it? Does it hold the attention? "Has it human value?" Or seem as if one had ever heard of "lucidity, force, and ease" or had any help from past thinkers? Is it subservient singsong or has it "muscles"?

La Fontaine's Fables. Professor Brower—if I am not inventing it—says a translator must have "depth of experience." The rhythm of a translation as motion, I think, should suggest the rhythm of the original, and the words be very nearly an equivalent of the author's meaning. After endless last choices, digressions, irrelevances, defiances, and futile imprudences, I am repaid for attempting to translate "The Grasshopper and the Ant" by hitting upon a substitute for an error, the most offensive and meaningless of a long list: "an't you please."

> —I sang for those who might pass by chance—
> Night and day, an't you please"

for which I am substituting "Night and day. Please do not be repelled," with the ant's reply, "Sang? A delight when someone has excelled." In harmonizing notes or words, there is more room for originality than in moralizing, and "the point," prefixed or appended to a tale irresistibly told, seems redundant. Although La Fontaine's primary concern was the poetry; even so, for him and for us, indifference to being educated has been conquered, and certain lessons in these fables contrive to be indelible: *Greed:* The owner of the hen that laid the golden eggs, "cut the magic chain and she'd never lay again. / Think this when covetous!" *Ingratitude:* The reanimated adder lunged at the farmer, "Its foster father who had been its rescuer. / . . . Two strokes made three snakes of the coil—/ A body, a tail, and a head. / The pestilent thirds writhed together to rear / But of course could no longer adhere." "Ingrates," La Fontaine says, "will always die in agony." *Be content with your lot:* A shepherd "was lured to part with his one and only flock / And invest all he'd earned, in a ship; but ah, the shock—/ Wrecked in return for all he'd paid."

Prose: mine will always be "essays" and verse of mine, observations. Of "Tedium and Integrity" the first few pages are missing—summarized sufficiently by: manner for matter; shadow for substance; ego for rapture. As antonym, integrity was suggested to me by a blossoming peach branch—a drawing by Hsieh Ho—reproduced above a *New York Times Book Review* notice of *The Mustard Seed Garden Manual of Painting* formulated about 500 A.D.—translated and edited by Miss Mai-mai Sze, published by the Bollingen Foundation in 1956 and as a Modern Library paperback in 1959. The plum branch led me to *The Tao of Painting*, of which "The Mustard Seed Garden" is a part, the (not "a") Tao being a way of life, a "oneness" that is tireless; whereas egotism, synonymous with ignorance in Buddhist thinking, is tedious. And the Tao led me to the dragon in the classification of primary symbols, "symbol of the power of heaven"—changing at will to the size of a silkworm; or swelling to the totality of heaven and earth;[1] at will invisible, made personal by a friend at a party—an authority on gems, finance, painting, and music—who exclaimed obligingly, as I concluded a digression on cranes, peaches, bats, and butterflies as symbols of long life and happiness, "O to be a dragon!" (The exclamation, lost sight of for a time, was appropriated as a title later.)

Verse: "Why the many quotation marks?" I am asked. Pardon my saying more than once, When a thing has been said so well that it could not be said better, why paraphrase it? Hence my writing is, if not a cabinet of fossils, a kind of collection of flies in amber.

More than once after a reading, I have been asked with circumspectly hesitant delicacy, "Your . . . poem, 'Marriage'; would you care to . . . make a statement about it?" Gladly. The thing (I would hardly call it a poem) is no philosophic precipitate; nor does it veil anything personal in the way of triumphs, entrapments, or dangerous colloquies. It is a little anthology of statements that took my fancy—phrasings that I liked.

Rhythm: The clue to it all (for me originally)—something built-in as in music.

> No man may him hyde
> From Deth holow-eyed.

I dislike the reversed order of words; don't like to be impeded by an unnecessary capital at the beginning of every line; I don't like, here, the meaning; the cadence coming close to being the sole reason for all that follows, the accent on "holow" rather than on "eyed," so firmly placed that the most willful reader cannot misplace it. "A fig for thee, O Death!"—meaning the opposite—has for me the same fascination. Appoggiaturas—a charmed subject. A study of trills can be absorbing to the exclusion of everything else—"the open, over-lapping, regular. . . ." A London *Times Literary Supplement* reviewer (perforce anonymous), reviewing *The Interpretation of Bach's Keyboard Works* by Erwin Bodky (Oxford University Press) on April 7, 1961, says, "phrasing is rarely marked by Bach . . . except as a warning that something abnormal is intended"—a remark which has a bearing, for prose and verse, on the matter of "ease" alluded to earlier. I like straight writing, end-stopped lines, an effect of flowing continuity, and after 1929—perhaps earlier—wrote no verse that did not (in my opinion) rhyme. *However*, when a friendly, businesslike, shrewd, valiant government official in a broadcast summarizes me in handsome style—a man who feels that in writing as in conduct I distinguish between liberty and license, agrees with me that punctuation and syntax have a bearing on meaning, and looks at human weakness to determine the possibilities of strength—when he says in conclusion, "She writes in free verse," I am not irascible.

Why an inordinate interest in animals and athletes? They are subjects for art and exemplars of it, are they not? minding their own business. Pangolins, hornbills, pitchers, catchers, do not pry or prey—or prolong the conversation; do not make us selfconscious; look their best when caring least; although in a Frank Buck documentary I saw a leopard insult a crocodile (basking on a river bank—head only visible on the bank)—bat the animal on the nose and continue on its way without so much as a look back. Perhaps I really don't know. I do know that I don't know how to account for a person who could be indifferent to miracles of dexterity, a certain feat by Don Zimmer—a Dodger at the time—making a backhand catch, of a ball coming hard from behind on the left, fast enough to take his hand off. "The fabric of existence weaves itself whole," as Charles Ives said (*Time*, August 22, 1960). "You cannot set art off in a corner and hope for it to have vitality, reality, and substance. My work in music helped my business [insurance] and my work in business helped my music."

I am deplored "for extolling President Eisenhower for the very reasons for which I should reprehend him." Attacked for vetoing the Farm Bill—April 1956—he said, "To produce more crops when we need less, squandering resources on what we cannot eat or sell . . . would it solve the problem? Is it in the best interests of all?" Anything reprehensible in that? While visiting Mr. Macmillan—London, May 6, 1959—he said, "Our strength is in dedication to freedom; . . . if we are sufficiently dedicated, we will discipline ourselves to make the sacrifices to do what needs to be done." He was not speaking to political aesthetes but to those who do not wish to join theorists in Suzanne Labin's *The Anthill:* those who farmed and were starved; the worker who was "overworked and underpaid"; thinkers who were "forced to lie"—a confederation in which "all were terrified" (*New York Herald Tribune*, December 25, 1960). "I think I might call you a moralist," the inquirer began, "or do you object?" "No," I said, "I think perhaps I am. I do not thrust promises or deeds of mercy right and left to write a lyric—if what I write ever is one"—a qualification received with smiles by a specialist (or proseur turned poseur)—(leopard and crocodile). "Poetry must not be drawn by the ears," Sidney says; in either the writing or the reading. T. S. Eliot is convinced that the work of contemporary poets should be read by students for enjoyment, not for credits; not taught formally but out of enthusiasm—with the classics as criterion (*New York Times*, December 30, 1960—printed a year earlier in Chicago). He is right about it, I think.

Prosody is a tool; poetry is "a maze, a trap, a web"—Professor Richards' epitome—and the quarry is captured in his own lines, "Not No" (in *Goodbye Earth*).

> *Not mine this life that must be lived in me.*
>
> Inside as out Another's: let it be.
> Ha, Skater on the Brink!
> > Come whence,
> > > Where go?
>
> Anywhere
> > Elsewhere
> > > Where I would not know
> *Not mine, not mine, all this lived through in me.*
>
> Who asks? Who answers? What ventriloquy!

My favorite poem? asked not too aggressively—perhaps recalling that Henry James could not name his "favorite letter of the alphabet or wave of the sea." The Book of Job, I have sometimes thought—for the verity of its agony and a fidelity that contrives glory for ashes. I do not deplore it that Sir Francis Bacon was often scathing, since he said, "By far the greatest obstacle . . . to advancement of anything is despair." Prizing Henry James, I take his worries for the most part with detachment; those of William James to myself when he says, "man's chief difference from the brutes lies in the exuberant excess of his subjective propensities. Prune his extravagance, sober him, and you undo him."

¹ The dragon as lord of space makes relevant Miss Mai-mai Sze's emphasis on "space as China's chief contribution to painting; the essential part of the wheel being the inner space between its spokes; the space in a room, its usefulness" in keeping with the Manual: "a crowded ill-arranged composition is one of the Twelve Faults of Painting"; as a man "if he had eyes all over his body, would be a monstrosity."

A Marianne Moore Reader. New York: Viking, 1961, pp. xiii–xviii.

A WRITER ON THE MOUND

A defeated pitcher—"a rather proud figure . . . peering into the depths of his glove"—and a passion for sport had planted in George "Prufrock" Plimpton a craving to pitch from the mound in the Yankee Stadium in an exhibition game. Much time on the phone had resulted in no more than "a snort at the other end" or a "Whazzat? Let's go through that again, hey," and the dream of participating in a game at championship level might have come to nothing if Toots Shor, when consulted, had not proposed a thousand-dollar prize set up by *Sports Illustrated* to be divided by the team which got the most hits— Plimpton pitching. *How to Play Baseball* (John McGraw) or *Pitching in a Pinch* (Christy Mathewson) or *It's Great to Be Alive* (Roy Campanella)— allowing for disparity in the year—might be an appropriate title for what follows.

George Plimpton had played last in a French meadow, with "a brightly colored beach ball which didn't travel far in the thick grass." However— "a fanatic about pitching" from boyhood, so obsessed that he would even throw stones at tree trunks, he says—he had "change of pace," a curve, "a sneaky submarine ball," and "of course I had a fast ball." Knowing better than to brave the inveterate superstition of ballplayers against lending, he provided himself with suit, accessories, and a glove. On the day of the game, a Sunday, the glove was missing—stolen from the car, which had not been locked. The quest for a substitute was fruitless until almost time for the batting contest, as players "bent to their labors" of autographing balls in the

Review of *Out of My League*, by George Plimpton, with photographs by Garry Winograd (Harper).

locker room. The reprieve must be read at leisure, not paraphrased. In the theft of the mitt, the inopportune arrival of President Eisenhower's motorcade at the Triborough Bridge, and similar dilemmas, Plimpton's stamina has a tincture of Charlie Chaplin's smile of agonized gratitude in acknowledgment of rebuffs.

Before consulting Toots Shor, Plimpton had said to *Sports Illustrated* of his project, "if it works out . . . perhaps I could do some more sports" (modest fellow); and after his stint on the mound he looked carefully around the deserted locker room, he says, "so that I could remember it, not to write about it as much as to convince myself that I had been there."

Out of My League copes with the problem of the imaginary nightmare of walking every batter and the glittering triumph (the shutout) of striking them out, one after the other. Afterward, hungry and thirsty, impatient to see the National League play the American, unrecognized as the pitcher for *Sports Illustrated*, neither ballplayer nor spectator, Plimpton found an empty seat in the upper deck of the stadium, bought two hot dogs, and was paying the vendor for a beer when evicted for having no ticket stub. He "crouched briefly in the aisle— . . . as nomadic as the youngsters who scuttle in without paying and are flushed like shorebirds and flutter down two or three sections to settle" until ushered further.

George Plimpton, as is already apparent, shines in simile—his great device; also in characterization. He has an ear for vernacular, says Willie Mays "has a pleasant face to start with," sometimes explodes in mighty laughter, and "his eyebrows [can] arch up," making him look "as if his manager had just finished addressing him at length in Turkish." Bob Friend, as magnetic as he was unaware that he was, said, "I don't feel all that much at home either," in reply to Plimpton's "It's all a little new."

Verisimilitude? In *Out of My League* it is not so much easy to find as it is impossible to avoid. "Frank Thomas' size made him look dangerous. . . . I imagined I heard the bat sing in the air like a willow switch." Ernie Banks, who had won a Most Valuable Player award for "his ability to lay off the bad pitches," was at the plate for such a long time that he "seemed to recede into the distance, along with [Elston] Howard [catching], until the two of them looked like figures viewed through the wrong end of a telescope." Elston Howard's detachment, in contempt of a stodgy task, had been painingly apparent to Plimpton. Then as Stan Lopata hit foul after foul, "lashing out like a cobra from his coil," Plimpton says, Howard "began to rise from his crouch after every pitch and fire the ball back . . . with an accuracy that mocked my control, harder than I was pitching it to him," inflicting "a deep bone bruise which discolored my left hand for over a week."

Christy Mathewson says, "a pitcher is not a ballplayer—he is a man in need of sympathy." Well . . . for a full-time man of letters, anonymity is a "role," and the reader's emotion is envy, envy of a man who retired his first two batters and later achieved the fine moment of his afternoon "when Mays hit that towering fly . . . forever available for recall." As Charles Poore says, "in a world where athletes are always signing ghost-written books this turn-about, with a writer ghosting an athlete, is fair play." If in *Out of My League* triumph does not dominate nightmare, something is wrong with the reader—if the performance by George Plimpton, his statistician, and photographer, Garry Winograd, has not earned them the triple crown with "rim tucked under," for poetry, biography, and drama.

New York Herald Tribune Book Review, 23 April 1961, p. 26; *A Marianne Moore Reader*.

MY CROW, PLUTO—A FANTASY

I T occurred to me one day to try a two-syllable-line, two-line-stanza piece about a crow—My crow / Pluto // the true / Plato // adagio—but I am changing to prose as less restrictive than verse. I had always wanted a crow and received a mechanical one for Christmas. Then Pluto, whose rookery is in Fort Green Park about a block from me, adopted me—a dream come true. He may have been attracted to my favorite hat, a black satin-straw sailor with narrow moire ribbon tied at the side, overlapping the nibs of crow feathers laid in a fan around the brim. If a feather blew away or partly detached itself, I had been dependent on a friend or relative to send me one in a letter. Now, I could salvage one almost any day from assiduous preenings—blue-green of the most ineffable luster. The hat—which had been bought me by my mother—was by Tappé, whose "creations" fascinated me, sketched and with descriptions published serially. Nor was the crow's intuition amiss, since he liked a great many kinds of food I like—honey, Anheuser-Busch high-potency yeast, dehydrated alfalfa, watercress, buckwheat cakes, fruit of all kinds.

Crows have a bad reputation as robbing songbirds' nests, fruit to be marketed, corn newly planted; even outdoing magpies in carrying off rings, gold thimbles, gems, loose or set; but since this crow lived with me most of the time, I acquired what he acquired; inconvenienced of course by having to restore what I could, with somewhat fraudulent explanations lest the culprit suffer. Although Chaucer has the phrase, "pull a finch," meaning filch, official investigation of crows' crops reveals comparatively innocent ravages of farm products. Is not the crow, furthermore, famed as an emblem of Providence, since ravens—certainly corvine—fed Elijah; and "of inspired birds, ravens were accounted the most prophetical," Macaulay says in his *History of St. Kilda.*

My crow was fanatically interested in detail—the pink-enameled heading on the stationery of *The Ladies' Home Journal* and the minuscule characters in *Harper's Bazaar* between the capital A's of *Bazaar* on that magazine's black-embossed pale blue stationery. I liked to take him with me on errands, although he attracted attention in a drugstore or store like Key Food, where I was allowed to bring him in if I kept an eye on him. He, however, had an eye for too much—cheese, grapes, nectarines, "party rolls," Fritos, and gadgets for the house. He was, happily, as literary as he was gastronomic— very fond of Doctor Zulli's 6:30 "Sunrise Semester" on Channel 2: "Landmarks in the Evolution of the Novel," and would perch on a brass knob at the foot of my bed as I took down the lecture, greatly convenienced by having a companion who could supply a word if I missed one. Also, because it was near the typewriter which interested him, he favored a bust as a perch—a bronze by Gaston Lachaise (cast and given me by Lincoln Kirstein)—but I could not induce him to say, "Nevermore." If I inquired, "What was the refrain in Poe's 'Raven,' Pluto?" he invariably would croak, "Evermore." He understood me, and I him from the first, even if our crow-Esperanto was not perfect; two squawks meant "no" and three "yes," a system a little like reading Braille raised dots, or guessing the word left out of a familiar text in Poetry Pilot contests, indicated by the number of letters omitted. Pluto— or Plato—as was inevitable from his habits and proficiencies, became alternates; choice depending on the vowel in the preceding word; after "eraser" it would be Pluto; after "cubic" it would be Plato. Pluto, from the perch on my head, could see and pick up anything I dropped, eraser or pencil. If I said, "Dictionary," he would fly to my case of miniature books in the front hall and bring me Webster's *Dictionary for the Vest Pocket*, 3 1/4 by 2 1/2 (1911), thumb-indexed and half an inch thick, containing "Rules for Spelling and Punctuation; of Parliamentary Law, of National Bankruptcy Law, Postal Rates, Etc."—heresy though it would be to mention Webster's Pocket rather than *New World Dictionary,* recently endorsed by me—if the Pocket really were Webster's "Latest & Best."

We should exemplify what we require of others and, having badgered a neighbor into returning a racoon to the woods where he got it, I asked one day, "Pluto, where were you born?" He said what sounded like "Correct account." I said, "Connecticut?" He cawed three times, so I took him to a Connecticut woods and liberated him—said, "Spread your wings. Fly," although "emancipated" is more accurate, since he was already free. "Fly?" Losing him was not simple but the spirit of adventure finally got the best of him. If what you have been reading savors of mythology, could I make it up? and if I could, would I impose on you? Remember, life is stranger than fiction.

Harper's Bazaar, 94 (October 1961), 184; *A Marianne Moore Reader*.

H. D.

H. D.'s first poems were published in 1912. Ezra Pound, in sending some of them to *Poetry, Chicago*, said "straight talk, straight as the Greeks!" H. D. contrived in the short line, to magnetize the reader by what was not said—to invest her work with the glow of romance; to give it the chiseled stateliness of Greek marble. When in New York in 1958, she remarked of some grapes—taken her by me—"Norman Douglas once said to me, 'you are like the Italians, you eat with your eyes.' " Of what she saw, her eyes made poems, stated with a lyric conciseness peculiarly hers, as in these lines from *What Do I Love?*

> A canoe slips from under a rhododendron-bush
> or is it Danielli's gondola,
> trailing its purple stuff?
> . . . .
> salamanders in the flame,
> heraldic wings surround the name
>
> Englé, Anglé, English . . .
>
> (May 1943)

May Sinclair said of her poems: "An austere ecstasy is in them. They have the quick beat of birds' wings, the rise and fall of big waves, the slow magical movement of figures in some festival of Demeter, or Dionysus carrying the sacra."

Evacuated to Switzerland after the first world war by her friend, Bryher— Winifred Ellerman—H. D. surmounted recurrent disabilities. On Wednesday, September 27th, she died in the Red Cross Hospital in Zurich. We say died, the word contradicted by her having left us much that lives that is herself.

Bryn Mawr Alumnae Bulletin, 42 (Fall 1961), 20.

WORTH OF RUE DE LA PAIX

IN this day of jets, blenders, and a page of print grasped at a glance, the perfected workmanship—inside and out—of a dress by Worth seems as unaccountable as the flawless replica—wrong side like right—of antennae, wing-spots, eyes and moth-fur, of Chinese embroidery on imperial satin: an abnormal calligraphy of the imagination-by-finger (finger in gold thimble, as one pictures it), faintly etched.

At the age of twenty, Charles Frederick Worth left London for Paris, and held court there with the needle until courtly fashion went out. At 7 rue de la Paix, in a world of after-theater parties, race meetings, masked balls and competitions in *travesti*, he became for ladies of title, counts, viscounts and royalty, a person to reckon with. It was not in that era considered effeminate for a man to wear a tied silk bow of one thickness, a shirt pleat with edge minutely embroidered, double rings on left little finger, and serpent watch chain—the tail ending in a hook, the head set with an emerald. Women wore pairs of bracelets with tiny guard-chain at the clasp; the giant cameo of Three Graces, say, cut white on shell pink. Cloisonné vinaigrettes and fans of rose-point on pierced ivory sticks were carried. The ebony shackle-necklace, of links the size of a dime, might be seen on a Renoir striped bodice or velvet straight jacket diverging from a broach at the neck. It was a day of white at the neck, the Basque collar set off by an edge of white stiffly starched, with white cuff edging the sleeve from inside. Impresarios were commemorated in food—pastry and whipped cream spiraled into a "lady-lock" or Napoleon.

The Worth concept of performance went deep, involving double dust ruffles of silk net; the high armhole and narrow sleeve with a forward motion; twenty to thirty adjoining buttons assuring snugness without a gap—every buttonhole hand-worked with self-matching twist that even in 1962 is not beginning to fray. You could put your hat on but could scarcely breathe. He might have created—fanatical impresario—who knows what eels if he had the neck-to-hem zipper at command. One is tempted to consult Vic Tanny with a view to reviving the spinach green afternoon dress of ribbed satin, the jacket prolonged in slim tapering swallowtails to the knees.

A half dozen jackets, each one of a kind, include an Aubrey Beardsley olive velvet with Medici collar and unbelievably huge leg-o'-mutton sleeves, ornamented with cut steel in backgammon points—a self-sustaining carapace almost simulating the medieval cuirass. Anyone, however, accustomed to its weight, or that of a cut velvet plum cloak to match a plum jet-beaded dress (the pair weighing two hundred pounds), should not hesitate about sacrificing lightness to drama.

Forsaking the armorers, the gem of the collection, I would say, is a featherweight azure tissue velvet jacket matching a ball dress, edged with snow leopard down, or at a guess, owl down bronzed by guard hairs ticked like Abyssinian cat fur, lined with China silk of the same blue, quilted in wide diagonals. As important as the Beardsley jacket, Mrs. Cheney's riding tunic with Chinese collar double jabot, and deep points traced in steel, has much going on; its severity, at the same time, recalling the Empress Eugénie side-saddle on a black horse—torso hard as a tenpin—with scoop hat tilted under the forward swirl of a black ostrich plume.

Among satins, the mighty Second Empire ball gown of Rhodamontine pink typifies C. F. Worth's devotion to basic design. Susceptible to enticements like dagging or outside stitching in parallel lines, he saw no substitute for the sweeping line—vary it as he did in countless ways, particularly in varieties of the overdrape, guaranteeing each customer something authoritatively original and indisputably personal. Never a duplicate, even in so massive an engineering project as the thousand dresses in a week he executed for the Princess Eugénie and her palace guests in 1866. Almost never—since the unique Rhodamontine pink ball gown appeared simultaneously in Boston, Providence and Hartford!

He worked his seams well—a craftsman of genius, Mr. Worth—especially in the monumental court presentation gown of ivory damask, preserving the elegance of the pattern by symmetry in the spacings; and by whaleboning, insuring an Elizabethan v-point and an inevitable firmness—as battens in slots stabilize the spread of a sail.

Then when the daughter of Charles Frederick Worth (fashion's Perseus intaglio with the light behind him, his fingers as shapely as those of a hawk) married Cartier, as should be, the picture was all of a piece.

Harper's Bazaar, 96 (April 1962), 106–11.

WILLIAM KIENBUSCH

THE sea, movement and sound here are equivalents in paint of prized moments—felt so deeply that nothing has been allowed to be overstated, guessed at or ambiguous.

In *Sound of the Gong Buoy # 2*, little hammers strike gongs as the buoy leans. The partial arc—upper left of the buoy—suggests the buoy swayed by the sea and made to clang. The hammers—small black oblongs side by side—achieve a kind of beat—a pictorial music. In *Sound of the Gong Buoy #5*, fog, island, a pine tree, rock and ocean, interlock; an x at the center suggesting the rocking and clanging. The small black objects are islands. A main impression for me in these Gong Buoy studies, as in *Island Wreck*, is of a fearless brush—secure and experienced; of texture never maltreated.

Much of the detail suggests music. In *Orange Grove #2*, the feature is a commotion created by wind—an all-orange equinox. *Concerning the Scarecrow* is a structure of rags—torn shreds of pearly white, moonshot and strange—wavered by wind into homogeneous similar thousands of very odd rhythms.

In *A Small Island Fire*—subdued as paint by comparison with the cerulean, ponsol, cobalt and ultramarine blues of the sea subjects—little gray New England clapboard houses are on fire at the far end of a field, a peaceful meadow of sunburnt Jaeger-brown grass. Again we have the sense of notes; the small square black windows seem a notation; you are aware of more and more going on as you get to the top of the painting—the excitement concentrated in a burst of pale gold tinged with pomegranate pink as the fire gains on the tinder-dry clapboard—a very *very* small fire, to which undivided attention must be devoted if one is to feel it expand, deadly and ravenous; the smoke "is a kind of shorthand for disaster."

These paintings capture the excitement of treasured perceptions, some preserved by the mind from early years till committed to paint. Contemporary art? Yes; but no *mélange moderne*. These are evocations.

In *William Kienbusch*. New York: Kraushaar Galleries. Catalogue of an Exhibition, January 28–February 16, 1963, p. 2.

E. E. CUMMINGS, 1894–1962

E. E. CUMMINGS was too distinctive a person to be subjected to in-
apposite comment. It is with diffidence that I speak—as Mr. Brooks and
Miss Geffen will corroborate.

"Art," E. E. Cummings said, "is pure personal feeling." His work says
it again—the painting, writing, drawing: especially the line drawings comprising curves, swirls, and leaning ellipses, like Chinese calligraphy which
does not hesitate. His art of economy has left its mark on us, making verbosity
seem suicidally crass. Instead of saying that the prison cell was six feet long
and four feet wide, he says it was six feet short and four feet narrow.

Ignorance to E. E. Cummings was a "monster, the collective pseudobeast." Nonentity as "the general menedjerr"

> . . . smoked a robert burns cigerr
> to the god of things like they err

A poem by E. E. Cummings has the sound of the voice:

> SNO [falls]
>   . . . . . .
>
> (on
>   air)
> don't speak

and

> i've come to ask you if there isn't a
> new moon outside your window saying if
>
> that's all, just if"

This grace with naturalness is best personified, I think, in the text by
E. E. Cummings to Marion Cummings' photographs entitled *Adventures in
Value:* "A wave . . . beginning—e-x-p-a-n-d-i-n-g UpReArInG—to": infin-
ity? he leaves us to say it. The cross-shadows in Patchin Place enshrine
reverence: "and nobody ever thought of touching them," the water-lilies Mrs.
Corkery, caretaker of Patchin Place, remembers in the fountain behind
Washington Square Arch.

One of the pictures is of a stone angel—a marvel of grace—superimposed on a grave, its wings closing about the grave in all-embracing compassion. "Death," E. E. Cummings said (in another connection), "as men call him, ends what they call men." The fact of it is dire. It makes of us orphans, waifs, mourners. Attempted consolation emphasizes the impossibility of consolation. For a positiveness, however, that is indivisibly undismemberable joy, it doesn't exist. At *The Dial*, we talked about "intensity" as a test for what purported to be art. What is this individual thing that lasts, that can not be counterfeited, this magician's secret that we call beauty—the result of hyper-care that is synonymous with affection? Henry McBride, our art critic for *The Dial*, said of the paintings by E. E. Cummings exhibited by the American-British Art Center, "They have the purities of mushrooms blooming in darkness." His oil, "Paris Roofs, rue de la Bûcherie" has this sacrosanctity of untainted naturalness; some of his poems have it. Two poems especially have made an indelible impression on me—the one about the Gravenstein apples, in its ability to evoke a place where apples grow by a wall in sunny grass:

> it's over a (see just
> over this) wall

There are further lines, returning like a fugue, to say:

> But over a (see just
> over this) wall
> the red and the round
> (they're gravensteins) fall
> with a kind of a blind
> big sound on the ground

The other poem is yet more the person. It has the unswerving individuality—better say, the unyielding vitality, of one who knew how "in an epoch of Unself" (of noneself) "to be ONEself":

> now (more near ourselves than we)
> is a bird singing in a tree,
> who never sings the same thing twice
> and still that singing's always his
> . . . .
> there never lived a gayer he;

> if earth and sky should break in two
> he'd make them one (his song's so true)

Proceedings of the American Academy of Arts and Letters and the National Institute of Arts and Letters. 2nd Series, No. 15 (1963), 285–87.

THE KNIFE

I have a knife held by two nails flat to the casing of my kitchen china closet. It has a blade about 8 inches long, of high-grade steel, joined to an ebony handle by a collar of brass—trade-marked Encore, Thomas Turner, Cutler to his Majesty—bought in Oxford in 1911 for cutting bread and cheese, by my mother and me who had lodgings in Magpie Lane, formerly Grove Street, not far from the Bodleian. Up a flight of stairs, above the reading room of the Library, among the exhibition cases containing objects congruous with the interests of studious persons, were trenchers on one of which the motto said,

> If thou be young then marry not yet.
> If thou be olde, then no wife get
> For young men's wives will not be taught
> And olde men's wives be good for naught.

I think this motto may have had a part in my dislike of the reversed order of words in verse which purports to be poetry.

My Turner knife is so sharp as to tempt use for cutting more than bread— for sectioning grapefruit, for slicing a lemon, a watermelon; for freeing honeycomb that has cemented itself almost permanently to the frame. The result: stains which indict hands too hurried to scour a knife with steel glow or Bon Ami—indication of housewifely status, as indisputable as the diamonds and rubies encrusting the massive gold swords provided by the king for each fairy invited to the christening of his daughter, the Princess, in Perrault's story of "The Sleeping Beauty."

A massive gold sword, as a paper knife, however, is less practical than tortoise shell, ivory, or the steel desk knife made by certain German manufacturers with a Mercury's head on the hilt and the word Victory. Metal is of course no match aesthetically for the beveled ebony Japanese paper cutter sold by Takahashi in San Francisco; or for a chinese ivory paper knife of the kind once given me—the handle diminishing in diameter from a short neatly rounded animal tail which appears to dive through the ivory from one side, while nose and ears come through on the other. Ivory seems the best edge for India paper—rather than a crazy sharp edge which could veer into the margin, or tear a corner off diagonally.

Yes, a knife is essential. As Admiral Roscoe F. Good observed, "A seafaring man without a knife is no sailor."

For correspondents with a security complex, who seal a flap shut to the last vestige of gummed edge, a tiny shop in Venice has exactly the blade: Ferigo Andrea, Cottelleria Arrotinaria, S. Marco 2358 Calle delle Ostreghe. The case of white bone is 1 1/16 inches long, secured by three brass rivets, with a red dot near the hinge. The blade, with thumb groove, has a ring and a point fine enough to enter an opening the size of a pinpoint. With a paper clip attached to the ring, this "bino" (*bambino*) need not be mislaid. This shop regards skinning knives as its specialty, but it has also a fruit knife and two-pronged fork of stainless steel, each with white composition handle. Using these as a substitute for the gigantic implements afforded by ships and hotels, one may rival the waiter paring a hard peach or apple without resting a finger on the part one would eat. I bought the pair; then was presented soon after with a Greek knife which has a 2-inch steel blade in a 2-inch grip, the blade engraved with a four-petaled flower on one side and on the other a fish carrying away a bit of fishline. Symmetrically warted by rivet heads that stabilize the blade, the brass handle of the knife has *repoussé* circles enclosing three small paste jewels—what appears to be a bloodstone between two garnets.

In size but not charm, my Greek flat sword is surpassed, naturally, by the watermelon knife which dominated the account by P. Papakoukas in the *Athens News* from the city's midsummer "watermelon front," which went more or less as follows:

> I once again deal with the so easily wielded instrument . . . which these days has reached a peak of activity. Two watermelon sellers got angry with a customer who didn't find the sliced watermelon . . . red enough, and treated him like a watermelon awaiting the knife.
>
> Every summer the color of this delicious fruit creates a multitude of misunderstandings which culminate in the police precinct. The scene is something like this: the watermelon seller with his pushcart . . . the innocent customer.
>
> "Are they red?"
>
> "If they're not, you don't take any. . . ." And the knife flashed forth. . . . "Fire couldn't be redder."
>
> "It's not red."
>
> "Not red?"
>
> An argument follows as to which is color blind. . . . At times experts

are called in. . . . "Excuse me, sir. Please, one minute of your time. . . . Is this watermelon red?" In about three minutes twenty experts gather, each shouting an opinion.

"It's red."

"No, it isn't, it's pink."

"White."

"Twenty years I've been selling watermelon and I know what I'm saying."

"I have been eating watermelons for forty years. . . ."

"Since I cut it, you have to buy it."

"If it isn't a watermelon but a marrow, what'll I do with it? Give it to the chickens? . . ."

"You're a marrow yourself . . . look like one."

There is no need for all this. Let the guessing as to the color be a question of technique, luck and extra-sense perception. . . . A police order on the matter could settle it once and for all.

We say he that lives by the sword shall die by the sword. The Roman, the Florentine and the Etruscan were not convinced of this. Could any warrior surpass in might an Etruscan holding up a 40-pound shield and long sword, under a helmet four or five feet long from crest to caudal tip? Giorgione's "A Soldier," in crimson, sword vertical, facing forward like a magistrate or philosopher, implies the opposite of bloodshed. Votes against Hippocrates when nominated for exile were never sufficient to exile him, as the count by *ostrakon* in Athens' Museum of the Agora shows. Fragments and little implements found where Phidias had his shop at Olympia as well as Charcot's triumph of surgery belong to the mythology of skill in which creative imagination (say, the soul) dwarfs any instance of triumph in combat.

That Praxiteles' Hermes should seem from the left to smile and from the right to ponder, baffles analysis. Marble cutting, manually, is becoming a lost art; as demonstrated in Michelangelo's David and in the Moses which was to be part of the tomb of Pope Julius II. The Moses—to the right of the chains which bound the Apostle Peter in the church named for him, San Pietro in Vinculi—is another proof that sculptors of saints are too often obstructed by unsaintly contemporaries. For the quarrymen of Carrara by their cupidity thwarted Michelangelo's dream of carving the tomb for Pope Julius II from Monte Borla marble. Michelangelo with two servants and horses, as his friend Condivi explains, spent eight months seeking the right vein of marble for the tomb, was then forced—with his Genoese sailors and their boat—to move south from Serraveza, from which the marble could have been loaded for transport to Ostia, up the Tiber to Rome. The tomb was never finished.

A ruder—say less elate—use of the chisel is afforded by architecture:

the Maidens of the Erectheum and their replicas with arms (made before the originals were damaged) beside the lake at Hadrian's Villa; the fast-eroding, benignly smiling Father Tiber at the end of the lake, Romulus and Remus nestled in his lap; the stone alligator which plants itself without a peer for naturalness in a semi S on the lake coping across from the Maidens, his jaws with sawtooth teeth parted rapaciously—or in a smile? The verity of the alligator has a counterpart in the rather unsimilar gargoyle alligator heads protruding from the band of stone which extends above the gate of the King's castle at Sintra—the gate itself overhung by a lion head which frowns and one which smiles; the approach shrouded at the base by dense maidenhair fern despite the sun-baked farmland below. Lions, recurring under many a king, we have again in the row of five or six with open mouths before what was the palace at Delos; also in Italy's lion fountains and in St. Mark's lion on the column beside the quay bordering St. Mark's Square.

A use of the chisel, seemingly more utilitarian than portraiture, is Italian intarsia-work depicting flowers, bees and butterflies—as in a notable table top in the castle drawing rooms at Montegufoni belonging to the Sitwell family; or as in the severely geometric olive, black and white intarsia screen setting apart the memorial chapel to Bishop Pantelone, founder of the church in Ravello. The pulpit is guarded by six bowlegged lions, each with a different face, three male, three female.

The stonecutter in Italy has brought to perfection the art of paving as seen in almost any Italian city: the concentric fan of street cobbles, the curbstone protruding in a half circle and mortised into the half eclipse of the adjoining one; not to mention the use of wall stones, protruding singly at intervals to form a stair such as reinforces the roadside wall up the nearly vertical hill road to Cortona; again in the nine- or ten-feet tall stone shutters still in use on the church at Torcello—each a single piece of stone and originally a protection against pirates.

This feeling for work with stone one sees in the floor mosaics from Herculaneum at the National Museum in Naples: black designs on white—a wall-of-Troy or interlinked eights enclosing separate symbols, the X, the axe, the box, the cross, the circle, the oval. A variant carried out in Greece in black and white pebbles constitutes a study in itself: the stair levels up the path to the citadel on Lindos, the spray of heliotrope, black on white, gracing the approach to the door of a formal home on Santorini.

Stonework in Italy is matched by engineering—by the tunnel, straight or sometimes a half serpentine; by the expedient to combat erosion: the arrow of implanted stone on a precipitous hillside; by the sheared rock precipice on the road from Perugia to Rome, where gorge after gorge is intersected by lesser ravines clad with vines like the vertical vineyards of Ravello. Home and grapes are often guarded by a wrought-iron gate at the top of a flight of steps cut from the rock. Such triumphs of hand labor are miniature, however, compared with the thirteen years' labor by 300,000 slaves in rearing the Temple to Zeus at Olympia. Even works of hand by the best stonecutters, one finds dwarfed by spirit, as symbolized by the grassy mound memorializing the dead at Marathon, near the stele of the Athenian soldier associated in one's mind with Phedippedes who, too excited after fighting at Marathon to lay aside shield, sword and leg guards, ran the twenty-six and a half miles to Athens in an hour to announce as he fell exhausted, "We won."

In valor, there is small room for egotism. As Confucius says, "If there be a knife of resentment in the heart, the mind fails to act with precision."

House and Garden, 123 (February 1963), 98–99, 140.

PROFIT IS A DEAD WEIGHT

OVERINITIATIVE has something to be said for it. With no resistance, a kite staggers and falls; whereas if it catches the right current of air it can rise, darting and soaring as it pulls and fights the wind. Overinitiative can take us somewhere. Humility is yet mightier, can sometimes retrieve a situation; as when the bear cub in Frank Buck's jungle camp escaped through a half-closed cage door, grew tired and hungry, hurried back, tripping over a python which looked like a fallen tree and reached camp safe, merely because the snake was asleep and moved but an inch or two. An exception doesn't prove the rule. The next python may not have just had a meal or may not be asleep.

I call these reflections "Profit is a Dead Weight"—a sentence I happened upon in my Italian dictionary: *lucro è peso morto*—because, although pride is usually regarded as the worst of the seven deadly sins, greed seems to me the vice of our century. Why should I pay "twenty dollars for the set" when I want *only* a portfolio, *no* paperknife and *no* brass gold pen? If I buy a chance and win a watch that was paid for by neighbors who bought a chance with hard-earned money needed for food, did I profit? The root of the struggle to win something for nothing is covetousness. Do we have to be like the man who killed the hen who laid the golden eggs? Overcome by greed to want all of them at once, he found "only what he would have found in an ordinary hen. He had cut the magic chain and she would never lay again."

Behavior: it all reduces to a moral issue. We must not want something from another so much that we steal it; cannot kill another and benefit. Of morals bearing on sex, I hear more than I used to; of trial marriage as reasonable and different from delinquency, an evasion of the moral law, I would say: no innovation and as old as mankind.

Among assets that one cannot ignore is the power of concentration. A preamble on television or snatch of phonograph music is not part of it. Are you able to ignore a disparaging comment, insult, slander? Smother your desire for revenge? Make allowance for the defiant salesman who writes, goes on writing and will not look up? The traffic man hardened to explanation? The asset of assets was summed up by Confucius when asked, "Is there a single principle that you can practice through life to the end?" He said, "Sympathy. What you don't want, don't inflict on others."

In the last war, as a man who had survived a bayonet charge was thinking he might somehow escape, he heard a groan; then, "Nigger, pull this bayonet out of my chest." Hardened by the term of disdain, he hesitated, then pulled the bayonet out for the victim and "drug him a mile," as the story was told to me. The surgeon treating the bayonet wound said, with a nod toward the Negro, "You owe your life to that man." The Negro and rescued man became friends after discharge from the army, shared dinners and holidays whenever possible. "And do you believe that faked-up story?" I was asked, of a friend's factual report. How discuss verity with cynics—cynicism being a plant with no fruit or interesting seed? As Confucius says, "If there be a knife of resentment in the heart, the mind fails to attain precision." Defamation, denigration, ridicule, are easy compared with the ability to portray magnanimity—defined by a commentator (via Webster) as "loftiness of spirit enabling one to bear trouble calmly, disdain revenge and make sacrifices for worthy ends."

And what are worthy ends? Knowledge made possible by an overpowering desire to possess it; usefulness—like that of Dr. Squibb, whose pure ether and reliable ether mask were "for use by all who needed them," never patented; conjoining bone and nerve ends of a boy's severed arm. Small (if small) ingenuities: one would like to have invented the zipper fastener, epoxy glue, the collapsible dustpan, figure-eight stitch closure of the hide cover of the baseball.

Sound technique is indispensable to the musician, painter, engineer, mechanic, athlete, fencer, boxer. One does not associate compassion, humility or modesty with boxing. Each could be "that talent which is death to hide" and a boy "wrapped up in it," speed-ball and pendulum, walking in heavy sand to strengthen the leg muscles; with an aptitude for "invention": a boy "coming up from a dungeon of darkness," in danger of being wasted, inhibited by false accusations—portrayed by Floyd Patterson in *Victory over Myself.* "It was a grind," he says, "but a way out for me and my family." The victory involved "application and concentration"—age-old formula for results in any kind of work, profession, art, recreation. "Powerful feeling and the talent to use it!"

"It should not be a case of sink or swim," Floyd Patterson says. "You have to learn to walk before you can run"; he (the pathos of it) having had to be *taught* to like being alive—at the Wiltwyck School in Esopus (New York), largely, he feels, by Miss Vivian Costen: "The only way I knew to thank her," he says, "was to be what she wanted me to be"; his repressiveness continuing a long, long time as "commensurate power" was emerging. Of coming to the Olympic Games he says, "I had to come four thousand miles to really begin to feel that I was like everybody else." Then, "When they handed out our official clothes, I could hardly believe my eyes. How do you describe the feelings somebody like myself can have at a time like that?" Having won the United States middleweight championship—never having bowed before—he says, "I placed one hand on my stomach and the other on my back . . . and bent low from the waist. . . . I don't know how long I remained in that pose. Long enough, anyhow, for somebody to say, 'All right now, Floyd.' Then I straightened up." The "feelings" are described "with perception at the height of passion"—letting Henry James say it for me. I doubt that anyone who is incurably interested in writing as I am, and always doing it, has had as much difficulty as I have in expressing what I fanatically find myself determined to say: How get it all in—compact, unmistakable—set down as if spontaneously? This book by Floyd Patterson with Milton Gross much intensifies my interest in writing—explicit, vivid, modest—every sentence enchaining the attention: "the dignity of equality" there on the page, for beginner or expert to examine at leisure.

After the conferring of contest awards for verse in a school which I visited, a teacher chiefly responsible for the zeal of the participants said in addressing the students: "You have daring, courage to believe in yourselves, craftly skill to produce that which is new and worthy of man as he was meant to be"; a combat warrant for scholastic effort applicable generally, one hopes.

"Recreation" can be punishment, and I have, like others, sometimes deplored television for misusing its possibilities. Sometimes, however, it has fired my imagination with gratitude as when I heard Andrés Segovia playing Boccherini, his fingers moving about among the strings of the guitar like hornet legs flickering here and there over a peach to determine its sweetness. I found absorbing also—although by no means similar—Mr. William Longendecker, an amateur of rhinoceros language, demonstrating his ability to mellow one of the animals by resting a hand on its head and imitating its speech.

Talent is a joyous thing—able to substitute the spirit of praise for the garment of heaviness; or so I thought when hearing—on television—Jean Renoir, son of the painter, interviewed at his home. Asked concerning childhood, "Would you say you were poor?" he said, "It depends on what you mean. My mother could do much with little. We were always surrounded by luxury in all that is done with the hand."

Talent, knowledge, humility, reverence, magnanimity involve the inconvenience of responsibility or they die. To the bonanza, the legacy, the professional hit, it would be well if our attitude were that of the Brazilian dazzled by unearthing a *calderião* (cluster of diamonds): "My Lord and Heavenly father, if this wealth endangers my soul, let it vanish." It is what every poem is about, as Robert Frost writes, "the triumph of the spirit over the materialism by which we are being smothered."

Example is needed, not counsel; but let me submit here these four precepts:

Feed imagination food that invigorates.

Whatever it is, do it with all your might.

Never do to another what you would not wish done to yourself.

Say to yourself, "I will be responsible."

Put these principles to the test, and you will be inconvenienced by being overtrusted, overbefriended, overconsulted, half adopted, and have no leisure. Face that when you come to it.

Seventeen, 22 (March 1963), 142, 165–66; *Tell Me, Tell Me*.

EDUCATION OF A POET

A main influence on my life as a writer was the Norcross family in Carlisle, Pennsylvania, where my childhood was spent. Dr. George Norcross was Pastor of the Second Presbyterian Church in Carlisle. Mrs. Norcross was Louise Jackson, whose brother, Dr. Sheldon Jackson introduced reindeer into Alaska. Of four daughters, three were graduates of Bryn Mawr and such was their attraction, scholastically and aesthetically, that I could not have imagined attending any other college. An unfanatical innate love of books, music, and "art," made Blake, Rembrandt, Giotto, Holbein, D. G. Rossetti and Christina Rossetti, Turner, Browning, Ruskin, Anthony Trollope, George Meredith, household companions of the family and their friends. (The Wicksteed Temple Dante was presented me by Mrs. Norcross on successive birthdays.) We were constantly discussing authors. When I entered Bryn Mawr, the College seemed to me in disappointing contrast—almost benighted. Theodore de Laguna created an appetite for philosophy and for dialectic as on occasion he took a few students walking under tall sycamores by a brook. Dr. David H. Tennent and Miss Randolph, demonstrator (almost inaudible but an expert of the scalpel) as said in my *Reader*, made biology and its toil, a pleasure and like poetry, "a quest."

M. Carey Thomas, President of Bryn Mawr at the time, had a genius for diction and unstereotyped thinking, her unintentional novelties of presentment in morning chapel were a criterion by comparison with which, the average speaker seemed labored and pathetic. Katharine E. McBride, now President of the College, is equally potent in a different way, making anything needlessly obscure, indirect or egotistical, seem old-fashioned, an educator whose atmosphere does not attract affectation. Simplicity and directness are the note.

After leaving Bryn Mawr, I came under the spell of the *English Review* edited by F. M. Ford (F. M. Hueffer) who wrote many of the book reviews— some of which I transcribed, having borrowed the copies. And *Blast*. The flavor of Wyndham Lewis meant a great deal to me: "Something in me says, 'Create, create, create. I designed a hat for Phillippone; she wears it to this day.' "

Professor Harry Levin, Irving Babbitt Professor of English at Harvard, has indelibly revised my concept of scholastic idealism, refusing remuneration for the slavish task of examining my translation of the La Fontaine Fables—Book by Book . . . saying to accept money "would make me professional and seem to know more than I do!"

Professor Henry A. Noss, Associate Professor of History at New York University, by his television lectures with occasional diagrams—has done more to enlarge my concept of history and the history of thought—of technology and of art, than any mere sentence is able to suggest.

As will have been inferred, the most important influence on my writing technically has been ethical—as my brother once said of a florid piece of description, "Starve it down and make it run." Moreover, his capacity for suffering in silence, has been an incalculable exponent of fiber. There is not a shred of sadism in his nature. My mother who first instructed us—my brother and me—in French and music (the piano) when we were very small, had a passion for books—finding gems amid the debris of book-sellers. She advantaged me more than by exciting texts, when she remarked under crushing disappointment, "Sursum corda; I will rejoice evermore."

Writer's Digest, 43 (October 1963), 35, 72.

OF BEASTS AND JEWELS

WHICH of us has not been stunned by the beauty of an animal's skin or its flexibility in motion? "Stupefied," Lucan was, he says, by Scitalis (*scitulus:* elegant) the bird-footed serpent, "winged and splendid. . . ." He mentions also "the fleet Jaculi that jump into trees and if any animal passes . . . fling themselves down and destroy it, whence they are called Jaculi, javelins." "There are in Arabia," the T. H. White *Book of Beasts* tells us, "certain snakes with wings known as Syrens that go faster than horses, their venom such that you die before you feel the pain of the bite." Also Dipsa has a poison equally fleet, so that "the face of the doomed man, even when death has already taken place, does not look sad." Having afforded us counsel, snakes—perhaps a lizard—could have an influence on what we wear. At the Villa Lante, one may be startled by a blaze of malachite green, the disguise worn by a long-tailed lizard amid ivied stones, moss and lichen— the dark filigree above its spine diminishing in width without loss of intricacy as it tapers to nothing. Van Cleef and Arpels have counterparts to the malachite lizard: a bracelet of emeralds and diamonds set in gold—its design a succession of triangles, each linked at the apex; and, finally, outer-encircled by an expert detail of narrow emeralds interrupted at short intervals by space. In it, Hiro, the photographer, has nested a live Everglades emerald snake—in size and color, it may not be irrelevant to say, identical with the all-alike snakes in Athena's necklace, knotted together, green with age, in the Museum of Antiquities in Piraeus.

Added to the mystery associated with serpents, we have, living on shore or in the water, "amphibia (*amphi:* both) such as seals, crocodiles, and hippos." The toad, not a swimmer, but dependent on moisture—moisture and shelter—is a veritable cosmos of jewels. Those of us who do not spend time in bogs, near ponds, or by streams, where water plants abound and gnats, newts and spiders hatch out, may be obliged to console ourselves with frogs and toads in replica—Verdura's frog of blistered gold, with emerald and diamond blazoned back and eyes of ruby; or an amethyst quartz

Chinese "sage and toad," or imperial embroidered bat; and may have to forgo the excitement of seeing an owl's amber and onyx eyes change with the changing light in dusky woodland ravines—too uninitiate to identify it even if we heard the "saw-whet" of the owl which uttered the cry for which it was named; unacquainted with the pale expanse under the dark spangles of the breast. We have had to become inured to the wearable derivative of the live animal, elegances of a knowing designer.

Sumptuous in a way quite other than Verdura's frog prince, is a necklace devised by Van Cleef and Arpels. Entirely of diamonds, it has the dazzle of Niagara Falls, shown against the flawless marine blue of pompano scales— encircling the "waist" of the live fish, which is accented by pale fins, like wings, tinted charcoal at the edge. Diminishing toward the clasp, the circlet is an architecture of contrasting shapes, in which uniformity is miraculously improved by the contrast of spindle-shaped marquise stones set aslant.

To the mythological world of animals, "art has contributed much confusion," combining the recognizable with the incompatible, quadrupeds with men's faces, and herbivorous tails with carnivorous bodies; to say nothing of centaurs and mermaids. Imagination hazarded as decorative: the Persian winged bull (Susa) fifth century B.C., and Assyrian winged bulls (Khorsabad) eighth century B.C.; the Minotaur of Crete. Of an elegance compatible with the gold and onyx bull-heads of antiquity, we have another contemporary necklace, now of diamonds and rubies. Harry Winston, masterly in rendering the heroic, poetic—and the massive, resilient—has been provided with the foreleg of a Black Angus bull as background for the necklace: a massive twist, like a wisteria cluster widening as it droops. Entwined with the diamonds, a double row of rubies emerges and crosses—rubies that become gigantic, then disappear before the necklace terminates with one tapered, exactly vertical diamond.

Only imagination that towers can reproduce evanescence and render rigidity flexible. Egyptian craftsmen had "hands," also animals to depict; the Renaissance had Cellini; France once had the fanatical purposefulness to produce spider-filament in platinum, and grass sparkling with dew. These craftsmen have rivals in the goldsmiths of 1963.

Harper's Bazaar, 97 (December 1963), 82–89.

MALVINA HOFFMAN

ORDERLY, handsome, encouraging—personally, domestically, professionally—Malvina Hoffman does not seem ever to need to sacrifice decency to chaos; seems indeed superior to disconcertingly disrupting digressions. Her walls or ceilings may fall; piles may burst; roof leak; she can be immobilized by coronary thrombosis, be told she most forego all manual exertion, yet produce a large bust of Thoreau and small replicas; bust of Dr. Hocking; design and execute medals involving close application—as when in the Near East making studies of racial types for the Field Museum Hall of Man, she noticed a sizable snake under her bed and—willing to favor another traveler, who might prefer a snake to a cockroach—said, "*Garçon, desservez moi de ce serpent.*"

In her house—one of two coach houses hers converted into three stories— the brass and silver shine: zebra stripes, of orange on black, mark a rise from entrance passage to studio—a room of proportions large enough to create a sense of perspective—its fireplace on one side facing on the opposite side a broad shelf extending half the length of the room, with a wall closet for tools at the end, exciting in their specialized excellence; while above that end of the studio a skylight the width of the room creates an even light for any kind of work. Her arrangements symbolize an instinct for performance; and "usefulness."

She hates malpractice, untidiness, bigotry, any proficiency that is excludingly stingy. I chanced once to deplore the fact that a reading knowledge of French, say, or German, Italian, or Spanish, is not also a speaking knowledge of the language. Miss Hoffman said, "You can learn—*study*"; and offered to share with me her Linguaphone records of Spanish to use with her, or borrow to take home.

Visiting her one summer when she had rented a house that had belonged to Mr. F. O. Matthiessen, I—as an appreciative guest—washed or dusted her car. Upon inspecting the result, she said, "You didn't do the wheels." Attempting a water color of the house, I could not get the chimney realistic. Miss Hoffman corrected my angles and after supper demonstrated for me the axiomatically interacting principles of perspective.

To-the-rescue is instinctive with her. The first involvement in rehabilitation for her when young and without resources of her own, was providing legs for a newsboy who, while clinging to the rear end of a trolley, was swung under the wheels in such a way that his legs were crushed. Knowing the surgeon of the hospital in which he was, she asked permission to see the boy, was told that he was expected to die, that no one might be admitted but his sister who was with him. She persisted and, when taken to him, said, "You will get well; don't despair. I shall have artificial legs made for you and you will earn money for your sister as you did." (He was an orphan.) Before leaving the hospital, she inquired what artificial legs might cost, and when told from three to five hundred dollars, she felt faint. Setting about earning a fund to purchase the legs, she let it be known if anyone taking her to a dance or concert thought of sending her flowers or candy, that five dollars for the fund would be preferable. One day the telephone rang and a voice said, "Miss Hoffman? You don't know who I am and no one will, but I am a customer of the Cantrell Shop—am a cripple—and am completing payment on the artificial legs you are providing the newsboy whose legs were amputated." The boy got well, wore the legs, finished his education, married, and each year at Christmas, made Miss Hoffman a visit.

Richard Hoffman, Miss Hoffman's father, was "soloist pianist" with the Philharmonic; and, pained by musicians' inability frequently to purchase an instrument for performance, Malvina Hoffman initiated a fund providing emergency aid for musicians, which she entitled The Trouble Bureau—a designation slightly embarrassing to the Fifth Avenue Bank, accustomed as it was to formality; but the name was not changed. The Music League of America was also initiated by Miss Hoffman, who stood a-tremble, she says, on the lion skin before the fireplace in Mrs. John H. Hammond's drawing room at Mount Kisco, New York, when she made a first appeal for subscriptions to establish the League; her effort resulting, need I say, in funds proffered enthusiastically.

With a passion for fundamentals—commissioned to provide the Field Museum in Chicago with a Hall of Man comprising types of racial groups throughout the world—Miss Hoffman stipulated that stone or bronze should be the materials in which the work was to be done rather than plaster as proposed. *Heads and Tails*, an account of her travels and work entailing four years in all, was a best seller; as a memoir now being edited I feel is bound to be also. *Sculpture Inside and Out*, is equally absorbing—a treatise which is required reading in college art departments—reprinted as soon as a current printing is exhausted. The specific nature of the book is irresistible—a revel for anyone with a feeling for tools and their uses, processes and reasons for them: bronze casting, treatment of iron; the lifting of the cover by the founder from the crucible in which molten bronze is being heated; the mending and finishing of a bronze; not to mention the remarkable tenacity of Riccardo Bertelli by whom the lost wax process was introduced to America—an ultrameticulous one. All this as told induces in the reader a sense of hopelessness for art if the artist does not *care;* likes to have the work done by others and would rather die than produce in marble four replicas of Houdon busts, as Miss Hoffman did when studying in Paris. It perhaps explains, also, how the instinct for mastery can make a fanatic of an artist— impel one to achieve in marble long strings of pearls like those worn by Mrs. H. E. Harriman in the portrait of her made by Malvina Hoffman; and create chain mail with every link indicated like that of the crusader in the Memorial Harvard Chapel, Cambridge.

Sculpture Inside and Out is a contribution to knowledge and to living— a conspectus of tasks not slighted—master work—primitive and later, which one hopes not to mislay. Shown in it are the animal monuments ornamenting the road to the Ming Tombs; the Chariot of the Moon (Angkor Vat); a crouching antelope from the Sudan, the horns grooved by closely adjacent horizontal incisions; Kurt Schwerdfeger's Zebra with high raised stripes and Pompon's Polar Bear in white marble. Malvina Hoffman is a specialist in animals, herself, especially elephants, one of which I have. (Ceramic.) My strongest debt, however, is to her marble heads of persons. The one of her mother, a pietà to me—accounts, if I am right, for many nobilities in those who knew her; Paderewski, 1925, incontrovertibly the person performing Chopin's great Polonaise in the Academy of Music, Philadelphia; Chopin and Schumann in Carnegie Hall, 1916; Pavlova in tinted wax dancing the Gavotte; a reproduction of which I removed, I think about 1910, from the almost prehistoric *Literary Digest* and mounted on a page of my album of "good art." The Marquis of Reading (to be found in the Sculpture book); also "Bill Working" (kneeling) flat waist narrowed to a keystone Egyptian waist, his arms expanded like calipers to grasp a great deal of work.

Miss Hoffman studied with Rodin four years. She received first prize at the Paris Salon for her "Russian Bacchanale," danced by Pavlova and Mord-kin—small figures—a large version of which was placed in the Luxembourg Gardens, later confiscated by the Nazis, 1941. She was appointed by the American Battle Monuments Commission to make the memorial to our dead in the Vosges Mountains after the Second World War—panels carved on the façade of the building designed by William A. Delano.

Miss Hoffman's friends are a book in themselves; her furniture also (refectory, French, and early American). Besides white and gold Napoleon "N" china, she has a pheasant-and-butterfly dinner set of the variety with design on strange semi-dark Lowestoft Chinese apple green. Her gilded ivory painted French sofa is covered with old Persian brocade, woven in a bird-and-flower-cluster design on green. Among her costume rarities, a square black corded cap from Tibet of "permanent" satin should be studied—in the hand; and her Tibetan wildcat fur coverlet—deep reddish fur, light as thistledown on a turquoise satin back. She has in the drawing room an oval silver box with a portrait of Napoleon *repoussé* on the lid, and a faded kingfisher blue *oiseau-*

mécanique which trills with a delayed-at-will tempo, making live cage birds seem negligible. In a case downstairs, with some modeling tools of Rodin's, there is the metal handle of a Javanese dagger ending in a bird—its strong angled claws grasping a snake—the bird's circular white eyes staring down on the upturned circular white eyes of the snake—a very emotional object. Carved paddles from New Guinea and the Solomon Islands are arranged side by side on the wall of the room devoted to typing and business.

Miss Hoffman is in sympathy with work by Brancusi, Gargallo, Lipchitz— his parallel planes stately early mode. As you will have inferred, however, she is not sorry that Houdon, Redouté, and Leonardo da Vinci were not abstractionists; nor is wishing that Paris laundresses would stop using the iron on Convent embroidery, demanding it be drip-dry. I am told that her house in Paris is a sculptor's dream—with white sculpture against green walls twenty feet high covered with ivy and Virginia creeper. She is through and through the artist. . . . such elegance, such modesty, such intellect; such élan. It is almost too good to be true.

Texas Quarterly, 7 (Spring 1964), 104–7.

MORTON DAUWEN ZABEL (1902–1964)

MORTON DAUWEN ZABEL's death in Billings Memorial Hospital, Chicago, on April 28th, deprives American letters of a valuable critic—our first exchange professor to Brazil, editor of the first anthology of American poetry in Portuguese, editor of many other anthologies—ours and foreign work—prose and verse. An authority on Henry James, Conrad, and on contemporary poetry, he was conspicuously brilliant in his shafts of wit as a book critic among the experts who wrote for Margaret Marshall during her literary editorship of the *Nation*.

"Teacher and Critic"—the heading for *The New York Times*'s notice of Dr. Zabel's death—is probably an accurate reflection of the impression made on those of his friends who were authors, and others of literary tastes: Robert Morss Lovett, Charles Trueblood, Van Wyck Brooks, Edmund Wilson, Wallace Fowlie, Hugh Kenner, Louise Bogan, Allen Tate, Malvina Hoffman, Eileen Tone, and T. S. Eliot. He was an almost lifetime friend of Miss Harriet Monroe, of Mrs. Donald F. Bond, librarian for many years of Chicago University's Poetry Library, and of Dr. Bond, Editor of the University's review, *Modern Philology;* long a friend of Miss Geraldine Udall, *Poetry*'s remarkable Secretary during Miss Monroe's and Dr. Zabel's editing of the magazine, for whom Dr. Zabel was instrumental in securing work appropriate to her later, when the need was crucial.

Honesty and probity are faint terms for Morton Zabel's trenchant exactitude. Capacity for friendship does not even suggest his chivalry in two senses—towards individuals and to letters. In speaking with me of Chicago, T. S. Eliot has more than once alluded to Dr. Zabel's extraordinary generosity of spirit, finding it possible to show him Maurice Browne's pioneer Little Theatre in the Fine Arts Building, of special interest to him, and other literary landmarks. Many a friend will recall similar generosities; meals at the University Club, visits to the Oriental Institute, the Art Institute, and to the Field Museum's Hall of Man collection of Malvina Hoffman's racial types, her study of typical specimens throughout the world. Upon one occasion, Morton Zabel was determined to find for me a scare-devil from the Nicobar Islands which I had seen formerly on an upper floor—tenaciously pursued till found by him in a miscellaneous collection in the basement of the Museum, awaiting placement. He was of extraordinary fortitude without self-emphasis or self-pity. On becoming aware of his sister's recurrent brain-tumors, which were to lead to her death, one could not forget his anxious daily visits to the hospital month upon month, consultations with specialists affording no hope, traveling from hospital to classroom—lecturing and examinations of candidates for degrees. One contemplates such ordeals with reverence.

Literary chivalries were commensurate. Having written at length an article summarizing Miss Monroe's career and achievements upon her retirement from the editorship of *Poetry*, Dr. Zabel hesitated to attempt a second conspectus after her death in South America; but since no one was so well equipped as he to do it, he wrote again: H. M.: IN MEMORY 1860–1936, an appreciation and résumé of her life—fourteen pages which appeared in the January issue of *Poetry*, 1961.

Requested to undertake a biography of Ruth Draper, he was reluctant to assume so difficultly delicate a task, but a sense of indebtedness to her gifts, nobility, and self-discipline overcame hesitation and, after exigent consultations with dramatic initiates and her friends, and others, he assembled what he felt was close to the facts yet an unintrusively reticent appreciation of her life and work. Then, "encountering what had been an extreme perplexity and distraction from the beginning by reason of hesitatings about the book and changes of feeling upon the part of her family," he was obliged, he felt, to "revise, rework, outline and recast endlessly" under stress which brought him to the verge of illness. "Persisting against fatigue," he rewrote the book. Self-discipline resulted in what seemed to impartial judges the right thing—deplored when published, for reticence—even rudely attacked by some for superficial treatment.

What Morton Zabel said of Miss Monroe as editor of *Poetry* was true of himself. He had "to exercise the vigorous eclecticism of choice which is always more difficult to maintain than a privileged selectivity." The magazine did not, with Miss Monroe as editor or with him, "indulge in unpaid accounts, bankruptcy, and aesthetic martyrdom." Devotion, patience, and unflagging kindness marked his attitude to contributors. "No resentments, grievances, arguments." His Notes in fine print which concluded issues of *Poetry*, summarizing items of current interest, constitute an index to poetry of that period. This initiate contribution on Morton Zabel's part is like his knowledge of and performance of music. A pupil of Leschetizsky in earlier years, he was ever finding with intense interest whatever good music was performed in Chicago. His fortitude and largeness of attitude have few counterparts. He was a person of high chivalry—a very great gentleman.

New York Review of Books, 2 (11 June 1964), 16–17.

ON WALLACE STEVENS

WALLACE STEVENS was a consummate refutation of the impression that life must be frantic. He was a lawyer, born in Reading, Pennsylvania, October 2, 1879, entered Harvard when eighteen and was a graduate of The New York Law School. In 1934, he became Vice-President of the Accident and Indemnity Company of Hartford, having been associated with the company while in New York previous to 1916, the year in which he moved to Hartford. He died August 2, 1955. He was in magnificent contrast with the two Dromios in *The Comedy of Errors*—"They must be bound and laid in some dark room." He was equipoise itself, although he could be displeased—in fact, angered by an imposter. People have a way of saying, "I don't understand poetry. What does this mean?" The query does not seem to me contemptible. However, Wallace Stevens did not digress to provide exegeses for bewildered readers. It should be known, I think, that fees which he received for lectures and readings, he gave anonymously to young poets whose ability and sincerity impressed him, or young magazines with a spirit he liked. He did not mix poetry with business. The more you feel a thing, he felt, the less excuse there is for being irresponsible. Phrases sometimes came to him on his way to the office in a taxi, he said, but you may be sure that "Frogs eat butterflies, snakes eat frogs" was not written in the office. Regarding "the sense of tragedy hanging over the world," he said, "What the poet has, is not a solution but some defense against it" (p. 697, *Lives of the Poets* by Louis Untermeyer). "My final point," he says in his book, *The Necessary Angel*, "is that imagination is the power that enables us to perceive the normal in the abnormal, the opposite of chaos in chaos."

Quoting "order is mastery" from the poem, "The Idea of Order at Key West," I have a picture in my mind of the office and desk of Wallace Stevens at the Hartford Accident and Indemnity Company. On my way home from New England one time, I had an errand at Trinity College—to save an English Department student the trouble of coming to Brooklyn to ask questions about a paper involving a degree. My brother that day was to take me to meet relatives, and finding me with half an hour to spare, said, "If you have shopping to do, there is a good store nearby; or is there anything else you might like to do?" I hesitated, then said, "I'd like to call on Wallace Stevens, but have no appointment." My brother said, "Here's a nickel; call him up." I said, "With Wallace Stevens, you aren't haphazard . . ." and deliberated. "He is formal." My brother stepped into a telephone-booth, saying, "*I'll* call him up." The door of the booth was open and I heard him say, "Have you had lunch, Mr. Stevens?" He came out. "What did he say?" I asked. "Said 'Come right over.' " The building where we were expected stood on a grassy eminence and has eleven or twelve white marble columns along the facade. (Mr. Stevens' offices previously had been at 125 Trumbull Avenue; he occupied the office where we saw him after 1921, the year in which the building was finished.) We were escorted down a wide corridor to his door which was open. His desk, of mahogany or other dark polished wood, had nothing on it—no pen stabbed into a marble slab at an angle. It faced two armchairs. The shade was half down, of a rather wide window. It was summer. Opening a drawer presently, Mr. Stevens brought out a post-card, a Paul Klee reproduction from Laura Sweeney (Mrs. James Sweeney) explaining that she was in Paris, said, "Such a pleasure she always is, don't you think?" and after other comment, when we said we must go, Mr. Stevens said, "Since this is your first visit, let me show you the building." We crossed the corridor and through a short connecting one, entering a large room with many windows, its desks not too near together and not too small. As we passed the many desks, each of the persons working on papers or at a typewriter looked up at Mr. Stevens with a pleased smile, reminding me of a visitor to a writing-conference I had attended who said when Hartford insurance was mentioned, "They aren't bothered with strikes there; the girls at the Hartford have it nice," and explained that she had a friend, a clerk in the Hartford Indemnity and Accident Company. We left by a door opposite the one by which we had entered, descended a few stone steps to a row of tall green arbor vitae at right angles to a drive. I said we had not wished to interrupt at a bad moment—that I owed the visit to my brother's initiative. Mr. Stevens said to him, "If you let me know when you are going to be here again, I'd like to take you for lunch to the Canoe Club, and to the house."

I first met Wallace Stevens in 1943 at Mount Holyoke where my mother and I were attending the Entretien de Pontigny, presided over by Professor Gustave Cohen, the medievalist. Mr. Stevens—sitting at a table under a tree—gave a lecture, "The Figure of the Youth as a Virile Poet" (included later in *The Necessary Angel*) about imagination, and spoke of Coleridge dancing on the deck of a Hamburg packet, dressed all in black, in large shoes and worsted stockings. Mr. and Mrs. Henry Church had brought Mr. Stevens in their car from the Lord Jeffrey Inn at Amherst at which all three had been staying. At luncheon, to which participants in the Conference were invited by the College, a moment of silence made conspicuous, this question—asked by a feminine aesthete: "Mr. Stevens, what do you think of the 'Four Quartets?' " The answer was quick; "I've read them of course, but I have to keep away from Eliot or I wouldn't have any individuality of my own"—an answer which in its scientific unevasiveness seemed a virtual self-portrait.

Henry Church was a *littérateur* whom Wallace Stevens liked—perhaps his favorite. He had inaugurated in Paris the magazine *Mésures*, to which Mr. Stevens and others of us contributed. He died in 1947. Some years later, Mrs. Church invited Mr. Stevens, Marcel Duchamp, Bernard Dubuffet, and me to luncheon. Anecdotes were mentioned which were considered amusing—one, about goats, which Mr. Stevens had told previously, and he was asked to tell it again. He shook his head—insistently begged to tell it—and said, "Do; I'd like to hear it." He said with almost intimidating emphasis, "You need not look at me with eyes of entreaty. I shall *not* tell it." "Order is mastery"—his own words; also, perceptiveness heightened, might describe him. *The Times Literary Supplement* (in London) complains that poets today lack maturity—adding that maturity includes, "governance of the emotions." You might say, I think, that Wallace Stevens was characterized by impassioned perceptiveness and governance of the emotions.

One other recollection, permissible perhaps because not induced—as descriptive of Mr. Stevens' diction. When I was leaving a reception given by Mrs. Church, Mr. Stevens detained me for a moment to inquire for my brother, adding, "Your brother is an ornament to civilization." Why? perhaps because my brother had suspected that it might be time to go, after having only recently come? Or had Mr. Stevens found visitors too self-determined to preface a visit by considerately inquiring, "Have you had lunch?"

Musically, "Wallace Stevens is America's chief conjuror" I felt, and said so long ago, in a book review[1] "as bold a virtuoso, with as cunning a rhetoric as we have produced." His "Bantam in Pine Woods" is the best example of alliteration that I know—the "inchling bristling" under pines, Mr. Stevens calls the bantam, to whom he says,

> Chieftain Iffucan of Azcan in caftan
> Of tan with henna Hackles, halt!

The bantam with henna hackles is standing on henna-red pine needles. Pictorially, we have in Wallace Stevens an opulence of jungle beauty, arctic beauty, marine beauty, hothouse beauty; and natural beauty. His "Domination of Black" depicts hemlocks "in which the sun can only fumble," that have the majesty of peacocks. He admired the blue-green of pines, could be called "the spokesman for pines," his own phrase. He brings alive "the green vine angering for life, meet for the eye of the young alligator." In 1935 he said in a Note on Poetry—in the Benét-Pearson *Anthology of American Poetry:*

> My intention in poetry is . . . to reach and express that which, without any particular definition . . . everyone recognizes to be poetry. And because I feel the need for doing it. I am rather inclined to disregard form. . . . The essential thing in form is to be free in whatever form is used. A free form does not assure freedom. . . . So that it comes to this, I suppose, that I believe in freedom regardless of form.

In "The Idea of Order at Key West," one has a clue to how poetic imagination works. Man "becomes an introspective voyager" for whom

> The lights on the fishing-boats at anchor there,
> As the night descended, tilting in the air,
> Mastered the night and portioned out the sea.

He cries,

> Oh! Blessed rage for order, pale Ramon.
> The maker's rage to order words of the sea, . . .
> And of ourselves and of our origins,
> In ghostlier demarcations, keener sounds.

He becomes a musician capable

> Of one vast, subjugating final tone,
> Polyphony beyond the baton's thrust.

Imagination is the musician, playing "what is beyond us, yet ourselves."

> They said, "You have a blue guitar,
> You do not play things as they are."

> The man replied, "Things as they are
> Are changed upon the blue guitar."

> And they said then, "But play you must,
> A tune beyond us, yet ourselves,

> A tune upon the blue guitar
> Of things exactly as they are."

Ourselves and yet beyond the baton's thrust. "The subject matter of poetry is life," as Wallace Stevens says. "The power of poetry leaves its mark on whatever it touches, unites the most disparate things, unites them all in its recognizable virtue" . . . "using the familiar to produce the unfamiliar," and thereby "helps people to lead their lives."

[1] See *Literary Opinion in America* by Morton Dauwen Zabel (Harper).

New York Review of Books, 2 (25 June 1964), 5–6.

THE POETRY OF ROBERT FROST

THIS study of Robert Frost was undertaken by Professor Brower "to bring out constellations of intentions" from the poems as stars. "He shows better than any critic has previously shown," Lawrence Thompson says, "just how intimately Frost's poems talk back and forth."

Recurrent emphasis is laid on Robert Frost "as one of the renewers of

Review of *The Poetry of Robert Frost: Constellations of Intention*, by Reuben A. Brower (Oxford University Press).

the speaking voice" and on the fact that his speech is not rustic speech. Professor Brower is careful to show that Robert Frost—" 'in favor of basing imagination and judgment on a knowledge of country things' "—"found in country knowledge" "intellectual sophistication," his main achievement being "a new blank-verse rhythm, [which] is hardly separable from his gift for drama and his wise insight into the human condition." Robert Frost's "commitment to oppositions" is made emphatic, his "temperamental bias seen in his love of irony and 'doubleness' " producing metaphors which in having two meanings at once, are puns. " 'The philosopher values himself on the inconsistencies he can contain by main force,' " he said. " 'They are two ends of a strut that keeps his mind from collapsing' ": this statement (in his introduction to Sarah Cleghorn's *Threescore*) affording a clue to his dramatic form, Professor Brower notes.

West-Running Brook, Mr. Brower feels (chap. viii), "best shows Frost 'all together' "—in its climatic opposites, "the '[white was] . . . flung backward,' riding 'the black forever' " as "the perpetual acting out of contrariety," the wave running "counter to itself," " 'The tribute of the current to the source.' " Of the swiftness of the current, Mr. Frost says in "The Master Speed":

> And you were given this swiftness, not for haste,
> Nor chiefly that you may go where you will,
> But in the rush of everything to waste,
> That you may have the power of standing still—

a "poem of faith . . . in mind and character," Mr. Brower calls it, "of firmness in the face of terror." We have an instance of this firmness in the official journey Robert Frost made to confer with Premier Khrushchev—accompanied by Secretary Udall, Mr. Frederick Adams, Director of the Morgan Library, and as friend and interpreter, Dr. F. D. Reeve, professor of Russian literature at Wesleyan University. Mr. Frost—overtaxed by a sense of the "responsibility of shaping the forces of power in the world"—was "suddenly extremely nervous," Mr. Reeve says in his account of the meeting (*Atlantic Monthly*, Sept. 1963): "Frost felt worse, he lay down. . . . [He] kept saying he couldn't go any farther," then rallied and proved able to do what he came for. He said to Premier Khrushchev that "the top thing a government could bestow was character"—that we are committed to "rivalry in sports, science, art, democracy" but we must "cease all pettiness, must be grand." He said "nobility of performance" was obligatory, and the Premier agreed.

Professor Brower is both formidable and persuasive; but I think he labors somewhat Robert Frost's resistance to being thought "religious." A "sober preference for not knowing too much" was basic in him but did he not affirm the only wholesome thing? "The strong are saying nothing till they see." Does not an evident sense of obstruction repeatedly, in alluding to what we cannot see, look like *Dominus Illuminatio Mea?* He resented meanings read into a thing, and very strongly. When "Stopping by Woods on a Snowy Evening" was overinterpreted to imply a thought of death, he said it was not about death. "If it had been about death, I would have said so." And when in Russia his reading of "Mending Wall" was "stretched [by an Associated Press reporter] into commentary on Berlin," he did not like it. One other query. I can not easily fit "A Masque of Reason" for which Mr. Brower finds an excuse—a parody on the Book of Job—into my Frost Unclassic Classics. Sympathizing with an experiment, we yet need not venerate the result. The serpent swallowing its tail in the "Masque" is an appropriate symbol of eternity. Still, Job—one does not parody the Book of Job.

For Professor Brower, nothing concerning poetic practice as bearing on Robert Frost is too much trouble to take into account; and writers considering possible influences on Robert Frost's work of poets who preceded him cannot overlook these Constellations of Intention. We are shown the importance for him of Wordsworth, Thoreau, William James, Arnold, Virgil, Catullus, and others; how he differed from Wordsworth in flexibility, constantly varying his rhyme scheme, and how in his attitude to the contemporary, he was philosophically deeper than Wordsworth. *North of Boston,* for instance, Professor Brower says—in a review of Robert Frost's letters to Louis Untermeyer—"is a book of people, not of poor people." Robert Frost was modern, not rustic. He followed with interest Thoreau's observation of nature; and the significant statement by Thoreau, " 'A true account of the actual is the rarest poetry,' " seems constantly borne out by him, as when he says of desolation,

> Now the chimney was all of the farm that stood
> Like a pistil when the petals fall.

He found "form and vision," Professor Brower says, in Emerson, who "left a mark on Frost's poetry" and "in 'The American Scholar' " came "close to writing the new poetry in prose." One of Professor Brower's strengths is his enriching of statement by his vividly enticing manner of quoting, reviving Emerson's contagion in his liking for "wild geese" and their "honking" when "flying by night," "the thin note of the companionable titmouse," "turpentine exuding from the tree," the realistic sigh of the book-deterred man of letters:

"How willingly we would . . . suffer nature to entrance us, and quit our life of solemn trifles"; the "trees begin to persuade us to live with them."

Professor Brower says of William James not that he influenced Robert Frost but that they moved "in the same intellectual climate"—James expressing a thought common to both when he said: "Salvation comes . . . only from the 'intrinsic promises and potencies' of 'the flux.'"

The "huckleberries and junipers" "pecker-fretted apple trees" aspect of Robert Frost endears him to us, the straight order of words, the "rhymes" falling "as if unplanned and without violence," in keeping with his saying that, of his poems, "The Mountain" is one of the "most perfect in form":

> And there I met a man who moved so slow
> With white-faced oxen in a heavy cart,
> It seemed no harm to stop him altogether.

Is not "Time Out," also, about another mountain, so similar in feeling as to be its twin?

> The mountain he was climbing had the slant
> As of a book held up before his eyes
> (And was a text albeit done in plant).

The mountain seems a prototype of the man himself—of "one acquainted with the night," of a piece with granite virility and Vermont ruggedness, of strength to surmount defeat by submitting to defeat; of one able to " 'take the spear-point' of tragedy 'in both hands to his breast,' " who yet raised naturalness to an art and could say of poetic achievement, "It begins in delight, inclines to impulse, and ends in a clarification of life."

Modern Philology, 62 (August 1964), 88–90.

POETRY AND CRITICISM

D o you see your work as having essentially changed in character or style since you began?

No; except that rhythm was my prime objective. If I succeeded in embodying a rhythm that preoccupied me, I was satisfied.

Uniform line-length seemed to me essential as accrediting the satisfactory model stanza and I sometimes ended a line with a hyphen, expecting the reader to maintain the line unbroken (disregarding the hyphen). I have found readers misled by the hyphen, mistaking it as an arcane form of emphasis, so I seldom use it today.

I am today much more aware of the world's dilemma. People's effect on other people results, it seems to me, in an enforced sense of responsibility— a compulsory obligation to participate in others' problems.

I s there, has there been, was there ever, a "revolution" in poetry, or is all that a matter of a few tricks? What is the relation of your work to this question: otherwise put, do you respond to such notions as The New Poetry, an American language distinct from English, the Collapse of Prosody, No Thoughts but in Things, The Battle between Academics and—What? (Others a fair field of corpses)?

The individuality and emotions of the writer should transcend modes. I recall feeling over-solitary occasionally (say in 1912)—in reflecting no "influences"; not to be able to be called an "Imagist"—but determined to put emphasis on what mattered most to me, a manner natural to me. I like end-stopped lines and depend on rhyme; but my rhymes are often hidden, and in being inconspicuous, escape detection. When beginning to write verse, I regarded flowing continuity as indispensable.

A Jellyfish

Visible, invisible,
  a fluctuating charm
an amber-tinctured amethyst
  inhabits it, your arm
approaches and it opens
  and it closes; you had meant
to catch it and it quivers;
  you abandon your intent.

Then when I came on Charles Sorley's "The Idea" (probably in *The Egoist*, London)—

It was all my own;
  I have guarded it well from
the winds that have blown
  too bitterly . . .—

I recognized the unaccented syllable (the light rhyme) as meant for me: as in "The Jerboa":

> . . . one would not be he
> who has nothing but plenty.
> . . . .
> closed upper paws seeming one with the fur
> in its flight from danger.

Having written the last stanza first, I had to duplicate it, progressing backward.

> Its leaps should be set
> to the flageolet;
> pillar body erect
> on a three-cornered smooth-working Chippendale
>   claw—propped on hind legs, and tail as third toe,
>   between leaps to its burrow.

In *Occasionem Cognosce*, the light rhyme is upside down:

> "Atlas"
> (pressed glass)
>
> looks best
> embossed.

Poetry is a magic of pauses, as a dog-valentine contrasting *pawses* and *pauses*—sent to me from Harvard where I had been discussing pauses—reminded me. I do not know what syllabic verse is. I find no appropriate application for it.

Might I say of the light rhyme, that T. S. Eliot's phrase in his Introduction to my *Selected Poems*, "the greatest living master of the light rhyme"—suggesting conscious proficiency or at most a regulatory art on my part—hardly deserves the term. Conscious writing can be the death of poetry. For me, what W. H. Auden says in the Preface to his *Collected Shorter Poems* is true: "In the eyes of every author, I fancy, his own past work falls into four classes. First, the pure rubbish which he regrets ever having conceived; second—for him the most painful—the good ideas which his incompetence or impatience prevented from coming to much (*The Orators* seems to me such a case of the fair notion fatally injured); third, the pieces he has nothing against except their lack of importance; these must inevitably form the bulk of any collection since, were he to limit to the fourth class alone, to those poems for which he is honestly grateful, his volume would be too depressingly slim." The slim seldom pieces are like a Gravenstein of the Hesperides, certainly, or a Sir Philip Sidney "medicine of cherries."

I should like to exonerate Mr. Auden of having selected me as a suitable translator of the La Fontaine *Fables*. Chivalry seems to have deterred him from flatly denying that he recommended me. He did approve, as advisor to a publisher, a retranslation of the La Fontaine *Fables* and perhaps under extortion, to name a specific translator, may tentatively have named me. Never have axioms seemed to me to have a more ever-current life than the morals of La Fontaine; and of all the lessons taught, the most valuable for me has been this one with wide application—from *The Rabbits:*

> When fables allure
> Rest assured that they are short.

"Strangeness is a quality," Howard Nemerov says, "belonging inseparably to language and vision" and—quoting Conrad, " 'It is above all, in the first place, to make you see,' said Joseph Conrad, of the object of art; and he said again, more formally, that the writer's object is 'to render the highest kind of justice to the visible world.' Seeing, and saying;—language is a special extension of the power of seeing, inasmuch as it can make visible not only the already visible world, but through it the invisible world of relations and affinities." The world of the soul? Difficult as it is to define the soul, "creativeness" is perhaps as near a definition as we can get. I recall the statement made in a sermon by Mr. Stanley Taylor, Co-ordinator of Inter-Urban Affairs of Protestant Churches in the Presbytery of Brooklyn-Nassau.

To sum up: poetry is not a thing of tunes, but of heightened consciousness—as in these lines, say, about the sea by Eric Schroeder:

> Element IV
> . . . .
> Haste waste and Haste the horror of the sea
> Downfall and trampling and swift yeasty reach,
> retreat, hoar tyranny-rearing dream, height, curling
> toppling, to another Hopeless Hurling
> Crashing and crawling
> *warning*
> the froth scuds
> the sky spatters
> the spume flies

And a bird comes downwind, rocking down the wind,
struggles, recovers, and sails and away goes
    wavering down the wind and away[1]

Is not Professor I. A. Richards always "new," as in this "Alpine Sketch":[2]

Swift flows the race,
Old Overshot wheels glittering o'er;
With no ill grace
The log draws through the saw;

his "Not No" being electric with spontaneity:

Ha, Skater on the Brink
        Come whence
            Where go?
Anywhere
    Elsewhere
        Where I would not know
Not mine, not mine, all this lived through in me.
Who asks? Who answers? What ventriloquy!

George Herbert's untampered-with-by-vanity "Heaven's Echo" also eludes vanity:

O who will show me those delights on high? *I.*
Thou, echo, thou art mortal, all men know. *No.*
Then tell me what is that supreme delight? *Light.*
Light to the mind: what shall the will enjoy? *Joy.*
But are there cares and business with the Pleasure? *Leisure.*
Light, joy and leisure; but shall they persever? *Ever.*

Lastly, John Bunyan's pre-statement about *The Pilgrim's Progress* provides us with manner-without-manner's true model:

I did not think
To show the world my pen and ink.
Nor did I undertake
Thereby to please my neighbor; no, not I
I did it mine own self to gratifie.

"Perhaps the last English book written without thought of a review," T. B. Fowler[3] says; "even of a possible reader," Bunyan said, himself. "Over

100,000 copies were sold in his lifetime. Between 1678 and 1778, thirty-three editions of Part One and fifty-nine editions of Parts One and Two together. Then the publisher stopped counting."

The Elegy for Mr. Valiant-for-truth

When Mr. Valiant "had this for a token that the summons was true, . . . that his pitcher was broken at the fountain, . . . Then said he, . . . 'though with great difficulty I have got hither, yet now I do not repent me of all the trouble I have been at to arrive where I am. My sword I give him that shall succeed me in my pilgrimage, and my courage and skill to him that can get it. My marks and scars I carry with me, to be a witness for me that I have fought His battles who now will be my rewarder.' . . . When the day that he must go hence was come, many accompanied him to the river-side, into which, as he went, he said, 'Death where is thy sting?' And as he went down deeper, he said, 'Grave, where is thy victory?' So he passed over, and all the trumpets sounded on the other side."

In the phrases of creativeness presented, we have maximum impact, it seems to me, unblurred and innate.

I see no revolution in the springs of what results in "poetry." No revolution in creativeness. Irrepressible emotion, joy, grief, desperation, triumph—inward forces which resulted in the Book of Job, Dante (the *Vita Nuova*, *Inferno*), Chaucer, Shakespeare—are the same forces which result in poetry today. "Endless curiosity, observation, research, and a great amount of joy in the thing," George Grosz, the caricaturist said, explained his art. These account for many other forms of art, I would say.

One's manner of objectifying feelings has many variants, of course. Governance of the emotions and impassioned perceptiveness seem to me "the artist." Thoreau said, "a true account of action is the rarest poetry." Flaubert's "Describe a tree so no other tree could be mistaken for it" is basic—exemplified by Leonardo da Vinci in his every sketch. Mannerism and pedantry have no place in art. Ezra Pound excludes much trivia when he says, "Use no word that under stress of emotion you could not actually say."

I do not make a distinction between the American and the English language.

I find that we become more and more concise—take for granted more and more as not needing to be explained.

DOES the question whether the world has changed during this century preoccupy you in poetry? Does your work appear to envision the appearance of a new human nature, for better or worse, or does it view the many and obvious changes as technological?

It preoccupies me, not as timely topics but fundamentally and continuously. Every day it is borne in on us that we need rigor,—better governance of the emotions. We behave like the companions of Ulysses who, "thinking that license emancipates one, were slaves whom they themselves had bound"; like the rout in *The Green Pastures*—like the people of Sodom, causing God to repent of having created man and to consider destroying mankind so that the angel Gabriel says, "Do dat Lawd, and start a new animal."

I think I see the beginning of a common understanding—some sincerity about "Justice for all."

Considering "the bomb," General Eisenhower and David Lilienthal remind us that "anxiety and imminent danger have been man's constant companions in many periods of history." As Adolf Berle says—"Let us all go to work in the little and in the greater affairs with which we have contact, putting potential danger out of the mind . . . dealing with situations which are within our grasp."

W H A T is the proper function of criticism? Is there a species you admire (are able to get along with)?

Criticism should stimulate an improved understanding of the subject discussed—"with a truce to politeness," as Montaigne says; unmannered and "without the pestilent filth of ambition."

Certain reviews of my work have been indispensable to me, not only in correcting uninitiate errors and affording information, but as models of writing. Dr. Johnson's critical observations and didacticisms throw light, or stimulate resistance. Emerson's "Representative Men," fearless in appraisal and comparisons, aid one in being affirmative yet not invariably encomiastic. Sir Kenneth Clark seems to me the ideal expositor—enabled to speak extempore safely because of knowledge that is objective.

There is an integrity of performance.

In his careful reasoning, Kenneth Burke demonstrates that it is well to take time if one wants results, lending emphasis to the axiom by noting that what to some authors are difficulties, the artist welcomes as opportunities.

Ford Madox Ford's book reviews in the *English Review* (1908–1912) were of inestimable value to me, as method. Wyndham Lewis in *Blast*, by his "heat" (massive energy) and skill, was instructive.

Criticism should animate the imagination, afford comparisons one had not thought of, should be affirmative with unequivocal gusto, like that of Ezra Pound in *The Spirit of Romance*.

[1] *Visions of Elements and Other Poems* (Freeport, Maine: The Bond Wheelwright Company).

² *Goodbye Earth and Other Poems* (Harcourt, Brace & Company).
³ *The English-Speaking World*, August, 1938.

Voice of America Poetry Series, published as *Poetry and Criticism: Response to Questions Posed by Howard Nemerov*. Cambridge, Mass.: Adams House and Lowell House Printers, 1965.

JEAN DE LA FONTAINE

LA FONTAINE, JEAN DE, 1621–95, French poet, born at Château-Thierry, eldest child of Françoise Pidoux and Charles de La Fontaine, a game and forest ranger. In the grammar school at Reims La Fontaine evidently studied enough Latin to read it easily and learned some Greek. In May, 1641, he entered the Oratory, and in October of that same year he entered Saint-Magloire; but in preparing for the priesthood he decided he had mistaken his vocation and turned for a time to the study of law. About 1646 he met François Maucroix (later abbé of Reims), his closest friend throughout life. In 1647 his father arranged his marriage to Marie Héricart, a pleasing girl of 16, and a son was born in 1653. Later La Fontaine and his wife separated, Marie's dowry reverting to her. Through her uncle, Jacques Jannart, La Fontaine was introduced to Fouquet, superintendent of the treasury, who provided him with 1,000 livres quarterly and residence in the Château. In honor of Fouquet, La Fontaine produced verse—in particular, *Le Songe de Vaux*, which described a tapestry, buried jewels, and the gardens of the château in imagined splendor of growth and told an animal story, a forerunner of fables to come. Fouquet, having incurred the king's displeasure, was sent to Limoges, accompanied by La Fontaine, who wrote letters to his wife that were full of detail and charm and were also considered important as literature (*Voyage en Limoges*).

The group of friends who made famous la Rue de Vieux Colombier—Racine, Boileau, Molière, and La Fontaine—was formed about 1664. The Stories (*Contes*) by La Fontaine were published beginning in 1664. Of *Adonis*, which appeared in 1669 and was much changed from Ovid's hunting piece, Paul Valéry says, "In its erudite, initiate lyric ingenuities, it is the height of art." The subjects, nearly all of which dealt with illicit love, were considered indecorous, but La Fontaine vigorously defended himself, saying that he had revived what was "earthy and racy," too light to be harmful.

La Fontaine was first attracted to verse, it is said, by Malherbe's poems, which were shown him by a soldier. The perfect storyteller, he holds the attention by his art of understatement, heightened by innuendo and subtle modesty. His first six books of fables came out in 1668; the next books appeared in 1671. These were derived mainly from Nevelet's *Mythologica Aesopica* and were the first fables written in verse with dialogue. The verse met with opposition from Lamartine, and although by 1682 La Fontaine was an appropriate candidate for election to the Académie, the king preferred Boileau. There were 16 votes for La Fontaine against 7 for Boileau, but the election was waived. Another vacancy occurring, he was elected to the Académie in 1684. His initiation presentation was a Discours à Madame de La Sablière (not to be confused with the last fable in Book IX), in which he praised her intuition, expressing gratitude for her discerning the "needs of his heart." Upon Fouquet's loss of royal favor, the duchess of Bouillon and d'Orléans (Mazarin's youngest niece) had invited La Fontaine to live in the Luxembourg palace with provision for meals and the title of equerry (*écuyer*). It was a happy time for him, but the duchess died in 1672. He found a rescuer in Madame de La Sablière. During a serious illness in 1692 he grew devout and, as a result of conversations with l'abbé Pouget, refused revenues from the *Contes*. Upon Madame de La Sablière's death in 1693, he devoted himself to religious works until he died on April 13, 1695.

La Fontaine alone represents independence from the formal rules for writing poetry that were widely accepted in the seventeenth century. Like the music of the lute that he loved and the airs he played on his harpsichord, his rhymes, in short lines, coming dazzlingly close together, reveal endless gusto. "His dexterity is not in the length of his lines," Professor Wadsworth says, "but in the grouping of dissimilar stanza forms, in run-on lines or unexpected pauses." His defiance is his glory, as when he sometimes uses a light rhyme at the end of a line despite Boileau's rules of versification, which insist that for an accented end rhyme, the matching rhyme must also be accented.

To La Fontaine animals are vehicles for his philosophy, not studies in natural history. He disliked pomposity, pride, "pushing persons," pedantry, avarice, greed, injustice. His "Animals Sick of the Plague" are a lethal indictment of the abuse of power. Most of all he hated war, and in 1689 he wrote a long letter to Prince de Conti, who was then at war, deploring love of military glory, "as though life were nothing" and "glory existed as a thing in itself." Deploring controversy as interfering with serenity, he called himself lazy and a daydreamer; whereas in fact his decorum in complicatedly intricate stanzas that could have been attained only by assiduous perseverance, his gifts of narration and satire even at his own expense, make him one of the best loved persons in literature.

BIBLIOGRAPHY: La Fontaine, *Fables; Conte et Nouvelles* (Bibliothèque de la Pléiade, 1959); *Selected Works of La Fontaine* (in French, ed. Philip A. Wadsworth, 1950); *The Fables of La Fontaine* (tr. by Marianne Moore, 1954; amended 1964 Compass Books, Viking Inc. Press); Monica Sutherland, *La Fontaine* (1953).

In *American People's Encyclopedia.* New York: Grolier, 1965. pp. 216–17.

DRESS AND KINDRED SUBJECTS

THE *Women's Wear Daily* series of interviews entitled, "It's Right To Be Proper" is admired first aid to those of us who deplore digressions from dignity in behavior and dress. It recalls Ruskin's statement that beauty of behavior is the finest of the fine arts; also, that in Venice—in accordance with "a tradition of noble behavior, in defense of children"—an ordinance, precipitated by an invasion of tourists wearing slacks, "forbids the citizen to wear dress too strangely shaped or scant."

"Solid values in dress" imply dignity and materials in keeping with it. Fashion may be at the mercy of whim. Style is basic and does not change with the year. For each person there is a skirt length that looks right; an area of bare neck that is not exhibitionist. Most women's leg-below-the-knee looks better than the leg-above-the-knee as currently on display in the subway.

Ease with naturalness is essential to style; accordingly the new skintight men's shirt looks restrictive, as if cut to save material. One should almost be able to reverse back and front of anything but a jacket; as the French and some Italians cut a shoe that fits either foot. Excessively high heels permit the foot to wobble—vary as balance does, with the individual arch. In any case, slightly higher than baby French heels are more elegant than six-inch vertical pipestems. Sandals require a thin White Rock fairy to wear them. Dog harness thongs are a subterfuge and look like knots in a string that has slipped from the package. Whatever the cut, width, or foot, the wearer should be able to step with assurance—as Dante says, like a crane— "come una crana." The military cape is the most graceful wrap we have— with Chinese straight-up collar.

Evening dress is a large subject, whether of wool, velvet or silk. For morning, afternoon or evening, one need not be intimidated by what someone "requires," but be guided by what feels right. I do not see the logic of removing half the bodice and all of the sleeves for a state occasion. The bodice should not be in imminent danger of slipping off the shoulder, and if a wide expanse of skin is favored, there could be a tulle, marabou, lace or fur border to divert the eye from banal skin and bone. Petticoats are not obsolete. Let no one mistake a wide skirt tapering to an hourglass at the ankle for elegance.

Hats. Wide brims and big bows disguise defects but cannot actually take the place of a sunshade. The Borsalino has stamina and suggests confidence—like the Stetson, especially with brim turned back to the crown at the side, military style.

Sportswear is entertaining; I like the tailored suit better. It can have ease, when the skirt line in the back has vertical continuity with the jacket; lent ease by pleats—especially inverted pleats, and a slim sleeve that does not look as if made of linoleum. Mr. Zuckerman is our wizard of the armhole—one which is roomy but snug—a study. Giving the sleeve freedom is not achieved by making the armhole too deep.

Makeup strictly is for the stage. To repair lipstick in company is not quite like fastening a garter on the street but is in the same category. The best cosmetic is lemon juice and sour cream (or fresh). Hair should not be synonymous with a hurricane. Now that men resort unabashed to the curling iron, the best one can hope for is the natural artificial effect and the time-honored rule, "Flat on top and close at the sides."

Dress is an adjunct and should conform with behavior—as illustrated by My Fair Lady's evolution. Madame Mensendieck should not be forgotten—she demonstrated that it is possible to occupy a chair, not droop from the edge like macaroni, then rise as in completing a court curtsey. Harry Golden is right about deference; it is, except in exceptional persons, a lost art. One should not be willing to be a pest, to keep a man standing, napkin in hand, while the meal gets cold which one interrupted to speak to his companion. One who smokes should not light cigarette after cigarette despite smoke continuously carried by the draught into another's eyes.

"He that ruleth his spirit is greater than he that taketh a city," applies to conversation. One is a pleasanter companion if one does not interrupt each statement with an anecdote livelier than the one being related. Brevity is an art; the best conversationalist is the best listener.

The period I admire most in fashion is the First Empire—the high-waisted bodice and long, slightly gathered straight skirt; with formal hair arrangement, and jewelry of intricate detail with no thought of time wasted in making.

Personalities I have admired? The Empress Eugénie in close-fitting riding-hat, with long, full black ostrich-plume curling forward to the ear at the left, sitting her horse with firm ease, as erect as Queen Elizabeth II at the Trooping of the Color. I admire the exactness with which Queen Elizabeth II has crown or tiara fit her coiffure naturally so as to seem one with the head and appear symmetrical from any angle. I thought Marie Bell a marvel of dexterous stateliness in draped Greek costume as Phaedre, influencing the skirt edge away from her foot, despite her impassioned swiftness, as the prow of a ship curls over billow after billow in its advance. I recall Pavlova's compassionate ardor of motion and un-self-centered esprit in her Gavotte reproduced by Malvina Hoffman in tinted wax, wearing a shade hat, catching her drapery at the right, upward in a curve, an absolute epitome of flawless élan. Remaining with me as the enticement attracting one at all costs to the City Center Ballet, I recall Tanaquil Leclerq's ardor accenting her intentionally creating of awkwardness into elegance. I was captivated by the naturalness and regal abandon in the voluminous bright-dark satin skirt folds worn by Madame Lavoisier, the wife of the chemist, in the life-size painting of her and her husband at the Rockefeller Institute. Greta Garbo's uncompromise and intensity seem to me to impart style to whatever she does; her flexible footwear whatever else others prescribe, is my most distinctive impression of her. I admired Madame Malraux's lace half-sleeve for evening, and bodice fairly high to the throat, when she was here, her unconcessiveness to extremes seeming to me eminence personified. A dramatic dress worn by Vera Zorina—reciting Ronsard in a Pro Musica Antiqua program—also looked comfortable. A long white grosgrain under a surcoat of black velvet, the edges diverging toward the hem; the only distraction being a single large diamond suspended from the neck, by a hairfine platinum chain.

My favorite possessions? I am not a collector, merely a fortuitous one. I have a silver seated rat mouse-size—a silver scissor sugar-tongs (a stork that contained a baby originally). Have a Japanese teak mouse, Austrian turquoise velvet one, and a bird embroidery framed in black and lemon lacquer (a long-shafted topaz lalibie with freckled breast and beak curved like a curlew's). A fly of amber with gold legs and a real fly in the amber of the big one—both given me by Miss Louise Crane. Have a Dresden leopard with green eyes standing on oval green grass; a mahout on an Indian brass elephant; a Chinese gilt-brass baby pheasant with head turning to look back; a mechanical elephant with gait that precisely mimics the lumbering gait of a live elephant; a mechanical crow that hops, squawks and flaps its wings. A Japanese monkey-painting kakemono by So Sen rolled on an ivory cylinder; a Japanese very old brass box with sliding lid; a snow leopard on a jewelbox lid painted by Dan Maloney; an iron firefly bootjack with gold wings, vermilion head and long curving antennae; an Aleutian Island small round basket with lid and design of "three rats" (or beavers) each following the other. A porcupine-quill birchbark round basket with quills woven into a square on the lid; a baby adderskin sewn by Alyse Gregory on a strip of lemon and silver Chinese brocade; an oil, entitled Zoo Picture, of a lion and three apes on trapezes by Mary Meigs, and also by her, five Plymouth Rock roosters and a watercolor of spruce woods in Maine; an Egyptian pale rhinoceros-skin whip; an ivory walrus tusk from the Greeley Expedition. And I received recently a veritable "King of the Castle," an Arctic ox of walrus ivory, carved by an Esquimau, Kay Hendrickson, for Mr. John Teal, Jr. to give me.

Recreation certainly is essential; but like Edward Bok, I usually find respite from one kind of work in another—sewing, cooking, mending and housework. The theater seems to me the ideal refuge from drudgery. And, of course, reading. I saw nothing to improve, in *The Madras House* by Granville Barker, in Disraeli played by George Arliss, or in *The Grass Harp* by Truman Capote. I like best, documentaries of animals and travel; *Elephant Boy* in which Sabu was featured, and (currently) *Bold Journey*, arranged by Jack Douglas; explorers' visits to Nepal, Tibet, Ethiopia, parts of this country, with travelers' commentary. Reading is my main recreation, outdoor sports when possible, tennis, sailing; travel by sea; and car journeys. I do plenty of walking but not for recreation.

Food, as we know, comprises protein, fats, sugar, minerals and enzymes. The readiest source of protein seems to be meat, cheese, fish, fowls, eggs, milk—cows', goats', "soymilk" and, as obtainable, asses'. Some gastronomists say two eggs a day are not a mistake; some, "if you can't bear eggs, don't eat them; an egg is the most putrefactive protein in existence." Some persons of hyper-protective mentality are unwilling to live by taking the lives of other animals, and will not wear shoes, gloves, or belts of leather or sanction use of leather upholstery. Irrespective of cruelty, some shrink from the sight of raw meat. One of my ancestors would not permit the ladies of the household to lay or hang flypaper in rooms that attracted flies. They concealed the strips till he had left for the office, and before his return.

An entomophagous diet augments the supply of food for some tribes, and snacks of dried grasshoppers and other unaugust forms of life—frogs, lizards, iguanas and snakes—seem to be a current fad. In a motion picture of the South Seas, a girl is seen eating a small fish wiggling as it is eaten. Childhood environment has a deep influence on imagination, and tolerance had best enter one's attitudes to others' habits. Some restaurants revenge themselves on the gourmet by serving farina as an exotic, disguised by tinting and shaping.

I am not voracious, eat regulation food, meat, cheese, vegetables and an additive when needed—brewer's yeast, powdered alfalfa, watercress, dehydrated potato and tomato as convenient—fisheggs of all kinds, raisins, honey and anything that purports to "make powerful animals." As for spirits, loyalty to brandy and whiskey, and certain wines, in signal emergencies, subdues intolerance on my part to alcohol, but I am simultaneously addicted to what Randall Jarrell in his book, *The Lost World*, calls "clear water, cold, so cold."

What makes a good life, a balanced life? Self-reliance, tolerance, adaptiveness. Gusto. As the fable says, if you want it done, do it yourself. Life is happiest, I am sure, when it is in some sense contributory, not wholly self-centered.

Dr. S. Parkes Cadman said, "One's chance of happiness is greater if one wants to do something than if one wants to have something." Apathy is defeat at the start. Whatever you do, put all you have in it. Let little things be little things. Don't mind embarrassment; forgive yourself when you make a mistake. Superiority is at the antipodes from insight. Beware of greed; it comes in many disguises. Don't strain to get something for nothing, avid to hit the jackpot.

Do not relive desperate experiences or anticipate others. Observe this rule and half one's troubles will vanish.

Much wisdom is epitomized by Confucius. Tze-Kung—asked if there is a single principle that you could practice through life to the end—said, "Sympathy"—analogous to our "Do unto others as you would have others do unto you." Confucius said, "If there be a knife of resentment in the heart, the mind fails to act with precision."

Don't despise mystics. As Martin Buber has said, "The free man believes in destiny—it has need of you."

Women's Wear Daily, February 17, 1965, pp. 4–5.

PRINCE CHURCHILL

WINSTON SPENCER CHURCHILL was the exemplification of courage—"in all its aspects," as Mr. Edward Russell says; in an age of conformity, he was "prepared to risk his whole political future on a decision." He epitomized the root meaning of the word courage—namely "heart": that in us which can quiver, as it is that which has the power "to conquer or go down fighting." It includes a capacity for affection above embarrassment—as when at Harrow, at a most self-conscious age for most boys, he invited his childhood nurse (whom he termed years later "my best and most intimate friend") to visit him, kissed her, and guided her about on his arm among his classmates. In the speech of May 13, 1940—"I have nothing to offer but blood, toil, tears, and sweat"—tears of his own became literal as well as metaphorical. "Can I," he said, "bring back the child beneath the debris?" shedding tears; and when an elderly woman "whose house had been demolished by a bomb, presented a 'posy,' he buried his head in his arms on the table, and wept."

Courage is a composite—all-caring in its infinitude. Winston Churchill's sense of responsibility was, as Sir Robert Menzies says, "massive and unremitting." It extended to every matter, however small: Should candy be rationed? the question received minute consideration; roller-skating by boys, at hazard to older persons, was *not* to be banned; those "in charge of tree-felling operations should keep in consideration the beauty of the English countryside."

"Search resolutely for practical solutions" was advice of which he was constantly and eloquently an example. "As a concomitant of resoluteness," Sir Robert says, "he incommoded himself on a mighty scale." When made First Lord of the Admiralty, Churchill spent eight months afloat on the Admiralty yacht *Enchantress*—"meeting commodores, captains, and crews; he visited naval installations, dock yards and every important ship. At the end he knew what everything looked like, where everything was, and how things fitted into one another." He converted the fleet from coal to oil, increasing speed and mobility. Admiral von Tirpitz admitted that he could not outbuild Britain.

As a component of his courage, Winston Churchill had foresight. "Bitter, when the *Royal Oak* was sunk by a U-boat at Scapa Flow after the *Courageous* had been sunk with six hundred dead, he reeled, murmuring to his staff and to Mrs. Churchill, 'if only they had taken notice of me a few years ago, this would not have happened.' " His Dardanelles strategy—which Clement Atlee called "the most imaginative strategy of the war," and Lord Ismay said would have shortened the war by two years—failed because Churchill was not supported. Yet it was he who bore the stigma of defeat.

When Churchill was dismissed, after having been acclaimed the greatest war minister since Pitt, he said, "The change from the intense activities at the Admiralty to the narrowly measured duties of a Councillor left me gasping. . . . Like a sea beast fished up from the depths, or a diver too suddenly hoisted, my veins threatened to burst. . . . I had to watch for six hateful months the great enterprises slowly and shamefully muddled and cast away."

Stamina: recovery under injustice is for the brave. His integrity of uncompromise was such that at the outbreak of the first war, he was still battling vicious unpopularity. Following every campaign in which he participated, he wrote a book telling the government what the plan of procedure should have been. This did not endear him to crusty senior officers.

"Throughout a career punctuated by disaster that would have broken the staunchest heart," one ally never wavered—the unconquerable Clementine Churchill, "who watched over and sustained him while he sustained the tottering world." She "fought her own Battle of Britain—the battle of her husband's health." "She has a tremendous sense of normality," her biographer says; it is this gift that "has given the whirlwind that is Winston its anchorage." She did not complement his force of character—she is its counterpart, we feel. Once, campaigning for him, she said, "He considers that in politics if you have something good to give, give it, a little at a time, but if you have something bad to get rid of, give it altogether and brace the recipient to receive it." "My marriage," Winston wrote, "was much the most fortunate and joyous event which happened to me in the whole of my long life, for what can be more glorious than to be united in one's walk through life with a being incapable of one ignoble thought."

A writer, admiring the wit, the brilliance, the overwhelming might of Winston Churchill's eloquence, should recall, as well, his finding of "practical solutions"—of procedure conducing to the result: in all his writing, five versions, never less, three spaces between typed lines, "the original dictated version lost in the end beyond recognition." He knew the weight of words: when the Ministry of Food inaugurated "Communal Feeding Stations," he said, "It is an odious expression suggestive of communism and the workhouse. I suggest you call them 'British Restaurants.'"

CHURCHILL SAID

When, early in his career, he went to a specialist about his lisp: "I can't be haunted by the idea that I must avoid every word beginning with an S."

To the younger generation: "Don't be frightened. Do not despair. Keep your head. Strength will be given when it is needed. We ought not to be afraid of running risks. Since when have we learned that we are entitled to security? The only way to avoid risks is never to have lived at all. To defeat, never give in—never, never, never, never—in nothing great or small. . . ."

In a War Cabinet meeting, in response to a proposal for giving a few weeks' holiday leave to senior civil servants: "Well, I suppose since you insist, that I must agree. But I confess, I do not understand how anybody privileged to play a part in this mighty struggle can bear to be separated from his duty, for even five minutes." (This seems to me a perfect illustration of Churchill's equipoise, his persuasive elegance, under non-concurrence.)

In 1941, in defiance of Hitler: "You do your worst and we will do our best."

At the moment of England's victory: "I felt as if I had been walking with destiny. My heart was filled with joy, and horror had drifted away. . . . A brighter radiance graced the imperial crown." (It is not from dictionaries, but from emotion that words flame from which we catch fire, words such as these.)

An imagination engaged and ignited, the courage of faith, the capacity for affection, and compulsions empowered by spiritual force, do not always make assent inescapable. How account for the fire at the center of the diamond? I feel it is this, as an associate said who knew him well: "He engendered in us a sense of participation in mysteries that ordinarily we feel are for others."

Harper's Bazaar, 98 (May 1965), 130–31.

EVOLUTION OF AN ARTIST

THIS memoir is a kind of true allegory in which a Mr. Valiant like the one in Bunyan's dream, encounters beings of similar valor, with strength "to seek, to find, and not to yield," prince of the spirit—some poor and anonymous; some a-glitter with honors and insignia of achievement. "It is not by what we have but by what we love," Malvina Hoffman says, "that we are known." Her life, exceptionally varied, is centralized throughout by fidelities—to art, sculpture, painting, music; to her parents, friends and a way of life. "There never was a time," she says, "when I was not glad to work, day after day, not from a sense of duty, but to explain something"—a scientist? I recall her implication of disdain, as of helpless contamination one time, in her rigorous cleaning of a dirty easel lent her with a Maine studio.

Integrity of performance on the part of her mother, father and their ancestors, seems to foreshadow achievements of her own. The youngest of five children, Malvina Hoffman was born June 15, 1885. When her grandparents

Review of *Yesterday Is Tomorrow: A Personal History*, by Malvina Hoffman (Crown).

objected to their daughter's marrying a music teacher and "public performer" and showed no signs of relenting, Fidelia and Richard Hoffman were married in 1869 at St. John's Chapel, Varick Street, of which Mr. Hoffman was organist, and rented a house on West 43rd Street opposite what is now Town Hall. Later, the son-in-law was found to be "a devoted husband and serious artist."

Malvina Hoffman's evolution as an artist is instructive. "I was always taking toys apart," she says, "to see how they worked." Her father explained the principles that govern music—needed in the practice of any art, "construction, rhythm, balance, harmony, and hard work," explained the importance of memorizing what one had seen, showing "how they put up a roof beam and beams slanting down, made frames and poured in concrete; held a level to line up the courses of a brick wall one time," Miss Hoffman says, "and made me see if I could break a brick with a trowel." "Affection blessed our family," she says—which included Paul and Ruth Draper who lived near.

There were no violent arguments. There was always a hopeful chance that animals from the Hippodrome would be led for an airing, elephants, zebras, ponies and occasionally a giraffe, as far as West Broadway and back. "A passion kept driving me—recording in pencil or ink the anatomy of horses," she says. James G. Crowell, headmaster of the Brearley School, said of seaweed and grasses he collected, "Many look at them. You must look into and through them and make them part of yourself." Malvina watched her cousin, Herbert Hazeltine, draw. He said, "There's a lot you don't keep."

Miss Hoffman attempted a three-quarter pastel, then bust, of her father. "Gutzon Borglum gave a thunderous look" (the shoulders having begun to slip), said, "Come with me; I'll show you how to build a decent armature." Anxious about her father's health, she says, "carving became a sort of salvation by obliteration." Her father took her to a Carnegie Hall matinee to hear Paderewski for the first time. He played the Schumann Fantasia and Chopin's Ballade in G Minor. Later Emma Eames, Scotti, Caruso "cast a spell by the force and convictions of their interpretations."

Miss Hoffman started "a trouble bureau"—to aid needy artists. The elderly directors of the Fifth Avenue Bank were puzzled by the informal title but wished not to lose accounts that included checks signed by two well-known men. She then initiated a trouble bureau of her own—providing legs for a newsboy who had swung under the rear wheels of a trolley. The boy's stamina had impressed her upon reading that one of his legs had been cut off, his other one crushed and that he had said to the surgeon in charge, "Take off the rest of the left leg and make a neater job." Since the boy had no money for artificial legs, she warned close friends who were in the habit of presenting flowers or candy when inviting her to a dance or a concert, they might instead contribute $5 to "the leg fund." Somewhat later, a pale young stranger called to see Mr. Hoffman, a violinist from England, and was invited to lunch the following Sunday, charmed them all, and Gutzon Borglum asked one day, "Why don't you model a head of this young man?" Eventually, "fated for each other," it seemed, Malvina and Samuel Grimson were married.

Having earned enough to take her mother to Europe, she was stirred, at Pompeii, by the fate of the guard faithful to the last breath, buried by lava, his spear held at attention; was spellbound before Michelangelo's Pietà; delighted by the Wellcome Medical Collection in London (medical data and anatomical specimens), filling notebook after notebook with drawings.

In Paris, after five attempts, she was able to see Rodin for whom she had left a letter of introduction from Gutzon Borglum. Reminded of it, Rodin confessed that he "was not much interested in letters." Obliged to accompany five or six "deputies" to a luncheon, he left Malvina in the studio. On his return—aware of the dampness—he threw fuel on the fire, wrapped his long cape about Malvina's shoulders, advising her "to care for her health above all things." He said, "accuracy, constancy, patience, are indispensable to any real accomplishment; to the art of living"; and in connection with a plaster figure broken by chance, said "capture the accidental and transform it into science."

Of interest in connection with Voltaire, a chapter of the memoir describes a spectacular find: a part, then all of the du Chatelet harpsichord built in Antwerp; rebuilt in 1770 by Pascal Taskin, identified by the letters P. T. carved at the back of each key. The pieces when brought to New York, took Mr. Grimson 16 months to restore. On the inside of the cover, the painting corresponded with the detail of Château de Cirey which Malvina and Mr. Grimson discovered after a baffling search; the keeper of the gatehouse sharing their excitement and showing them the Voltaire wing. They entered the garden where Voltaire would retire each morning to write, under trees with trunks clothed by ivy and moss. Iturbi in New York, hearing of the restoration, wished to see the harpsichord, exclaimed it a delight, playing on it Scarlatti and a Bach fugue. It is now in the Yale Museum of Musical Instruments.

The most comprehensive project offered her, Miss Hoffman says, was the Hall of Man, in what is now the Field Museum, Chicago—studies made in Africa, Indo-China, Java, and other parts of the world. For types represented, the material was to be plaster, painted. "I completed a specimen," she says, was determined to have the figures bronze—two or three heads to be in stone or marble—Mr. Field saying in surprise, "What does this mean?" But he acquiesced. For the result of the undertaking, the Field Museum is renowned.

Miss Hoffman, while visiting the Schellings in Switzerland, mentioned that she was writing an ending for an account of her world trip. Paderewski, also a guest, said it must be a beginning, that she must concentrate each day on the book and he would read the result. The narrative became *Heads and Tails*—followed by a second book—urgently suggested by W. W. Norton: *Sculpture Inside and Out*.

Miss Hoffman was commissioned to design a facade for the William Delano memorial in the Vosges mountains at Epinal, honoring Army, Navy and Air Force. In 1964 she received the Medal of Honor of the National Sculpture Society; has made portraits (busts) of Thomas Paine, William Hocking, Thoreau, and others. Certain photographs in this book are in themselves art—the Seven Lamson sisters, Richard Hoffman at the piano, as a boy—engraved from a daguerreotype, Pavlova (The Gavotte); Miss Hoffman at Bush House 90 feet above the ground, or in the battle to live; behaves instead as if the dead had eyes; as if she had wings and carried a torch.

The New York Times Book Review, 7 November 1965, pp. 30, 32, 34.

A BURNING DESIRE TO BE EXPLICIT

ALWAYS, in whatever I wrote—prose or verse—I have had a burning desire to be explicit; beset always, however carefully I had written, by the charge of obscurity. Having entered Bryn Mawr with intensive zeal to write, I examined, for comment, the margin of a paper with which I had taken a great deal of trouble and found, "I presume you had an idea if one could find out what it is."

Again—recently! In a reading of my verse for a women's club, I included these lines from "Tell me, tell me":

> I vow, rescued tailor
> of Gloucester, I am going
> to flee: by engineering strategy—
> the viper's traffic-knot—flee
> to metaphysical newmown hay,
> honeysuckle or woods fragrance. . . .

After the program, a strikingly well-dressed member of the audience, with equally positive manner, inquired, "*What* is metaphysical newmown hay?" I said, "Oh, something like a sudden whiff of fragrance in contrast with the doggedly continuous opposition to spontaneous conversation that had gone before." "Then why don't you *say* so?" the impressive lady rejoined.

Although prepared for an "element of the riddle" in any poem, an even somewhat experienced person is not irked by clues to meaning. Attempting to provide a foreword to the catalogue of an exhibition of paintings by William Kienbusch at the Kraushaar Galleries in 1964, I referred to *Sound of the Gong—Buoy No 2*. Mr. Kienbusch, himself present, remarked, "The partial arc—upper left of the buoy—suggests the buoy swayed by the sea and made to clang."

This expository aid made me profoundly grateful—like the following one concerning another composition entitled *A Small Island Fire:* "The smoke is a kind of shorthand for disaster."

I can scarcely be called *avant-garde*, and might say that "My Crow Pluto" is narrative, not an attempt at abstract writing. It says that crows entertain me, that the tame one perched on the shoulder of Barnaby Rudge lends Barnaby attraction for me; but that the bird has wings and should be finding his own food, not be encouraged to think he is a person.

My lines "Marriage," beginning:

> This institution,
> perhaps one should say enterprise

in no sense suggest a philosophy of marriage; are but a little anthology of terms and phrases that had entertained me, which I did not wish to lose and conjoined as best I might.

When John Freeman asked Lord Birkett (the British judge), "Why did you leave your father's business, to study law?" he said, "I think it was the fascination of using words in a way that would be effective"—true indication of indigenous talent. Ezra Pound indicates "passion" as at the root of the matter: no "addled mosses dank": "say nothing—nothing—that you couldn't in some circumstances, under stress of emotion, actually say."

Writing is a fascinating business. "And what should it do?" William Faulkner asked. "It should help a man endure by lifting up his heart." (—Admitting that his might not always have done that.) *It should.*

The Christian Science Monitor, 11 January 1966, p. 10; *Tell Me, Tell Me.*

MALVINA HOFFMAN: 1885–1966

MALVINA HOFFMAN had a passion for exactitude. As a child she was always taking things apart to see how they worked, impelled by a curiosity relevant to her masteries. She despised half-measures. Her comment when I had been over-persuaded by an editor to write something of her house in Paris and her studio in New York, was—"Well, it's a description; I wouldn't call it an essay."

In her tool cabinet on the wall of her New York studio there were carbon-tipped chisels, forged and hardened to hold an edge, forceps, hammer and mallets, an architect's rare set of measuring tools. To students of sculpture, she says in her manual, "The pupil should learn to temper and sharpen tools. The edge must be watched and kept in perfect condition. . . . When you stop working in clay, wash your tools and dry them. Do not leave them in a pail to soak. Have a modeling stand with a revolving top. There should be a wet sponge on the stand to keep your hands clean. Have a rack for tools just over the workbench."

Her parents, in their 43rd Street house, gave her a room at the top as a studio. "I had a passionate consciousness," she says, "that if I could do a good portrait of my father (a pianist), something of his art and integrity might be caught in my own art and never leave me. Then suddenly one night the inadequate armature gave way, the neck had broken and half the clay had slipped down. The door opened and a friend came in accompanied by a stranger who turned out to be Gutzon Borglum. He said, 'Come along with me to my studio at once, and I'll show you how to make a good armature.' "

The bust of her father in marble and one of Samuel Grimson in bronze, were the examples of her work that she carried to Rodin to convince him of the seriousness of her wish to study with him. That she was "a sculptor" is self-evident—the verisimilitude of portraits subsequently achieved: of Lord Reading, of Pavlova (the Gavotte), of Paderewski, of her studio-man Bill, of Ubangi women, of Rita de Acosta Lydig, of Dr. Cushing, of her mother in marble. Some studies reveal her art of catching a fleeting expression, notably of an intention to smile. Her recent portrait of Dr. William Ernest Hocking so pleased him that he had three replicas made for his family.

Commissioned by Chicago's Field Museum in 1930 to create "The Hall of Man," each racial type to be represented in plaster, Miss Hoffman insisted that the approximately 100 heads and life-size figures be bronze or stone. Despite official hesitation, the costlier materials were used.

Never complacent regarding her own skill, her one question was, "Could it be better?" She admitted that replicas of a bust by Houdon, made as training, required patience; that reproducing with a chisel links of chainmail for her crusader in Harvard's Memorial Chapel, was not easy.

Her proficiencies in art were matched by her generosities. Reading in the paper that a newsboy's leg had been cut off by the wheels of a streetcar, and that he was not expected to live, she insisted on seeing him, restoring incentive by telling him that she would get him artificial legs. For paraplegics under the supervision of Dr. Rusk, she made model charts which patients could copy, furthering their efforts toward independence and rehabilitation. She devoted much time to making models for medical studies in pre-natal care.

Miss Hoffman was grateful to France for making her a member of the Legion of Honor and proud of the Medal of Honor which the National Sculpture Society bestowed on her. As Gilmore Clarke's "In Memoriam" sonnet to her says, "Nobly you lived, beauty the guiding spirit of your life; with consummate skill you fashioned inert clay." She is revered by foundations, governments, academies, experts in medicine, and students of aesthetics. Malvina Hoffman is a notable figure in American art, and in a literary way important by reason of her books—*Heads and Tales* (1930), recounting her travels in connection with the Hall of Man; *Sculpture Inside and Out* (1939) and *Yesterday Is Tomorrow* (1965).

Sculpture Inside and Out, a manual for students of sculpture, is preeminently vital, providing specifications minutely detailed, diagrams and master photographs of master art. Few persons have the capacity to record what has been learned in a lifetime in such a way that the picture of experience becomes another kind of masterpiece. *Sculpture Inside and Out* is a working book, expounded with intensive care, and at the same time, a clue, I feel, to Miss Hoffman's life—a kind of monument which had become, for me, her own self-portrait.

National Sculpture Review, 15 (Fall 1966), 7, 30.

FOREWORD

Fellow-citizens,

We are privileged that Mr. Clay Lancaster—like Thomas Jefferson— assists us to be intelligent and to love beauty. He says as Kuo Hsi said, "a virtuous man in a rustic retreat . . . may meet fishermen, woodcutters and hermits; . . . haze, mist and the haunting spirits of the mountains are what human nature seeks, and yet can rarely find."

Asher Durand's painting, "Kindred Spirits," so "rested me" and was synonymous with "out of doors," that given copies by "Time Magazine" which I requested, I was unable to resist framing one, on my wall ever since, the personalities of the two men, made incomparably vivid—depicted on a projecting table of rock, gazing down upon the stream and toward surrounding verdure.

I am vague; Mr. Lancaster is specific. Readers would be short-sighted not to read of the great white oak, felled as a barrier to British troops in the Revolutionary War. Some may remember our three-cent violet stamp, The Battle of Brooklyn, on which Washington directs the Battle from his white horse—high on the ridge.

Mr. Lancaster is a selective writer; his pages are art. I envy this book. The Chinese concept of nature for man to *enjoy* captivates me like Mr. Lancaster's exact, careful but unstilted writing.

May 16, 1967

In *Prospect Park Handbook*, by Clay Lancaster. New York: Walton H. Rawls, 1967, p. 7.

CROSSING BROOKLYN BRIDGE AT TWILIGHT

ASSETS tempt comparison, but I realize that my venerations are tinctured with materialism.

When I arrived in Brooklyn from New York in 1929, the first submarine— or, say, an early submarine—entitled The Intelligent Whale, weighing about ten tons, lay inside the Cumberland Street Gate of the Navy Yard. It was a shapely little cylinder of clamshell gray, like a pig. The Squibb Laboratory was in use—memorialized later by Squibb Park, with a tower and lighted clock, an accommodation greatly welcomed by motorists, marking the end of the Brooklyn Bridge. Dr. Squibb was a Quaker but had been assured by an aunt that it was permissible for him to be a Navy doctor since he would not be killing anybody. Brooklyn has been called the City of Churches and, one might add, of preachers. Lyman Abbott was pastor of the Plymouth

Church and editor of *The Outlook*. Dr. Phillips Eliot, pastor of the First Presbyterian Church of Brooklyn, in a vesper series of lectures, Great Preachers of the Past, included Dr. S. Parkes Cadman, who, when asked what conduces to happiness, said, "A chance of happiness is better if we want to do something than if we want to have something." *The Brooklyn Daily Eagle* was hospitable to writers resident or on the wing, and quick to detect talent. . . . The evening classes at Brooklyn College attract lively attendance. The Williamsburg Savings Bank clock-tower has minutes on its face a foot wide that are visible for miles. . . . High-school boys, my neighbors, acquired out-of-date tennis technique from me, on the Fort Greene tennis courts, which are free. Brooklyn has trees—a group of massive English elms in Fort Greene Park, and sycamores arching over South Portland Avenue; but its crowning curio is the Camperdown Elm in Prospect Park not far from the boathouse, planted in 1872. It has eighteen cavities, is in need of cleaning and bracing under its heavy horizontal limbs. Funds could make it serve as an outdoor classroom, demonstrating techniques of tree care. Will it be here in 1972? (Camperdown Fund, 171 Congress Street, Brooklyn, Mrs. Graff.)

New York has a waterfront. It has a Mayor of Presidential caliber. It has books: Rizzoli's of international Old World grandeur, and the Gotham Book Mart's new compactness with Miss Steloff, Philip Lyman and Don Smith in charge on 47th Street. "Wise Men Fish Here" the sign says, and they do. I have food nearby—a family of relatives named Montvori who wrap the items and buy the best. They may be praised or not. They are businessmen and not vain. There is the unicorn tapestry in the Cloisters of the Metropolitan Museum; the Museum of Primitive Art on 54th Street; Audubon's crossfox is in the Museum of the City of New York. Some time ago the museum exhibited white sapphires, woven wind scarves and Tippoo's tiger with victim, the Victoria and Albert's automaton. Brooklyn had a ball team. Roy Campanella and Dazzy Vance. The Mets to begin with had Casey Stengel—a master of restraint and elegant comportment when I made his acquaintance. The Yankees are having an off season, but their timber is there. As *The Boston Transcript* said of the Harvard crew, "Win or lose, their speed is marvelous." The club with princely food and ball field to match should enable them to flower.

The Pierpont Morgan Library is directed by Frederick B. Adams. Its corridor of notable drawings, calligraphy, illuminated manuscripts, its lectures and music make it exceptional. The Museum of Natural History has a blue whale weighing sixty tons. Asked, "Can I take the Ninth Avenue Elevated to the Museum of Natural History?" the policeman on duty said, "Don't take it. The city needs it."

I like Santa Barbara, Vancouver, British Columbia; have an incurable fondness for London. But of any cities I have seen, I like New York best.

The New York Times, 5 August 1967, p. 22.

RANDALL JARRELL

LIKE Randall Jarrell's bats, we live by hearing, by vibrations; by having heard what makes us happy—by his way of saying what he says. I cannot think of anyone who gives me more incentive than Randall Jarrell, as I read him or think about him.

Even a touch of affectation would have spoiled it—what he says in "The Lost World" of himself as a child, reading at bedtime, "Forced out of life into / Bed." Safe in his naturalness, he says, "I'm not afraid," and goes on in his glow of gratitude to existence.

> There off Sunset, in the lamplit starlight
> A scientist is getting ready to destroy
> The world. "It's time for you to say good night,"
> Mama tells me; I go on in breathless joy.
> "Remember, tomorrow is a school day,"
> Mama tells me; I go on in breathless joy.
> . . . .
> Then I go back
> To my bedroom; I read as I undress.
> The scientist is ready to attack.
> Mama calls out, "Is your light out?" I call back, "Yes,"
> And turn the light out.

Randall Jarrell's evaluation of others is descriptive of himself. He says, ". . . the poems of Miss Bishop or Mr. Williams or Mr. Graves are a lonely triumph of integrity, knowledge, and affection."

War engulfs him. "The engines rise to their blind laboring road."

> "The great drake
> Flutters to the icy lake—
> The shotguns stammer in my head.
> I lie in my own bed,"
> He whispers, "dreaming"; and he thinks to wake.
> The old mistake.

. . . .
The tags' chain stirs with the wind; and I sleep
Paid, dead, and a soldier. Who fights for his own life
Loses; loses: I have killed for my world, and am free.

No; the dead are not afraid, cannot refute

The grave's cross, the grave's grass, the grave's
        polished granite
THESE DIED THAT WE MIGHT LIVE
        —That I may live!—

Like Jonah, the soldier is vomited into life from the grave—not bitter or
with uncertainty but with emphasized comprehension.

"Integrity, knowledge, and affection." Of these attributes it seems as
though affection, affection unaided, might have demonstrated the abounding
unsnobbishness of his heart. He says, "In my / Talk with the world,"

how strange that I
Know nothing, and yet it tells me what I know!—
I appreciate the animals, who stand by
Purring. Or else they sit and pant. It's so—
So *agreeable.*

One might say here something about an art of appreciation that does not
estrange the beneficiary from the giver. Randall Jarrell could invest a creature
with romance which makes it seem the counterpart of a luna moth with
seagreen wings that have violet crescents on them—a creature that was a
worm, and that only respects compliments which respect modesty.

Randall Jarrell's integrity is inescapably graphic in the testfire of anom-
olous associates described by him in his *Pictures from an Institution.* The
institution was Benton College; and Dwight Robbins was its President. He
had inherited Miss Camille Batterson, teacher of creative writing, "and there
was nothing he could do about her. Nothing, that is, that wouldn't have been
cruel and inexpedient. . . . the University of Iowa, or Illinois, or Indiana . . . had offered Miss Batterson a better job, a Chair in fact. . . . [The
President] hid the joy he felt, and expressed . . . the sorrow he did not
feel."

The Head of the Department that had made the offer "was the informing
intelligence of the committee that revised the English curriculum of the
secondary schools of his state." "His field was Cowper." "When you pronounce Cowper properly, you say Cooper. . . . But when people who didn't

know how to pronounce Cowper heard the head referred to by people who did . . . *they* thought him an authority on Cooper and spoke of him as such."
". . . before long he and his wife were spending evenings with deans."
". . . it did no good to remind himself that Cowper had been, for a good deal of his life, insane."

"Nobody except the English Department thought it sensible of him to be interested in Cowper; now everybody thought it sensible of him to be interested in the English Department. Each member of the Department did something that seemed to the world impractical at best, idiotic at worst; to be in charge of the whole idiocy and impracticality seemed impractical or idiotic to no one."

His wife was a daughter and granddaughter of Justices of the Supreme Court of Virginia. "She was Miss Batterson's oldest and dearest friend. She . . . had heard Ellen Glasgow refer to Miss Batterson as 'a woman of the finest sensibility.' " After she left Benton, Miss Batterson sent postcards "home to Benton." "It was as if she were attending the University, not teaching at it."

"In March, the first spring after she left Benton, she died." "The next day, when the first girls came to Dr. Rosenbaum's office for their conferences, there was only a note on the door postponing these. . . . Dr. Rosenbaum was looking out the window of a plane . . . on his way to a funeral."

Dr. Gottfried Rosenbaum and Mrs. Rosenbaum seem the most lovable residents of Benton. "And [yet] they did not like America so well as one would have wished them to like it; . . . Irene, for instance, had a name that is pronounced *i RA ne,* more or less, over most of Europe; here in America she was called I REEN." Dr. Rosenbaum "had published three volumes of an immense work showing how content gets expressed in, and modified by, the forms of its time." He was composer in residence, known for his *Joyous Celebration of the Memory of the Master Johann Sebastian Bach.*

One cannot degrade the Rosenbaums' house by calling it exotic. ". . . there were, badly arranged on its rarely dusted bookshelves, books in English, German, Russian, French, Latin, Greek—all the languages of the earth . . . printed scores, photostats of scores, scores in manuscript, scores in Esperanto, almost . . . a pale engraving of Vivaldi, Beethoven and Liszt letters in stand-up frames, glass on both sides so that one could see both sides of the page. There was no end to the confusion and richness of the house." A student friend "would close her eyes, and then open them again and look at the Rosenbaums 'like puzzled urchin on an aged crone / Who keepeth closed a wond'rous riddle-book.' " Gertrude Johnson (English Department) was a spoiled one, spoiled beyond repair, marred forever in the making—a novelist who "listened only as A Novelist." Her books "did not murder to dissect, but dissected to murder. The blush on the cheek of Innocence is really—one learned this from Gertrude—a monomolecular film of giant levorotatory protein molecules, and the bonds that join them are bonds of self-interest."

In Randall Jarrell, we have an author who somehow unshackled himself from *self* and could have a good time; have as companions a bat, a chipmunk, a bird. This was in the South and a mockingbird frequented the yard. He was somewhat mercurial. ". . . on his bad days he'd dive on everything that came into the yard—on cats and dogs, even. . . . The day the bat went to him the mockingbird was perched on the highest branch of the big willow by the porch, singing with all his might . . . every part of him had a clear, quick, decided look about it. He was standing on tiptoe . . . sometimes he'd spring up into the air. This time he was singing a song about mocking-birds."

"The bat fluttered to the nearest branch, hung upside down from it, and listened; finally when the mockingbird stopped for a moment he said in his high little voice: 'It's beautiful, just beautiful! . . . I could listen to you every night. Every day too. I—I . . . could listen to you forever.' " [The bird was pleased.] " 'I'll sing it for you again.' . . . When the mockingbird had finished, the bat thought: 'No, I just can't say him mine. Still, though—' "

Later, "the bat said: 'Sometimes when I wake up in the daytime I make up poems. Could I—I wonder whether I could say you one of *my* poems?' "

"Till a bat is two weeks old he's never alone: the little naked thing . . . clings to his mother wherever she goes. After that she leaves him at night; . . . almost dreaming, the bat began to make up a poem about a mother and her baby."

A bat is born
Naked and blind and pale.
His mother makes a pocket of her tail
And catches him:
. . . .
She lives by hearing.
The mother eats the moths and gnats she catches
In full flight; in full flight
The mother drinks the water of the pond
She skims across. Her baby hangs on tight.
. . . .
      at daybreak
The tired mother flaps home to her rafter.
The others are all there.
. . . .
Bunched upside down, they sleep in air.

The bat-poet's art is like Randall Jarrell's—never forced, but a thing of integrity, knowledge, affection. The weak rhymed foot not always matching the strong foot ("the moonlight" and "beak is bright"); "through the night / Doubling and looping, soaring, somersaulting"—as inconspicuous as prose; or "In full flight; in full flight / . . . Her baby hangs on tight," emphasized as if giving directions to an inexperienced child.

(After seeing Maurice Sendak's pictures of Randall's animals—of the bat fleeing from the owl, while "the night holds its breath" as the owl "calls and calls"; or a mother possum with all her baby possums holding tight to her, in the moonlight where apples have fallen under the apple tree—I am sure that if he were not an artist, he would not work for an exterminator.)

"The X-Ray Waiting Room in the Hospital," "In Galleries," *The Bat-Poet,* "They All Go"—no "steps echoing along the corridor." These story-dramas are not labored; they ignite imagination and just stop; they have no end. But the magic *never* ends.

The Atlantic Monthly, 220 (September 1967), 96–98; *Randall Jarrell, 1914–1965,* edited by Robert Lowell, Peter Taylor, and Robert Penn Warren. New York: Farrar, Straus & Giroux, 1967, pp. 125–32.

IN FASHION, YESTERDAY, TODAY AND TOMORROW

SOME phase of altitude manifests itself in every age. Dante says Beatrice walked like a crane—*come una crana.* And in Jacopo Amigoni's painting entitled "The Embarkation of Helen of Troy," Helen is wearing a long dress, holding by the hand a child in a miniature long dress. They were not depicted in mini-skirts or tennis-net square-mesh stockings. In fact, the mere tip of Helen's foot shows.

In keeping with a tradition of noble behavior, for the defense of children Venice by ordinance forbids the citizen to wear dress too strangely shaped or scant. A narrow sheath or pant (if I may use the word) does not set a hippomoid figure off to advantage. The sound-hole in a cello, an upper-case Caslon Old-style S, an approaching swan, a swiftly twirling sea-lion reversing direction, fifty elephants with heads touching the ground as honoring majesty in Thailand—these symbolize fashion rightness as unfreakishly right as Siam is distant from Manhattan. In an exhibition of historic designs in the Brooklyn Museum not long ago, dresses or a wrap by the House of Worth was as pleasant to wear or try on as any dashing innovation in an uptown shop on Madison Avenue.

I have a tintype, taken about 1880, of eminently dressed Philadelphians. The men wore boating straws with university bi-colored ribbons; the ladies' basques have sleeves that *fit*, which make our current blouses look like dressing-gowns. One synonym of aplomb among the ladies in the tintype wears a silk basque, tightly fastened by about twenty-nine bullet buttons almost touching, and a close-fitting small hat covered by stiff ribbons ended diagonally. Nor did they slouch.

The greatest change in fashion from Victorian times is in boys' clothes— long trousers instead of knickers. The yachtman's double-breasted Navy jacket, and cap with white flannels or ducks are the man's most effective garb, I think. (These modifying words are appropriate to any dogmatism expressed here by your fashion reporter.) Ballplayers' uniforms seem to me not so trim as formerly. They should not look like babies' sleepers or snow-suits. Not only potential buyers applauded S. Klein's Mink Maids when exhibited there. A 19-year-old electric utility clerk said, "It sure breaks the monotony of lunch-hour," as the Mink Maids paraded mink stoles, jackets, and a mink trench-coat. An elderly Manhattan widow kept murmuring af-terward, "Beautiful, beautiful. I wonder if they have any seconds that they're giving away." The most expensive coat in the show ($3,987) was a floor-length white mink with a detachable flounce. This coat I view with partisan interest, since I am an incurable sufferer of thrift. If I were not the recipient of a donated French brocade emerald jacket and purple velvet skirt of papal quality I could be mistaken for a mere citizen of Times Square at the rush hour.

May I digress to shoes? Fontana of Rome makes a pale elephant's breath suede blucher with cotton tie that might well be standard. At least, *did* make. The cuffless trouser ought not to draw attention to itself—should be worn by a connoisseur of legs. Vests, slowly coming back, omitted to save cloth during the war, add four pockets to the suit and an inside one to carry a billfold. Men's hats are still to be seen abroad. The New Haven between Stamford, Greenwich and New York is said to carry 40,000 commuters and the New York Central the same; and not a hat to be seen, except with a uniform. A Stetson or wide-brimmed Panama should not be merely an or-nament, cost what it may! Sir Winston Churchill had nine hats. The New Guinea Tari tribeman's bunch of leaves at the back, steadied by a vine-string, is perhaps the least hampering concession to fashion.

Today? We are menaced by inexplicable epidemics of violence. Mr. Ortega y Gasset, quoted on television by Prof. Floyd Zulli, sees violence, such as the stoning of cars and the defacing of churches by between-age girls and boys, as caused by empty minds—vacuity is interpreted as nobility that is action. But how can probity or fashion be instilled by parents who find sacrifices too inconvenient in providing children a home?

Tomorrow? The Italians have a saying: "It's a queer bee that makes honey only for itself." To what life and fashion principle may one adhere? Confucius, translated by Ezra Pound, said, "Sympathy."

The New York Times, 4 November 1967, p. 32.

INTRODUCTION

AS early as 1836, William Cullen Bryant said in the *New York Evening Post* that the City of New York should reserve our forest and woodland for shade and refreshment as a park. He recalled that "at the beginning of the Century, anyone had been able to walk in half an hour from his home to the open fields that soon would be covered with brick and mortar." In London a year later than his original suggestion, Bryant requested for a park, "a central reservation in New York" and today, we have that very thing, designed by Frederick Law Olmsted and Calvert Vaux, keeping Bryant's original words, Central Park.

As one comes down Fifth Avenue in early May, the air itself seems a delicate green by reason of the multitude of tiny leaves that appear to have come out overnight. Entering the park at 72nd Street, one pauses to admire the ancient, small-leafed Chinese elm, one of the original planting, the largest Chinese elm in America. Just ahead, we have an example of Frederick Olmsted's genius; he makes the path turn so that as one looks back, one has lost the city and sees only a mass of green: lindens, oaks, elms and maples.

From the terrace above the Bethesda Fountain, one descends the wide steps, pausing for a moment to examine the accurately realized, square-framed, sculptured subjects, such as pears or a lotos pod, dogwood blossoms and a bird about to pick up a worm (a rather large worm lest it be overlooked). On the left, a tree towers over the stairway, a tall paulownia, or is it a catalpa? One notices then that the angel hovering over the pool is really hovering, without touching the water. A bird lights on her wing. One may catch the scent of mowed grass and see boats emerge from under Bow Bridge, which rises to an ellipse at the center that no oarsman need scrape the underside. This bridge is faded by weather to an ideal Oriental bleached blue.

Crossing Bow Bridge, of broad pale timbers, one comes to a wilder area—masses of rock showing striations of the glacier, and in what direction the mass moved. Roots of large trees clasp the rocks of the moraine, forming a passage for water trickling down. At some places, brush has intentionally been left for songbirds and one is startled by the note of a titmouse, "Peter? Peter? Peter?" A step farther, one hears the sound of a waterfall.

Near 100th Street and Central Park West, there are Osage oranges and a bald cypress and sweetgum trees with a leaf that is deeper cut than a maple's. On the hillside are towering tulip trees worthy of study. The smooth shaft of the trunk rises like a column of steel. If it is spring, as the eye turns up it catches the brilliance of flowers, greenish yellow and orange. A petal falls, lending excitement when examined. Benches can be found along the walk, and lamp posts designed by Henry Bacon, the post rising from a stylized vine at the base.

Spring: masses of bloom, white and pink cherry blossoms on trees given us by Japan. Summer: fragrance of black locust and yellow-wood flowers. Autumn: a leaf rustles. Winter: one catches sight of a skater, arms folded, leaning to the wind—the very symbol of peaceful solitude, of unimpaired freedom. We talk of peace. This is it.

New York City, July 20, 1968

In *Central Park Country: A Tune Within Us,* edited by David Brower, text by Mireille Johnston. San Francisco: Sierra Club, 1968, pp. 18–19.

THE LIBRARY DOWN THE STREET IN THE VILLAGE

JEFFERSON MARKET COURTHOUSE at the southwest corner of West Tenth Street and Sixth Avenue—now the main Greenwich Village branch of the New York Public Library—stood for two years with the hands of the clock at twenty minutes after two. Then devoted and persistent citizens saved the building from threatened demolition, transforming a particularly awkward architectural elephant into the mascot of Greenwich Village.

Never was there a Village project that had such unanimity. Mrs. Margot

Gayle was chairman of the committee of neighbors to get the clock on Jefferson Market Courthouse started. Philip Wittenberg was chairman of the Committee for a Library in Jefferson Market Courthouse. The Hon. Eugene E. Hult was the Mayor's deputy when the library was officially opened on November 27, 1967.

The Jefferson Market Courthouse was built in 1876 and designed by Frederick C. Wither and Calvert Vaux, who with Frederick Law Olmsted was co-designer of Central Park.

The saga of Jefferson Market Courthouse is a true fairy tale of the transformation of our Venetian High Victorian Ruskinian Gothic relic into our chic Village Square Library. Cleaned, or rather "refreshed," was the word of the architect, Giorgio Cavaglieri. In 1963 the Committee for the Clock paid off their $3,400 debt, having provided the clock with an electric motor. The clock was given new hands, its four faces were repaired, each face eight feet in diameter. As the clock struck twelve, Greenwich Villagers on the balcony of the Jefferson Market Courthouse tower could be seen throwing streamers and waving flags.

There is an extensive reference room in the library basement. Precaution was taken that the air-conditioning at the top of the building would not be visible from the street and spoil the skyline. What was the Second District Court is now the Children's Room. Elevators connect two staff lounges by a bridge or balcony above the east end of the main reading room. The underside of the spiral stairs to the first floor, simulating an unfurling fan effect, is worth more than a glance—reminding one of the medieval cathedral fan-vaulting.

A further reason for pausing when descending the stair, a reminder of Jefferson Courthouse days, are the following sharply chiseled words in Gothic script on the curving stone of the wall: "The precepts of the law are these: to live correctly, to do an injury to none and to render everyone his due."

The liberality of the library staff affords a counterpart to those statements, although who knows what correctness is? The foregoing item could not have existed if two much-incommoded librarians, Miss Smith and Mrs. McCullough, in custody of frail clippings had not trusted the public and rendered users of Old Jeff a great deal more than their due.

Leaving the building, I saw a long line of children, each with a book to be charged. Every book was protectively covered by cellophane or plastic. They were ideally neat by comparison with the library books in 1923, when I advised boys asking advice in the Hudson Park Children's Room, and might suggest John McGraw's *How to Play Baseball* and Christy Mathewson's *Pitching in a Pinch*.

The young readers did not incommode me or one another and I like my neighborhood very much; whereas in other libraries or city museums I have frequently had to avoid schoolbooks made use of as missiles or shields for the head.

I recalled from my recent Village reading that in early days children glanced up at Old Jeff Tower clock and got to school on time, and I wondered if Paul Freeman, Assistant Secretary of the Neighborhood Committee and Clockkeeper, may still not have become weary of fund-raising. I felt that it would be the final triumph of the restoration of Old Jeff if the big bell on the Courthouse Tower could strike the hours again, serving tradesmen, postmen, drugstores and laggards like me who neglect mealtimes when under pressure.

If only the clapper of the great clock on the library tower would continue to afford us its sonorously encouraging harmonies, and go on vibrating through the sometimes quiet streets of Village Square!

The New York Times, 4 May 1968, p. 38.

ONE POET'S PITCH FOR THE CARDINALS TO WIN THE SERIES

THE difference of a hair, in offense or defense, could mean success, I feel, for the Cardinals or the Tigers, in this World Series. The teams are so nearly matched in talented personnel that individual effort under stress is going to make the difference when the first ball is thrown out this Wednesday. Bob Gibson and Dennis McLain are pitchers of outstanding caliber. Each of these gentlemen may be expected to win two games. One may say that when things are at their worst they are at their best. They have a will to win, indispensable to victory.

The Cardinals' manager, Red Schoendienst, overcame tuberculosis—odds so great that most people looked on his ball days as over. In his will to win over this dread menace he exhibited a fortitude and courage great enough to conquer the disease, the very kind of stamina needed in all human endeavor. Orlando Cepeda, Cardinal first baseman, has been pivotal in a World Series already. He had to overcome a leg so crooked it had to be broken by a surgeon and reset. His leg was then so weak from the surgery that for months he had to wear a 22-pound shoe to build extra strength into the leg. It is well known that a player can put forth super-effort—even at damage to himself—in a crisis that would be all but impossible in day-to-day playing. Both these players suffered injustice for "not trying" but had the fortitude to ignore such blame with a matchless courage that will count in the World Series. This season, when batting failed, the glove men performed wonders in the field. Such resources may tip the scales for victory even if other teams have them—but not to the degree of the Cardinals.

Cepeda said in his book, "One of the things that makes baseball so fascinating to me is the number of non-standard plays—plays you're seeing for the first time—that occur in baseball. Stan Musial said that even after twenty years in the game you constantly keep seeing things you have never seen before, which makes baseball a lot different than so many other sports."

I've been talking about fortitude. In Lawrence Ritter's biography of Richard Marquard, known as Rube, he says Marquard had a letter from a catcher, Howard Wakefield, from Cleveland. It said, "We could use a left-handed pitcher and if you make good we'd reimburse you for transportation and give you a contract." No letter came, says Marquard. He had never been away from home before. It took him five days and five nights riding freight trains, sleeping in the open fields, to reach his destination. The next year—1908—he went to spring training with the Indianapolis club. He was already warming up when a couple of Cleveland players yelled at him, "Are you the bat boy?" "No," he said, "I'm the pitcher—ask Bill Bradley. . . . I'm going to pitch against you and I'm going to beat you." "Beat us! Busher, you couldn't beat a drum!" Rube played in the big leagues for eighteen years.

There are approximately 40,000 athletic scholarships given out annually. Roy Campanella prefers scholarship to glamour. He said through a public address system to a baseball clinic for boys in the Bronx playground, "Look, the head of Cheshire Academy once told me that the average boy will put out 100 percent on a ball field while he will put out only 50 percent in the classroom." As for the clinic, Roy views his pupils as a partisan: "You don't have to throw so hard. The first baseman may need his teeth."

World champions are not to be acclaimed by the eminence reached but by the obstacles overcome. Glenn Cunningham was so burned as a youth by an autumn-leaf fire doctors said he would never walk again. He resolved to be a track champion and became a miler, holding the record for several years. Johnny Weismuller, the famous swimmer, overcame tuberculosis. Ben Hogan, the golf champion, was so injured in an auto crash, they said he would never play another game! Such courage is inspirational and contagious—especially among those possessing championship talent, making them invincible.

The Times may not favor prophecies from laymen, who hazard opinions diffidently, but it looks to me as if the St. Louis Cardinals are going to win.

The New York Times, 28 September 1968, p. 32.

APPENDIX

LETTERS TO THE EDITOR

Sir:

L. A. G. Strong's article, "English Poetry Since Brooke," is of great interest to me as subject matter; and somewhat curiously, might I say, dogmatic in presentment though it is, it induces cooperation. I am aware, however, of fire in Padraic Colum that the word "innocent" scarcely conveys; it is a great thing to be able to express strong truths quietly. And for me John Masefield has more illusion than apparently he has for Mr. Strong; also, though I don't object to it, ". . . humanitarianism and an intense love of animals are not easy to express in poetry" is to me an arresting statement.

Very pleasing aspects of the article are the proprietarial impartiality of the observations, the conciseness in connection with extensiveness of survey, and at various points an ability to state with delicacy certain insights which are difficult to express; for example that W. H. Auden's "achievement hitherto is semiprivate, in the sense that those who know him personally have a better chance of understanding it than those who do not." One also concurs very earnestly with Mr. Strong's implication that proficiency apologizes for singularity, and that "in contemplating nature" a man can live "as intensely as when he is contesting an election on the Communist ticket."

Mr. Strong has made his statements so emphatically as to excite interest in modern poetry and he obliges one to infer a certain continuity of poetic development. Either feat is not very usual it seems to me.

American Mercury, 36 (June 1935), 251–52.

Editor, *View*:

I am opposed to any kind of censorship that says in an official way that we must not speak in a personal way. As for *View*, the readers of *View* have been exposed to demoralizing strangeness from the cradle up, and are not going to be harmed by anything that anyone with a gift for novelty, offers them.

I am indebted to *View* for making me somewhat closely acquainted with the work of Joseph Cornell; and am full of gratitude to you and Parker Tyler for defending me to a public, that if it is aware of me at all, is likely to regard me as a drawback. But I look upon *View* as not in good health. There is usually in each issue something I wish to keep, and I ask myself as I ponder the whole content, why can one not have something acutely irresistible without having it negatived by what is intolerable? Why may one not be a matchless rugmaker of Daghestan without being a woman of Daghestan who has never washed? Why, on a dare or under a vow, does one mask as a leper so perfectly as to earn commiseration upon one's mortal affliction?

The sense of your generosity has led me to read *View* with dozing optimism, hoping for the best, and would have kept me from thrusting on you my dissatisfactions, but since you ask me how I feel about the paper, I answer.

View, Ser. 4, No. 1 (Spring 1944), 23.

Dear Mr. Weiss:

It is a hardship not to be helpful . . . but I have nothing to offer—prose or verse—beyond what you have. . . . My versions of La Fontaine are as yet tentative and should not be presented as final. Certain of La Fontaine's precepts, however, reiterated throughout the fables, have made on me so deep an impression, they begin to assume for me a character of a command. Might you care to publish the following?—placing first what has a thousand variants—"Be content with your lot" and, "we deceive ourselves but cannot deceive God and can rarely deceive man, so let there be no lies, even of expediency":

> "Like what you have, don't tell a falsehood;
> That is safest; but would you if you strove
> By lies to secure some kind of good,
> Ever get it? You cannot deceive Jove."

Do as you would be done by.

If in a slough,
Strive too, and Heaven shows you how.

Settle your troubles at home; don't bear grudges.

You cannot make peace with dishonest foes.

Murder does not make a matter better.

Greed is its own punishment.

Humor is delightful? not when forced or self-centered.

Don't be irreconcilable.
The better the mind is, the more adaptable.

Demand too much and have none usually.
Superciliousness is folly.

Doctors and wives had better be good ones.

> "Don't be covetous;
> During recent years, what multitudes we have seen,
> Who in one day lost all, hoping to have been
> Prematurely prosperous."

> "Advantage is bought at too much cost
> When what was worth most is lost."

Patient work and time can do more than strength and anger can.
Moreover, there are instances in which wholesome toil
  has been more curative than medicine.

Look before you leap, when taking a walk, when choosing a livelihood, when
falling in love.

Wisdom is wealth that is not burdensome.

Don't attribute to Fate, misfortune resulting from neglect.

Modesty is a good symptom and mercenariness, a bad one. "There's my frog,
that little goose who tried to be an ox, she was so grandiose."

Don't be garrulous. Save my life, then tell me what you have to say.

Be efficient:

> "I, when alone, tower so tall the bravest shiver;
> I crush and see Persian emperors suffer;
> I am a king, an idol;
> My head is hid by showers of diadems:
> Then the king's affairs by some unjust reversal,
> Are but La Fontaine's problems."

Be yourself, wolfish, or gentle. "A wolf is a wolf and he had best seem what he
is; that is wisest."

> "A snare though well woven
> At times may snare the weaver

And treachery how often
Betrays the deceiver."

Few are wise; few are fit to wear a diadem; nothing so rare as a friend.

—M. M.

Quarterly Review of Literature, 4, No. 2 (1948), 122–23. In a special Marianne Moore issue.

April 24, 1953

Dear Mr. Carter:

I am *sorry* not to help, supposing what I wrote might be a help. I enclose a poem Jaime de Angulo wrote (to me) when I was making an effort to get the Viking Press to publish the *Indian Tales*. It may not supplement well material you had thought of using, of course. I am merely catching at a straw, to be in some sense of use to you. I am indeed enthusiastic about the *Tales* and about Don Gregorio—especially Don Gregorio (in *Nine*) and the drawings for the *Indian Tales*. You have on the jacket of the *Tales* what I said to Mr. Wyn.[1]

In writing the Whitney Foundation for assistance in publishing the *Tales*, I said what is mild but what is as follows:

As I see it, there is health in the work; it is entertaining (to me) and, as an untainted contribution to ethnology, is rare, in my experience.

I am tempted to try to comment on the *Tales* but must not.

[1] "I am charmed by the book—text and pictures. It is no effort, of course, to be pleased by the sure touch—stories and animal drawings that are poetry, innate, humorborn, and wise." From the jacket of *Indian Tales* by Jaime de Angulo. A. A. Wyn, 1953.

Shenandoah, 4 (Summer–Autumn 1953), 117.

New-York, 10 novembre 1955

Cher Monsieur.

La sensibilité avec laquelle vous parlez d'Adrienne Monnier—et, en particuliar, de sa mort—me fait souhaiter de pouvoir vois adresser, en hommage à sa mémoire, quelque chose de rare. Les mots me manquent, mais laisez-moi exprimer mon affection pour elle, elle et son art d'hospitalité au renfort de gens comme moi—de gens qui sentaient qu'ils avaient un chez-soi littéraire à l'adresse: 7, rue de l'Odéon—si même l'on y fut ombre, et jamais présence.

Touchante, en vérité, cette générosite qui se manifestait dans des conditions dont elle, héroïque, ne se plaignait pas, de sorte que ses dons m'ont toujours paru grandis par sa façon de ne compter que sur elle-même, et par sa ferme résolution de ne demander aucune aide.*

*New York, November 10, 1955

Dear Sir:
    The sensitivity with which you speak of Adrienne Monnier—and, particularly, of her death—makes me pleased to be able to write to you in homage to her memory, something so rare. Words fail me, but let me express my affection for her, and the awareness of a debt to her: she and her art of hospitality were a comfort to people like me—people who felt that they had a literary home-away-from-home at the address: 7, rue de l'Odéon—even if one were present there only in spirit, not in person.
    One was indeed touched by that generosity which showed itself in certain circumstances of which she, heroically, never complained—of a kind that always made her gifts seem to me heightened by her manner of self-reliance, and by her firm insistence on not asking for help.

*Letter printed in French as translated by the editors; no original English version survives.

Mercure de France, No. 1109 (1 January 1956), 17.

You are very kind to wish to include me in your Brooklyn Heights Supplement but several tasks I have undertaken make anything more out of the question.
    I feel the charm of the Heights every time I am there; the Hill on which I live is mundane by comparison.
    I am sorry not to make the trouble you have taken, worth something to you.

"The Literary Heights," supplement to *The [Brooklyn] Heights Press,* 18 June 1959, n.p.

To The Editor:
    Strange reading—the disaffected, disaffectingly written review by Ruth Chat-

terton. For a gem of a book one expects a gem of a review, not a *crapaud*, a book read with corroborating relish by close friends of Ruth Draper, members of her family, experts of the stage, writers for it, and initiates of biography.

The New York Times Book Review, 3 July 1960, p. 13. Concerning *The Art of Ruth Draper* by Morton Dauwen Zabel.

I implore Mr. Newbold Morris to allow our boathouse in Prospect Park to remain. We in Brooklyn admire it. No substitute for it would appease us.

Civic News: Official Monthly Bulletin of the Park Slope Civic Council, 28 (January 1965), 1.

Dear Editor:
I feel that George Grosz (the caricaturist) was right when he said, "What makes the artist?; endless curiosity, observation, research and a great amount of joy in the thing."
In current verse, I dislike the kind that whines and wanders and merely ceases, instead of concluding. A writer should blaze with life from within. Do we have to be cynical toward parents, arrogant toward moral standards, satirical toward duty, skeptical of every advantage?
Like John Cheever, "I have an impulse to bring glad tidings. My sense of literature is one of giving, not diminishing."

Writer's Digest, 46 (January 1966), 15.

Sir:
I think Svetlana Alliluyeva's contagion for good, irresistible. Very moving indeed, her message to Pasternak.

The Atlantic Monthly, 220 (August 1967), 20.

To the Editor:
I am much enheartened by what Daniel Hoffman has said of me ("Two Ladies of Legend," *The Reporter*, December 28). But may I say of Dame Edith Sitwell that my strongest impression of her is of compassion—two instances of making

amends for harsh judgment—of notable hospitality, at the St. Regis and in London. Her last words to me, after detaining me for tea, were "See you in New York."

In her so-called Autobiography, she gives a most misleading impression of herself, I was sad to see (I think too, uncompromise is better than overconcessiveness).

The Reporter, 38 (25 January 1968), 8.

DUST JACKET BLURBS

There is much help for one in the strong feeling and unspoiled directness. I am much aware of being your debtor. Your book is a great gift.

Sidney Salt, *Christopher Columbus and Other Poems*, Bruce Humphries, 1937.

William Jay Smith's "Cupidon" is a permanence, a rare felicity.

William Jay Smith, *Poems*, Banyon Press, 1947.

H. D. is a poet of color heightened by color, of overtones of sound and meaning—e.g., Rosemary, Rose-of-Mary and ros maris; and of uninsisted upon implications. . . .

H. D., *By Avon River*, Macmillan, 1949.

One envies a self-awareness which managed to be both explicit—through understatement—and concise.

Theodore Spencer, *An Acre in the Seed*, Harvard University Press, 1949.

This is a book I would not wish to be without. I have learned more from Ezra Pound about writing than from anyone else—more that I value—and I think these letters suggest why. His disinterested focused zeal is, in my experience, unparalleled.

The Letters of Ezra Pound, edited by D. D. Paige. Harcourt, Brace & World, 1950.

These poems . . . reveal a kind of composite hero; uncompromising, discerner, and poet with a sense of the unity of the rhythm of a poem—something that looks one right in the eye.

Horace Gregory, *The Selected Poems of Horace Gregory*, Viking, 1951.

Miss Greeff is an observer who "ties outer to inner act,"—is as gallant as she is perceiving.

Adele Greeff, *Love's Argument*, Macmillan, 1952.

Iberica is resolute and undeceived—one unequivocally disinterested voice, raised on behalf of civic honesty and the cause of free men.

Iberica Magazine, 1955.

Pretensions to omniscience and apathy toward moral insight—these contemporary hobgoblins are here laid bare by Mr. Jarrell. While busy at his mighty task, how gay he seems; how gay we are as we look on! How can we ever thank him?

Randall Jarrell, *Pictures from an Institution*, Alfred A. Knopf, 1954.

This collection is to me extraordinary—impassioned, unforced, and masterly in a technical way, almost without exception. There are in the style traces of W. B. Yeats and Thomas Hardy, but the overall effect is unique, of indigenous originality . . . the work is above praise.

Charlotte Mew, *Collected Poems*, Macmillan, 1954.

I was startled by this achieved writing and rare content— and humor, interior humor. As verisimilitude in depicting nature and behavior, this book is a performance. Stolid obsessed fleshly episodes impart to the book a grisly note.

Charles Neider, *The White Citadel*, Twayne, 1954.

I am instructed, enheartened, entertained; arrested on every page by live touches which the interested translation keeps alive; not to mention the Introduction—a treasury of sensibility as lasting as the tales themselves.

Henri Pourrat, *A Treasury of French Tales*, Houghton Mifflin, 1954.

. . . A notable book—A pleasure.

Norman MacCraig, *Riding Lights*, Macmillan, 1956.

. . . indispensable. . . . the interstitial matter has a great deal of charm. Comprehensive, with interacting references, and terms conspicuously set apart for quick use, it is truly a handbook, both for beginner and expert.

Babette Deutsch, *Poetry Handbook: A Dictionary of Terms*, Funk & Wagnalls, 1957.

The work is aglow with feeling, with conscience . . . embodied in appropriate diction.

Ted Hughes, *The Hawk in the Rain*, Harper and Row, 1957.

I am delighted that *No Special Pleading* is to have a sequel. . . . her work is synonymous to me with ability, sensibility and good sense.

Mary Ballard Duryee, *This Instant Joy*, Pageant Press, 1958.

Hugh Kenner, upon technicalities of the trade, is commanding; and when intent upon what he respects, the facets gleam. Entertaining and fearless, he can be too fearless, but we need him.

Hugh Kenner, *Gnomon: Essays on Contemporary Literature*, McDowell Obolensky, 1958.

You are a wizard about Cummings.

Charles Norman, *The Magic-Maker: E. E. Cummings*, Macmillan, 1958.

I Wanted to Write a Poem is an engrossing book; in its verity and at the same time in having the attraction of fiction—*certain* fiction.

William Carlos Williams, *I Wanted to Write a Poem*, reported and edited by Edith Heal, Beacon Press, 1958.

E. E. Cummings is a concentrate of titanic significance, "a positive character"; and only ingenuousness could attempt to suggest in a word the "heroic" aspect of his paintings, his poems, and his resistances. He does not make aesthetic mistakes.

100 Selected Poems by E. E. Cummings, Grove Press, 1959.

The more I use *Webster's New World Dictionary*, the better I like it. It does not define a word merely in variants of the same word. It is a true etymological-general combination dictionary. It takes account of slang, lists places, names of really important persons, scientific terms recently formulated; and—to me— a prime feature is its one listing, an incalculable advance over listing by categories.

Webster's New World Dictionary of the American Language, World Publishing Company, 1958.

Impassioned feeling, accurate observation, conscience, sensibility, have combined to make Stanley Kunitz's undeceived presentation of life hardy. I doubt that anyone could take more interest in the work of Stanley Kunitz than I do. I value his "poetic eye" and trenchant speech.

Stanley Kunitz, *Selected Poems, 1928-1958*, Little, Brown, 1959.

I read with reverence *anything* that Father Berrigan writes.

Daniel Berrigan, *Encounters*, World Publishing Company, 1960.

Mildred Capron's film-programs are the best I know—pictorially and interpretively. Her portrayal of living and livelihoods, domestic arts, terrain, animals, agriculture, crop-detail, climate and sports, her grasp of history; her capturing the charm of a place or a person, of spirit and beliefs—amid the drama of color of stones or town or country—seems both factual and inspired; and the moral effect is as great as the visual. One couldn't say enough.

Mildred Capron, flyer for documentary film *Ireland*, Washington, Pennsylvania, 1960.

A valuable book . . . with an originality of interpretation which at times matches an unstereotyped and phenomenally interested kind of research. [Mr. Norman] has done us a service—the curious and those of us who really care about poetry, and about Ezra Pound.

Charles Norman, *Ezra Pound*, Macmillan, 1960.

Not only in primary purport but in light which it throws on Vachel Lindsay, the book is invaluable.

Margaret Haley Carpenter, *Sara Teasdale*, Schulte Publishing Company, 1960.

The wonderful selectiveness, the allure, the judgment with which the use of the sophisticated alternates with averageness, preserving the verity: consummate!

Frederick Prokosch, *A Ballad of Love*, Farrar, Straus and Cudahy, 1960.

A studious, ardent, truly expository study of La Fontaine. A pleasure to me and lexicon as well.

Margaret Guiton, *La Fontaine: Poet and Counterpoet*, Rutgers University Press, 1961.

I find him prepossessing.

John Ashbery, *The Tennis Court Oath*, Wesleyan University Press, 1962.

Mr. Grucci's poem "Rhine Burial" is haunting and ineffaceable.

Joseph Leonard Grucci, *The Invented Will*, Mayer Press, 1962.

. . . captures the feel of romance . . . indeed intimates drama and her sense of rhythm is such that her words seem to lend the page notes.

Henrietta Fort Holland, *Grace after Meat and Other Verses*, Wake-Brook House, 1962.

Compassionate, dextrous, knowledgeable Miss Deutsch . . . one contemplates her depth, range, straightness, and commanding stature as a poet.

Babette Deutsch, *The Collected Poems of Babette Deutsch*, Doubleday, 1963.

Throughout these various revelations, poems are embedded in the words, attesting indigenous, contagious, deep-rooted poetic imagination.

Ruth Stephan, *Various Poems*, Gotham Book Mart, 1963.

Perfection, with Cape Ann woodlands and quarry pools ennobled page on page, and every touch vivid.

Gudron S. Worcester, *The Singing Flute*, Ivan Obolensky, 1963.

I cherish the personal book-shop. What an elysium is a shop of which the owner reads some of the items he sells! One double-owns anything which he . . . sells.

Phoenix Book Shop, Catalog # 68, 1964.

Louis and Celia Zukofsky's *Bottom on Shakespeare* communicates its passion for music and its passion for Shakespeare. Shakespeare is emphasized here by an anthology of comparisons. Louis and Celia Zukofsky are talented in the device of interruption to make text emphatic; and the University of Texas knows how to print. An item!

Louis Zukofsky, *Bottom on Shakespeare*, with music by Celia Zukofsky, University of Texas Press, 1964.

. . . gives point to publishing, in a day of too many books.

Robert Francis, *Come Out into the Sun*, University of Massachusetts Press, 1965.

I can safely say to my little nephews for whom I shall be ordering a copy: the bat-poet's poems are really true to life—bat life, bird life, and child life.

Randall Jarrell, *The Bat-Poet*, Farrar, Straus and Giroux, 1965.

"The Mocking Bird," "Well Water," "Bats,"—and many others of the pieces startle me into felicity. Randall Jarrell is a revelation of how pleasing, how ingenious as words, poetry can be.

Randall Jarrell, *The Lost World: New Poems*, Macmillan, 1965.

He is an accomplished artist.

David Shapiro, *January: A Book of Poems*, Holt, Rinehart and Winston, 1965.

Dry Summer in Provence, "poetry": it is Provence intently observed, with an occasional line of plain prose—which does no harm. You have perched villages "hill-hung." "The Citadelle was built in the Twelfth Century"; "stone walls slit for spying"; "blackberries blur the boulders"; "the inverted L of hoeing with a mattock crooks his back."

The French call American windows guillotines;
    theirs open out
    so
    no screens
    the bugs flock in.

If the phrases sound right to you, read it all; do, and come on some terms with special meanings perhaps. It is a careful replica of a place; a devout book, tuned to miracles.

Millen Brand, *Dry Summer in Provence: Poems of a Place*, Clarkson N. Potter, 1966.

To begin with, a poet. His absence of affectation is one of the rarest things on earth. *Towards a Better Life* is a book to annotate. Un-stodgy *he!*

Kenneth Burke, *Towards a Better Life: Being a Series of Epistles, or Declamations*, University of California Press, 1966.

He has talent. For me, the final section of this book portends much.

Jeffrey Kindley, *The Under-Wood*, Phoenix Book Shop, 1966.

A vigilant sports observer and contagious narrator.

George Plimpton, *Paper Lion*, Harper & Row, 1966.

I am exhilarated by this departure from ordinary tributes—involving days upon days of research and rare familiarity with books and persons who have brought the sea alive in their writings. *The Bottom of the Sea* is a beautiful achievement . . . a beautiful book.

A. M. Sullivan, *The Bottom of the Sea*, Dun & Bradstreet, 1966.

It offsets a great deal for me . . . induces hope. I hope [Mr. Burns] continues to express what he is expressing here—and doing it concisely.

Robert Grant Burns, *Quiet World*, Charles A. McBride, 1967.

Music should be directed by the ear; poetry by the imagination. . . . Jean Garrigue must have heard of the Philistines, might have spoken to one. If so, no imprint of any such meeting has been left on her.

Jean Garrigue, *New and Selected Poems*, Macmillan, 1967.

Ivanov Seven creates an appetite for life. I am rereading it.

Elizabeth Janeway, *Ivanov Seven*, Harper & Row, 1967.

I consider Kraus Reprint Corporation's reprinting of early little magazine contents invaluable in making available to contemporary writers what predecessors have written and also available to living writers what they themselves produced.

Kraus Reprint Corporation, *The Little Magazines*, 1967.

I venerate George MacDonald, and Maurice Sendak has never done a scene I like better than the one with the crow and the tree and the thatched roof.

George MacDonald, *The Golden Key*, Farrar, Straus & Giroux, 1967.

Judging by portions I have read of Michael Reck's *Close-Up* of Ezra Pound, . . . by my several visits to St. Elizabeth's, and by my correspondence with Ezra Pound, and by his always helpfulness and generosities, I welcome the *Close-Up*. But more than all, his terse, pithy, compacted self-statements are verity itself—unmodified. One could ask nothing better.

Michael Reck, *Ezra Pound: A Close-Up*, McGraw-Hill, 1967.

I'd rather read Cosmicomics than go to the moon.

Italo Calvino, *Cosmicomics*, Harcourt, Brace & World, 1968.

Daniel Hoffman is an observer; and what he finds, the rhythm does not contradict. He "thinks"—and what he thinks has substance.

Daniel Hoffman, *A Little Geste*, Oxford University Press, 1968.

The verity of his writing is a pleasure.

Julian Mazor, *Washington and Baltimore*, Alfred A. Knopf, 1968.

Sie Thao: an ancient poet grieves, and Nature's beauty is a language that the reader cannot resist. Only the translator can effect such magic . . . a poet of Mary Kennedy's sensibility.

Mary Kennedy, *I Am a Thought of You: Poems by Sie Thao (Hung Tu)*, Gotham Book Mart, 1968.

. . . graphic, horrifying, strengthening. . . .

Hugh Nissenson, *Notes from the Frontier: An American's Experiences on a Border Kibbutz, Summer 1965 / June 1967*, The Dial Press, 1968.

Sensibility and chivalry do characterize her work. . . . She is a relief from the callous spirit of these times. . . . I take this book to heart.

Lenore Marshall, *Latest Will: New and Selected Poems*, W. W. Norton, 1969.

It is surely a remarkable and remarkably perfected piece of work. The effect of actuality, courage and idealism is invaluable.

Laurence Stapleton, *Yushin's Log and Other Poems*, A. S. Barnes, 1969.

I find remarkable Daniel Hoffman's *Striking the Stones*. . . . Who has the complacence to evaluate the verity of these poems as he reads?

Daniel Hoffman, *Striking the Stones*, Oxford University Press, 1970.

Reverent, scrupulous—keeping the mood and selectiveness of the original.

Rainer Maria Rilke, *The Duino Elegies*, translated by Stephen Garmey and Jay Wilson, Harper & Row, 1972.

MISCELLANEOUS SHORT PIECES

An attitude, physical or mental—a thought suggested by reading or in conversation—recurs with insistence. A few words coincident with the initial suggestion, suggest other words. Upon scrutiny, these words seem to have distorted the concept. The effort to effect a unit—in this case a poem—is perhaps abandoned. If the original, propelling sentiment reasserts itself with sufficient liveliness, a truer progress almost invariably accompanies it; and associated detail, adding impact to the concept, precipitates an acceptable development. To illustrate: a suit of armor is impressively poetic. The movable plates suggest the wearer; one is reminded of the armadillo and recalls the beauty of the ancient testudo. The idea of conflict, however, counteracts that of romance, and the subject is abandoned. However, the image lingers. Presently one encounters the iguana and is startled by the paradox of its docility in conjunction with its horrific aspect. The concept has been revived—of an armor in which beauty outweighs the thought of painful self-protectiveness. The emended theme compels development.

In *Everyman's Genius*, by Mary Austin. New York: Bobbs Merrill, 1925, p. 339.

•

In some quarters there is doubt about why these things of mine exist, let alone should be reprinted but if—with Mr. Cummings—you are willing to stand by "A Grave," do include it. It is from *Observations*. My favorite short poems by E. E. Cummings are a painting of two children dancing in the street near a horse-drawn merry-go-round; and the phrase, "Dirry me" from his play, *him*. But I should add that I have not seen Mr. Cummings for years, so this is not a *rendre à vous*.

As for "A Grave," it has a significance strongly apart from the literal origin, which was a man who placed himself between my mother and me, and surf we were watching from a "middle" ledge of rocks on Monhegan Island after a storm. ("Don't be annoyed," my mother said. "It is human nature to stand in the middle of a thing.") Since you are not publishing a guide-book, I should stop here but I am tempted to say a word about pre-artist days at Monhegan, when we reached the island by a sail-boat called *The Effort*. It usually got becalmed and we arrived at a mooring out from the fish-beach at low tide, midnight, and we hobbled over stones and slippery objects by lantern-light—our luggage accompanying us on a wheelbarrow—but next morning looked out of a gabled attic-room in a fisherman's cottage, on a pile of split birch-wood and an expanse of sea rising from a jagged line of fir-tops.

In *Fifty Poets*, edited by William Rose Benét. New York: Duffield & Green, 1933, pp. 84–85.

•

For either verse or prose, I feel that Sterne's advice might be followed: "Write anything and write it any how, so it but comes from yᵣ heart." The question then presents itself how valuable is the heart which writing from the heart will reveal?—through individuality, predilections, reading, sense of color, scene— even selfishness, and the qualities which hinder aspiration.

If, however, the thought in your inquiry concerned idiosyncrasies of technique, may I say that I am interested in precision, and feel that one should regard no amount of trouble taken too great to ensure making the meaning clear; admitting too that a concept as one exposits it, is so predominantly what is in one's mind that one sometimes fails to detect inadvertencies.

I dislike affectation. The unaccented rhymed syllable has an attraction for me as it had for Longfellow, Whittier, and others; and as a phase of unaccent, I tend to like a poem which instead of culminating in a crescendo, merely comes to a close; and though one cannot score words as one does notes there is an inevitable connection, I feel, between poetry and music.

Quoted by Alice Hunt Bartlett in "Dynamics of American Poetry: LVI," *The Poetry Review*, 26 (September 1935), 404.

•

I tend to write in a patterned arrangement, with rhymes; stanza as it follows stanza being identical in number of syllables and rhyme-plan, with the first stanza. (Regarding the stanza as the unit, rather than the line, I sometimes divide a word at the end of a line, relying on a general straightforwardness of treatment to counteract the mannered effect.) I have a liking for the long syllable followed by three (or more) short syllables,—"ly*ing on the* air *there is a* bird," and for the inconspicuous or light rhyme,—"let" in flageolet, for instance, being rhymed with "set" in the lines,

> Its leaps should be set
> to the flageolet.

I try to secure an effect of flowing continuity and am more and more impressed by the many correspondences between verse and instrumental music. I am against the stock phrase and an easier use of words in verse than would be tolerated in prose. I feel that the form is the outward equivalent of a determining inner conviction, and that the rhythm is the person.

In *The Oxford Anthology of American Literature*, edited by William Rose Benét and Norman Holmes Pearson. New York: Oxford University Press, 1938, p. 1319.

•

Wallace Stevens: the interacting veins of life between his early and later poems are an ever-continuing marvel to me. He seems to live in an unspoiled cosmos of his own, in which under surprises or alien pressure he is so constitutionally incapable of self-treachery that his poetry becomes for us a symbol of hope,— a kind of incorruptible Eleazer of the Apochrypha.

The Harvard Advocate, 127 (December 1940), 31.

•

"What Are Years?" partly written in 1931 and finished in 1939, is elegiac.

The desperation attendant on mortal fallibility is mitigated for me by admitting that the most willed and resolute vigilance may lapse, as with the Apostle Peter's denial that he could be capable of denial; but that failure, disgrace, and even death have now and again been redeemed into inviolateness by a sufficiently transfigured courage.

Marianne Moore

Brooklyn, N.Y.
March 22, 1942.

Dear Whit:
    Again, "What Are Years?" Again, Bach plays back Bach.

Marianne

N.Y. 1968

In *This Is My Best*, edited by Whit Burnett. New York: The Dial Press, 1942, p. 645, and Doubleday, 1970, p. 913.

•

E. E. Cummings is a concentrate of titanic significances, "a positive character"; and only ingenuousness could attempt to suggest in a word, the "heroic" aspect of his paintings, his poems, and his resistances. He does not make aesthetic mistakes.

The Harvard Wake, 5 (Spring 1946), 24.

•

"A poem to or about him might be very illuminating." Yes, if one could divest the mind of this or that better poem *by* him. I can only say that for me, lacklusterness and aesthetic mildew vanish under the burning-glass of real poetry, and William Carlos Williams is the real thing.

"With Regard to William Carlos Williams," *Briarcliff Quarterly*, 3 (October 1946), 192.

•

Alfred Stieglitz had no gift for subterfuge. He was almost queer in his inability to approximate counterfeit. His horses in a blizzard did not have to be zebras. The blacks and whites of his portraits are as businesslike as printing. It is impossible to forget the eternal aspect of what Alfred Stieglitz published when at 291. Even the envelopes made a robber of visitors, so much was given them. A distinctive place was 291—an American Acropolis so to speak, with a stove in it, a kind of eagle's perch of selectiveness, and like the ardor of fire, in its completeness.

Exhibiting is hard work, but Alfred Stieglitz did not weary of his ever new virtuosi. Advertising is also arduous, and whereas derogation has the attraction of not being extorted, devising testimonials is not so simple; yet if Mr. Stieglitz could say a word about ability such as Loren MacIver's or Benjamin Kopman's, he was willing to be an advertiser. He knew everything there is to know about selling, when he concluded that nothing can be paid for, can only be given. He was an en"thus"iast, not exactly a theologian but a godly man; and he was right; a thing is remembered, not for its shadows but for itself.

In *Stieglitz Memorial Portfolio, 1864–1946*, edited by Dorothy Norman. New York: Twice a Year Press, 1947, p. 35.

•

With regard to Mr. McBride and his Modern Art commentary in *The Dial*, mere fact in the way of editorial gratitude has the look of extravagance. It is hard to credit Mr. McBride's innate considerateness as synonymous with his unfailing afflatus, thought so substantial as coincident with gaiety, and so wide a range of authority as matched by ultra-accuracy.

Each month, usually in the morning, Mr. McBride would bring his three pages of Modern Art commentary to *The Dial*, visit without hurry, but briefly, and infect routine with a savor of hieratic competence. The word "competent" may have connotations of mildness, but not in this connection. Mr. McBride and insight are synonymous. You may have gone to the fair and come away with a gross of green glasses but not Mr. McBride. As he said of Elie Nadelman: "Directly in proportion to the vitality of an artist's work is the reluctance of the public to accept it."

You may have premonitions but Mr. McBride has the data, is succinct and matter-of-fact,—be your investigations in what field they may—: houses, furniture, dress, printing, painting, dancing, music, verse, sculpture; the camera, movies, the drama. Wit that is mentality does not betray itself and Henry McBride is adamant to the friend of a friend desiring encomiums.

He is not susceptible to self-eulogy. Where feeling is deep it is not a topic. Reverence that is reverence is a manifestation, as has never been proved better than by Mr. McBride.

In *To Honor Henry McBride*, by Lincoln Kirstein. New York: Knoedler Galleries, 1949, pp. 2–3.

•

Ezra Pound is that rarity, an artist who is a preceptor by *example:* a master or "sage," whose inexhaustible virtuosity has made and is making his verse and criticism an archive of poetic wisdom.

Quarterly Review of Literature, 5, No. 2 (1949), 146.

•

Material for *The Dial* was assembled with gusto, with an unwaveringly ardent interest in creativeness. The proprietors felt that diffuseness is synonymous with dullness: they felt they were without prejudice; they had a conscience concerning the injustice of rejecting what was better than what they had published. Exhilaration and incentive never, it would seem, subside into weary fortitude.

The *faux bon*—deprecated in *Dial* advertisements—is constantly encroaching upon talent: and talent however fertile, can stumble into ancient pitfalls. The ferocity of contributors toward one another and toward editors is a commonplace; art enterprises abound in surprises that are not conducive to peace of mind, and the staff of *The Dial* found the emancipated liberality of the owners instructive. A passion for the positive is like the unicorn; violence is no match for it. To be loyal was not necessary; to have disliked *The Dial* from the inside would have been impossible.

"Symposium on Little Magazines," *Golden Goose*, Series 3, No. 1 (1951), 18.

•

I was born in Missouri in 1887, was graduated from Bryn Mawr in 1909 and live in Brooklyn in a six-story yellow brick and lime-stone apartment house on what is known as The Hill.

My recreations are the theater, tennis, sailing, reading and the movies—animal documentaries, travelogues, an occasional French film, and the newsreel.

I like country fairs, roller-coasters, merry-go-rounds, dog shows, museums, avenues of trees, old elms, vehicles, experiments in timing like our ex-Museum of Science and Invention's two roller-bearings in a gravity chute, synchronized with a ring-bearing revolving vertically. I am fond of animals and take an inordinate interest in mongooses, squirrels, crows, elephants. I read few magazines but would be lost without the newspaper. My favorite authors, I think, are Chaucer, Molière and Montaigne. I am attached to Dr. Johnson; also like Xenophon, Hawthorne, Landor and Henry James. I take an interest in trade journals, books for children, and never tire of Beatrix Potter. My favorite reading is almost any form of biography—Ellen Terry, Cellini, Mr. Churchill's war memoirs, Capt. Corbett's *Man Eaters of Kumaon*, E. E. Cummings' *Eimi*, Wallace Fowlie's *Pantomime*, Sir Osbert Sitwell's *Escape with Me*.

I work best in the morning but usually keep on, afternoon and evening. I seldom use a desk, (write on a pad or portfolio). I seem to myself an observer, an interested hack rather than an author, but am an extremist with regard to exact statement; am quoted as having said, "I write exercises in composition"; perhaps said, "I look on my verse as exercises in composition." When I have finished a thing it is, so far as I know, the last thing I shall write; but if taken unaware by what charms or stirs me up, I may write again.

It is a great deal to me that there are in the world a few real enemies of enslavement and that some of them are generals—General Eisenhower, General MacArthur and General de Tassigny; that there are a few men of Socratic wisdom among us, like Professor Macmurray, Professor Niebuhr and Professor Hocking; that a few real artists are alive today—Casals, Soledad, E. McKnight Kauffer, Hans Mardersteig, Alec Guinness, the Lippizan horsemen.

"Some of the Authors of 1951 Speaking for Themselves," *New York Herald Tribune Book Review*, 7 October 1951, pp. 14, 16.

•

To be trusted is an ennobling experience; and poetry is a peerless proficiency of the imagination. I prize it, but am myself an observer; I can see no reason for calling my work poetry except that there is no other category in which to put it. Anyone could do what I do and I am the more grateful that those whose judgment I trust should regard it as poetry.

Someone at a poetry conference at which I was present, complained of modern poetry and said he could not read it. He could only read Dante; and R. P. Blackmur said, "But we don't come in that big size." A pleasing statement; yet perspective occasionally does come in large sizes and Wallace Stevens in his book, *The Necessary Angel*, puts his finger on this thing poetry, it seems to me, where he refers to "a violence within that protects us from a violence without." We have it in Chaucer's heady epitome: "I think I thirst the more the more I drink"—an intensity which finds a way of surpassing intensity—in which "I think" means I know and understatement is emphasis. In poetry, metaphor substitutes compactness for confusion and says the fish moves "on winglike foot." It also says—and for "it" I had better say Confucius—"If there be a knife of resentment in the heart, the mind will not attain precision." That is to say, poetry watches life with affection. In poetry the light touch is the strong touch as when La Fontaine says:

> And if I have failed to give you real delight,
> My excuse must be that I had hoped I might.

I could cite contemporary counterparts to these instances of what I think of as poetry. The thing certainly has not died with Dante, nor has courtesy died with King Arthur, as is apparent in the chivalry of this audience, listening patiently to me as I speculate on the "secret experimental activities" which are responsible for the art of poetry. "Secret experimental activities" is, I should say, a phrase of Harold Rosenberg's.

I am much aware of the luster shed by preceding recipients of this award upon those who follow, and thus upon myself. I am more indebted to the judges than I know how to say, for regarding potential achievement in the instance of my work as synonymous with performance. As already implied, tremendous incentive is afforded one in being trusted by those whose judgment one trusts. And we have a very great debt, I feel, to the National Book Award Committee, for its liberality in caring to create in our midst, an atmosphere conducive to poetry.

"A Felicitous Reponse," *The Christian Science Monitor*, February 7, 1952, p. 7. Remarks on the acceptance of the National Book Award.

•

Queen Juliana said to us when here, "In the world-conscious respect for the freedom of others lies a great mental power which is yours."

Thinking of what she expressed, I would say that the John Simon Guggenheim Memorial Foundation, in liberating the mind and enabling it to understand beauty, is cause for pride to our city and to this country, revered the more for its modestly quiet manner of giving, which is personified by its president, Mrs. Simon Guggenheim, who has consented to be with us today.

Giving is good, but when the manner of giving is itself a gift, then it is better— benevolence in this instance as anonymously unrestrictive as Deity's—I can but say with fervor and personal gratitude of my own to the Foundation.

The Council of the Institute proffers this award of 1952 in recognition of Mrs. Guggenheim's profound helpfulness to human achievement in establishing with her husband, the late Senator Simon Guggenheim, the John Simon Guggenheim Memorial Foundation, and her continuing leadership and generosity in providing fellowships in music, literature and the arts.

Indeed, I find it impossible to restrain myself from alluding to the exhilaration and gratitude stirred in us by Mrs. Guggenheim's own special gifts to the public of favorite works of art such as Rousseau's "The Sleeping Gypsy" in the Museum of Modern Art, Tchelitchew's "Hide and Seek," and classic examples of Maillol and Lachaise.

The affectionately intensive devotion embodied by Senator and Mrs. Guggenheim in the Foundation is so much a part of the Memorial, I should like to read the purposes of the Foundation as stated in 1925 in Senator Guggenheim's first letter of gift, as follows:

"We strongly hope that this Foundation will advance human achievement by aiding students to push forward the boundaries of understanding, and will enrich human life by aiding them in the cultivation of beauty and taste. If, at the close of our lives, looking both backward and forward, we can envision an endless succession of scholars, scientists, and artists aided by the John Simon Guggenheim Memorial Foundation, devoting themselves to these purposes, we shall feel that, with the help of our associates, we shall have accomplished the aim which we had set before us in memory of our son."

I would not detract from the depth of these words by adding to them, but would ask you, Mrs. Guggenheim, if we may present you, with the love and unanimity of the Institute, this Award of 1952 for Distinguished Service to the Arts.

"Presentation to Mrs. Simon Guggenheim of the Award for Distinguished Service to the Arts," *Proceedings of the American Academy of Arts and Letters,* Second Series, No. 3 (1953), 18–19.

•

The Church has been a miracle, Mr. McCandless says, in bringing unity to warring nations and antagonistic races. Now conscience is central, is it not, in the matter of obligations as part of the rights we enjoy?

Bushmen in the Kalahari Desert, I am told by Mrs. Laurance Marshall the anthropologist, have no predisposition to combat. They assume good intention on the part of approaching strangers. Indeed, in their fairness, they approximate the Christian ideal of humility and faith.

Theodore Parker, in his *Journal*, recalls an incident in childhood. "A rhodora in full bloom," he says, "a rare plant in the neighborhood, attracted my eye. I saw a little spotted tortoise sunning himself in the shallow water at the root of the glowing flower and lifted a stick I had in my hand, to strike it—as I had seen other boys attack birds, squirrels or small animals. But all at once a voice said within me clear and loud, 'It is wrong.' I hastened home to my mother and asked what had told me it was wrong. She said, 'Some call it conscience; I prefer to call it the voice of God in the soul. If you listen and obey, it will speak clearer and clearer, and always guide you aright; but if you turn a deaf ear or disobey, then it will fade out little by little and leave you alone in the dark, without a guide. Your life depends on your heeding this little voice.' I am sure," he says, "no event in my life left so deep an impression."

Socrates throughout his trial constantly referred to his Inner Voice as the guide of all his actions.

This potential of greatness, manifested in Socrates, Polycarp, Giordano Bruno, Abraham Lincoln, and in men in our own time, has come to us, we might say, as the over-ruling power of the Moral Law, combined through the Grace of God, with human experience, from the days of our first parents to the present time— codified by Moses in the Ten Commandments; expanded and modified when tested by reason, from potentiality or spiritual apperception, into what we call a sense of duty. We sometimes forget conscience, or feel that it can be controlled. But on a day, we may find it our master.

What is conscience? Alban Butler, the hagiologist (1700–1773) said, "There is in man a faculty which takes into consideration the springs of action. And to this a religious sanction is added, which results not only in a sense of duty, but a sense of security in following it and a sense of danger in departing from it. Virtue," he says, "consists in following this law of nature"—or thing we call conscience.

Awareness of this directive is powerfully present in the work of W. H. Auden. The impact of his work largely derives, I would say, from the recurrent emphasis in it on *choice*. In his *New Year Letter*, the Devil is personified as equivocation, the Double Man—perpetually baffling his victim with "either-or," a clouder of the eye of conscience.

We say that Russia substitutes self for God and makes experience, Deity. Mr. Auden's interpretation of Grimm's Fairy Tales is an amplification of practice that is the opposite. "From tale after tale," he says, "we learn not that wishing is a substitute for action, but that wishes for good and evil are terribly real. The son who marries the Princess and inherits the kingdom is not a superman with exceptional natural gifts. He succeeds not through merit, but through the as- sistance of a Divine Grace. His contribution is firstly a humility which admits that he cannot succeed without Divine Grace; and secondly, a faith which believes that Grace will help him, so that when the old beggar asks for his last penny . . . when, humanly speaking, he is dooming himself to fail, he can give it away; and, lastly, he succeeds through willingness to accept suffering."

To summarize: Choice is inescapable; and with the aid of humility in subordinating self-will to God's will—to the voice of the ages alive in us through Christ—the spirit attains *true* freedom, in which it continues to live and not die.

"Conscience," *Church of the Epiphany Bulletin*, 4 October 1953, pp. 5–6.

•

In reading an author who has "made us a gift of truth," Proust says, we have "a friend without formalities. But if we put to him questions that he cannot answer, we ask for answers that would not instruct us. . . . All he can do is give us desires . . . by making us contemplate beauty, . . . the mirage that constitutes a vision."[1]

These observations apply, for me, to Wallace Stevens, who "wears a deliberately commonplace costume," studies "the interior of a parasol," and by various tactful feints, provides us with a "place in which it would be pleasant to spend a holiday." Amid grandeurs the more spectacular for not being grandiose, he conjures up for the reader, harmonies special to himself—scenes and sounds that are communicated by only a very great musician.

[1] Proust: "Days of Reading" in *Essays on Language and Literature*, edited by J. L. Hevesi (Allan Wingate).

"A Tribute," *Trinity Review*, 8 (May 1954), 11.

•

He was true to his gift and he had a mighty power, indigenously accurate like nature's. And his mechanism at times is as precise as the content.

"Tribute to Dylan Thomas," *Yale Literary Magazine*, 122 (November 1954), 6.

•

If medals were awarded for diffidence, nothing could be more appropriate than the decision of the Institute to present its 1953 medal for poetry to me.

It is for achievement, however, that honors are bestowed, and we are indebted to various of my associates for achievements that are epic. This being the case, I can but do what the members of the Institute have done—waive logic and assure them that undeserved honors shall not make me La Fontaine's Aesopian frog,

a little goose
who tried to be an ox, she was so grandiose.

Illogical idealism can be as powerful in implementing effort as if it were reasonable. Permit me to testify that this is so; and to say that I shall double diligence in the hope that I may yet justify the confidence which the members of the Institute have expressed in me.

"Acceptance of the Gold Medal for Poetry," *Proceedings of the American Academy of Arts and Letters*, Second Series, No. 4 (1954), 13.

•

Yes, I believe in prayer—as a mystery which can endow one with more power perhaps than any other spiritual mystery, yet a mystery which cannot be exposited to the point where it is not a mystery. That Alexis Carrell's, Glenn Clark's, Richard C. Cabot's and others' statements about prayer, are applicably potent, and real, certainly is not a contradiction of what I have just said.

As when the apostle Peter objected, "Lord, depart from me for I am a sinful man," the paradox of faithful distrust, surely leads one to an apprehension of "faith." With regard to the efficacy of prayer "in communicating new courage" to the detached observer, however, courage to be derived from prayer will only be derived by those who make a trial of it.

"I Believe in Prayer," in *How Prayer Helps Me*, edited by Samuel Duff McCoy. New York: The Dial Press, 1955, p. 96.

•

Ezra Pound does not age; nor do I tire of saluting the newness, the incisiveness, the poetic potencies of his verse, his translations, his criticism, and his counsel. The poetic scene would be desert without him.

In *Ezra Pound at Seventy*. Norfolk, Conn.: New Directions, 1956, p. 6.

•

In 1957, the Lafayette Avenue Presbyterian Church will be a hundred years old. Preceded by Dr. Cuyler, Dr. Gregg, Dr. McAfee and Dr. Albertson, Dr. Magary has for more than twenty-six years, steadfastly and with power, been answering the plea embodied literally in the structure of our pulpit, "Sir, we would see Jesus." Christianity as expounded by Dr. Magary has made real to us principles of faith which constitute a portrait of the Christian; and since these precepts, recurrently emphasized by Dr. Magary, seem to various of his parishioners, to afford a conspectus of his ministry, it has been suggested that certain of them be embodied in this resolution as follows:

"God has given us the spirit not of fear but of power" that we may show forth the light vouchsafed us in the Gospel; that we may "do justly, love mercy, and walk humbly before our God"; that we may say with the Psalmist, "When my heart is overwhelmed: lead me to the rock that is higher than I," that we may know right from wrong by the fact that "the right things are creative; the wrong things, destructive."

The Bible is a book of remembrance—of God's mercy accorded men through no merit of their own, a memorial of escape from bondage, not because they were few but because the Lord loved them: a book in which no command is more frequent than that ye proclaim liberty to the captive—a proclamation inspiring hope that all may be free and no man the property of another.

The Bible is a book inspiring a faith which—beyond the power of self-discipline—growing from darkness, leads to the place of understanding; as the Patriarch Job said, "Behold the fear of the Lord, that is wisdom." As the Apostle Paul stood before King Agrippa, and Christ before Pilate, the man of faith is able to face the man of power and prevail.

As enjoined upon the congregation by Dr. Magary throughout his ministry among us, "nothing is more unprofitable than the assumption that life is easy." And—as the Apostle Paul, essaying to be a rabbi, became a Christian missionary and, threatened by shipwreck, said, "When the ship could no longer bear up into the wind, we let her drive," trusting to a compass not seen but of faith— "frequently we are Columbus sailing for one port and arriving at another." As the Apostle did not consider himself a finished Christian, and the Apostle Peter exclaimed, "Lord, depart from me for I am a sinful man," "persecuted but not forsaken, cast down but not destroyed," shall we not take heart, reminded by Dr. Magary that the heroes of the Bible are, indeed, "saints without halos."

It has been impressed upon us by Dr. Magary that we may be obedient to the heavenly vision, yet be unprofitable servants if we do only our duty. Dr. and Mrs. Magary in their joint ministry to the bereaved, the ill and those in perplexity, have not merely participated in the life of the church but have taken upon themselves duties far beyond any to be anticipated: Mrs. Magary as pianist and not infrequently supper hostess for meetings of the Young People's Association; Dr. Magary for three successive years conducting on Sunday evenings a class in Bible study: an exposition of the Book of Job; a history of the Jews with commentary; and currently, a study of the Epistles of the Apostle Paul.

Solicitous for the young and temptations which may beset them, concerned for those under the strain of failing health, and for those whom the burden of years threatens to be too great, Dr. Magary has been to us Pastor, teacher, and friend. He has rescued the Gospel from theology and made creed personal. He is, as was said by Dr. Elliot, our Moderator of the congregational meeting on October 24, "a man with the mark of Christian genius upon him."

When times are auspicious, when the membership of a church is strong and self-renewing and the neighborhood one promising stability, optimism is easy. With conditions the reverse, Dr. Magary has stood firm, inspiriting the Church by his devotion and courage. That he may be enheartened by the conviction that his work "has not been in vain in the Lord," is the prayer of this Church— a message personal to Dr. and Mrs. Magary as part of this resolution.

"Resolution on Dr. Magary's Retirement," *The Lafayette Record* (Bulletin of the Lafayette Avenue Presbyterian Church, Brooklyn, New York), March 1957, pp. 4–5.

•

If we may write to enhearten one another, Robert Frost is a titan—better say a near-deity—to his writer friends. I treasure him; I wish I might benefit him— GIVE him something—not merely be saying that I do.

Beloit Poetry Journal, Chapbook Number Five (Summer 1957), [1].

•

George Lynes—in a way that is emphasized by absence—contributed to my knowledge of art; not art merely, but to my knowledge of art as behavior. His ironic idiosyncrasy of understatement made preliminaries painless, professionally and socially. His understanding of light and impatience with retouching as a substitute for focus, imparted to his work a glow in which naturalness is not sacrificed to verisimilitude. He had style—created style; this impression strengthens with time.

In *New York City Ballet: Photographs from 1935 through 1955 taken by George Platt Lynes 1907–1956*. New York: The New York City Center of Music and Drama, 1957, [p. 4].

•

The National Book Award affected me as a *person*—gave me confidence in my work and a feeling of optimism as regards the public. The Award indeed has been a lasting encouragement to me, has lent my work value to myself and is an eternal incentive.

"What NBA Means to Some Past Winners," *New York Herald Tribune Book Review*, 1 March 1959, pp. 2, 11.

•

I thrive on experiment—have never knowingly written two pieces in the same meter and am charged continually with obscurity; so the role of censor dare not be mine.

The defiant steady down sometimes, into what is beneficial, if not beneficent. I always can see in non-conformists aspects of imagination. Might we say that the reader's interest is the court by which the writer is judged. The writer must hold the attention—poet, novelist, dramatist—whatever he is. If the writer invents an obstructiveness of technique or subject matter too great for the reader to feel in any degree rewarded, the reader automatically turns to what "says more" and "says it better." How overcome indifference is the problem. The burden of proof is on the writer. "Do I overcome the reader's indifference?" he may ask; or let him ask nothing and risk a restricted restricted reciprocity— even neglect.

To deny the effect of comparison is not workmanlike, is it?

P. S. Ezra Pound is not prim; nor is he always lucid, yet he feels that it is a fair test of a poem to ask, "Has it human value?"

In "Symposium: The Beat Poets," *Wagner Literary Magazine* (Spring 1959), 18.

•

Robert Frost's "continuity" in spirit and performance is a thing for which to give thanks in our unending battle with materiality. His "complementarity" has a vigor that never wears thin; the verse, a dexterity that never seems forced— that never loses its craftly fascination:

(A Lone Striker—1934)

He knew another place, a wood,
And in it, tall as trees, were cliffs;
And if he stood on one of these,
'Twould be among the tops of trees, . . .

His e's and be's and he's and trees do more than keep out of one another's way; they say something. His consonants and rhymes do more than chime neatly:

(Two Tramps in Mud Time—1936)

But yield who will to their separation,

My object in living is to unite
My avocation and my vocation
As my two eyes make one in sight. . . .

In 1934 or 5 after he had read at the Brooklyn Academy, I thanked him. He had a heavy cold, was being solicitously and rapidly conducted along the corridor from the offices to an elevator, implored not to delay on any pretext. He insisted on stopping, however, and said, "I want to say something" and asked me if anything of mine had been printed as a book. I said no. He said, "Well, I am going to do something about it." I said, "O but I must explain; I *am* going to have a book. Macmillan and Faber & Faber—at the same time—say they would like to issue for me a book of Selected Poems. So you mustn't do anything about me." "O well then," he said (and in a very unhurried manner as he turned away with his guide) "that's all right."

In *Robert Frost: Trial by Existence*, by Elizabeth Shepley Sargent. New York: Holt, Rinehart & Winston, 1960, pp. 417–18.

•

A writer
is trying to express something so well that it could not be expressed better.

Assets: power of observation
   inexhaustible perseverance
   gusto—a great amount of joy in the thing;

bearing in mind two "Imagist don'ts:"
   "Direct treatment
   no unnecessary word."

No mannerisms; you are not seeking notoriety or a fortune;
you are a student of art.

Whatever it is—poem, play, story, memoir, business letter—
it must hold the attention.

"Poetry as Expression," *The Writer*, 75 (April 1962), 35.

•

Generous friends, ingeniously finding time to make it possible to be here:
   It is hardly considerate, it seems to me, to invite friends to gather for an evening's reciprocity which they may not be at leisure to spend, unless one has something of great technical interest to offer or novelty of art for the occasion, treasurable or not.
   My observations, as usual, are borrowed. I am asked why I quote rather than say things in my own words. (I feel that when a thing has been said so well that

it could not be said better, why paraphrase it?) So may I quote—as to writers—what was said long ago and is vehemently now reiterated by Ezra Pound: "Use no word which does not contribute to the presentation." And another thought of his—new to me—that the parenthesis, circuitously prolonged, "as an American art form," is the distinctively "Jamesian contribution."[1]

Two thoughts of late, in their possible bearing upon us, have come to me with great force, the matter of leisure, in connection with hospitality. Sebastian de Grazia in a book entitled *Of Time, Work, and Leisure*, published by the Twentieth Century Fund, says: "The Romans, who were paragons of constructive activity," were accustomed to spend the afternoon resting and still do. Could we manage this, "even if the local climate is not favorable to it?"

Hospitality—say generosity—as I discern it, is giving what you could profitably use yourself; golden examples of which abounded in the parts of Italy and Greece in which I was last summer; exemplified by ship companies, inns, and even very poor persons: the white rose and spray of lemon verbena spontaneously given by a museum guard who had it on his table; five pomegranates glowing scarlet in the afternoon sun, like apples of the Hesperides, given five itinerants by a large family with food scarce; a little heap of pins for the use of clerks, in a shop in Athens, presented in a glazed white gold-edged box "with the compliments of the shop" when a patron proposed buying ten or so.

As a novelty or "work of art"—a kind of ceremonial bow to those who have incommoded themselves to be present, the few lines which follow have tried with schoolboy diligence to make themselves clear: an allegory involving an elephant, a dog, and a carpet of flowers—a fifteenth-century Flemish or French scene in the spirit of the Cluny unicorn tapestry, entitled "Charity Overcoming Envy."

> Have you time for a story
> (depicted in tapestry)
> Charity, riding an elephant,
> on a "mosaic of flowers," faces Envy,
> the flowers "bunched together, not rooted."
> Envy, on a dog, is worn down by obsession—
> his greed, since of things owned by others,
> he can only take *some*.
> . . . .
> He is saying, "O Charity, pity me; Deity!
> O pitiless Destiny
> what will become of me,
> maimed by Charity—Caritas—sword unsheathed
> over me yet? Blood stains my cheek. I am hurt."
> In chest-armor over chain mail, a steel shirt
> to the knee, he repeats, "I am hurt."

The elephant, at no time borne down by self-pity,
    convinces the victim
that Destiny is not devising a plot.

The problem is mastered—insupportably
tiring when it was impending.

Deliverance accounts for what sounds like an axiom,

    The Gordian knot need not be cut.

Charity Overcoming Envy: late fifteenth-century tapestry (Flemish or French),
Glasgow Art Gallery and Museum, The Burrell Collection.

[1] Ezra Pound, interviewed by Donald Hall; *Paris Review*—Summer–Fall, 1962.

*Proceedings of the American Academy of Arts and Letters and the National Institute
of Arts and Letters.* 2nd Series, No. 15 (1963), 280–81. Remarks delivered at
a dinner in honor of her seventy-fifth birthday.

•

Incomparable Isak Dinesen—the Baroness Blixen, whose motto when seventeen
was "Navigare," and more recently, "Je responderay"—the latter, a friend's
motto adopted by the friends presented to her. Are not these mottoes insignia?
A description of Isak Dinesen's gifts of mind and heart—of her dignity, warmth,
esprit—her consummate gallantry?

In *Isak Dinesen: A Memorial*, edited by Clara Svendsen. New York: Random
House, 1964, p. 96.

•

I Am the Greatest, if meant seriously is comic and if meant comically, is comic.
It is romantic comedy, it is poetic drama, it is poetry. If it savors of diatribe,
consider: "I worry not the danger; I have archly crossed the moor." These rhyming
couplets are a mode of verse, the *New York Times* says, for which more has
been done here than by anyone else since Alexander Pope. At a crucial moment—rather often indeed—altitude is saved by a hair from being the flattest,
peanuttiest, unwariest of boastings; saved might one say with Shakespeare, by
"one of Caesar's hairs."
    I Am the Greatest or *Much Ado about Cassius* has structure. Its hero, The
Greatest—though a mere youth—has snuffed out "more dragons than Smokey
the Bear hath." Mighty-muscled and fit, he is confident, he is sagacious; even

so, he *trains*, he fights; he is not ring-rusty. He acquires a title, a crown, a purse; a king's daughter is bestowed on him as a fiancée—a princess. He is literary—in the tradition of Sir Philip Sidney, defender of Poesie. His verse is ornamented by alliteration. An official voice calls him: "Come forth, Cassius Clay." A knight, a king of the ring, a mimic, a satirist, he calms his opponent: "Of course you're tired and irritable. Control yourself!" He has aplomb sufficient to impersonate Presidential "vigah." He is not even deterred by "the small volks dragons." He has a fondness for antithesis, will not only "give fighting lessons but falling lessons." As The Greatest, he is of course, master of hyperbole: his "punch raises his opponent clear out of the ring. The crowd is getting frantic. A radar station has picked him up. He is over the Atlantic." Admittedly the "classiest and brassiest," when asked, "How do you feel about the British calling you Gaseous Cassius," his reply is one of the prettiest in literature: "I do not resent it." He is a master of concision. Asked, "Have you ever been in love," he says, "Not with anyone else." Note this: beat grime revolts him. How not! Has any champion charm when beclouded by grime? He is neat, spruce; debonaire with manicure; his brow is high. If beaten—since mortal—he still is not "beat." Might he, as winner, be Tel-elusive? Not so. He will be seen win or lose—in normal motion and slow. Could MUCH ADO, could The Greatest, disappear in desert air? "Anywhere at all?" Might "eight trillion" copies of *I Am the Greatest* be enough? No. He fights and he writes. Is there something I have missed? He is a smiling pugilist.

Record jacket for *I Am the Greatest!* by Cassius Clay, Columbia Records, 1963.

•

January 23, 1963.

Sylvia Beach,—how do justice to one with impact so great as hers, and unfailing delicacy? Who never allowed logic to persuade her to regret over-charity to a beneficiary; ardent, restive, forever exerting herself, to advantage and give pleasure to one who had, as she felt, benefited her. During sixty years and more, this has been my impression of her.

"How Do Justice . . . ," *Mercure de France*, 349 (August–September 1963), [13].

•

When I wake at six or seven—I drink a glass of water—write a résumé in a little 2 1/2 by 3 1/2 Swiss calendar-diary, given to me by a friend, of the previous day, any special name or fact I mustn't forget—hang on my trapeze for a moment or two—whether infirm or not, read a few lines calculated to counteract infirmity, from the Bible usually, as stabilizing "the innocency of our lives and the constancy of our faith"—impatient to work but pause for breakfast—bring it to my room—half a grapefruit or orange juice, honey, an egg, hard-boiled or scrambled, a piece of Pepperidge white toast—may eat a chocolate leaf if I have one—in winter, dark hot chocolate with marshmallow or whipped cream, in summer perhaps no egg—hearing meanwhile what Bob Hite has to say about the weather—dress and go on answering correspondence of the day before, interrupted constantly by the telephone.

"How They Start the Day," *Glamour*, 61 (September 1963), 179.

•

I am proud of Kenyon College, Mr. Ransom, and each of you.

"John Crowe Ransom, Gentleman Teacher, Poet, Editor, Founder of the Kenyon Review: A Tribute from the Community of Letters," *The Kenyon Collegian*, Supplement to Vol. 2, No. 7 (1964), 55.

•

Words, phrases, remembered epithets, elude the vehemence of my gratitude to R. P. Blackmur: to his tonic unaggressive instinctive unswerving uncompromise of exactitude, making explicit the integrity of his single focus on verity of effect; on his reciprocal sense of human indebtedness—exempt from egotism of revenge or sense of injustice to his work; hospitably "at ease"—"liberal"—"kind to the presumptuous young" as G. S. Fraser says; a man of letters; yes—of mind.

"On R. P. Blackmur," *Nassau Literary Magazine* (May 1965), 8.

•

Pound is the most contagious teacher I have known—deadly in earnest, at the same time, indigenously piquant. "You might have more fun with rhymes," concerning a flat line as equivalent for a French one. How indisputably right; "consecutive work toward an avowable end." "A coherent paragraph in plain English. The rule? Subject, predicate, object." AND, "ask the solid of yourself; the trifle of others."

Agenda, 4 (October–November 1965), 22.

•

Generosity is giving what you could use yourself.

Reader's Digest, 88 (April 1966), 205.

•

My grandfather was a Presbyterian minister and was present during the Battle of Gettysburg. He was a pastor there, and his wife, my grandmother, died of typhoid fever as a result of the battle, since conditions in Gettysburg were very unwholesome.

My brother was born in Massachusetts; I in Missouri. As young children we lived with my aunt and grandfather, my grandfather being pastor of a Presbyterian church in Kirkwood, Missouri. He had a little white manse with a porch and about five white buildings surrounding it.

There were oak trees and bluejays in the churchyard. An aunt had sent me a little alligator as a pet, and we had numerous kittens. There were flowers along the fence between the yard and the adjoining one, with crimson roses and white clematis along the fence which separated the two yards—in the autumn, chrysanthemums—and there was spatterdock in tubs by the back door.

We children attended a kindergarten and carried a small market basket holding an orange and butter-thin biscuits.

We then went to live in Pennsylvania. My brother attended high school, and I, Metzger Institute. My mother taught English there. She prepared me for Bryn Mawr and spoiled me badly.

I was diffident when I was sixteen, intimidated by sleigh rides, barn dances, and such parties. I was interested in animals and sports, and after school I read books like *Captains Courageous* and *Stories Mother Nature Told Her Children*, *For Freedom's Cause* and one about Scotland. I was always reading or preparing lessons. I was over-anxious when sixteen. I'd be uncertain whether I'd pass this or that subject. My main thought was to know English and French—I'd read Carlyle. But I couldn't take French at Metzger and I couldn't take English, not elective, that is, so I was badly disappointed. Then later on I wanted very much to go to Bryn Mawr. I did go there. I was one of two girls in the Latin course, the only girl in French.

I also took piano lessons, but I've forgotten it by now. I'm very fond of music. I even took singing lessons—not because I could sing, because I could *not*. I had a very dutiful teacher. She was really a precisionist and did me a lot of good. We had chapel and had to sing "Onward, Christian Soldiers." I used to sing it like this: "Onward, Christian Sold-i-e-rs." My teacher said, "You must never do that. Cut the long note out." I admired that. She was articulate.

I never cared much for poetry then, though I did read the classics—Spenser, Tennyson, the early English poets. I was plagued, of course, by having to master subjects to get into college. There wasn't the pressure of today, but I wanted to. People said to me, "Why don't you go to Dickinson College? It's coeducational, and you and your brother can both go." But I had met some graduates of Bryn Mawr who seemed to me very talented and unusual. I thought I'd like to be like them.

When I got there, the teams of girls were coming up from the athletic field and were far from beautiful. Their hair hung down over their faces, their hockey skirts were dragging. Otherwise we wore velveteen. There were different colors for each class—yellow, blue, darker blue, green and red. The color of my class was red. We made up a song:

> Ruber ruber ruber rex
> DCCCCIX

Later on, I gave a course in Contemporary Poetry there, in 1953, second semester.

My brother went to Yale. He was very self-reliant. I was homesick, very. I'd never been anywhere. Oh, to Boston, and before I was in college my mother took us to Florida, to see historic sites, the Fountain of Eternal Youth, and the compositions of rock and shell walls characteristic of old towns in Florida. I heard about Pizarro and Ponce de León and saw a Spanish dungeon. The prisoners were lowered into the prison through a high window; food was let down to them. They were never released.

I was always reading then. I read Dickens from one end to the other; I was getting ready for college. When I was in college, Kipling and Henry James. But more to the point, *now* I am reading Augustus Buell's *Life of John Paul Jones*, from which I am learning a great deal. He is someone who can write.

Now I regret that I didn't study chemistry and Greek in college. But I didn't. When I was sixteen, I felt as old and decisive as when I was fifty or sixty. Especially when I was fifteen to twenty, I rarely listened to reason. I think you should be open-minded and as grateful to people as you can be. We should judge ourselves by the least that we are, and judge others by the most that they are. Rate other people as high as we can. People ask me, "How do you think of things to write about?" I don't. *They* think of *me*. They become *irresistible*. I was looking at my little book, the one just out:

> Tell me, tell me
> where there might be a refuge for me
> from egocentricity.

I would say, "Don't think about yourself from morning to night." As for egotism, paranoia and putting pressure on others, most people say you have to be inconsiderate or you won't get anywhere. I've always felt that pushiness and pushy people are obnoxious.

To me, growing up means being able to change from a fixed opinion. When you become liberalized in your judgment, then you are growing up. You are grown up when you make a sacrifice on behalf of another person and don't call it a sacrifice. I do not like slacks on women, let's say. But there's something to be said for them. I was amazed when a friend of mine and I went to the country together. She had on canvas britches. I thought, "Maybe she ought to wear a skirt." But I changed my mind—there were brambles, blackberries and wire to surmount. As *Punch* said, "How do you know whether our 'striplings' are boys or girls?" Don't belittle yourself. Change or be at home with yourself. If you fail, better have it that way.

I like to read. I like *The Glory of Their Times* by Lawrence Ritter, a baseball book about early players. If I begin one of these accounts, I just have to read right on to the end. It was the same with the *Life of Wilkie Collins* by Kennett Robinson. (Collins wrote *The Moonstone* and *The Woman in White*.) Sometimes people ask me which I like best of the ballplayers now playing. I could give a guess, but I do not like preferences, comparisons.

I am also asked, "What do you see in animals?" They are not self-conscious, are consummately graceful and knowing sometimes. Ted Atkinson, the jockey, said about Tom Fool, "He was the most intelligent horse I ever rode." That interests me.

I like anything connected with horses. Have you seen the horse show at Madison Square Garden? And I like the theater, though I haven't been to a play for some time. What I really like is to be out in the open air, play tennis, go sailing. I have my trapeze, but neglect it. I didn't use to.

I lived in Brooklyn until recently. We used to have there, at the Brooklyn Institute, the cream of the museum experts, Dr. Bailey, Dr. Ripley and others. I took notes on what they said about penguins, cormorants, ducks.

As I said to John Mason Brown at the National Book Awards, when he asked, "What would you say about your writing?" "Well, the only reason for calling it poetry is there is no other category in which to put it." That's true, I say it still. So if someone wants to write, I would say, "By all means, do. Nothing could be better if you don't expect everything to be a masterpiece."

I notice that most new writers remind us of other writers. Once at Sarah Lawrence College, R. P. Blackmur said to a man, "I see that you don't agree with me." The man said, "I don't read poetry—only read Shakespeare and Dante." Mr. Blackmur said, "We don't come in that big size."

"I don't like verse that is self-conscious and haughty. I think we ought to be natural. And it always puts me off when I come on the reversed order of words. But one piece I was fascinated by begins:

No man may him hyde
From Deth holow-eyed.

Accents. Rhythm was my whole interest in verse in the beginning. But strive for the natural. As you know, you're not supposed to rhyme an *ac*cented and an *un*accented syllable. Well, the *Fables* of La Fontaine *inebriated* me by the way in which La Fontaine broke rules. I hadn't even read him before I translated his *Fables*.

Someone once said to me, "You must be a very brave person because you always do what you are afraid of doing." I was very pleased because I am somewhat "schizoid." But why not? Why expose myself? Why can't I be private?

Last evening I spent an hour and a half just opening my letters. In the morning I look at them. Sometimes in the past I didn't eat until about noon, I was so determined to get my mail answered. Now I eat as soon as I wake up—cereal, fruit juice. If there is a really urgent letter, I answer it first. Someone may be in a hurry for a book for Christmas and wants it signed: "Could you let me have it before Christmas?" I say, "If you accompany it with a jiffy bag, I'll do it." At present, though, my signature is rather scratchy.

Well, I think it's natural for people who like a thing to want to know all they can about the author. I wanted very much, once, to meet Thomas Hardy. But nothing could induce me to go to Max Gate [his home in England] and say, "I just want to speak to you." In proportion as you value a person, you ought to protect the person.

What has made most impression on me in recent years was going to Venice and Greece. And the next year going to Cornwall and Ireland, to Belfast, North Ireland, then South Ireland. Everything I had read in books came to life. Have you been to Greece, seen the olive trees and the goats, and the magpies flitting and hopping? Then in England, that grayish misty countryside and the hills. And going to battlefields in Greece. I brought home some laurel from Marathon. I keep it in this box made of olive wood. I even visited the olive tree under which Plato sat, a high excitement. I wish I could go again, to see the real and tangible Discobolos and various other statues reproduced, as it were, forever, the Calf-bearer, the Gladiator, Laocoön. And then the Acropolis!

I was also at a little folk museum at Piraeus. We ate octopus and little clams by the waterside. Well, I brought home four or five, they were so beautifully formed. I wanted to go up Santorini on a donkey, and did. Then I was determined to buy me a donkey bell, but the driver couldn't understand English. I said, "You promised to get me one, I must have it!"—and he cut the bell right off the donkey. I gave him about twice what he wanted for it, and I do have much amusement from it.

I have it, and a little walrus-ivory ox carved by an Eskimo in Alaska, Kay Hendrickson. . . .

John J. Teal, Jr., is raising musk ox on his farm in Vermont. He showed a film of musk ox at Abercrombie's in their top story. You could sit in a window seat or a chair and see this film. It showed how they captured an ox under great difficulties. Well, the plane companies aren't allowed to carry animals, but thought a few muskrats might be permitted. He faced them with enormous creatures weighing two or three hundred pounds. They are still growing. Let us hope they won't multiply till they have to be thinned out. They are very gentle animals and produce more wool than Australian cashmere rams do. You can make seven men's suits out of the wool of one ram, can shear and spin oxdown. Mr. Teal wrote an article, "Golden Fleece of the Arctic," from which I derived one of my poems. When my brother heard the poem, he said, "It sounds just like an advertisement."

"Well," I said, "it is."

In *When I Was Sixteen*, edited by Mary Brannum. New York: Platt and Munk, 1967, pp. 223–31. Transcribed from an interview.

•

As I think of Margaret Fuller's and Emerson's *Dial*, the fortnightly *Dial*, the sepia-covered monthly *Dial;* of the gold-leaf lettering on the ground floor windows of Scofield Thayer's and Sibley Watson's *Dial* at 152 West 13th Street, with now and then dinners served by a Japanese butler on the top floor; of the somewhat narrow thickly padded carpet of the stair, the pleasant pair of editorial offices on the second floor, I cannot imagine our classic, daring, reclusive, selectly worded, culture-obsessed pages, inconsistently modest, argus-eyed monthly *Dial* without: S. Foster Damon.

New York, January 24, 1968

In *A Birthday Garland for S. Foster Damon*, edited by Alvin Rosenfeld and Barton St. Armand. Providence: Brown University, 1968, p. 21.

•

Who so well embodied art and life in words as Vernon Watkins? As in his "Against Controversy?" Who so well expressed the sea? As in "The Mermaid of Zennor?" Who so exactly portrayed Cornwall?

> A thousand tides, a thousand tides,
> And bridals on the hill.
> The sunken ships with broken sides
> Lean over and are still.
> A granite church the seaweed hides
> Its aisles the fishes fill.
>
> The mermaid knows what no man knows,
> The secrets of a shell,
> The pearl on fire, the breaking rose,
> The murmuring, foundered bell
> Whose sound through singing chambers goes
> Crossed by the tingling swell.

In *Vernon Watkins: 1906–1967*, edited by Leslie Norris. London: Faber and Faber, 1970, p. 44.

•

Christopher Smart's energy

> originality
> innate resourcefulness
> in choice of diction
> and rhythm

Make him one of my favorite poets.

In *Christopher Smart*, by Frances E. Anderson. New York: Twayne, 1974, p. 123.

BOOKLISTS

1. T. Corbière: *Les Amours jaunes.*
2–4. J. Cocteau: *Poèmes; Théâtre; Essais critiques.*
5. A. Dumas: *Les Trois Mousquetiers.*
6. J.-H. Fabre: Souvenirs entomologiques.
7. Littré.
8. Molière: *Théâtre.*
9. Montaigne: *Essais.*
10. Pascal: *Pensées.*
11–12. Saint-John Perse: *Éloges; Exil.*
13. M. Proust: *The Maxims of* (Columbia University Press).
14. C. Perrault: *Contes.*
15–17. Stendhal: *Le Rouge et le Noir; De l'Amour; Mémoires d'un Touriste.*
18–21. P. Valéry: *La Soirée avec M. Teste; Poèmes; Variété; Introduction à la Méthode de Léonard de Vinci.*
22. Voltaire: *Correspondance.*
23. Sainte-Beuve: *Portraits contemporains.*
24. Comtesse de Ségur: *Les Malheurs de Sophie.*
25. Flaubert: *Madame Bovary.*
26. Plato: *The Dialogues.*
27. Plutarch.
28. Seneca.
29–31. Xenophon: *On Hunting; Hipparchicus; On Horsemanship.*
32–33. Chaucer: *Troilus and Cressida; Canterbury Tales.*
34. Henryson: *Poems and Fables.*
35–36. Donne: *Letters; Poems.*
37–38. Sidney: *Defense of Poesie; Poems.*
39–42. Shakespeare: *Sonnets; Midsummer Night's Dream; Hamlet; Macbeth.*
43. Christopher Smart: *Poems.*
44. Pope: *Essay on Criticism.*
45. Samuel Johnson: *Lives of the Poets.*
46–48. Goldsmith: *Vicar of Wakefield; Plays; Poems.*
49–50. Swift: *Gulliver; Journal.*
51. Blake: *Poems.*
52–53. Coleridge: *Poems; Biographia Literaria.*
54–55. Keats: *Letters; Poems.*
56. Byron: *Letters.*

57. Charles Lamb: *Letters*.
58. Edmund Burke: *Speeches*.
59–60. Hawthorne: *Notebooks;* Fiction.
61–62. Melville: *Poems;* Short novels.
63–65. Henry James: Prefaces; *Letters;* Novels.
66–67. A. Trollope: *Autobiography; Phineas Finn*.
68–70. Thomas Hardy: *Poems; Tess of the d'Urbervilles; A Pair of Blue Eyes*.
71. Lewis Carroll: *Alice's Adventures in Wonderland*.
72. Edward Lear: *The Owl and the Pussycat*.
73–74. George Saintsbury: *A Short History of English Literature; The English Novel*.
75. D. G. Rossetti: *Italian Poets before Dante*.
76–77. Beatrix Potter: *Peter Rabbit; Squirrel Nutkin*.
78–81. W. H. Auden: *The Double Man; Collected Shorter Poems; Introduction to the Oxford Book of Humorous Verse; Introduction to the Greek Reader* (Viking Press).
82–83. E. E. Cummings: *Eimi; Poems*.
84–86. T. S. Eliot: *Poems;* Plays; *The Use of Poetry and the Use of Criticism*.
87. Horace Gregory: *Criticism*.
88–89. G. M. Hopkins: *Poems; Letters*.
90–93. Harry Levin: *Studies of Joyce; Stendhal; Flaubert; Balzac*.
94–96. James Joyce: *Poems;* Novels; *Dubliners*.
97. Ogden Nash: *Poems*.
98–101. Ezra Pound: *Translations of the Analects of Confucius; Poems; Guido Cavalcanti's "Donna Mi Prega."*
102–103. Wallace Stevens: *Poems;* Prose commentaries.
104–105. Gertrude Stein: *The Making of Americans; The Geographical History of America*.
106–107. Edmund Wilson: *Joyce; Axel's Castle*.
108. Reinhold Niebuhr: *The Dilemma of Modern Man* (in *The Nation*'s Series *A Faith to Live By*).
109–110. Jacques Maritain: in Series: *A Faith to Live By;* "Religion and the Intellectuals" (*Partisan Review* Symposium).
111–112. Dante: *The Divine Comedy; La Vita Nuova*.

In *Pour une Bibliothèque Idéale*, edited by Raymond Queneau. Paris: Gallimard, 1956, pp. 228–32.

I may have been inattentive, but I am inclined to think that *Symbol and Metaphor in Human Experience* by Martin Foss (Princeton University Press, 1949) has not been sufficiently emphasized in the press.

In answer to a query: what book published during the past quarter century do you believe to have been the most undeservedly neglected? *The American Scholar*, 25 (Autumn 1956), 488.

•

New Orleans, by Oliver Evans; *The Screens, and Other Poems*, by I. A. Richards; *Ezra Pound*, by Charles Norman.

"Books I Have Liked," *New York Herald Tribune Book Review*, 4 December 1960, p. 36.

•

La Fontaine: Poet and Counterpoet, by Margaret Guiton; *Out of My League*, by George Plimpton; *Snake Man*, by Alan Wykes.

"Books I Have Liked," *New York Herald Tribune Book Review*, 5 December 1961, p. 12.

•

Victory over Myself, by Floyd Patterson and Milt Gross; *The Heart to Artemis*, by Bryher; *The Points of My Compass*, by E. B. White.

"Books I Have Liked," *New York Herald Tribune Book Review*, 2 December 1962, p. 5.

•

Beechnut, Grimkie, Florence and John and the Rollo books, by Jacob Abbott.
The works of Oliver Goldsmith and William Cowper with pictures by Randolph Caldicott.
Pilgrim's Progress, by John Bunyan.
The Red Fairy Book, The Blue Fairy Book, The Yellow Fairy Book, etc., by Andrew Lang.
David Copperfield, by Charles Dickens.
Plays: Pleasant and Unpleasant, by George Bernard Shaw.
The music criticism of George Bernard Shaw.
The Barchester series, *Phineas Finn* and *Autobiography*, by Anthony Trollope.

Tess of the D'Urbervilles, *Under the Greenwood Tree* and other novels by Thomas Hardy.
Psychology, by William James.
The letters and early novels of Henry James.
I and Thou, by Martin Buber.

"What Books Did Most to Shape Your Vocational Attitude and Your Philosophy of Life?" *The Christian Century*, 18 (1 May 1963), 583.

•

The Magic Lantern of Marcel Proust, by Howard Moss.
Greek Meter, by P. Mass.
Images of Truth, by Glenway Wescott.

"A Cornucopia of 1963 Favorites," *New York Herald Tribune Book Review*, 1 December 1963, p. 18.

•

To what book published in the past ten years do you find yourself going back— or thinking back—most often?

I think I revert most often to special sayings in the Analects of Confucius, translated by Ezra Pound—*The Great Digest:* analogous to the Golden Rule, quoted in my *Predilections* 82-83: Tze-kung, asked if there was a single principle that you could practice through life to the end, said, "Sympathy; what you don't want, don't inflict on another" (Book Fifteen, XXIII); "Require the solid of yourself, the trifle of others" (Book Fifteen, XIV).
Great Digest: "If there be a knife of resentment in the heart or enduring rancor, the mind will not attain precision."
. . . Practice five things: "sobriety (*serenitas*), magnanimity, sticking by one's word, promptitude . . . kindliness (*caritas*)." As "for the problem of style. Effect your meaning. Then stop" (Book Fifteen, XL).
My Early Life by Winston S. Churchill and *John Paul Jones* by Augustus C. Buell are two other books to which I revert for the same reason, refusal to compromise on the part of the person depicted.

The American Scholar, 36 (Summer 1965), 186, 188.

•

As a teenager, I liked: Howard Pyle's *The Merry Adventures of Robin Hood*; *Kidnapped* and *Treasure Island* by R. L. Stevenson; *Lorna Doone* by Blackmore;

Grimm's *Fairy Tales*; Lang's *Fairy Books* (the *Red* and *Yellow* in particular); the Brownie books by Palmer Cox; *Captains Courageous* by Kipling; *Rebecca of Sunnybrook Farm* by Kate Douglas Wiggin; *The Child's Bible*; Bunyan's *The Pilgrim's Progress*; nearly all of G. A. Henry—*For Freedom's Cause, The Lion of the North* (Venice in her glory), *Beric the Briton, The Young Carthagenian, For the Temple* (Jerusalem), *By Pike and Dyke* (Holland); *What Mother Nature Told Her Children*; Hawthorne's *Tanglewood Tales*; *The Pied Piper of Hamelin*; *Hans Brinker and the Silver Skates*; Dickens' *David Copperfield*; Goldsmith's *Mad Dog*; Cowper's *John Gilpin's Ride*; and *The House that Jack Built*. Here are only a few; I was always reading—, many books about animals and travel.

Attacks of Taste, compiled by Evelyn B. Byrne and Otto M. Penzler. New York: Gotham Book Mart, 1971, pp. 31–32.

•

I think well of Denise Levertov, Daniel Hoffman . . . and George Starbuck; [and among English poets of] Charles Tomlinson, Stevie Smith, and Hal Summers.

"Poet as Patron," *Wilson Library Bulletin*, 19 (January 1962), 371.

QUESTIONNAIRES

Q. What should you most like to do, to know, to be? (in case you are not satisfied).
A. To do the kind of work that I am doing; to know what might lend it impetus; to be more efficient in it.

Q. Why wouldn't you change places with any other human being?
A.

Q. What do you look forward to?
A.

Q. What do you fear most from the future?
A. Unless I delude myself, I am not conscious of fear with regard to present or future.

Q. What has been the happiest moment of your life? The unhappiest? (if you care to tell).
A. My life has not been signalized by catastrophes or triumphs and has been for the most part happy.

Q. What do you consider your weakest characteristic? Your strongest? What do you like most about yourself? Dislike most?
A. Weakest characteristic, unsociability; strongest, perseverance.

Q. What things do you really like? Dislike? (nature, people, ideas, objects, etc. Answer in a phrase or a page, as you will).
A. (Like) reading; outdoor sport; (dislike) selfishness, affectation, inquisitiveness, acquisitiveness.

Q. What is your attitude toward art today?
A.

Q. What is your world view? (Are you a reasonable being in a reasonable scheme?)
A. International fraternity.

Q. Why do you go on living?
A. The surrender of life doesn't seem to be demanded of me.

"Confessions—Questionnaire," *The Little Review*, 12 (May 1929), 64.

•

Q. Do you intend your poetry to be useful to yourself or others?
A. Myself.

Q. Do you think there can now be a use for narrative poetry?
A. Yes; but not as a species of prose narrative.

Q. Do you wait for a spontaneous impulse before writing a poem; if so, is this impulse verbal or visual?
A. If aware of an insistently urgent bit of poetic material, in my consciousness or outside it—word, phrase, sentence, or concept—I make a written note of it; not usually being at the moment at leisure to go further.
　The working out: intentional, not spontaneous.
　I doubt that the impulse is not always both (verbal and visual).

Q. Have you been influenced by Freud and how do you regard him?
A. I have respect for Freud, but don't know his work well enough to know to what extent I may have been influenced by him.

Q. Do you take your stand with any political or politico-economic party or creed?
A. No, but I am conservative; opposed to regimentation.

Q. As a poet what distinguishes you, do you think, from an ordinary man?
A. Nothing; unless it is an exaggerated tendency to visualize; and on encountering manifestations of life—insects, lower animals, or human beings—to wonder if they are happy, and what will become of them.

"Answers to an Enquiry," *New Verse*, 1 (October 1934), 16.

•

Q. Are you for, or are you against Franco and fascism? Are you for, or are you against the legal government and the people of Republican Spain?
A. I am for the legal government and the people of Loyalist Spain; against Franco, against fascism; against any suppression of freedom by tyranny masked as civilization.

Writers Take Sides: Letters about the War in Spain from 418 American Authors. New York: The League of American Writers, 1938, p. 43.

•

Q. Do you think a representative "American poetry" exists now, distinct from English poetry, that an "American tradition" is in process of creation? To put the question another way, do you think the American Renaissance of 1912 and the following years had permanent value?
A. Certain "established American poets" (Wallace Stevens, E. E. Cummings, William Carlos Williams, for instance—acknowledged experts here) seem not to be well known in England and fortuitously in that respect, American poetry *is* distinct from English poetry, I would say; but this is an anomaly, much to be deplored, I feel. "The American Renaissance of 1912" revived a reading interest in poetry and gave impetus to experiment and had permanent value, I feel.

As for American tradition, although childhood associations dye the imagination and a thing that is one's own can double the use of it, as Henry James said of Hawthorne (T. S. Eliot and Ezra Pound being conspicuously American in that respect), I do not see that there can be a distinctive poetry without a distinctive rhythm, such as one has in Irish, Russian, or Spanish music, or in American-Indian tribal or African tribal music.

Q. Do you regard yourself as part of the "American tradition," as an American poet, regional or national; or as a poet simply, dissociated from nationality?
A. Yes; as implied above, an American chameleon on an American leaf.

Q. Do you think the poetry written by Americans during the last ten years shows any signs of development (progression)?
A. Impatience with bunkum and a desire to be as nearly as possible one's self, I think is, with us, the distinguishing trend.

"Enquiry," *Twentieth Century Verse*, No. 12/13 (October 1938), 114.

•

Q. Is it nonsense to talk of a typical American poem? If not, what, in your opinion, are the qualities which tend to distinguish a poem as "American"?
A. American verse presents variety so extreme, I do not see how one can speak of "a typical American poem." A tendency to defy convention does seem to me typically American; but when American verse disregards rules and defies precedent and yet is poetry, it is so, surely, despite turns of speech and subject matter peculiar to this country. It is poetry because depth of experience, imagination, and "ear," make it so; because it is stamped by firmness of personality.

Q. Do you consider that the language of American poetry (vocabulary, use of vocabulary, metric, cadences, syntax, punctuation) differs notably from that of

English poetry? Is this difference (if any) fortuitous or does it correspond to some underlying difference of sensibility?

A. When American poetry differs "notably" from English poetry, in being illiterate or because the author has not read any but his own work, I do not care to concede that the work is typically American!

Q. Has American poetry been affected by those trends in English poetry in the thirties typified by the work of Auden, Spender, Day Lewis and MacNeice? Has American poetry been affected by the romanticism now prevalent in English poetry, and represented in varying ways by the work of Dylan Thomas, George Barker, The New Apocalypse, Personalism, and the later poetry of Miss Edith Sitwell?

A. W. H. Auden's influence on American work is very marked, and general; Dylan Thomas is to some extent an influence; one encounters a modern archaism occasionally that could perhaps be attributed to Vernon Watkins; I have now and again recognized a cadence of Miss Sitwell's war poetry.

"American and English Poetry: A Questionnaire," in *Modern American Poetry (Focus Five)*. London: Dennis Dobson, 1950, pp. 182–83.

•

Q. From a naturalistic point of view, all events (including those of history) have their causes, and the present revival of religion would not be an exception. What do you think are the causes of the present trend? Is it due to the worldwide failure and defeat of a real radical movement in politics? To a renunciation of hopes for any fundamental social improvement? Or to some kind of breakdown in the organization of modern society, to which religion would seem to supply a remedy?

A. The helplessness of individuals and of society, I attribute to breakdown in the individual.

Q. Granting that social changes or catastrophes may bring people to consider religion more sympathetically, the fact still remains that the trend in question here is one among intellectuals, who have undergone a change in *convictions*. What has happened to make religion more credible than it formerly was to the modern mind? The credibility of certain religious mysteries like the Incarnation and the Trinity would certainly not seem to be changed by any new data, scientific or otherwise; but there may be other parts of religion whose general credibility is changed by fundamental changes in the climate of opinion. Do you consider these latter changes valid?

Does this new trend imply that the scientific attitude of mind is being forsaken? Or that drastic limits are being set to it? Or is some readjustment necessary, by which the scientific attitude will be given new place in the intellectual hierarchy?

A. Catastrophe conduces to contrition. Convictions, however, are the result of experience. Corroborated by the thinking of others—and the moral law (which is self-demonstrating, most of us admit)—experience is almost certain to accept the fact that mystery is not just a nut which diligence can crack.

Mystical belief which is not unthinking belief, seems to find that science does not discredit the supernatural but reinforces it. That is to say, we see that reverence for science and reverence for the soul can interact.

Q. Religion and culture. Can culture exist without a positive religion? To what extent must this religion be organized as an institution? The distinctions have been made between prophetic and institutional religion: Do you think that enduring values in society can be carried by the former?

Certain writers in this century (the Frenchman Maurras would be an example) have sought to justify religion simply as a social institution—a safeguard for civilized tradition as a means of social discipline. What do you think of such justification? Is a return to religion necessary in order to counter the new means of social discipline that we all fear: totalitarianism?

If we are to have an integral religious culture again, can its tradition be purely Christian? Will not the religious tradition of any civilization have to be essentially pluralistic?

A. Can culture exist without a positive religion? Culture so far, has not existed without religion and I doubt that it could.

Religion that does not result first of all in self-discipline will never result in "social discipline" and could be the prey of any form of tyranny.

Can culture be purely Christian? It partakes of varied cultural elements.

Q. Religion and literature. The revival of religion has perhaps been most noticeable in the literary world. Does this imply some special dependence of the literary imagination upon religious feeling and ideas? Is the present emphasis upon myth among literary theorists connected with the renewed interest in religion?

A. Correspondences in contrasting religions make it instinctive to examine comparatively, myth, literature, and religion—in which examination one is impressed by the findings of mythographers as demarcating worship from ingenuity.

Q. Certain writers have attempted to separate the religious consciousness (as an attitude toward man and human life) from religious beliefs. Thus the philosopher Heidegger, and in his recent writings the novelist Malraux, both attempt to make viable certain attitudes that were formerly aspects of the religious consciousness while at the same time rejecting traditional religious beliefs. Is this separation possible? Is there a valuable religious consciousness that can be maintained without an explicit credo postulating the supernatural? Assuming that in the past religions nourished certain vital human values, can these values now be maintained without a widespread belief in the supernatural?

A. If everything literary were deleted, in which there is some thought of deity, "literature" would be a puny residue; one could almost say that each striking literary work is some phase of the desire to resist or affirm "religion."

That belief in God is not easy, is seemingly one of God's injustices; and self-evidently, imposed piety results in the opposite. Coercion and religious complacency are serious enemies of religion—whereas persecution invariably favors spiritual conviction. But this is certain, any attempted substituting of self for deity, is a forlorn hope.

"Religion and the Intellectuals," *Partisan Review,* 17 (February 1950), 6–7, 48.

•

Q. Has the net result of woman's "coming out of the kitchen" been helpful or detrimental to society?

A. The net result of woman's "coming out of the kitchen" has been helpful, I think. Who could regard in any other light the activities of such women as Florence Nightingale, Susan B. Anthony, Helen Keller, Jane Addams, Katharine E. McBride, Millicent Carey McIntosh, Margaret A. Clapp, Elizabeth Gray Vining, Marie Curie, Florence Sabin or Eleanor Bliss?

With regard to careers outside the home, delegated motherhood can be a threat, for I believe that our integrity as a nation is bound up with the home. Good children are not the product of mothers who prefer money or fame to the well-being of their families. Did not the Apostle Paul, in his ardor to afford Timothy a steadying influence, bid him remember his mother, Eunice, and his grandmother, Lois?

We dare not regress by suppressing intelligence or forbidding women to be useful. But steadfastness, conscience and the capacity for sacrifice, on the part of both parents, are basic to good family relations which, in turn, are basic to the well-being of society in general.

Encyclopedia Year Book: The Story of Our Time. New York: The Grolier Society, 1957, pp. 155–56.

•

Q. What should be done with Ellis Island, the famous landmark in New York Harbor?

A. The hospital buildings could, at one end, house the harbor police. (The police in England have such housing.) The other end could be divided into little units for aged couples.

Retired artists could be quartered in one end of the buildings. We have no attractive, congenial accommodations for retired artists such as they have at Nogent-sur-Marne in France. The location of the island makes the place a potential paradise.

Certainly nothing is more needed than recreation facilities for hemmed-in, deprived children; facilities such as the Children's Zoo in the Bronx or in Central Park. But the expense of maintaining a ferry service and staff supervision might be prohibitive.

An information center for all America is another suggestion—perhaps too luxurious for practical consideration.

Perhaps the most practical suggestion about the use of Ellis Island is that musicians—retired musicians or active musicians who cannot afford suitable surroundings—be given studios there where practicing could be done and "noise" made by them not be a main problem.

"Ellis Island: Park, Youth Center, Shrine or—?" *The New York Times Magazine*, 25 May 1958, p.16.

•

Line of work: Writing.

But what would you really rather do? The same.

Mainspring: Be of use—doing some kind of work that I would enjoy doing even if I were not paid for doing it.

Most paradoxical quality: Like to be inconspicuous but look well.

Chinks in the armor: Resent injustice, to others and to myself.

Boiling point: Malevolence that cannot be controlled; mob violence; buying a dog to make life pleasant, then turning it loose without its collar and going south in winter or north in summer.

Personal panacea: God and family.

Persisting superstitions: I hang things on doorknobs or walk under ladders insouciantly, but I don't sew black hooks on a white dress.

The terrible temptation: To subside and not persevere.

Unfounded fears: That I may forget to be cautious in crossing streets or that the car won't perform in a crisis.

Secret satisfaction: That a ballplayer, just after I had been told by a writer that it was affectation for me to pretend to be interested in baseball, entitled a piece,

"An Hour Well Spent," in which he said, "She speaks to our condition as ballplayers."

"Marianne Moore," *Esquire*, 58 (July 1962), 99.

•

Which play, book, painter, food, film, musical work, celebrity, activity, virtue, place, mental attitude, type of humor has seemed to you dismal, disastrous and distasteful?

Play: *Desire Under the Elms* (original production): a gigantic inability to proceed, of which one cannot remember the detail. Equally dismal, *La Plume de ma Tante*; I cannot think of anything more risqué, hackneyed, or more uncomplimentary to an audience.

Book: *The Prince* by Machiavelli: so dull; the advice, obvious (win the obstacle's favor, enslave, or extirpate has not been working very well). Whereas the *History of Florence* says all by implication and sparkles like a diamond.

Painter: Mary Cassatt: A near-Renoir without Renoir's novelty; a kind of pictorial breakfast food.

Food: Cold soup—vichyssoise or bean.

Film: Gushing little girl sirens in adult roles rescued by a bloodhound galloping out of dark woods, climbing an alp and jumping into space, finding refuge in a kind of Graybar Building.

Musical work: A certain andante cantabile (I don't know what opus) by Tchaikovsky for trio, with undulant theme, repeating itself with nondescript contrast at too short intervals to infinity.

Celebrity: Mike Wallace with no more concept of Deity or touch of compassion than to ask Roy Campanella if he thought God meant to punish him by allowing him to disable himself.

Activity: Complying with the inconsiderate R. S. V. P. which omits the proviso: "If you are able to be present."

Virtue: Persistent humanitarian compassion which asks, "Why don't you ever say 'no'; you are wearing yourself out." "Why don't you retire?" *Madonna mia!*

Place: The prosaic approach to the Hall of Fame.

Mental attitude: Apathy.

Type of humor: Jeweled thousand-dollar out-of-scale animal lapel ornaments with human aptitudes: scotties, kittens, skunks, orangs or pelicans.

Anti-dote in a category of my own: A really rough sea in a middle-sized ship that is thought to be seaworthy.

"Antidotes," *Harper's Bazaar*, 96 (19 July 1963), 74.

•

Dear Mr. Plimpton: The questions:

Q. Why do you wear two watches?
A. Partly because I have a security obsession, I think—to be sure I know the time and not have to be late—along with a touch of vanity. I like trifles to harmonize. My gold watch is a Hamilton, given me by my brother (selected by me), rather pale gold, the color of a pin I usually wear, with a rosette (French set) of small diamonds at the center—the clasp curled into a half-twist, so secure it needs no safety catch—bought for himself in New Orleans by my grandfather, William Moore, an iron-founder in Portsmouth, Ohio, who had lived in Mississippi before the Civil War and said, I am told, "I'll never get my money out of the Confederacy; I might as well buy diamonds."

My other watch is an Eternamatic given me by Dr. and Mrs. J. S. Watson: the case, of an alloy that an engraver in Bermuda said was the hardest substance he had, so far, engraved. A hair-fine revolving hand for timing is superimposed on the two other hands which have triangular radiumized centers of katydid green, just below five gold dots signifying water-proof, shock-proof, temperature-proof, automatic, and another thing, I forget what. The Hamilton ticks louder than the Eternamatic, so I don't need to hold it to my ear to know it is going, but it is a trifle erratic. Since it was given me by my brother, I am attached to it. It might possess potency—like an elephant-hair. I don't feel dressed without it.

Q. You had a large handbag with you at the [Yankees World Series] game. What was in it?
A. A Hermes address book with an extensible very thin silver pencil; and two other pencils—a black ball-point (my name stamped in gold), retractable, made by a veteran who is paralyzed below the chest, who makes and sells a variety of eye-catchers as a living—Hal McColl, 101 West Club Boulevard, Durham, North Carolina. I occasionally order a pen set of him since it doesn't scratch or exude spiders. In case it gave out, I had a Dixon Ticonderoga with brass cap; had a Standard ring-topped notebook and a little thing of fifteen pages with a glazed white cover, souvenir of Unz & Co., Stationers, 24 Beaver Street, New York City—given me for a trip but saved for a single special event. Then I had a miniature pair of black plastic binoculars weighing an ounce and three-quarters—bought by mail to watch a bluejay that for two or three years had preempted a catalpa tree in a backyard adjacent to my back windows. I like to startle it

by imitating it, so that it gives a sharp look round and answers uncertainly. It stays all winter.

Q. Why were you and James Thorpe walking down the railroad tracks?
A. I was in charge of the Commercial Department (of the United States Industrial Indian School in Carlisle, Pennsylvania). The class had been given the day off with me responsible for its behavior, and I was taking it to the circus by a shortcut—was walking with two Indians, James Baker and James Thorpe, who were talking to me and watching that I didn't stumble on the ties. It threatened rain and I had with me a man's big cherry-handled cotton umbrella. James Thorpe, noting the heavy umbrella, said, "Miss Moore, may I carry your parasol for you?" I said, "Thank you, James"—never called him "Jim" (as too familiar) though everyone else did. I never use an umbrella for sun; was entertained by the paraphrase—also touched by the courtesy of the question. On Memorial Day we were provided with sickles and went as a body to the School cemetery to cut grass—tall and dry on the graves; a by no means solemn occasion!

Q. Did you ever watch him play football? Was he idolized in the school?
A. He was liked by all—*liked* in italics, rather than venerated or idolized—unless perhaps privately admired by "Pop" Warner, he was such an all-round phenomenon—"Jim." He was off-hand, modest, casual about anything in the way of fame or eminence achieved. This modesty, with top performance, was characteristic of him, and no back-talk. The charge of professionalism was never popular in the Olympic world; everyone felt it should not be held against him, since any violation was accidental rather than intentional.

I used to watch football practice on the field after school sometimes; signals for passes; little starts with the ball; kicks for goal; and often watched track sports in spring—throwing the hammer, at which James was adept, taking hurdles—the jump. He had a kind of ease in his gait that is hard to describe. Equilibrium with no strictures; but crouched in the lineup for football he was the epitome of concentration, wary, with an effect of plenty in reserve. I never saw him irascible, sour, or primed for vengeance. In the classroom he was a little laborious, but dependable; took time—head bent earnestly over the paper; wrote a fine even clerical hand—every character legible; every terminal curving up—consistent and generous. I don't mention team trips away for I know nothing about them; but celebrations involving liquor (reputedly) can't be good for any athlete.

Q. Could you say something about *style* and the athlete?
A. An animal—also an athlete—in command of a skill should glory in it; but the manner, probably, is inadvertent. To attain nicety, deliberateness at some point in performance is obligatory. The halves of the body should have some practice in compensating for each other. Then when experience has lent confidence, opportunity seems like destiny.

A sense of ability and prime strength safeguarded by caution—with a recollection of success—a Goliath-like brashness tamed by near-misses—should, I feel, conduce to form. Not knowing how to hold back by perhaps a second seems to account for many a failure—many a ball in tennis, shot into the net, resulting in the cheerful insult "too anxious" or "still with you." Taking a Blue Ridge bus from Washington to Hagerstown one time, I saw through the window a handful of boys taking turns swinging on a rope from a tree branch over a creek—each letting go the rope exactly at the right moment to hit the pool like a cast at a trout. And in San Francisco once, I saw from a window overlooking a backyard a cat—black Siamese—catching hummingbirds. From a motionless crouch on a fence half-shaded by flowers, the body lunged in a long horizontal pounce—a kind of chameleon-tongue striking a fly.

Restraint seems to be the key to form as equilibrium. The most spectacular instance of equilibrium that I recall was a slack-rope walker in the Great Sensational Swedish Circus shown on International Showtime television, January 30, 1964. The performer, gliding forward in long slow strides without parasol or wand, rested his head on the wire, raising his legs till vertical, stood on his head for some time, supported by a tip of a forefinger on the wire at each side of the head, then sprang lightly down. Also, I have seen a girl ascend a ladder with a glass of wine balanced on her forehead. On the glass rested an oblong parallelogram tray on which six small-stemmed glasses of wine stood. She descended the ladder, without having spilled a drop, and in conclusion before bowing, took one glass up and drank the wine. The pleasantest instance of dexterity to watch that I have seen recently was the jumping of a horse with a name like Exceptional (no mention of it in the *Times* the next day, that I could find) by a girl in the International Contest at Madison Square Garden. Launched for the jump, the horse looked self-automated as it floated up out over the barrier, with ease as if liking the airlift—forelegs flattened to the body but with no rectangular carousel bend of the knee. Seurat's "Standing Horse" in the Guggenheim Museum has a stance that says it all—ears forward, legs sloping almost imperceptibly forward, and level back.

Q. And now perhaps something of the relationship between the athlete and the animal?

A. I am sure that stricture interferes with form, and with dexterity. A gibbon in a flying leap seems to have no joints; and an orangutan can lie stretched out, high up on a level pipe, with one arm under its head eating an orange with the other hand, and a knee drawn up as a man might lie on a couch. The little gray poodle in *Flipper* (Walt Disney) before his dive into the pool, straining up erect on thin hind legs, jubilant to go, and otters shown at the top of a snow-slide, were not afflicted with muscle kinks. Aptitude without zeal is not much. Next to the manse we lived in, in Chatham, New Jersey, a small brindled bulldog had ears fringed with scars; staggering from a last encounter, if he saw a sizable dog across the street, he had to be forcibly restrained from limping out to fight—

as Cassius Clay in being reminded of Sonny Liston, said, "I can't wait to get at him; it took two policemen to keep me off him. Don't mention him no more."

Manipulating an implement involves nicety. It seems to me that aptitude for mobility is at a peak in the elephant. I have seen in a movie an Asian elephant edging a lawn beside a pavement, using the finger of its proboscis as daintily as if it were a razor; have also seen an elephant slowly push flat a good-sized tree, as in pulling and piling teak.

Mrs. Thrale, with friends comparing people and their likenesses to some animal or other said, "We pitched upon the elephant for his resemblance:" (Dr. Johnson)—adding that "the proboscis of that creature was like his mind, most exactly strong to buffet even the tiger and pliable to pick up even the pin."

Q. Why is baseball the particular sport that has held your interest as a poet? Or have others? Football?
A. Roy Campanella roused, I should say revived, my interest in baseball in 1953 or 1954, at Ebbets Field. Karl Spooner was pitching. Roy Campanella, who was catching, walked out to the mound, and after a few earnest words to Karl came briskly back to the plate after a parting encouraging slap or pat on Karl's rear. His brisk, confident little roll was very prepossessing and I thought, "I guess I'll have to keep an eye on him." His experienced crouch with no sign of reluctance, and the fact that he never missed a foul, corroborated the pleasing impression. But the notable thing about him was his vim. It belongs with the remark in his book, *It's Good to Be Alive*, that he enjoyed the game so much, he would gladly play even if he didn't get paid.

Football seems scientifically tactical nowadays—not so conglomerate as fifty years ago, with fewer mounds of bodies and victims exanimately breathless at the bottom of the pile.

Tennis is the game that I liked from the first and always have. We played on a dirt court by a giant willow belonging to the school we attended till grammar-school age and I till entering college. My brother is tall and hard to get past, playing net. I am no athlete, tire soon, seldom achieve a decisive shot, have no whirlwind serve, but can place the ball "where they ain't."

One day a youngster, a great-nephew of the principal of the school, arrived for a visit and had a new racquet. He magnanimously lent it to me while waiting a turn—a Harry C. Lee Dreadnaught Driver, strung in red and blue gut (rather gaudy, I thought). It had a slotted throat, disparaged by some as a sales feature, but it tightened the grip and weighted the top in my opinion. I improved so that I could think of nothing else; my mother got me one, and from then on my brother and I considered any day wasted when we did not play. Thanks to the new weapon, we welcomed adversaries but seldom could beat two men (friends who lived nearby—older than we—one of whom reclusively read the *Figaro* by the willow when not playing). Twenty-five or so years later, for me an accidental thrill came in a small tennis competition in which Personnel in the Puget Sound Navy Yard entered my brother and me in 1922. The score was 3-6, 7-5, 6-3.

Seven pairs. A tough hand-ornamented score-sheet was thumbtacked to a tree. The final set of a three-set series with the finalists went to seven deuces. My face began to burn and I could hardly swallow but dared not fail my brother. It was my serve. I heard a murmur—a curious battle cry, "Now cuckoo; to-gether," caught a fractional glance back, fortunately took my opponent off-balance; and the feeble return, my brother angled out of our competitor's reach. Our matching opponent sprang over the net, shook hands, and said, "Well—I guess that's curtains."

Much later—in Brooklyn—I had no one to play, selected a boy and got him a racquet at Davega's. He took no interest and had no ability. Another boy who had sat at our door in aggrieved disgust as the recruit accompanied me to the courts, came to the rescue and had everything but experience. We had to procure permits from Lefferts Mansion—some distance away—but nothing deterred two more boys from joining us, and a benevolent Parkman winked at interlopers, one of whom owned a bicycle entitled Colleen in bold script along the back of the saddle, with foxtails flowing from the handlebars. The boys are now in the Coast Guard, Air Force, or thriving businessmen (married to Yvonne, or Betty, or Helene).

Q. Have you met, or known, many athletes? McGraw? Or Mack?
A. Near the Fence, on my first visit to Yale, I met Ray Biglow (Lucius Horatio Biglow), Captain of 1907's football team. He was All-American right tackle, and Varsity Captain in 1907. Yale never lost a game to Harvard or Princeton while he was at right tackle; also had a Y for rowing. He was commensurately modest. He never went on the field loaded with pads and armor—was the picture of solid know-how; had not much to say but spoke with great exactness and sensibility—with no self-consciousness; no affectations. Professor Jack Reed said he was the only member of his class in Nineteenth Century Poets to hand in the written assignment the day before his last game against Harvard.

My brother—John Warner Moore (Captain, Chaplain Corps, USN, Ret.) was sailing officer on each of the ships on which he served, and crews trained by him for Fleet Regattas consistently won. My nephew, John Warner Moore, was a Yale Varsity swimmer for three years.

One of my pleasantest memories of Harvard was meeting—in November, 1962—members of Lowell House who were athletes: Jamie Hoyt '65—a mid-dleweight boxer and football player; Eugene Kinasewich, Varsity and all-Ivy League hockey player from Alberta; John Carroll, Varsity Lacrosse player who has taught in Tanganyika, as surgical assistant and assistant in carpenter work with natives. "Tanganyikan soccer," he says, "is the most agreeable integration of sport with daily life I have ever witnessed. At all levels soccer is played in one's street clothes—bare feet, baggy shorts, and tattered undershirt—and they can really boom the ball on their bare calloused feet. Pickup games spread like fire. Schoolboys, washing their only clothes in the icy stream, race naked after a floppy rag against a raw wind from the high mountains. Nothing can express the exultation that comes with sport played like this."

When teaching at the Carlisle Indian School, Charles (Chief) Bender, the pitcher, was a respected figure whom I often saw—the perfect model of a pitcher, proportioned much like Ty Cobb but taller; and anything but common property, his patrician aspect modified by the fact that he was not so lofty as to despise chewing gum. I had in my department, besides James Thorpe, Joel Wheelock, Gus Welsh, Alex Arcasa—all indispensable on the football team.

John McGraw and Connie Mack? I used to thrust John McGraw's *How to Play Baseball* on little boys in the Hudson Park Branch of the New York Public Library when they came asking what they should read. Connie Mack went to Buckthorn, Kentucky, looking for a left-handed pitcher. Dr. Elmer Gabbard was showing him the Buckthorn School—a magnificent effort in compensating for broken homes, feuding fathers, and moonshiners—when they met a boy who had a string of squirrels he had stoned for the family dinner—stoned, he said, with his left hand. Connie Mack hired him, but on the mound the boy used his right hand. Asked why he had stoned the squirrels with his left hand instead of his right, the boy said, "If I used my right hand, I was afraid I might bruise them."

Q. What are the aspects of baseball that particularly appeal to you?
A. Dexterity—with a logic of memory that makes strategy possible. Phil Rizzuto observed that for Elston Howard, not just any ball would do—that he could have had the batting crown if it hadn't been for a regulation: "You have to pitch him in tight, so he can't get the best part of the bat on it." And Mudcat (Jimmy) Grant's apparent ferocity and abandon are worth watching—seeing him leap up to pull down a speedy liner hit over the mound. I admire, too, Minnie Minoso's fury; and certainly the Yankee pitcher Al Downing (Alphonse Erwin Downing) has (as Arthur Daley says) "all the ingredients." His left arm goes up in a jug-handle curve, his right lies across him like a barrel stave—left leg trailing to right, kneeling—the right leg as prop—so he can't fall. In 1961 against the Senators, Arthur Daley says, "he struck out two, walked batters, hit batters, batters hit him, so that after an inning and a third, Ralph Houk, the manager, saved him from further embarrassment and took him out." But as Elston Howard says, "He has the best arm on the ballfield. He has been close to no-hitters and has got to make it sometime. Curves and fancy pitches can be learned, but no one can teach a man how to throw a fast ball." Hope of scoring seems focused in the pitcher, and I think a "pleasant" mound may have something to do with inducing an intimation of triumph.

One of the handsomest things about the game, I think, is accuracy that looks automatic in fielding fast balls. I never tire of a speedy ball from the catcher finding the glove of the pitcher, when half the time he isn't even looking at it.

A record, it seems to me, doesn't compare with "from-time-to-time good plays by uncelebrities." I went to the Yankee Stadium one time to see Babe Ruth.

He could bat, but his pigeon-toed, stubbed little trot lacked beauty. The batter I like to watch is Willie Mays. Vim marks every action—an effect of knowing he has what it takes, without being conceited. Responsibility and talent; calling it enough. There's a moral to it. I can always last in a drawn-out game—to wait for Elston Howard at bat. Two little boys, perhaps taking him for an umpire, detained my brother one time and said, "Did you see that home run? My Daddy did that."

A thing I don't like about baseball is the veteran who hazes the rookie—such as nailing Ty Cobb's spikes to the clubhouse floor, and sawing his bat through. It's not funny, but a heavy thought to me that when Honus Wagner was asked why he smiled happily after saying, "Nice hit," to Ty Cobb and being told "Go to hell," he said: "I liked that remark. He was the first major leaguer ever to speak to me."

Roger Maris, in being victim of the batting competition, suffered in being a cause of worry it seemed to me—while in people's concept of him, he was a star; then revealed a touch of embarrassment in being party to a commercial. Infrarub should not harm him but it doesn't lend a ball player luster exactly. He then regained my sympathy by admitting that the only privacy he could count on was when taking his place on the ball field.

We like home runs but Mickey Mantle is a beautiful outfielder and I think I like him catching flies better than I like him hitting them. Some of his spectacular incalculable catches do not fade from the mind. In any case, it is most pleasing that two such battling fielders as Roger Maris and Mickey Mantle have at no time been diminished by internecine jealousies. Their series of ailments by no means estrange one—at least not me, who am prone to any impairment— sprained a right middle finger playing basketball, I was hit on the eye at close range by a tennis ball, made only second teams in hockey and Lacrosse in college, and was momentarily in danger of being spilled when two or three classmates and I rented polo ponies from an ex-army-officer and would dash about the lanes and woodlands of Bryn Mawr.

Q. What other pets than Elston Howard (your alligator) have you? Was there a crow there? Haven't I read that you have a crow?
A. Yes, I always wanted one after seeing one in the Hippodrome, bunting ping-pong balls; and hearing one at the Sportsman's Show "answering" questions. I was given a mechanical one that hops, flaps its wings, and caws, have it still. I like a crow's harsh voice that differs with circumstances; also its businesslike waddle. From Fort Greene Park, I see a handful sometimes speeding past my windows; so when *Harper's Bazaar* asked me for a fantasy, I thought I might have one adopt me, sleep in the Park or wherever it goes at night, come to see me, wait on me if I wanted my pocket dictionary or an eraser or handkerchief. I wrote the piece, had the crow go to market with me, the drugstore, and listen to the 6:30 Sunrise Semester with me—supplying a word if I missed one; liberated it in the end but had hard work detaching it! Alice Morris of *Harper's*

Bazaar improved the piece till it could be used. The crow caught the eye of my doctor's husband, who is a dentist. Happening to be going down in the elevator when I did, he said, "Miss Moore, *where* is that crow of yours?" I said, "In my mind." He said, "You *deceived* us? I couldn't have *imagined* you would do such a thing." I said, "If you could see and hear him hop, flap his wings, and caw, you wouldn't be so indignant."

Other animals? I have a mechanical elephant with plush skin, named Seneca, given me by Loren MacIver and Lloyd Frankenberg. I have a bronze elephant and mahout (Chinese and old) and a bronze baby pheasant (Chinese) with its head turned back the opposite way from the way it is sitting, also old; a ceramic elephant made by Malvina Hoffman; have an ebony elephant from Ceylon; ebony llama and lambs-wool llama—ears tied with scarlet silk to designate ownership; black clay Zuni turtle; Chinese brass lizard; green bronze Italian lizard with two tails, a Dresden leopard from Nice; an amber fly with a fly in it, entwined with gold—to wear—given me by Louise Crane who gave me my nutria coat which you mention—my poor maligned nutria, worn against possible freak winds; a Burmese gilt owl given me by Chester Page; a teak mouse (Japanese) named Natasha for Faith Morrow's mouse, Natasha, whose mother is named for me; a Radcliffe mouse; a rat with carnelian eyes—sitting up, its tail curled around its hind legs; a Peter Rabbit who brought his book with him from Winding Lane, Leetsdale, Pennsylvania. I did not give myself any of these animals except Elston Howard. I have many more. But I've not yet been up to see Mr. Teal's oxen. It's intolerable.

Best Wishes,

M. M.

"Ten Answers: Letters from an October Afternoon, Part II," *Harper's*, 229 (November 1964), 91–98.

•

Q. What influence have the Greek and Latin classics had upon your creative and/or critical work? Has that influence been good or bad, extensive or insignificant? Has it grown or declined in the course of your career?
A. A strengthening effect—becoming wider and more unmistakable.

Q. Would you advise a young writer or critic to get himself a classical education? If yes, why? And what kind of classical education would you recommend?
A. By all means; ignorance of originals is suicide.

Q. Claims are still made for a living continuity between Graeco-Roman civilization and our own. If these claims are anything more than familiar cultural

gestures, at what levels, and in what contexts, can they still be valuably made?
A. Opportunity to compare standards of beauty and acquire initiate speech.

Q. How far can the classics live meaningfully within our culture, and our literature, when so few people have a real command of Greek and Latin? Can translations take the place of the original texts? (Obviously, not absolutely. But is there some sort of sliding scale—i. e., Plato and the historians can survive in translation; the dramatists and lyric poets cannot?) What value is there in the kind of knowledge of Greek and Latin which a literary man may acquire for himself, as he learns German or Italian? Is there any real value in struggling ignorantly through a difficult ancient text?
A. We have the Loeb Library and contemporary talent working busily; it is suicide to take no interest, not to enrich one's own writing.

Q. If the classics can to some extent survive in translation (see question 4 above), what sort of translation do we mainly want? Translations which offer "an English poem" for a Greek or Latin one? Or translations which offer a literal account of what the original "says"?
A. Two kinds of comparison—literal meaning and attempted poignancy of the original.

Q. If it is true, or arguable, that modern criticism (i. e., criticism after Pound and Eliot) has functioned with only slight reference to Greek and Roman literature, is this because the classics are not deeply relevant to modern literary and literary-critical problems? Or because there have been so few to urge their relevance?
A. It's a case of individual affinity; any genius is three-fourths curiosity. Most people doze.

Q. Since the Romantic period, Greece has provided the cultural myths which had previously been provided by Rome. Is this still a Greek period? Or has there been anything in the way of a Roman comeback?
A. Rome is the fashion, gaining disciples.

Q. European writers and artists spent many centuries working over, domesticating, "imitating" the various modes and genres of Roman literature (and Greek, to a lesser extent). Is there anything still to be done? Or have the classics simply been used up?
A. Originals are *never* "used up."

Q. Much of this struggle (see question 8 above) went into finding *formal equivalents* for classical forms (e. g., the Spanish *lira* or Marvellian stanza for the Horatian stanza; the heroic couplet for the elegiac of hexameter line, etc.). Is this in any way relevant to the modern writer's formal interests?
A. Talent should go on, attempting equivalents.

Q. In the past, Greece and Rome have provided valid cultural myths. Can these myths, or any new comparable mythologizations of the ancient world, survive our much greater historical knowledge?

A. Myths are primal—do not die.

Q. What has been the effect of the Musee Imaginaire metaphor by which Greece and Rome are no longer two uniquely privileged, paradigmatic father-cultures, but simply two cultures among many? Liberating, or destructive?

A. ? ? ?

Q. Students were formerly taught Greek and Latin literature, but not English literature. English literature has now taken their place, so that where people once read Homer and Horace at school and then found them echoed in Milton and Pope, they now read Milton and Pope at school and painfully work their way back to Homer and Horace. What are the effects of this altered perspective?

A. English literature has not taken their place. Substitutes at best result in lack of intensity.

Q. What one Greek or Latin author do you personally, as man or writer, turn to most often?

A. Dante; but I get obsessed with Homer on any slight ground.

Q. Who in your opinion is the biggest, most inflated Greek or Latin bore?

A. E. P. said Pindar is the greatest windbag of all time. Any pastoral seems to pall.

Q. How valuable in your opinion is the classical education offered today at both the undergraduate and graduate level in the American (or British) university? Is the instruction offered pertinent to the needs of the able student who is not *professionally* interested in Classics (i. e., who wants a good general education and has no intention of becoming a classicist)? What are its merits? Its deficiencies?

A. You get interested in roots and derivations, become more exact, but too soon get enough. Inspired teaching of both plodder and genius is the answer.

Q. Classical studies are sometimes accused of being so concerned with philological skills (text criticism, literary history, etc.) that they neglect literary questions altogether. If this is true, does it matter? What, in your opinion, should be the relation between scholarship and criticism at the graduate level?

A. Vanity of pedagogy is fatal. Enjoyment has to be achieved or study is useless.

"An *Arion* Questionnaire: The Classics and the Man of Letters," *Arion*, 3 (Winter 1964), 3–4, 65–66.

•

Q. Are you for, or against, the intervention of the United States in Vietnam? How, in your opinion, should the conflict in Vietnam be resolved?
A. Does it *have* to be "Give me death or liberty"? It is shortsightedly irresponsible, I think, to permit Communist domination and acquiesce in the crushing of the weak by the strong. *Can* negotiation be imposed by force? Winston Churchill thought appeasement solved nothing.

In *Authors Take Sides On Vietnam*, edited by Cecil Woolf and John Bagguley. New York: Simon & Schuster, 1967, p. 54.

•

Q. What would you do if you were president?
A. I'd do away with forced retirement. I would let people work as long as they can. The country needs their knowledge and experience, and they should have the joy of being productively employed, useful.

Pure water and pure air seem to me needed above all else. This would require vigorous efforts toward pollution control.

Some women are overlooked who have capacity for service—as mathematicians, as scientists. I wish this could be given intensive thought.

I would encourage more government support of projects to save or restore historic houses and landmarks. Road and tree care seem important. Mrs. Johnson has aroused much incentive toward making scenery inspiring. I wouldn't overlook the beauties of Brooklyn. There, Mrs. Millar Graff's appeal for aid to historic trees has borne fruit by salvaging the beautiful Camperdown Elm in Prospect Park, planted in 1872.

The government is doing much for musicians, composers, and writers. I'd continue this help.

McCall's, 95 (January 1968), 52.

•

Q. What constitutes a modern classic?
A. No current classic comes to mind, but I submit several (as I think) classic epigrams: Kenneth Burke says that what some writers deplore as difficulties, "the artist regards as opportunities." Djuna Barnes, in her novel *Nightwood*, wrote, "When she touched anything, her hand seemed to take the place of an eye." Roger Shattuck says Igor Stravinsky "starts creating all over again from scratch, annually." Benjamin Franklin said, "I have not yet indeed thought of a remedy for luxury." And Captain J. W. Moore (aged 83), my brother, said,

"I have found it true that if one never gives up an intention—though much menaces it—in the end it prevails."

"Tomorrow's Classics," *Avant Garde* (January 1969), 31.

•

Q. What is inward beauty?
A. Inward beauty affords you contentment. Compensates you for miserable things you see and read about, the happenings and unnecessary mistakes in life that worry you. Good will and concern for the other person; inward beauty—it contradicts bad behavior and ill will.

Bettie Wysor, "The Mystery of Inner Beauty," *Harper's Bazaar*, 103 (August 1970), 128.

INDEX

Grateful acknowledgment is made for permission to reprint the following material:

"Charlotte Brontë" in *The Criterion*, issue of July 1932; "The Warden," July 1933; "A Draft of XXX Cantos," April 1934; "Ideas of Order," January 1936; and "Who So Well" in *Vernon Watkins 1906–1967* edited by Leslie Norris are reprinted by permission of Faber and Faber Limited.

"High Thinking in Boston" in *Saturday Review*, November 6, 1948. © 1948 Saturday Review Magazine. Reprinted by permission.

"Worth of Rue de la Paix" in *Harper's Bazaar*, issue of April 1962; "Of Beasts and Jewels," December 1963; "Prince Churchill," May 1965; and a portion of "The Mystery of Inner Beauty," August 1970, are reprinted courtesy of *Harper's Bazaar*. Copyright 1962, 1963, 1965, 1970 by The Hearst Corporation.

"The Poetry of Robert Frost" in *Modern Philology*, August 1964. Reprinted by permission of the University of Chicago Press.

"Randall Jarrell" in *Randall Jarrell, 1914–1965* edited by Robert Lowell, Peter Taylor, and Robert Penn Warren. This work first appeared in *The Atlantic*. Copyright © 1967 by Farrar, Straus & Giroux, Inc.

Letter to Elizabeth Shepley Sargent in *Robert Frost: Trial by Existence* by Elizabeth Shepley Sargent, Henry Holt and Company, 1960.

Excerpts from "A Lone Striker" and "Two Tramps in Mud Time" from *The Poetry of Robert Frost* edited by Edward Connery Lathem. Copyright 1936 by Robert Frost. Copyright © 1964 by Leslie Frost Ballantine. Copyright © 1969 by Holt, Rinehart and Winston. Reprinted by permission of Henry Holt and Company.

Liner notes for "I Am the Greatest!" by Cassius Clay, Columbia Records, 1963.

"A Note" (on Ezra Pound) in *Agenda*, October-November 1965. Reprinted with permission.

A portion of *A Birthday Garland for S. Foster Damon* edited by Alvin Rosenfeld and Barton St. Armand, Brown University, 1968. Reprinted with permission.

"An Arion Questionnaire: The Classics and the Man of Letters" in *Arion* magazine, Winter 1964. Reprinted with permission.